John Willis
Theatre World
1988–1989 SEASON

VOLUME 45

DISCARD

CROWN PUBLISHERS, INC.
201 EAST 50TH STREET
NEW YORK, NEW YORK 10022

LIBRARY OF CONGRESS CATALOG CARD NO. 73-82953.
ISBN 0-517-57715-1

Quality printing and binding by
Courier Company Inc.
Pleasant Street
Westford, MA 01886 U.S.A.

T O
N E I L   S I M O N

the most prolific and commercially successful playwright of this century, with gratitude for the many hours of entertainment he has given his audiences. May his great talent continue to fill our theatres for many years.

Broadway Productions: **Come Blow Your Horn (1961), Little Me (1962), Barefoot in the Park (1963), The Odd Couple (1965), Sweet Charity (1966), The Star-Spangled Girl (1966), Plaza Suite (1968), Promises, Promises (1968), The Last of the Red Hot Lovers (1969), The Gingerbread Lady (1970), The Prisoner of Second Avenue (1971), The Sunshine Boys (1972), The Good Doctor (1973), God's Favorite (1974), California Suite (1976), Chapter Two (1977), They're Playing Our Song (1979), I Ought to Be in Pictures (1980), Fools (1981), Little Me (1981/revised), Brighton Beach Memoirs (1983), Biloxi Blues (1984/Tony Award), The Odd Couple (1985/female version), Broadway Bound (1986), Rumors (1988)**

CONTENTS

Dedication: Neil Simon 2

The Season in Review 5

Broadway Calendar:
    Productions that opened June 1, 1988 through May 31, 1989 6
    Productions from previous seasons that played through this season 37
    Productions from previous seasons that closed during this season 45

Off-Broadway Calendar:
    Productions that opened June 1, 1988 through May 31, 1989 46
    Productions from previous seasons that played through this season 69
    Off-Broadway Companies Series 74

National Touring Companies 109

Professional Regional Companies 119

Award-winning Productions: Pulitzer, New York Drama Critics Circle, 1989 "Tony" Awards   186

Theatre World Award recipients of 1989 187

1989 Theatre World Awards presentations 190

Previous Theatre World Award recipients 192

Biographical Data on This Season's Casts 194

Obituaries from June 1, 1988 through May 31, 1989 227

Index 233

EDITOR: JOHN WILLIS
Assistants: Tom Lynch, Herbert Hayward, Jr., Doug Holmes, Barry Monush,
Stanley Reeves, Giovanni Romero, John Sala
Staff Photographers: Bert Andrews, Michael Riordan, Evan Romero, Michael Viade, Van Williams
Designer: Peggy Goddard

Joan Allen and Boyd Gaines in "The Heidi Chronicles," Winner of Pulitzer, NY Drama Critics Circle, and "Tony" for Best New Play *(Gerry Goodstein Photo)*

REVIEW OF THE SEASON
June 1, 1988–May 31, 1989

The worst Broadway season ever! That is, in every way except box office grosses. In spite of a declining audience, the cash intake broke records. The increase in ticket prices is responsible for this phenomenon. According to *Variety,* the average paid admission was $33.90 with a record high of $55 for ducats to "Jerome Robbins' Broadway." It was the first production to have a 22 week rehearsal period with a cast of 62. Each of the numbers was from a different Robbins show, necessitating different sets for each reproduction. Although the rise in price of admission has been appreciable, there was a greater increase in production costs and in cost of living. Production costs for the extravagant musical make it difficult to mount and finance, but the audience has come to demand the extravaganza rather than a simpler less expensive production. The long recoupment period is not attractive to investors. The playgoer wants to see a "megamusical" for the "big bucks" he has to spend for tickets. Many unforeseen technical problems also contribute to mounting costs. The dearth of productions has created a crisis for theatre owners. The Nederlander organization announced that it was leasing the beautiful Mark Hellinger Theatre to the Times Square Church for 5 years—a shock to the theatre community.

During this dismal season, new productions were at an all-time low: only 29 opened. There were more new plays but fewer musicals than in past years. There were only 6 new musicals and 1 revival, 12 new plays and 9 revivals. Concert attractions were Joan Jett, Lou Reed, Kenny Loggins, and Barry Manilow, but star performers did not guarantee an audience unless they were from other media: television, recording or films.

Eugene O'Neill's centenary was celebrated with excellent revivals of "Long Day's Journey into Night" and "Ah, Wilderness!" both with Jason Robards and Colleen Dewhurst giving their always memorable performances. The First New York International Festival of the Arts (Martin Segal, President) sponsored the unforgettable production of Dublin Gate Theatre's "Juno and the Paycock." Other productions worth mentioning were "Night of the Iguana" with Jane Alexander and Nicolas Surovy, "Checkmates" with Ruby Dee and Denzel Washington, "Eastern Standard," "Spoils of War," "The Devil's Disciple" with Philip Bosco and Victor Garber, and "Ain't Misbehavin' " with its complete original cast.

This season's "Tony" Awards were celebrated and televised on Sunday, June 4, 1989 in the Lunt-Fontanne Theatre with Angela Lansbury, a charming hostess for such a dreary affair. "Jerome Robbins' Broadway" received 6 "Tonys," including Best Musical, Best Performance by a Leading Actor in a Musical (Jason Alexander) and Featured Actress and Actor in a Musical (Debbie Shapiro/Scott Wise). Ruth Brown was voted Best Actress in a Musical ("Black and Blue"). Boyd Gaines received Best Actor in a Play ("The Heidi Chronicles") that garnered Best Play to add to its Pulitzer Prize. Its playwright, Wendy Wasserstein, became the first woman to win a "Tony" for an original play. Philip Bosco was rewarded for Best Actor in a Play ("Lend Me a Tenor"), Pauline Collins received Best Actress in a Play ("Shirley Valentine"), and Christine Baranski for Best Featured Actress in a Play ("Rumors"). "Our Town" was cited as Best Revival. Its producer (Lincoln Center Theater Co.) was having such success with previous productions that it was forced to rent a Broadway house for the run. This season no "Tonys" were given for Best Book nor for Best Score of a Musical. "Jerome Robbins' Broadway" and "Black and Blue" were ineligible because their music had been used previously. Again, efforts were made to have Off-Broadway productions declared eligible, and again unsuccessfully. So the "Tony" Awards remain strictly for excellence on Broadway, not in New York theatres, not in U.S. Theatres.

In addition to those named above, other Broadway actors who gave noteworthy performances are Joan Allen, Dylan Baker, Mikhail Baryshnikov (making his Broadway legitimate debut), Bunny Briggs, Avery Brooks, Joanne Camp, Nell Carter, Andre DeShields, Tovah Fledshuh, Peter Frechette, Savion Glover, Linda Hopkins, Bill Irwin, Madeline Kahn, John Kavanagh, Sally Mayes, Donal McCann, Sharon McNight, Armelia McQueen, Penelope Ann Miller, Kate Nelligan, Ken Page, Faith Prince, Linda Ronstadt, John Rubinstein, Campbell Scott, Kyra Sedgwick, Eric Stoltz, Leslie Uggams, Eli Wallach, Julie Wilson, Paul Winfield, Charlaine Woodard.

Praiseworthy Off-Broadway performers are Ernest Abuba, Kevin Anderson, Robin Bartlett, Suzanne Bertish, Ivar Brogger, Nial Buggy, Dan Butler, Amelia Campbell, Thom Christopher, Kevin Conway, Keene Curtis, Joan Cusack, Blythe Danner, Loren Dean, Mia Dillon, John Dossett, Roma Downey, Patrick Fitzgerald, Pauline Flanagan, Gloria Foster, Beth Fowler, Peter Francis-James, Daniel Gerroll, Anita Gillette, Bob Gunton, Anthony Heald, Eileen Heckart, Michael Jeter, Leilani Jones, Judy Kaye, Kevin Kline, Nathan Lane, Edmund Lewis, Joseph Maher, Nancy Marchand, Paul Mardirosian, Steve Martin, Barry McGovern, Jennie Moreau, Haviland Morris, Matt Mulhern, Carrie Nye, John Pankow, Estelle Parsons, Lonny Price, Paul Provenza, Scott Renderer, Elaine Rinehart, Esther Rolle, Mercedes Ruehl, Tony Shalhoub, John Shea, Howard Spiegel, Lewis J. Stadlen, Russ Thacker, John Turturro, Christopher Walken, Joanne Whalley-Kilmer, Robin Williams, Irene Worth.

Off-Broadway productions deserving a visit were musicals "Blues in the Night," "Forbidden Broadway," "Gifts of the Magi," "The Hired Man," "Middle of Nowhere," "Sweeney Todd," "The Taffetas," and "The Ten Percent Revue." Plays include "Amulets against the Dragon Forces," "Aristocrats," "Brilliant Traces," "The Cocktail Hour," "Coriolanus," "Florida Crackers," "The Film Society," "Italian-American Reconciliation," "The Kathy & Mo Show," "Love Letters," "Nasty Little Secrets," "The Night Hank Williams Died," "Only Kidding," "Other People's Money," "Reckless," "Saved from Obscurity," "Stars in the Morning" from Leningrad's Maly Theatre, "Wallem & Tolem," and "What the Butler Saw."

Off-Broadway showcases (average 35 per month) do not have expensive sets, props and costumes, but do have directorial freedom and a rapport with their audiences. However, rising rentals are endangering the future of both Off-Broadway and Off-Off-Broadway productions and companies. The lack of affordable space is the current great problem for non-profit theatres. Rising ticket prices will tend to lose an audience who cannot afford it, so reports the Alliance of Resident Theatres (130 members).

More touring companies than in recent seasons were extending Broadway across the U.S. They also hit a new record for boxoffice receipts. Regional audiences were becoming more adamant about seeing Broadway hits almost immediately. Although the number of working Actors Equity members held about even with last season's tally, the average income for working members rose to $9,858 or 9.6%, but there was a slight decrease in membership this year.

BROADWAY PRODUCTIONS

(June 1, 1988 through May 31, 1989)

LONG DAY'S JOURNEY INTO NIGHT

By Eugene O'Neill; Director, Jose Quintero; Scenery, Ben Edwards; Costumes, Jane Greenwood; Lighting, Jennifer Tipton; Sound, Alan Stieb; Presented by Ken Marsolais, Alexander H. Cohen, The Kennedy Center for the Performing Arts in association with Yale Repertory Theatre, Richard Norton, Irma Oestreicher, Elizabeth D. White; Casting, Meg Simon/Fran Kumin; General Management, Barbara Carrellas, Denise Cooper; Props, James Fedigan; Hair, Ron Frederick; Wardrobe, Nancy Schaefer; Technical Supervisor, Neil A. Mazzella; Presented as part of the First New York International Festival of the Arts; Stage Managers, Mitchell Erickson, John Handy; Press, Burnham-Callaghan/Edward Callaghan, Jacqueline Burnham, Owen Levy, Matthew Cole, Jill Larkin, Catherine Lippincott, Stacie Rauch, Tony Vargas. Opened at the Neil Simon Theatre on Monday, June 6, 1988*

CAST

James Tyrone ....Jason Robards
Mary Cavan Tyrone, his wife ....Colleen Dewhurst
James Tyrone, Jr. ....Jamey Sheridan
Edmund Tyrone, younger son ....Campbell Scott
Cathleen, second girl ....Jane Macfie

STANDBYS: William Cain (James Tyrone), Jeff Hayenga (James, Jr.), Louise Roberts (Cathleen)

A drama in 4 acts performed with one-intermission. The action takes place in the living-room of the Tyrones' summer home in August of 1912.

*Closed July 24, 1988 after 28 performances and 3 previews, in repertory with "Ah, Wilderness!" For original Broadway production, see *Theatre World* Vol. 13. The cast included Fredric March, Florence Eldridge, Jason Robards, Jr., and Bradord Dillman.

Peter Cunningham, Gerry Goodstein Photos

Jamey Sheridan, Campbell Scott
Top Right: Jason Robards, Colleen Dewhurst

6

AH, WILDERNESS!

By Eugene O'Neill; Director, Arvin Brown; Scenery, Michael H. Yeargan; Other credits same as for "Long Day's Journey into Night"; Mounted originally by Yale Repertory Theatre (Lloyd Richards, Artistic Director; Benjamin Mordecai, Managing Director). Opened in the Neil Simon Theatre on Wednesday, June 17, 1988*

CAST

Tommy Miller	Nicholas Tamarkin
Mildred Miller	Jennifer Dundas
Arthur Miller	Campbell Scott
Essie Miller	Colleen Dewhurst
Lily Miller, Nat's sister	Elizabeth Wilson
Sid Davis, Essie's brother	George Hearn
Nat Miller, owner of local paper	Jason Robards
Richard Miller	Raphael Sbarge
David McComber, dry-goods merchant	William Cain
Norah	Jane Macfie
Wint Selby, classmate of Arthur	Steven Skybell
Belle	Annie Golden
Bartender	Jamey Sheridan
Salesman	William Wise
Muriel McComber	Kyra Sedgwick

STANDBYS: William Cain (Nat), Robbie Dekelbaum (Tommy), Jeff Hayenga (Bartender/Salesman), Jane Macfie (Belle), Louise Roberts (Mildred/Muriel/Norah), William Wise (Sid Davis/David McComber).

A comedy in 3 acts and 7 scenes. The action takes place on July 4, 1906 in Connecticut in the Miller home, a bar, and on a strip of beach along the harbor.

*Closed July 24, 1988 after 12 performances and 6 previews in repertory with "Long Day's Journey into Night." The original production opened Oct. 2, 1933 in the Guild Theatre and ran for 289 performances.

Peter Cunningham Photos

Colleen Dewhurst, Campbell Scott, Jason Robards

Elizabeth Wilson, George Hearn

Annie Golden, Raphael Sbarge

AN EVENING WITH ROBERT KLEIN

Conceived and Written by Robert Klein; Musical Director, Bob Stein; Vocalists, Betsy Bircher, Catherine Russell; Company Manager, Susan Elrod; Press, Merle Debuskey, Leo Stern; Presented by Circle in the Square Theatre (Theodore Mann, Artistic Director; Paul Libin, Producing Director) as part of the First New York International Festival of the Arts (Martin E. Segal, Chairman). Opened in the Circle in the Square Theatre on Sunday, June 19, 1988*

CAST
ROBERT KLEIN

*Closed June 27, 1988 after limited engagement of 3 performances.

Robert Klein

Linda Ronstadt, Daniel Valdez

CANCIONES DE MI PADRE
(Songs of My Father)

Directed and Choreographed by Michael Smuin; Setting, Tony Walton; Lighting, Jules Fisher; Presented By Ira Koslow for Asher/Krost Management; Assistant Set Designer, Charlie Beal; Assistant Lighting Designer, Peggy Eisenhauer; Costumes, Arturo Ceballos, Manuel; Maestro, Ruben Fuentes; Stage Managers, Lonnie McKenzie, Roy Snyder, Randy Post; Hair, Milton Buras; Make-Up, Julie Purcell; Management, Peter Asher, Jose Delgado; Press, Peter Cromarty, Rob Murray. Opened in the Minskoff Theatre Tuesday July 12, 1988.*

CAST
Linda Ronstadt

Mariachi Vargas De Tecalitan	Ballet Folklorico de La Fonda
Danny Valdez	Gilberto Puente
Sal Lopez	Urbanie Lucero
Mary Louise Diaz	Elsa Estrada
Luis Valdez	Lalo Garcia

A musical revue in two acts. The setting is a romantic evening in old Mexico.

*Closed July 30, 1988 after a limited run of 18 performances.

Bob Blakeman Photos

8

THE NIGHT OF THE IGUANA

By Tennessee Williams; Director, Theodore Mann; Scenery, Zack Brown; Lighting, Richard Nelson; Costumes, Jennifer von Mayrhauser; Production Stage Manager, Michael F. Ritchie; Stage Manager, Wm. Hare; Presented by Circle in the Square Theatre (Theodore Mann, Artistic Director; Paul Lubin, Producing Director) as part of The First New York International Festival Of The Arts; Casting, Hughes Moss Casting; Press, Merle Debuskey, Leo Stern. Opened in the Circle in the Square Theatre on Sunday June 26, 1988.*

CAST

Pancho	Mateo Gomez
Maxine Faulk	Jane Alexander
Pedro	Mark Damon
Reverend T. Lawrence Shannon	Nicolas Surovy
Hank	Jonathan Mann
Herr Fahrenkopf	Christopher Martin
Hilda	Chandra Lee
Wolfgang	Peter Lang
Frau Fahrenkopf	Kathleen Marsh
Miss Judith Fellowes	Pamela Payton-Wright
Hannah Jelkes	Maria Tucci
Charlotte Goodall	Marita Geraghty
Nonno (Jonathan Coffin)	William LeMassena
Jake Latta	Tom Brennan

UNDERSTUDIES: Robert Emmet (Jake/Hank/Rev. Shannon/Herr Fahrenkopf/Wolfgang), Chandra Lee (Frau Fahrkopf/Charlotte), Jonathan Mann (Pancho/Pedro), Kathleen Marsh (Maxine Faulk/Hannah Jelkes/Judith Fellows/Hilda)

A drama in two acts. The action takes place in the Costa Verde Hotel in Puerto Barrio, Mexico during the summer of 1940.

*Closed September 4, 1988 after 81 performances and 11 previews. For original production see *Theatre World* Vol. 18.

Martha Swope Photos

Nicolas Surovy, Jane Alexander
Top Right: Jane Alexander, Maria Tucci

JUNO AND THE PAYCOCK

By Sean O'Casey; Director, Joe Dowling; Scenery, Frank Hallinan Flood; Costumes, Consolata Boyle; Lighting, Rupert Murray; General Manager, George Elmer; Associate Manager, Patricia Berry; Incidental Music, Jim Doherty; Stage Managers, Bill McComb, Lita O'Connell; Company Manager, Susan Elrod; Press, Merle Debuskey, Leo Stern; A Gate Theatre Dublin production presented by Circle in the Square Theatre (Theodore Mann, Artistic Director; Paul Libin, Producing Director) as part of the First New York International Festival of the Arts. Opened in the John Golden Theatre on Tuesday, June 21, 1988*

CAST

Mary Boyle	Rosemary Fine
Juno Boyle	Geraldine Plunkett
Johnny Boyle	Joe Savino
Jerry Devine	Tony Coleman
Captain Jack Boyle	Donal McCann
Joxer Daly	John Kavanagh
Charles Bentham	Garrett Keogh
Maisie Madigan	Maureen Potter
Mrs. Tancred	Stella McCusker
Needle Nugent	Seamus Forde
An Irregular Mobilizer	Anto Nolan
Coal-Block Vendor	Brendan Laird
Sewing Machine Man	Michael Egan
Furniture Removal Men	Enda Oates, Donagh Deeney
Neighbour	Eithne Dempsey

A drama in three acts. The action takes place in 1922 in the living apartment of a two-roomed tenancy of the Boyle family, in a tenement house in Dublin.

*Closed July 2, 1988 after a limited engagement of 12 performances and 6 previews.

Tom Lawlor Photos

**Left: John Kavanagh, Donal McCann
Top: Maureen Potter, Geraldine Plunkett, Donal McCann,
John Kavanagh**

Donal McCann, Maureen Potter

Geraldine Plunkett

Marsha Jackson, Denzel Washington
Top Right: Paul Winfield, Ruby Dee, Marsha Jackson,
Denzel Washington
Right: Paul Winfield, Ruby Dee

CHECKMATES

By Ron Milner; Director, Woodie King, Jr.; Scenery, Edward Burbridge; Costumes, Judy Dearing; Lighting, Ronald Wallace; General Manager, Roy A. Somlyo; Stage Managers, Robert Bennett, Ed LeShae; Company Manager, Lauren Somlyo; Assistant Scenic Designer, Don Jensen; Assistant Lighting Designer, Mark Schwentner; Wardrobe, Elonzo Dann; Sound, Otts Munderloh; Casting, Lynda Watson; Presented by James M. and James L. Nederlander, Philip Rose, Michael Harris, Hayward Collins by arrangement with The New Federal Theatre of New York; Press, Joshua Ellis Office/Adrian Bryan-Brown, Chris Boneau, Tim Ray, Jackie Green, Susanne Tighe. Opened in the Forty-Sixth St. Theatre on Thursday August 4, 1988.*

CAST

Sylvester Williams	Denzel Washington
Mattie Cooper	Ruby Dee
Frank Cooper	Paul Winfield
Laura McClellan-Williams	Marsha Jackson

STANDBYS: Gilbert Lewis (Frank), Yvette Hawkins (Mattie), Darnell Williams (Sylvester), Elizabeth Van Dyke (Laura)

A comedy in two acts. The action takes place in Detroit, or just about any other American metropolis.

*Closed January 1, 1989 after 177 performances and 17 previews.

Martha Swope Photos

Denzel Washington, Marsha Jackson

AIN'T MISBEHAVIN'

Conceived and Directed by Richard Maltby, Jr.; Musical Staging and Choreography, Arthur Faria; Music Supervision and Arrangements, Luther Henderson; Associate Director, Murray Horwitz; Vocal and Musical Concepts, Jeffrey Gutcheon; Vocal Arrangements, William Elliott, Jeffrey Gutcheon; Casting, Johnson-Liff & Zerman; Sets, John Lee Beatty; Costumes, Randy Barcelo; Lighting, Pat Collins; Sound, Tom Morse; Conductor/Pianist, Luther Henderson; Presented by The Shubert Organization, Emanuel Azenberg, Dasha Epstein, Roger Berlind; Based on an idea by Murray Horwitz, Richard Maltby, Jr.; General Managers, Berg/Birkenhead; Production Stage Manager, Scott Glenn; Stage Managers, Tracy Crum, Peter Lawrence; Press, Bill Evans & Associates, Sandy Manley, Jim Randolph. Opened in the Ambassador Theatre on Monday, August 15, 1988*

CAST

Nell Carter †1
Andre De Shields †2
Armelia McQueen †3
Ken Page †4
Charlaine Woodard †5
Luther Henderson

STANDBYS: Kecia Lewis-Evans, Jackie Lowe, Eric Riley, Ken Prymus

MUSICAL NUMBERS: Ain't Misbehavin', Lookin' Good But Feelin' Bad, 'T Ain't Nobody's Biz-ness If I Do, Honeysuckle Rose, Squeeze Me, Handful of Keys, I've Got a Feeling I'm Falling, How Ya Baby, The Jitterbug Waltz, The Ladies Who Sing With the Band, Yacht Club Swing, When the Nylons Bloom Again, Cash For Your Trash, Off-Time, The Joint Is Jumpin', Spreadin' Rhythm Around, Lounging at the Waldorf, The Viper's Drag, Mean to Me, Your Feet's Too Big, That Ain't Right, Keepin' Out of Mischief Now, Find Out What They Like, This Is So Nice, Fat and Greasy, Black and Blue, I'm Gonna Sit Right Down and Write Myself a Letter, Two Sleepy People, I've Got My Fingers Crossed, I Can't Give You Anything But Love, It's a Sin To Tell a Lie

A musical based on the music of Thomas "Fats" Waller performed in two acts.

*Closed January 15, 1989 after 176 performances and 8 previews. For original production see *Theatre World,* Vol. 34.

†Succeeded by: 1. Terri White, 2. Eric Riley, 3. Patti Austin, 4. Ken Prymus, 5. Jackie Lowe

Martha Swope Photos

Right: Nell Carter, Armelia McQueen
Above: Ken Page, Andre DeShields
Top: McQueen, Page, Charlaine Woodard, DeShields, Nell Carter

Luther Henderson, Jackie Lowe

Terri White, Ken Prymus

GEORGIAN STATE DANCERS

Artistic Director/Choreographer, Tengiz Sukhishvili; Director of the School of The Georgian State Dance Company, Tamaz Gogoteshvili; Chief Choreographer, Nina Ramishvili; Founders of the Company, Nina Ramishvili, Iliko Sukhishvili; Costumes, Simon Virsaladze; Presented by James M. Nederlander in association with Classical Artists International; Executive Producer for the Nederlander Organization, Peter H. Russell; Wardrobe Supervisor, Emzari Gabeliya; Head of Production, Pyotr Dgvepadze; Press, Jan Morgan, Cromarty & Co/Peter Cromarty, David Gersten, Kevin Brockman, Joe Wolhandler; General Manager, Arthur Rubin; Production Stage Manager, Roger Franklin, Opened in the Mark Hellinger Theatre on Tuesday, August 16, 1988.*

SOLOISTS: Besik Bakuradze, Rusudan Berianidze, Soso Dekanoidze, Nugzer Dzhikuri, Tamara Eliozishvili, Vladimir Gabeliya, Dzeheiran Goginava, Nelli Khazhomiya, David Khozashvili, Teimuraz Khozashvili, Nana Mukeria, Gia Nadareishvili, Nodar Pliev, Gulnara Sikharulidze, Roland Tatishvili, Inga Tevzadze

PROGRAM: Partsa, Kartuli, Khorumi, Kasbeksky Dance, Georgian Suite, Invitation, Dances of the Khevsuri, Dolebi, Narnari, Mkhedruli, Dance from the Hills, Samaya, Khandjluri, Tzkarostan, Lelo, Karachokheli, Davluri, Kintauri, Simd, Competition

*Closed September 4, 1988 after 24 performances.

Georgian State Dancers

Georgian State Dancers

MOSCOW CIRCUS '88

U.S. Producer of the Moscow Circus, Steven E. Leber; Deputy Director, Yuri Matveev; Presented in association with Radio City Music Hall Productions; Executive Producers, Steve Leber, Scott Sanders; Press, Patricia Robert, Kimberly Hollfield, Moss International, Inc. Opened in the Radio City Music Hall on Wednesday, September 14, 1988.*

PERFORMERS: The Flying Cranes, The Zolkins, Alexander Frish, Nikolai Pavlenko, Gregory Popovich, Tamerlan Nugzarov, Mednikovi and Abakorovi, Margulyan and Podchufarov, The Alexandrovs, Ukranian Amusements, The Shahnini

*Closed October 9, 1988 after 44 performances.

Patricia Lanza Photos

Moscow Circus

PAUL ROBESON

By Phillip Hayes Dean; Director, Harold Scott; Musical Direction, Ernie Scott; Special Arrangements/Orchestration, Eva C. Brooks; Original Choreography, Dianne McIntyre; Stage Manager, Doug Hosney; Lights, Shirley Prendergast; Sets/Costumes, Michael Massee; Presented by Eric Krebs, in association with South Street Theatre; General Management, Eric Krebs Theatrical Management/Whitbell Productions, Inc.; Press, Shirley Herz Associates/Glenna Freedman, David Roggensack, Sam Rudy, Pete Sanders; Company Manager, Gail Bell; Associate Manager, Paul Morer. Opened in the Golden Theatre on Wednesday, September 28, 1988.*

CAST

Paul Robeson .... Avery Brooks
(Matinees: Herb Downer)
Lawrence Brown .... Ernie Scott
STANDBY: Herb Downer

A drama in two acts.

*Closed October 30, 1988 after 28 performances and 8 previews. It had previously played 26 performances off Broadway in The South Street Theatre. For the original production see *Theatre World* Vol. 34

Avery Brooks as Paul Robeson
Left: Ernie Scott,
Avery Brooks

MICHAEL FEINSTEIN IN CONCERT:

Production Stage and Supervised by Christopher Chadman; Musical Director/Conductor, Joel Silberman; Sets, Andrew Jackness; Lighting, Beverly Emmons; Sound, Daryl Bornstein; Special Material, Bruce Vilanch; Orchestrations, Ian Finkel; Additional Orchestrations, Joseph Gianono, Larry Hochman, Pete Levin, Johnny Mandel, John Oddo; Presented by Ron Delsener, Jonathan Scharer; Press, The Joshua Ellis Office/Adrian Bryan-Brown, Jackie Green, Susanne Tighe, Tim Ray, Chris Boneau; Production Manager, Sam Ellis; Production Stage Manager, Kenneth Cox; Wardrobe, Cleon Byerly; Special Arrangements, Stan Freeman, Joel Silberman. Opened in the Booth Theatre on Wednesday, October 5, 1988.*

CAST

MICHAEL FEINSTEIN

Performed with one intermission.

*Closed November 6, 1988 after 39 performances.

Marc Bryan-Brown Photos

Michael Feinstein

CAFE CROWN

By Hy Kraft, Director, Martin Charnin; Scenery/Costumes, Santo Loquasto; Lighting, Richard Nelson; Casting, Rosemarie Tichler/Nancy Piccione; Joseph Papp's New York Shakespeare Festival production is presented by LeFrak Entertainment, James M. Nederlander, Francine LeFrak, James L. Nederlander, Arthur Rubin; Associate Producer, Jason Steven Cohen; General Management, Joseph Harris, Peter T. Kulok; Props, Joseph Harris, Jr., Frances Smith; Wigs/Hair, Frida Aradottir/Paul Huntley; Stage Managers, Thomas A. Kelly, Lisa Buxbaum; Press, Shirley Herz, Richard Kornberg. Opened in the Brooks Atkinson Theatre on Saturday, Feb. 18, 1989*

CAST

Kaminsky/Looie	Mitchell Jason
Rubin	Jack Kenny
Sam	Fyvush Finkel
Jacobson	Bernie Passeltiner
Kaplan	Felix Fibich
Mendel Polan	David Margulies
Mrs. Perlman	Tresa Hughes
Hymie	Bob Dishy
Walter	David Carroll
Beggar Florist/Western Union Messenger	Sidney Armus
Toplitz	George Guidall
Lester Freed	Steven Skybell
Norma Cole	Laura Sametz
Ida Polan	Marilyn Cooper
David Cole	Eli Wallach
George Burton	Walter Bobbie
Lipsky	Carl Don
Anna Cole	Anne Jackson

UNDERSTUDIES: Rose Arrick (Ida/Anna/Mrs. Perlman), Jack Kenny (Lester/George), George Guidall (David Cole), Jack Aaron (Mendel/Rubin/Jacobson), Susan Bruce (Norma), Maggie Burke (Ida/Mrs. Perlman)

A comedy in 3 acts. The action takes place during 1940 in the Cafe Crown on Second Avenue and Twelfth Street in New York City.

*Closed March 28, 1989 after 45 performances. It had previously played 56 performances and 32 previews in the Public/Newman Theater (Off Broadway). Originally presented Jan. 23, 1942 in the Cort Theatre where it played 141 performances with Morris Carnovsky, Sam Jaffe and Jay Adler. Recipient of 1989 "Tony" for Best Scenic Design.

Martha Swope Photos

Right: Eli Wallach, Anne Jackson, Bob Dishy (standing)
Top: David Carroll, Laura Sametz, Anne Jackson,
Steven Skybell

David Carroll, Marilyn Cooper, Harry Goz, Carl Don

Eli Wallach, Anne Jackson

KENNY LOGGINS ON BROADWAY

Presented by James M. Nederlander, James L. Nederlander, Arthur Rubin; Production Manager, Skip Rickert; Tour Manager, Denny Jones; Lighting/Set, Michael Ledesma; Sound, Clair Bros. Audio; Press, Cromarty & Co./David Gersten, Kevin Brockman, Jim Baldassare; General Manager, Arthur Rubin. Opened in the Neil Simon Theatre on Tuesday, November 1, 1988.*

CAST
KENNY LOGGINS
CRAIG SHOEMAKER

*Closed November 6, 1988 after a limited run of 8 performances.

Kenny Loggins

SPOILS OF WAR

By Michael Weller; Director, Austin Pendleton; Set, Andrew Jackness; Costumes, Ruth Morley; Lighting, Paul Gallo; Sound, Gary and Timmy Harris; Casting, Meg Simon/Fran Kumin; Hair, Antonio Soddu; Presented by Ed and David Mirvish, in association with The Second Stage Theatre/Robyn Goodman, Carole Rothman; General Management, Gatchell & Neufeld, Ltd./R. Tyler Gatchell, Jr., Peter Neufeld, Nina Lannan; Company Manager, J. Anthony Magner; Stage Managers, Pamela Edington, James Harker; Press, The Joshua Ellis Office/Adrian Bryan-Brown, Susanne Tighe, Tim Ray, Jackie Green, Chris Boneau. Opened in the Music Box Theatre on Thursday, November 10, 1988, after playing 64 performances Off-Broadway at the Second Stage Theatre.*

CAST

Martin	Christopher Collet
Andrew	Jeffrey De Munn
Elise	Kate Nelligan
Penny	Marita Geraghty
Emma	Alice Playten
Lew	Kevin O'Rourke

STANDBYS: Laurie Kennedy (Elise), Stephen Rowe (Andrew/Lew), Jonathan Del Arco (Martin), Gloria Biegler (Penny/Emma)

A drama in two acts. The action takes place in New York City in the 1950s.

*Closed December 10, 1988 after 36 performances and 14 previews.

Susan Cook and Roy Mitchell Photos

Top Left: Kate Nelligan, Christopher Collet, Jeffrey DeMunn

Kevin O'Rourke, Kate Nelligan
Above: Jeffrey DeMunn, Marita Geraghty, Christopher Collet

THE DEVIL'S DISCIPLE

By George Bernard Shaw; Director, Stephen Porter; Scenery and Costumes, Zack Brown; Lighting, Curt Ostermann; Hair and Wigs; Paul Huntley; Stage Managers, Wm. Hare, Bill Braden; Casting, Hughes Moss; Company Manager, Susan Elrod; Presented by Circle in the Square Theatre (Theodore Mann, Artistic Director; Paul Libin, Producing Director); Press, Merle Debuskey, Leo Stern. Opened in the Circle in the Square on Sunday, November 13, 1988.*

CAST

Mrs. Dudgeon	Rosemary Murphy
Essie	Marguerite Kelly
Christy	Adam LeFevre
Anthony Anderson	Remak Ramsay †1
Judith Anderson	Roxanne Hart
Lawyer Hawkins	Richard Clarke
William Dudgeon	David Cryer
Mrs. William Dudgeon	Carol Goodheart
Titus Dudgeon	Russell Leib
Mrs. Titus Dudgeon	Chandra Lee
Richard Dudgeon	Victor Garber †2
Sergeant	Paul Ukena, Jr.
Major Swindon	Bill Moor
General Burgoyne	Philip Bosco †3
Officers	David Cryer, Russell Leib
Brudenell	David Cryer
Soldiers	J. Grant Albrecht, Robert Emmet
Townspeople	Connie Roderick, Tom Sminkey

UNDERSTUDIES: Robert Emmet (Richard Dudgeon), Richard Clarke (Gen. Burgoyne), David Cryer (Anthony), Carol Goodheart (Mrs. Dudgeon), Russell Leib (Hawkins/Swindon), Chandra Lee (Judith/Essie), Tom Sminkey (William/Brudenell/Titus), J. Grant Albrecht (Sergeant/Christy), Connie Roderick (Mrs. Dudgeon/Mrs. Titus Dudgeon).

A comedy in two acts. The action takes place in Websterbridge, New Hampshire in 1777.

†Succeeded by: 1. John Cunningham, 2. Philip Casnoff, 3. Lee Richardson

*Closed February 19, 1989 after 113 performances and 26 previews.

Martha Swope Photos

Right: Victor Garber, Roxanne Hart
Above: Robert Emmet, J. Grant Albrecht, Roxanne Hart,
Paul Ukena, Victor Garber Top: Chandra Lee, Carol
Goodheart (seated), Russell Leib, Roxanne Hart (seated),
Richard Clarke, David Cryer (seated), Adam LeFevre, Remak
Ramsay, Rosemary Murphy (seated), Victor Garber,
Marguerite Kelly (foreground)

Philip Bosco, Bill Moor

Philip Bosco, Victor Garber, Remak Ramsay, Roxanne Hart

(from top) Andre Gregory, Jessica Walter, Joyce Van Patten, Ken Howard, Ron Leibman, Lisa Banes, Christine Baranski, Mark Nelson

(Descending the stairs) Larry Linville, Dick Latessa, Lisa Emery, Jessica Walter, Joyce Van Patten, Ron Leibman, Christine Baranski, Richard Levine, Charles Brown, Cynthia Darlow
Right: Ron Leibman, Jessica Walter

RUMORS

By Neil Simon; Director, Gene Saks; Scenery, Tony Straiges; Costumes, Joseph G. Aulisi; Lighting, Tharon Musser; Sound, Tom Morse; Casting, Jay Binder; Presented by Emanuel Azenberg; Originally presented by the Old Globe Theatre, San Diego (Jack O'Brien, Artistic Director; Tom Hall, Managing Director); Stage Managers, Peter Lawrence, John Brigleb; Company Manager, Leslie Butler; Asst. Company Manager, Sammy Ledbetter; Consultant, Jose Vega; Sound, Michael Lynch; Wardrobe, Penny Davis; Asst. Set Design, Richard Jaris; Press, Bill Evans & Associates (Sandy Manley/Jim Randolph). Opened in the Broadhurst Theatre on Thursday, November 17, 1988.*

CAST

Chris Gorman	....	Christine Baranski †1
Ken Gorman	....	Mark Nelson †2
Claire Ganz	....	Jessica Walter †3
Lenny Ganz	....	Ron Leibman †4
Cookie Cusack	....	Joyce Van Patten †5
Ernie Cusak	....	Andre Gregory †6
Glenn Cooper	....	Ken Howard †7
Cassie Cooper	....	Lisa Banes †8
Welch	....	Charles Brown
Pudney	....	Cynthia Darlow †9

STANDBYS: Kandis Chappell (Chris/Cassie/Pudney), Gibby Brand (Ken/Lenny/Welch), Cynthia Darlow (Claire/Cookie), Timothy Landfield (Ernie/Glenn)

A farce in three acts. The action takes place at the present time in a house in Sneeden's Landing, N.Y., during June.

†Succeeded by: 1. Kandis Chappell, Catherine Cox, 2. Richard Levine, 3. Veronica Hamel, 4. Greg Mullavey, 5. Alice Playten, 6. Dick Latessa, Dan Desmond, 7. Larry Linville, Timothy Landfield, 8. Lisa Emery, 9. Kathleen Marsh

*Still playing May 31, 1989. "Tony" was awarded Christine Baranski for Best Performance by a Featured Actress in a Play.

Martha Swope & Assoc. Photos

Dan Desmond, Alice Playten
Above: Veronica Hamel, Greg Mullavey

OUR TOWN

By Thornton Wilder; Director, Gregory Mosher; Musical Director, Michael Barrett; General Manager, Steven C. Callahan; Production Manager, Jeff Hamlin; Sets, Douglas Stein; Costumes, Jane Greenwood; Lighting, Kevin Rigdon; Stage Managers, Michael F. Ritchie, Gary Natoli; Executive Producer, Bernard Gersten; Presented by Lincoln Center Theatre; Company Manager, Sally Campbell; Wardrobe Supervisor, Don Brassington; Hair Stylist, Ann Miles; Press, Merle Debuskey, William Schelble. Opened in the Lyceum Theatre on Sunday, December 4, 1988.*

CAST

Stage Manager	Spalding Gray †1
Dr. Gibbs	James Rebhorn
Joe Crowell	Joey Shea †2
Howie Newsome	W. H. Macy †3
Mrs. Gibbs	Frances Conroy
Mrs. Webb	Roberta Maxwell
George Gibbs	Eric Stoltz †4
Rebecca Gibbs	Lydia Kelly †5
Wally Webb	Shane Culkin
Emily Webb	Penelope Ann Miller †6
Professor Willard	Bill Alton
Mr. Webb	Peter Maloney
Woman in the balcony	Marilyn Hamlin
Man in the auditorium	Steven Goldstein
Lady in the box	Katharine Houghton †7
Simon Stimson	Jeff Weiss
Mrs. Newsome	Mary McCann
Mrs. Soames	Marcell Rosenblatt
Constable Warren	Tom Brennan
Si Crowell	Christopher Cunningham, Jr. †2
Baseball Players	Steven Goldstein, Todd Weeks, Jordan Lage
Sam Craig	Roderick McLachlan
Joe Stoddard	William Preston
Farmer McCarty	Patrick Tovatt †8
Mr. Carter	John Griesemer †9
Mr. Greenough	Michael Barrett †10

UNDERSTUDIES: Bill Alton (Joe Stoddard), Christopher Cunningham, Jr., Devin Doherty (Joe Crowell), Steven Goldstein (Howie Newsome), John Griesemer (Dr. Gibbs/Prof. Willard/Mr. Webb/Constable Warren), Marilyn Hamlin (Mrs. Gibbs), Katharine Houghton, Joan MacIntosh (Mrs. Webb/Mrs. Soames), Jordan Lage (Man in auditorium/Sam Craig/Farmer McCarty/Mr. Carter), Mary McCann (Emily Webb/Woman in balcony/Lady in the box), Roderick McLachlan (Simon Stimson), Joey Shea, Devin Doherty (Si Crowell/Wally Webb), Ron Parady, Patrick Tovatt (Stage Manager), Amanda Weeden, Lydia Kelly (Rebecca Gibbs), Todd Weeks (George Gibbs), Thomas Kopache (Prof. Willard/Constable Warren/Farmer McCarty)

A drama in three acts. The action takes place in Grover's Corners, New Hampshire.

†Succeeded by: 1. Don Ameche, 2. Atticus Brady, 3. John Griesemer, 4. Jason Gedrick, 5. Amanda Weeden, 6. Helen Hunt, 7. Joan MacIntosh, 8. Ron Parady, 9. Thomas Kopache, 10. Evans Haile.

*Closed April 1, 1989 after 135 performances and 27 previews. The original production opened in the Henry Miller Theatre on Feb. 4, 1938 and ran for 336 performances. Recipient of 1989 "Tony" for Best Revival.

**Top Right: Eric Stoltz, Peter Maloney, Penelope Ann Miller
Right: Eric Stoltz, Spalding Gray, Penelope Ann Miller**
(Brigitte LaCombe Photos)

Eric Stoltz, Penelope Ann Miller

(foreground) Frances Conroy, Penelope Ann Miller

LEGS DIAMOND

Music/Lyrics, Peter Allen; Book, Harvey Fierstein, Charles Suppon; Based on the Warner Bros. motion picture "The Rise and Fall of Legs Diamond"; Director, Robert Allan Ackerman; Musical Numbers Choreographed by Alan Johnson; Scenery, David Mitchell; Costumes, Willa Kim; Lighting, Jules Fisher; Sound, Peter J. Fitzgerald; Black Art Effects Consultant, Ted Shapiro; Hair, Howard Leonard; Musical Director/Vocal Arrangements, Eric Stern; Assistant Conductor, Tim Stella; Orchestrations, Michael Starobin; Dance Music Arrangements, Mark Hummel; General Manager, Gary Gunas/Joey Parnes; Casting, Meg Simon/Fran Kumin; Musical Coordinator, John Monaco; Stage Managers, Peter B. Mumford, Gary M. Zabinski, Robert B. Gould; Company Manager, Nina Skriloff; Presented by James M. and James L. Nederlander, Arthur Rubin, The Entertainment Group, George M. Steinbrenner III, in association with Jonathan Farkas and Marvin A. Krauss; Associate Producer, Kathleen Raitt; Props, Charles Zuckerman; Wardrobe, Gayle Patton; Press, Shirley Herz Assoc./Glenna Freedman, Pete Sanders, Sam Rudy, Miller Wright. Opened in the Mark Hellinger Theatre on Monday, December 26, 1988.*

CAST

Jack Diamond	Peter Allen
Convict/Latin Dancer/Boy from Bay Ridge/A.R.'s Gang	Adrian Bailey
Convict/Gangster/A.R.'s Gang	Quin Baird
Convict/Latin Dancer/Taxi Dancer/Jack's Gang	Frank Cava
Convict/Latin Dancer/Chinese Waiter/Jack's Gang	Norman Wendall Kauahi
Convict/Latin Dancer/Gangster/Taxi Dancer/ Boy from Bay Ridge/A.R.'s Gang	Bobby Moya
Convict/Latin Dancer/Gangster/Jack's Gang/Policeman	Paul Nunes
Convict/Latin Dancer/Jack's Gang	Keith Tyrone
Prison Guard/Tuxedo Dancer/Gangster/Jack's Gang	Stephen Bourneuf
Prison Guard/Gangster/Boy from Bay Ridge/ A.R.'s Gang/F.B.I. Man	Rick Manning
Madge	Brenda Braxton
Cigarette Girl/Hotsy Totsy Girl	Deanna Dys
Bones	Christian Kauffmann
Augie	Raymond Serra
Kiki Roberts	Randall Edwards
Devane	Pat McNamara
Hotsy Totsy Announcer/Gangster/Barber	Mike O'Carroll
Flo	Julie Wilson
Hotsy Totsy Girl/Champagne Girl	Carol Ann Baxter
Hotsy Totsy Girl/Showgirl	Colleen Dunn
Hotsy Totsy Girl/Champagne Girl/Burlesque Woman	Gwendolyn Miller
Hotsy Totsy Girl/Showgirl/Burlesque Woman	Wendy Waring
Moran	Jim Fyfe
Arnold Rothstein	Joe Silver
Tropicabana Announcer/Gangster/F.B.I. Man	James Brandt
Tuxedo Dancer/Gangster/A.R.'s Gang	Jonathan Cerullo
Tuxedo Dancer/Taxi Dancer/Jack's Gang	K. Craig Innes
Tuxedo Dancer	Kevin Weldon
Mourner	Ruth Gottschall
Jack Diamond's Secretary	Shelley Wald
Swings	Dan O'Grady, Jennifer Rymer, Steven Scionti

UNDERSTUDIES: Ruth Gottschall (Flo), Colleen Dunn (Kiki), Mike O'Carroll (Rothstein), Adrian Bailey (Bones), Mike O'Carroll (Devane), Frank Cava (Moran)

A musical in two acts. The action takes place in and around New York during the 1920s.

*Closed February 19, 1989 after 64 performances and 72 previews.

Martha Swope Photos

Above: Wendy Waring, Gwendolyn Miller, Carol Ann Baxter, Peter Allen, Deanna Dys, Colleen Dunn
Center: K. Craig Innes, Colleen Dunn, Adrian Bailey, Randall Edwards (C), Keith Tyrone, Wendy Waring, Bobby Moya

Top: Peter Allen with company

Peter Allen

EASTERN STANDARD

By Richard Greenberg; Director, Michael Engler; Sets, Philipp Jung; Costumes, William Ivey Long; Lighting, Donald Holder; Sound, Jan Nebozenko; Casting, Lyons/Isaacson; General Management, Kingwill/Goossen; Presented by Jessica Levy and the Manhattan Theatre Club; Originally presented by the Seattle Repertory Theatre; Stage Managers, Pat Sosnow, Tammy Taylor; Production Assistants, Tim Salamandyk, Tim Vasen, Jenny Besch, Jim Sandefur, Michael Chybowski; Production Supervisor, Larry Morley; Wardrobe, Jean Steinlein; Props, Carie Kramer; Press, David Powers. Opened in the John Golden Theatre on Thursday, January 5, 1989 after playing 66 performances off-broadway at the Manhattan Theatre Club.*

CAST

Stephen Wheeler	Dylan Baker
Drew Paley	Peter Frechette
Ellen	Barbara Garrick
Phoebe Kidde	Patricia Clarkson
Peter Kidde	Kevin Conroy
May Logan	Anne Meara

UNDERSTUDIES: Angela Pietropinto (May), Colette Kilroy (Phoebe/Ellen), Michael McKenzie (Stephen/Drew/Peter)

A comedy in two acts. The action takes place in Manhattan and the Hamptons during the spring and summer of 1987.

*Closed March 25, 1989 after playing 92 performances and 20 previews.

Gerry Goodstein Photos

Left: Barbara Garrick, Peter Frechette, Kevin Conroy

Above: Frechette, Conroy, Dylan Baker, Patricia Clarkson
Top: Anne Meara, Barbara Garrick

Dylan Baker, Patricia Clarkson

Anne Meara, Patricia Clarkson

BLACK AND BLUE

Entire production Conceived, Designed and Directed by Claudio Segovia and Hector Orezzeli; Choreographers, Cholly Atkins, Henry Letang, Frankie Manning, Fayard Nicholas; Assistant, Diane Walker; Musical Supervision, Arrangements, Orchestrations, Sy Johnson; Additional Arrangements and Orchestrations, Luther Henderson; Lighting, Neil Peter Jampolis, Jane Reisman; Sound, Abe Jacob; Presented by Mel Howard and Donald K. Donald; Associate Producer, Marilynn LeVine; General Management/Norman E. Rothstein, Robert A. Buckley, Julie Crosby; Casting, Julie Hughes/Barry Moss/Jessica Gilburne; Technical Supervisor, Peter Fulbright; Hair/ Makeup, Jean Luc, Don Vito; Props, Dennis Randolph; Wardrobe, Dolores Gamba, Dave Olin Rogers; Stage Managers, Alan Hall, Ruth E. Rinklin, Jack Gianino, Tamara K. Heeschen; Press, P.R. Partners/Marilynn LeVine, Kevin McAnarney, Phil Santora, Barbara Cavargna. Opened in the Minskoff Theatre on Thursday, January 26, 1989*

CAST

THE SINGERS: Ruth Brown †, Linda Hopkins, Carrie Smith
THE HOOFERS: Bunny Briggs, Ralph Brown, Lon Chaney, Tina Pratt, Jimmy Slyde, Diane Walker
THE DANCERS: Rashamella Cumbo, Tanya Gibson, Germaine Goodson, Angela Hall, Kyme, Valerie Macklin, Deborah Mitchell, Valerie E. Smith, Frederick J. Boothe, Eugene Fleming, Ted Levy, Bernard Manners, Van Porter, Kevin Ramsey, Ken Roberson, Melvin Washington, Ivery Wheeler
THE YOUNGER GENERATION: Cyd Glover, Savion Glover, Dormeshia Sumbry
MUSICAL NUMBERS: *Act I:* Blues a Capella, I'm a Woman, Hoofers a Capella, Royal Garden Blues, St. Louis Blues, Everybody Loves My Baby, After You've Gone, If I Can't Sell It I'll Keep Sittin' on It, I Want a Big Butter and Egg Man, Rhythm Is Our Business, Mystery Song, Stompin' at the Savoy, I've Got a Right to Sing the Blues, Black and Tan Fantasy, Come Sunday, Daybreak Express, 'Tain't Nobody's Business if I Do, That Rhythm Man *Act II:* Swinging to Wednesday Night Hop, Cry Like a Baby, Memories of You, Body and Soul, I'm Confessin', East St. Louis Toodle-oo, Am I Blue, I Can't Give You Anything But Love, In a Sentimental Mood, Black and Blue, Finale.

†During Miss Brown's absence in previews her numbers were sung by Melba Joyce, Carrie Smith and Dakota Staton

*Still playing May 31, 1989. Recipient of 1989 "Tonys" for Best Performance by a Leading Actress in a Musical (Ruth Brown), Best Costume Design, and Best Choreography.

Martha Swope Photos

Right: Dancers Above: Carrie Smith, Eugene Fleming, Kevin Ramsey, Ted Levy
Top: Linda Hopkins (L), Ruth Brown (R)

Savion Glover

Bunny Briggs

Kyme, Kevin Ramsey, Ted Levy, Fred Boothe, Bernard Manners

Franklin Cover, Madeline Kahn, Ed Asner,
Daniel Hugh Kelly

Right: Ed Asner

BORN YESTERDAY

By Garson Kanin; Director, Josephine R. Abady; Production Supervised by John Tillinger; Set, David Potts; Costumes, Ann Roth; Lighting, Jeff Davis; Sound, Lia Vollack; Hair, J. Roy Helland; Casting, Michael Doyle Fender; Presented by Jay H. Fuchs, Columbia Artists Management, A. Joseph Tandet and the Cleveland Play House (Josephine R. Abady, Artistic Director; Dean R. Gladden, Managing Director) in association with Little Prince Productions Ltd; Associate Producer, Martha Wilson; General Management, Gatchell & Neufeld; Associate, Nina Lannan; Company Manager, Douglas C. Baker, Florie Seery; Props, Robert Saltzman; Wardrobe, Anne Appolito; Fight Choreographer, Terry Hinns; Stage Managers, Don Walters, Peggy Peterson; Press, Jeffrey Richards/Irene Gandy, Maria Somma, Susan Chicoine, Diane Judge. Opened in the 46th Street Theatre on Sunday, Jan. 29, 1989*

CAST

Helen, a maid	Heather Ehlers
Bellhops	Gregory Jbara, Paul Hebron
Paul Verrall	Daniel Hugh Kelly
Eddie Brock	Joel Bernstein
Assistant Manager	Ron Johnston
Harry Brock	Edward Asner
Billie Dawn	Madeline Kahn
Ed Devery	Franklin Cover
Barber	Paul Hebron
Manicurist	Charlotte Booker
Bootblack	Gregory Jbara
Senator Norval Hedges	John Wylie
Mrs. Hedges	Peggy Cosgrave
Waiter	Paul Hebron

STANDBYS & UNDERSTUDIES: Charlotte Booker (Billie), Robert Murch (Harry Brock/Ed Devery), Pamela Pascoe (Helen/Mrs. Hedges/Manicurist), Paul Hebron (Paul Verrall), Ron Johnston (Hedges), Gregory Jbara (Eddie Brock)

A comedy in 2 acts and 3 scenes. The action takes place in a hotel suite in Washington, D.C., during 1945.

*Closed June 11, 1989 after 153 performances and 13 previews. Original production opened in the Lyceum Theatre, Feb. 4, 1946 and played 1642 performances. Leading players were Paul Douglas, Judy Holliday, Gary Merrill. See THEATRE WORLD Vol. 3.

Peter Cunningham Photos

Ed Asner, Madeline Kahn

SHIRLEY VALENTINE

By Willy Russell; Director, Simon Callow; Design, Bruno Santini; Lighting, Nick Chelton; Presented by The Really Useful Theatre Co. and Bob Swash; General Management, Gatchell & Neufeld/Nina Lannan; Company Manager, Wendy Orshan; Technical Supervisors, Theatre Services; Props, George Green, Jr., Andrew Acabbo; Wardrobe, Adelaide Laurino, David Hemenway; Stage Managers, Jeff Lee, Michael McEowen; Press, Philip Rinaldi, James Morrison. Opened Thursday, February 16, 1989 in the Booth Theatre*

CAST

Shirley Valentine .... Pauline Collins†
Standby: Patricia Kilgarriff

A comedy in two acts. The action takes place at the present time.

†Succeeded by Patricia Kilgarriff, Ellen Burstyn

*Closed Nov. 25, 1989 after 324 performances and 8 previews. Miss Collins received a 1989 "Tony" for Best Actress in a Play.

Catherine Ashmore Photos

**Left: Pauline Collins,
also below**

HIZZONER!

By Paul Shyre; Director, John Going; Set, Eldon Elder; Costumes, Patrizia Von Brandenstein; Lighting, John McLain; Sound, Abe Jacob; General Manager, Ralph Roseman; Production Assistant, Doug Lange; Company Manager, Alan R. Markinson; Technical Director, Jeremiah J. Harris; Props, Sal Sclafani; Wardrobe, June Wolfe; Stage Managers, Michael A. Bartuccio, Betsy Nicholson; Press, Joshua Ellis/Adrian Bryan-Brown, Jackie Green, Susanne Tighe, Tim Ray, Chris Boneau, Shannon Barr. Opened in the Longacre Theatre on Thursday, February 23, 1989*

CAST

Fiorello H. LaGuardia .... Tony Lo Bianco

A play in two acts. The action takes place in the office of Mayor Fiorello H. LaGuardia in New York City Hall on his last day in office in 1945.

*Closed March 5, 1989 after 12 performances and 13 previews.

Martha Swope Photos

Tony Lo Bianco

JEROME ROBBINS' BROADWAY

By James M. Barrie, Irving Berlin, Leonard Bernstein, Jerry Bock, Sammy Cahn, Moose Charlap, Betty Comden, Larry Gelbart, Morton Gould, Adolph Green, Oscar Hammerstein II, Sheldon Harnick, Arthur Laurents, Carolyn Leigh, Stephen Longstreet, Hugh Martin, Jerome Robbins, Richard Rodgers, Burt Shevelove, Stephen Sondheim, Joseph Stein, Jule Styne; Direction/Choreography, Jerome Robbins; Co-Director, Grover Dale; Scenic Designer, Robin Wagner; Scenery, Boris Aronson, Jo Mielziner, Oliver Smith, Robin Wagner, Tony Walton; Supervising Costume Designer, Joseph G. Aulisi; Costumes, Joseph G. Aulisi, Alvin Colt, Raoul Pene du Bois, Irene Sharaff, Tony Walton, Miles White, Patricia Zipprodt; Musical Director, Paul Gemignani; Assistants to Choreographer, Cynthia Onrubia, Victor Castelli, Jerry Mitchell; Sound, Otts Munderloh; Lighting Design, Jennifer Tipton; Hair/Makeup, J. Roy Helland; Casting, Jay Binder; Orchestrations, Sid Ramin, William D. Brohn; Musical Continuity, Scott Frankel; Produced in association with Pace Theatrical Group; Presented by The Shubert Organization (Gerald Schoenfeld, Chairman; Bernard B. Jacobs, President), Roger Berlind, Suntory International Corp., Byron Goldman and Emanuel Azenberg; General Manager, Leonard Soloway; Production Supervisor, Charles Blackwell; Company Manager, Brian Dunbar; Technical Supervision, Theatrical Services, Inc.; Props, Jan Marasek, Tommy Thomson; Wardrobe, Joe Busheme, Richard Ruiz; Assistant General Manager, Abby Evans; Stage Managers, Beverley Randolph, Jim Woolley; Press, Fred Nathan/Bert Fink, Merle Frimark, Scott Taylor, Marc P. Thibodeau, Thomas Naro. Opened in the Imperial Theatre Sunday, February 26, 1989*

COMPANY

Jason Alexander, Richard Amaro, Dorothy Benham, Jeffrey Lee Broadhurst, Christophe Caballero, Mindy Cartwright, Irene Cho, Jamie Cohen, Charlotte d'Amboise, Camille de Ganon, Donna Di Meo, Donna Marie Elio, Mark Esposito, Susann Fletcher, Scott Fowler, Angelo H. Fraboni, Ramon Galindo, Nicholas Garr, Gregorey Garrison, Carolyn Goor, Michael Scott Gregory, Andrew Grose, Alexia Hess, Nancy Hess, Louise Hickey, Eric A. Hoisington, Barbara Hoon, JoAnn M. Hunter, Scott Jovovich, Pamela Khoury, Susan Kikuchi, Michael Kubala, Robert La Fosse, Mary Ann Lamb, Jane Lanier, David Lanier, David Lowenstein, Michael Lynch, Greta Martin, Joey McKneely, Julio Monge, Troy Myers, Maria Neenan, Jack Noseworthy, Steve Ochoa, Kelly Patterson, Luis Perez, Faith Prince, James Rivera, Tom Robbins, George Russell, Greg Schanuel, Debbie Shapiro, Renee Stork, Mary Ellen Stuart, Linda Talcott, Leslie Trayer, Ellen Troy, Andi Tyler, Scott Wise, Elaine Wright, Barbara Yeager, Alice Yearsley

MUSICAL NUMBERS

ACT I: Overture, New York New York, Sailors on the Town, Ya Got Me, Charleston, Comedy Tonight, I Still Get Jealous, Suite of dances from "West Side Story"
ACT II: The Small House of Uncle Thomas, You Gotta Have a Gimmick, I'm Flying, On a Sunday by the Sea, Mr. Monotony, Fiddler on the Roof, Some Other Time, Finale

*Still playing May 31, 1989. Recipient of "Tonys" for Best Musical, Best Performance by a Leading Actor in a Musical (Jason Alexander), Best Performance by a Featured Actor and Actress in a Musical (Scott Wise, Debbie Shapiro), Best Direction of a Musical, Best Lighting Design.

Martha Swope Photos
Right: "The Small House of Uncle Thomas"
Above: Charlotte d'Amboise (C) in "America"
Top: Susann Fletcher, Faith Prince, Debbie Shapiro, Mary Ann Lamb in "You Gotta Have a Gimmick"
Below: wedding from "Fiddler on the Roof"

Jason Alexander, Scott Wise, Joey McKneely, Michael Kubala

Finale

LEND ME A TENOR

By Ken Ludwig; Director, Jerry Zaks; Setting, Tony Walton; Costumes, William Ivey Long; Lighting, Paul Gallo; Sound, Aural Fixation; Hair, Angela Gari; Casting, Johnson-Liff & Zerman; Music Coordinator, Edward Strauss; Presented by Martin Starger and The Really Useful Theatre Co. (Bridget Hayward, Andrew Lloyd Webber, Keith Turner); General Manager, Robert Kamlot; Company Manager, Lisa M. Poyer; Technical Supervision, Theatrical Services (Arthur Siccardi, Peter Feller, Sr.); Props, George Wagner; Wardrobe, Karen Lloyd; Production Assistant, Richard Hester; Stage Managers, Steven Beckler, Clifford Schwartz; Press, Joshua Ellis/Adrian Bryan-Brown, Jackie Green, Susanne Tighe, Tim Ray, Chris Boneau, Shannon Barr. Opened in the Royale Theatre on Thursday, March 2, 1989*

CAST

Maggie, Max's girl friend ....J. Smith-Cameron†1
Max, assistant to Saunders .... Victor Garber†2
Saunders, Maggie's father, General Manager of the Cleveland Opera Co
....Philip Bosco
Tito Merelli, world-famous tenor, known as Il Stupendo to fans .....Ron Holgate
Maria, Tito's wife .... Tovah Feldshuh†3
Bellhop .... Jeff Brooks
Diana, a soprano ....Caroline Lagerfelt†4
Julia, Chairman of the Opera Guild .... Jane Connell

STANDBYS & UNDERSTUDIES: David Cryer (Saunders/Tito), Michael Waldron (Max/Bellhop), Jane Cronin (Maria/Julia), Eileen Dunn (Diana/Maggie)

A farce in 2 acts and 4 scenes. The action takes place in a hotel suite in Cleveland, Ohio, in 1934.

*Still playing May 31, 1989. Recipient of 1989 "Tonys" for Best Performance by a Leading Actor in a Play (Philip Bosco), and Best Direction of a Play (Jerry Zaks).

†Succeeded by: 1. Wendy Makkena, 2. Patrick Quinn, 3. Chris Callen, 4. Jane Summerhays

Martha Swope Photos

Right: Victor Garber, Philip Bosco

Above: Caroline Lagerfelt, Victor Garber

**Top: Jane Connell, Philip Bosco, Jeff Brooks,
J. Smith-Cameron**

**Victor Garber, Tovah Feldshuh, Ron Holgate, Jane Connell,
Philip Bosco**

Ron Holgate, Victor Garber

THE PAJAMA GAME

Book, George Abbott, Richard Bissell; Lyrics/Music, Richard Adler, Jerry Ross; Based on novel "7½ Cents" by Richard Bissell; Director/Choreographer, Theodore Pappas; Conductor, Peter Howard; Sets, Michael Ananta; Costumes, Marjorie McCown; Lighting, Ken Tabachnick; Chorus Master, Joseph Colaneri; Assistant Stage Directors, David Pfeiffer, Christian Smith; Musical Preparation, Stephen Sulich, William Barto Jones; Associate to Mr. Pappas, Debra Dickinson; Assistant Choreographer, Carol Schuberg; Technical Director/Production Manager, Rik Kaye, Chuck Giles; Stage Managers, Stephen Chaiken, Joseph Gasperec, John Knudsen; Props, David Fletcher, Maggie Kuypers; Hairstylist, Monserrate Alvarez; Makeup, Robert Baker; Press, Susan Woelzl, Dale Zeidman. Opened in Lincoln Center's New York State Theater on Friday, March 3, 1989*

CAST

Hines	Avery Saltzman
Prez	David Green
Joe	Jim Borstelmann
Hasler	Steve Pudenz
Gladys	Lenora Nemetz
Mae	Susan Nicely
Brenda	Joyce Campana
Poopsie	Lillian Graff
Sid Sorokin	Richard Muenz
Charlie	Louis Perry
First Helper	Scott Robertson
Second Helper	David Koch
Mabel	Brooks Almy
Babe Williams	Judy Kaye
Max	Don Yule
Pat	Paula Hostetter
Pop	William Ledbetter
Steam Heat Boys	Jim Borstelmann, David Koch

STANDBYS: Susan Terry (Babe), Karen Ziemba (Gladys), Mark Jacoby (Sid), Scott Robertson (Hines)

MUSICAL NUMBERS: Overture, The Pajama Game, Racing with the Clock, A New Town Is a Blue Town, I'm Not At all in Love, I'll Never Be Jealous Again, Hey There, Her Is, Sleep-Tite, Once in a Year Day, Small Talk, There Once Was a Man, Steam Heat, Think of the Time I Save, Hernando's Hideaway, Jealousy Ballet, Seven and a Half Cents

A musical in two acts. The action takes place in a small town in the Midwest in June of 1957.

*Closed April 16, 1989 after 51 performances. For original Broadway production see *Theatre World* Vol. 10.

Martha Swope Photos

Right: Judy Kaye, Richard Muenz
(also above center)
Top: Avery Saltzman (C)

David Green, Judy Kaye

Avery Saltzman

METAMORPHOSIS

Based on a story by Kafka; Adapted and Directed by Steven Berkoff; Musical Director, Larry Spivack; Costumes, Jacques Schmidt; Supervisor, Susan O'Donnell; Lighting, Brian Nason; Casting, Pat McCorkle; Presented by Lars Schmidt and Roger L. Stevens; General Manager, Ralph Roseman; Company Manager, Michael Lonergan; Technical Director, Jeremiah Harris; Wardrobe, Kathleen Gallagher; Stage Managers, Patrick Horrigan, Brian Meister; Press, David Powers, David Roggensack. Opened in the Ethel Barrymore Theatre on Monday, March 6, 1989*

CAST

Gregor, the son	Mikhail Baryshnikov
Mr. Samsa, his father	Rene Auberjonois
Mrs. Samsa, his mother	Laura Esterman
Greta, his sister	Madeleine Potter
Chief Clerk, his employer	Mitch Kreindel
The Lodger	T. J. Meyers

Music performed by Larry Spivack

UNDERSTUDIES: Joanna Peled (Greta/Mrs. Samsa), T. J. Meyers (Mr. Samsa/Chief Clerk), Mitch Kreindel (The Lodger)

Performed without an intermission.

*Performances suspended May 6, 1989; resumed Monday, June 12, and closed July 1, 1989, after a total of 97 performances and 5 previews.

Martha Swope Photos

Laura Esterman, Madeleine Potter, Mikhail Baryshnikov, Rene Auberjonois, Mitch Kreindel
Top Left: Mikhail Baryshnikov

RUN FOR YOUR WIFE!

By Ray Cooney; Director, Mr. Cooney; Set Supervision, Michael Anania; Costumes, Joseph G. Aulisi; Lighting, Marilyn Rennagel; Don Taffner, Paul Elliott, and Strada Entertainment Trust present the Theatre of Comedy production; General Manager, Leonard Soloway; Company Manager, Richard Berg; Production Supervision, Theatrical Services; Sound, Brian Lynch; Props, Jan Marasek; Wardrobe, Jennifer Nichols; Casting, Stuart Howard, Amy Schecter; Stage Manager, Travis Decastro; Press, Jeffrey Richards/Irene Gandy, Maria Somma, Diane Judge, Susan Chicoine, Kathryn Frawley, Jillana Devine, John Wilcox, Robert V. Thurber, Tony Armento. Opened Tuesday, March 7, 1989*

CAST

John Smith	Ray Cooney
Detective Sgt. Troughton	Gareth Hunt
Barbara Smith	Hilary Labow
Detective Sgt. Porterhouse	Dennis Ramsden
Bobby Franklyn	Gavin Reed
The Reporter	Doug Stender
Mary Smith	Kay Walbye
Stanley Gardner	Paxton Whitehead

UNDERSTUDIES: Doug Stender (John Smith/Porterhouse/Bobby), Ian Stuart (Stanley/Troughton/Reporter), Alexandra O'Karma (Barbara/Mary)

A farce in two acts. The action takes place at the present time in the Wimbledon flat of John and Mary Smith, and simultaneously in the Streatham flat of John and Barbara Smith.

*Closed April 9, 1989 after 39 performances and 15 previews.

Paxton Whitehead, Ray Cooney, Gareth Hunt

Top: Ray Cooney, Hilary LaBow, Paxton Whitehead, Kay Walbye, Dennis Ramsden

THE HEIDI CHRONICLES

By Wendy Wasserstein; Director, Daniel Sullivan; Set, Thomas Lynch; Costumes, Jennifer von Mayrhauser; Lighting, Pat Collins; Sound, Scott Lehrer; Projection Design, Wendall Harrington; Casting, Daniel Swee; Presented by the Shubert Organization, Suntory International Corp., and James Walsh in association with Playwrights Horizons; General Manager, James Walsh; Company Manager, Florie Seery; Production Coordinator, Carl Mulert; Technical Supervisors, Theatre Services; Props, Karen Caton; Wardrobe, Barbara Hladsky; Hairstylist, David H. Lawrence; Wigs, Paul Huntley; Stage Managers, Roy Harris, Mary Fran Loftus; Press, Fred Nathan Co/Marc P. Thibodeau, Philip Rinaldi, Bert Fink, Merle Frimark, Scott Taylor, Tom Naro. After 99 performances at Playwrights Horizons, it opened in the Plymouth Theatre on Thursday, March 9, 1989*

CAST

Heidi Holland	Joan Allen†1
Susan Johnston	Ellen Parker†2
Chris Boxer/Mark/TV Attendant/Waiter/Ray	Drew McVety†3
Peter Patrone	Boyd Gaines†4
Scoop Rosenbaum	Peter Friedman†5
Jill/Debbie/Lisa	Anne Lange
Becky/Clara/Denise	Cynthia Nixon†6
Fran/Molly/Betsy/April	Joanne Camp†7

UNDERSTUDIES: Laura Hicks (Heidi/Susan), Amanda Carlin (Misses Lang, Camp, Nixon), Stephen Stout (Chris/Peter/Scoop)

A play in 2 acts and 11 scenes. The action takes place from 1965 to 1989 at various locations.

†Succeeded by: 1. Christine Lahti, Brooke Adams, 2. Amy Aquino, 3. Tony Carlin, 4. David Pierce, 5. Tony Shalhoub, 6. Marita Geraghty, 7. Deborah Hedwall.

*Still playing May 31, 1989. Recipient of Pulitzer Prize, New York Drama Critics Circle Citation, Drama Desk, Dramatists Guild, Outer Critics Circle, and "Tony" for Best New Play. Boyd Gaines also received a "Tony" for Best Featured Actor in a Play.

Gerry Goodstein, Peter Cunningham Photos

Right: Joan Allen, Boyd Gaines

Above: Joan Allen, Peter Friedman

Top: Cynthia Nixon, Anne Lange, Joanne Camp, Joan Allen, Ellen Parker

Joan Allen

Boyd Gaines, Joan Allen, Peter Friedman, Joanne Camp

CHU CHEM

Book, Ted Allan; Music, Mitch Leigh; Lyrics, Jim Haines, Jack Wohl; Director, Albert Marre; Scenery, Robert Mitchell; Costumes, Kenneth M. Yount; Lighting, Jason Sturm; Sound, Gary M. Stocker; Musical/Vocal Direction, Don Jones; Orchestrations, Michael Gibson; Production Supervisor, Dwight Frye; The Mitch Leigh Company and William D. Rollnick present the Jewish Repertory Theatre production; General Management, Niko Associates (Manny Kladitis/Abbie M. Strassler); Props, James Caufield; Wardrobe, Sydney Smith; Hair, George Fraggos; Casting, Stephanie Klapper; Assistant Company Manager, Erich Hamner; Stage Managers, Geraldine Teagarden, Larry Smith, David Stoll; Press, Shirley Herz Associates/Pete Sanders, Glenna Freedman, Sam Rudy, Miller Wright. After 20 performances Off Broadway, opened in the Ritz Theatre on Friday, April 7, 1989*

CAST

The Prince	Kevin Gray†1
The Elder	Alvin Lum
Hong Ho, the Governor	Chev Rodgers
The Prince's Brother	Hechter Ubarry
Daf-ah-Dil/Concubine/Villager	Zoie Lam
The Prompter	Timm Fujii
Na Mi/Concubine/Villager	Simone Gee
Lei-An/Concubine/Villager	Keelee Seetoo
Shu-Wo/Propman/Villager	Kenji Nakao
Ho-Ke/Propman/Villager	Jason Ma
Nu-Wo/Propman/Villager	Paul Nakauchi
Chueh-Wu/Propman/Guard	Nephi Jay Wimmer
Chu Chem	Mark Zeller
Lotte	Emily Zacharias†2
Yacob	Irving Burton

STANDBYS & UNDERSTUDIES: Michael Ingram (Chu Chem/Yakob/Hong Ho), Mary Munger (Lotte), Paul Nakauchi (Prince/Prince's Brother), Nephi Jay Wimmer (Elder), Jason Ma (Prompter/Guard), Simone Gee (Daf-ah-Dil), Christine Toy (Concubines/Ladies/Na-Mi/Lei-An), David Stoll (Propmen)
MUSICAL NUMBERS: Orient Yourself, What Happened?, Welcome, You'll Have to Change, Love Is, I'll Talk to Her, Shame on You, It Must Be Good for Me, The River, We Dwell in Our Hearts, Goodbye Love, Re-Orient Yourself, I Once Believed, It's Possible, Our Kind of War, Boom!, Finale

    A play in two acts with music. The action takes place some six hundred years ago in China.

†Succeeded by: 1. Thom Sesma, 2. Mary Munger

*Closed May 14, 1989 after 45 performances and 24 previews.

Martha Swope/Carol Rosegg Photos

Right: Thom Sesma, Emily Zacharias
Above: Nephi Jay Wimmer, Chev Rodgers
Top: Emily Zacharias, Mark Zeller

Mark Zeller

Timm Fujii, Mark Zeller

WELCOME TO THE CLUB

Music, Cy Coleman; Lyrics, Cy Coleman/A. E. Hotchner; Book, A. E. Hotchner; Director, Peter Mark Schifter; Musical Numbers Staged by Patricia Birch; Scenery, David Jenkins; Costumes, William Ivey Long; Lighting, Tharon Musser; Sound, Otts Munderloh; Orchestrations, Doug Katsaros; Vocal Arrangements, Cy Coleman/David Pogue; Musical Director, David Pogue; Casting, Deborah Aquila/Don Pemrick; Hair, Angela Gari; Presented by Cy Coleman, A. E. Hotchner, William H. Kessler, Jr., Michael Weatherly in association with Raymond J. Greenwald; Associate Producer, Robert R. Larsen; General Management, Richard Seader/Sylrich Management; Company Manager, Paul B. Berkowsky; Props, Heather Herbert, Alan Stern; Wardrobe, Alyce Gilbert; Dance Captain, Terri White; Production Assistant, Emily Adler; Stage Managers, John C. McNamara, Victor Lukas; Press, Jeffrey Richards Associates/Irene Gandy, Diane Judge, Susan Chicoine, Maria Somma, Kathryn Frawley, Jillana Devine, Tony Armento, Robert Thurber, Michael Trent. Opened in the Music Box on Thursday, April 13, 1989*

CAST

Arlene Meltzer	Marilyn Sokol
Milton Meltzer	Avery Schreiber
Gus Bottomly	Bill Buell
Aaron Bates	Scott Wentworth
Bruce Aiken	Samuel E. Wright
Kevin Bursteter	Scott Waara
Betty Bursteter	Jodi Benson
Carol Bates	Marcia Mitzman
Eve Aiken	Terri White
Winona Shook	Sally Mayes

UNDERSTUDIES: Joanna Glushak (Arlene/Betty/Carol), Sal Mistretta (Gus/Bruce), Walter Hudson (Aaron/Kevin)

MUSICAL NUMBERS: Overture, A Place Called Alimony Jail, Pay the Lawyer, Mrs. Meltzer Wants the Money Now!, That's a Woman, Piece of Cake, Rio, Holidays, The Trouble with You, Mother-in-Law, At My Side, Southern Comfort, The Two of Us, It's Love! It's Love!, The Name of Love, Miami Beach, Guilty, Love Behind Bars, It Wouldn't Be You

A musical in two acts. The action takes place at the present time in a section of a New York City jail exclusively reserved for alimony delinquents.

*Closed April 22, 1989 after 12 performances and 20 previews.

Peter Cunningham Photos

Left: Terri White, Marcia Mitzman, Scott Wentworth, Jodi Benson
Above: Mitzman, Sokol, Benson, White, Avery Schreiber
Top: Wentworth, Wright, Waara, Sokol

Avery Schreiber, Marilyn Sokol, Bill Buell

Avery Schreiber, Scott Waara, Scott Wentworth, Marilyn Sokol, Samuel Wright

Barry Manilow

BARRY MANILOW
AT THE GERSHWIN

Presented by Garry C. Kief, James M. Nederlander, James L. Nederlander, Arthur Rubin; Director, Production Created and Produced by Joe Gannon; Written by Ken and Mitzie Welch, Roberta Kent, Barry Manilow; Designer, Jeremy Railton; Lighting, J. T. McDonald; Music Director/Drums, Bud Harner; Music Director/Keyboards, Ron Pedley; Vocals, Debra Byrd; Production Manager, Gary Speakman; Stage Manager, Jed DeFillipis; Production Associates, Randy Doney, Kathy Carey; Wardrobe, Philip Dennis; Press, Solters/Roskin/Friedman, Keith Sherman, Susan DuBow. Opened in the Gershwin Theatre on Tuesday, April 18, 1989*

CAST

BARRY MANILOW

Vanessa Brown (Percussion/Vocals), Debra Byrd (Vocals), Billy Kidd (Keyboards/Vocals), Marc Levine (Bass Guitar/Vocals), Joe Melotti (Keyboards/Vocals), John Pondel (Guitar/Vocals), Dana Robbins (Woodwinds/Vocals)

Performed with one intermission.

*Closed June 10, 1989 after 44 performances.

THE PLAYERS CLUB
CENTENNIAL SALUTE

Producer, Terry Hodge Taylor; Director, Tony Stevens; Musical Conductor, Linda Twine; Written by Bill Rosenfield; Lighting, Marc B. Weiss; Music Coordinator, John Monaco; Costumer, David Toser; Stage Manager, John Bonnani; Press, Richard P. Pheneger. Produced and Presented by Hodge Taylor Associates in the Shubert Theatre for one performance only Sunday, April 23, 1989.

CAST

Jose Ferrer (Master of Ceremonies), Cindy Adams, Debby Boone, Betty Comden, Carmen de Lavallade, Andre DeShields, Ron Devito Dancers, Dolores Gray, Jack Gilford, Adolph Green, Geoffrey Holder, George S. Irving, Werner Klemperer, Juliette Koka, Emily Loesser, Robert Merrill, Patrice Munsel, Phyllis Newman, Lee Roy Reams, Arthur Rubin, Jo Sullivan, Julie Wilson; Induction of the first women members: Theoni V. Aldredge, Lauren Bacall, Bridgett Brodkin, Carol Burnett, Betty Comden, Jean Dalrymple, Agnes De Mille, Nancy Evans, Elizabeth Falk, Lillian Gish, June Havoc, Helen Hayes, Beth Holland, Sylvia Fine Kaye, Florence Klotz, Angela Lansbury, Lucille Lortel, Dina Merrill, Ruth Mitchell, Mary Tyler Moore, Toni Morrison, Phyllis Newman, Jane Pauley, Leontyne Price, Marian Seldes, Sylvia Sidney, Liz Smith, Isabelle Stevenson, Gwen Verdon, Eudora Welty, escorted by Dick Cavett, Howard Cosell, Alfred Drake, Jack Gilford, Morton Gottlieb, Vartan Gregorian, Al Hirschfeld, Barnard Hughes, Garson Kanin, James MacArthur, Burgess Meredith, Harold Prince, Jason Robards, John Rubinstein, Vincent Sardi, Gerald Schoenfeld, Willard Swire, Eli Wallach, Arthur Whitelaw

Miss Helen Hayes was inducted as the first woman member and was presented with the first Edwin Booth Award for Lifetime Achievement in the Theatre.

Jose Ferrer, Helen Hayes, Burgess Meredith

STARMITES

Music and Lyrics, Barry Keating; Book, Stuart Ross, Barry Keating; Directed and Staged by Larry Carpenter; Choreography, Michele Assaf; Assistant Choreographer, T. C. Charlton; Sets, Lowell Detweiler; Costumes, Susan Hirschfeld; Lighting, Jason Kantrowitz; Sound, John Kilgore; Musical Direction/Dance Arrangements, Henry Aronson; Orchestrations/Sound Effects, James McElwaine; Vocal Arrangements/ Associate Musical Director, Dianne Adams; Casting, Julie Hughes, Barry Moss; Presented by Hinks Shimberg, Mary Keil, Steven Warnick; Associate Producers, Peter Bogyo, John Burt, Severn Sandt; General Manager, Albert Poland; Company Manager, Mitchell A. Weiss; Dance Captain, John-Michael Flate; Production Assistant, Jennifer Brown; Special Effects, Gregory Meeh; Technical Direction, Jeremiah Harris Associates; Hairstylist, John Quaglia; Wardrobe, Dawn Walnut; Stage Managers, Zoya Wyeth, Mary Ellen Allison, John-Michael Flate; Press, Shirley Herz Associates/Glenna Friedman, Pete Sanders, Sam Rudy, Miller Wright. Opened the new Criterion Center Stage Right on Thursday, April 27, 1989*

CAST

ON EARTH:
Eleanor .... Liz Larsen
Mother ....Sharon McNight
INNERSPACE:
Shak Graa .... Ariel Grabber
Spacepunk .... Brian Lane Green
Trinkulus ....Gabriel Barre
STARMITES:
Ack Ack Ackerman .... Bennett Cale
Herbie Harrison .... Victor Trent Cook
Dazzle Razzledorf ....Christopher Zelno
Diva ....Sharon McNight
Bizarbara .... Liz Larsen
BANSHEES:
Shotzi ....Mary Kate Law
Canibelle ....Gwen Stewart
Balbraka ....Freida Williams
Maligna ....Janet Aldrich
Droids ....John-Michael Flate, Ric Ryder

UNDERSTUDIES: Wendy-Jo Vaughn (Eleanor/Bizarbara/Banshees/Droid), Janet Aldrich (Mother/Diva), John-Michael Flate (Shak Graa/Spacepunk/Trinkulus), Ric Ryder (Starmites)

MUSICAL NUMBERS: Superhero Girl, Starmites, Trink's Narration, Afraid of the Dark, Little Hero, Attack of Banshees, Hard to Be a Diva, Love Duet, The Dance of Spousal Arousal, Finaletto, Bizarbara's Wedding, Milady, Beauty Within, The Cruelty Stomp, Reach Right Down, Immolation, Finale

A musical in 2 acts and 9 scenes with a prologue and epilogue. The action takes place now on earth and in Innerspace.

*Closed June 18, 1989 after 60 performances and 35 previews.

Martha Swope Photos

Right: Sharon McNight, Liz Larsen; Brian Lane Green
Above: Green, Christopher Zelno, Bennett Cale,
Victor Treat Cook
Top: Green, Larsen, Sharon McNight (standing)

Liz Larsen

Brian Lane Green, Liz Larsen

GHETTO

or "The Last Performance in the Vilna Ghetto" by Joshua Sobol; Translated by David Lan; Director, Gedalia Besser; English Lyrics, Jeremy Sams; Musical Direction/Arrangements, William Schimmel; Movement, Nir Ben Gal, Liat Dror; Fight Direction, B. H. Barry; Set, Adrian Vaux; Costumes, Edna Sobol; Lighting, Kevin Rigdon; Casting, Julie Hughes/Barry Moss; Presented by Circle in the Square Theatre (Theodore Mann, Artistic Director; Paul Libin, Producing Director); Company Managers, Susan Elrod, William Schaeffer; Props, Frank Hauser; Wardrobe, Claire Libin; Stage Managers, Wm. Hare, A. Robert Scott; Press, Merle Debuskey, Leo Stern. Opened in the Circle in the Square Theatre on Sunday, April 30, 1989*

CAST

Srulik, a ventriloquist	Avner Eisenberg
Kittel	Stephen McHattie
Hayyah	Helen Schneider
The Dummy	Gordon Joseph Weiss
Gens	George Hearn
The Hassid	Jerry Matz
Weiskopf	Donal Donnelly
Kruk	Jarlath Conroy
Haiken	Marshall Coid
Reed Player	David Hopkins
Guitar Player	Barry Mitterhoff
Accordion Player	William Swindler
Miriam	Julie Goell
Ooma, Dr. Weiner	Alma Cuervo
The Rich Man	Richard M. Davidson
Dr. Gottlieb	Jerry Matz
A Judge	David Rosenbaum
Luba	Andrea Clark Libin
Yankel	Jon Rothstein
Yitzhak Geivish	Matthew P. Mutrie
Elia Geivish	Jonathan Mann
Dessler	William Verderber
Jewish Policeman Averbuch	Ahvi Spindell
Jewish Policeman Levas	Angelo Ragonesi
A Woman	Julie Anne Eigenberg
German Soldiers	Brian Maffitt, Spike McClure

UNDERSTUDIES: William Verderber (Gens), Spike McClure (Kittel), Julie Anne Eigenberg (Hayyah/Dr. Weiner), Ahvi Spindell (The Hassid/Dr. Gottlieb), Jerry Matz (Srulik), David Rosenbaum (Kruk)

A drama in two acts. The action takes place in and around the theatre in the Vilna ghetto under the Nazi occupation from September 1941 to its liquidation two years later.

*Closed May 28, 1989 after 33 performances and 25 previews.

Martha Swope Photos

Top Right: George Hearn, Donal Donnelly, Stephen McHattie
Right: Helen Schneider, Stephen McHattie

Avner Eisenberg, Gordon Joseph Weiss, Helen Schneider

Jarlath Conroy, Stephen McHattie

LARGELY NEW YORK

Written and Directed by Bill Irwin; Scenic Design, Douglas Stein; Costumes, Rose Pederson; Lighting, Nancy Schertler; Sound, Bob Bielecki; Video Design, Dennis Diamond/Video D Studios; Collaborator/Production Stage Manager, Nancy Harrington; Original Steps/Routines, Margaret Eginton, Leon Chesney and Steve Clemente; Choreography, Bill Irwin/Kimi Okada; Presented by James B. Freydberg, Kenneth Feld, Jerry L. Cohen, Max Weitzenhoffer, the John F. Kennedy Center for the Performing Arts, and the Walt Disney Studios; Executive Producer, Robin Ullman; General Management, Fremont Associates; James B. Freydberg, Dana Sherman; Producing Associate, Susan West; Company Manager, Dana Sherman; Dance Captain, Lori Vadino; Props, Nicholas Laudano; Wardrobe, Jean Steinlein; Stage Managers, Anna Jo Gender, Mitchell Hamilton; Press, Fred Nathan Co./Marc P. Thibodeau, Bert Fink, Merle Frimark, Scott Taylor, James Morrison. Opened in the St. James Theatre on Monday, May 1, 1989*

CAST

The Post-Modern Hoofer .... Bill Irwin
The Poppers .... Leon Chesney, Steve Clemente
The Soloist ....Margaret Eginton
The Videographer ....Dennis Diamond
The Video Assistant .... Debra Elise Miller
The Dean ....Jeff Gordon

ENSEMBLE: Michael Barber, Jon E. Brandenberg, Chris Quay Davis, Patti Dobrowolski, Raymond Houle, Amy Mack, Karen Omahen, Lori Vadino, Cindy Sue Williams, Toni Wisti, Christina Youngman
UNDERSTUDIES: Christina Youngman (Soloist), John Christian (Poppers), Michael Barber (Dean), Mitchell Hamilton (Videographer/Assistant)

Recipient of New York Drama Critics Circle Special Citation.

*Closed Sept. 2, 1989 after 157 performances and 11 previews.

Joan Marcus, Bob Marshak Photos

Left: Steve Clemente, Leon Chesney, Bill Irwin
Top: Margaret Eginton, Jeff Gordon, Steve Clemente,
Leon Chesney, Bill Irwin

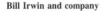

Bill Irwin and company

Bill Irwin

BROADWAY PRODUCTIONS FROM PREVIOUS SEASONS THAT PLAYED THROUGH THIS SEASON

A CHORUS LINE

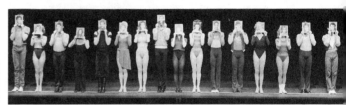

Conceived, Choreographed and Directed by Michael Bennett; Book, James Kirkwood, Nicholas Dante; Music, Marvin Hamlisch; Lyrics, Edward Kleban; Co-choreographer, Bob Avian; A New York Shakespeare Festival Production presented by Joseph Papp in association with Plum Productions; Musical Direction/Vocal Arrangements, Don Pippin; Orchestrations, Bill Byers, Hershy Kay, Jonathan Tunick; Setting, Robin Wagner; Costumes, Theoni V. Aldredge; Lighting, Tharon Musser; Sound, Abe Jacob; Music Director, Jerry Goldberg; Music Coordinator, Robert Thomas; Associate Producer, Bernard Gersten; Original Cast Album by Columbia Records; Assistant to Choreographers, Baayork Lee; Company Manager, Robert Reilly; Dance Captain, Troy Garza; Wardrobe, Alyce Gilbert; Stage Managers, Tom Porter, Ronald Stafford, Morris Freed, Fraser Ellis; Press, Merle Debuskey, William Schelble; Opened in the Shubert Theatre on Friday, July 25, 1975*

CAST

Roy	Dale Stotts
Kristine	Flynn McMichaels
Sheila	Dana Moore †1
Mike	Danny Herman †2
Val	Wanda Richert †3
Butch	Michael-Pierre Dean †4
Larry	J. Richard Hart †5
Maggie	Dorothy Tancredi †6
Richie	Bruce Anthony Davis †7
Tricia	Robin Lyon
Tom	Frank Kliegel †8
Zach	Robert LuPone †9
Mark	Andrew Grose †10
Cassie	Laurie Gamache
Judy	Cindi Klinger †11
Lois	Julie Tussey
Don	Michael Danek
Bebe	Karen Ziemba †12
Connie	Sachi Shimizu
Diana	Denise DiRenzo †13
Al	Tommy Re †14
Frank	William Mead
Greg	Bradley Jones †15
Bobby	Ron Kurowski
Paul	Wayne Meledandri †16
Vicki	Cynthia Fleming
Ed	Morris Freed †17
Jarad	Troy Garza
Linda	Niki Harris
Douglas	Gary Chryst †18
Herman	Fraser Ellis
Hilary	Arminae Azarian †19

MUSICAL NUMBERS: I Hope I Get It, I Can Do That, And. . . ., At the Ballet, Sing!, Hello 12 Hello 13 Hello Love, Nothing, Dance 10 Looks 3, The Music and the Mirror, One, The Tap Combination, What I Did for Love, Finale

A musical performed without intermission. The action takes place in 1975 during an audition in this theatre.

†Succeeded by: 1. Susan Danielle, 2. Michael Gruber, 3. Diana Kavilis, 4. Kevin Chinn, Glenn Turner, 5. Kevin Neil McCready, 6. Dorothy Dybisz, Michele Pigliavento, Susan Santoro, 7. Gordon Owens, 8. Carlos Lopez, 9. Scott Pearson, Randy Clements, Robert LuPone, 10. Matt Zarley, 11. Angelique Ilo, 12. Beth Swearingen, Christine Maglione, 13. Arminae Azarian, 14. Stephen Bourneuf, 15. Ron Navarre, 16. Drew Geraci, 17. Tom Kosis, 18. Frank Kliegel, 19. Kathleen Moore, Donna M. Pompei

*Still playing May 31, 1989. Cited as Best Musical of 1975 by NY Drama Critics Circle, winner of 1976 Pulitzer Prize, and 1976 "Tonys" for Best Musical, Book, Score, Direction, Lighting, Choreography, Best Actress in a Musical (Donna McKechnie), Best Featured Actor and Actress in a Musical (Sammy Williams, Kelly Bishop), and a Special Theatre World Award was presented to each member of the creative staff and original cast. See *Theatre World* Vol. 31. On Thursday, Sept. 29, 1983 it became the longest running production in Broadway history.

Martha Swope Photos

Right Center: Laurie Gamache

Drew Geraci (center)

CATS

Based on "Old Possum's Book of Practical Cats" by T. S. Eliot; Additional Lyrics, Trevor Nunn, Richard Stilgoe; Music, Andrew Lloyd Webber; Director, Trevor Nunn; Associate Director/Choreographer, Gillian Lynne; Presented by Cameron Macintosh, The Really Useful Co., David Geffen, The Shubert Organization; Executive Producers, R. Tyler Gatchell, Jr., Peter Neufeld; Design, John Napier; Lighting, David Hersey; Sound, Martin Levan; Musical Directors, Stanley Lebowsky, Jack Gaughan, David Caddick; Casting, Johnson-Liff & Zerman; Orchestrations, David Cullen, Andrew Lloyd Webber; Original cast album by Geffen Records & Tapes; Production Supervisor, Jeff Lee; Dance Supervisor, Richard Stafford; Company Manager, James G. Mennen; Assistant Choreographer, Jo-Anne Robinson; Makeup, Candace Carell; Wigs, Paul Huntley; Associate Conductor, Bill Grossman; Production Assistant, Nancy Hall; Props, George Green, Jr., Merlyn Davis; Wardrobe, Adelaide Laurino, Rachele Bussanich; Hairstylists, Leon Gagliardi, Frank Paul; Stage Managers, Sally J. Jacobs, Dan Hild, Peggy Peterson; Press, Fred Nathan/ Merle Frimark, Bert Fink, Marc P. Thibodeau, James Morrison, Scott Taylor. Opened in the Winter Garden Theatre on Thursday, October 7, 1982*

CAST

Alonzo	Scott Taylor
Bustopher Jones/Asparagus Growlinger	Stephen Hanan [1]
Bombalurina	Marlene Danielle
Cassandra	Julietta Marcelli
Coricopat	Johnny Anzalone
Mungojerrie	Ray Roderick
Demeter	Patricia Ruck [2]
Grizabella	Loni Ackerman
Jellylorum/Griddlebone	Bonnie Simmons
Jennyanydots	Anna McNeely [3]
Mistoffelees	Kevin Poe [4]
Munkustrap	Robert Amirante
Old Deuteronomy	Larry Small
Plato/Macavity/Rumpus Cat	Jamie Patterson
Pouncival	John Joseph Festa
Rumpleteazer	Paige Dana [5]
Rum Tum Tugger	Frank Mastrocola
Sillabub	Susan Santoro [6]
Skimbleshanks	Robert Burnett [7]
Tantomile	Sandy Leigh Leake [8]
Tumblebrutus	Jay Poindexter
Victoria	Claudia Shell
Cats Chorus	Michael DeVries, Jay Aubrey Jones, Bryan Landrine, Susan Powers, Heidi Stallings

STANDBYS & UNDERSTUDIES: John Aller/Brian Andrews/Jack Magradey/ Greg Minahan (Alonzo), Bryan Landrine (Bustopher/Asparagus/Growltiger), Rebecca Timms/N. Elaine Wiggins (Bombalurina), Rebecca Timms/N. Elaine Wiggins/Lily-Lee Wong (Cassandra), John Aller/Wade Laboissonniere/Jack Magradey/ Greg Minahan (Coriocopat), Rebecca Timms/N. Elaine Wiggins (Demeter), Heidi Stallings/Beth Swearingen (Grizabella), Marcy DeGonge/Susan Powers (Jellylorum/Griddlebone), Marcy DeGonge/Susan Powers/Suzanne Viverito (Jennyanydots), Johnny Anzalone/John Joseph Festa/Richard Stafford (Mistoffelees), Brian Andrews/Wade Laboissonniere/Jack Magradey/Greg Minahan (Mungojerrie), John Aller/Jack Magradey/Scott Taylor (Munkustrap), Jay Aubrey Jones/Bryan Laudrine (Old Deuteronomy), Brian Andrews/Wade Laboissonniere (Pouncival), Suzanne Viverito/Lily-Lee Wong (Rumpleteazer), John Aller/Jack Magradey/Greg Minahan (Rum Tum Tugger).
MUSICAL NUMBERS: Jellicle Songs for Jellicle Cats, The Naming of the Cats, Invitation to the Jellicle Ball, The Old Gumbie Cat, The Rum Tum Tugger, Grizabella the Glamour Cat, Bustopher Jones, Mungojerrie and Rumpleteazer, Old Deuteronomy, The Awefull Battle of the Pekes and Pollicles, Marching Songs of the Pollice Dogs, The Jellicle Ball, Memory, Moments of Happiness, Gus the Theatre Cat, Growltiger's Last Stand, Skimbleshanks, Macavity, Mr. Mistoffelees, Journey to the Heavyside Layer, The Ad-Dressing of Cats

A musical in 2 acts and 12 scenes.

*Still playing May 31, 1989. Winner of 1983 "Tonys" for Best Musical, Book, Score, Direction, Supporting Musical Actress (Betty Buckley as Grizabella), Costumes, and Lighting. For original production, see *Theatre World* Vol. 39.

†Succeeded by: 1. Paul Harman, 2. Beth Swearingen, 3. Marcy DeGonge, 4. Michael Barriskill, 5. Kristi Lynes, 6. Dana Walker, 7. Richard Stafford, 8. Lisa Dawn Cave

Top Right: Larry Small, Loni Ackerman
Martha Swope Photos

INTO THE WOODS

Music/Lyrics, Stephen Sondheim; Book, James Lapine; Presented by Heidi Landesman, Rocco Landesman, Rick Steiner, M. Anthony Fisher, Frederic H. Mayerson, Jujamcyn Theaters; Associate Producers, Greg C. Mosher, Paula Fisher, David Brode, The Mutual Benefit Companies/Fifth Avenue Productions; Executive Producer, Michael David; Settings, Tony Straiges; Lighting, Richard Nelson; Costumes, Ann Hould-Ward; Magic Consultant, Charles Reynolds; Sound, Alan Stieb, James Brousseau; Hairstylist, Phyllis Della Illien; Costumes, based on original concepts by Patricia Zipprodt, Ann Hould-Ward; Orchestrations, Jonathan Tunick; Musical Director, Paul Gemignani; Musical Staging, Lar Lubovitch; Casting, Joanna Merlin; General Management, David Strong Warner Inc./Michael David, Edward Strong, Sherman Warner; Company Manager, Sandra Carlson; Production Supervisor, Peter Feller, Sr.; Props, Liam Herbert, Michael Fedigan; Wardrobe, Nancy Schaefer; Production Assistant, Chris Felder; Stage Managers, Frank Hartenstein, Johnna Murray, Marianne Cane, James Dawson, Karen Armstrong, Donna A. Drake; Press, Joshua Ellis Office/Adrian Bryan-Brown, Jackie Green, Leo Stern, Bill Shuttleworth, Susanne Tighe, David Fuhrer, Tim Ray, Chris Boneau, Kevin McAnarney. Opened in the Martin Beck Theatre on Thursday, November 5, 1987*

CAST

Narrator	Tom Aldredge †1
Cinderella	Kim Crosby
Jack	Ben Wright †2
Baker	Chip Zien †3
Baker's Wife	Joanna Gleason †4
Cinderella's Stepmother	Joy Franz
Florinda	Kay McClelland †5
Lucinda	Lauren Mitchell †6
Jack's Mother	Barbara Bryne
Little Red Riding Hood	Danielle Ferland †7
Witch	Bernadette Peters †8
Cinderella's Father	Edmund Lyndeck
Cinderella's Mother	Merle Louise
Mysterious Man	Tom Aldredge †9
Wolf	Robert Westenberg
Rapunzel	Pamela Winslow †10
Rapunzel's Prince	Chuck Wagner †11
Grandmother	Merle Louise
Cinderella's Prince	Robert Westenberg
Steward	Philip Hoffman †12
Giant	Merle Louise
Snow White	Jean Kelly †13
Sleeping Beauty	Maureen Davis

MUSICAL NUMBERS: Into the Woods, Hello Little Girl, I Guess This Is Goodbye, Maybe They're Magic, I Know Things Now, A Very Nice Prince, Giants in the Sky, Agony, It Takes Two, Stay with Me, On the Steps of the Palace, Ever After, So Happy, Lament, Any Moment, Moments in the Woods, Your Fault, Last Midnight, No More, No One Is Alone, Children Will Listen

A musical in two acts.

†Succeeded by: 1. Dick Cavett, Tom Aldredge, 2. Jeff Blumenkrantz, Ben Wright, 3. Philip Hoffman, Chip Zien, 4. Mary Gordon Murray, Cynthia Sikes, Kay McClelland, 5. Susan Gordon Clark, 6. Teresa Burrell, 7. LuAnne Ponce, 8. Phylicia Rashad, Betsy Joslyn, Nancy Dussault, Joy Franz, 9. Edmund Lyndeck, Tom Aldredge, 10. Marin Mazzie, 11. Dean Butler, 12. Greg Zerkle, Adam Grupper, 13. Heather Shulman, Cindy Robinson

*Closed Sept. 3, 1989 after 764 performances and 43 previews. Winner of 1988 "Tonys" for Best Book of a Musical, Original Score, Leading Actress in a Musical (Joanna Gleason).

Top Right: (L) Phylicia Rashad
(R) Nancy Dussault
Right Center: Chip Zien, Betsy Joslyn, Mary Gordon Murray

Cynthia Sikes, Robert Westenberg

LES MISERABLES

Book, Alain Boublil, Claude-Michel Schonberg; Based on novel of same title by Victor Hugo; Music, Claude-Michel Schonberg; Lyrics, Herbert Kretzmer; Additional material, James Fenton; Orchestral Score, John Cameron; Musical Supervision/Direction, Robert Billig; Sound, Andrew Bruce/Autograph; Associate Director/Executive Producer, Richard Jay-Alexander; Executive Producer, Martin McCallum; Casting, Johnson-Liff & Zerman; General Management, Alan Wasser; Design, John Napier; Lighting, David Hersey; Costumes, Andreane Neofitou; Presented by Cameron Mackintosh; Directed/Adapted by Trevor Nunn, John Caird; Original Cast recording on Geffen Records/Tapes/Discs; Production Supervisor, Sam Stickler; Technical Manager, John H. Paull III; Props, Timothy Abel; Wardrobe, Adelaide Laurino, John Laurino; Assistant Conductor, Jay Alger; Company Managers, Mark S. Andrews, Harriett Kittner; General Managers, Alan Wasser, Allan Williams; Associate Production Manager, Marie Barrett; Stage Managers, Marybeth Abel, Deborah Clelland, Michael John Egan; Press, Fred Nathan Co./Marc Thibodeau, Merle Frimark, Bert Fink, Philip Rinaldi, Scott Taylor, James Morrison. Opened in the Broadway Theatre on Thursday, March 12, 1987*

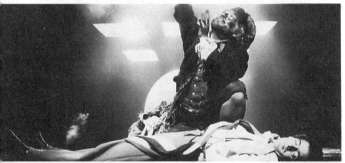

CAST

Prologue: 1815, Digne. Colm Wilkinson †1 (Jean Valjean), Terence Mann †2 (Javert), Tim Shew, Joel Robertson, Stephen Bogardus, John Dewar, Leo Burmeister, Joseph Kolinski, Ray Walker, Bruce Kuhn, Michael Maguire †3, J. C. Sheets, Tom Zemon, Ed Dixon, Hugh Panaro, Jordan Leeds (Chain Gang), Jesse Corti †4 (Farmer), Bruce Kuhn (Labourer), Susan Goodman (Innkeeper's Wife), John Norman Thomas (Innkeeper), Norman Large †5 (Bishop), Marcus Lovett, Steve Shocket †6 (Constables)
1823 Montreuil-sur-Mer: Randy Graff †7 (Fantine), Joel Robertson (Foreman), Jeffrey Clonts, John Dewar, Jessica Molaskey, Olga Merediz, Cissy Rebich, Jean Fitzgibbons (Workers), Ann Crum †8 (Factory Girl), Jordan Leeds, J. C. Sheets, John Dewar (Sailors), Anne Marie Runolfsson, Jean Fitzgibbons, Cissy Rebich, Natalie Toro, Susan Goodman, Lisa Ann Grant, Tracy Shayne, Gretchen Kingsley-Weihe (Whores), Cindy Benson †9 (Old Woman), Olga Merediz (Crone), Steve Schocket (Pimp/Fauchelevent)
1823 Montfermeil: Donna Vivino, Daisy Eagan, Shanelle Workman (Young Cosette), Jennifer Butt (Mme. Thenardier), Leo Burmeister †10 (Thenardier), Shanelle Workman, Daisy Eagan (Young Eponine), Jeffrey Clonts (Drinker), Bruce Kuhn, Gretchen Kingsley-Weihe (Young Couple), John Norman Thomas (Drunk), Pete Herber, Jean Fitzgibbons (Diners), Steve Schocket, Tom Zemon, J. C. Sheets, Jessica Molaskey, Susan Goodman, Anne Marie Runolfsson (Drinkers), Joseph Kolinski †11 (Young Man), Cissy Rebich, Lisa Ann Grant (Young Girls), Olga Merediz, John Dewar (Old Couple), Joel Robertson, Willy Falk (Travelers)
1832 Paris: Danny Gerard (Gavroche), Susan Goodman (Old Beggar), Anne Marie Runolfsson (Young Whore), John Norman Thomas (Pimp), Frances Ruffelle (Eponine), Bruce Kuhn, Willy Falk, J. C. Sheets, Steve Schocket (Thenardier's Gang), Michael Maguire †3 (Enjolras), Ray Walker †12 (Marius), Judy Kuhn †13 (Cosette), Joel Robertson (Combeferre), Jordan Leeds (Feuilly), Jeffrey Clonts (Courfeyrac), John Dewar (Joly), Tom Zemon (Grantaire), Pete Herber (Lesgles), John Norman Thomas (Jean Prouvaire)

MUSICAL NUMBERS: Prologue, Soliloquy, At the End of the Day, I Dreamed a Dream, Lovely Ladies, Who Am I?, Come to Me, Castle on a Cloud, Master of the House, Thenardier Waltz, Look Down, Stars, Red and Black, Do You Hear the People Sing?, In My Life, A Heart Full of Love, One Day More, On My Own, A Little Fall of Rain, Drink with Me to Days Gone By, Bring Him Home, Dog Eats Dog, Turning, Empty Chairs at Empty Tables, Wedding Chorale, Beggars at the Feast, Finale

A dramatic musical in 2 acts and 4 scenes with a prologue.

† Succeeded by: 1. Gary Morris, Tim Shew, William Solo, Craig Schulman, 2. Anthony Crivello, Norman Large, Herndon Lackey, Peter Samuels, 3. Joseph Kolinski, 4. Jeffrey Clonts, 5. Anthony Crivello, Steve Schocket, 6. Pete Herber, 7. Susan Dawn Carson, Laurie Beechman, 8. Janene Lovullo, Anne Marie Runolfsson, 9. Jessica Molaskey, 10. Ed Dixon, 11. Jordan Leeds, 12. Hugh Panaro, 13. Tracy Shayne

Bob Marshak, Peter Cunningham Photos
Left Center: Laurie Beechman, Herndon Lackey

Above: Ed Dixon Top: Tim Shew

Leo Burmester, Jennifer Butt

M. BUTTERFLY

By David Henry Hwang; Director, John Dexter; Presented by Stuart Ostrow, David Geffen; Scenery/Costumes, Eiko Ishioka; Lighting, Andy Phillips; Hairstylist, Phyllis Della Illien; Music, Giacomo Puccini, Lucia Hwong; Casting, Meg Simon/Fran Kumin; Peking Opera Consultants, Jamie H. J. Guan, Michele Ehlers; General Management, Joseph Harris Associates/Steven E. Goldstein, Peter T. Kulok, Nancy Simmons; Technical Supervision, Jeremiah J. Harris Associates; Props, Joseph Harris, Jr.; Wardrobe, Barrett Hong; Musical Director, Lucia Hwong; Management Associate, Gerri Higgins; Sound, Peter J. Fitzgerald; Make-up, Joe Compayno; Music Coordinator, John Miller; Live Music arranged by Jason Hwong, Yukio Tsuji; Stage Managers, Bob Borod, Barry Kearsley; Press, John Springer, Gary Springer. Opened in the Eugene O'Neill Theatre on Sunday, March 20, 1988*

CAST

Kurogo ....Alec Mapa †1, Chris Odo †2,
....H. J. Guan †3
Rene Gallimard ....John Lithgow †4
Song Liling ....B. D. Wong †5
Marc/Man 2/Consul Sharpless ....John Getz †6
Renee/Woman at party/Girl in magazine ....Lindsay Frost †7
Comrade Chin/Suzuki/ShuFang ....Lori Tan Chinn †8
Helga ....Rose Gregorio †9
M. Toulon/Man 1/Judge ....George N. Martin †10

A drama in three acts with one intermission. The action takes place in a Paris prison in 1988, and in recall: The years 1960–1986 in Beijing and Paris.

†Succeeded by: 1. Chris Odo, 3. Alan Ariano, 4. David Dukes, John Rubinstein, Tony Randall, 5. Alec Mapa, 6. Richard Poe, Curt Karibalis, 7. Kathryn Layng, Lolita Lesheim, 8. Ann Harada, 9. Pamela Payton-Wright, 10. Tom Klunis, George Martin

*Still playing May 31, 1989. "Tonys" were awarded for Best Play, Best Featured Actor in a Play (B. D. Wong), Best Direction of a Play.

**Left: Alec Mapa (L), George Martin (C), John Rubinstein (R)
Top: Alec Mapa, John Rubinstein**

John Rubinstein, Alec Mapa

Tony Randall, Alec Mapa

ME AND MY GIRL

Book and Lyrics, L. Arthur Rose, Douglas Furber; Music, Noel Gay; Book Revision, Stephen Fry, Mike Ockrent; Director, Mike Ockrent; Presented by Richard Armitage, Terry Allen Kramer, James M. Nederlander; Stage Promotions Ltd.; Choreography, Gillian Gregory; Sets, Martin Johns; Costumes, Ann Curtis; Lighting, Chris Ellis, Roger Morgan; Musical Direction, Stanley Lebowsky; Sound, Tom Baker; Casting, Howard Feuer; General Manager, Ralph Roseman; Company Manager, Robb Lady; Technical Director, Jeremiah Harris; Props, Joseph Harris, Jr., Ted Wondsel; Wardrobe, Linda Berry, Cissy Obidowski; Dance Captain, Tony Parise; Wigs, Tiv Davenport, Antonio Belo; Make-up, Margaret Sunshine; Hairstylist, Paul Huntley; Associate Music Director, Tom Helm; Stage Managers, Steven Zweigbaum, Arturo E. Porazzi, Tracy Crum; Press, Jeffrey Richards/C. George Willard, Ben Morse, Susan Lee, Marie-Louise Silva, Ken Mandelbaum, Audrey Scheiderman. Opened the new Marquis Marriott Theatre on Sunday, August 10, 1986*

CAST

Lady Jacqueline Carstone .... Jane Summerhays †1
Honorable Gerald Bolingbroke .... Nick Ullett †2
Lord Battersby ....Eric Hutson †3
Lady Battersby .... Justine Johnston †4
Stockbrokers .... Cleve Asbury †5, Randy Hills,
Barry McNabb †6
Footman ....Larry Hansen
Herbert Parchester .... Timothy Jerome
Sir Jasper Tring ....Leo Leyden
Maria, Duchess of JDJene .... Jane Connell †7
Sir John Tremayne .... George S. Irving †8
Charles Heathersett, butler .... Thomas Toner
Bill Snibson .... Robert Lindsay †9
Sally Smith ....Maryann Plunkett †10
Pub Pianist ....John Spalla
Mrs. Worthington-Worthington .... Gloria Hodes
Lady Diss .... Elizabeth Larner †11
Lady Brighton/Lambeth Tart .... Susan Cella †12
Bob Barking .... Kenneth H. Waller †13
Telegraph Boy ....Bill Brassea †14
Constable ....Eric Johnson †15
Mrs. Brown .... Elizabeth Larner †16

MUSICAL NUMBERS: A Weekend at Hareford, Thinking of No One but Me, The Family Solicitor, Me and My Girl, An English Gentleman, You Would if You Could, Hold My Hand, Once You Lose Your Heart, Preparation Fugue, The Lambeth Walk, The Sun Has Got His Hat On, Take It on the Chin, Song of Hareford, Love Makes the World Go Round, Leaning on a Lamppost, Finale

A musical in 2 acts and 9 scenes with a prologue. The action takes place in the late 1930's in and around Hareford Hall, Hampshire, Mayfair and Lambeth.

†Succeeded by: 1. Dee Hoty, 2. Edward Hibbert, Nick Ullett, 3. Herb Foster, Merwin Goldsmith, 4. Eleanor Glockner, 5. Bobby Longbottom, 6. John MacInniss, 7. Sylvia O'Brien, 8. Jay Garner, 9. Jim Dale, James Brennan, 10. Ellen Foley, Judith Blazer, 11. Donna Monroe, 12. Ann Heinricher, 13. J. B. Adams, 14. Jamie Torcellini, John M. Wiltberger, 15. John Jellison, 16. Eleanor Glockner

*Closed Dec. 31, 1989 after 1420 performances and 11 previews. 1987 "Tonys" were awarded Robert Lindsay and Maryann Plunkett (Best Actor and Actress in a Musical), and Gillian Gregory for Best Choreography.

Peter Cunningham Photos

Top Right: James Brennan, Judy Blazer

James Brennan (C)

OH! CALCUTTA!

Devised by Kenneth Tynan; Conceived/Directed by Jacques Levy; Presented by Hilliard Elkins, Norman Kean; Production Supervisor, Ron Nash; Authors/Composers, Robert Benton, David Newman, Jules Feiffer, Dan Greenburg, Lenore Kandel, John Lennon, Jacques Levy, Leonard Melfi, Sam Shepard, Clovis Trouille, Kenneth Tynan, Sherman Yellen; Music/Lyrics, Robert Dennis, Peter Schickle, Stanley Walden; Conductor, Tim Weil; Scenery/Lighting, Harry Silverglat Darrow; Costumes, Kenneth M. Yount; Sound, Sander Hacker; Assistant to Director, Nancy Tribush; Choreography, Margo Sappington; Projections, Gardner Compton; Live Action Film, Ron Merk; Company Manager, Doris J. Buberl; Producer, Norman Kean; Executive Producer, Maria Productions; Production Associates, Karen Nagle, Nancy Arrigo; Assistant General Manager, Tobias Beckwith; Assistant Musical Conductor, Dan Carter; Wardrobe, Mark Bridges; Stage Managers, Maria DiDia, Ron Nash; Press, Les Schecter, John Murphy. Opened at the Eden Theatre on Friday, June 17, 1969 and at the Edison Theatre on Friday, September 24, 1976*

CAST

Cheryl Hartley	Samuel D. Cohen
Danielle P Connell	Philip Gibson, Norman Dutweiler
Jacqueline Fay	Peter J. Lanigan
Amy Fortgang	William Thomas
Katherine Miller	Cheryl Hartley
† Ann Neville	

MUSICAL NUMBERS & SKITS: Taking Off the Robe, Will Answer All Sincere Replies, Playin', Jack and Jill, The Paintings of Clovis Trouille, Delicious Indignities, Was It Good for You Too?, Suite for Five Letters, One on One, Rock Garden, Spread Your Love Around, Four in Hand, Coming Together Going Together

An erotic stage musical in two acts and 14 scenes.
†Miss Hartley, a veteran of over 10 years and 5000 performances, holds the record for the longest run by a performer in a play or musical.

*Closed Sunday, August 6, 1989 after 5959 performances. For original production, see *Theatre World* Vol. 26.

THE PHANTOM OF THE OPERA

Music, Andrew Lloyd Webber; Lyrics, Charles Hart; Additional Lyrics, Richard Stilgoe; Book, Richard Stilgoe, Andrew Lloyd Webber; Director, Harold Prince; Musical Staging/Choreography, Gillian Lynne; Presented by Cameron Macintosh and The Really Useful Theatre Company; Production Design, Maria Bjornson; Lighting, Andrew Bridge; Sound, Martin Levan; Musical Supervision/Direction, David Caddick; Orchestrations, David Cullen, Andrew Lloyd Webber; Casting, Johnson-Liff & Zerman; Assistant Director, Ruth Mitchell; Dance Captain, Denny Berry; Props, Timothy Abel, Michael Bernstein, Victor Amerling; Wardrobe, Adelaide Laurino, Alan Eskolsky; Associate Conductors, Jack Gaughan, Jeffrey Huard, Paul Schwartz, Kristen Blodgette; Production Assistant, Rachel Abroms; Stage Managers, Mitchell Lemsky, Fred Hanson, Bethe Ward. Mark Rubinsky; Company Manager, Michael Gill; Technical Manager, John H. Paul III; General Manager, Alan Wasser; Props, Timothy Abel; Press, Fred Nathan Co./Merle Frimark, Bert Fink, Scott Taylor, Marc Thibodeau, James Morrison. Opened in the Majestic Theatre on Tuesday, January 26, 1988*

CAST

The Phantom of the Opera ....Michael Crawford †1
Christine Daae .... Sarah Brightman †2
(Thursday evenings/Saturday matinees) Patti Cohenour
Raoul, Vicomte de Chagny .... Steve Barton
Carlotta Guidicelli .... Judy Kaye †3
Monsieur Andre ....Cris Groenendaal †4
Monsieur Firmin ....Nicholas Wyman
Madame Giry ....Leila Martin
Ubaldo Piangi ....David Romano
Meg Giry ....Elisa Heinsohn
Monsieur Reyer .... Keter Kevoian †5
Auctioneer ....Richard Warren Pugh
Porter/Marksman .... Jeff Keller †6
Monsieur Lefevre ....Kenneth Waller
Joseph Buquet ....Philip Steele
Don Attilio (IL MUTO)/Passarino ....George Lee Andrews
Slave Master (Hannibal) ....Luis Perez †7
Flunky/Stagehand ....Barry McNabb
Policeman ....Charles Rule
Page (Don Juan) ....Olga Talyn
Porter/Fireman ....William Scott Brown
Page (Don Juan) .... Candace Rogers Adler †8
Wardrobe Mistress/Confidante ....Mary Leigh Stahl
Princess (Hannibal) ....Rebecca Luker †9
Madame Firmin .... Beth McVey †10
Innkeeper's Wife (Don Juan) ....Jan Horvath
Ballet Chorus of the Opera .... Irene Cho, Nicole Fosse,
Lisa Lockwood, Lori MacPherson,
Dodie Pettit, Catherine Ulissey,
Tenor Brown, Alina Hernandez
Ballet Swing ....Denny Berry †11
Swings .... Frank Mastrone, Alba Quezada,
Keith Buterbaugh, Paul Laureano

UNDERSTUDIES: Jeff Keller (Phantom), Keith Buterbaugh/David Cleveland (Raoul), George Lee Andrews/Paul Laureano (Firmin), George Lee Andrews/Frank Mastrone (Andre), Jan Horvath (Christine/Carlotta), Mary Leigh Stahl (Mme. Giry), William Scott Brown/Richard Warren Pugh (Piangi), Dodie Pettit/Catherine Ulissev (Meg), Barry McNabb (Slave Master/Solo Dancer)

MUSICAL NUMBERS: Think of Me, Angel of Music, Little Lotte/The Mirror, The Phantom of the Opera, The Music of the Night, I Remember/Stranger Than You Dream It, Magical Lasso, Notes, Prima Donna, Poor Fool Makes Me Laugh, Why Have You Brought Me Here, Raoul I've Been There, All I Ask of You, Masquerade, Why So Silent, Twisted Every Way, Wishing You Were Somehow Here Again, Wandering Child, Bravo Bravo, Don Juan Triumphant, The Point of No Return, Down Once More, Track Down This Murderer, Finale

A musical drama in 2 acts and 19 scenes. The action takes place in the Paris Opera House in 1911, and Paris in 1881.

†Succeeded by: 1. Timothy Nolen, Cris Groendendaal, 2. Patti Cohenour, Rebecca Luker, Dale Kirstein, Katharine Buffaloe, 3. Marilyn Caskey, 4. Jeff Keller, 5. Frank Mastrone, 6. David Cleveland, 7. David Loring, 8. Rhonda Dillon, 9. Raissa Katona, 10. Dawn Leigh Stone, 11. Lori MacPherson.

*Still playing May 31, 1989. Recipient of 1988 "Tonys" for Best Musical, Leading Actor in a Musical (Michael Crawford), Featured Actress in a Musical (Judy Kaye), Scenic Design, Costume Design, Lighting, Direction of a Musical.

Clive Barda/Bob Marshak Photos
Top Right: Patti Cohenour, Leila Martin

Below: Steve Barton, Patti Cohenour

Cris Groenendaal, Rebecca Luker

ANYTHING GOES!

Music/Lyrics, Cole Porter; Original Book, Guy Bolton, P. G. Wodehouse, Howard Lindsay, Russel Crouse; New Book, Timothy Crouse, John Weidman; Sets/Costumes, Tony Walton; Lighting, Paul Gallo; Musical Director, Edward Strauss, Jim Coleman; Musical Supervisor, Edward Strauss; Orchestrations, Michael Gibson; Dance Arrangements, Tom Fay; Sound, Tony Meola; Choreography, Michael Smuin; Assistant, Kirk Peterson; Production Manager, Jeff Hamlin; General Manager, Steven C. Callahan; Director, Jerry Zaks; Company Manager, Company Managers, Lynn Landis, Edward Nelson; Assistant Director, Lori Steinberg; Props, C. J. Simpson; Wardrobe, Joseph Busheme, Don Brassington; Hair Stylist, Sonia Rivera; Associate Conductors, Joshua Rosenbaum, Philip Kern; Wigs, Paul Huntley; Stage Managers, George Darveris, Chet Leaming, Leslie Loeb; Dance Captains, Alice Anne Oakes, Robert Ashford; Cast Album by RCA; Press, Merle Debuskey, William Schelble, Bruce Campbell, Leo Stern. Opened in the Vivian Beaumont Theater on Monday, Oct. 19, 1987 and closed Sept. 3, 1989 after 804 performances and 44 previews.*

CAST

Louie	Eric Y. L. Chan †1
Elisha Whitney	Rex Everhart
Fred	Steve Steiner
Billy Crocker	Howard McGillin †2
Reno Sweeney	Patti LuPone †3
Young Girl	Michele Pigliavento †4
Sailor	Alec Timerman †5
Captain	David Pursley
Purser	Gerry Vichi
Reporter #1	Robert Kellett
Photographer	Gerry McIntyre †6
Reporter #2	Larry Cahn †7
Purity	Daryl Richardson †8
Chastity	Barbara Yeager †9
Charity	Maryellen Scilla
Virtue	Jane Lanier †10
Minister	Richard Korthaze
Luke	Stanford Egi †11
John	Toshi Toda
Hope Harcourt	Kathleen Mahony-Bennett †12
Mrs. Evangeline Harcourt	Anne Francine †13
Lord Evelyn Oakleigh	Anthony Heald †14
G-Men	Dale Hensley, Leslie Feagan
Erma	Linda Hart †15
Moonface Martin	Bill McCutcheon
Woman in Bathchair	Jane Seaman
Her Niece	Alice Anne Oakes
Countess	Pat Gorman
Thuggish Sailors	Mark Chmiel, Lloyd Culbreath, Dan Fletcher, Lacy Darryl Phillips †17
Swings	Robert Ashford, Paul Geraci †18, Amy O'Brien, Michelle O'Steen

Bill McCutcheon, Linda Hart, Anthony Heald, Kathleen Mahony-Bennett, Anne Francine, Rex Everhart
Top: Patti LuPone (L), Leslie Uggams

MUSICAL NUMBERS: I Get a Kick out of You, No Cure Like Travel, Bon Voyage, You're the Top, Easy to Love, I Want to Row on the Crew, Sailors Chantey, Friendship, It's Delovely, Anything Goes, Public Enemy #1, Blow Gabriel Blow, Goodbye Little Dream, Be Like the Bluebird, All through the Night, The Gypsy in Me, Buddie Beware

A musical in 2 acts and 13 scenes. The action takes place on board a passenger ship in the Atlantic Ocean.

*Recipient of 1988 "Tonys" for Best Revival, Choreography, and Featured Actor in a Musical (Bill McCutcheon). Original production opened in The Alvin Theatre on Nov. 21, 1934 and played 420 performances.

†Succeeded by: 1. Marc Oka, 2. Gregg Edelman, 3. Linda Hart, Leslie Uggams, 4. Jane LaBanz, 5. Dale Hensley, 6. Dan Fletcher, 7. Ken Shepski, Larry Cahn, 8. Karen E. Fraction, 9. Michaela Hughes, 10. Kim Darwin, 11. Ronald Yamamoto, 12. Nancy Opel, 13. Ellen Hanley, 14. Walter Bobbie, 15. Jane Seaman, 16. Joe Deer, 17. Garry Q. Lewis, 18. Gib Jones.

Brigitte Lacombe Photos

PRODUCTIONS FROM PREVIOUS SEASONS THAT CLOSED DURING THIS SEASON

Title	Opened	Closed	Performances
Broadway Bound	12/4/86	9/25/88	756 + 12 preview
Cabaret	10/22/87	6/4/88	262 + 19 preview
Dandy Dick	5/11/88	6/26/88	54
42nd Street	8/25/80	1/8/89	3485 + 6 preview
Frankie and Johnny in the Claire de Lune	10/14/87	3/12/89	525
Godspell	5/31/88	12/31/88	225 + 15 preview
Romance! Romance!	4/20/88	1/15/89	297 + 10 preview
Sarafina!	9/25/87	7/2/89	597 + 11 preview
V & V Only	5/25/88	7/3/88	46
A Walk in the Woods	2/28/88	6/26/88	136 + 22 preview

OFF BROADWAY PRODUCTIONS
(June 1, 1988 through May 31, 1989)

(The Cubiculo) Thursday, June 2–12, 1988 (10 performances) The National Shakespeare Co. (Elaine Sulka, Artistic Director) presents in repertory:
THE IMPORTANCE OF BEING EARNEST by Oscar Wilde; Director, June Pyskacek, and **A MIDSUMMER NIGHT'S DREAM** by William Shakespeare; Director, Elaine Sulka; Sets, Vaughn Patterson; Lighting, Blu; Costumes, Renee Sykes CAST: Matthew Blomquist, Kay Bourbiel, Amy Brentano, Alison Lani Broda, Pierre Brulatour, Leone Fogel, Jim Hogue, James Karcher, Vernard Lunon, Steve Mehmert, Jerry Perna, Elizabeth Slaby

(Judith Anderson Theatre) Friday, June 3–25, 1989 (21 performances) The Writers Theatre presents:
RESISTANCE by D. Keith Mano; Director, Linda Laundra; Set, Bobby Berg; Lighting, Vivien Leone; Costumes, Margarita Delgado; Original Music, Patricia Lee Stotter; Producer, John P. Whitesell; Stage Managers, Sarah E. Donnelly, Jenny Peek CAST: Don Chastain (Frederick Cassidy), Colin Fox (Josip Sulka), Laurie Kennedy (Noelle Turner), Michael Luciano (Peter Flett), Thomas Nahrwold (Stephen Cassidy), Aideen O'Kelly (Kathleen Cassidy), Patrick Rameau (Manuel), Rachel West (Thryn Turner).
The action takes place in a prison cell block on a Caribbean Island that has fallen to a Communist regime.

(Actors Playhouse) Tuesday, June 7–Nov. 6, 1988 (176 performances and 16 previews)
TEN PERCENT REVUE with words and music by Tom Wilson Weinberg; Director, Scott Green; Producer, Laura Green; Choreography, Tee Scatuorchio; Costumes, Kevin-Robert; Musical Arrangements, Tom Wilson Weinberg, Lisa Bernstein; Backdrop, Edwin Perez-Carrion; Lighting, Joshua Starbuck; Press, Peter Cromarty and Co./Robert Murray, Tom Bollinger CAST: Lisa Bernstein, Rainie Cole, James Humphrey, Helena Snow, Robert Tate, Understudies: Wendy Binkowitz, John Corker, Tom Wilson Weinberg.
MUSICAL NUMBERS: Flaunting It, Best Years of My Life, Threesome, Wedding Song, If It Were/I'd Like to Be, Gay Name Game, Home, Not Allowed, Personals, Safe Sex Slut, Homo Haven Fight Song, Turkey Baster Baby, High Risk for Afraids, Obituary, And the Superemes, Before Stonewall, Write a Letter, We're Everywhere
A revue in two acts.

(INTAR) Wednesday, June 8–July 10, 1988
INTAR Hispanic-American Arts Center (Max Ferra, Artistic Director; Dennis Ferguson-Acosta, Managing Director) as part of the First New York International Festival of the Arts presents:
WELCOME BACK TO SALAMANCA with Book and Lyrics by Migdalia Cruz; Music, Fernando Rivas; Director, George Ferencz; Set, Loy Arcenas; Lighting, Beverly Emmons; Costumes, Sally J. Lesser; Musical Director, Jeremy Kahn; Magic Design, Peter Samelson; Casting, Ellen Novack; General Manager, James DiPaola; Production Manager, Robert L. Anderson; Stage Manager, Jon Roger Clark; Press, Bruce Cohen, Kathleen von Schmid CAST: Sheila Dabney (Maria), Willie C. Barnes (Shank), Carlos Arevalo (Brisket), Humberto Alabado (Flank), Alexis Reyes (Lorenzo), John Steber (Rondo), Steven Bland (Cuchi)
MUSICAL NUMBERS: Blood, Secret Jungle, Give Us the Story, Making It Happen, I'm the Meat Man, The Food Chain, 1999, Cuchi, Magic, Sweet China Eyes, Island, Maria's Lament, The Pot, Finale
A musical in one act. The action takes place during the winter of 2000 A.D. in a Meateasy in New York City.
ALMA with Book and Lyrics by Ana Maria Simo; Music, Fernando Rivas; Director, Paul Zimet; Choreography, Rocky Bornstein CAST: Irma-Estel LaGuerre (Elena), Nancy Sorel (Rolando/Alma), Al DeCristo (Diego)
MUSICAL NUMBERS: Wake Up, The Strike-Song, Good Morning Cousin, Handsome as a Man, Alma Means Soul, When You Want a Woman, I've Got a Life of My Own, Come Back, Rolando, Alma's Return
A musical in one act. The action takes place on September 1, 1939 in a New York City Tenement near Union Square.

Top: Robert Tate, Lisa Bernstein (front), Rainie Cole, James Humphrey, Helena Snow (back) in "Ten Percent Revue"
(Martha Swope Photo)
Below: Nancy Sorel, Irma Estel La Guerre in "Alma"
(Carol Rosegg Photo)

(Ensemble Studio Theatre) Wednesday, June 8–July 18, 1988 (48 performances) The Ensemble Studio Theatre (Curt Dempster, Artistic Director) presents:
MARATHON '88: 12 one-act plays in three series. **SERIES A:** Sets, Ann Sheffield; Lighting, Greg MacPherson; Costumes, Deborah Shaw; Sound, Bruce Ellman; Stage Manager, Ken Simmons; An event of the First New York International Festival of the Arts. "Neptune's Hips" by Richard Greenberg; Directed by Christopher Ashley; "Buster B and Olivia" by Shirley Kaplan; Director, Billy Hopkins; "Something about Baseball" by Quincy Long; Director, Risa Braman; "A Poster of the Cosmos" by Lanford Wilson' Director, Jonathan Hogan. CAST: Leslie Ayvazian, Macaulay Culkin, John Fiedler, Richard Grusin, Ellen Hamilton Latzen, Leslie Lyles, Bruce MacVittie, Andrew McCarthy, Tom Noonan, Park Overall, Mercedes Ruehl, Steven Weber, William Youmans
SERIES B: "Juliet" by Romulus Linney; Director, Peter Maloney; "Mango Tea" by Paul Weitz; Director, Curt Dempster; "Human Gravity" by Stuart Spencer; Director, Evan-Yionoulis; "Door to Cuba" by James Ryan; Director, Charles Richter. CAST: Bill Cwikowski, Peter Friedman, Thomas Gibson, Ernesto Gonzalez, Priscilla Lopez, Rob Morrow, Robin Moseley, James Murtaugh, Keith Reddin, Sam Schacht, Victor Slezak, Lois Smith, Marisa Tomei, Jennifer Van Dyck, Bradley Whitford
SERIES C: "Diphthong" by Michael B. Kaplan; Director, Lisa Peterson; "Slaughter in the Lake" by Jose Rivera; Director, Joan Vail Thorne; "The Man Who Climbed the Pecan Trees" by Horton Foote; Director, Curt Dempster; "Singing Joy" by Oyamo; Director, Peter Wallace. CAST: Kevin Davis, Dan Desmond, Horton Foote, Jr., Zach Grenier, Patrick John Hurley, Robert Jetter, Katherine Leask, James G. Macdonald, James McDaniel, Robin Miles, Anne O'Sullivan, James Rebhorn, James E. Reynolds, Grant Shaud, Lois Smith, Richard Topol, Pamala Tyson

(Cherry Lane Theatre) Sunday, June 12–27, 1988 (12 performances) Stages Trilingual Theatre (Artistic Director, Paul Verdier; Managing Director, Judith Lamb) presents as part of the First New York International Festival of the Arts: **PAVLOVSKY MARATHON** three plays by Argentine playwright Eduardo Pavlovsky; Production Superviser, Gioras Fischer; Press, Peter Cromarty. "*Slowmotion*" translated and directed by Paul Verdier; Set, Jim Sweeters; Lighting, Philip Allen; Sound, Bill O'Shaugnessy; Assistant Director, Judith Alonso; Costumes, Emily Payne; Stage Manager, Sindy Slater. CAST: Tony Abatemarco (Dagomar, an ex-boxer), Hal Bokar (Amilcar, his former manager), Grace Zabriskie (Rosa, a neighbor friend). The action takes place at the present time in Buenos Aires. "*Potestad*" directed by Norman Brisky; Music, Martin Pavlovsky; Lighting, Philip Allen; Stage Manager, Sindy Slater. CAST: Eduardo Pavlovsky (El Hombre), Susana Evans (Tita). The action takes place at the present time in Buenos Aires after the end of military repression. "*Pablo*" translated and directed by Paul Verdier; Lighting, Kevin Mahan; Stage Manager, Sindy Slater. CAST: Hal Bokar (L), Tony Maggio (V). The action takes place during the late 1970's in a room of a "Safe House" in Buenos Aires.

(Cathedral of St. John the Divine) Tuesday, June 14–25, 1988 (10 limited performances) Cathedral Arts presents as part of the First New York International Festival of the Arts, the New York premiere of Poland's Theatre Association Gardzienice (Stanislaw Kral, Administrative Director) **GATHERING and ARCHPRIEST AVVAKUM: THE LIFE WRITTEN BY HIMSELF** adapted by the company from a book written in a 17th Century Russian prison by Archpriest Avvakum before being burned at the stake. GATHERING is based on the primeval ritual of people gathering to share and celebrate their common experiences. Direction and Scenario, Wlodzimierz Staniewski. CAST: Anna Zubrzycki, Mariusz Golaj, Jadwiga Rodowicz, Tomasz Rodowicz, Henryk Andruszko, Dorota Porowska, James Ennis, Slawomir Tomala, Grzegorz Bral, Jacek Ostaszewski

Top Right: Hal Bokar, Tony Maggio in "Pablo"

Below: "Stars In The Morning Sky" *(Valery Plotnikov Photo)*

(American Place Theatre) Monday, June 20–July 2, 1988 (16 performances). Maly Productions (Ken Marsolais, President) presents the Leningrad Maly Drama Theatre (Lev Dodin, Artistic Director) in:
STARS IN THE MORNING SKY by Alexander Galin; Director, Lev Dodin; Co-Director, Tatyana Shestakova; Set, Alexei Porai-Koshitz; Lighting, Oleg Kozlov; English translation, Michael Stronin, Elise Thoron; Associate Producer, Elizabeth D. White; In association with the USSR Union of Theater Workers; General Management, Barbara Carrellas; Stage Manager, Maureen F. Gibson; Press, Burnham-Callaghan Associates/Ed Callaghan, Owen Levy CAST: Galina Filimonova (Valentina, caretaker responsible for fire safety in the mental asylum), Sergei Kozyrev (Nikolai, her son), Natalya Akimova (Maria, 15, beloved of Nikolai), Irina Seleznyova (Lora, from the Crimean coast), Marina Gridasova (Klara, girl from Moscow), Tatiana Shestakova (Anna, citizen of Moscow), Vladimir Osipchuk (Alexander, asylum patient)

The action takes place on the eve of the 1980 Olympic Games in an old derelict barracks which once served as an asylum for the mentally handicapped. Performed without intermission.

(St. Ann's Arts Center) Sunday, June 21–26, 1988 (6 performances) The Arts at St. Ann's presents the first contemporary theatre troupe from Indonesia to appear in the U.S. as part of The First New York International Festival of the Arts
THE RITUAL OF SOLOMON'S CHILDREN conceived, visualized and directed by W. S. Rendra; Assistant Director, Udin Mandarin; Art Director, Ken Zuraida; Set, Daniel Talpers; Costumes, Ken Zuraida; Masks, Agus Jolli; Lighting, Tom Andrews; Composer/Music Director, Tonny Prabowo; Press, Bruce Cohen, Kathleen von Schmid. CAST: Nyai Dewi Pakis (Joker), Udin Mandarin, Sawung Jabo, Awan Sanwani, Dudy Anggawi (Male Dancers), Lily Suardi, Ken Zueaida, Pipien Putri (Female Dancers), Johnie Waromi (Mama), Ria Rondang Pardede (Clown), Adi Kurdi (Headman), W. S. Rendra (Suto), Endang Talipaksa (1st Reptile), Afrion (2nd Reptile), Tita Indriati (Female Reptile), Otig Pakis (Bib-Bob), Amien Kamil (ZZZ), Ken Zuraida (Fatima)

(American Theatre of Actors) Friday, June 24–July 10, 1988 (11 performances and 4 previews). The New Punctuation Army presents:
TWO FOR THE SHOW by Gayden Wren who directed; Production Design, Janette Kennedy; Props, Elissa Maria Tomasetti; Lighting, Anna Ibe; Press, Henry Luhrman Associates/Terry M. Lilly, David Lotz, Naomi Grabel, Tom LaPointe CAST: Barbara Acey (Maureen), Robert F. Amico (Raoul), Paul Birnbaum (Bennie), L. B. Chanin (Archie), Robert Diefendorf (Tony/Marvin), Thomas Gardner (Derek Dangerfield), Daniel A. Nordstrom (Milo), Andrew Olivo (Andrew), Tim O'Neil (Tim), Karen Pope (Sandra Clark), Tailer Reed (Bobby), David Sennett (Bernard Bettman), Elissa Maria Tomasetti

A comedy in three acts. The action takes place at the present time and follows the course of a play from rehearsal to opening night.

Karen Pope, David Sennett, Thomas Gardner in "Two For The Show" *(Janette Kennedy Photo)*

Above: "The Ritual of Solomon's Children"

47

"Ti Daro' Quel Fior . . ."
Above: Richard Tabor, Grover Zucker, Malcolm Stephenson
in "King Henry IV, Part One"

(Ohio Theatre) Friday, June 24–July 9, 1988 (14 performances) The Manticore Theatre (Bob Verini, Executive Director) presents:
KING HENRY IV, Part One by William Shakespeare; Director, Bob Verini; Set, Peter R. Feuche; Costumes, Susan DeMasi; Lighting, Don Guyton; Props, Deborah Scott; Fight Choreography, David Brimmer; Sound, Kevin Barry; Casting, David S. Cohen; Stage Manager, Elizabeth B. Davis; Press, Canaan Communications CAST: Kevin Barry, Mary Boyer, George Cambus, Jamie Cheatham, Chris Eigeman, Andrew Jarkowsky, Jon Krupp, Richard Lemerise, Michael Oberlander, Alec Phoenix, Alfred Preisser, Robyn Rose, Malcolm Stephenson, Richard Tabor, Kenneth Talberth, Bruce Van Cott, Eloise Watt, Grover Zucker

(Cherry Lane Theatre) Wednesday, June 29–July 11, 1988 (16 performances). Stages Trilingual Theatre (Artistic Director, Paul Verdier; Managing Director, Judith Lamb) presents:
ENGLISH MINT (L'Amante Anglaise) by Marguerite Duras; Director, Paul Verdier; Set, Jim Sweeters; Costumes, Emily Payne; Lighting, Kevin Mahn; Production Supervisor, Gioras Fischer; Production Assistant, Judith Alonso; Press, Peter Cromarty, Robert Murray CAST: Hal Bokar (Pierre Lannes), Grace Zabriskie (Claire Lannes), Paul Verdier (The Interrogator)

(Hunter College Playhouse) Wednesday, June 29–July 3, 1988 (5 performances). The John D. Calandra Italian American Institute of CUNY as part of the First New York International Festival of the Arts presents:
TI DARO QUEL FIORE/"I'll Give You That Flower" by Marco Mete; Organized by Bea Boscardi; Costumes, Camilla Righi; Pianist, Alfredo Messina; Press, Peter Cromarty, Rob Murray CAST: Gennaro (Gustavo DeFloris), Renato Campese (Inspector Vecchiato), Maria Cristina Fioretti (Dolores DeFloris)
A musical in two acts.

(Hunter College Playhouse) Wednesday, July 6–9, 1988 (4 limited performances). The First New York International Festival of the Arts, and John D. Calandra Italian American Institute of CUNY present:
LA NUOTATTICE TURCA/The Turkish Swimmer by Fabrizio Caleffi; Directed by the author; Press, Peter Cromarty, Rob Murraxy CAST: Fabrizio Caleffi (Victor Strongfort), Donata D'Alistal (The Singer), Cristina Gentile (The Woman)
A comedy of an Italian-American who goes to Italy thinking it is heaven.

Geoff Edholm, Kevin Madden in "AIDS Alive"
(Richard Wilson Photo)

(Don't Tell Mama) Wednesday, July 6–Nov. 26, 1989 (25 performances) The People with Aids Theater Workshop (Nick Pippin, Founding Director; Sylvia Stein, Producing Director) presents:
AIDS ALIVE by Lanie Robertson; Director, Carter Inskeep; Press, Andy Shearer, Peter Cromarty CAST: Nico Angelo, Frank Brown, Geoff Edholm, Tom Lutz, Mark Fotopoulos, Kevin Madden, Tom Sullivan, Tony Torres, Nick Pippin

(South Street Theatre) Friday, July 8, 1988–South Street Theatre in association with Erick Productions presents:
GUILTY CONSCIENCE by Richard Levinson and William Link; Director, Vincent Bossone; Set, Wade Battley; Costumes, Debi Thibeault; Lighting, Alan Sporing; Production Stage Manager, Andrew Sterrer; Press, Jeffrey Richards Associates/Ben Morse CAST: Steve Weiser (Arthur Jamison), Julann Rosa (Louise Jamison), Tom Gebbie (Prosecutor), Wendy Parks (Jackie Willis)

(Shandol Theatre) Wednesday, July 13–31, 1988 (16 performances) The Village Theatre Company presents:
THE HOT L BALTIMORE by Lanford Wilson; Director, Henry Fonte; Set, Edmond Ramage; Lighting, John Paul Szczepanski; Sound, Richard L. Sirois; Costumes, Mary O'Dowd; Props, Zach Zito; Stage Managers, Elaine R. O'Donnell, Jodi Feldman; CAST: Randy Kelly (Bill Lewis), Barbara Berque (Girl), Sylvia Davis (Millie), Sally Hamilton (Mrs. Bellotti), Julia McLaughlin (April Green), Keith Michl (Mr. Morse), Susan Farwell (Jackie), David McConnell (Jamie), Michael Hill (Mr. Katz), Donnah Welby (Suzy), Howard Thoresen (Suzy's John), Michael Curran (Paul Granger III), Pat Squire (Mrs. Oxenham)
A play in three acts. The action takes place on Memorial Day 1972 in the run-down Hotel Baltimore.

(The Cubiculo) Friday, July 15, 1988–   The Open Space Theatre Experiment (Lynn Michaels, Artistic Director) presents:
KNEPP by Jorge Goldenberg; Translated by Judith Leverone; Director, Susan Einhorn; Set, Michael Boak; Lighting, Dan Wagner; Costumes, Jeffrey Ullman; Sound, Phil Lee; Stage Manager, Christien Wagner; Press, Bruce Cohen, Kathleen von Schmid CAST: Ellen Barber, David Little, Annie Murray, Michael O'Gorman, Richard Riehle
A psychological political suspense play

Randy Kelly, David McConnell, Julia McLaughlin
in "Hot L Baltimore" (Nina Krieger Photo)

48

(Apple Corps Theatre) Sunday, July 17–Aug. 21, 1988 Apple Corps Theatre (Founder/director, John Raymond) presents:

GEORGE WASHINGTON SLEPT HERE by Moss Hart, George S. Kaufman; Director, John Raymond; Set, Alex Polner; Costumes, MaryAnn D. Smith; Lighting, William J. Plachy; Sound, Neal Arluck; Technical Director, Tom Carroll; Props/Production Assistant, Lauren Helpern; Wardrobe, Amy Henriquez; Stage Managers, Myra Oney Weferling, Benmio Easterling; Press, Francine L. Trevens, Aviva Cohen, Robert J. Wewton, Mike Kopelow. CAST: Christina Campanella (Miss Wilcox), Maria Cellario (Annabelle), Bob Del Pazzo (Mr. Kimber), Frank Dowd (Tommy Hughes), Benmio Easterling (Steve), Arthur French (Kimber), Angela Logan (Rena Leslie), Sakina Jaffrey (Hester), Sherman Lloyd (Uncle Stanley), Helen Marcy (Mrs. Douglas), Lorraine Morin-Torre (Madge Fuller), Kenny Price (Raymond), Jamie Lynn O'Brien (Sue Barrington), Eddie Sambucci (Leggett Frazer), Michael Tolan (Newton Fuller), Charles Turner (Clayton Evans/Mr. Prescott)

(Perry Street Theatre) Wednesday, Aug. 3–Sept. 9, 1988 Ron Lesser & Tom Mazziotti present:

SLASHER written by Michael Hillyer, Biff Paruolo, Bill Wheeler; Music & Lyrics, Michael Calderwood; Musical Direction, Jan Callner; Director, Tom Mazziotti; Choreography, Susan Stroman; Executive Producer, Gerald A. Davis; Associate Producer, Angela Bowen; Set, Bryan Johnson; Costumes, Vicki R. Davis; Lighting, Jennie Ryan; Special Effects, Peter Barbieri, Jr.; Sound, Jordan Pankin; Fight Staging, Simon Brooking; Stage Manager, Vickie Verner; Press, Pamela Giddon CAST: Marla Cahan, Carl T. Evans, Lori Fischer, Mitchell Fleiss, Morgan LaVere, Peter-Michael Marino, Lisa Sellers, Frank Stewart, Caron Treger, Bill Wheeler

(William Redfield Theatre) Wednesday, Aug. 3–14, 1988 (12 performances). Doctor Hasty presents:

MACBETH by William Shakespeare; Director, Simon Doctor; Lighting, Cynthia Dorrell; Stage Manager, Alene Guenther CAST: Grace Jordan (Witch 1), A. Lee Massaro (Witch 2), Jacqueline McNally (Witch 3), Jack Ryan (Duncan/Doctor/Siward), Mark Tankersly (Malcolm), Robert Laconi (Sgt./Old Man/Monteith), Chris Cappiello (Lennox/1st Murderer), Robert Maniscalco (Ross), Matt Mitler (Macbeth), Paul Bolger (Banquo), David Johnston (Angus/2nd Murderer), Nancy Hasty (Lady Macbeth), Lenny Gross (Messenger/Porter), Daniel Guenther (Fleance), Jeff Zeichner (Macduff), Lawrence Preston (Donalbain/Young Siward), Melanie Oakes (Lady Macduff/Hecate), Eric Guenther (Macduff's Son), Drew Murphy (Seyton) Performed with one intermission.

Top: Michael Tolan, Angela Logan, Maria Cellario in "George Washington Slept Here" *(Austin Trevett Photo)*
Below: Karen Curlee, Jody Abrahams, Tia Speros, Melanie Mitchell in "The Taffetas"

(Cherry Lane Theatre) Friday, Aug. 5, 1988–Jan. 1, 1989 (166 performances and 5 previews; Moved to the Village Gate Wednesday, February 1–April 9, 1989 for 67 additional performances). Arthur Whitelaw & James Shellenberger in association with Select Entertainment present:

THE TAFFETAS, A Musical Journey through the Fabulous Fifties; Conceived by Rick Lewis; Director, Steven Harris; Staging/Choreography, Tina Paul; Musical Direction/Vocal Arrangements, Rick Lewis; Associate Producer, Adam Sternberg; Scenery, Evelyn Sakash; Costumes, David Graden; Lighting, Ken Billington; Sound, Raymond Schilke; Production Assistant, Maureen May; Stage Managers, Allison Sommers, Jean Tait; Press, Henry Luhrman Associates/Terry M. Lilly, David Lotz, Russ Gustafson, Tom LaPointe CAST: Jody Abrahams, Karen Curlee, Melanie Mitchell, Tia Speros, Understudy: Jean Tait
Presented in two acts.

(SouthStreet Theatre) Sunday, Aug. 7–Oct. 9, 1988 (20 performances and 6 previews). Eric Krebs in association with the South Street Theatre presents:

PAUL ROBESON By Phillip Hayes Dean; Director, Harold Scott; Choreography, Dianne McIntyre; Set/Costumes, Michael Massee; Lighting, Shirley Prendergast; Sound, Rob Gorton; Arrangements/Orchestrations, Eva C. Brooks; Stage Manager, Doug Hosney CAST: Avery Brooks (Paul Robeson), Ernie Scott (Lawrence Brown)

(Riverwest Theatre) Friday, Aug. 12–Sept. 3, 1988 (16 performances) CHS Productions and Dina & Alexander E. Racolin in association with Riverwest Theatre (Director, Andy Jordan) present:

LUNATIC AND LOVER by Michael Meyer; Direction & Design, Andy Jordan; Lighting, Alan Baron; Costumes, Lisa LoCurto; Set, Patrick Eagleton; Sound, David Lawson; Production Coordinator, Paul A. Kochman; Stage Managers, Nancy Wernick, Catalina Castells; Press, Chris Boneau CAST: Richard M. Davidson (August Strindberg), Eileen Dunn (Siri), Tessie Hogan (Frida), Diana LaMar (Harriet), Joseph McKenna (Father), Robert Mason (Director).
Performed without intermission. The action takes place in various part of Europe during the years 1857–1912.

(St. Clement's Church) Tuesday, Aug. 23, 1988–   The Soupstone Project presents:

UNCOUNTED BLESSINGS three one-act comedies: *"Hidden in This Picture"* by Aaron Sorkin; Director, David Saint; Lighting, Matt Berman; Original Music/Sound Design, Kenn Dovel; Production Manager, Susan P. Lewis. *"Hidden in This Picture"* by Aaron Sorkin; Director, David Saint; CAST: Nathan Lane, Wally Dunn, Aaron Sorkin, Rick Lawless. *"Stacey Elizabeth Tries to Climb out of Her Nightmare"* by David Rush; Director, Avril Hordyk; CAST: Maggie Scott, Michael Rush. *"Forget Him"* by Harvey Fierstein; Director, Neile Weissman; CAST: William Haynes, Tom Starace, Jerry Cole

Richard Davidson, Diana LaMar in "Lunatic and Lover"
(Paul Yuen Photo)

(Minetta Lane Theatre) Tuesday, Aug. 30–Oct. 23, 1988 (61 performances and 16 previews) M Square Entertainment and TV Asahi present:
BLUES IN THE NIGHT Conceived and Directed by Sheldon Epps; Set/Costumes, Michael Pavelka; Lighting, Susan A. White; Sound, Charles Bugbee III; Musical Direction/Additional Arrangements, David Brunetti; Music Supervisor/Arranger/Orchestrator, Sy Johnson; Assistant Director, Patricia Wilcox; Casting, Mark Simon; Co-Producers, Joshua Silver, Victoria Maxwell; Associate Producers, Colin Hooper, Betsy Lifton and Showpeople Ltd. Company Manager, Patricia Berry; Technical Director, Mark Vogeley; Wardrobe, Rachael Cusnetz; Stage Managers, Bruce Lumpkin, Rob Babbitt; Press, Peter Cromarty & Co./David Gersten, Kevin Brockman. CAST: Carol Woods (Lady from the road), Brenda Pressley (Woman of the world), Leilani Jones (Girl with a date), Lawrence Hamilton (Man in the saloon), C. E. Smith (understudy for Mr. Hamilton)

The action takes place in the late 1930's in a cheap hotel with three women and a saloon singer recalling memories and music that get them through the night. Performed with one intermission.

(Theatre East) Tuesday, Sept. 6, 1988–May 31, 1989 Jonathan Scharer presents:
FORBIDDEN BROADWAY with Concept/Parody Lyrics/Direction by Gerard Alessandrini; Choreography, Roxie Lucas; Costumes, Erika Dyson; Production Consultant, Pete Blue; Associate Producers, Arthur B. Brown, Chip Quigley; General Management, Margay Whitlock, Kevin Dowling; Technical Supervisor, Will Knapp; Wardrobe, Sabado Lam; Stage Managers, Jerry James, Philip George; Press, Glenna Freedman/Shirley Herz Associates/Pete Sanders, David Roggensack, Sam Rudy, Miller Wright CAST: Toni DiBuono, Philip Fortenberry, Roxie Lucas, David B. McDonald, Michael McGrath, Understudies: Dorothy Kiara, Philip George

A parody of Broadway musicals in two acts.

(Greene Street Cafe) Friday, Sept. 9, 1988–
ONE MAN BAND a musical odyssey with Book by James Lecesne; Music, Mark Eliot, Larry Hochman; Lyrics, Marc Eliot; Press, Tony Origlio CAST: James Lecesne, Geri Winbar, Stephanie Madden

(South Street Theater) Monday, Sept. 12–   Eric Krebs and South Street Theater (Artistic Directors, Jean Sullivan/Michael Fischetti) present:
A MURDER OF CROWS by Ed Graczyk; Director, Edward Stern; Set, Ursula Belden; Costumes, Kathryn Wagner; Lighting, Daniel Stratman; Casting, Joseph Abaldo; General Managers, Gail Bell/John Ann Washington; Company Manager, Paul Morer; Stage Manager, Patricia Flynn; Press, Shirley Herz/David Roggensack CAST: Terry Layman (Corey Woodson), Susan Greenhill (Doris Woodson), Kim Hunter (Jennie Woodson), Michael Higgins (Harley Woodson), Jay Devlin (Luther "Digger" Briggs), Evelyn Page (Velma Mackey)

A play in two acts. The action takes place in Wallace, Ohio, during 1984.

(Provincetown Playhouse) Thursday, Sept. 15–Oct. 23, 1988 (22 performances). Moved Thursday, Nov. 10, 1988 to Theatre Off Park and still playing there May 31, 1989. Theatre in Limbo presents:
I COULD GO ON LIP-SYNCHING conceived and developed by John Epperson and Justin Ross; Direction/Choreography, Justin Ross; Puppets, Harry Rainbow, Mike Thomas; Gowns, Anthony Wong; Set, John-Eric Broaddus; Lighting, Vivien Leone CAST: John Epperson (Lypsinka)

Performed without intermission.

(Kittredge Club) Thursday, Sept. 15–Oct. 8, 1988 (11 performances and 5 previews) Apple Acting/New American Theatre presents:
DODGER BLUE by Elizabeth Heffron Herring; Director, Jayne Brookes; Assistant Director, Sarah Daly; Set, Stan Pippin; Lighting, Rob Zanfagna; Costumes, Kathryn Graves; Sound, George Edwards; Props, Laura Sewell; Press, Chris Boneau CAST: Marjorie Austrian, Laura Brutsman, Gerald Campbell, Manuel Santiago, Michael Storck, J. D. Swain, Martin Treat

A play in two acts about an aging waitress in a Los Angeles diner.

(Criterion Center Stage Left) Sunday, Sept. 25–Dec. 4, 1988 (81 performances and 23 previews) Richard Redlin, Will Roberson, Bryan Scott, Norma and David Langworthy present:
SUDS: The Rock '60's Musical Soap Opera; Created and Written by Melinda Gilb, Steve Gunderson, Bryan Scott; Musical/Vocal Arrangements, Steve Gunderson; Director, Will Roberson; Choreography, Javier Velasco; Set, Alan Okazaki; Costumes, Gregg Barnes; Lighting, Kent Dorsey; Sound, Adam Wartnik; Musical Director, William Doyle; General Management, Brent Peek Productions; Management Associate, Danny Stewart; Company Manager, Sally Campbell; Wigs, Frank Bowers; Wardrobe, Todd Tomarrow; Makeup, Charles Barry; Stage Managers, Mark Baltazar, Laura Kravets; Press, Jeffrey Richards Associates/Ben Morse, Irene Gandy, Susan Chicoine, Diane Judge, Jillana Devine, Roger Lane, Mark McBride, Lapacazo Sandoval CAST: Christine Sevec (Cindy), Melinda Gilb (Marge), Susan Mosher (Dee Dee), Steve Gunderson (Everyone Else), Understudies: Jeanine Morick, Julie Waldman, Bob Stromberg

A musical in two acts. The action takes place in a laundramat in the 1960's.

Brenda Pressley, Lawrence Hamilton, Carol Woods, Leilani Jones in "Blues in the Night" *(Martha Swope Photo)*

Toni DiBuono, Michael McGrath, David B. McDonald, Roxie Lucas in "Forbidden Broadway" *(Carol Rosegg Photo)*

Steve Gunderson, Melinda Gilb, Susan Mosher, Christine Sevec in "Suds" *(Ken Howard Photo)*

(47th Street Theatre) Tuesday, Sept. 27– Good Omen Productions presents:
THE LEGEND OF SHARON SHASHANOVAH by Alexander Francis Horn; Director, Sharon Gans; Set, Lauren Sherman; Lighting, Mary Lou Geiger; Costumes, Susan Herschfeld; Puppets, Susan Stein CAST: Sharon Talbot, Bronwen Barnett, Christofer Deoni, Linda Froehlich, Michael Horn, Frank Natasi, Irma St. Paule, Jeremiah Sullivan

(45th Street Theatre) Thursday, Sept. 29–Oct. 29, 1988 (20 performances) Dina and Alexander Racolin and Lily Turner present:
MOTHER BICKERDYKE AND ME by Antoinette Kray; Director, Edward Berkeley; Production Design, Don Jensen; Lighting, John Michael Deegan; Stage Manager, Don Hamptgon; Press, David Rothenberg, Terence Womble CAST: Ruth Adams (Josie), Cynthia Kaplan (Eva), Anita Keal (Gracie), Lori March (Ruth). The action takes place on an empty stage in a theatre with one intermission.

Friday, Sept. 30–Oct. 22, 1988 (20 performances). CHS Productions & Stab Stab Stab Partners in association with Riverwest Theatre present:
DESIRE by Paul Coates; Director, Dennis Deal; Set, Curt Schnell; Lighting, Norman Coates; Costumes, Patric McWilliams; Sound, Greg Sutton; Original Music, Marjorie Poe; Hairstylist, Bobby Grayson; Production Coordinator, Paul A. Kochman; Stage Managers, John Rainwater, Angela Foley; Technical Director, Patrick Eagleton; Press, Chris Boneau CAST: Dan Erickson (Drew Cole), Sheri Galan (Cricket Cole), Rex Hays (Dr. Wesley Cole), Laura Kenyon (Margo Featherway), Lisby Larson (Faith Featherway), Mark McCoy (Jack Lawrence), Wendy Radford (Summer Covington), Constance Shulman (Announcer), Nancy J. Sullivan (Desiree Featherway).
A play in two acts. The action takes place at the present time in various locales in and around Allison Bay, a small town north of Boston.

(Westbeth) Thursday, Oct. 6–30, 1988 (16 performances). Westbeth Theatre Center (Producing Director, Arnold Engelman; Associate Producer, Juda Youngstrom) presents:
GET ANY GUY THRU PSYCHIC MIND CONTROL OR YOUR MONEY BACK by Cherie Bennett; Director, Linda Burson; Set, Venustiano Borromeo; Sound, Aaron Winslow; Lighting, Wendy Bozdin; Musical Direction, Tim Howard; Choreography, Jerry Yoder; Stage Managers, Amy Huggans, Joan Valentina. CAST: Jeff Gottesfeld (Sky/D.J./), Maggie Greer (Sissy Anne Jamison), Rita Jenrette (Dora-Lee), Jeanne Jones (Jamella Mae Jamison), Paige Alenius (Faith Jamison), Richard McWilliams (Genesis Tyler), Michael Gilpin (Ernest Bear), Matthew Shiner (Singing Voice of Cutter Red). The action takes place at the present time in the Rev. Earl Park in Nashville, Tennessee.

Lisby Larson, Mark McCoy in "Desire" *(Martha Swope Photo)*
Above: Ruth Adams, Anita Keal in "Mother Bickerdyke and Me" *(Marvin Einhorn Photo)*

Bruce Davison, Nancy Marchand, Keene Curtis, Holland Taylor in "The Cocktail Hour" *(Martha Swope Photo)*
Above: Richard Backus, Holland Taylor, Nancy Marchand, Keene Curtis (standing) in "The Cocktail Hour" *(Martha Swope Photo)*

(Actors Outlet Theatre) Thursday, Oct. 6–29, 1988 (13 performances and 5 previews). Actors Outlet (Eleanor Segan, Executive Director; Ken Lowstetter, Artistic Director) by special arrangement with Randy Charnin presents:
THE GREEN DEATH written and directed by Peter Mattaliano; Set, Charles E. McCarry; Lighting, Randall Etheredge; Costumes, Joseph A. Cigliano; Choreography, Patricia Wilcox; Fight Director, Brandon E. Doemling; General Manager, Barbara J. Hodgen; Stage Manager, Juliann Flynn CAST: Nelson Avidon, Ralph Buckley, Frank Dahill, Janis Dardaris, Stephani Hardy, Suzy Hunt, Steve Robinson
A "black comedy for blue times" in two acts.

(Promenade Theatre) Friday, Oct. 7, 1988–still playing May 31, 1989 Roger L. Stevens, Thomas Viertel, Steven Baruch, Richard Frankel present the Old Globe Theatre production:
THE COCKTAIL HOUR by A. R. Gurney; Director, Jack O'Brien; Set/Costumes, Steven Rubin; Lighting, Kent Dorsey; General Manager, Ralph Roseman; Associate Producer, Thomas Hall; Company Manager, Susan Gustafson; Props, Ted Wallace; Wardrobe, Anne-Marie Wright; Stage Managers, Douglas Pagliotti; Patrick Horgan; Press, David Powers, Mary Bryant, David Roggensack CAST: Keene Curtis (Bradley), Nancy Marchand (Ann, his wife), Bruce Davison succeeded by Richard Backus (John, his son), Holland Taylor (Nina, his daughter)
A comedy in two acts. The action takes place during early evening in early fall in the mid-'70's in a city in upstate New York.

(Kaufman Theater) Wednesday, Oct. 12–23, 1988 (6 performances and 8 previews) Martin R. Kaufman presents:
MY UNKNOWN SON by Daniel Curzon; Director, Sal Trapani; Set, Philip Baldwin; Costumes, Arnall Downs; Lighting, Michael Chybowski; Music, Jim Farmer; Casting, Pat McCorkle/Richard Cole; General Management, Marshall B. Purdy Stage Managers, Melissa L. Burdick, Alice King; Press, Henry Luhrman Associates/Terry M. Lilly, David Lotz, Russell Gustafson CAST: David Proval (The Father), Lorraine Lanigan (The Midwife), Stephen Hamilton (The Son), Understudy: Alice King (Midwife)
Performed without intermission

Matthew Vipond, Marisa Tomei in "Sharon and Billy"
(Martha Swope Photo)

Above: Anthony Chisholm, Howard Mungo, Reg E. Cathey in
"Back in the World" *(Susan Cook Photo)*

(Apple Corps Theatre) Tuesday, Oct. 18–30, 1988 (13 performances and 8 previews)
The Women's Project and Productions (Julia Miles, Artistic Director) presents:
MA ROSE by Cassandra Medley; Director, Irving Vincent; Set, Philip Baldwin; Costumes, Judy Dearing; Lighting, Pat Dignan; Sound, Aural Fixation; Technical Director, Tom Carroll; Wardrobe, Amy Correia; Props, Lauren Halpern; General Manager, Donna Campbell; Stage Manager, Ken Simmons; Press, Fred Nathan Co./Merle Frimark CAST: LaTanya Richardson (Rosa), Lizan Mitchell (Vera), Pawnee Sills (Ethel), Herb Lovelle (Wayman), Rosanna Carter (Ma Rose)
A play in 2 acts and 10 scenes. The action takes place in mid-December of 1980 in a small midwestern town.

(TNT Playhouse) Thursday, Oct. 20–Nov. 20, 1988 (16 performances) The New Theatre of Brooklyn (Deborah J. Pope and Steve Settler, Artistic Directors) presents:
ANNULA, AN AUTOBIOGRAPHY written and directed by Emily Mann; Set, Marjorie Bradley Kellogg; Lighting, Donald Holder; Costumes, Jennifer von Mayr-hauser; Sound, Tom Gould; Dialect Coach/Text Consultant, Nora-Dunfee; Stage Manager, Casandra Scott CAST: Linda Hunt (Annula), Karen Ludwig (Young Woman's Voice)
Performed without intermission.

(Holy Trinity Church) Thursday, Oct. 20–Nov. 13, 1988 (16 performances) The Triangle Theatre Co. (Executive Director, Michael Ramach; Associate Executive Director, Molly O'Neil; Production Manager, Anne M. Cantler) presents:
RHAPSODY TACHISTE by Mary Gail; *World Premiere;* Director, Michael Ramach; Set, Bob Phillips; Costumes, Amanda J. Klein; Lighting, Danianne Mizzy; Technical Director, Ed Ramage; Stage Manager, Anne M. Cantler; Press, Chris Boneau, Tim Ray. CAST: Danielle Fayne (Fay), Judy Dodd (Francine), Monica Merryman (Muriel), Don Fischer (Pyrrhus), Krista Helferrich (Lucy)

(Judith Anderson Theatre) Wednesday, Oct. 12–Nov. 27, 1988 (26 performances and 20 previews) Vietnam Veterans Ensemble Theatre Company (Thomas Bird, Artistic Director) presents:
BACK IN THE WORLD by Stephen Mack Jones; Director, Pat Julian; Production Supervisor, Thomas Bird; Set, Jim Youmans; Lighting, Terry Wuthrich; Sound, Scott David Sanders; Associate Producer, Susan P. Lewis; Stage Managers, John M. Atherlay, Kira Coopersmith; Press, Bruce Campbell CAST: Leo V. Finnie III (The Man), Norman Matlock (Sgt. Major Hannibal A. Bellsen), Howard Mungo (Pvt. 1st Class Maurice T. Morton), Anthony Chisholm (SP4 Anthony "Jam" Brazil), Reg E. Cathey (Cpl. James Norton Stephens), Understudy: Randy Frazier
A drama in two acts. The action takes place at the present time.

(Westbeth Theatre Center) Thursday, Oct. 13–30, 1988 (16 performances) Westbeth Theatre Center (Arnold Engelman, Producing Director; Juda Youngstrom, Associate Producer) presents:
CRYSTAL CLEAR devised by Phil Young; Director, Ted Snowdon; Set, Bob Phillips; Costumes, Joanie Canon; Lighting, Nancy Collings; Sound, Aaron Winslow; Technical Director, Michael J. Kondrat; Props, Kira Coopersmith; Stage Managers, Michael Musick, Kira Coopersmith; Press, David Lotz CAST: Armand Schultz (Richard), Elaine Rinehart (Thomasina), Robin Poley (Jane). The action takes place in Richard's London flat in the early 1980's.
Performed in 5 scenes without intermission.

(Nat Horne Theatre) Friday, Oct. 14–Nov. 17, 1988 (14 performances for each play) Manhattan Class Company (Executive Director, Robert LuPone; Executive Director, Bernard Telsey) present in repertory:
SHARON AND BILLY by Alan Bowne; Director, W. D. Cantler; Set, Gregory Mercurio; Lighting, John Hastings; Production Manager, Laura Kravets; Co-Producer, Maggie Lear; Stage Manager, Lori Culhane; Press, G, Theodore Jilmer. CAST: Marisa Tomei (Sharon), Sonja Lanzener (Mom), Mathew Vipond (Billy), Richard Grusin (Dad)
A play in 2 acts and 7 scenes. The action takes place in the late 1950's in a tract home of a blue collar suburb of Los Angeles, California.
FUN by James Bosley; Director, Brian Mertes; Costumes, Sam Fleming; Sound, John Wise; Casting, Laurel Smith; Associate Producer, Rona Carr; Stage Manager, Cheryl Zoldowski; Press, G. Theodore Killmer; Composer, Chris Kowanko; Props, Georgia Accola CAST: Amelia Campbell (Bonnie), Kelly Wolf (Hillary), Ian Shupeck/Ken Marks (John), Maryann Urbano (Jane)
Performed without intermission.

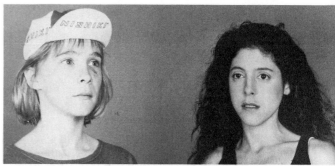

Herb Lovelle, La Tanya Richardson, Pawnee Sills, Lizan
Mitchell in "Ma Rose" *(Martha Holmes Photo)*
Above: Amelia Campbell, Kelly Wolf in "Fun"
(Martha Swope Photo)

(INTAR Theatre) Thursday, Nov. 3–13, 1988; moved to the 47th Street Theatre Nov. 17 and closed The Heritage Players present:
THE HIRED MAN by Melvyn Bragg and Howard Goodall; Producer/Director, Brian Aschinger; Musical Director, Ann Crawford; Musical Staging, Rodney Griffin; Set, Tamara Kirkman; Costumes, Patricia Adshead; Lighting, Leon Di Leone; Dialect Coach, Margaret Schenck; Stage Managers, David Sitler, David M. Beris, Marilyn Firment; Press, Jeffrey Richards Associates/Ben Morse. CAST: Paul Avedisian (John), David M. Beris (Josh), Gloria Boucher (Sally), Christopher Boyd (Chairman/Alec), Ray Collins (Isaac), Keith Cooper (Tom), Nick Corley (Seth), Tom Freeman (Dan), Ray Luetters (Jackson), Richard Lupino (Pennington/Vicar), Aimee Luzier (Beth), Bruce Mackillip (Bob), Len Matheo (Joe Sharp/Alf), James O'Neill (Harry), Carolyn Popp (Emily), Corliss Preston (May), Robin Smith (Landlady), Larry Stotz (Recruiting Officer), Bob Wilkens (Blacklock), Marilyn Firment (Standby for Emily)
MUSICAL NUMBERS: Song of the Hired Man, Fill It to the Top, Now for the First Time, Work Song: It's All Right for You, Who Will You Marry Then? Time Passing, Get Up and Go Lad, I Wouldn't Be the First, Fade Away, Hear Your Voice, What a Fool I've Been, If I Could, Men of Stone, You Never See the Sun, Interlude: Jackson, What Would You Say to Your Son?, Union Song, Gathering of Soldiers, Farewell Song, So Tell Your Children, Crossbridge Dance, No Choir of Angels, Finale
A musical in 2 acts and 14 scenes. The action takes place in 1896 and in 1914 in England.

(Folksbiene Playhouse) Saturday, Oct. 22, 1988–March 12, 1989 (48 performances). The Folksbiene Playhouse (Ben Schecter, Managing Director; Morris Adler, Chairman) presents:
THE BIG WINNER by Sholom Aleichem; Adapted by I. D. Berkowitz; Director, Rina Elisha; Music, Haim Elisha; Lyrics, Miriam Kressyn; Costumes, Nancy Palmatier; Set, James Feng; Lighting, Scott Wolfeil; Stage Manager, Beth Lord; Press, Max Eisen, Madelon Rosen CAST: David Rogow (Shimele Soroker), Zypora Spaisman (Eti Meni), Mina Bern (Perl/Golda Fein), I. W. Firestone (Solovychik), Sandy Levitt (Soloman Fein), Richard Carlow (Kopl), Michael Krauss (Motl), Amy Gordon (Beylke), Yosi Sokolsky (Koltun), Herman Abrams (Mendl), Richard Silver (Goldenthaler), Herbert Scherzer (Usher Feyn), English narration: Simcha Kruger
A comedy with music in 2 acts and 4 scenes.

(Riverwest Theatre) Friday, Oct. 28–Nov. 19, 1988 (20 performances) CHS Productions and Dina & Alexander E. Racolin and John Scarfeo in association with Riverwest Theatre present:
REACHING OUT by Mary Rysuk; Director, Apollo Dukakis; Set, Lewis Folden; Lighting, David Higham; Costumes, Donna Marie Larsen; Original Music, Regan Ryzuk; Production Coordinator, Paul A. Kochman; Stage Managers, Annie Devish, Liz Engelhardt; Press, Chris Boneau CAST: Barbara Joy Spiegel (Lee), Marjorie Austrian (Thema), John Corey (Bacio), Christina Zorich (Jill), Joseph Massa (John), Gregory Henderson (Stan)
A "romantic comedy" in two acts. The action takes place at the present time on Lee's sun-porch and backyard somewhere in Queens, New York City.

(Symphony Space) Wednesday, Nov. 2–6, 1988 (6 limited performances) The National Foundation for Jewish Culture presents the Haifa Municipal Theatre's New York debut in:
SOUL OF A JEW by Joshua Sobol; Director, Gedalia Besser; Music/Musical Direction, Yoni Rechter; Set, Adrian Vaux; Costumes, Edna Sobel; Lighting, Yehiel Orgal CAST: Doron Tavori (Otto Weininger), Giora Shammai (Leopold), Leora Rivlin (Adelaide/Adela), Gury Segal (Berger), Noa Goldberg (Clara), Ilan Toren (Teitz/Strindberg/Mobius), Michael Kfir (Freud), Tchia Danon (Prostitute)
A drama performed in Hebrew. The action takes place in Vienna at the turn of the century.

(Village Theatre) Thursday, Nov. 3–13, 1988 (20 performances and 9 previews). The Village Theatre Company presents:
WHAT WOULD ESTHER WILLIAMS DO IN A SITUATION LIKE THIS? by Don Werbacher, Rich Werbacher; Director, Judd Silverman; Set, Bryan Johnson; Sound, Jimmy Flynn; Lighting, Tracy Lee Wilson; Costumes, Kerri Lea Robbins; Hairstylist, George Kuhn; Stage Manager, Jodi Feldman; Press, Peter Cromarty & Co./Kevin Brockman, Jim Baldassare, David Gersten. CAST: Michael Curran (Walter Sparks), Milton Elliott (Gordon), Susan Farwell (Doris Sparks), James Fleming (Commodore), Randy Kelly (Tony), Julia McLaughlin (Muriel Sparks), Keith Michl (Pops Sparks), Howard Thoresen (George Sparks)
A comedy in three acts. The action takes place in the living-room of the Sparks' home in lower New York Bay on the Shores of Staten Island, late in the afternoon in the summer of 1945.

(Actors Space) Thursday, Nov. 3, 1988–   The Actors Space (Alan Langdon, Artistic Director, Sheila Wood, Managing Director) presents:
SHOOTING STARS by Molly Newman; Director, Richard Maynard; Set, Robert Briggs; Lighting, Ken Posner; Costumes, Martha Hally; Sound, Michael Cohen; Stage Manager, Margaret Curry CAST: Yvonne Campbell (Butch), Karen Biderman (Tammy), Melissa Randel (Shelby), Elizabeth Browning (Wilma), Judith Barnett (Birdie), Stephen Bradbury (Cassius), Elizabeth C. Loftus (Gay), Joan Rosenfels (Charlene)

(West Bank Downstairs Theatre) Thursday, Nov. 3–5, 1988 (3 limited performances)
MORTAL FRIENDS by Katharine Houghton; Director, Lucien Douglas; Production Assistant, Cece Donoghue; Lighting/Stage Manager, Judy Avioli CAST: Schuyler Grant (Sky), Gwyllum Evans (Alan), Jim Stubbs (Waiter)
The action takes place in the present surreal in the Palm Court of the Plaza Hotel in New York. Performed without intermission.

Top: Mina Bern, David Rogow, Zypora Spaisman in "The Big Winner" *(Martha Swope Photo)*

Center: Carolyn Popp, Ray Luetters in "The Hired Man" *(Ernest Hoitsma Photo)*

Bottom: Susan Farwell, Randy Kelly in "What Would Esther Williams Do in a Situation Like This?" *(Nina Krieger Photo)*

(Orpheum Theatre) Saturday, Nov. 5–20, 1988 (12 performances and 8 previews) Jacob Salzman presents:

THE FAITHFUL BRETHREN OF PITT STREET by Philip Lamb; Director, Ethan Taubes; Set/Lighting, Jeffrey Schissler; Costumes, Marianne Powell-Parker; Sound, Aural Fixation; General Manager, Arthur Cantor Associates; Company Manager, Alexander Fraser; Technical Director, Rick A. Shrout; Stage Managers, William Castleman, Philip Shultz; Press, Henry Luhrman Associates/Terry M. Lilly, Russell Gustafson, David Lotz, Eleanore Anderson CAST: David Hurst (Joseph Knaitsch), Sol Frieder (Zalman Zudick), Norman Kruger (Myles Bocktzein), Michael Marcus (Shimshen Boorvis), Victor Arnold (Murray Significado), Ward Saxton (Alfred Russell), Debra Stricklin (Ella Pagira), Allen L. Rickman (Jerry), Carl J. Frano (Gregory)

A comedy in 3 acts. The action takes place at the present time on the stage of the National Yiddish Art Theater.

(Actors Outlet) Wednesday, Nov. 9–Dec. 3, 1988 (11 performances and 5 previews). Time and Patience Unlimited presents:

ON THE PROWL directed by Tony DiBenedetto; Music/Book/Lyrics, John Chibbaro, Claudia-Jo Allmand; Assistant Director/Stage Manager, Juliann Flynn; Set/Lighting, Randall Etheredge; Musical Director, Bernard Purdie; Musical Staging/Dances, Marvin Gordon; Costumes, Donna Marie; Casting, Ginger Friedman; Assistant Stage Manager, Allison Shuker; Press, Henry Luhrman/Terry M. Lilly, David Lotz, Russ Gustafson, Eleanor Anderson CAST: Lucinda Adams (Crazy Lady), Claudia-Jo Allmand (Becky), Kim Cea (Nikki), Jeanie Columbo (The Voice), Tony DiBenedetto (Anthony), Mark Enis (Ralphie), Christina Faye (Crazy Lady), Cher Ranae Kimbrew (Crazy Lady), Gail Lou (Diana), Alfred Preisser (Robert), Jessica Wicken (Anna/Becky's Mom)

MUSICAL NUMBERS: Crazy, On the Prowl, If I Say Yes, Closer to Me, We're Just Like Children, I Cry Tears, I Forget about Romance, Tailpipe, Once There Was Love in Me, Dancing Alone, Tell Me, Please Let Me Prove, This Is What I'll Do

A musical in two acts. The action takes place at the present and ten years past.

(Studio Theatre 603) Thursday, Nov. 10–20, 1988 (8 performances). The Directors Company (Michael Parva, Artistic/Producing Director; Victoria Lanman Chesshire, Artistic/Managing Director) presents the Passage Theatre Company of New Jersey's production of:

BOB'S GUNS by Jim McGrath; Director, Stephen Stout CAST: Barry Cullison (Bob), Anne O'Sullivan (JoBeth), David Doty (Frank), Becky Gelke (Saucy, Bob's wife), Ritchie Marron-Montgomery (Bob's nephew, Roddy), Tom Stechschulte (Buck)

A dark comedy set in a family-run Dallas gun shop on the day of John F. Kennedy's assassination.

(Raft Theatre) Tuesday, Nov. 15–Dec. 6, 1988 (11 performances). Quaigh Theatre Will Lieberson, Producing Director) presents:

BATTING PRACTICE by Paul Gleason; Director, Will Lieberson; Set, Kricker James; Sound/Lights, Bob Mahnken; Producer, James Rosin; Stage Manager, Wink Powers CAST: Kricker James (Possum Badger), James Rosin (Les Miller)

The action takes place at the present time during early spring outside a neglected little ball park on the outskirts of a small town in Central Florida.

(45th Street Theatre) Thursday, Nov. 17–Dec. 10, 1988 (20 performances) Primary Stages Company (Casey Childs, Artistic Director; Janet Reed, Associate Artistic Director) presents:

NASTY LITTLE SECRETS by Lanie Robertson; Director, Stuart Ross; Producing Associate, Herbert H. O'Dell; Co-Producers, Dina and Alexander E. Racolin; Dialect Coach, Howard Samuelson; Costumes, Bruce Goodrich; Associate Designer, Deborah Scott; Sound, C. E. Slisky; Casting, Marilyn McIntyre/James Harper; Production Assistant, Chris Pagoota; Stage Managers, James Stephen Sulanowski, Patti Saraniero; Press, Shirley Herz Associates/Miller Wright, Chris Boneau CAST: Scott Renderer (Joe Orton), Craig Fols (Kenneth Halliwell), Colin Fox (Mr. Willoughby), John C. Vennema (Carnes)

A drama in two acts. The action takes place in the bed-sitting room of Halliwell/Orton in the Islington section of London from the Fall of 1952 through late summer of 1967.

(Astor Place Theatre) Thursday, Nov. 17–Dec. 11, 1988 (24 performances). Frank Basile, Lewis Friedman, Tom O. Meyerhoff, Albert Nocciolino present:

THE MIDDLE OF NOWHERE based on songs by Randy Newman; Conceived and Written by Tracy Friedman; Direction/Choreography, Tracy Friedman; Set, Loren Sherman; Costumes, Juliet Polcsa, Loren Sherman, Lighting, Phil Monat; Sound, Christopher "Kit" Bond; Musical Supervisor/Arrangements/Orchestrations, Robby Merkin; Musical Director/Conductor, Jonny Bowden; Casting, David Cady; Associate Choreographer, Richard Stafford; General Manager, KL Management; Technical Director, Richard Booth; Props, Lynn Johnson; Wardrobe, Rebecca Kreinen; Stage Managers, Ellen Raphael, Christine Gaudet; Press, Joshua Ellis/Adrian Bryan-Brown, Jackie Green, Susanne Tighe, Tim Ray, Chris Boneau CAST: Roger Robinson (Joe), Vondie Curtis-Hall (G.I.), Michael Arkin (Salesman), Diana Castle (Girl), Tony Hoylen (Redneck), Understudies: Rudy Roberson (Joe/G.I.), Nick Searcy (Salesman/Redneck), Christine Baudet (Girl)

MUSICAL NUMBERS: I Think It's Going to Rain, Simon Smith, Yellow Man, Davy the Fat Boy, Political Science, Lonely at the Top, Lover's Prayer, Old Kentucky Home, Tickle Me, Maybe I'm Doing It Wrong, They Just Got Married, Short People, Song for the Dead, Baltimore, I'm Different, It's Money That I Love, Sigmund Freud's Impersonation, Sail Away, You Can Leave Your Hat On, Old Man, Marie, Rednecks, Mr. President, Louisiana 1927.

A musical performed without intermission. The action takes place in 1969 somewhere on the back roads of Louisiana.

(Courtyard Theatre) Friday, Nov. 18–Dec. 18, 1988 (120 performances. It had previously played 12 weeks prior to its formal Off-Broadway opening). The Glines presents:

ON TINA TUNA WALK by John Glines; Director, Peter Pope; Set, Matthew Moore; Costumes, Charles Catanese; Lighting, Tracy Dedrickson; Associate Producers, William Castleman, Dennis Dane, Bill Repicci; Press, FLT/Francine L. Trevens, Mike Kopelow, Robert J. Weston. CAST: Eddie Cobb (Eddie), Jeff Herbst (Michael), Cy Orfield (Russell), John Speredakos succeeded by Peter Pope (J.J.), Tom Donoghue (Paul)

A play in 2 acts and 3 scenes. The action takes place at the present time on the front deck of Eddie's house on Tina Tuna Walk in The Pines on Fire Island, NY.

(Theatre at St. Peter's Church) Sunday, Nov. 20, 1988–Jan. 15, 1989 (54 performances and 10 previews). Golden Glow Unlimited presents:
THE MAJESTIC KID by Mark Medoff; Director, Derek Wolshonak; Set, Lewis Folden; Costumes, Debra Stein; Lighting, Scott Pinkney; Music, Jan Scarbrough; Lyrics, Mark Medoff, Jan Scarbrough; Sound, The Sound Spa; Production-Manager, Marion Vaccaro; Assistant to Director, Kathleen Mary; Production Assistant, Matthew Ellis; Stage Manager, Sheri Kane; Press, Cromarty & Co./Peter Cromarty, David Gersten, Kevin Brockman, Douglas J. Morse CAST: Stuart Zagnit (Aaron Weiss), Michael Cullen (Judge Wm. S. Hart Finlay), Kay Walbye (A. J. Pollard), Juliette Kurth (Lisa Belmondo), Alex Wipf (The Laredo Kid), Eliza Berry (Grip), Rande Mele (Grip)
   A comedy in two acts. The action takes place out West, not very long ago.

(Joyce Theater) Tuesday, Nov. 22–27, 1988 (8 limited performances). IPA in association with the Joyce Theater Foundation presents:
ARIADNE OBNOXIOUS by Ethyl Obnoxious; Music composed and performed by Peter Golub; Costumes, Gerard Little/Mr. Fashion; Lighting, Dan Kotlowitz; Technical Director, Marc Warren; Production Coordinator, Eric Osbun; Stage Managers, Matt Baylor, Phillip Warner; Press, Susan Bloch Co./Ellen Zeisler, Alison Sherman, Bradley Daves CAST: Black-Eyed Susan, Ethyl Eichelberger
   Performed with one intermission.

(Lamb's Theatre) Friday, Nov. 25–Dec. 31, 1988 (37 performances and 15 previews). Lamb's Theatre Company (Carolyn Rossi Copeland, Producing Director) presents:
THE GIFTS OF THE MAGI based on the O. Henry stories; Book/Lyrics, Mark St. Germain; Music/Lyrics, Randy Courts; Director, Sonya Baehr; Set, Michael C. Smith; Costumes, Hope Hanafin; Lighting, Heather Carson; Choreography, Ricarda O'Conner; Musical Director, Randy Courts; Original Incidental Music, Steven M. Alper; Technical Director, Paul Grigoridis; Wigs, Tina Delafield; Stage Managers, Robin Anne Joseph, Vivian Lamar; Press, Cromarty & Co./Peter Cromarty, Kevin Brockman, David Gersten CAST: Michael Calkins (Him), Rebecca Renfroe (Her), Adam Bryant (Willy), Scott Waara (Jim), Jessica K. Beltz (Della), Gabriel Barre (Soapy)
MUSICAL NUMBERS: Star of the Night, Gifts of the Magi, Jim and Della, Christmas Is to Blame, How Much to Buy My Dream, The Restaurant, Once More, Bum Luck, Greed, Pockets, The Same Girl, The Gift of Christmas
   A musical performed without intermission. The action takes place in New York City, December 23–25, 1905.

Claiborne Cary, John Rothman, Rodney Scott Hudson,
Marilyn Sokol in "Faith, Hope and Charity"
(Anita/Steve Shevett Photo)
Above: Stuart Zagnit, Alex Wipf in "The Majestic Kid"

Cy Orfield, John Speredakes in "On Tina Tuna Walk"
(Gerry Goodstein Photo)
Above: Rebecca Renfroe, Gabriel Barre, Michael Calkins in
"Gifts of the Magi" (Martha Swope Photo)

(Our Studios) Wednesday, Nov. 30–Dec. 11, 1988 (16 performances). Masque Productions present:
THE ELEPHANT MAN by Bernard Pomerance; Director, Mark Harborth; Original Music, Paul Weiss, Bob Scheffler, Jim Kratzer; Scenic Drops, Jeff Bretl; Stage Manager, Todd E. Adams; Press, Kevin P. McAnarney CAST: T. C. Burtt, Jr. (Treves/Policeman), Patricia Cucco (Pinhead/Nurse Sandwich/Princess Alexandra), Tom Crow (Ross/Bishop How/Snork), Holly Hawkins (Pinhead/Mrs. Kendal/Countess), Gary Kerr (John Merrick), Roy Owsley (Carr Gomm/Conductor), Doug Smith (Pinhead Manager/Policeman/Porter/Lord John)
   A drama in two acts. The action takes place in London and Belgium Brom 1884 to 1890.

(Ensemble Studio Theatre) Wednesday, Nov. 30–Dec. 18, 1988 (20 performances). The Ensemble Studio Theatre (Curt Dempster, Artistic Director) presents:
THE PROMISE by Jose Rivera; Director, David Esbjornson; Set, Ann Sheffield; Lighting, Greg MacPherson; Costumes, Toni Leslie James; Sound, Bruce Ellman; Choreographer, Kate Gyllenhaal; Stage Manager, Camille Calman; Producer, Kate Baggott CAST: Jaime Sanchez (Guzman), Socorro Santiago (Lilia), Donald Berman (Carmelo/Hiberto), Ivonne Coll (Lolin/Woman in shroud), Rene Moreno (Milton), Kate Gyllenhaal (Malinche), Yusef Bulos (Alegria/Priest)
   A play in two acts. The action takes place at the present time in Patchogue, Long Island, NY.

(South Street Theatre) Wednesday, Dec. 7, 1988–Jan. 8, 1989 (24 performances and 21 previews, including 8 previews at the Triplex Theatre). Max Daniels in association with Hospital Audiences Inc. presents:
FAITH, HOPE, AND CHARITY three one-act plays directed by Edward Berkeley; Sets, Patricia Woodbridge; Lighting, Jane Reisman; Costumes, Martin Pakledinaz; Wigs/Makeup, Elsen Associates; Casting, Thomas Lee Sinclair; Sound, Paul Bang; General Manager, Max Daniels; Technical Director, Kevin Durkin; Props, Gina Rubino, Production Assistant, David Frutkoff; Stage Managers, Tom Roberts, Angela Nevard; Press, Ruth Rothbart Mayer CAST: "Faith" by Israel Horovitz; with Claiborne Cary (Jackie), Rodney Scott Hudson succeeded by Alex Molina (Ted), Angela Nevard (Faith), Marilyn Sokol (Agatha), John Rothman (Roger). "Hope" by Terrence McNally; with Angela Nevard (Faith), John Rothman (Toby), Claiborne Cary (Sister Bonta), Rodney Scott Hudson succeeded by Alex Molina (Raymond Whitcomb), Marilyn Sokol (Hope Bregman). "Charity" by Leonard Melfi; with Claiborne Cary (Alice Brown), Angela Nevard (Carolina Doe), Marilyn Sokol (Enda Ford), John Rothman (Gregory House), Rodney Scott Hudson succeeded by Alex Molina (Ingonna Johnson).
   The action for all three plays takes place at the present time in New York City's Central Park.

John Shea, Suzanne Bertish in "Rosmersholm"
(Marc Bryan-Brown Photo)

(Actors Playhouse) Wednesday, Dec. 7, 1988—   Will You Remember Productions presents:
SWEETHEARTS: Nostalgic Musical Memories of Jeanette MacDonald and Nelson Eddy; Conductor/Pianist, David Wolfson; Arrangements, Don Chan; Costumes, Josie Gardner, Ethel Anderson; Lighting, Paul Lindsay Butler; General Manager, Steven M. Levy; Technical Director, Ellen Kurrelmeyer; Technical Coordinator, Pamela C. Ross; Wardrobe, Judith Strawn; Wigs, Wayne Gerou; Stage Manager, David G. O'Connell; Press, Robert Ganshaw CAST: Antoinette Mille, Walter Adkins
    A musical in two acts reviewing the careers of Jeanette MacDonald and Nelson Eddy.

(Actors Outlet) Wednesday, Dec. 7, 1988—   The Beacon Project presents:
THE REVENGER'S TRAGEDY by Cyril Tourneur; Director, Elizabeth Huffman; Set, Miguel Lopez Castillo; Lighting, Tracy Lee Wilson; Costumes, Elizabeth Huffman; Choreographer, Dane Akers; Wigs/Hairstylist, Jonathan Lippman; Dramaturge, Stuart Laurence; Stage Manager, Elaine O'Donnell CAST: Lisa Bansavage, Cynthia Bock, Richard Bowden, Leah Cartmell, Michael Fife, Darroch Greer, Joseph Haj, Jane Hamilton, Tom Dale Keever, Stuart Laurence, Anthony John Lizzul, Brian Markinson, Marc Nohe, Larry Reinhardt-Meyer, Robert L. Rowe, Bronwyn Truex, Warren Watson
    A drama in two acts.

(Charles Ludlam Theater) Thursday, Dec. 8, 1988–July 14, 1989 (performances) On April 28, 1989 it was joined in repertory by "Salome". The Ridiculous Theatrical Company (Everett Quinton, Artistic Director) presents:
A TALE OF TWO CITIES adapted by Everett Quinton from the novel by Charles Dickens; Director, Kate Stafford; Set, Jan Bell, James Eckerle, Daphne Groos; Costumes, Susan Young; Lights, Richard Currie; Technical Director, Jan Bell; Stage Manager, James Eckerle; Press, Steven Samuels CAST: Solo performance by Everett Quinton

(William Redfield Theatre) Thursday, Dec. 8–18, 1988 (12 performances). The Third Step Theatre Company presents:
THE CHRISTMAS BRIDE by Margit Ahlin; Based on "The Battle of Life" by Charles Dickens; Music/Lyrics, Noel Katz; Director, Al D'Andrea; Musical Direction, Michael H. Lavine; Set, Barbara Wolfe; Lighting, Richard Schaefer; Costumes, Julia Maines; Choreography/Assistant Director, Seth Walsh; Supervsing Producer, Melody Brooks; Stage Manager, Greg Weiss; Press, Kendall Korsgaard CAST: David Arthur Bachrach, Richard P. Gang, Lynellen Kagen, Kate Konigisor, Joanne Lessner, Susan Morgenstern, Marilyn Olsen, Robert Shampain, Bob D. White, Lee Winston, Zenon Zelenich
    A musical romance.

(LaMama E.T.C. Annex) Thursday, Dec. 8–30, 1988 (18 performances) La Mama E.T.C. (Ellen Stewart, Artistic Director, Wickham Boyle, Executive Director) presents:
ROSMERSHOLM by Henrik Ibsen; Translation, Frank McGuinness; Director, Sarah Pia Anderson; Set, Roger Glossop; Music/Sound, Mike Figgis; Set, David Adams, Jun Maeda, Brad Phillips, Mark Tambella; Lighting, Carol Mullins; Sound, Richard Kirshner; Casting, Ellen Novack; Production Manager, Jonathan David; Stage Managers, MaryBeth Ward, Virlana Tkacz; Press, Susan Bloch Co./Ellen Zeisler, Alison Sherman, Bradley Daves CAST: Suzanne Bertish (Rebekka West), Carol Morley (Mrs. Helseth), Ted vanGriethuysen (Rector Kroll), John Shea (John Rosmer), Gwyllum Evans (Ulrik Brendel), Peter McRobbie (Peder Mortensgaard)
    A drama in 4 acts with one intermission. The action takes place during the summer in the living room and study of Rosmersholm.

(Beacon Theatre) Wednesday, Dec. 14–20, 1988 (8 performances). The Real Events Company presents:
1000 AIRPLANES ON THE ROOF written by David Henry Hwang; Composed by Philip Glass; Set/Projections, Jerome Sirlin; Sound, Kurt Munkacsi; Musical Director, Martin Goldray; Lighting, Robert Wierzel; Director, Philip Glass; Producers, Robert LoBianco, Jedediah Wheeler; Sound, Euphorbia Productions; Movement, Mary Ann Kellogg; Wardrobe, Winsome McKoy; Technical Director, Jerry Marshall; Projection, Ray Myslewski; Tour Manager, Susan West; Stage Managers, Michele Steckler, Kristina Kinet; Press, Susan Bloch Co./Ellen Zeisler, Bradley Daves, Alison Sherman CAST: The Philip Glass Ensemble: Martin Goldray, Jon Gibson, Jack Kripi, Dora Ohrenstein, Richard Peck, Phillip Bush, Dan Dryden, Bob Bielecki and Patrick O'Connell as "M"
    Performed without intermission.

(Theater for the New City) Thursday, Dec. 15, 1988–Jan. 8, 1989 The Theater for the New City (Artistic/Managing Director, George Bartenieff; Executive/Artistic Director, Crystal Field) presents:
HEATHEN VALLEY by Romulus Linney; Set, Mark Marcante; Lighting, Anne Militello; Stage Manager, Francesca Mantani Arkus CAST: Jim Ligon (Billy), Robert Hock (Bishop), Scott Sowers (Starns), J. Joseph Houghton (Harlan), Ann Sheehy (Cora), Julie Follansbee (Juba)
    A drama set in an incredibly remote region of North Carolina during the 1840's.

(Ohio Theatre) Tuesday, Dec. 20–23, 1988 (4 performances)
BEHIND THE HEART by Sande Zeig; Adapted from the stories "Cassation" and "The Grande Malade" by Djuna Barnes; Director, Lucille King; Set, Andrea Dorman; Costumes, Susie Levi; Lighting, Roma Flowers; Movement, Joan Nicholason; Music, Paul Spong; Props, Rebecca Kurtz; Sound, Lee Daly; Technical Director, Terry Dame; Producer, La Compagnie; Associate Producer, Lake Ivan Performance Group; Stage Manager, Pamela De Carlo; Press, Jeffrey Wise CAST: Julia Sheehy (Julia), Joan Nicholson (Madame), Sande Zeig (Katya), Abigail Pogrebin (Moydia), John McIlveen (Monsieur X), Paul Amodeo (Baron), Bina Scharif (Gaya)
    Performed with one intermission.

"Behind the Heart" Above: Everett Quinton in "A Tale of Two Cities" *(Anita & Steve Shevett Photo)*

56

(Westbeth Theatre Center) Wednesday, Jan. 4–22, 1989 (16 performances) Westbeth Theatre Center in association with Donal Egan presents:

WOMEN ALONE two short plays by Dario Fo and Franca Rame; Director, Sheldon Deckelbaum; Set, Zipora Schulz; Lighting, Kim T. Sharp; Music, Aural Fixation; Stage Manager, Paul A. Kochman

COMING HOME takes place in a modern middle class Italian Housing project.

ULRIKE MEINHOF takes place in a contemporary European prison.

Performed by Lynne McCollough

(45th Street Theatre) Thursday, Jan. 5–28, 1989 (16 performances). The Phoenix Ensemble (Mary Jasperson, Artistic Director; Stacey Gladstone Managing Director; Kim Hubbard, Producing Director) presents:

WORKING MAGIC by Margaret Hunt; Director, Gail Kellstron; Lighting, Richard Currie; Special Effects, Anthony Ferrer; Magic Consultant, Jeff Sheridan; Sound, Matt Berman; Stage Manager, Jonathan Gelman; Press, Shirley Herz Associates/Sam Rudy. CAST: Michael Varner (Harry Houdini Grant), Stacey Gladstone (Lila Grant), Kate Coyle (Charlene Maxwell), Fred Velde (Moses Booth), Paul Ravich (Joey/Leon/Lentz/Others), Kerry Metzler (Nettie/Jackie/Mrs. King/Others), Vicki Hirsch (Waitress/Receptionist/Others), Jeff Vaughn (Vinnie/DiAngelo/Cooper/Others), Kim Highland (Malcolm Maxwell)

The action takes place at the present time in New York City and environs. Performed with one intermission.

(Downstairs at the Trocadero) Tuesday, Jan. 10–25, 1989 (8 performances) Cat & Mouse Productions presents:

STARK'S CAFE by Art Mortensen; Produced and Directed by Robert J. Geary CAST: Gail Barle, Wanda Bimson, Bridget Cronson, David Pincus, Jeff Shoemaker, Robert Winston

A comedy in two acts.

(Judith Anderson Theatre) Jan. 10–Feb. 26, 1989 (performances). Manhattan Punch Line Theatre (Steve Kaplan, Artistic Director) presents the fifth annual:

FESTIVAL OF ONE ACT COMEDIES: Evening A: "Wonderful Party" by Howard Korder; Director, Val Hendrickson; "The Gettysburg Sound Bite" by Ted Tally; Director, Louis Scheeder; "One Monday" by Matt Cutugno; Director, Scott Rubsam; "Seven Menus" by David Ives; Director, Fred Sanders; "Sex Lives of Superheroes" by Stephen Gregg; Director, Paul Lazarus. Evening B: "The News from St. Petersburg" by Rich Orloff; "Seeing Someone" by Laurence Klavan; Director, Steve Kaplan; "Requiem for a Heavyweight" by Mark O'Donnell; Director, Robin Saex; "Pillow Talk" by Peter Tolan; Director, Jason McConnell Buzas; "Good Honest Food" by Bill Bozzone; Director, Steve Kaplan Sets, James Wolk; Lighting, Danianne Mizzy; Costumes, Fontilla Boone, Michael Schler; Sound, Scott David Sanders; Casting, Jeffery Passero; Stage Managers, Janet Clancy, Padraic Lee Fisher, Angela Foster, Beth G. Shery, Stephen Spulick, Cathy Tomlin, Michael David Winter, Jay McManigal, Jonathan D. Secor; Production Manager, Bernita Robinson CAST: Peter Basch, Brad Bellamy, Larry Block, Bill Cohen, Jaffe Cohen, Gary Cookson, Ead Daniels, Kenwyn Dapo, Dan Desmond, Ellen Dolan, Sarah Eckhardt, Steven Gilborn, Daniel Hagen, Tessie Hogan, Cady Huffman, Jack Kenny, David Konig, Amy Lanzet, Neal Lerner, Nicholas Levitin, Steven Marcus, George Melrod, Edmund J. McCormick, Jr., Christiane McKenna, Barry Miller, Susan Monagan, Michael Piontek, Elaine Rinehart, Kathrin King Segal, Pamela Jean Shaddock, Constance Shulman, Victor Slezak, Dan Strickler, Debra Stricklin, Carl Sturmer, Ann Talman, Lois Taylor, Andrea Weber, Melissa Weil, Andrew Winkler

Elaine Rinehart, Matt Cutugno in "One Monday"
(Carol Rosegg Photo)
Above: Fred Velde, Michael Varna, Kim
Highland in "Working Magic" *(Judith Kirtley)*

(City Center Theater) Wednesday, Jan. 11–15, 1989 (3 limited performances). The New York Opera Repertory Theatre (Leigh Gibbs Gore, Founder) presents the world premiere of:

DESIRE UNDER THE ELMS based on the play by Eugene O'Neill; Music, Edward Thomas; Libretto, Joe Masteroff; Conductor, Leigh Gibbs Gore; Director, David Gately; Set, Michael Anania; Costumes, Gregg Barnes; Lighting, Kirk Bookman; Wigs/Makeup, Tom Watson; Props, Alice M. Forrester; Hats, Woody Shelp; Stage Manager, Timothy J. Ocel; Press, Hale & Husted/Alan Hale CAST: Robert Paul Heimann (Simeon), William Livingston (Peter), James Schwisow (Eben), Nicholas Solomon (Ephraim Cabot), Judy Kaye (Abbie Putnam Cabot), Burton Fitzpatrick (Sheriff), Ensemble: Colette Black, Jim Curtin, Joe Fitzpatrick, Debbi Fuhrman, John Lynch, Heidi Mollenhauer, Stephanie Paul, Jacob Terry

An American folk opera in 3 acts and 8 scenes.

(Samuel Becket Theater) Thursday, Jan. 12, 1989–   Wayne Martens in association with the Harold Clurman Theater presents:

ULYSSES IN NIGHTTOWN adapted from a chapter of James Joyce's novel "Ulysses"; Dramatized by Marjorie Barkentin; Director, Wayne Martens; Assistants to Director, Monique Miller, James Sullivan; Lighting, Edward R. F. Matthews; Technical Director, Betsy J. Wingfield; Stage Manager, Carol Venezia CAST: Leslie Block, Stephen Vincent Brennan, James Burke, Cheryl Clifford, Steve Coats, Jayne Amelia Larson, Joseph McKenna, Erin McLaughlin, Robert Molnar, David Teschendorf, Steve Varnum, Carol Venezia, Michele Winslow, Kurt Ziskie

Judy Kaye, Nicholas Solomon in "Desire Under the Elms"
(Beatriz Schiller Photo)

(Chelsea Hotel) Thursday, Jan. 12–Feb. 5, 1989 (10 performances). En Garde Arts (Anne Hamburger, Producer) presents:
AT THE CHELSEA: Director, Lisa Berlin; Press, Ted Killmer. "Room 302" by Stephan Balint; with Alexandra Auder, Rebecca Major, Stephan Balint; "Room 322" by and with Penny Arcade; "Room 502" by David Van Tieghem; with Tina Dudek; "Room 102" by Frank Maya; "Room 302" by Ann Carlson

(Peter Xantho Theatre) Thursday, Jan. 12, 1989 and still playing May 31, 1989. Nico Hartos and Vincent de Angelis present the premiere of the Pyramid Group Theatre Company (Nico Hartos, Artistic Director) production of:
BUNNYBEAR by Nico Hartos; Directed by the author; Design, D. C. Glenn/Marc Umile; Sound/Lighting, Winifred Powers; Costumes, Emmanuel Xuereb, Sophie Xuereb; Stage Managers, Hudson Plumb, Emmanuel Xuereb; Press, FLT/Francine L. Trevins/Mike Kopelow, Charlie Eisenberg CAST: Laura Fay Lewis (Sandy), Richard Flynn (Jack).
   A drama in two acts. The action takes place in Jack and Sandy Hunter's one-bedroom apartment on the upper west side of Manhattan, New York City.

(Apple Corps Theatre) Wednesday, Jan. 18–29, 1989 (12 performances). The Apple Corps Theatre (Michael Tolan, Chairman) presents:
AMERICAN VOICES an evening of four Short Plays performed with one intermission; Scenery, Philip Baldwin; Costumes, Thom Heyer, Kevin Brainerd; Lighting, Deborah Constantine; Sound, Neal Arluck; Artistic Director, John Raymond; Technical Director, Tom Carroll; Wardrobe, Rachel True; Props, Lauren Helpern; Press, Aviva Cohen
Program: "June Moon" by Ring Lardner/George S. Kaufman; Director, Michael Tolan; with William Christian (Fred), Cordelia Richards (Edna). The action takes place in a parlor car during the 1920's. "The Footsteps of Doves" by Robert Anderson; Director, Caymichael Patten; with Matthew Gottlieb (Salesman), Carmen de Lavallade (Harriet), Michael Tolan (George), Charlotte Maier (Jill). The action takes place in the basement of a bed store in the recent past. "Queens of France" by Thornton Wilder; Director, Caymichael Patten; with Monique Cintron (Marie-Sidonie Cressaux), Matthew Gottlieb (M'su Cahusac), Carment de Lavallade (Mme. Pugeot), Charlotte Maier (Mamselle Pointevcin). The action takes place in a lawyer's office in New Orleans during 1869. "Hello Out There" by William Saroyan; Director, Elinor Renfield; with William Christian (Young Gambler), Cordelia Richards (Girl), Neal Arluck (Husband), Michael Tolan (Another Man), Monique Cintron (Wife); Prologue by Kevin O'Connor. The action takes place in a little jailhouse in Matador, Texas in 1940.

(Riverwest Theatre) Friday, Jan. 20–Feb. 11, 1989 (16 performances) Dina & Alexander E. Racolin and CHS Productions in association with Riverwest Theatre present:
OUR OWN RED BLOOD by Cecil Jenkins; Director, Stephen Jobes; Set, Patrick Eagleton; Lighting, Amy A. C. Coombs; Costumes, Thomas Heyer; Sound, Lou Piccirillo; Technical Director, Yung Tam; Stage Managers, Andrea Nugit, Victoria Tejeda; Press, Chris Boneau CAST: George Bamford (Dr. Grant), John Juback (Delaney)
   A drama in 2 acts and 7 scenes. The action takes place at the present time in Grant's study, and in a basement shelter.

(Courtyard Theatre) Wednesday, Jan. 25–Feb. 12, 1989 (16 performances) The Actors Collective presents:
THE VISIT by Friedrich Durrenmatt; Director, Warren Manzi; Set, Jay Stone; Lighting, Ben Solotaire; Costumes, Maud Kernsowski; Sound, David Lawson; Producer, Catherine Russell; Technical Director, Jay Stone; Stage Manager, Tom Canary; Press, Becky Flora & Company. CAST: James Farrell (Man 1/Doctor), Ken Martin (Man 2), Jim Quinlivan (Man 3), Kaarin Raup (Man 4/Sexton), Michael O. Maher (Painter), Nicholas Saunders (Mayor), Jed Krascella (Schoolmaster), Marcus Powell (Priest), Jeffrey Hyatt (Bailiff), Drew Eliot (Alfred III), Francine Farrell (Claire Zachanassian), Joseph Mantello (Ticket Inspector/Gymnast/Second Reporter), Paul Wiley (Moby/Hoby/Zoby), Howard Katz (Boby), Shawn McGuire (Mixed Choir/Cameraman/Coffin Bearer), Francesca Fordiani (Miss Louisa/Mixed Choir), Richard Bassin (Director/Mixed Choir/Coffin Bearer), Hill Carrie Jiler (Hermione/3rd Reporter), Morgan Williams (Policeman), John Hunkele (Toby), Rocco Matone (Roby), Hugh Paine (Koby), Joseph Scott (Loby), Nancy Russell-Tutty (Mrs. Ill), Elizabeth Diamond (Mrs. Mayor), Kevin McGinn (Karl), Marian Chamow (Otillie), Jenny Martel (1st Woman/1st Reporter), Denise McCarthy (2nd Woman/Radio Commentator)
   A drama in two acts. The action takes place in Guellen during 1955.

(Actors Outlet) Thursday, Jan. 26–Feb. 26, 1989 (20 performances). The Working Theatre/Gloucester Stage Company presents:
HENRY LUMPER by Israel Horovitz; Director, Grey Cattell Johnson; Set, David Condino; Costumes, Jose Rivera; Lighting, Douglas Kirkpatrick; Stage Managers, Elizabeth Heeden, Douglas Gettel, Elaine O'Donnell; Press, Bruce Cohen/Kathleen von Schmid CAST: Roger Serbagi, Joseph Jamrog, Brian Delate, Paul O'Brien, Carol Bradley, Jordan Lund, Ralph Bell, Cullen Johnson, Robert Arcaro, Randy Frazier, Kilian Ganly, Anthony Gentile, Luis Guzman, Honor Molloy, Rocco Santo, Monte Russell, Bill Gillogly

Top: **Michael Tolan, Carmen De Lavallade in**
"American Voices"
Below: **Laura Fay Lewis, Richard Flynn in**
"Bunnybear" *(Ken Howard Photo)*

Cathy Reinheimer, Brian Delate, Beverly Dretzel in "Henry Lumper" *(Carol Rosegg Photo)*
Above: George Bamford, John Jubak in "Our Own Red Blood" *(Paul Yuen Photo)*

(Westside Arts Theatre/Downstairs) Opened Saturday, Jan. 28, 1989, and still playing May 31, 1989. Kenneth F. Martel, Ellen M. Krass in association with Home Box Office and Kenneth M. Weinstock present the Martel Media Enterprises production of:
THE KATHY & MO SHOW: PARALLEL LIVES written and performed by Mo Gaffney and Kathy Najimy; Director, Paul Benedict; Set, David Jenkins; Costumes, Gregg Barnes; Lighting, Frances Aronson; Executive Producer, James B. Freydberg; General Management, Fremont Associates; Company Manager, Dana Sherman; Hair/Makeup, Charles Joseph Berry; Production Supervisor, Michael Baden; Wardrobe, Virginia D. Patton; Stage Managers, Brian A. Kaufman, Kate Riddle; Press, Cromarty & Co./Peter Cromarty, Kevin Brockman, David Gersten. CAST: Mo Gaffney, Kathy Najimy
A series of sketches performed with one intermission.

(Broadway Playhouse) Wednesday, Feb. 1–12, 1989 (11 performances). Quinapalus Theatre (Artistic Directors: Tony Rust, Thomas Rice, Denise Dalfo) presents:
MOBY DICK by Herman Melville; Adapted/Directed by Tony Rust; Designers, Peter R. Feuche, Deirdre E. Donohue; Technical Director, Anthony Ferrer; Lighting, Stephen Petrilli; Assistant Director/Costume Coordinator, Denise Dalfo; Stage Manager, Susan Feurzeig CAST: Thomas Rice (Capt. Ahab), Tim Zay (Ishmael), Matthew Shiner (Starbuck), John R. Little (Stubb), John Moss (Father Mapple/Capt. Boomer), Kevin Hills (Peleg/Dr. Bunger), Oliva Le'Auanae (Queequeg), George H. Croom (Dagoo/Cook), Reed Payne (Landlord), Jimmy Blackman (Elijah), Nick Lindsay (Carpenter)
A drama in two acts.

(Minetta Lane Theatre) Tuesday, Feb. 7, 1989 and still playing May 31, 1989. Jeffrey Ash and Susan Quint Gallin in association with Dennis Grimaldi present the Hartford Stage Company production of:
OTHER PEOPLE'S MONEY by Jerry Sterner; Director, Gloria Muzio; Set, David Jenkins, Costumes, Jess Goldstein; Lighting, F. Mitchell Dana; Sound, David Budries; Casting, Judy Henderson; General Management, George Elmer, Patricia Berry; Production Manager, Steven Ehrenberg; Props, Kirk Lawrence; Wardrobe, Joanna Viverta; Stage Managers, Stacey Fleischer, Peter Jack Tkatch CAST: Kevin Conway (Lawrence Garfinkle), James Murtaugh (William Coles), Arch Johnson (Andrew Jorgenson), Scotty Bloch succeeded by Lenka Peterson (Bea Sullivan), Mercedes Ruehl succeeded by Janet Zarish (Kate Sullivan)
A play in two acts. The action takes place at the present time in New York and Rhode Island.

Mo Gaffney, Kathy Najimy (also above) in "The Kathy and Mo Show" *(Martha Swope Photo)*

(Primary Stages) Thursday, Feb. 9–March 4, 1989 (21 performances). Primary Stages Company and Dina and Alexander Racolin present:
ALGERIAN ROMANCE by Kres Mersky; Director, Casey Childs; Set, Andrew Greenhut; Lighting, Deborah Constantine; Costumes, Bruce Goodrich; Props, Deborah Scott; Composer, Bob Kelmenson; Sound, Paul Garrity; Artistic Director, Casey Childs; Associate Artistic Director, Janet Reed; Producing Associate, Herbert H. O'Dell; General Manager, Gordon Farrell; Stage Manager, Sally Plass; Press, Anne Einhorn, Chris Boneau CAST: Gregg Almquist (Bob), Lloyd Battista (Juan), Ralph Marrero (Guard One), Michael Galardi (Guard Two), Lonnie Quinn (Steve), Eleanore Reissa (Vocalist)
A farce without intermission. The action takes place at the present time in a room of a hotel that caters to American tourists in the small Central American nation of Casa Luna, somewhere behind Honduras.

(All Souls Fellowship Hall) Friday, Feb. 10–26, 1989 (14 performances) All Souls Players present:
SPIDER'S WEB by Agatha Christie; Director, Jeffery K. Neill; Set, Robert Edmonds; Costumes, Chas E. Roeder; Lighting, Michael Aguilar; Producers, Marie Landa, Harry Blum, Joseph Aronica; Props, Laurie Pink; Wardrobe, Mary Jane Gocher, Laurie Pink; Stage Managers, Marlene Greene, Foster Rhalse, Tina Grey; Press, Tran Wm. Rhodes CAST: Regis Bowman (Hugo Birch), Philip Dennis DiCristina (Elgin), Sam Goodyear (Henry Hailsham-Brown), Wilbur Edwin Henry (Insp. Lord), Kate Konigisor (Clarissa Hailsham-Brown), Jenny R. Mather (Pippa Hailsham-Brown), George Millenbach (Jeremy Warrender), John Otis (Sir Rowland Delahaye), Florence Rupert (Mildred Peake), Grant Stevens (Oliver Costello), Eric Walden (Constable Jones)
A mystery in 3 acts and 4 scenes. The action takes place in the drawing-room of Copplestone Court, the Hailsham-Brown home in Kent, England on an evening in March.

(The Space at St. Clement's) Tuesday, Feb. 14–March 4, 1989 (18 performances and 4 previews) Music-Theatre Group (Lyn Austin, Producing Director; Diane Wondisford, Mark Jones, Associate Producing Directors) and Thought Movement Motor (Charles Moulton, Artistic Director) present:
DANGEROUS GLEE CLUB conceived, choreographed and directed by Charles Moulton; Conceived and composed by Steve Elson; Lighting, Debra Dumas; Costumes, Eileen Lynch; Stage Managers, Steven Ehrenberg, Brian DuGay CAST: Bruce Bell, Rick Ford, Allysaon Green, Aaron Heick, Bill Ruyle, Lissy Trachtenberg
Performed without intermission.

Scotty Bloch, James Murtaugh, Mercedes Ruehl, Arch Johnson in "Other People's Money"
Above: Kevin Conway, Ruehl in "Other People's Money"
(Peter Cunningham Photos)

(Triplex Performing Arts Center) Thursday, Feb. 16–March 5, 1989 (18 performances) Mabou Mines and INTAR Hispanic American Arts Center (Max Ferra, Artistic Director) in association with the Boston Musica Viva presents:
SUENOS adapted by Ruth Maleczech from the writings of Sor Juana Ines de la Cruz, Eduardo Galeano and Homero Aridjis; Music Composed by Herschel Garfein; Original Lyrics, Ruth Maleczech, George Emilio Sanchez, Herschel Garfein; Choreographer, Pat Hall Smith; Music Director/Conductor, Richard Pittman; Director, Ruth Maleczech; Lighting, Clay Shirky; Sound, L. B. Dallas; Costumes, Toni-Leslie James; Set, Michael Deegan; Birds/Masks, Barbara Pollitt; Technical Director, David Brune; Assistant Music Director, Jonathan Knight; Company Manager, David Baron; Stage Managers, Anthony Gerber, Stephanie Bond; Press, Ellen Jacobs & Co. CAST: John Arrucci, Luz Bermejo, Eduardo Carrillo, James Coelho, Eric Culver, Charles Davis, Jeffrey Dooley, Rotzo B. Morris, Lorraine Hunt, Clinton Chinyelu Ingram, Itabora, Irma-Estel LaGuerre, Maribel Lizardo, Julissa Marquez, Barbara Martinez, Tomas Milian, Christina Ann Nater, Theresa Patton, Erica Payne, Gustavo Pereiro, Claudio Rogozzi, William Reinerl, Isabel Soez, Renoly Santiago, Nairobi Smith, Roger Guenveur Smith, Rohan Smith, Eduardo Uribe, Terence Yancey
  Performed with one intermission.

(Newfoundland Theater) Thursday, Feb. 16–March 12, 1989 (16 performances). Odyssey Theater Company presents an original adaptation of:
THE GAMBLER by Fyodor Dostoevsky; Director, Mary Wolford; Composer, David Simons; Set, Andrew Arnault; Costumes, Ann R. Emo; Lighting, Paul Koestner CAST: Alana Adena, Andrew Arnault, Bob Caccomo, Michael Gnat. Robert Laconi, Valorie Niccore, David Glenn Stern, Vivian Stern, Fred Sugarman, Julie Green, Denman Maroney, David Simons

(Billie Holiday Theatre) Friday, Feb. 17, 1989—Marjorie Moon presents:
OVER FORTY with Book by Celeste Walker; Music/Lyrics/Musical Arrangements/Direction by Weldon; Director, Mikell Pinkney; Set/Costumes, Felix E. Cochren; Lighting, Christian Epps; Stage Manager, Avan; Press, Howard Atlee; CAST: Eunice Newkirk (Gwen Matthews), Janyse M. Singleton (Patricia Ellen Shaw), Marisa Francesca Turner (Beryl Paige), Lady Peachena (Annie Ruth Johnson).
MUSICAL NUMBERS: Over Forty, When We Were Young, Oldies Melody, Why Did We Part, Ignite My Love, Another Life to Come, Arms in Revolt, We Shall Overcome, We Need Our Men, Someone to Say I Love You, Beat the Clock, Workin' Girls, A Little Age Sits Well, Since I Laid My Burdens Down, In My Life.
  Performed with one intermission.

Top: Marisa Francesca Turner, Lady Peachena, Eunice Newkirk, Janice M. Singleton (sitting) in "Over Forty"
(Jessica Katz Photo)

Below: Emily Loesser, Colin Romoff, Jo Sullivan, Douglas Romoff in "Together Again For the First Time"
(Anita/Steve Shevett Photo)

(Kaufman Theatre) Friday, Feb. 17–March 26, 1989 (30 performances and 13 previews). Martin R. Kaufman presents:
TOGETHER AGAIN FOR THE FIRST TIME conceived by Barry Kleinbort and Colin Romoff; Director, Barry Kleinbort; Musical Staging, Donald Saddler; Musical Direction and Arrangements, Colin Romoff; Scenery, Philip Baldwin; Costumes, William Ivey Long; Lighting, Ted Mather; Sound, Sandor Margolin; Bass, Douglas Romoff; General Manager, Marshall B. Purdy; Company Manager, Richard Biederman; Technical Director, David L. Bornstein; Stage Manager, Elizabeth Heeden; Press, Henry Luhrman Associates/Terry Lilly, David Lotz, Jim Randolph, Russ Gustafson CAST: Jo Sullivan, Emily Loesser in a two part celebration of the Broadway Musical.

(Nat Horne Theatre) Thursday, Feb. 23, 1989–   Manhattan Class Company (Robert LuPone, Bernard Telsey, Executive Directors) presents its annual:
ONE-ACT PLAY FESTIVAL: Sets, Dan Conway, Gregory Mercurio; Lighting, John Hastings; Costumes, Dianne-Finn Chapman; Sound, Lia Vollack; Production Manager, Laura Kravets; Associate Producers, Maggie Lear, Eric Berkal; General Manager, W. D. Cantler; Press, Shirley Herz Associates
Series A: "The Lost Colony" by Wendy MacLeod; Director, Michael Greif; with Ken Marks, Robin Morse, Joe Ponazecki, Jane Summerhays. "Red Sheets" by Erik Ehn; Director, Daniel Wilson; with Kent Adams, Cara Buono, Jarlath Conroy, Melora Walters. "Bikini Snow" by Anna Theresa Cascio; Director, Jimmy Bohr; with Mark W. Conklin, Linda Larson, Stephen Schnetzer, Leif Tilden
Series B: "Dakota's Belly, Wyoming" by Erin Cressida Wilson; Director, Brian Mertes; with Victor Slezak, Gordana Rashovich, Kyra Sedgwick. "Catfish Loves Anna" by Constance Ray; Director, Kevin Kelley; with Constance Ray, Cass Morgan. "Prelude and Liebestod" by Terrence McNally; Director, Paul Benedict; with Larry Bryggman, Leslie Denniston, Panchali Null, Simon Brooking, Domenic Cuskern

(Actors Outlet) Saturday, Feb. 25–March 18, 1989 (24 performances). Don Saxon, Robert R. Blume, William Roudebush, Malcolm Allen present:
THE DIETRICH PROCESS by Leo Rost; Director, William Roudebush; Set, Bob Barnett; Costumes, Pamela Scofield; Lighting, Susan Y. Roth; Makeup/Hairstylist, Robert Baker; Sound, Gary and Timmy Harris; Technical Director, E. F. Morrill; Props, Paul Carter; Stage Manager, Bill McComb; Press, Max Eisen, Madelon Rosen CAST: Joe Pichette (Andrew White), Paul Mulder (Timothy), Natalie Ross (Mrs. S. C. "Maggie" Rouge), Tom Flagg (Jake Rosen), Bruce B. Morton (Boyd Travis), Dieter Himmel (Dr. Dietrich)
  A "wicked play" in 2 acts and 4 scenes. The action takes place in the private sitting room of Mrs. S. C. Rouge in Westchester County, NY.

Joe Pichette, Natalie Ross, Paul Mulder in "The Dietrich Process" *(Martha Swope Photo)*

(INTAR Theatre) Thursday, March 2–18, 1989 (16 performances). The Classic Theatre (Nicholas John Stathis, Executive Director) in association with Manticore Theatre (Bob Verini, Executive Director) presents:
PHILOCTETES by Sophocles; Translated by E. F. Watling; Director, Kevin Barry; Set/Lighting, Tim Saternow; Costumes, Sam Fleming; Combat Choreography, Jamie Cheatham; Stage Manager, Elizabeth Brady Davis CAST: Andrew Jarkowsky (Odysseus), Jon Krupp (Neoptolemus), Barry Kramer (Sailor/Merchant), Austin Pendleton (Philoctetes), Charles Mandracchia (Heracles), Sailors: Keith Glover, Brian Price, Malcolm Stephenson
    The action takes place on the island of Lemnos during the tenth year of the siege of Troy. Performed without intermission.

(Actors Playhouse) Thursday, March 2–May 28, 1989 (85 performances). Ellen M. Krass and Home Box Office Inc. present:
RENO IN RAGE AND REHAB written and performed by Reno; Director, John Ferraro; Lighting, Jackie Manassee; Associate Producer, Jacqueline Judd; Executive Producer, James B. Freydberg; General Management, Fremont Associates; Company Manager, Terry Byrne; Production Supervisor, Peter Etcheto; Stage Manager, Scott Rodabaugh; Press, Jeffrey Richards Associates, Philip Rinaldi. CAST: Reno in a solo performance without intermission.

(The Arts at St. Ann's) Monday, March 6–19, 1989 (18 performances).
BRIGHTNESS FALLING by Hilary Blecher; Director, Miss Blecher; Set/Costumes, Wilhelm Hahn; Lighting, Bill Armstrong CAST: Barnaby Spring, Pamela Gien, Joseph McKenna, Stephen Mellor, George Taylor, Dana Bate, Julie Follansbee, Seth Sibanda, Paula van der Merve, Aodoulaye N'Gom

Top: (left) Assurbanipal Babilla, Katherine Shepard in
"Grand Central Paradise" *(Yvette Raby Photo)*
Top: (right) Reno in "Reno: In Rage and Rehab"
(Lois Greenfield Photo)

Below: Frederick Neumann, Jane Fleiss, Helen Stenborg in
"Niedecker" *(Martha Holmes Photo)*

(Westbeth Theatre) Tuesday, March 7–Apr. 9, 1989 (30 performances), The Meridian Theater presents:
GRAND CENTRAL PARADISE by Assurbanipal Babilla; Producer/Director, Hamid Fardjad; Costumes, Mariam Touzie; Design, Hamid Fardjad; Music, Mehrdad Jenabi; Press, Donna Linderman, Behnam Nateghi CAST: Katherine Shepard, Assurbanipal Babilla, Judson Camp, Dana Ertischek, Jed Krascella, Donna Linderman, Ken Threet

(Apple Corps Theatre) Tuesday, March 7–26, 1989 (13 performances and 8 previews) The Women's Project and Productions (Julia Miles, Artistic Director) presents:
NIEDECKER by Kristine Thatcher; Director, Julianne Boyd; Set, James Noone; Costumes, Deborah Shaw; Lighting, Frances Aronson; Sound, Bruce Ellman; Technical Director, Tom Carroll; Wardrobe, Evelyn Radinson; Production Assistants, Cheryl Klim, Paul. A. Kochman; Stage Manager, Linda Carol Young; Press, Fred Nathan Co./Merle Frimark CAST: Helen Stenborg (Lorine), Mary Diveny (Ginny), Jane Fleiss (Mary), Frederick Neumann (Al)
    A play in 2 acts and 8 scenes. The action takes place from November 1963 to February 1970, in and around a small cabin just outside Fort Atkinson, Wisconsin, where the Rock River runs into Lake Koshkonong.

(The Village Theatre) Wednesday, March 8–26, 1989 (16 performances). The Village Theatre Company presents:
YOU NEVER CAN TELL by George Bernard Shaw; Director, Henry Fonte; Set, Bryan Johnson; Lighting, Tracy Lee Wilson; Sound, Jimmy Flynn; Costumes, Ismael Hernandez, Jillian Maslow CAST: Barbara Berque, Milton Elliott, Marjorie Feenan, Christie Harrington, Michael Hill, David McConnell, Julia McLaughlin, Patrick Turner, Howard Thoresen

(Ensemble Studio Theatre) Wednesday, March 8–26, 1989 (20 performances)
THE MAGIC ACT by Laurence Klavan; Director, Peter Zapp; Set, Brian Martin; Lighting, David Higham; Costumes, David Sawaryn; Sound, Bruce Ellman; Stage Manager, Jana Llynn CAST: Anne O'Sullivan (Mona Kale), Rick Lawless (Young Alan/Todd), Cordelia Richards (Young Annabelle/Linda), Frederica Meister (Mother/Older Annabelle/Newswoman), Sam Schacht (Father/Older Alan/Newsman)
    A play in two acts. The action takes place at the present time and in the past.

(Lamb's Theatre) Thursday, March 9–25, 1989 (6 performances and 4 previews) Lamb's Theatre Company (Carolyn Rossi Copeland, Producing Director) presents:
THE REVELATION OF JOHN by and with Tom Key; Set, Michael C. Smith; Lighting, Jeff Schissler; Production Manager, Denise Nations; General Manager, Stephen W. NebgenPress, Peter Cromarty & Co./Kevin Brockman, David Gersten
    A solo performance without intermission.

Tom Key in "The Revelation of John"
(Reis Birdwhistell Photo)

61

(Perry Street Theatre) Friday, March 17–Apr. 19, 1989 (25 performances). New York Theatre Workshop (James C. Nicola, Artistic Director; Nancy Kassak Diekmann, Managing Director) presents:
NERO'S LAST FOLLY by and with LEO BASSI. A solo performance.

(INTAR Theatre) Saturday, March 18–Apr. 8, 1989 (16 performances and 4 previews) New Arts Theatre (Joshua Astrachan, Artistic Director) presents:
SLEEPING DOGS by Neal Bell; Director, Thomas Babe; Set, Michael Boak; Lighting, Greg MacPherson; Costumes, Claudia Brown; Sound, Tom Gould; Casting, Wendy Ettinger/Virginia Addison; Assistant to Director, Roger Raines; Props, Jessica Lanier; Technical Director, Ben Jacobs; Stage Manager, Jess Lynn; Press, Cromarty & Co. CAST: Richmond Hoxie (Park), Christopher Fields (Sling), Leslie Lyles (Sally), Cynthia Kaplan (Nana), John P. Connolly (Miner), Jodie Markell (Evelyn Keestro), David Briggs (Bartender), Richard Council (Capp)
A dark comedy performed without intermission. The action takes place in summer during the earliest years of the Reagan administration in and around the Fidelity Building in Manhattan, and at Park's home in Connecticut.

(Promenade Theatre) Monday, March 27, 1989—still playing May 31, 1989 on Sundays and Mondays only. Roger L. Stevens, Thomas Viertel, Steven Baruch, Richard Frankel present:
LOVE LETTERS by A. R. Gurney; Director, John Tillinger; Lighting, Dennis Parichy; General Management, Richard Frankel Productions/Marc Routh; Company Managers, Marc Routh, Linda Wright; Stage Manager, William H. Lang; Press, Joshua Ellis Office/Tim Ray, Jackie Green, Shannon Barr CAST: (weekly change) Kathleen Turner/John Rubinstein, Swoosie Kurtz/Stephen Collins, Katherine Kerr/George Hearn, Swoosie Kurtz/Bruce Davison, Stockard Channing/Bruce Davison, Holland Taylor/A. R. Gurney, Dana Ivey/Victor Garber, Swoosie Kurtz/Richard Backus, Marsha Mason/John Heard, Blythe Danner/Christopher Walken, Maria Tucci/Christopher Reeve, Dana Ivey/James Naughton, Katherine Kerr/John Rubinstein, Nancy Marchand/Paul Sparer, Joanna Gleason/Richard Thomas, Blythe Danner/John Rubinstein, Jane Curtin/Stephen Collins, Elaine Stritch/Jason Robards, Frances Sternhagen/Remak Ramsay, Patricia Elliott/Josef Sommer, Debra Mooney/John Cunningham, Barbara Barrie/George Grizzard, Joan Van Ark/John Rubinstein, Rochelle Oliver/Fritz Weaver, Mary Beth Hurt/Anthony Heald, Frances Sternhagen/Philip Bosco, Julie Harris/Richard Kiley, William Hurt/Pamela Reed
A play in two acts. Performed by two actors seated at a table and reading directly from correspondence chronicling a lifelong relationship.

Top Left: Leo Bassi in "Nero's Last Folly"
(Paula Court Photo)
Top Right: John P. Connolly, Jodie Markell in "Sleeping Dogs" *(Martha Swope Photo)*
Below Left: Kathleen Turner
Below Right: Bruce Davison

(Theatre at St. Clement's) Tuesday, March 28–Apr. 22, 1989 (23 performances and 7 previews). Music-Theatre Group (Lyn Austin, Producing Director) and The Women's Project and Productions (Julia Miles, Artistic Director) present:
LADIES by Eve Ensler; Director, Paul Walker; Music, Joshua Shneider; Set, Victoria Petrovich; Lighting, Debra Dumas; Costumes, Donna Zakowska; Sound, John Kilgore; Production Manager, Steven Ehrenberg; Stage Manager, Michele Steckler; Press, Cromarty & Co. CAST: Margaret Barker (Dot), Denise Delapenha (Prince), Alexandra Gersten (Alpha), Allison Janney (Nickie), Marcella Lowery (Allegro), Isabell Monk (Mary), Novella Nelson (Monetty), Ching Valdes/Aran (Rosa), Beverly Wideman (Ama)
A play without intermission about nine homeless women.

(Judith Anderson Theatre) Saturday, Apr. 1–23, 1989 (11 performances and 5 previews) Quantum Leap and Pamela Phillips present:
HAMLET by William Shakespeare; Director, Caroline Arnold; Set, Philip Hanson; Costumes, Kerri Lea Robbins; Lighting, Bruce R. Kahle; Sound, Phil Lee; Fight irection, Joe Pritchard; Assistant Director, Oliver Arnold; Technical Director, Dennis Sullivan; Props, Brian Pride; Stage Managers, Denise Laffer, Sean Havens; Press, Cromarty & Co/Kevin Brockman CAST: Gregory Lamont Allen (Voltemand/Lucianas/Sailor), Anthony M. Brown (Laertes), Kristofer Batho (Fortinbras), Pierre Brulatour (Marcellus/Player/Captain), Murray Changar (Osric), Donovan Dietz (Ghost/Player/Gravedigger), J. Frank Lucas (Polonius), Lynellen Kagen (Ophelia), Dan Martin (Claudius), Robert Lee Martini (Horatio), Craig Mathers (Barnardo/Servant/Player), Kathe Mull (Player Queen/Lady in Waiting), Joseph O'Brien (Rosencrantz), Andrew Prosky (Guildenstern), Marie Puma (Gertrude), Rainard Rachelle (Francisco/Priest/Cornelius/Guard/Ambassador), Shan Sullivan (Hamlet)

(Actor's Outlet Upstage) Saturday, Apr. 1–22, 1989 (20 performances). Actor's Outlet Theatre (Eleanor Segan, Executive; Ken Lowstetter, Artistic Director) presents:
DOUBLE TAKES by Miklos Vamos; Directors, Ken Lowstetter, Pamela Caren Billig; Set, Eugene Brogyanyl; Costumes, Donna Marie; Sound, Kenn Dovel; Lighting, Stephen Edelstein; General Manager, Barbara J. Hodgen; Technical Director, Leif Smith; Stage Manager, Carol Dorn; Press, Max Eisen, Madelon Rosen CAST: Part I–"Somebody Else" directed by Ken Lowstetter; a play in four scenes; with Russell Stevens (Lala), Lezlie Dalton (Olga), Deborah LaCoy (Gabi). Part II–"Mixed Doubles" directed by Pamela Caren Billig; a play in four scenes; with David H. Sterry (Cornis/Black Rhinocerus), Cornelia Mills (Kid/Cameroonian Goat), Jeannie Dobie (Babe/Turtle)

Russell Stevens, Lezlie Dalton in "Double Takes"
(Martha Swope Photo)

(Cooper Square Theatre) Wednesday, Apr. 5–May 7, 1989 (24 performances and 6 previews). The Shaliko Company (Leonardo Shapiro, Artistic Director) presents:
WHIRLIGIG by Mac Wellman; Direction/Design, Leonardo Shapiro; Music, Charlie Morrow; Set/Lighting, Kyle Chepulis; Producer, Maryellen Kernaghan; Scenic Artist, Polly Walker; Stage Managers, Cathy Biro, Tess Kahmann; Press, David Rothenberg Associates CAST: Cathy Biro (Hun), Tess Kahmann (Hun), Geza Kovacs (Xuphus), Cecil MacKinnon (Sister), Elena Nicholas (Girl), Michael Preston (Busman)

(Interart Theatre) Thursday, Apr. 6–May 21, 1989 (26 performances and 5 previews) Interart Theatre (Margot Lewitin, Artistic Director) presents:
BRIMSTONE AND TREACLE by Dennis Potter; Director, Rosemary Hay; Set, Christina Weppner; Lighting, Frances Aronson; Costumes, Martha Bromelmeier; Sound, Vito Ricci; Assistant Director, John Bjostad; Supervising Producer, Richard Husson; Props, Nancy Swartz; Production Assistant, Rosalyn Evans; Wigs, Denise O'Brien; Stage Manager, Debora E. Kingston CAST: Shula Van Buren (Pattie), Maggie Soboil (Mrs. Bates), Frank Lazarus (Mr. Bates), Rudy Caposaro (Martin)
A play in four acts with one intermission. The action takes place in the Bates' home in a North London suburb.

(Hartley House Theatre) Friday, Apr. 7–23, 1989 (12 performances). On Stage Productions (Lee Frank, Artistic Director; Randolf Pearson, Associate Artistic Director; Jesse Ramos, Producing Director) presents:
TWO BY TWO with music by Richard Rodgers; Lyrics, Martin Charnin; Book, Peter Stone; Based on play "The Flowering Peach" by Clifford Odets; Director, Monica M. Hayes; Choreographer, Carol Cornicelli; Wayne Blood, Musical Director; Costumes/Set, Carol Wiederrecht; Special Effects, R. Robere; Lighting, Anna Bezzola; Artistic Consultant, Martin Charnin; Stage Manager, Nancy Hornecker CAST: Robert J. Gardner (Noah), Virginia Wing (Esther), John F. Higgins (Japheth), Carmine Manicone (Shem), Lucille DeCristofaro (Leah), Lawrence Clayton (Ham), Cynda Williams (Rachel), Leslie Hyland (Goldie), Understudies: Carol Cornicelli, Cindy Matthews, Norm Rotkowitz
MUSICAL NUMBERS: Why Me?, Put Him Away, Something Somewhere, You've Got to Have a Rudder on the Ark, Something Doesn't Happen, An Old Man, Ninety Again, Two by Two, I Don't Know a Day I Did Not Love You, When It Dries, You, Forty Nights, The Golden Ram, Poppa Knows Best, As Far As I'm Concerned, Hey Girlie, The Covenant
A musical in 2 acts and 19 scenes. The action takes place before, during and after The Flood, in and around Noah's home, and on the ark atop Mt. Ararat.

(Village Theatre) Saturday, Apr. 8–May 14, 1989 (32 performances). M. Ellen Mahonev and Rene Savich present:
THE RUG OF IDENTITY by Jill W. Fleming; Director, Pat Golden; Set, Nancy Deren; Costumes, Sharon Lynch; Lighting, Robert W. Rosentel; Sound, Rita Houston; Props, Lisa Daniello; Stage Managers, Elizabeth Heeden, John Himmel; Press, Jacksina Co/Judy Jacksina, Brig Bernev CAST: Anne Capron (Laurie), Yvonne Clifford (Mona/Mugger), Shelly Colman (Prison Officer/Hot Dog Seller/Mugger), Joyce Sozen (Mrs. Proctor), Deborah Wren (Joanna)
A play in 2 acts and 4 scenes. The action takes place at the present time on Death Row, in Laurie's flat, and at Charing Cross Station in London.

Top: Michael Preston, Geza Kovacs (sitting), Elena Nicholas in "Whirligig" *(Bob Marshak Photo)*

Below: Gretchen Cryer in "Back in My Life" *(Susan Cook Photo)*

(Stage Left) Monday, Apr. 10–22, 1989 (13 performances). Criterion Center (Charles B. Moss, Jr., Producer) presents:
BACK IN MY LIFE by and with Gretchen Cryer, assisted by Robin Cryer and pianist Michael O'Flaherty; Press, Bill Evans/Jim Baldassare PROGRAM: Back in My Life, Mary Margaret's House in the Country, Reckless, Do Whatcha Gotta Do, Changing, Let the Chips Fall, You Can Kill Love, The American Dream, The News, Cavalier, Natural High, Smile, Dear Tom, Captain of Industry, Precious Days, Wilfred Academy, Strong Woman Number, Celebrate, Old Friend

(Carnegie Hall) Thursday, Apr. 13–16, 1989 (5 limited performances). The Princess Theatre Ensemble presents:
SITTING PRETTY IN CONCERT with Book and Lyrics by Guy Bolton and P. G. Wodehouse; Director-Conductor, John McGlinn CAST: Paul V. Ames (Judson Waters), Kim Criswell (Dixie Tolliver), Dillon Evans (Roper), Davis Gaines (Bill Pennington), Jason Graae (Horace), Beverly Lambert (Babe LaMarr), James Mahady (Horace), Robert Nichols (Uncle Jo), Paige O'Hara (May Tolliver), Richard Woods (Mr. Pennington), Linda Milani (Wilhelmina Pennington), Mike Harmon (Otis Pennington), Sally Ann Swarm (Wilhelmina II), Carrie Wilder (Jane), Paula Laurence (Mrs. Wagstaff/Mrs. Waters), Ensemble: Deborah Cole, Linda Milani, Sally Ann Swarm, Carrie Wilder, Keith Bernardo, Mike Harmon, James Mahady, Robert Vincent Smith

(William Redfield Theatre) Thursday, Apr. 13–May 6, 1989 (16 performances). The Phoenix Ensemble (Mary Jasperson, Artistic Director; Kim Highland, Producing Director) presents:
SECRET THIGHS OF NEW ENGLAND WOMEN by Jan Paetow; Director, Gail Kellstrom; Set, Jeff Vaughn; Lighting, Richard Currie; Sound, Greg Sutton; Stage Manager, Fred Velde; Press, Shirley Herz Associates/Sam Rudy CAST: Paul Ravich (Daniel Gordon), Dru-Ann Chuchran (Merrilee), Robert Sonderskov (Doc Drew), Judith Kirtley (Millie Drew Gordon), Mary Jasperson (Aunt Mercy), Blanche Cholet (Grace Gordon)
The action takes place at the present time in a small town in coastal New England.

Paul Ravich, Dru-Ann Chuchran, Judith Kirtley in "Secret Thighs of New England Women" *(T. L. Boston Photo)*

Paul Spencer, Emily Riddle, John Elejalde in "Justice"
(Martha Swope Photo)

(All Souls Church) Thursday, Apr. 20–May 14, 1989 (19 performances). All Souls Players (Tran William Rhodes, Producer) presents:
OUT OF THIS WORLD with Music and Lyrics by Cole Porter; Book, Dwight Taylor, Reginald Lawrence; Directed and Choreographed by Jeffery K. Neill; Musical Direction/Special Arrangements, Wendell Kindberg; Set, Robert Edmonds; Costumes, John Michel; Lighting, Jenny Ryan; Stage Manager, Court Sweeting CAST: Lynn Alice Webster (Juno), Andrew Hammond (Jupiter), Branch Woodman (Mercury), Teri Bibb (Helen O'Malley), Alfred Schmitz (Art O'Malley), Regis Bowman (Niki Skolianos), Donna Lynn Burns (Chloe), Ginni Terry (Aurora), Mirla Criste Agnir (Night), Larry Raben (Adonis), Grant Stephens (Bacchus/Harry), Andrew Alloy (Neptune), John Bransdorf (Cupid), Steve Correia (Apollo), Jerry Goehring (Mars), Kathleen Dodson (Vulcania), Roxanne Fay (Diana), Rosalind Hurwitz (Venus), Patty Noonan (Minerva), Ruth Rome (Flora/Fauna)
MUSICAL NUMBERS: I Jupiter I Rex, Use Your Imagination, Hail, Juno's Ride, I Got Beauty, We're on the Road to Athens, Maiden Fair, Where Oh Where, From This Moment On, They Couldn't Compare to You, What Do You Think about Men?, You Don't Remind Me, I Sleep Easier Now, I Am Loved, Hush, Midsummer Night, Climb Up the Mountain, Oh It Must Be Fun, No Lover for Me, Cherry Pies, Hark to the Song of the Night, Nobody's Chasing Me, Finale.
   A musical in 2 acts. The action takes place in Heaven, Manhattan and Greece.

(Westbeth) Friday, Apr. 21–30,1989 (12 performances and 2 previews) The Westbeth Theatre Center in association with Walnut Street Theatre Company presents:
FINDING DONIS ANNE by Hal Corley; Director, Granville Burgess; Set, Melinda Oblinger; Costumes, Pattilynne Meadows; Lighting, DeVida Jenkins; Stage Managers, Micheal Musick CAST: Janis Dardaris (Rachel), James Hassett (Darryl), Daryl Edwards (Luther), Maura Swanson (Claire)
   The action takes place at the present time just outside Richmond, Virginia, and then in and around Washington, D.C. Performed with one intermission.
Friday, Apr. 28–May 21, 1989 (14 performances and 4 previews)
A MATTER OF TONE by Gordon C. Osmond; Director, Linda Burson; Set, Bob Phillips; Lighting, Nancy Collings; Costumes, Joanie Canon; Sound, Richard Dunning; Stage Managers, Dominique J. Cook, David Warehime CAST: Michael Alan Gregory (Benjamin Jons), Sal Provenza (Malcolm Honet), Michelle Hurd (Joanne Leigh)
   A play in two acts. The action takes place at the present time in the living-room of the Jons-Honet home in Bel-Air, California, and in the TV studio of the Pan-Pacific Cable Network.

(Joyce Theater) Tuesday, Apr. 25–May 7, 1989 (16 performances) American Ballroom Theater (Pierre Dulaine & Yvonne Marceau, Artistic Directors) presents:
RENDEZVOUS WITH ROMANCE with Choreography by Pierre Dulaine, Yvonne Marceau, Gary Pierce, Willie Rosario; Costumes/Decor, Eduardo Sicangcao; Lighting, Thomas R. Skelton; Production Supervisors, Graciela Daniele, Tina Paul; General Managers, Deirdre Valente, Lisa Booth; Production Manager, William Schaffner; Wardrobe, Kyle Larson-Cardee, Thea Stevens; Cromarty & Co./Peter Cromarty, Kevin McAnarney, David Gersten, Kevin Brockman CAST: Gary Pierce & Shelley Freydont, Willie Rosario & Dee Quinones, Danny Carter & Gaye Bowidas, Patrick Taverna & Judy Sabrina Carr, Stanley McCalla & Jennifer, Eddie Simon & Lori Brizzi
   A dance program in 2 acts and 4 scenes: Spring in Hollywood, Summer in Havana, Autumn in Paris, Winter in Vienna

(Apple Corps Theatre) Friday, Apr. 14–30, 1989 (12 performances). The Source Foundation (Susan Flakes, Artistic Director) presents:
SERIOUS COMPANY: AN EVENING OF ONE-ACT PLAYS; Director, Susan Flakes; Sets, Shelley Barclay; Lighting, Joshua Starbuck; Costumes, Jennifer Straniere; General Manager, Michael Stotts; Stage Manager, Gigi Rivkin CAST: "Swan Song" by Anton Chekhov; with Conrad L. Osborne (Vasily), Frank Geraci (Nikita). "The Stronger" by August Strindberg; with Katina Cummings (Mlle. Y), Diane Salinger (Mrs. X), Gigi Rivkin (Waitress). "Hughie" by Eugene O'Neill; with Austin Pendleton (Erie Smith), Frank Geraci (Night Clerk)

(Ernie Martin Studio) Friday, Apr. 14–May 2, 1989 (12 performances) MAMAW Productions presents:
JUSTICE by Terry Curtis Fox; Director, L. R. Hults; Set, Arthur M. Reese; Lighting, Gerhart Brandner; Props, Ron Casidine; Stage Manager, Gretta McCarron; Press, Dolph Browning CAST: Paul Spencer (Roger Ackerman), Robert Wagner (Daniel Kalen), G. Tom Swift (Philip Skylar), John Elejalde (John Fidello), Emily Riddle (Barbara Walters), Ralph Remington (Cleland Jones), Cheryl Black (Cathy Hart), Antonia Banewicz (Voice of Roseanne DeVito)
   A play in two acts. The action takes place in Chicago during July of 1978.

(Criterion Center Cabaret) Sunday, Apr. 16–30, 1989 (6 limited performances). Criterion Center (Brent Peek, President/Managing Director; Michael O'Flaherty, Cabaret Director) presents:
STREETSONGS directed by Richard Maltby, Jr.; Musical Direction/Arrangements, Stanley Wietrzychowski; Vocal Direction, Andy Thomas Anselmo; Costumes, Bill Walker; By special arrangement with Alan Eichler; Press, Bill Evans/Jim Baldassare CAST: Geraldine Fitzgerald
MUSICAL NUMBERS: Underneath the Arches, Forget-Me-Not-Lane, Pirate Jenny, She's Funny That Way, The Poor People of Paris, Danny Boy, She's Leaving Home, Swanee, It's Not British to Deny Your Poor Old Mother, The Pig Song, Saturday Night at the Rose and Crown, Who's This Geezer Hitler?, Smile, Pack Up Your Troubles, When You're Smiling, The White Cliffs of Dover, Side by Side, Fitzy Rag
   Performed without intermission.

Stanley McCalla, Jennifer Ford, Judy Sabrina Carr, Patrick Taverna, Gary Pierce, Shelly Freydont in "Rendezvous With Romance" *(Jack Mitchell Photo)*
Above: Michael Francis Boyle, Brenda Thomas in "Crossin' the Line" *(Martha Swope Photo)*

Michael Alan Gregory, Sal Provenza in "A Matter of Tone"
(Carol Rosegg Photo)

Above: Welker White, Lee Brock, Erika Goodman in "Three Sisters" *(Cathy Blaives Photo)*

(Opera Ensemble Theatre) Wednesday, May 3–21, 1989 (9 limited performances). The Opera Ensemble of New York (John J. D. Sheehan, Executive Director; Jonathan Tunick, Music Director) presents:
SHE LOVES ME based on play by Miklos Laszlo; Book, Joe Masteroff; Music, Jerry Bock; Lyrics, Sheldon Harnick; Production Director, John J. D. Sheehan; Music Director, Jonathan Tunick; Choreographer, Lavinia Plonka; Set, Russell Metheny; Costumes, Susan Branch; Lighting, Don Guyton; Orchestrations, Don Walker; Hairstylist, Goran Sparrman; Production Executive, Howard R. McBride; Assistant Musical Director, Ben Schaechter; Technical Director, Jason Townley; Props, Janet Smith; Wardrobe, Meghan Burdui, Christopher DelCoro; Stage Managers, John M. Atherlay, John R. Stattel CAST: Ciro Barbaro (Ladislav Sipos), Franc D'Ambrosio (Arpad Laszlo), Annie McGreevey (Ilona Ritter), Davis Gaines (Steven Kodaly), Gregg Edelman (Georg Nowack), Charles Goff (Maraczek), Elizabeth Walsh (Amalia Balash), Mark Lainer (Headwaiter), Ensemble: J. Andrew Clark, Loriana DeCrescenzo, Christine Elliott, Bonnie Hess, Randall E. Lake, Jeanine Pardey, Michael Soncrant, Alesia Sullivan, Mark Traxler
MUSICAL NUMBERS: Good Morning Good Day, Sounds While Selling, Thank You Madame, Days Gone By, No More Candy, Three Letters, Tonight at Eight, I Don't Know His Name, Perspective, Goodbye Georg, Will He Like Me?, Ilona, I Resolve, A Romantic Atmosphere, Tango Tragique, Dear Friend, Try Me, Where's My Shoe?, Vanilla Ice Cream, She Loves Me, A Trip to the Library, Grand Knowing You, 12 Days of Christmas, Finale.
A musical in two acts. The action takes place in and around Maraczek's Parfumerie in a city in Europe during the 1930's.

(Academy Theatre) Thursday, May 4–28, 1989 (22 performances and 7 previews). John Stuart presents:
LEGENDS IN CONCERT created and directed by John Stuart; Choreography, Inez Mourning; Musical Director, Kerry McCoy; Lighting/Production Consultant, Dennis Condon; Costumes, Betty Lurenz; Technical Consultant, Ron Popp; Multi-Media Design, Media Innovations/Joseph Jarred; Technical Director, Alan Murphy; Lasers, Mark Fisher; Supervisor in charge of production, Steve Yuhasz; Associate Producers, Don Saxon, Robert R. Blume, Malcolm Allen; Assistant Choreographer, Angelo Molo; Wardrobe, Jimm Halliday, Carol Etkin; General Management, Saxon-Blume Productions/Malcolm Allen; Press, Joshua Ellis Office/Adrian Bryan-Brown, Jackie Green, Susanne Tighe, Tim Ray, Chris Boneau CAST: Eddie Carroll (Jack Benny), Clive Baldwin (Al Jolson), George Trullinger (Buddy Holly), Daryl Wagner (Liberace), Katie LaBourdette (Marilyn Monroe), Donny Ray Evins (Nat King Cole), Julie Sheppard (Judy Garland), Randy Clark (John Lennon), Tony Roi (Another Guest), Singer/Dancers: Renee Chambers, Troy Christian, Vincent D'Elia, Elena Ferrante, Debby Kole, Gary LaRosa, Michael Roberts, Marrielle Monte
Presented with one intermission.

(Space 603) Thursday, Apr. 27–May 21, 1989 (20 performances). The Barrow Group (Seth Barrish, Artistic Director) presents:
THE THREE SISTERS by Anton Chekhov; Translated by Lanford Wilson; Director, Seth Barrish; Costumes, Nina Canter; Scenic Coordinator, Jeff McDonald; Lighting, Bill Simmons; Technical Director, Bonnie McDonald; Scenic Artist, Katie Maxie; Sound, William Castleman; Props, G. A. Howard, Greg Hansen; Production Manager, Kris Shaw; Stage Manager, John Handy; Press, Philip Rinaldi CAST: Barbara Bradish (Anfisa), Lee Brock (Masha), Regina Corrado (Maid/Production Assistant), Tom Farrell (Andrei), Martha French (Natasha), Erika Goodman (Olga), Nicolas Glaeser (Fedotik), Jacob Harran (Tuzenbach), Nate Harvey (Solyony), James Lish (Rodez), Mark Shannon (Vershinin), Vasek C. Simek (Chebutykin), Edward Stevlingson (Feraponot), Robert Keith Watson (Kulygin), Welker White (Irina)
A drama in 4 acts with one intermission. The action takes place in the Prozorov's house at the turn of the Century in Russia.

(Lamb's Little Theatre) Tuesday, May 2–June 10, 1989 (40 performances and 7 previews). Lamb's Theatre Company (Carolyn Rossi Copeland, Producing Director) presents:
CROSSIN' THE LINE by Phil Bosakowski; Director, Sonya Baehr; Set, Michael C. Smith; Lighting, Dave Feldman; Costumes, Debra Stein; General Manager, Stephen Nebgen; Props, Clark C. Reiman; Production Assistant, Tony Morello; Stage Managers, Denise Nations, Clark C. Reiman; Press, Cromarty & Co./Peter Cromarty CAST: Michael Francis Boyle (Sgt. Martin/Richie), Judy Malloy (Bette), Josh Mosby (Hayden Doyle), Talia Paul (Trudee Waits), John Speredakos (Mitch Kohler), Brenda Thomas (Ellie Burke)
Performed without intermission.

Julie Sheppard (Judy Garland), Daryl Wagner (Liberace), Donny Ray Evins (Nat King Cole), Katie LaBourdette (Marilyn Monroe), Randy Clark (John Lennon) in "Legends in Concert"

Above: Elizabeth Walsh, Gregg Edelman in "She Loves Me"
(Beatriz Schiller Photo)

(Judith Anderson Theatre) Friday, May 5–21, 1989 (12 performances and 4 previews). Manhattan Punch Line (Steve Kaplan, Artistic Director) presents three plays by women playwrights:
EQUAL WRIGHTS: "The Agreement" by Janet Neipris; Director, Steve Kaplan; with Susan Pellegrino (Sybil Natchett), Richmond Hoxie (Sigmund Matchett), Ilana Levine (Alicia), Pat Nesbit (Alice Bailey), Brian Keeler (Lester Ostermeyer), David Wasson (Boris/Judge). The action takes place at the present time in California and New York. "Marathons" by Terri Wagner; Director, Robin Saex; with Ellen Tobie (She), Michael French (He). The action takes place Nov. 6, 1988 in the five burroughs of New York City. "How It Hangs" by Grace McKeaney; Director, Melia Bensussen; with Caris Corfman (Rowdy), Robin Groves (Girlene), Beth Dixon (Sister), Peggity Price (Doll Fox), Miles Herter (Bob Moore). The action takes place at the present time at the weekly meeting of the battered women's group on the outskirts of Lusk, Wyoming. Stage Managers, Cathy D. Tomlin, Denise Laffer.

(Criterion Center/Stage Left) Friday, May 5–17, 1989 (3 performances and 12 previews). Roger Berlind, Franklin R. Levy and Gregory Harrison present:
BLAME IT ON THE MOVIES! The Reel Music of Hollywood; Director, David Galligan; Musical Staging/Choreography, Larry Hyman; Musical Direction/Arrangements, Ron Abel; Original Music/Lyrics, Billy Barnes; Musical sequences compiled and conceived by Ron Abel, Billy Barnes, David Galligan from an original idea by Franklin R. Levy; Set, Fred Duer; Costumes, Bonnie Stauch; Lighting, Michael Gilliam; Sound, Jon Gottlieb; Musical Conductor, John McDaniel; Casting, Jeffery Passero; General Manager, Rodger H. Hess; Company Manager, Jean Rocco; Production Coordinator, Charles A. Smolsky II; Wardrobe, Laura Benyo; Technical Director, Steven Loehle; Props, Charlie Eisenberg; Dance Captain, Dan O'Grady; Production Assistant, Julie Michael Thomas; Stage Managers, Elsbeth M. Collins, Andrea Iovino; Press, Joshua Ellis Office/Adrian Bryan-Brown, Jackie Green, Susanne Tighe, Tim Ray, Chris Boneau, Shannon Barr CAST: Sandy Edgerton, Kathy Garrick, Bill Hutton, Christine Kellogg, Peter Marc, Dan O'Grady, Barbara Sharma, Patty Tiffany, Understudies: Ivy Austin, Frank DiPasquale PART I: Blame it on the Movies, The Forties, The War Years, Foreign Film Tribute, Fox in Love PART II: Entr'acte, Saturday Matinee, Oscar Losers, A Tribute to the Hollywood Film Score: A Place in the Sun Ballet, Finale

(Arts Common at St. Peter's Church/Edmund Anderson, Executive Director) Sunday, May 7–Aug. 6, 1989 (85 performances). Zev Guber and Sanford H. Fisher, Beluga Entertainment Corp. present:
LAUGHING MATTERS written by Linda Wallem, Peter Tolan; Director, Martin Charnin; Music/Lyrics, Peter Tolan; Scenery/Lighting, Ray Recht; Costumes, Jade Hobson; General Management, Robert V. Straus Productions; Sound, Abe Jacob; Company Manager, David Handley; Associate Producer, Iva Mendelowitz; Props, Sean Haven; Stage Managers, Jonathan Dimock Secor, Sally Plass; Press, Joshua Ellis Office/'Adrian Bryan-Brown, Jackie Green, Susanne Tighe, Tim Ray, Chris Boneau CAST: Linda Wallem, Peter Tolan PROGRAM: Weird Interlude, Inner Thoughts, The 10% Solution, Inner Thoughts II, The Gap, Bridge over Troubled Daughters, John Loves Mary, When You Live in New York, Max, Next Season on Broadway, Reunion, Back in Champaign-Urbana, Inner Thoughts

Linda Wallem, Peter Tolan in "Laughing Matters"
(Martha Swope Photo)

Above: Bill Hutton, Barbara Sharma in "Blame it on the Movies!" *(Marc Bryan-Brown Photo)*

Anthony Ponzini, Kate Hurd in "The Understanding"
(Kurwin McCarthy Photo)

(William Redfield Theatre) Tuesday, May 9–June 4, 1989 (28 performances). Third Step Theatre Company presents:
SIDEWAYS GLANCE by Roberto Cordovani and Alejandre Guibert; Performed by Roberto Cordovani, founder-artistic director of Arte Livre Do Brasil. This work was developed out of an interest in the private, public and political life of Greta Garbo.

(INTAR Theatre) Tuesday, May 9–28, 1989 (22 performances and 2 previews) DS Productions presents:
DANNY CURTIS: WALLS OF CHANCE written by Danny Curtis; Additional Material, Howard Berger; Directors, Danny London, Donald Swartz; Orchestrations/Musical Director, Peter Candela; Sound Recordings, Bob Suede; Lighting, Jeffrey Glovsky, Joseph Goshert; Wardrobe, WilliWear/WilliSmith; Associate Producer, Vincent Donato; Executive Director, Norman Opper; General Manager, Donald Swartz; Press, Cromarty & Co./Peter Cromarty, Kevin Brockman CAST: Danny Curtis

A musical in 2 acts and 6 scenes. The action takes place at the present time, backstage in the dressing room of a Broadway theatre, five minutes before finale, with flashbacks to other times and places.

(South Street Theatre) Tuesday, May 9–June 18, 1989 (39 performances and 3 previews). Eric Krebs presents:
THE UNDERSTANDING by William Mastrosimone; Director, Joe Brancato; Set, Bill Stabile; Costumes, Mary Ann Smith; Lighting, Denny Moyser; Press, Shirley Herz Associates/Miller Wright CAST: Anthony Ponzini, John Cygan, Kate Hurd
A drama in two acts.

(Ubu Repertory Theatre) Wednesday, May 10–20, 1989 (8 performances). The UBU Repertory Theatre (Francoise Kourilsky, Artistic Director) presents:
ALIVE BY NIGHT by Reine Barteve; Translated from the French by Alex Gross; Director, Francoise Kourilsky; Set/Lighting, Watoku Ueno; Music/Sound, David Simons; Costumes, Carol Ann Pelletier; Stage Manager, Lamis Khalaf; Press, Jonathan Slaff CAST: T. Scott Lilly (Ray/Geslin), Joseph McKenna (Nick/Beaurepaire), Corliss Preston (Marina/Cecile Dudion), Thomas Carson (The Watchman), Rene Houtrides (Margot/DeLalance)

(Theater for the New City) Thursday, May 11–28, 1989 (12 performances). The Theater for the New City (George Bartenieff, Executive Director; Crystal Field, Artistic Director) presents:
THE HEART OUTRIGHT by Mark Medoff; Director, Mike Rutenberg; Set, Peter R. Feuche; Costumes, Traci DiGesu; Lighting, K. Robert Hoffman; Production Assistant, Francesca Mantani Arkus; Technical Director, E. F. Morrili; Fight staged by K. Robert Hoffman; Stage Managers, Kathleen Mary, Anya Drulovic; Press, Jonathan Slaff CAST: David Andrews (Stephen (Red) Ryder), Anjanette Comer (Angel Childress), Kim McCullum (Dickie Turpin), Kevin O'Connor (Ray Fowler)
A play in 2 acts. The action takes place in 1977 in the lobby of a restored movie theatre (Act I) and in 1981 in a small town bus station in Southern New Mexico.

(Westbeth Theatre) Thursday, May 11–28, 1989 (16 performances). Don Schatzberg Productions presents:
CHERI by Anita Loos; Based on novel by Colette; Direction/Design, James Esterly; Lighting, Ron Burns; Wigs, Paul Huntley; Affiliate Producer, Neil Jacob; Technical Adviser, Ron Burns; Props, JD Productions; Produced in association with Brooklyn Playworks; Stage Manager, Uriel Menson; Press, Jacksina Co./Judy Jacksina, Julianne Waldheim, Patricia Kane, Laura Leinweber, Brig Berney, Jennifer Ackerman CAST: Taina Elg (Lea DeLonval), Matte Osian (Cheri), Lucille Patton (Charlotte Peloux), Susanna Clemm (Baroness de la Berche), Brenda Gardner (Rose), Peter Lang (Butler), Terry Londeree (Count Bertellmy), Peggy Miley (Lili), Natalie Norwick (Coco), Quin Pierrot (Marie-Laure), Erin Tavin (Edmee)
A play in 3 acts and 5 scenes with a prologue. The action takes place in Paris and Neuilly, France, from 1905 to 1910.

Top: David Andrews, Kevin O'Connor in "The Heart Outright" *(Jonathan Slaff Photo)*
Below: Taina Elg, Matte Osian in "Cheri" *(Lorin Klaris Photo)*

Mark Sawyer (front), Donna Murphy, Douglas Bernstein, Veanne Cox in "Showing Off" *(Martha Swope Photo)*

(The Cubiculo) Friday, May 12–27, 1989 (6 performances). The National Shakespeare Company (Elaine Sulka, Artistic Director) presents in repertory:
AS YOU LIKE IT directed by Anthony Naylor; **OEDIPUS REX** directed by Elaine Sulka; **TWELFTH NIGHT** directed by Anthony Naylor; Producing Director, Lenny Bart; Sets, Richard A. Kendrick; Costumes, Renee Sykes; Lighting, Laura Perlman; Musical Directors, Deena Kaye, Adam Morrison CAST: John Berlind (Silvius/Dennis/Lord/Palace Messenger/Chorus/Sebastian), Kay Bourbiel (Celia/Sphinx/Antigone/Chorus/Viola), Benjamin Chelsea (Adam/Tiresius/Chorus/Sir Andrew Aguecheek), Jamie Gomer (Rosalind/Jocasta/Olivia), Dennis Grant (Oliver/Amiens/Mar/Chorus/Valentine/Antonio), James Haskins (Orlando/Chorus/Sea Captain/Priest/Officer), Mark Homan (Touchstone/Chorus/Corinthian Messenger/Sir Toby Belch), Jerry Kann (The Dukes/Narrator/Chorus), Marybeth Regan (Lord/Phebe/Chorus/Ismene/Maria), Dan Snow (Charles/Corin/Audrey/Creon/Orsino), Mark Waterman (LeBeau/Jacques/Oedipus/Malvolio)

(45th Street Theatre) Friday, May 12–June 4, 1989 (17 performances and 3 previews). Primary Stages Company (Casey Childs, Artistic Director) presents:
ANCIENT HISTORY by David Ives; Director, Jason McConnell Buzas; Producing Associate, Herbert H. O'Dell; General Manager, Gordon Farrell; Set, Philipp Jung; Lighting, Deborah Constantine; Costumes, Claudia Stephens; Sound, David Ferdinand; Stage Managers, Greg Weiss, Tony Luna; Press, Shirley Herz Associates/Miller Wright CAST: Beth McDonald (Ruth), Christopher Wells (Jack)
A comedy in two acts. The action takes place at the present time in Ruth's bedroom.

(Steve McGraw's) Monday, May 15–Oct. 15, 1989 (172 performances and 11 previews). Suzanne J. Schwartz and Jennifer Manocherian present:
SHOWING OFF a musical revue by Douglas Bernstein, Denis Markell; Director, Michael Leeds; Set/Props, Joseph Varga, Penny Holpit; Costumes, Jeanne Button; Lighting/Sound, Josh Starbuck; Musical Director, Stephen Flaherty; Associate Producer, Howard Deutsch; Hairstylist, Antonio Soddu; General Management, Entertainment Ink; Company Manager, Barbara Barnett; Production Associate, Martin Teitel; Stage Manager, Robin Rogers; Press, Patt Dale, David Rothenberg CAST: Douglas Bernstein, Veanne Cox, Donna Murphy succeeded by Bebe Neuwirth, Mark Sawyer, Understudies: Kristopher Antekeier, Laura Turnbull PROGRAM: Showing Off, 72nd Street, Native New Yorkers, I Don't Get It, S.I.P., Showbiz Rabbi, They're Yours, Mightier Than The Sword, Michele, Raffi: The Concert Movie, Rental Cruelty, Joshua Noveck, Ninas, How Things Change, Take de Picture, Old Fashioned Song
Performed with one intermission.

(Cherry Lane Theatre) Monday, May 15–June 18, 1989 (38 performances and 8 previews). Comco Productions presents:
S. J. PERELMAN IN PERSON by Bob Shanks; Based on the published works of S.J. Perelman; Director, Ann Shanks; Set, Wes Peters; Costumes, Deon I. Brauner; Lighting, Mal Sturchio; General Manager, Kevin Dowling; Company Manager, Jeff Capitola; Assistant Director, Jeffrey Howard; Technical Director, James Eckle; Stage Manager, Morgan Kennedy; Press, Shirley Herz Associates/Glenna Freedman, Pete Sanders, Sam Rudy, Miller Wright CAST: Lewis J. Stadlen (S. J. Perelman), Standby: Mitchell Greenberg
Performed with one intermission. The action takes place during the 1950's in a study in New York City.

(165 West 86th Street) Thursday, May 18–June 5, 1989 (16 performances). The Riverside Shakespeare Company (Timothy W. Oman, Artistic Director) presents:
HAMLET by William Shakespeare; Director, Linda J. K. Masson; Set, Sarah Edkins; Costumes, Sasha Thayer; Lighting, Stephen Petrilli; Fight Choreographer, Todd Loweth; Stage Managers, Rachel S. Levine, Stephen Weths; Press, Leslie Carroll CAST: R Bruce Elliott (Polonius), Robert Emmet (Horatio), Paula Eschweiler (Player Queen/Attendant), Andrew Jarkowsky (Claudius), Richmond Johnson (Ghost/Player King/2nd Ambassador), Sonja Lanzener (Gertrude), Todd Loweth (Laertes), Lisa Nicholas (Ophelia), Austin Pendleton (Hamlet), Gay Reed (Marcellus/Priest), Gene Santarelli (Guildenstern/Pallbearer), Woody Sempliner (Rosencrantz), William Schenker (Bernardo/2nd Gravedigger/Sailor/Pallbearer), Jeff Shoemaker (Francisco/1st Gravedigger/Osric/Player)
    A tragedy performed with one intermission.

(Marymount Manhattan Theatre) Monday, May 22–June 4, 1989 (16 performances in repertory).
THE ACTING COMPANY: John Houseman, Founder; Margot Harley (Executive Producer; Gerald Gutierrez, Artistic Director; Elizabeth Smith, Voice/Speech Consultant; Company Manager, Laura Delano Weekes; Technical Director, David W. Chapman; Lighting, Jonathan G. Terry; Wardrobe, Doug Hansen; Props, Kevin J. Hoffman; Staff Repertory Director, Jennifer McCray; Stage Managers, C. A. Clark, Richard Feldman; Press, Fred Nathan Co/Bert Fink
REPERTOIRE:
LOVE'S LABOUR'S LOST by William Shakespeare; Director, Paul Giovanni; Set, Robert Klingelhoefer; Costumes, Jess Goldstein; Dance Consultant, Patricia Birch; Songs/Incidental Music, Bruce Adolphe. **BOY MEETS GIRL** by Bella and Samuel Spewack; Director, Brian Murray; Set, Derek McLane; Costumes, Jennifer von Mayrhauser; Music, Bruce Pomahac; Lighting, Stephen Strawbridge. **THE PHANTOM TOLLBOOTH** by Susan Nanus; Based on book by Norton Juster; Director, Jennifer McCray; Set, Russell Parkman; Costumes, Constance Romero; Music, Robert Waldman CAST: Spencer Beckwith (King of Navarre/Rodney Bevan/King Azaz, Whetherman), Anthony Cummings (Costard/Larry Toms/Wordsnatcher), Gayla Finer (Jacquenetta/Peggy, Nanny, Nurse/Soundkeeper), Larry Green (Dumaine/Robert Law/Dr. Dischord), John Greenleaf (Moth/Rosetti/Senses Taker), Douglas Krizner (Don Armado/J. Carlyle Benson/Terrible Trivium), Michael MacCauley (Dull/Dr., Announcer, Maj. Thompson/Dodecahedron), Theresa McCarthy (Maria/Nurse/Dynne), Alison Stair Neet (Rosaline/Green/Princess Reason), Laura Perrotta (Princess of France/Susie/Princess Rhyme), David Rainey (Boyet/Slade/Mathemagician), Ken Sawyer (Longaville/Young Man/Studio Officer/Milo), Gary Sloan (Berowne), Martha Thompson (Katherine/Miss Crews/Tock), John Tillotson (Holofernes/C. Elliott Friday), Gregory Wallace (Sir Nathaniel/Cutter/Humbug)

(Raft Theatre) Thursday, May 25–June 24, 1989 (21 performances and 6 previews). Sharkskin Productions presents:
SIMON SAYS. . . . by Joseph James; Director, Jeff Mousseau; Set, Jack Dunlea; Costumes, Roseann Forde; Lighting, Jed Stiles; Production Manager, Lark Hackshaw; Technical Director, Jan Bell; Sound, Peter Golub; Stage Manager, Stephanie Mooney; Press, Cromarty & Co./Peter Cromarty, Kevin Brockman CAST: Jim O'Malley (Joe Simon), John McGrane (Bobby Morgan), Laura Rogers (Elaine), Paul Vernet (Mike Plaza)
    Performed without intermission. The action takes place at the present time in New York City.

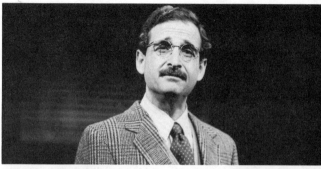

Top Right: Lewis J. Stadlen in "S.J. Perelman . . . in Person"
(Cynthia DeGrand Photo)

Below: The Acting Company in "Love's Labour's Lost"
(Peter Cunningham Photo)

(Ensemble Studio Theatre) Thursday, May 25, 1989–   . The Ensemble Studio Theatre (Curt Dempster, Artistic Director) presents:
MARATHON '89: Producer, Kate Baggott; Associate Producer, Peter Glatzer; Sets, Maurice Dana; Lighting, Greg MacPherson; Costumes, Deborah Shaw; Sound, Gayle Jeffrey; Stage Manager, Stephen Vallillo SERIES A: "The Essence of Margrovia" by Jenny Lombard; Director, Lisa Peterson; with Cody Conklin (Lizzy), Lizabeth Zindel (Terry). "Self-Torture and Strenuous Exercise" by Harry Kondoleon; Director, Max Mayer; with Donald Berman (Carl), John Michael Higgins (Alvin), Alexandra Gersten (Bethany), Caroline Aaron (Adele). "Wink-Dah" by William Yellow Robe, Jr.; Director, Richard Lichte; with Kohl Miner (Two Shoe), Randy Mantooth (Death), Philip Moon (Virgil), Eagle-Eye Cherry (Jeremy), Cochise Anderson (Earnest), Frank Girardeau (Victor). SERIES B: "Woman Floating Out a Window" by Jacklyn Maddux; Director, Charles Karchmer; with Carmen de Lavallade (Parker), Jody Gelb (Meredith), Sam Gray (Oswald). "Pathological Venus" by Brighde Mullins; Director, Jimmy Bohr; Music, Charles Goldbeck; with Merri Blechler (Venus), Susan Greenhill (Betty Butchko), John Scanlan (Kenwigs). "The Open Boat" by Neal Bell; Director, Curt Dempster; Phillip Casnoff (John-John), John Ottavino (Marcus), Debra Stricklin (Jane), John MacKay (Vincent). SERIES C: "Outside the Radio" by Kermit Frazier; Director, Oz Scott; with Herb Downer (Wilbur), Seret Scott (Iris), Tamika Tamara-Tucker-Cole (Rachel), Katherine Leask (Arlene). "Big Frogs" by David Golden; Director, Matthew Penn; with Barry Sherman (Dennis), Thomas Kopache (Harley). "Water Music" by Michael Erickson; Director, Beth A. Schachter; with Zach Grenier (Lutz), Tyrone Wilson (Abungi), James G. Macdonald (Charles)

(Judith Anderson Theatre) Friday, May 26–June 25, 1989 (20 performances). Manhattan Punch Line (Steve Kaplan, Artistic Director) presents:
FRIENDS by Lee Kalcheim; Director, Mr. Kalcheim; Set, Richard Meyer; Lighting, Steve Rust; Production Manager, Chris A. Kelly; Sound, Janet Kalas; Stage Manager, Denise Laffer CAST: Richard Lenz (Howard "Okie" Peterson), David Spielberg (Mel)
    Performed without intermission. The action takes place at the present time in a cabin in Vermont.

(Village Theatre) Wednesday, May 31–June 11, 1989 (12 performances). Quinapalus Theatre Co. (Tony Rust, Thomas Rice, Denise Dalfo, Artistic Directors) presents a reverse-gender production of:
THE TAMING OF THE SHREW by William Shakespeare; Director, Tony Rust; Assistant Director, Thomas Rice; Lighting/Scenic Coordinator, Peter R. Feuche; Technical Director, Anthony Ferrer; Costume Coordinator/Set Decoration, Douglas Hout; Stage Manager, Gina Andreoli CAST: Tim Zay (Katrino), Denise Dalfo (Petruchia), John Touhey (Bianco), Kay Rothman (Lucentia), Laura Gillis (Gremia), Patricia Denny (Hortensia), Susan McBrien (Trania), Kathleen Brant (Grumia), Bonnie Kalisher (Baptista Minola), John Moss (Curtis/Tailor/Widower), Janet Rust (Biondella), Denni Lee Heiges (Vincentia), Pier Lisa (Pedant). Music by Cole Porter and Ella Fitzgerald
    Performed with one intermission.

OFF-BROADWAY PRODUCTIONS FROM PAST SEASONS THAT PLAYED THROUGH THIS SEASON

THE FANTASTICKS

Book & Lyrics, Tom Jones; Music, Harvey Schmidt; Suggested by Edmond Rostand's play "Les Romanesques"; Director, Word Baker; Presented by Lore Noto; Original Musical Direction/Arrangements, Julian Stein; Production Design, Ed Wittstein; Co-Producer, Don Thompson; Associate Producers, Sheldon Baron, Dorothy Olim, Jules Field; Assistant Producer, Michael Yarborough; Current Musical Director, Dorothy Martin; Original Stage Manager, Geoffrey Brown; Current Stage Managers, James Cook, Steven Michael Daley; Production Consultant, Tony Noto; Press, Ginnie Weidmann. Opened in the Sullivan Street Playhouse on Tuesday, May 3, 1960, and still playing May 31, 1989.

CAST

The Narrator/El Gallo ....Robert Vincent Smith*
The Girl ....Glory Crampton †1
The Boy ....Neil Nash †2
Girl's Father ....William Tost*
Boy's Father ....Dale O'Brien †3
Old Actor ....Bryan Hull*
Man Who Dies/Indian ....John Thomas Waite †4
The Mute ....Matthew Eaton Bennett †5
At the piano ....Dorothy Martin*
At the harp ....Joy Plaisted*

UNDERSTUDIES: Anne Fisher (The Girl), Steven Michael Daley (The Boy), William Tost (Boy's Father), Neil Nash (Narrator) succeeded by Mathew Eaton Bennett

MUSICAL NUMBERS: Overture, Try to Remember, Much More, Metaphor, Never Say No, It Depends on What You Pay, Soon It's Gonna Rain, Rape Ballet, Happy Ending, This Plum Is Too Ripe, I Can See It, Plant a Radish, Round and Round, They Were You

The world's longest-running musical is performed with one intermission.
*30th anniversary cast

†Succeeded by: 1. Kate Suber*, 2. Howard Lawrence, Neil Nash, Mathew Eaton Bennett*, 3. Ron Kidd*, 4. Earl Aaron Levine*, 5. Steven Michael Daley*

Steve Young Photos

Bill Tost, Neil Nash, Glory Crampton, Dale O'Brien
(Charlyn Zlotnik Photo)

Robert Vincent, Kate Suber *(Steve Young Photo)*
Above: Steven Michael Daley, Robert Vincent, (middle) Bryan Hull, Kate Suber, Mathew Eaton Bennett, (bottom) Bill Tost, Earl Aaron Levine, Ron Kidd *(Steve Young Photo)*

DRIVING MISS DAISY

By Alfred Uhry; Director, Ron Lagomarsino; Set, Thomas Lynch; Costumes, Michael Krass; Lighting, Arden Fingerhut; Sound, Joshua Starbuck; Incidental Music, Robert Waldman; General Management, Richard Frankel/Marc Routh; Company Manager, Marshall B. Purdy; Production Associate, Kate Clark; Technical Director, Albert W. Webster; Props, Barbara Lee; Wardrobe, Cathy Lee Cawley; Casting, Pat McCorkle; Hairstylist, Randy Mercer; Stage Managers, Franklin Kaysar, Daniel S. Lewin; Press, David Powers. Originally presented by Playwrights Horizons in its theatre for 80 performances from March 31–June 7, 1987. It was then transferred to the John Houseman Theatre, opening there on Friday, July 24, 1987 and still playing there on May 31, 1989*

CAST

Daisy Werthan ....Dana Ivey †1
Hoke Coleburn .... Morgan Freeman †2
Boolie Werthan ....Ray Gill †3

Performed without intermission. The action takes place in Atlanta, Georgia, from 1948 to 1973.

†Succeeded by: 1. Frances Sternhagen, 2. Earle Hyman, Arthur French, 3. Anderson Matthews

*Recipient of 1988 Pulitzer Prize.

Top Right: Frances Sternhagen, Anderson Matthews, Arthur French in "Driving Miss Daisy"

NUNSENSE

Written and Directed by Jan Goggin; Musical Staging/Choreography, Felton Smith; Presented by the Nunsense Theatrical Co. in association with Joseph Hoesl, Bill Crowder, Jay Cardwell; Scenery, Barry Axtell; Lighting, Susan A. White; Musical Direction, Ethyl Will; Casting, Joseph Abaldo; Musical Arrangements, Michael Rice; General Management, Roger Alan Gindi; Company Manager, Jim Singlar; Technical Supervisor, Ted Kent Wallace; Stage Managers, Mary E. Lawson, Paul Botchis; Cast Album by DRG Records; Press, Shirley Herz/Pete Sanders, Peter Cromarty, Glenna Freedman, David Rossensack, Miller Wright. Opened in the Cherry Lane Theatre on Tuesday, Dec. 3, 1985, moved Monday, Feb. 27, 1986 to the Circle Repertory Theatre, and to the Douglas Fairbanks Theatre on Monday, September 8, 1986*

CAST

Sister Mary Regina ....Marilyn Farina †1
Sister Mary Hubert .... Vickie Belmonte †2
Sister Robert Anne .... Christine Anderson †3
Sister Mary Amnesia .... Semina DeLaurentis †4
Sister Mary Leo ....Suzi Winson †5
Understudies: Anne Allgood, Patti Whipple

MUSICAL NUMBERS: Nunsense Is Habit-Forming, A Difficult Transition, Benedicte, The Biggest Ain't the Best, Playing Second Fiddle, So You Want to Be a Nun, Turn Up the Spotlight, Lilacs Bring Back Memories, Tackle That Temptation with a Time Step, Growing Up Catholic, We've Got to Clean out the Freezer, Just a Coupl'a Sisters, Soup's On (The Dying Nun Ballet), I Just Want to Be a Star, The Drive In, I Could've Gone to Nashville, Gloria in Excelsis Deo, Holier Than Thou

A musical comedy in two acts. The action takes place at the present time in Mt. Saint Helen's School auditorium in Hoboken, NJ.

†Succeeded by: 1. Travis Hudson, Mary-Pat Green, Julie J. Hafner, 2. Edwina Lewis, Nancy Johnston, 3. Helen Baldassare, 4. Nancy Johnston, Susan Gordon-Clark, Nancy Hillner, Lynne Wintersteller, Sarah Knapp, 5. Jane Potter, Valerie DePena

*Still playing May 31, 1989.

Helen Baldassare, Marilyn Farina, Julie J. Hafner, Valerie De Pena, Sarah Knapp in "Nunsense" *(Martha Swope Photo)*

STEEL MAGNOLIAS

By Robert Harling; Director, Pamela Berlin; Set, Edward T. Gianfrancesco; Lighting, Craig Evans; Costumes, Don Newcomb; Hairstylist, Bobby H. Grayson; Sound, Aural Fixation; Stage Managers, Karen Moore, Bryan Burch; General Manager, Albert Poland; Company Manager, Marion Finkler; Wardrobe, Brionna McMahon; Press, Jeffrey Richards Associates. Opened at the Lucille Lortel Theatre on Friday, June 19, 1987*

CAST

Truvy .... Margo Martindale †1
Annette .... Constance Shulman †2
Clairee .... Kate Wilkinson †3
Shelby .... Betsy Aidem †4
M'Lynn .... Rosemary Prinz †5
Ouiser .... Mary Fogarty †6

A play in two acts and four scenes. The action takes place at the present time in Chinquapin, Louisiana.

†Succeeded by: 1. Susan Mansur, Suzy Hunt, 2. Dorrie Joiner, 3. Betty Moore, 4. Stacy Ray, Cynthia Vance, 5. Maeve McGuire, Rosemary Prinz, 6. Anna Minot, Anne Pitoniak, Anna Minot, Bette Henritze

*Still playing May 31, 1989. Originally presented by the WPA Theatre for 29 performances from March 11, 1987–April 19, 1987.

Martha Swope Photos
Top Right: (Clockwise from bottom right) Dorrie Joiner, Anna Minot, Rica Martens, Suzy Hunt, Jennifer Parsons, Rita Gardner

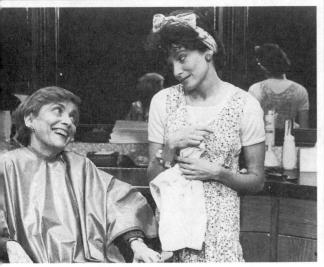

Rita Gardner, Dorrie Joiner
Above: Bette Henritze, Cynthia Vance

Suzy Hunt, Jennifer Parsons

OIL CITY SYMPHONY

By Mike Craver, Mark Hardwick, Debra Monk, Mary Murfitt; Director, Larry Forde; Set, Jeffrey Schissler; Sound, Otts Munderloh; Lighting, Natasha Katz; Presented by Lois Deutchman, Mary T. Nealon, David Musselman; Associate Producers, Thomas DeWolfe, Little Prince Productions, George Gordon; General Management, Newave Management; Assistant Manager, James Jay Wilson; Press, Joshua Ellis Office/ Adrian Bryan-Brown, Jackie Green, Bill Shuttleworth, Leo Stern, Susanne Tight, David Fuhrer, Tim Ray, Chris Boneau, Shannon Barr. Opened in Circle in the Square Theatre on Tuesday, November 3, 1987*

CAST

Mike Craver	Mark Hardwick
Debra Monk †1	Mary Murfitt †2

Standbys: Carol Sharar, Richard Jenkins, Mary Ehlinger

MUSICAL NUMBERS: Count Your Blessings, Czardas, Musical Moments, A Classical Selection, A Popular Selection, Ohio Afternoon, Baby It's Cold Outside, Beaver Ball at the Bug Club, Beehive Polka, Musical Memories, A Patriotic Fantasy, Dueling Pianos/Dizzy Fingers, Introductions, Iris, The End of the World, A Tribute, Coaxing the Ivories, Bus Ride, In the Sweet By and By, My Old Kentucky Rock and Roll Home

A recital in two acts with refreshments afterward.

†Succeeded by: 1. Michelle Horman, 2. Kathy Beaver

*Closed May 7, 1989 after 626 performances and 11 previews.

Mike Craver, Mary Murfitt, Mark Hardwick, Debra Monk in
"Oil City Symphony"

TAMARA

By John Krizane; Director, Richard Rose; Executive Producer, Moses Znaimer; Associate Producers, Lawrence N. Dykun, Barrie Wexler; Conceived by Richard Rose, John Krizane; Associate Director, Phil Killian; Design, Robert Cheecchi; Music, William Schallert; Choreography/Fight Direction, Gary Mascaro; Costumes, Gianfranco Ferre; Assistant Director, George Rondo; Casting, Johnson-Liff/Zerman; Lighting, Brian Bailey; Hairstylist, Bobby H. Grayson; General Management, Maple Interactive Entertainment Ltd.; Company Managers, Melinda P. Bloom, L. Glenn Poppleton III; Technical Director, David Kennedy; Props, Tom Swift, Douglas Kane, Nancy Greenstein; Wardrobe, Briona McMahon, Mary Lou Rios; Dance/Fight Captain, Norb Joerder; Dialect Coach, Sam Chwat; Stage Managers, Bruce Kagel, Cosmo P. Hanson; Press, Jeffrey Richards Associates. Opened in the Park Avenue Armory on Wednesday, December 2, 1987 and still playing May 31, 1989*

CAST

Tamara de Lempicka	Sara Botsford †1
Luisa Baccara	Lally Cadeau †2
Carlotta Barra	Cynthia Dale †3
Emilie Pavese	Roma Downey †4
GianFrancesco de Spiga	Patrick Horgan †5
Aelis Mazoyer	Marilyn Lightstone †6
Dante Fenzo	Leland Murray †7
Gabriele d'Annunzio	Frederick Rolf †8
Aldo Finzi	August Schellenberg †9
Mario Pagnutti	Jack Wetherall †10

A melodrama in two acts with dinner served at intermission. The action takes place on two successive days of 1927 in Il Vittoriale, the country retreat of Gabriele d'Annunzio.

†Succeeded by: Anna Katarina, Christine Dunford, Anne Swift, Elke Sommer, 2. Laura Esterman, Wanda Bimson, 3. Terri Hawkes, Lyn Vaux, Isabelle Fokine, 4. Sue Giosa, Monique Fowler, Ronnie Farer, 5. Sam Tsoutsouvas, William McCauley, 6. Judith Roberts, 7. Ray DeMattis, Joe Zaloom, 8. George Morfogen, Philip Pleasants, George Morfogen, 9. Thom Christopher, Christopher Goutman, John Bourgeois, Michael O'Gorman, 10. Mark Lewis, John Wesley Shipp, Marc Kudisch

*Still playing May 31, 1989.

Christine Dunford in "Tamara" *(T.L. Boston Photo)*

**Dea Lawrence, Theresa McElwee, Howard Samuelsohn in
"Vampire Lesbians of Sodom"** *(T.L. Boston Photo)*

TONY 'N' TINA'S WEDDING

By Artificial Intelligence; Conception, Nancy Cassaro; Director, Larry Pellegrini; Choreography, Hal Simons; Design/Decor, Randall Thropp; Costumes/Hair & Make-up Design, Juan DeArmas; Producers, Joseph Corcoran, Daniel Corcoran; General Manager, Leonard A. Mulhern; Company Manager, James Hannah; Stage Manager, Teresa Hagar; Press, David Rothenberg Associates/Terence Womble. Opened in the Washington Square Church & Carmelita's on Saturday, Feb. 6, 1988*

CAST
(alternating)

Valentina Lynne Nunzio, the bride .... Nancy Cassaro/Kelly Cinnante
Anthony Angelo Nunzio, the groom ....Mark Nassar/Ron Eldard
Connie Mocogni, maid of honor ....Chase Winton/Judy Sheehan
Barry Wheeler, the best man .... Mark Campbell/Bruce Kronenberg
Donna Marsala, bridesmaid ....Patty Granau/Debi Toni
Dominick Fabrizzi, usher ....James Altuner/George Shifini
Marina Gulino, bridesmaid .... Patricia Cregan/Aida Turturro
Johnny Nunzio, usher/groom's brother ....Eli Ganias/James DuMont
Josephine Vitale, mother of the bride .... Susan Varon/Roseanna Mineo
Joseph Vitale, brother of the bride ....Thomas Michael Allen/Billy Joe Young
Luigi Domenico, bride's great uncle .... Jacob Harran/Kirk Duncan
Rose Domenico, bride's aunt .... Jennifer Heftler/Kelly Ebsary
Sister Albert Maria, bride's cousin .... Elizabeth Herring/Jean Synodinos
Anthony Angelo Nunzio, Sr., groom's father ..... Chris Fracchiolla/Rick Shapiro
Madeline Monroe, his girl friend .... Leila Kenzle/Liliane DuRae
Grandma Nunzio, groom's grandmother .... Denise Moses/Bonnie Marcus
Michael Just, Tina's ex-boyfriend ....Jack Fris/Eric Cadora
Father Mark, parish priest .... Vincent Floriani/David Carr
Vinnie Black, caterer ....Kevin A. Leonidas/Tom Karlya
Loretta Black, his wife ....Joanna Cocca/Victoria Constan
Mick Black, their son ....Gary Schneider/William Marsilii
Nikki Black, his daughter ....Judy Sheehan/Cathryn de Prume
Mitzi Black, caterer's sister ....Carrie Gordon
Mikie Black, another son ....John Allen Goffredo
Pat Black, another sister .... Merri Biechler
Rick DeMarco, video man .... Neil Monaco/Patrick Smith
Sal Antonucci, photographer .... Daniel Maher/John Fulweiler
Vlasik ....Randall Thropp
Donny Dulce, band leader ....Tony Dowdy/Michael Visconti
Celeste Romano, keyboards ....Kia Colton/Debra Barsha
Carlo Cannoli, bass ....Charlie Terrat/Jim Dillman
Rocco Caruso, drums .... Towner Galaher

An environmental theatre play. The action takes place at the present time at Tony and Tina's wedding and reception.

*Still playing May 31, 1989, after moving to St. John's Church and Vinnie Black's Coliseum.

VAMPIRE LESBIANS OF SODOM

By Charles Busch; Director, Kenneth Elliott; Presented by Theatre in Limbo, Kenneth Elliott, Gerald A. Davis; Choreography, Jeff Veazey; Casting, Stuart Howard; Wigs, Elizabeth Katherine Carr; Company Manager, Richard Biederman; Wardrobe, Alee Ralph; Production Assistant, Loretta Grande; Stage Managers, Jim Griffith, Jeff Barneson; Press, Shirley Herz, Sam Rudy, Pete Sanders, Glenna Freedman, Miller Wright. Opened in the Provincetown Playhouse on Wednesday, June 19, 1985, and still playing May 31, 1989.

CAST

"Sleeping Beauty" or *"Coma"*
Miss Thick .... Chuck Brown †1
Enid Wetwhistle ....Carol Monferdini †2
Sebastian Lore .... Brick Hartney †3
Fauna Alexander ....David Drake †4
Ian McKenzie .... Nick Kaledin †5
Anthea Arlo .... Beata Baker †6
Barry Posner .... Jeff Barneson †7
Craig Prince .... A. J. Vincent †8

The action takes place in and around London in the 1960's.

"Vampire Lesbians of Sodom"
Ali a guard/P. J. a chorus boy .... Jeff Barneson †7
Hujar a guard/Zack a chorus boy .... A. J. Vincent †4
A Virgin Sacrifice/Madeleine Astarte ....David Drake †4
The Succubus/LaCondessa a vamp .... Carole Monferdini †2
King Carlisle a movie idol ....Nick Kaledin †5
Butler Etienne/Danny a chorus boy ....Paul Kassel †1
Renee Vain, starlet/Tracy a singer .... Beata Baker †6
Oatsie Carewe a gossip columnist ....Brick Hartney †3

UNDERSTUDIES: Heather Ehlers, Kari Jenson, Lisa Bansavage, Mark Hamilton, John St. Angelo

Performed with three scenes: Sodom in days of old, Hollywood in 1920 in La Condessa's mansion, and in a Las Vegas rehearsal hall today.
†Succeeded by: 1. Paul Kassel, Charles Kelly, 2. Carole Monferdini, Holly Felton, Dea Lawrence, 3. Brick Hartney, Roy Cockrum, 4. David Drake, Tom Aulino, Charles Busch, Howard Samuelsohn, 5. Matt Bradford Sullivan, Roger Bart, Laurence Overmire, 6. Monica Horan, Theresa McElwee, 7. Jeff Barneson, Robert Carey, 8. A. J. Vincent, Doug Tompos, Matt McLanahan

**Pat Cregan, Elizabeth Dennehy, Moira Wilson, Mark Nassar,
Nancy Cassaro, Mark Campbell, James Altuner, Eli Ganias
in "Tony N' Tina's Wedding"** *(Martha Swope Photo)*

OFF-BROADWAY COMPANIES SERIES

AMAS REPERTORY THEATRE

Twentieth Season

Founder/Artistic Director, Rosetta LeNoire; General Manager, Jeffrey Solis; Administrator, Eric M. Schussel; Production Manager, Christophe Pierre; Development, Ellen O'Neil; Wardrobe, Migdalia Ferrand; Press, Fred Nathan Company/Scott Taylor

Thursday, Oct. 13–Nov. 6, 1988 (17 performances)
BLACKAMOOR with Book by Joseph George Caruso, Helen Kromer; Lyrics, Helen Kromer; Music, Ulpio Minucci; Musical Director, Amy Engelstein; Arrangements, Buck Brown; Set, Steve Caldwell; Costumes, Jana Rosenblatt; Lighting, Phil Monat; Choreography/Musical Staging, Barry McNabb; Director, Kent Paul; Stage Manager, Tom Moseman; Based on novel "I, Juan de Pareja" by Elizabeth Borton de Trevino CAST: Tony Clarke (Carlos), Edouard DeSoto (Velasquez), Brian Fisher (Dancer), Guillermo Gonzalez (Luis), Ruthanna Graves (Mirl), Carolyn Heafner (Dona Miranda), Lon Hurst (Dancer), Christopher Innvar (Romero), David Jackson (Juan de Pareja), Lorenzo (Loll), Evan Matthews (Pablo), Herman Petras (King Felipe IV), Keelee Seetoo (Dancer), Lynette Tompkins (Trini)
MUSICAL NUMBERS: Spanish Serenade, In Madrid, We Do Absolutely Nothing, I Like to Paint by Early Light, Home with the King, We Can't Turn Back, Satisfied with Very Little Miri Miri, It's All Over for Us, Will I Be Caught?, The King's Law, More Sauce, He's Got You Busy, You're Wearing the Autumn So Well, I Don't Want to Send Her Away, Had We Been Free, Black Is, Remembrance, Free
A musical in 2 acts and 28 scenes. The action takes place in Madrid in the mid-Seventeenth Century.

Thursday, Feb. 16–March 19, 1989 (24 performances)
STEP INTO MY WORLD conceived and developed by Ronald G. Russo; Music/Lyrics, Micki Grant; Musical Director, George Caldwell; Musical Arrangements, William McDaniel; Lighting, Jeffrey Hubbell; Costumes, Mary Ann Lach; Production Manager, Christophe Pierre; Wardrobe, Migdalia Ferrand; Choreography, Jeffrey Dobbs; Director, Ronald G. Russo; Stage Manager, Teri Thorpe CAST: Jean Cheek, Ellen DeVerne, Martron Gales, David Girolmo, Evan Matthews, Deborah Woodson, Jennifer Bell, Jeffrey Dobbs
MUSICAL NUMBERS: Step into My World, This Time, How to Say Goodbye, Togetherness, It's Lonely, Waterfaucet Blues, The Women, Fetch Me Watah, Like a Lady, I've Still Got My Bite, They Keep Coming, We're Gonna Have a Good Time, Back Home, Mysteries and Miracles, Fighting for the Pharoah, The World Keeps Going Round, American Dream, Bright Lights, Who's Gonna Teach the Children, First Born, I Ain't Had My Fill, Workin', for the Man, Cleanin' Woman, Lovin' Al, Burn Out, Look at That Sky, Keep Steppin'
A musical in 2 acts and 6 scenes. The action takes place at the present time, in and around the city.

Wednesday, April 26–May 21, 1989 (20 performances)
PRIZES with Music and Lyrics by Charles DeForest; Book, Raffi Pehlivanian; Director, Lee Minskoff; Choreography, Margo Sappington; Musical Direction/Arrangements, Ned Ginsburg; Set, Jane Sablow; Lighting, Beau Kennedy; Production Manager, Christophe Pierre; Costume Coordinator, Robert Griggs; Stage Manager, John Rainwater CAST: Luther Fontaine (Ransom "Shoo-Fly" Lewis), Martron Gales (Ransom Jr.), Nancy Groff (Leda Farrell), Paul Hoover (Hank Morris), Allen Walker Lane (Milton Gershe), Heidi Mollenhauer (Eddie Winters), Doug Okerson (Jess Lincoln), Mary Stout (Ida Gershe), Darcy Thompson (Diana Evans), Karen Ziemba (Maggie Lincoln), Alan Gray (Understudy), Ensemble: Bruce Barbaree, Nick Corley, Natania Cox, Peter Ermides, Dexter Jones, Kari Nicolaisen, Rita Renha, Troy Rintala
MUSICAL NUMBERS: Awards, Thank You Very Much, It Always Worked, I'm Not Ready for You, Shoo-Fly, Run a Little Faster, Lonely at the Top Is It?, Is There Any Other Way to Live, All the Rest Is Bullshit, I Am the One, Leda's Song, Who Can Dance Like You?, I Don't Need Anybody, Dance!, Trio, Know What I've Learned, Thank You Very Much, Prizes
A musical in two acts.

Gilbert Johnson Photos
Top Right: David Jackson, Herman Petras in "Blackamoor"

Bruce Barbaree, Nick Corley, Morton Gales, Peter Ermides, Troy Rintala, Dexter Jones in "Prizes"

Above: Evan Matthews, Ellen De Verne in "Step Into My World"

AMERICAN JEWISH THEATRE

Fifteenth Season

Artistic Director, Stanley Brechner; General Manager, David Lawlor; Development, Norman Golden; Technical Director, Mike Kondrat; Press, Peter Cromarty (Theatre Guinevere) Wednesday, Sept. 7, 1988
Laocoon Production Company and the American Jewish Theatre present:
THE GOLDEN LEG by David Glikin; Directed by Mr. Glikin; Set, Bonnie Brinkley; Lighting, George B. Kelly; Stage Manager, JoAnn Minsker; Press, Jeffrey Richards Associates/Diane Judge CAST: Robert Silver (Konstantin Ivanovich), Joseph V. Francis (Revolutsinner), Lucille Rivin (Raisa), Robert Austin (Lord)
A play in two acts. The action takes place in Russia in the mid-1970's.

(Susan Bloch Theatre) Saturday, Oct. 10–Dec. 11, 1988 (49 performances and 11 previews) Re-opened Friday, April 14, 1989 in the Westside Arts Theatre and still playing there May 31, 1989. Presented by special arrangement with Bruce Lazarus, Richard Vos and Patrick Hogan.
ONLY KIDDING! by Jim Geoghan; Director, Larry Arrick CAST: Larry Keith (Jackie Dwayne), Michael Jeter (Sheldon Kelinski), Ethan Phillips (Tom Kelly), Paul Provenza (Jerry Goldstein), Sam Zap (Sal D'Angelo)
A play in three scenes with one intermission. At Westside Arts Theatre, Michael Jeter and Ethan Phillips were succeeded by Howard Spiegel and Andrew Hill Newman, respectively.

(Westside Arts Theatre) Friday, April 14–Dec. 31, 1989 (300 performances). Bruce Lazarus and Patrick Hogan present:
ONLY KIDDING! by Jim Geoghan; Director, Larry Arrick; Sets, Karen Schulz; Lighting, Debra Dumas; Costumes, Jeffrey L. Ullman; Sound, Paul Garrity; Associate Producer, Richard Vos; Production Coordinator, Heather Holmberg; General Manager, Albert Poland; Company Manager, Marcia Goldberg; Stage Managers, Zane Weiner, Lori Culhane; Press, Jeffrey Richards Associates/Irene Gandy, Diane Judge; Susan Chicoine, Maria Somma, Kathryn Frawley, Jillana Devine CAST: Larry Keith (Jackie Dwayne), Howard Spiegel (Sheldon Kelinski), Andrew Hill Newman (Tom Kelly), Paul Provenza succeeded by Ralph Macchio (Jerry Goldstein), Sam Zap (Sal D'Angelo), Peter Waldren (Voice of Buddy King), Standbys: Jerry Grayson, Robb Pruitt
A comedy in 2 acts and 3 scenes. The action takes place in the Catskill resort, in a nightclub basement, and the "green room" of the Buddy King Show.

(Susan Bloch Theatre) Saturday, Jan. 28–Feb. 26, 1989 (34 performances and 9 previews).
THE IMMIGRANT: a Hamilton County Album by Mark Harelik; Conceived by Mark Harelik and Randal Myler; Director, John Driver; Set, Randy Benjamin; Lighting, Susan A. White; Costumes, Victoria Lee; Sound, J. Wise; Language/ Dialect Coach, Ari Roussimoff; Stage Manager, Rick Lucero CAST: Ann Hillary (Ima Perry), Lonny Price (Haskell Harelik), Nesbitt Blaisdell (Milton Perry), Lisa Pelikan (Leah Harelik)
The action takes place from 1909 to the present in and around Hamilton, a tiny agricultural community in Texas.

Saturday, March 25–May 21, 1989 (67 performances and 11 previews).
THE EDUCATION OF H*Y*M*A*N K*A*P*L*A*N with Book by Benjamin Barnard Zavin; Based on stories of Leo Rosten; Music/Lyrics, Oscar Brand, Paul Nassau; Director, Lonny Price; Musical Director, Nicholas Levin; Set, Randy Benjamin; Costumes, Gail Cooper-Hecht; Lighting, Betsy Adams; Production Coordinator, Lisa Forman; Assistant Director, Daisy Prince; Props/Wardrobe, Jocelyn Pursley; Stage Manager, Jon Roger Clark CAST: Neal Ben-Ari (Yissel Fishbein/Plonsky), Norman Golden (Pinsky), Jack Hallett (Hyman Kaplan), Stephen McNaughton (Parkhill), Laura Patinkin (Rose Mitnick), Michael Shelle (Wilkomirski/Callahan/Judge Mahon), Molly Stark (Sadie Moskowitz/Mrs. Mitnick)
MUSICAL NUMBERS: The Adult Class, Strange New World, Ooee Ooere, Anything Is Possible, Lieben Dich, Loving You, Love Will Come, Spring in the City, An Old-Fashioned Husband, Shakespeare, I Never Felt Better in My Life, When Will I Learn, All American
A musical in 2 acts. The action takes place on the Lower East Side of New York.

Monday, May 8, 1989 (limited 2 performances)
SHELLEN LUBIN IN MOTHER/CHILD a solo performance; written by Miss Lubin; Additional Lyrics, Elliot Meyers, Elsa Rael; Director, Jane Whitehill in performance with AMERICAN PARLOR SONGS OF THE 19th CENTURY sung by Naomi Lewin.

Martha Swope, Gerry Goodstein Photos
Top Right: Paul Provenza, Andrew Hill Newman in
"Only Kidding"

Below: Andrew Hill Newman, Larry Keith, Howard Spiegel in
"Only Kidding"

Ralph Macchio in "Only Kidding" (L); Jack Hallett in
"Education of Hyman Kaplan" (R); Above: Lonny Price, Lisa
Pelikan in "The Immigrant"

AMERICAN PLACE THEATRE

Twenty-fifth Season

Director, Wynn Handman; General Manager, Mickey Rolfe; Business Manager, Joanna Vedder; Literary Manager, Chris Breyer; Press, Fred Nathan Co./Marc P. Thibodeau, Fifi Schuettich

Saturday, Sept. 24–Oct. 9, 1988 (13 performances)
CALVIN TRILLIN'S UNCLE SAM written and performed by Calvin Trillin; Production Design, John M. Lucas

Sunday, Oct. 31–Nov. 13, 1988 (21 performances)
A BURNING BEACH by Eduardo Machado; Director, Rene Buch; Set, Donald Eastman; Lighting, Anne Militello; Costumes, Deborah Shaw; Sound, Daniel Moses Schreier; Technical Director, John M. Lucas; Stage Managers, Rebecca Green, Jeffrey L. Pearl CAST: Lillian Garrett (Marta), Ivonne Coll (Ofelia), Seret Scott (Maria), George Lundoner (Juan), Liann Pattison (Constance), Mateo Gomez (Un Hombre)
A drama in two acts. The action takes place in 1895 in Cuba.

Thursday, Feb. 9–19, 1989 (19 performances)
THE UNGUIDED MISSILE by David Wolpe; Director, Fred Kolo; Set/Lighting, Holger; Costumes, Gail Cooper-Hecht; Audio/Visual Producer, Matthew Heineman; General Manager, Mickey Rolfe; Wardrobe, Deborah Hurst; Technical Director, George Zegarsky; Stage Managers, Richard Hester, Charles D. Cissel CAST: Estelle Parsons (Martha Mitchell), Jerome Dempsey (John Mitchell), Nick Searcy (Photographer/Alan Webster/Others), Barry Cullison (Mike Madden/Todd Peterson/Others), Lezlie Dalton (Sherri Peterson), Mary Jo Salerno (Cathy Reid/Dr. Kramer/Others)
A drama in two acts. The action begins on June 17, 1972, the date of the Watergate break-in.

Thursday, May 11–28, 1989 (21 performances)
THE BLESSING by Clare Coss; Director, Roberta Sklar; Set, Donald Eastman; Costumes, Sally J. Lesser; Lighting, Frances Aronson; Sound, Daniel Moss Schreier; General Manager, Mickey Rolfe; Technical Supervisor, George Zegarsky; Wardrobe, Lena Berry; Stage Managers, Richard Hester, Carol Dawes CAST: Kelly Bishop (Nan), Leila Boyd (Marilyn), Beth Fowler (Kathleen), Anita Gillette (Restive), Louisa Horton (Claudine), Olga Merediz (Flora), Anne Shropshire (Miss Mary)
A play in two acts. The action takes place during the summer of 1987 in the Lerner Adult Home on the South Shore of Long Island, NY.

Martha Holnes Photos
Top Left: Calvin Trillin in "Calvin Trillin's Uncle Sam"

Estelle Parsons, Jerome Dempsey in "The Unguided Missile"
Above: Ivonne Call, Lillian Garrett in "A Burning Beach"

Kelly Bishop, Anita Gillette in "The Blessing"

Cast of "Green Card"
Top Right: Cast of "Six Characters In Search of an Author"
Center Right: Pamela Gein, Priscilla Smith, Alvin Epstein in
"Six Characters in Search of an Author"

AMERICAN THEATER EXCHANGE

Third Season

(Joyce Theater) Monday, June 13–18, 1988 (15 performances) The Joyce Theater
Foundation (Cora Cahan, Vice President; Lisa A. Lawer, General Manager) and
AT&T: On Stage present as part of The First New York International Festival of the
Arts, the Mark Taper Forum/Center Theatre Group (Artistic Director/Producer,
Gordon Davidson; Managing Director, Stephen J. Albert) production of:
GREEN CARD written and directed by Joanne Akalaitis; Assistant Directors, Linda
Callahan, Elizabeth Diamond; Set, Douglas Stein; Costumes, Marianna Elliott;
Lighting, Frances Aronson; Choreography, Carolyn Dyer; Sound, Jon Gottlieb; Slide
Projection/Photography, Craig Collins; Associate Producer, Madeline Puzo; Hair/
Makeup, Bobby Miller; Production Manager, Julia Gillett; Stage Managers, Mireya
Hepner, Caryn Shick; Press, Ellen Jacobs CAST: Abraham Alvarez, Raye Birk, Jesse
Borrego, Rosalind Chao, Pamela Dunlap, George Galvan, Jim Ishida, Josie Kim,
Dana Lee; Alma Martinez, Jesse Nelson
   Act I: Prologue, Success Story, Customs and Costumes, Work, English, Natives,
Immigration, California, Act II: Prologue, Religion, Colonialism, Culture, CIA, A
Glossary, Testimony, Dead Letters, Dying in Your Dream, Waiting

(Joyce Theater) Friday, July 1–30, 1988 (16 performances). The Joyce Theater
Foundation and AT&T: On Stage present as part of the First New York International
Festival of the Arts the American Repertory Theatre (Robert Brustein, Artistic
Director; Robert J. Orchard, Managing Director; Richard Riddell, Associate Direc-
tor) production of:
BIG TIME: SCENES FROM A SERVICE ECONOMY by Keith Reddin; Direc-
tor, Steven Schachter; Sets, Bill Clarke; Costumes, Ellen McCartney; Lighting,
Thom Palm; Sound, Stephen D. Santomenna; Stage Managers, Anne S. King, Abbie
H. Katz, Hallie Kuperman; Press, Ellen Jacobs CAST: William Converse-Roberts
(Paul), Cherry Jones (Fran), Peter Crombie (Peter), Thomas
Derrah (Ted), Harry S. Murphy (Hassan). In repertory with: Wednesday, July 6–26,
1988 (15 performances)
SIX CHARACTERS IN SEARCH OF AN AUTHOR by Luigi Pirandello;
Adapted and Directed by Robert Brustein; Set/Costumes, Michael H. Yeargan;
Lighting, Frank Butler CAST: (The Company) John Grant-Phillips (Jack, Stage
Manager), Tom Rooney (Rooney, Assistant Stage Manager), Sandra Shipley (San-
dra, an actor), Thomas Derrah (Tommy, an actor), Jeremy Geidt (Jeremy, the senior
actor), Peter Gerety (Peter, an actor), Harry S. Murphy (Harry, an actor), (The
Characters) Pamela Gien (Stepdaughter), Priscilla Smith (Mother), Alvin Epstein
(Father), Benjamin Evett (Son), Matthew Dundas (Little Brother), Dawn Kelly
(Little Sister), Michael Balcanoff (Emilie Paz).
   The action takes place during a rehearsal by the American Repertory Theatre
company at the Joyce Theater, New York City. Performed without an intermission.

Richard Feldman Photos

William Converse-Roberts, Sandra Shipley in "Big Time"

BROOKLYN ACADEMY OF MUSIC

(BAM/Opera House) Wednesday, June 8–16, 1988 (8 limited performances) The Brooklyn Academy of Music (Harvey Lichtenstein, President/Executive Producer) presents the Royal Dramatic Theatre of Sweden in:
HAMLET by William Shakespeare; Director, Ingmar Bergman; Scenery and Costumes, Goran Wassberg; Music, Jean Billgren, Christian Falk; Managing/Artistic Director, Lars Lofgren; Technical Director, Bernt Thorell; Lighting, Hans Akesson; Assistant Director, Richard Looft; Producer, Katarina Sjoberg; Stage Managers, Tomas Wennerberg, Kaj Forsgardh, Per Hoglund, Bertil Österberg; Press, Peter B. Carzasty, Karen Goldman, Robert Boyd CAST: Borje Ahlstedt (Claudius), Peter Stormare (Hamlet), Per Myrberg (Ghost of Hamlet's Father), Gunnel Lindblom (Gertrude), Ulf Johanson (Polonius), Pierre Wilkner (Laertes), Pernilla Ostergren (Ophelia), Jan Waldekranz (Horatio), Johan Lindell (Rosencrantz), Johan Rabaeus (Guildenstern), Orjan Ramberg (Bernardo), Johan-Rabaeus (Marcellus), Dennis Dahlsten (Francisco), Johan Lindell (Osric), Marie Richardson (Court Lady), Oscar Ljung (Priest), Ulf Johanson (Gravedigger), Orjan Ramberg (Fortinbras), Per Myrberg (Player King), Marie Richardson (Player Queen), Oscar Ljung (Lucianus), Gerd Hagman (Pelageia), Ivan Ossoinak (Flautist), Michael Vinsa (Drummer), Dennis Dahlsten (Captain), and Peter Anderson, Jonas Erkman, John Svensson, Staffan Fridman, Stefan Larsson, Benoit Malmberg, Magnus Mark, Jan Olsson, Thomas Strand, Paula Ternstrom, Ralf Tjernlund, Thomas Wrisemo.
   Performed with one intermission.

(BAM/Majestic Theatre) Thursday, July 7–10, 1988 (5 performances). Brooklyn Academy of Music presents as part of the First New York Festival of the 87 Arts and Inter-Arts, NY (Noriko Sengoku, Producer) Yume no Yuminsha's:
COMET MESSENGER-SIEGFRIED written and directed by Hideki Noda; English translation, Don Kenny; Set, Masahiro Iwai; Lighting Design, Takashi Kitakizaki Kitakazaki; Sound Design/Associate Director, Yukio Takatsu; Choreography, Tamae Sha; Costumes, Masami Hara; Stage Manager, Mitsumasa Tsuda; Company Manager, Hiroshi Takahagi; Company Manager, Takashi Nakashima; Production Manager, Andrew Feigin; Press, Ellen Jacobs CAST: Hideki Noda (Flying Sawyer), Yasunori Danta (Huckleberry Finn Lizard), Shozo Uesugi (Galileo/Prof. Ikigami/God), Akiko Takeshita (Tamiko/Sleeping Princess), Kazuyuki Asano (Nostradamus/Merchant of Penis), Aaya Enjoji (Val/Enigmatic Nun 1), Shinobu Kawamata (Rie/Nun 2), Sachiko Matsuura (Nun 3), Ryosei Tayama (Prof. Ikibotoke), Nobuyoshi Uedi (Asst. Shinigami), Kaoru Mukai (Mrs. Galileo/God's Wife), Toshia Toyama (Bird-ancestor), Yuichi Haba (Fish-ancestor), Kenta Satoi (Bird-ancestor), Toshio Monma (Ninja Fujimaru), Sugie Watanabe (Ninja Kunoichi), Hideyuki Sugita (Nagashima), Masayuki Hamano (Believer 1), Masahiro Totani (Believer 2), Jun Shionishi (Believer 3), Katsuya Kobayashi (Narrator). Performed in 2 acts and nineteen scenes.

(BAM/Majestic Theatre) Wednesday, Oct. 19–30, 1988 (15 performances) Brooklyn Academy of Music (Harvey Lichtenstein, President/Executive Producer), Yale Repertory Theatre, Colonus Inc. (Liza Lorwin, Producing Director) present:
THE WARRIOR ANT (Book I and the conclusion of Book III) Poem and Lyrics, Lee Breuer; Music, Bob Telson; Scenery/Paintings, Alison Yerxa; Lighting, Julie Archer; Costumes, Ghretta Hynd; Sound, Ron Lorman; Conceived and Directed by Lee Breuer; General Manager, Laurel Ann Wilson; Company Manager, Frier McCollister; Technical Manager, Rhys Williams; Presented in association with American Music Theatre Festival, Spoleto Festival, U.S.A., and Mabou Mines; Choreography, Pat Hall-Smith, Estelle Eichenberger, Kevin Davis, Carmen deLavallade CAST: Yoshida Tamamatsu, Kanju Kiritake, Sam Butler, Jr., Denise Delapenha, Jevetta Steele, Frederick Neumann, Isabell Monk, Leslie Mohn, Ruth Maleczech, Randy Carfagno, Patrick Kerr, John Ludwig, Eren Ozker, Barbara Pollitt, Elena, Hassan Halkmoun, Christian Ward, Bryan Brooks, Bev Brown, Ronald Burton, M. Afida Derby, Asma Feyijinmi, Errol Grimes, Amy Pivar, Sam Yipp, Mark Stephen Pickett, Duran Gordon, Jason Bailey, Toby White, James Geddie, Empire Loisaida Escola de Samba, Little Village, Moods Pan Groove, Simon Shaheen Near East Ensemble
   A musical in two acts.

(Opera House) Friday, Dec. 2–10, 1988 (8 limited performances)
THE FOREST by Robert Wilson and David Byrne; Book/Design/Direction, Robert Wilson; Music, David Byrne; Text, Heiner Muller, Darryl Pinckney; Assistant Director, Julia Gillett; Choreography, Suzushi Hanayagi; Set, Tom Kamm, Robert Wilson; Costumes, Frida Parmeggiani; Lighting, David Byrne, Jimmie Haskell; Hair/Makeup, Vito Mastrogiovanni; Dramaturg, Christopher Ruter, Hans-Werner Kroesinger; Assistant Directors, Katharina Seidel, Steven Valk; Props, Reinhard Bichsel, Alain Thomas; Technical Director, Hans-Jurgen Hageneuer; Special Effects, Margit Billib; Stage Manager, Lisa Riedl CAST: Peter Fitz, Frank Hentschker, Gunter Ehlert, Beate Pilar von Pilchau, Michel Honesseau, Corin Curschellas, Lucia Hartpeng, Claudia Jakobshagen, Jezy Milton, Anita Kohler, Simon Newby-Koschwitz, Martin Peter, Vera Schrankl, Monika Tahal, Olaf Drauschke, Florian Fritz, Bill Maceri, Geno Lechner, Martin Wuttke, Eva-Marie Meineke, Howie Seago, Ashley St. Thomas, Alexander Serafin.
   A play in 7 acts and 11 scenes, with 2 intermissions.

Bengt Wanselius, Daizaburo, Martha Swope,
Gerhard Kassner Photos
Top Right: Pierre Wilkner, Peter Stormare in "Hamlet"
Below: Hideki Noda in "Comet Messenger-Siegfried"

"The Forest"
Above: "The Warrior Ant"

CIRCLE REPERTORY THEATRE

Twentieth Season

Artistic Director, Tanya Berezin; Associate Artistic Director, B. Rodney Marriott; Resident Director/Casting, Mark Ramont; Literary Manager, Adrienne Hiegel; General Manager, Paul R. Tetreault; Marketing, Jan Ohye; Development, Ellen Mittenthal; Production Manager, Jody Boese; Technical Director, Larry Springer; Props, Stephanie Lessen; Wardrobe, Carrena Lukas, Jane Loranger; Press, Gary Murphy

(Circle Repertory Theatre) Wednesday, Sept. 14, 1988–Jan. 1, 1989 (125 performances)
RECKLESS by Craig Lucas; Director, Norman René; Sets, Loy Arcenas; Costumes, Walker Hicklin; Lighting, Debra J. Kletter; Sound, Chuck London/Stewart Werner; Stage Managers, Fred Reinglas, Jodi Manners CAST: Robin Bartlett (Rachel), Michael E. Piontek (Tom/Tom, Jr.), John Dossett (Lloyd), Welker White (Pooty/Talk Show Guest), Kelly Connell (Roy/Tim/Talk Show Host), Susan Blommaert (Trish/Woman Patient), Joyce Reehling (Doctor 1 through 6)
   A comedy in two acts.

(Cherry Lane Theatre) Friday, Jan. 20–March 12, 1989 (61 performances)
BRILLIANT TRACES by Cindy Lou Johnson; Director, Terry Kinney; Set, John Lee Beatty. Costumes, Laura Crow; Props, Carrena Lukas CAST: Kevin Anderson (Henry Harry), Joan Cusack (Rosannah DeLuce)
   Performed without intermission; The action takes place at the present time in the State of Alaska in the middle of nowhere.

Wednesday, Jan. 25–March 5, 1989 (46 performances)
DALTON'S BACK by Keith Curran; Director, Mark Ramont; Set, William Barclay; Costumes, Susan Lyall; Stage Manager, Denise Yaney CAST: John Dossett (Dalton Possil), Colleen Davenport (Teresa MacIntyre), Matt McGrath (Dalty), Lisa Emery (Mom), Jayce Bartok (Hiram), Understudies: Dan Wantland (Dalton), Stephanie Lessem (Teresa), Robert Gladding (Dalty), Lynn Battaglia (Mom), Scott Constantine (Hiram)
   A play in two acts. The action takes place at the present time in Dalton's rooms.

Wednesday, March 22–May 7, 1989 (52 performances)
AMULETS AGAINST THE DRAGON FORCES by Paul Zindel; Director, B. Rodney Marriott; Set, David Potts; Costumes, Walker Hicklin; Lighting, Dennis Parichy; Original Music, Norman L. Berman; Fight Director, Rick Sordelet; Production Manager, Jody Boese; Amulet Sculptures, Kate Conklin; Props, Jane Loranger, James Gregory; Stage Managers, M. A. Howard, Robert Gladding CAST: Jerome Preston Bates (Attendant #1/Leroy), Loren Dean (Harold), Deborah Hedwall (Mrs. Boyd), Robert Gladding (Richie), Ruby Holbrook (Mrs. DiPardi), Carrena Lukas (Rosemary), Matt McGrath (Chris), James Greogry Smith (Roochie), John Spencer (Floyd), John Viscardi (Attendant 2/Joey)
   A drama in two acts and seven scenes. The action takes place on Staten Island, NY in 1955.

Wednesday, May 17–June 25, 1989 (46 performances)
FLORIDA CRACKERS by Wm. S. Leavengood; Director, John Bishop; Set, John Lee Beatty; Costumes, Connie Singer; Lighting, Dennis Parichy; Sound, Chuck London/Stewart Werner; Music, Jonathan Brielle; Technical Director, Tim Hamilton; Props, Stephanie Lessem, Jane Loranger; Wardrobe, Lynn Battaglia; Stage Managers, Fred Reinglas, Scott Constantine CAST: Joel Anderson (Dean), Cyndi Coyne (Tracey), Kim Flowers (Lori), Brian Jensen (Strings), John C. McGinley (Joe), Michael Piontek (Grant), Scott Rymer (Russell)
   A drama in 2 acts and 7 scenes. The action takes place during the summer of 1979 in St. Petersburg Beach, Florida.

Gerry Goodstein, Bob Marshak Photos
Top Right: Robin Bartlett, John Dossett, Welker White in "Reckless"

Below: Joan Cusack, Kevin Anderson in "Brilliant Traces"

Loren Dean, Matt McGrath in "Amulets Against The Dragon Forces"
Above: John Dossett, Lisa Emery in "Dalton's Back"

79

CSC REPERTORY LTD.

The Classic Stage Company

Artistic Director, Carey Perloff; Managing Director, Ellen Novack; General Manager, Dara Hershman; Production Manager, Jeffrey Berzon; Literary Associate, Suzanne Collins; Production Assistant, Bill Blank; Press, Peter Cromarty & Co./ David Gersten, Jim Baldassare, Kevin Brockman
(CSC Repertory Theatre) Tuesday, Oct. 11–Nov. 20, 1988 (30 performances)
RAMEAU'S NEPHEW by Denis Diderot; Translation/Adaptation, Shelley Berc, Andrei Belgrader; Director, Andrei Belgrader; Set, Anita Stewart; Costumes, Candice Donnelly; Lighting, Robert Wierzel; Sound, William Uttley; Casting, Ellen Novack; Stage Managers, Kate Riddle, Bill Blank; Wigs, Paul Huntley; Wardrobe, Dominique J. Cook CAST: Nicholas Kepros (Moi), Tony Shalhoub (Lui)
Performed with one intermission.

(CSC Repertory Theatre) Saturday, Dec. 10, 1988–Jan. 15, 1989 (28 performances and 8 previews). The Classic Stage Company (Carey Perloff, Artistic Director; Ellen Novack, Managing Director) presents:
PHAEDRA BRITANNICA by Jean Racine; Adapted by Tony Harrison; Director, Carey Perloff; Set, Donald Eastman; Costumes, Gabriel Berry; Lighting, Frances Aronson; Composer, Elizabeth Swados; Voice/Text Consultant, Nancy Lane; Casting, Ellen Novack; Production Manager, Jeffrey Berzon; Wardrobe, Christine Verleny; General Manager, Dara Hershman; Stage Managers, Richard Hester, Bill Blank; Press, Cromarty & Co./Peter Cromarty, David Gersten, Kevin Brockman CAST: Jack Stehlin (Thomas Theophilus), David Riehle (Burleigh), Rajika Puri (Ayah), Caroline Lagerfelt (Governor's Wife), John Wendes Taylor (ADC to Governor), Sakina Jaffrey (Lilamani), Mehr Tatna (Tara), Michael Jayce (Chuprassie), Winter Mead, Jill Williams (Servants), Bob Gunton (Governor)
A play in two acts. The action takes place in British India in the 1850's, a few years before the Indian Mutiny.

(CSC Theatre) Tuesday, Mar. 21–Apr. 30, 1989 (29 performances and 15 previews). The Classic Stage Co. (Carey Perloff, Artistic Director; Ellen Novack, Managing Director) and INTAR Hispanic American Arts Center (Max Ferra, Artistic Director; James DiPaola, Managing Director) present:
DON JUAN OF SEVILLE by Tirso de Molina; Translated by Lynne Alvarez; Director, Carey Perloff; Set, Donald Eastman; Costumes, Gabriel Berry; Lighting, Frances Aronson; Composer, Elizabeth Swados; Movement, Mark Taylor; Production Manager, Jeffrey Berzon; Technical Director, David Brune; Wardrobe, Christine Verleny; Stage Managers, Richard Hester, Carol Dawes CAST: Royce M. Becker (Courtier/Wedding Guest/Servant), Sara Erde (Courtier/Servant/Aminta), Ron Faber (Don Pedro/King Alphonso), Don Gettinger (Guard/Courtier/Wedding Guest/Fabio/Servant), Michael Jayce (Guard/Courtier/Batricio), Norberto Kerner (King of Naples/Don Diego/Gaseno), Robert Langdon Lloyd (Don Gonzalo), Winter Mead (Coridon/Wedding Guest/Servant), Denise B. Mickelbury (Isabella), Jeffrey Nordling (Don Juan), Hope Nye (Anabella/Wedding Guest/Belisa/Courtier), Michael Perez (Catalinon), Al Rodriguez (Ripio/Courtier/Marquis de la Mota), Jack Stehlin (Octavio), John Wendes Taylor (Anfriso/Courtier), Jill Williams (Servant/Wedding Guest/Courtier), Sarah Williams (Courtier/Dona Ana/Servant), Kim Yancey (Tisbea)
A play in two acts. The action takes place in Naples and Seville, and many places on the road in between.

Paula Court Photos
**Top L: Richard Riehle, Jack Stehlin, Rajika Puri,
(seated) Bob Gunton, Caroline Lagerfelt in
"Phaedra Britannica"
Top R: Rajika Puri, Caroline Lagerfelt in "Phaedra Britannica"**

**Sara Erde, Michael Perez, Jeffrey Nordling, Kim Yancy,
Denise Burse-Mickelbury in "Don Juan of Seville"
Above: Tony Shalhoub, Nicholas Kepros in
"Rameau's Nephew"**

HUDSON GUILD THEATRE

Fourteenth Season

Artistic Director, Geoffrey Sherman; Associate Director, Steven Ramay; General Manager, Paul Hutchison; Artistic Associate, John Daines; Production Manager, Patrick J. Scully; Stage Manager, Fredrick Hahn; Development, Linda Scott; Press, Jeffrey Richards Associates/Ben Morse, Irene Gandy, Diane Judge, Roger Lane, Susan Chicoine, John Wilcox, Michael Trent, Jillana Devine.

Saturday, June 11–July 3, 1988 (17 performances and 17 previews)
IN PERPETUITY THROUGHOUT THE UNIVERSE by Eric Overmyer; Director, Stan Wojewodski, Jr.; Set, Christopher Barreca; Costumes, Robert Wojewodski; Lighting, Stephen Strawbridge; Sound, Janet Kalas; Produced in association with Center Stage, Baltimore. CAST: Troy Evans (Mr. Ampersand Qwerty/Oscar Rang), Arthur Hanket (Lyle Vial), Tzi Ma (Dennis Wu/Tai-Tung Tranh), Carolyn McCormick (Christine Penderecki), Jennifer Harmon (Marla Montage/Claire Silver), Laura Innes (Buster/Miss Peterson/Jaculatrix)

A play in two acts. The action takes place at the present time very late at night in a series of rooms and offices in Manhattan, NYC.

Wednesday, Oct. 19–Nov. 13, 1988 (28 performances)
TEA WITH MOMMY AND JACK by Shela Walsh; Director, Lawrence Sacharow; Set, Donald Eastman; Lighting, Paul Wonsek; Costumes, Marianne Powell-Parker; Sound, Aural Fixation; Original Music, Peter Gordon; Props, Catherine Policella; Stage Manager, Fredrick Hahn CAST: David Groh (Jack), Sylvia Miles (Mommy), Caris Corfman (Josie)

A comedy in 2 acts and 6 scenes. The action takes place in late Spring of 1963 in Mommy's parlour on Long Island.

Wednesday, Nov. 30–Dec. 31, 1988 (33 performances)
ALMOST PERFECT by Jerry Mayer; Director, Geraldine Fitzgerald; Set, James D. Sandefur; Lighting, Phil Monat; Costumes, Pamela Scofield; Sound, Aural Fixation; Props, Catherine Policella, Sarah Harper; Lingerie, Miss Elaine; Stage Managers, Fredrick Hahn, Beth Franco CAST: Ivar Brogger (Mike Apple), Chevi Colton (Mom), Cathy Lee Crosby (Boots), Mia Dillon (Jenny Apple), Ethan Phillips (Buddy Apple), Bill Nelson (Dad)

A comedy in two acts. The action takes place at various locations in St. Louis, MO.

Wednesday, Feb. 1–26, 1989 (28 performances)
WITHOUT APOLOGIES by Thom Thomas; Director, Edgar Lansbury; Set, John Wulp; Lighting, Paul Wonsek; Costumes, Karen Hummel; Incidental Music, Tamara Kline; Choreography, Jerry Yoder; Props, Catherine Policella, Sarah Harper; Assistant Director, Neil Wilson; Stage Managers, Fredrick Hahn, Peter Ficht CAST: Kurt Knudson (Algy Beaumont), Pauline Flanagan (His Wife Gwen), Peter Pagan (Ernie Beaumont), Carrie Nye (Cecily, his wife), Laura Brutsman (Brenda, their daughter), Edmund Lewis (Willie Jukes)

A comedy in 2 acts and 4 scenes. The action takes place in the front parlor of the Beaumont residence on Camden Road in London, England, in 1933, 1937 and 1940.

Wednesday, March 29–April 23, 1989 (31 performances)
WALKERS by Marion Isaac McClinton; Directors, Steven Ramay, Mr. McClinton; Set/Lighting, Paul Wonsek; Costumes, Elsa Ward; Sound, Craig R. Zaionz; Stage Manager, Fredrick Hahn CAST: Terry E. Bellamy (Walker Gillette Walker), Iona Morris (Woman), Faye M. Price (Annalisa Walker), Ron Dortch (Boston Westinghouse "Wes Jr" Walker), John Henry Redwood (Boston Westinghouse Walker, Sr.), James A. Williams (Danny Skynner)

A drama in two acts. The action takes place in an interrogation room.

Wednesday, May 24–June 18, 1989 (28 performances)
UP 'N' UNDER by John Godber; Director, Geoffrey Sherman; Set/Lighting, Paul Wonsek; Costumes, Pamela Scofield; Sound, Craig R. Zaionz; Assistant Director, Pete Ficht; Wardrobe, Mary Ellen Waters; Stage Managers, Gary M. Zabinski, Megan Burdy, Sherry Stuart CAST: Ivar Brogger (Frank Rowely), Ray Collins (Phil Hopley), John Curless (Arthur Hoyle), Fredrick Hahn (Tony Burtoft), Edmund Lewis (Reg Welsh/Steve Edwards), Elaine Rinehart (Hazel Scott)

A play in two acts. The action takes place at the present time in Yorkshire, England.

Gerry Goodstein Photos

Top Right: David Groh, Caris Corfman, Sylvia Miles in "Tea with Mommy and Jack"
Below: Cathy Lee Crosby, Ethan Phillips in "Almost Perfect"

John Curless, Fredrick Hahn, Ivar Brogger, Edmund Lewis
in "Up 'N' Under"
Above: Kurt Knudson, Peter Pagan, (seated) Carrie Nye,
Pauline Flanagan in "Without Apologies"

EQUITY LIBRARY THEATRE

Forty-sixth Season

Producing Director, George Wojtasik succeeded by Jeffrey Costello; Assistant, Suzanne O'Connor; Business Manager, Gerard Mawn; Development, Bonni-Faith Byrnes; Production Manager, Randy Becker; Technical Director, Randolph Alexander; Wardrobe, Carole Cuming; Stage Managers, Mark Wagenhurst, Michael David Winter, Mary Ellen Waters; Press, Lewis Harmon

(Master Theatre) Thursday, Sept. 29–Oct. 16, 1988 (24 performances)
THE MALE ANIMAL by James Thurber and Elliott Nugent; Director, Geoffrey C. Shlaes; Set, Warren Karp; Costumes, Stephen L. Bornstein; Lighting, Kenneth J. Lapham; Sound, Hal Schuler CAST: Regis Bowman (Ed Keller), Robert Fass (Reporter/Radio Announcer), Lori Galante ("Nutsy" Miller), Patricia Guinan (Blanche), Jona Harvey (Myrtle), James Kiberd (Joe Ferguson), James Lish (Michael Barnes), Robert McFarland (Dean Damon), Louise Mike (Cleota), Sandy Rowe (Ellen), Robert Shampain (Tommy Turner), Kathleen Weber (Patricia Stanley), Patrick White (Wally Myers)

A comedy in three acts. The action takes place during 1939 in the living-room of Prof. Thomas Turner in a midwestern university town.

Thursday, Oct. 27–Nov. 20, 1988 (30 performances and 2 previews)
FIORELLO! with Book by Jerome Weidman, George Abbott; Music, Jerry Bock; Lyrics, Sheldon Harnick; Director, Bob Nigro; Costumes, Ken Brown; Lighting, Mark Andrew; Set, John Kenny; Musical Director, Alkiviades Seriopoulos; Choreographer, Ken Prescott; Stage Managers, Jerry Nadal, Bernita Robinson, Carmen Suarez; Props, Brendan Smith; Wardrobe, Carole Cuming CAST: David Cleveland (Floyd), Elizabeth Darrett (Mrs. Pomerantz), Joe Dispenza (Fiorello), Felicia Farone (Dora), Wayne Gordy (Neil), Mark Goldbaum (Morris), Kathryn Kendall (Mitzi), Paul Laureano (Ben Marino), Campbell Martin (Card Player), Ron Meier (Card Player), Mark James Morris (Card Player), Mia Randall (Marie), G. Tom Swift (Card Player), Eli Tray (Card Player), Jane Wasser (Thea), Richard Whelan (Zappetella/Card Player), Ensemble: Angelo Adkins, Penny Jay, Cara McCarthy, David McKeown, Shannon McGough, Wendy Perelman, Peter Romero

A musical in 2 acts and 17 scenes, with a prologue. The action takes place in New York City shortly before World War I and ten years later.

Thursday, Dec. 1–18, 1988 (22 performances)
PEG-O' MY HEART by J. Hartley Manners; Director, D. J. Maloney; Set, Robert McBroom; Costumes, Martha Bromelmeier; Lighting, Pat McGillicuddy; Sound, Paul Garrity; Props, Betty Berkowitz; Hairstylist, Joy Prignon, Alyson Marek; "Mecushla" sung by Kevin Alvey; Stage Managers, Jay McManigal, Carol Venezia CAST: Yvette Edelhart (Mrs. Chichester), Stephen Gabis (Christian Brent), Tim Gail (Jerry), Russell Goldberg (Alaric), George Holmes (Jarvis), Judith McIntyre (Peg), Marjorie Ann Miller (Ethel), Arland Russell (Montgomery Hawkes), Johnette Sullivan (Bennett)

A comedy in 3 acts and 4 scenes. The action takes place during early summer of 1930 in the living room of Regal Villa, the Tudor estate of Mrs. Monica Chichester in Scarborough, England.

Thursday, Jan. 5–29, 1989 (24 performances)
TOMFOOLERY the words, music and lyrics of Tom Lehrer; Adapted by Cameron Mackintosh, Robin Ray; Director/Choreographer, Pamela Hunt; Musical Director, Bob McDowell; Scenic Coordinator, Wilber Ball; Costumes, Thomas Lee Keller; Lighting, Kenneth J. Lapham; Musical Arrangements, Chris Walker, Robert Fisher; Additional Arrangements/Orchestrations, Bob McDowell; Stage Manager, Jon Roger Clark CAST: Don Bradford, Jack Doyle, Patricia Masters, John Remme, Bob McDowell (Piano), Paul Johnson (Second Piano), Andy Hasen (Percussion)

The songs of Tom Lehrer performed with one intermission.

Thursday, Feb. 9–26, 1989 (24 performances)
FIFTH OF JULY by Lanford Wilson; Director, Andrew Glant-Linden; Set, Richard Ellis; Lighting, A. C. Hickox; Costumes, Hilarie Blumenthal; Sound, Steven Osgood; Fight Coordinator, Gilbert Cruse; Production Assistant, Deborah Natoli; Stage Managers, Jon Roger Clark, John Frederick Sullivan, John Flak, Ron Casidine CAST: Jack L. Davis (Kenneth Talley, Jr.), Laurence Overmire (Jed Jenkins), Rebecca Hoodwin (June Talley), Cate Damon (Shirley Talley), Kevin Jeffries (John Landis), Susanna Frazer (Gwen Landis), Don Weingust (Weston Hurley), Joan Mann (Sally Friedman)

A play in two acts. The action takes place on the Talley farm near Lebanon, Missouri, on Independence Day of 1977 and the following morning.

Ned Snyder Photos
Top Left: Regis Bowman, Robert Shampain, Robert McFarland, Sandy Rowe, Kathleen Weber, James Lish in "The Male Animal"

Below: Joe Dispenza in "Fiorello"

Don Bradford, Jack Doyle, John Remme, Patricia Masters in "Tomfoolery"

Thursday, Mar. 9–Apr. 2, 1989 (32 performances)
LEAVE IT TO JANE with Music/Lyrics, Jerome Kern; Book, Guy Bolton, P. G. Wodehouse; Staged and Choreographed by Lynnette Barkley, Niki Harris; Musical Director, Ethyl Will; Conductor, Paul Johnson; Set, John Shimrock; Lighting, Kenneth Posner; Costume Coordinator, M. Christine Shank; Sound, Hector Melia; Assistant to Director, Douglas Hall; Stage Managers, John Frederick Sullivan, Lori Culhane, Christine Catti, Betty Berkowitz CAST: Liz Amberly (Ensemble/Josephine Barclay), Tom Brown (Ollie Mitchell), Elisa Carnahert (Ensemble/Martha Abbott), Nick Corley (Stubby Talmadge), Rob Donohoe (Dr. Witherspoon), R. Bruce Elliott (Coach Marty McGowan), David Hibbard (Ensemble/Jimsle Hopper), Adrienne Hurd (Ensemble/Cissie Summers), Rusty Jacobs (Ensemble/Happy Jones), Susan Hartley (Bessie Tanner), Michael Iannucci (Prof. Talbot), Heidi Joyce (Flora Wiggins), Matt Lenz (Ensemble/Dick McAllister), Nancy Melius (Ensemble/Cora Jenks), Sandy Mulvihill (Ensemble/Bertha Tyson), Wendy Oliver (Jane Witherspoon), Marcus Powell (Hiram Bolton), Peter Reardon (Billy Bolton), Carroll Van Cleave (Silent Murphy), David Vincent (Ensemble/Mickey Larabee)
MUSICAL NUMBERS: Good Old Atwater, Peach of a Life, Wait Till Tomorrow, Just You Watch My Step, Leave It to Jane, Siren's Song, Cleopaterer, Dancing Time, There It Is Again, The Crickets Are Calling, Whoop-de-doodle-do, Nervous, What I'm Longing to Say, Sir Galahad, The Sun Shines Brighter, Land Where the Good Songs Go
A musical in two acts. The action takes place at Atwater College.

Thursday, April 13–30, 1985 (24 performances)
THE THIRTEENTH CHAIR by Bayard Veiller; Director, Maggie Jackson; Set, James A. Bazewicz; Lighting, Douglas Cox; Costumes, Lisa LoCurto; Sound, Hector, Milia; Stage Managers, Carol Venezia, Lauren Helpern, Kim McNutt, Michael David Winter; Hair/Wigs, Kevin Brainerd; Special Effects, Gregory Erbach CAST: Peter Blaxill (Howard Standish), Hewitt Brooks (Ins. Tim Donohue), Bernard Ferstenberg (Sgt. Dunn), Babs Hooyman (Rosalie LaGrange), Bob Horen (Edward Wales), Mare Kenney (Mary Eastwood), Rosemary Keough (Helen Trent), Mike Kimmel (Policeman/Doolan), Malia Ondrejka (Helen O'Neill), Daniel Nalbach (Roscoe Crosby), El len Orchid (Grace Standish), David Rose (Braddish Trent), Joseph Scott (Pollock), T. Ryder Smith (Will Crosby), Tom Spivey (Philip Masdon), Maxine Taylor-Morris (Mrs. Crosby), Alison Trattner (Elizabeth Erskine)
A mystery in three acts. The action takes place in 1916 in the drawing-room in the home of Mr. and Mrs. Roscoe Crosby of New York City.

Thursday, May 11–June 4, 1989 (32 performances)
GIGI with Book and Lyrics by Alan Jay Lerner; Music, Frederick Loewe; Based on novel by Colette; Director, Gerard Alessandrini; Choreography, John Carrafa; Musical Direction, Paul Johnson; Set, Nicholas Lundy; Costumes, Bruce Goodrich; Lighting, Nancy Collings; Company Manager, Suzanne O'Connor; Props, Ron Considine, Jennifer Wolfson; Wardrobe, Maureen Frey CAST: Nicholas Augustus (DuFresne), Lynette Bennett (Aunt Alicia), Kevin Brunner (Victor), John Byron (Charles/Butler), Jonathan Cerullo (Jacques/Receptionist), Russell Costen (Honore), Bob Cuccioli (Gaston), Terrence DuBay (Jean-Paul), D'Yan Forest (Mamita), Bernard Granville (Manuel), Julie Jirousek (Michelle), Kathleen LoGuidice (Albertine/Giselle), Andrea Lyman (Jacqueline), Jamie Martin (Claudine), Marylin Monaco (Mme. DuMard), Robert Paolucci (Baron Ephraim), John Patti (DuClos/Telephone Installer), Joanna Polinsky (Juliette), Gilbert Marc Polt (Leon), Donna Ramundo (Liane), Toby Reivant (Sandomir), Pamela Shafer (Gigi), Lin Snider (Mme. Laverne), Eileen Woods (Madeleine)
MUSICAL NUMBERS: Thank Heaven for Little Girls, It's a Bore, I Don't Understand the Parisians, Paris Is Paris Again, Waltz at Maxim's (She's Not Thinking of Me), The Night They Invented Champagne, I Remember It Well, I Never Want to Go Home Again, Telephone Installer Song, Gigi, The Contract, I'm Glad I'm Not Young Anymore, In This Wide, Wide World
A musical in 2 acts and 17 scenes. The action takes place in Paris during May of 1901.

Top: Peter Reardon, Nick Corley, Wendy Oliver, Susan Hartley in "Leave It To Jane"
Center: Laurence Overmire, Jack L. Davis in "Fifth of July"
Bottom: Babs Hooyman in "The Thirteenth Chair"

IRISH REPERTORY THEATRE

First Season

Producing Director, Ciaran O'Reilly
(18th Street Playhouse) Thursday, Sept. 15–Oct. 9, 1988 (16 performances)
THE PLOUGH AND THE STARS by Sean O'Casey; Director, Charlotte Moore; Set, Dana DeVille; Sound, Mike Lamberton; Stage Manager, Kathy Mull; Production Assistants, Patricia Heitman, Noon Gourfain; Press, Janet Noble. CAST: Ron Bottitta (Sgt. Tinley), Pom Boyd (Rosie), Brian Calloway (Peter), Chris Carrick (Barman), Donald Creedon (Capt. Brennan), Paddy Croft (Bessie), Thomas Delaney (Covey), Patrick Fitzgerald (Langon), Errol Landis (Jack), Carmel O'Brian (Mrs. Grogan), Ciaran O'Reilly (Voice of Speaker), Anne Sullivan (Nora), Peter Rogan (Fluther), Neville Wells (Cpl. Stoddart)

A play in four acts, performed with one intermission. The action takes place in 1915–1916 in and around the Clitheroe flat in a Dublin tenement.

Thursday, Jan. 12–Feb. 5, 1989 (16 performances)
I DO NOT LIKE THEE, DR. FELL by Bernard Farrell; Director, Charlotte Moore; Set, David Raphel; Lighting/Sound, Richard Clausen; Costumes, Natalie Walker; Stage Manager, Chris Kelly CAST: Chris Carrick (Peter), Paula Kenny (Maureen), Kathe Mull (Suzy), Denis O'Neill (Paddy), Ciaran O'Reilly (Joe), Enid Rogers (Rita), Timothy Thomas (Roger). Performed with one intermission. The action takes place at the present time on a Saturday evening in a third story room in Dublin.

(Public Theater) Sunday, March 19–22, 1989 (4 performances) and Monday, April 17, 1989 (1 performance)
YEATS: A CELEBRATION . . . in his own words!; Conceived and Directed by Charlotte Moore; Set, Patricia Heitman; Lighting, Richard Clausen; Harpist, Deidre Danaher. Performed by Pauline Flanagan, Bernard Frawley, Kitty Sullivan, Patrick Fitzgerald, Paula Kenny, Ciaran O'Reilly with one intermission.

Thursday, May 25–June 18, 1989 (16 performances)
A WHISTLE IN THE DARK by Thomas Murphy; Director, Charlotte Moore; Set, Patricia Heitman; Sound/Lighting, Richard Clausen; Costumes, Natalie Walker; Stage Manager, Kathe Mull. CAST: Ron Borrirra (Hugo), W. B. Brydon (Dada), Patrick Fitzgerald (Des), Chris A. Kelly (Iggy), Denis O'Neill (Mush), Ciaran O'Reilly (Harry), Jean Parker (Betty), Maurice Sheehan (Michael).

A drama in three acts performed with one intermission. The action takes place at the present time in Michael Carney's home in Coventry, England.

Len Tavares, Eric Baer Photos
**Top Right: Paddy Croft, Peter Rogan in "The Plough
and the Stars"**
**Below: Timothy Thomas, Kathe Mull, Ciaran O'Reilly in
"I Do Not Like Thee, Dr. Fell"**

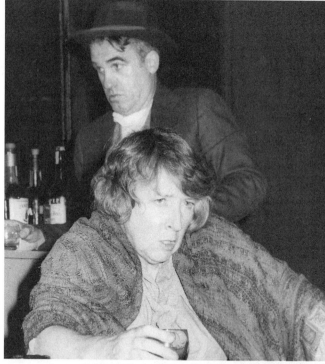

Deidre Danaher in "Yeats: A Celebration"

**Maurice Sheehan, Denis O'Neill, Ciaran O'Reilly in
"A Whistle in the Dark"**

JEWISH REPERTORY THEATRE

Fifteenth Season

Artistic Director, Ran Avni; Associate Director, Edward M. Cohen; Casting, Stephanie Klapper; Development, Bruce Fagin; Press, Shirley Herz Associates/Pete Sanders, David Roggensack, Glenna Freedman

Tuesday, June 14–
THE GRAND TOUR with Music and Lyrics by Jerry Herman; Book, Michael Stewart, Mark Bramble; Director, Ran Avni; Musical Numbers Staged by Helen Butleroff; Musical Direction, Andrew Howard; Sets, Jeffrey Schneider; Costumes, Karen Hummel; Lighting, Dan Kinsley; Sound, Ken Schwartz; Stage Manager, Geraldine Teagarden; Play is based on play by Franz Werfel, "Jacobowsky and the Colonel," and the American play by S. N. Behrman based on the same. CAST: Stuart Zagnit (Jacobowsky), Paul Ukena, Jr. (The Colonel), Steven Fickinger (Szabuniewicz), Ray Wills (Man with pince-nez/Groom/Others), Patti Mariano (Mme. Bouffier/Mme. Clairon/Others), Steve Sterner (Chauffeur/Papa Clairon/Others), Jeanne Montano (Claudine/Others), Patricia Ben Peterson (Marianne), Don Atkinson (S. S. Captain). *Musical Numbers:* I'll Be Here Tomorrow, For Poland, I Belong Here, Marianne, We're Almost There, Less and Less, One Extraordinary Thing, Mrs. S. L. Jacobowsky, I Think, Mazeltov, You I Like, Finale

A musical in 2 acts. The action takes place from June 13th to June 18th, 1940 between Paris and the Atlantic coast of France.

Saturday, Oct. 8–Nov. 13, 1988 (20 performances). Re-opened in the Lamb's Theatre on Tuesday, Feb. 14, 1989 and closed
CANTORIAL by Ira Levin; Director, Charles Maryan; Set, Atkin Pace; Costumes, Lana Fritz; Lighting, Brian Nason; Sound, Gary & Timmy Harris; Casting, Jim Meaux; Props, Paul M. Carter; Production Assistant, Robert Brycon; Wardrobe, Helena Knego; Stage Managers, Catherine A. Heusel, Mimi Moyer CAST: Anthony Fusco (Warren Ives), Lesly Kahn (Lesley Rosen), Woody Romoff (Morris Lipkind), James DeMarse (Philip Quinn), Joan Howe (Donna Quinn), Robert Nichols (William Ives)

A play in two acts. The action takes place at the present time in a home that formerly was a synagogue, on the lower east side of Manhattan, New York City.

Thursday, Dec. 22, 1988–Jan. 8, 1989 (20 performances)
CHU CHEM with book by Ted Allan; Music, Mitch Leigh; Lyrics, Jim Haines, Jack Wohl; Director, Albert Marre; Choreographer, Rosalind Newman; Set, Bob Mitchell; Costumes, Ken Yount; Lighting, Jason Sturm; Musical Director, Don Jones; Associate Musical Director, Joseph Baker; Production Coordinator, Adam A. Marre; Production Manager, David Schaap; Production Assistant, David Stoll; Props, Melissa Stephens; Stage Managers, Geraldine Teagarden, Gregg Fletcher CAST: Irving Burton (Yakob), Timm Fujii (Prompter), Simone Gee (Na-Mi), Zoie Lam (Daf-ah-Dil), Alvin Lum (The Elder), Kenji Nakao (Tsu-Hoke), Marc C. Oka (Izu-Lo-Yeh), Chev Rodgers (Hong Ho), Keelee Seetoo (Lei-An), Thom Sesma (The Prince), Hechter Ubarry (Prince's Brother), Emily Zacharias (Lotte), Mark Zeller (Chu Chem)
MUSICAL NUMBERS: Orient Yourself, Rain, What Happened, Welcome, You'll Have to Change, Love Is, I'll Talk to Her, Shame on You, It Must Be Good for Me, The Wise, The River, We Dwell in Our Hearts, Re-Orient Yourself, I Once Believed, It's Possible, Our Kind of War, Boom!, Finale

A musical in two acts. The action takes place some 600 years ago in the village of Kai Feng, China.

Saturday, Jan. 28–Feb. 26, 1989 (20 performances)
BITTER FRIENDS by Gordon Rayfield; Director, Allen Coulter; Set, Michael C. Smith; Costumes, Laura Drawbaugh; Lighting, Dan Kinsley; Stage Manager, D. C. Rosenberg CAST: Ben Siegler (David Klein), Farryl Lovett (Rachel Klein), Sam Gray (Rabbi Arthur Schaefer), Yosi Sokolsky (Ambassador Ezra Ben-Ami), Viola Harris (Helen Klein), Bill Nelson (Congressman Wingate Whitney), Dan Pinto (Wingate Whitney), Andrew Thain (Embassy Employee/Headwaiter/Guard)

A play in two acts. The action takes place in various locations in Washington, DC, New York City, Philadelphia and Virginia.

Jeffrey Schneider, Martha Swope Photos
Top: Paul Ukena, Jr., Steven Fickinger, Stuart Zagnit in "Grand Tour"

Below: Woody Romoff, Lesly Kahn, Anthony Fusco in "Cantorial"

Bottom: Lee Wallace, Bernie Passeltiner in "The Sunshine Boys"

Above: Emily Zacharias, Mark Zeller in "Chu Chem"

Saturday, April 29–May 28, 1989 (20 performances)
THE SUNSHINE BOYS by Neil Simon; Director, Marilyn Chris; Sets, Ray Recht; Costumes, Karen Hummel; Lights, Dan Kinsley; Sound, Jonathan Rigg; Stage Managers, Saylor Creswell, Patrick Cognetta CAST: Edwin Bordo (Phil Schaefer/Patient), Miriam Burton (Roxie O'Neill/R.N.), Patrick Cognetta (Eddie), Fred Einhorn (Ben Silverman), Amy Gordon (Nursey), Bernie Passeltiner (Al Lewis), Lee Wallace (Willie Clark)

A comedy in two acts. The action takes place in the late fall of 1972 in Willie's apartment on the Upper West Side of New York City.

Saturday, June 17–July 16, 1989 (27 performances)
DOUBLE BLESSING by Brenda Shoshanna Lukeman; Director, Edward M. Cohen; Set, Ray Recht; Costumes, Karen Hummel; Lighting, Dan Kinsley; Sound, Paul Garrity; Original Music, Marsdhall Cold; Stage Manager, D. C. Rosenberg CAST: Victor Raider-Wexler (Manny Hagoodnick), Rosalind Harris (Martha Snitofsky), Helen Greenberg (Chana Snitofsky), Mark Ethan (Morris Blavatsky)

A play in two acts. The action takes place at the present time in the parlor of a brownstone in Borough Park, Brooklyn, New York.

85

LINCOLN CENTER THEATER

Fourth Season

Gregory Mosher, Director; Bernard Gersten, Executive Producer; General Manager, Steven C. Callahan; Company Manager, Lynn Landis; Production Manager, Jeff Hamlin; Press, Merle Debuskey

(Mitzi E. Newhouse Theater) Friday, June 10–July 24, 1989 (39 performances) **I'LL GO ON** based on the novels *Molloy, Malone Dies,* and *The Unnamable* by Samuel Beckett; Adapted by Gerry Dukes and Barry McGovern; Director, Colm O'Briain; Design, Robert Ballagh; Lighting, Rupert Murray; The Gate Theatre Dublin production presented by arrangement with Ken Marsolais and Patricia Daily as part of the First New York International Festival of the Arts; Stage Managers, Sean Burke, Liz Small; Press, Merle Debuskey, Mary Bryant

CAST
BARRY McGOVERN

(La Mama E.T.C. Annex) Thursday, July 14–Sept. 18, 1988 (62 performances and 15 previews). Lincoln Center Theater (Gregory Mosher, Director; Bernard Gersten, Executive Producer) and La Mama E.T.C. (Ellen Stewart, Artistic Director; Wickham Boyle, Executive Director) present:
ROAD by Jim Cartwright; Director, Simon Curtis; Sets and Costumes, Paul Brown; Lighting, Kevin Rigdon; Sound, Daniel Schreier; Production Manager, Jeff Hamlin; General Manager, Steven C. Callahan; Company Manager, Hugh Barnett; Assistant Director, Adrienne J. Weiss; Wardrobe, Helen Toth; Props, Marc Duncan, Sarah Manley; Stage Managers, Jack Doulin, Gary Natoli; Press, Merle Debuskey, Bruce Campbell CAST: Jack Wallace (Scullery), Joan Cusack (Louise/Clare), Kevin Bacon (Louise's Brother/Brink/Joey), Jayne Haynes (Brenda/Molly/Helen), Betsy Aidem (Carol), Gerry Bamman (Eddie's Father/Jerry), Michael Wincott (Skin-Lad/Eddie) Understudies: Debra Cole (Clare/Louise/Carol), Robin McKay (Brenda/Molly/Helen), Jake Weber (Brink/Eddie/Skin-Lad/Joey)
A play in two acts. The action takes place tonight on a road in a small Lancashire town.

(Mitzi E. Newhouse Theater) Tuesday, Oct. 11–Nov. 27, 1988 (25 performances and 31 previews)
WAITING FOR GODOT by Samuel Beckett; Director, Mike Nichols; Set, Tony Walton; Costumes, Ann Roth; Lighting, Jennifer Tipton; Sound, Tom Sorce; Makeup, J. Roy Helland; General Manager, Steven C. Callahan; Production Manager, Jeff Hamlin; Props, C. J. Simpson; Production Assistant, Sarah Manley; Wigs, Paul Huntley; Stage Managers, Bill Buxton, Gwendolyn M. Gilliam; Press, Merle Debuskey, Bill Evans CAST: Robin Williams (Estragon), Steve Martin (Vladimir), Bill Irwin (Lucky), F. Murray Abraham (Pozzo), Lukas Haas (A Boy), Understudies: James Lally (Estragon/Vladimir), David Pierce (Lucky), Dan Butler (Pozzo), Atticus Brady (Boy)
A play in two acts. The action takes place on a road.

(Mitzi E. Newhouse Theater) Friday, Feb. 3–May 7, 1989 (69 performances and 36 previews)
MEASURE FOR MEASURE by William Shakespeare; Director, Mark Lamos; Set Costumes, John Conklin; Lighting, Pat Collins; Sound, David Budries; Original Music, Mel Marvin; Assistant Director, Rob Bundy; Props, George T. Green, Jr.; Wardrobe, Mary P. Eno; Production Assistant, John Kirman; Stage Managers, Wendy Chapin, Fredric H. Orner CAST: Mario Arrambide succeeded by Anthony Crivello (Father Thomas/Barnardine), Jonathan Baker (Secretary/Officer), Robert Bella (Secretary), Kate Burton (Isabella), Deryl Caitlyn (Provost), Len Cariou (Vicentio), Joel Chaiken (Boy), Gabriella Diaz-Farrar (Juliet), Paul S. Eckstein (Officer), Ethyl Eichelberger (Froth), Marcus Giamatti (1st Gentleman/Varius), George Hall (Escalus), Marceline Hugot succeeded by Lois Markle (Francisca), Thomas Ikeda (Elbow), Don Mayo (Friar Peter/Justice), Reggie Montgomery (Lucio), Philip Moon (Abhorson/2nd Gentleman), Jonathan Nichols (Officer), Koji Okamura (Secretary), Campbell Scott (Angelo), Ascanio Sharpe (Officer), Lois Smith succeeded by Marceline Hugo (Mistress Overdone), Lorraine Toussaint succeeded by Kim Staunton (Mariana), Jack Weston succeeded by Wayne Knight (Pompey)
Performed with one intermission.

Brigitte Lacombe Photos
Top Left: Barry McGovern in "I'll Go On"
Top Right: Jayne Haynes, Joan Cusack in "Road"
Below: Michael Wincott, Joan Cusack, Betsy Aidem, Kevin Bacon in "Road"

Len Cariou, Campbell Scott in "Measure For Measure"
Above: Len Cariou, Kate Burton in "Measure For Measure"

Robin Williams, Steve Martin in "Waiting for Godot"
Above: F. Murray Abraham, Robin Williams, Steve Martin,
Bill Irwin in "Waiting for Godot"
Top Right: Robin Williams, Steve Martin, F. Murray
Abraham, Bill Irwin in "Waiting for Godot"

(Newhouse Theater) Tuesday, May 23–July 16, 1989 (25 performances and 31 previews).
UBU by Alfred Jarry; Adapted by Larry Sloan, Doug Wright; Based on literal translation by Jacqueline de la Chaume; Director, Larry Sloan; Original Score, Greg Cohen; Set, Douglas Stein; Costumes, Susan Hilferty; Lighting, Stephen Strawbridge; Sound, Bill Dreisbach; Musical Director/Orchestrations, Greg Cohen; Production Manager, Jeff Hamlin; Production Assistant, Bill Wrubel; Props, Sam Parrish, George T. Green, Jr.; Wardrobe, Mary P. Eno; Hairstylist, Larry Boyette; Movement, Tim Carryer; Stage Managers, Matthew T. Mundinger, Sarah Manley CAST: Bill Alton (King Venceslas/Stanislas Leczinski/General Lasky), Tom Aulino (The Nobles/Nicola Rensky), Ramiro Carrillo (Pile), Christopher Durang (Ubu's Conscience), K. Todd Freeman (Boleslas/Michel Federovitch/Russian Soldier), Patrick Garner (The Imagemaker/Younger Peasant), Trip Hamilton (Cotice), Olek Krupa (Capt. Bordure), Jodie Markell (Mere Ubu), Ralph Marrero (Ladislas/The Czar/Bear), Barnabas Miller (Bougrelas), Kristine Nielsen (Queen Rosamund), Oliver Platt (Pere Ubu)

Performed without an intermission.

Ramiro Carillo, Trip Hamilton, Jodie Markell, Olek Krupa,
Oliver Platt in "Ubu"
Above: Christopher Durang, Oliver Platt in "Ubu"

87

MANHATTAN THEATRE CLUB

Seventeenth Season

Artistic Director, Lynne Meadow; Managing Director, Barry Grove; General Manager, Victoria Bailey; Artistic Associates, Jonathan Alper, Michael Bush; Casting, Lyons/Isaacson; Development, Janet Harris; Press, Helene Davis, Linda Feinberg, Clay Martin; Production Manager, Michael R. Moody; Technical Director, Betsy Tanner

(City Center Stage I) Tuesday, Oct. 11–Dec. 4, 1988 (66 performances). Moved to Eastern Standard Golden Theatre Monday, Dec. 19, 1988. See Broadway calendar. (City Center Stage II) Tuesday, Oct. 18–
ITALIAN AMERICAN RECONCILIATION by John Patrick Shanley; Set, Santo Loquasto; Costumes, William Ivey Long; Lighting, Peter Kaczorowski; Sound, John Gromada; Wardrobe, Elizabeth Valsing; Production Assistant, Marc Goldsmith; Stage Managers, Ruth Kreshka, William Joseph Barnes CAST: John Turturro (Aldo Scalicki), John Pankow (Huey Maximilian Bonfigliano), Laura San Giacomo (Teresa), Helen Hanft (Aunt May), Jayne Haynes (Janice)

A comedy in two acts. The action takes place in "Little Italy" during the Spring.

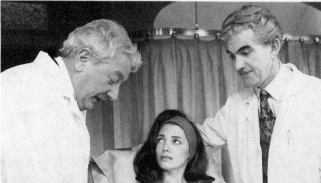

(City Center Stage I) Tuesday, Dec. 20, 1988–Feb. 5, 1989 (51 performances)
ONE TWO THREE FOUR FIVE with book by Larry Gelbart; Music/Lyrics, Maury Yeston; Director, Gerald Gutierrez; Set, Douglas Stein; Costumes, Ann Hould-Ward; Lighting, Pat Collins; Sound, Otts Munderloh; Orchestrations, Harold Wheeler; Choral Composition/Musical Continuity, Maury Yeston; Choreography, Larry Hyman; Musical Direction, Tom Fay; Special Effects, Greg Meeh; Hairstylist, Robert DeNiro; Stage Managers, Ed Fitzgerald, Ara Marx CAST: Seda Azarian (Swing), Pamela Blair (Maylis), Darrell Carey (Pheti/Ensemble), Frank DiPasquale (Swing), Mickey Freeman (Zymah), Davis Gaines (Avi), Jonathan Hadary (Dack), Philip Hoffman (Kol), Damien Jackson (Raab/Avi's Son/Ensemble), Tom Lloyd (Sammel/Ptapateepa/Ensemble), Celeste Mancinelli (Mrs. N/Ensemble), Kenneth L. Marks (Romer), Barbara McCulloh (Ensemble), Tammy Minoff (Noma/Ensemble), Lauren Mitchell (Ariel), Martin Moran (Avi's Son/Ensemble), Brenda Pressley (Cynia), Jennifer Smith (Ensemble), Mary Testa (Taradee), Henrietta Valor (Bmmhe)

(Stage I) Wednesday, Feb. 15–May 10, 1989 (98 performances)
WHAT THE BUTLER SAW by Joe Orton; Director, John Tillinger; Set, John Lee Beatty; Costumes, Jane Greenwood; Lighting, Ken Billington; Sound, John Gromada; Assistant to Director, Jordan Merkur; Props, Carol Silverman; Wardrobe, Teresa Purcell; Production Assistant, Lisa Ostrow; Stage Managers, James Harker, Camille Calman CAST: Charles Keating (Dr. Prentice), Joanne Whalley-Kilmer succeeded by Marisa Tomei (Geraldine Barclay), Carole Shelley succeeded by Angela Thornton (Mrs. Prentice), Bruce Norris (Nicholas Beckett), Joseph Maher (Dr. Rance), Patrick Tull (Sergeant Match)

A farce in two acts.

(Theatre Four) Thursday, April 11–Sept. 24, 1989 (186 performances)
ARISTOCRATS by Brian Friel; Director, Robin Lefevre; Set, John Lee Beatty; Costumes, Jane Greenwood; Lighting, Dennis Parichy; Sound, John A. Leonard; Wardrobe, Jonathan Green; Production Assistant, Michael Feigin; Stage Managers, Tom Aberger, G. Roger Abell cast; John Christopher Jones (Willie Diver), Peter Crombie succeeded by Michael O'Neill (Tom Hoffnung), Thomas Barbour (Uncle George), Niall Buggy (Casimir), Margaret Colin succeeded by Maryann Plunkett (Alice), John Pankow (Eamon), Haviland Morris succeeded by Tracy Sallows (Claire), Kaiulani Lee succeeded by Robin Moseley (Judith), Joseph Warren (Father), Roma Downey (Anna's Voice)

A drama in three acts with one intermission. The action takes place during a summer of the mid-1970's at Ballybeg Hall, the home of District Judge O'Donnell, overlooking the village of Ballybeg, County Donegal in Ireland.
The New York Drama Critics Circle cited "Aristocrats" as the Best Foreign Play of the season.

Right Center: John Pankow, Kaiulani Lee in "Aristocrats"
Above: Joseph Maher, Joanne Whalley-Kilmer,
Charles Keating in "What the Butler Saw"
Top: Jayne Haynes, John Turturro in "Italian American
Reconciliation" *Gerry Goodstein Photos*

Margaret Colin, Niall Buggy in "Aristocrats"

(Stage II) Tuesday, Feb. 28–March 26, 1989 (32 performances)
THE TALENTED TENTH by Richard Wesley; Directed by M. Neema Barnette; Sets, Charles McClennahan; Costumes, Alvin B. Perry; Lighting, Michael R. Moody; Sound, David Lawson; Wardrobe, Jonathan Green; Production Assistant, Gina Fried-Miller; Stage Managers, Diane Ward, Lloyd Davis, Jr. CAST: James E. Gaines (Sam Griggs), Roscoe Orman (Bernard), Marie Thomas (Pam), Richard Gant (Marvin), LaTanya Richardson (Rowena), Elain Graham (Irene), Rony Clanton (Ron), Akosua Busia (Tanya)

A play in two acts. The action takes place during the 1980's.

(Stage II) Tuesday, April 25–May 28, 1989 (32 performances)
ELEEMOSYNARY by Lee Blessing; Director, Lynne Meadow; Set, John Lee Beatty; Costumes, William Ivey Long; Lighting, Dennis Parichy; Stage Manager, Ruth Kreshka CAST: Eileen Heckart (Dorothea, a woman of some means), Joanna Gleason (Artie, her daughter), Jennie Moreau (Echo, her granddaughter)

The action takes place in 1989 and before. Performed without intermission.

(Stage I) Tuesday, May 23–July 2, 1989 (49 performances)
THE LISBON TRAVIATA by Terrence McNally; Director, John Tillinger; Set, Philipp Jung; Costumes, Jane Greenwood; Lighting, Ken Billington; Sound, Gary/ Timmy Harris; Fight Staging, B. H. Barry; Props, Shelley Barclay; Stage Manager, Pamela Singer CAST: Anthony Heald (Stephen), Nathan Lane (Mendy), Dan Butler (Mike), John Slattery (Paul)

A play in two acts.

(Stage II) Tuesday, June 6–July 2, 1989 (32 performances)
THE LOMAN FAMILY PICNIC by Donald Margulies; Director, Barnet Kellman; Set, G. W. Mercier; Costumes, Jess Goldstein; Lighting, Debra J. Kletter; Music, David Shire; Musical Director, Mark Goodman; Sound, Aural Fixation; Choreography, Mary Jane Houdina; Hairstylist, Bobby Grayson; Wardrobe, Jacqueline French; Stage Managers, Renee Lutz, Laura Kravets CAST: Marcia Jean Kurtz (Doris), Michael Miceli (Mitchell), Judd Trichter (Stewie), Larry Block (Herbie), Wendy Makkena (Marsha)

A play in two acts. The action takes place in a middle-class high-rise apartment in Coney Island, Brooklyn, New York, around 1965.

Right: Nathan Lane, Dan Butler, Anthony Heald in "Lisbon Traviata"
Above: Joanna Gleason, Jennie Moreau, Eileen Heckart in "Eleemosynary"
Top: LaTanya Richardson, Marie Thomas, Elain Graham in "The Talented Tenth"
Gerry Goodstein Photos

Marcia Jean Kurtz, Michael Miceli in
"The Loman Family Picnic"

Marcia Jean Kurtz, Larry Block in "The Loman
Family Picnic"

89

MUSICAL THEATRE WORKS

Marianne Tatum, James Hindman, Panchali Null in "Passionate Extremes" *(Rita Katz Photo)*

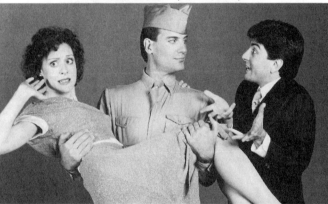

Donna English, James Pyecka, Ray Wills in "Kiss Me Quick . . ." *(Carol Rosegg Photo)*

Paul E. Ukena, Jr., Mary Bracken Phillips in "Cradle Song"

Artistic Director, Anthony J. Stimac; Associate Artistic Director, Mark S. Herko; General Manager, Marilyn Stimac; Business Manager, Denys Baker; Administrative Associate, Pamela Kaplan; Press, Peter Cromarty & Co./Jim Baldassare, David Gersten, Kevin Brockman (Theatre at St. Peter's Church) Wednesday, Oct. 26–Nov. 13, 1988 (21 performances and 8 previews)

KISS ME QUICK BEFORE THE LAVA REACHES THE VILLAGE with Music by Peter Ekstrom; Book, Steve Hayes; Lyrics/Story, Peter Ekstrom, Steve Hayes; Director, Anthony J. Stimac; Choreography, Frank Ventura; Set, James Noone; Lighting, Richard Latta; Costumes, Amanda J. Klein; Casting, Mark S. Herko; Musical Director/Arranger, Albert Ahronheim; Production Manager, David Schapp; Wardrobe, Blair Winston; Production Assistant, Tanya Elder; Stage Michael Schmalz, Carla Crowe CAST: Donna English (Dottie Rogers), Ray Wills (Nick Tyler), Maria Bostick (Grace Townsend), Bill Buell (Wally Gruber), Skip Lackey (Ted Randall), David Barron (Minister), Ensemble: Mana Allen, Tom Farrell, Suzanne Hevner, Wade Howard, Kristine Nevins, Nicola Stimac, Bill Walters

MUSICAL NUMBERS: Lava Line, Look at Me!, Dottie's Song, When Dottie Makes It Big in Hollywood, Make You a Star, Not Yet, Bring Me a Man, Lailuni Lie, Never Alone Again, Off We Go!, I Always Get de Man in de End, Will She Still Love Me Now?, Roll Me Over, Rosie and Ruthie, Boom Boom Boom, Tell Me Moon, Battle Hymn, God Bless a Boy That I Love

A musical in two acts and 8 scenes. The action takes place at the present time in Greenwich Village and in Hollywood.

(Midtown Arts Common/St. Peter's Church) Wednesday, Sept. 28–Oct. 16, 1988 (13 performances and 8 previews)

PASSIONATE EXTREMES with Music by George Cochran Quincy; Libretto, Thayer Q. Burch; Director, Mark S. Herko; Set, James Noone; Lighting, Kendall Smith; Costumes, Amanda J. Klein; Musical Director, Eric Barnes; Production Manager, David Schaap; Wardrobe, Blair Winston; Production Assistants, Tanya Elder, Scott Fried; Stage Manager, David Allen Butler CAST: Steve Mattar (Narrator), Ruthann Curry (Narrator), Sarah Knapp (Carlotta McClure), Steve Watkins (Umberto Blake), Panchali Null (Lotte McClure), James Hindman (Otto McClure), Marianne Tatum (Dr. Bluebird), SuEllen Estey (Prana Yopatha Swann)

MUSICAL NUMBERS: Prologue, Ocean Liner Aria, Kiss, Gibbous Moon Quartet, Love! Love!, Duet Magical, New York State of Devotion, Maternal Memories, Disputation, Otto's Agony, The Roschach Tango, The Outrage Trio, Computer Duet, Aria of Desperate Measures, My Innocent Boy, Triple Vision Trio, I Can See the Light, Carlotta's Awakening, Sick Trio, I'll Make Her Happy, Beloved's Blues, When You Find a Love, Climactic Octet

Performed without an intermission.

(Theatre at St. Peter's Church) Wednesday, Mar. 8–Apr. 2, 1989 (21 performances and 8 previews)

CRADLE SONG with Book/Lyrics by Mary Bracken Phillips; Music, Jan Mullaney; Director, Anthony J. Stimac; Arrangements/Orchestrations, Keith Levenson; Set, Richard Ellis; Lighting, Clarke W. Thornton; Costumes, Amanda J. Klein; Sound, Daryl Borenstein; Musical Directors, Keith Levenson, Jan Mullaney; Production Manager, Michael Schmalz; Wardrobe, Jennifer Ehmann; Assistant Conductor, Andrew Wilder; Production Assistant, Michelle Jacobi; Stage Manager, Sandra M. Franck CAST: Mary Bracken Phillips (Paula), Paul E. Ukena, Jr. (Jonathan), Keith Charles (Harding), Carole Schweid (Susan)

MUSICAL NUMBERS: Rational Lovesong, Father's Day, Choices, Beautiful Baby, Beautiful Eyes, Hickory Dickory Dock, Lovely Child, He Was Just Here, Kick the Machine, Is It Anybody's Business but My Own, I Believe, Nobody's Perfect, I Wouldn't Trade a Minute

A musical in 2 acts and 13 scenes.

Wednesday, April 12–30, 1989 (21 performances and 8 previews)

YOUNG RUBE book by George W. George and Matty Selman; Music/Lyrics, Matty Selman; Director, Mark Herko; Choreographer, Margie Castleman; Musical Director, Bryan Louiselle; Set, David Mitchell; Lighting, Richard Latta; Costumes, Amanda J. Klein; Production Manager, Michael Schmalz; Production Assistant, Zak Tucker; Stage Manager, Alan Fox; Press, Cromarty & Co/Kevin McAnarney CAST: Adinah Alexander (Gallus Mag/Liberty Undaunted), Maria Bostick (Tillie/Pearl), Kenneth Boys (Woodward/Newsboy/Mike), Hal Hudson (Ike), Joan Jaffe (Hannah Goldberg/Medjulla Oblongata), Gary Kirsch (Abrams/Mayor Hyland/McStammer), Skip Lackey (Rube Goldberg), Mike O'Carroll (Max Goldberg/Prof. Butts), Robert Polenz (Harry Mayo Bunker/Zump), Keith Savage (Boob McNutt), Don Stephenson (Smith/Abe Rueff/Orderly/McSnark), Miki Whittles (Lala Palooza)

MUSICAL NUMBERS: Boob McNutt, Funny, Corrections, Melody, Everybody's Here Tonight, My Crazy Right Hand, A Real Torch Song, We're Counting on You, Big Parade, Candy Kid, Lowell High, Mixing Metaphors, Your Crazies, Do It the Hard Way

A musical in two acts.

Maureen Silliman, William Mooney, Hattie Winston in
"Prince"
Top Left: Brenda Denmark, LaTanya Richardson, Gwen
Roberts-Frost in "Mississippi Delta"
Below: (L) Samuel Jackson, Michelle Shay in "Sally" (R)
Cynthia Bond, O. L. Duke in "Sally"

NEGRO ENSEMBLE COMPANY

(Theatre Four) Friday, Aug. 12–Oct. 23, 1988 (77 performances and 8 previews) The
Negro Ensemble Company (President, Douglas Turner Ward; Producing Director,
Leon B. Denmark) presents:
FROM THE MISSISSIPPI DELTA by Dr. Endesha Ida Mae Holland; Director, Ed
Smith; Set, Steven Perry; Costumes, Judy Dearing; Lighting, William H. Grant III;
Sound, Jacqui Casto; General Manager, Susan Watson Turner; Company Manager,
Lauren Yates; Wardrobe, Ale Turns; Stage Manager, Sandra L. Ross; Press, Howard
Atlee CAST: Gwen Roberts-Frost (Woman One), Brenda Denmark (Woman Two),
Latanya Richardson succeeded by Saundra McClain (Woman Three)

Performed without intermission. The action takes place from the early 1950's
through the mid-1980's.

(Theatre Four) Wednesday, Nov. 9, 1988–Feb. 26, 1989 (41 performances and 19
previews). The Negro Ensemble Company (Douglas Turner Ward, President; Leon
B. Denmark, Producing Director) presents:
WE: PART I-SALLY/PART II-PRINCE: by Charles Fuller; Director, Douglas
Turner Ward; Set, Charles McClennahan; Costumes, Judy Dearing; Lighting, Arthur
Reese; Sound, John T. Cherry; General Manager, Susan Watson Turner; Company
Managers, Lauren Yates, Beverly Jenkins; Wardrobe, Freda L. Thomas; Production
Assistants, Samuel Moses, John Wooten; Business Manager, Gary Halcott; Stage
Managers, Wayne Elbert, Sandra Ross; Press, Howard Atlee CAST: Michele Shay
(Sally), Alvin Alexis (Yockum), Samuel Moses (Pell), Samuel L. Jackson (Prince),
O. L. Duke (Vendross), Carl Gordon (Sutton), Ed Wheeler (Washington), Cynthia
Bond (Jonquil), Rosanna Carter (Becky), William Mooney (General), Larry Sharp
(Lt. Cable), Raynor Scheine (Reporter)

A play in two acts. The action takes place in Beaufort, South Carolina, during the
winter of 1862–63.

(Theatre Four) Saturday, Dec. 3, 1988–Feb. 26, 1989 (41 performances and 15
previews). The Negro Ensemble Co. (Douglas Turner Ward, President; Leon B.
Denmark, Producing Director; Susan Watson Turner, General Manager) presents:
WE by Charles Fuller; PART II: PRINCE; Director, Douglas Turner Ward; Set,
Charles McClennahan; Costumes, Judy Dearing; Lighting, Arthur Reese; Sound,
John T. Cherry; Company Managers, Lauren Yates, Beverly Jenkins; Wardrobe,
Freda L. Thomas; Production Assistants, Samuel Moses, John Wooten; Stage Man-
agers, Wayne Elbert, Sandra Ross; Press, Howard Atlee CAST: Samuel L. Jackson
(Prince), Alvin Alexis (Norman), Carl Gordon (Quash), Carla Brothers (Tiche),
Peggy Alston (Mary), Ed Wheeler (Burner), Rosanna Carter (Carrie), Graham
Brown (Stubbs), Pirie MacDonald (Dr. Bernard), Hattie Winston (Lu), Larry Sharp
(Duffy), Raynor Scheine (Proter), William Mooney (Kellogg), Maureen Silliman
(Hannah), Sam Moses, John Wooten (Soldiers)

A play in two acts. The action takes place in the fall and early winter of 1864 in
Virginia, in various locales of the Union Army.

William Mooney (C) in "Prince"

Bert Andrews Photos

NEW FEDERAL THEATRE

Woodie King, Jr., Producer; For Henry Street Settlement: Daniel Kronenfeld, Executive Director; Barbara Tate, Director Arts for Living Center; Linda Herring, Company Manager; Pawnee Sills, Assistant to the Producer; Victoria Jeter, Technical Director; Press, Max Eiseb, Madelon Rosen Solomon (Marry DeJur Playhouse) Thursday, June 30–July 31, 1988 (30 performances). Henry Street Settlement's New Federal Theatre (Woodie King, Jr., Producer), as part of the First New York International Festival of the Arts presents:
JIKA written and directed by Maishe Maponya; Set, Terry Chandler; Lighting, William H. Grant III; Costumes, Karen Perry; Sound, Carmen Whiip; Nantsi i-Bazooka Dance, Welcome Msomi; Stage Manager, Dwight R. B. Cook; Company Manager, Linda Herring; Technical Director, Victoria A. Jeter; Wardrobe, Harriet Foy; Props, Lisa Watson CAST: Fana Kekana, Jerry Mofokeng. Performed in five scenes. The action takes place in South Africa.

(Harry De Jur Henry Street Settlement Playhouse) Thursday, Oct. 20–Nov. 20, 1988 (30 performances)
GOOD BLACK by Rob Penny; Director, Claude Purdy; Set, Ken Ellis; Costumes, Karen Perry; Lighting, William H. Grant III; Sound, Jacqui Casto; Stage Manager, Major Hudson; Press, Max Eisen, Madelon Rosen CAST: Dorothi Fox, Kenneth J. Green, Fern Howell, Amber Kain, Marcus Naylor, Alicia Rene Washington, Judi Ann Williams, Mel Winkler

(Harry DeJur Playhouse) Saturday, Jan. 14–Feb. 12, 1989 (30 performances)
'TIS THE MORNING by Ruth Beckford, Ron Stacker Thompson; Director, Ron Stacker Thompson; Set, Kerry Sanders; Costumes, Rubee Taylor; Lighting, Ernest Baxter; Sound, Ron Stacker Thompson; Technical Director, Peter Covell; Wardrobe, Ileana Peyton; Props, Celeste Welch; Stage Manager, Jacqui Casto CAST: Ruth Beckford (Rixue), Billy Hutton (Ken), Margarette Robinson (Dottie), Melvin Thompson (Wayne, Jr.), Inez Norman (Janice)
Performed with one intermission. The action takes place at the present time in California.

(Harry DeJur Playhouse) Tuesday, March 14–25, 1989 (8 performances). Zebra Promotions (Julian Ellison, Executive Producer; Herman LeVern Jones, Assistant American Producer) presents The Royal National Theatre of Great Britain in repertory; Director, Nick Ward; Designer, Fred Pilbrow; Fights Director, Malcolm Ranson; Assistant Designer, Rumi Matsui; Stage Managers, Sonia Friedman, Sarah Cornelia Koeppe; Music, Richard Heacock; Voice Work, Geoffrey Connor
MACBETH by William Shakespeare. CAST: Alan Bennion (King Duncan/ Seyward/Scottish Doctor/Old Man), Amelda Brown (Lady Macbeth/Witch), Katrin Cartlidge (Witch/Donalbain/Fleance/Lady Macduff/Gentlewoman), Ken Drury (Macbeth), Paul Higgins (Witch/Malcolm/Son of Macduff/Porter/Murderer), Cyril Nri (Banquo/Seyton/Messenger), Matthew Scurfield (Captain/Macduff/Murderer), Paul Stacey (Lennox/Ross/Young Seward/Murderer).
Performed without intermission.
APART FROM GEORGE by Nick Ward. CAST: Matthew Scurfield (George Sutton), Katrin Cartlidge (Linda Sutton), Amelda Brown (Pam Sutton), Alan Bennion (Arthur Loveless/John Grey).
Performed without intermission.

(Louis Abrons Arts for Living Center) Saturday, April 29–May 28, 1989 (30 performances)
A THRILL A MOMENT: Song Book, William "Mickey" Stevenson; Director-Choreographer, Edward Love; Musical Director, Grenoldo Frazier; Set, Richard Harmon; Costumes, Fontella Boone; Lighting, William H. Grant III, Jerry Forsyth; Assistant Choreographer, Kiki Shepard; Wardrobe, Bashari; Stage Manager, Lisa L. Watson. CAST: Adrian Bailey, Irene Datcher, Dwayne Grayman, Kelly Rice, Kiki Shepard, Gina Taylor, Allison Williams
MUSICAL NUMBERS: Nothings Too Good for My Baby, Motoring, He Was Really Saying Something, Needle in a Haystack, Jamie, Playboy, Devil with the Blue Dress, Pride and Joy, Stubborn Kind of Fellow, Beechwood 4-5789, Danger Heartbreak Dead Ahead, One of These Days, Love Me All the Way, Got to Be a Miracle, Dancing in the Street, Hitchhike, Wild One, My Baby Loves Me, You Been in Love Too Long, Truly Yours, Ask the Lonely, Just Loving You, A Thrill a Moment, It Takes Two.
The action takes place at the present time in Mickey's Place (bar and restaurant) and is performed with one intermission.

Bert Andrews Photos
Top: Jerry Mofokeng, Fana Kenana in "Jika"
Below Left: Matthew Scurfield, Katrin Cartlidge in "Apart From George"
Below Right: Amelda Brown, Ken Drury in "Macbeth"

Kiki Shepard, Irene Datcher, Gina Taylor, Allison Williams in "A Thrill A Moment"
Above: Ruth Beckford, William Hutton in " 'Tis the Morning"

NEW YORK SHAKESPEARE FESTIVAL

Twenty-second Season

Producer, Joseph Papp; Associate Producer, Jason Steven Cohen; General Manager, Bob MacDonald; Company Manager, Mary C. Miller; Plays and Musical Development, Gail Merrifield; Casting, Rosemarie Tichler; Development, Steve Dennin; Executive Assistant to Mr. Papp, Barbara Carroll; Production Manager, Andrew Mihok; Technical Director, Mervyn Haines, Jr.; Props, James Gill, J. L. Marshall; Press, Richard Kornberg, Reva Cooper, Carol Fineman, Warren Anker.

(Public/Newman Theater) Tuesday, June 14–July 10, 1988 (31 performances) Presented in association with Spoleto Festival, U.S.A., and part of The New York International Festival of the Arts.

MIRACOLO D'AMORE conceived and directed by Martha Clarke; Created with the company; Composed by Richard Peaslee; Sets/Costumes, Robert Israel; Lighting, Paul Gallo; Vocal Director, Jeff Halpern; Assistant to Director/Stage Manager, Elizabeth Sherman; Technical Supervisor, Joshua Weitzman; Wardrobe, George Erdman; Props, Elizabeth Valsing CAST: Peter Becker, Rob Besserer, Felix Blaska, Marshall Coid, Larrio Ekson, Marie Fourcaut, Alexandra Ivanoff, David Jon, John Kelly, Francine Landes, Nina Martin, Adam Rogers, Paola Styron, Elisabeth Van Ingen, Nina Watt

(Public/Shiva Theater) Friday, June 17–July 16, 1988

THE IMPERIALISTS AT THE CLUB CAVE CANEM by Charles L. Mee, Jr.; Director, Erin B. Mee; Set, Albert Webster; Costumes, Lissy Walker; Lighting, Josh Starbuck; Music, Guy Yarden. CAST: Victoria Chickering, Terence Cranendonk, John Guerrasio, Kevin McMillan, Chuck Montgomery, Kathleen Tolan, Lissy Walker, Guy Yarden, and the Second Hand Dance Company.

(Public/Anspacher Theater) Friday, June 17–July 10, 1988 (16 performances and 13 previews) Presented as part of The First New York International Festival of the Arts; A project of Festival Latino 1988 (Oscar Ciccone/Cecilia Vega, Directors).

THE DEATH OF GARCIA LORCA by Jose Antonio Rial; Translated by Julio Marzan; Director, Carlos Gimenez; Scenery/Costumes, Rafael Reyeros; Lighting, Carlos Gimenez; Props, Lisa Venezia; Wardrobe, Mark Niedzolkowski, Ira Rosenbaum; Stage Managers, K. Sibohan Phelan, Roylan Diaz CAST: Mario Arranbide (Sgt/DeFalla/Dioscoro), Emilio Del Pozo (Falangist/Valdez), Herbert Duarte (1910 Lorca), Sara Erde (Esperanza/Girl in black/Shoeshine Boy), Cesar Evora (Luis Rosales), Patricia Falkenhain (Mother), Kevin Gray (Vicente Alexandre/Secretary to Valdez), Margarita Irun (Angelina), Maria Cristina Lozada (Concha), Gonzalo Madurga (Ramon Ruiz Alonzo), Roberto Medina (Arcollas/Rafael Alberti), Rene Morena (Gerardo Diego/Pepe/Galadi), Joseph Palmas (Pablo Neruda/Gabriel Perea/Customer in Cafe), Tim Perez (Murillo/Gitano), Lionel Pina (Photographer/1920 Lorca), Jorge Luis Ramos (Jorge Guillen/Guard), Judith Roberts (Tia Luisa), Al Rodriguez (Miguel/Salvador Dali), Bernard White (Federico Garcia Lorca).

A drama in two acts.

(Delacorte Theater/Central Park) Friday, June 24–July 31, 1988 (30 performances). Presented by the New York Shakespeare Festival (Joseph Papp, Producer) in association with New York Telephone, and with the cooperation of the City of New York (Edward I. Koch, Mayor; Mary Schmidt Campbell, Commissioner of Cultural Affairs; Henry J. Stern, Commissioner of Parks & Recreation)

MUCH ADO ABOUT NOTHING by William Shakespeare; Director, Gerald Freedman; Scenery, John Ezell; Costumes, Theoni V. Aldredge; Lighting, Thomas R. Skelton; Music, John Morris; Choreography, Tina Paul; Fights, B. H. Barry; Associate Producer, Jason Steven Cohen; Stage Managers, Michael Chambers, Pat Sosnow CAST: Augusta Allen-Jones (Ensemble/Beatrice), N. Richard Arif (Ensemble/Friar), Dylan Baker (Borachio), Holly Baumgardner (Ensemble/Ursula), Ethan T. Bowen (Ensemble/Don John), Andre Braugher (Ensemble/Benedick), Dan Butler (Conrade), Phoebe Cates (Hero), Blythe Danner (Beatrice), MacIntyre Dixon (Verges), Brian Dykstra (Ensemble/Sexton), Leslie Geraci (Margaret), Robert Gerringer (Leonato), Larry Green (Ensemble/Borachio), George Hall (Antonio), Kevin Kline (Benedick), Meghan Rose Krank (Ensemble/Hero), David Landon (Sexton), David Letwin (Ensemble/Leonato), Michael Louden (Ensemble/Claudio), Don Mayo (Balthasar), Daniel Markel (Ensemble/Boy), Brian Murray (Don Pedro), David Pierce (Don John), William Preston (3rd Witch), Don Reilly (Claudio), Steve Routman (2nd Witch), Laura Sametz (Ensemble/Margaret), Matt Servitto (Ensemble/Balthasar), Jerry Stiller (Dogberry), Kate Wilkinson (Ursula), Graham Winton (Ensemble/Conrade), Richard Woods (Friar), Joe Zaloom (1st Witch).

Performed with one intermission.

(Various theatres) Wednesday, Aug. 3–27, 1988 (64 performances)

FESTIVAL LATINO (Joseph Papp, Producer; Oscar, Ciccone, Cecilia Vega, Directors; Press, Richard Kornberg, Reva Cooper, Julio Marzan

Festival Latino began in 1976 to introduce U.S. audiences to the artistic achievements in Latin countries, in theatre, music, film and television.

Martha Swope, Javier Guerrero Photos
Top: Blythe Danner, Kevin Kline in
"Much Ado About Nothing"
Below: Paola Styron, Nina Watt, (standing) Larrio Ekson,
Rob Besserer in "Miracolo D'Amore"

Luis Fernando Gomez, Carmen Bunster in
"El Martirio del Pastor"
Above: Bernard White, Cesar Evora in
"The Death of Garcia Lorca"

93

NEW YORK SHAKESPEARE FESTIVAL
(continued)

(Delacorte Theater/Central Park) Aug. 5–Sept. 4, 1988 (13 performances) The New York Shakespeare Festival in association with New York Telephone and with the cooperation of the City of New York presents:
KING JOHN by William Shakespeare; Director, Stuart Vaughan; Scenery, Bob Shaw; Costumes, Lindsay W. Davis; Lighting, John Gleason; Music, Peter Golub; Fights Staged by B. H. Barry; Associate Producer, Jason Steven Cohen; Technical Director, Joshua Braun; Wardrobe, Tony Powell; Wigs/Hair, Manuela La Porte; Stage Managers, Karen Armstrong, John J. Toia CAST: Ron Bottitta (Ensemble/Lewis), Teagle F. Bougere (Ensemble/Bandulph), Ethan T. Bowen (Ensemble/Monk), Andre K. Braugher (Herald/Messenger), Deryl Caitlyn (Ensemble/Austria), Andrew Colteaux (Ensemble/Lord Melun), Kevin Conway (King John), Joseph Culliton (Melun), Michael Cumpsty (Pembroke), Steven B. Dominguez (Ensemble/Faulkinbridge), Herb Downer (Citizen/Abbot), Tom Dunlop (Lord Bigot/Faulconbridge), Brian Dykstra (Ensemble/Messinger), Paul Eckstein (Ensemble), Alison Edwards (Lady in Waiting), Larry Green (Ensemble/Salisbury), Moses Gunnandulph), Mariette Hartley (Constance), John Hickey (Ensemble/Henry), Rob LaBelle (Gurney/Monk), Michael Louden (Lewis), Jordan Lund (Duke of Austria), Christopher McHale (Earl of Salisbury), Devon Michaels (Arthur), John J. Miskulin (Ensemble/Bastard), Joe Morton (Hubert), Robin Moseley (Lady Faulconbridge), Joyce O'Connor (Blanch), Wade Raley (Henry/Arthur), Gary Dean Ruebsamen (Ensemble/Messenger), Laura Sametz (Lady in waiting), Jay O. Sanders (Philip), Matt Servitto (Ensemble/Monk), Rex Slate (Ensemble/Gurney), Richard Venture (King Philip), David Wheeler (Ensemble/Pembroke), Jane White (Queen Elinor), Graham Winton (Herald/Soldier)
Performed with one intermission.

(Public/Susan Stein Shiva Theater) Tuesday, Aug. 9–Sept. 4, 1988 (18 performances and 2 previews)
STRANGER HERE MYSELF with songs of Kurt Weill; Director, Christopher Alden; Set, Paul Stenberg; Lighting, Anne Militello; Music Director/Pianist, Christopher Berg; English Translations, Michael Feingold; Hair/Make-up, Randy Dobbin; Stage Manager, Jennifer Gilbert CAST: Angelina Reaux.
Performed with one intermission.

(Public/Susan Stein Shiva Theater) Tuesday, Oct. 11–Dec. 4, 1989 (50 performers and 8 previews) Joseph Papp presents the Ontological-Hysteric Theater production of:
WHAT DID HE SEE? written, directed and designed by Richard Foreman; Lighting, Anne Militello; Associate Producer, Jason Steven Cohen; Technical Director, David Nelson; Stage Managers, David Herskovitz, Cass Rodeman CAST: Lili Taylor, Rocco Sisto, Will Patton

(Public/Anspacher Theater) Tuesday, Nov. 8, 1988–Jan. 15, 1989 (63 performances and 15 previews)
CORIOLANUS by William Shakespeare; Director, Steven Berkoff; Set, Loren Sherman; Costumes, Martin Pakledinaz; Lighting, Steven Berkoff; Music, Larry Spivak; Props, Evan Canary; Wardrobe, Tony Powell; Stage Managers, James Bernardi, Buzz Cohen CAST: Andre Braugher (Junius Brutus), Larry Bryggman (Sicinius Vellutus), Ashley Crow (Virgilia), Keith David (Tullus Aufidius), Moses Gunn (Cominius), Paul Hecht (Menenius Agrippa), Thomas Kopache (Titus Lartius), Christopher Walken (Coriolanus), Sharon Washington (Valeria), Irene Worth (Volumnia), Ensemble: Ethan T. Bowen, Deryl Caitlyn, Albert Farrar, Tom McGowan, Joseph C. Phillips, Armand Schultz, Roger Guenveur Smith, Matt Bradford Sullivan, John Madden Towey
A drama in 5 acts and 24 scenes performed with one intermission. The action takes place in Rome.

(LuEsther Hall) Tuesday, Nov. 29, 1988–Jan. 22, 1989 (8 performances and 50 previews).
GENESIS: MUSIC AND MIRACLES from the Medieval Mystery Plays; Book/Lyrics, A. J. Antoon/Robert Montgomery; Music, Michael Ward; Choreography, Lynne Taylor-Corbett; Director, A. J. Antoon; Scenery/Costumes, John Conklin; Lighting, Jan Kroeze; Sound, David A. Schnirman/Gene Ricciardi; Dance Captain, Patrick Cea; Props, John Masterson, Janice Kijner, Barbara Lynn Rice; Wardrobe, Karen Perry; Associate Choreographer, Rodney Griffin; Stage Managers, Bonnie Panson, Gregory Johnson CAST: Stephen Bogardus (Adam/Noah/Abraham), Bill Christopher-Myers (Angel/Abel/Japhet), Mindy Cooper (Angel/Martha), Braden Danner (Angel/Townsperson/Isaac), Raymond G. del Barrio (Angel/Townsperson), Melissa De Sousa (Angel/Mary), Ty Granaroli (Angel/Adam/Ham), David Patrick Kelly (Angel/Cain/Shem), Mary Munger (Eve/Nesta/Sarah), Tina Paul (Angel/Eve/Gossip Goodbody), Russ Thacker (Lucifer/Satan/Garcio/Bishop/Beggar), Christine Toy (Angel/Cherubim/Miriam), Understudies: Patrick Cea, Nan Friedman, Mindy Cooper, Joel Fredericks, Juliet Lambert, Devon Michaels, Raymond G. del Barrio
A musical performed without intermission.

Martha Swope, George Joseph Photos
Top: Mariette Hartley in "King John"
**Below: Rocco Sisto, Will Patton, Lili Taylor in
"What Did He See?"**

Stephen Bogardus, Mary Munger in "Genesis"
Above: Christopher Walken, Keith David in "Coriolanus"

(Public/Martinson Hall) Tuesday, Dec. 13, 1988–Jan. 22, 1989 (16 performances and 30 previews).

FOR DEAR LIFE by Susan Miller; Director, Norman René; Set, Loy Arcenas; Costumes, Walker Hicklin; Lighting, Arden Fingerhut; Dance, Theodore Pappas; Fight, B. H. Barry; Piano Teacher, Rusty Magee; Props, Kevin Brannick, Cass Rodeman, Brian Moran; Wardrobe, Marcia Belton, June Kushner, Beth Pratt; Hairstylist, Manuela LaPorte; Stage Managers, K. Siobhan Phelan, Scott Rodabaugh CAST: Tony Shalhoub (Jake), Bellina Logan (Maggie), Laila Robins (Catherine), Christine Estabrook (Dottie), Joseph Lambie (Peter), Stephen Mailer (Sam), Jennifer Aniston (Emily)

A play in three acts. The action takes place at the present time and some years later in Jake and Catherine's New York City apartment and Jake's studio.

(Public/Susan Stein Shiva Theater) Saturday, Jan. 17, 1988–May 21, 1989 (134 performances and 8 previews)

SONGS OF PARADISE based on the biblical poetry of Itsik Manager; Book, Miriam Hoffman, Rena Berkowicz Borow; Music, Rosalie Gerut; Director, Avi Hoffman; Music Arrangements, Bevan Manson; Musical Direction/Additional Arrangements, James Mironchik; Musical Staging, Eleanor Reissa; Set, Steven Perry; Lighting, Anne Militello. A production of the Joseph Papp Yiddish Theater (Sherry P. King, Mendl Hoffman, Producers) in association with the YIVO Institute for Jewish Research. CAST: Adrienne Cooper, Rosalie Gerut, Avi Hoffman, David Kener, Eleanor Reissa Understudies: Betty Silberman, Richard Silver

Musical Numbers: The Twilight, Khave and the Apple Tree, Odem and Kjhave Duet, Avrum and Sore's Duet, Hoger and the Turks, Song of Blessings, Hoger's Lament, Sore's Lullaby, Yankev and Rokhl Duet, Yosef's Tango, The Farewell Song

A musical in two acts and 8 scenes.

(Public/Newman Theater) Tuesday, Jan. 17–March 5, 1989 (14 performances and 41 previews). Seventh production of the Shakespeare Festival Marathon.

LOVE'S LABOR'S LOST by William Shakespeare; Director, Gerald Freedman; Set, John Ezell; Costumes, James Scott; Lighting, Natasha Katz; Music, John Morris; Choreography, Tina Paul; Stage Managers, Richard Costabile, Michael Chambers CAST: Peter Carlton Brown (Attendant), Ronn Carroll (Nathaniel), Andrew Colteaux (Attendant), William Converse-Roberts (Berowne), Joseph Costa (Holofernes), Roma Downey (Rosaline), Christine Dunford (Princess of France), Brian Dykstra (Forester), Kate Fuglei (Maria), Michael Gerald (Attendant), Julia Gibson (Jaquenetta), Davis Hall (Marcade), John Horton (Boyet), Mark Hymen (Longaville), Juliette Kurth (Katharine), Richard Libertini (Don Adriano de Armado), Spike McClure (Dumaine), Mark Moses (King of Navarre), P. J. Ochlan (Moth), Steve Ryan (Dull)

Performed with one intermission.

(Anspacher Theater) Tuesday, Feb. 21–Apr. 9, 1989 (24 performances and 31 previews).

THE WINTER'S TALE by William Shakespeare; Director, James Lapine; Set, John Arnone; Costumes, Franne Lee; Lighting, Beverly Emmons; Music, William Finn/Michael Starobin; Music Coordinator, Seymour Red Press; Musical Director, David Evans; Choreography, Diane Martel Stage Managers, Karen Armstrong, Buzz Cohen CAST: Jesse Bernstein (Mamillius), Rob Besserer (Harlequin), Graham Brown (Antigonus), Michael Cumpsty (Time/Lord), MacIntyre Dixon (Archidamus), Jennifer Dundas (Perdita), Albert Farrar (Cleomenes), Denise Faye (Ensemble), Peter Jay Fernandez (Dion), Cynthia Friberg (Ensemble), Bertina Johnson (Emilia/Dorcas/2nd Lady), Raymond Kurshal (Ensemble), Tom McGowan (Clown), Kathleen McNenny (Mopsa/1st Lady), James Olson (Camillo), Mandy Patinkin (Leontes), Frank Raiter (Jailer/Officer/Servant), Christopher Reeve (Polixenes), Rocco Sisto (Autolycus), Graham Winton (Florizel), Alfre Woodard (Paulina)

The action takes place in the kingdoms of Sicilia and Bohemia in the late Eighteenth Century. Performed with one intermission.

Martha Swope Photos
Top: Laila Robins, Tony Shalhoub, Christine Estabrook, Joseph Lambie in "For Dear Life"
Below: Avi Hoffman, Rosalie Gerut, David Kener, Adrienne Cooper, Eleanor Reissa in "Songs of Paradise"

Right Center: Mark Hymen, Spike McClure, William Converse-Roberts, Mark Moses, Roma Downey, Juliette Kurth, Christine Dunford, Kate Fuglei in "Love's Labour's Lost"

Jennifer Dundas, Graham Winton, Mandy Patinkin, Alfre Woodard, James Olson, Christopher Reeve, Diane Venora in "The Winter's Tale"

NEW YORK SHAKESPEARE FESTIVAL
(continued)

(Martinson Hall) Tuesday, Mar. 7–Apr. 16, 1989 (9 performances and 39 previews). The Wilma Theater production of:
TEMPTATION by Vaclav Havel; Translated by Marie Winn; Director, Jiri Zizka; Set, Jerry Rojo; Costumes, Hiroshi Iwasaki; Lighting, Jerold R. Forsyth; Music, Adam Wernick; Sound, Charles Cohen; Projection Design, Jeffrey S. Brown; Choreography, Raymond G. del Barrio; Production Assistant, Michael Stein; Dramaturg, Michael Ladenson; Props, John Masterson, Janine Kijner; Wardrobe, Marcia Belton; Stage Managers, Donald Christy, Chris Sinclair CAST: Larry Block (Deputy Director), Bille Brown (Fistula), Angel David (Lover), Raymond G. del Barrio (Dancer), Annie Rae Etheridge (Lover), Margaret Gibson (Wilma), Katherine Hiler (Marketa), Tanny McDonald (Dr. Libby Lorencova), Sarah Melici (Mrs. Mulch), Joel McKinnon Miller (Dr. Neuwirth), Bill Moor (Director), David Schechter (Dr. Kotrly), David Strathairn (Dr. Foustka), Marla Sucharetza (Petrushka), Ronnie West (Special Secretary)

A play in 2 acts and 10 scenes. The action takes place at the Institute, in Foutska's apartment, and Vilma's apartment.

(Public/LuEsther Hall) Tuesday, March 14–June 4, 1989 (70 performances and 26 previews)
THE FORBIDDEN CITY by Bill Gunn; Director, Joseph Papp; Set, Loren Sherman; Costumes, Judy Dearing; Lighting, Peter Kaczorowski; Music Supervision, Sam Waymon; Props, James Gill, John DeVito; Technical Director, Mervyn Haines, Jr.; Production Manager, Andrew Mihok CAST: Erika Alexander (Loretta), William Cain (Hodge), Demitri Corbin (David), Guy Davis (Abel), Frankie R. Faison (Nick Sr.), Gloria Foster (Molly), Mansoor Najee-Ullah (Whistlin' Billy), Cortez Nance, Jr. (Cupid), Akili Prince (Nick Jr.), P. Jay Sidney (Ivan), Allie Woods, Jr. (Smitty)

A drama in 2 acts and 4 scenes. The action takes place during 1936 in the Nick Hoffenburg home, and in a room in the Worcestershire Hotel.

(Public/Newman Theater) Tuesday, May 9–June 25, 1989
CYMBELINE by William Shakespeare; Director, JoAnne Akalaitis; Design, George Tsypin; Costumes, Ann Hould-Ward; Lighting, Pat Collins; Original Music, Philip Glass; Music Direction, Alan Johnson; Projections, Stephanie Rudolph; Fight Direction, David Leong; Choreography, Diane Martel; Stage Managers, Steven Ehrenberg, Pat Sosnow; Hair/Makeup, Bobby Miller CAST: George Bartenieff (Cymbeline), Jesse Borrego (Guiderius), Teagle F. Bougere (British Captain), Ethan T. Bowen (Roman Captain), Don Cheadle (Arviragus), Michael Cumpsty (Iachimo), Joan Cusack (Imogen), Ton Fervoy (1st Lord), Clement Fowler (1st Gentleman/1st Jailer), Richard Hicks (2nd Gentleman/British Lord), Earl Hindman (Caius Lucius), Peter Francis James (Pisanio), Tom Dale Keever (British Captain), Wendy Lawless (Lady/Soldier), Joan MacIntosh (Queen), Devon Michaels (1st Brother), David Neumann (Belarius), Jeffrey Nordling (Posthumus), David Ossian (Frenchman/Soldier), William Parry (Sicilius Leonatus), Mary Beth Peil (Ghost Mother), Wendell Pierce (Cloten), Rajika Puri (Soothsayer), Stefan Schnabel (Cornelius), John Madden Towey (Philario/2nd Jailer), Sharon Washington (Lady Helen/Soldier), Eloise Watt (2nd Brother), Jacob White (Jupiter), Joe Zaloom (2nd Lord)

Performed with one intermission.

(Anspacher Theatre) Wednesday, May 31–June 18, 1989 (19 performances)
ROMANCE IN HARD TIMES written and composed by William Finn; Director, David Warren; Choreography, Marcia Milgram Dodge; Set, James Youmans; Costumes, David C. Woolard; Lighting, Peter Kaczorowski; Sound, John Kilgore; Orchestrations, Daniel Moses Schreier; Musical Direction/Vocal Arrangements, Ted Sperling CAST: Rufus Bonds, Jr., Lawrence Clayton, Victor Trent Cook, Vondie Curtis Hall, Andi Henig, Peggy Hewett, Timothy Jerome, Alix Korey, Michael Mandell, Chiara Peacock, Melodee Savage, John Sloman, James Stovall, Lillias White

A musical in two acts. The action takes place in a New York soup kitchen during the Great Depression.

Martha Swope Photos

Top: Cast of "Temptation"

Below: Gloria Foster, Akili Prince in "The Forbidden City"

Right Center: David Neumann, David Ossian,
Ethan T. Bowen, Jeffrey Nordling, John Madden Towey,
Michael Cumpsty in "Cymbeline"

Jesse Borrego, Frederick Neumann, Don Cheadle, Joan Cusack in "Cymbeline"

NEW YORK THEATRE WORKSHOP

Artistic Director, James C. Nicola; Associate Artistic Director, Maria Gillen; Managing Director, Nancy Kassak Diekmann; Dramaturg, Nina Mankin; Marketing, Esther Cohen; Production Manager, William H. Lang; Technical Director, Tom Carroll; Props, Susan Benjamin; Press, Gary Murphy

(Perry Street Theatre) Thursday, Oct. 27–Nov. 5, 1988 (17 performances)
L'ILLUSION by Pierre Corneille; Adapted by Tony Kushner; Director, Brian Kulick; Set, Stephan Olson; Costumes, Claudia Brown; Lighting, Pat Dignan; Composer/Sound, Mark Bennett; Producing Dramaturg, Nina Mankin; Casting, Jason Lapadura; Production Manager, William H. Lang; Stage Manager, Richard Hester CAST: Stephen Spinella (The Amanuensis), Victor Raider-Wexler (Pridamant), Isiah Whitlock, Jr. (Alcandre), Michael Galardi (Calisto/Clindor/Theogenes), Socorro Santiago (Elicea/Lyse/Clarina), Neil Maffin (Pleribo/Adraste/The Prince), Regina Taylor (Melibea/Isabelle/Hippolyta), Arthur Hanket (Matamore)

The action takes place in a magician's cave in the late 18th Century. Performed without an intermission.

(Perry Street Theatre) Wednesday, Nov. 16–Dec. 18, 1988 (30 performances)
EMERALD CITY by David Williamson; Director, R. J. Cutler; Set, James Youmans; Costumes, Michael Krass; Lighting, Kenneth Posner; Sound, John Gromada; Dialect Coach, Nadia Venesse; Casting, Jason LaPadura; Stage Manager, Suzanne Hauser Weiss CAST: Daniel Gerroll (Colin), Doris Belack (Elaine), Gates McFadden (Kate), Dan Butler (Mike), Alice Haining (Helen), Jerry Manning (Malcolm)

A play in two acts. The action takes place at the present time in Sydney, Australia.

Wednesday, Feb. 8–26, 1989 (13 performances)
MERCEDES by Thomas Brasch; Translated from the German by Becke Buffalo; Director, Cheryl Faver; Sets, Rob Murphy; Costumes, Marina Draghici; Lighting, Pat Dignan; Sound Mark Bennett; Casting, Jason LaPadura/Natalie Hart; Production Manager, William H. Lang; Stage Manager, Carol Fishman CAST: Sharon Brady (Oi), Larry Bazzell (Sakko), Bruce Katzman (Man in car)

Performed without intermission
In repertory with:
THE NEST by Franz Xaver Kroetz; Translated from the German by Roger Downey; Director, Bartlett Sher; Stage Manager, Elizabeth Valsing CAST: Alma Cuervo (Martha), Matt Craven (Kurt), Justin Musumeci or Michael Pryor (Stefan)

Performed without intermission. The action takes place in West Germany.

(Perry Street Theatre) Wednesday, May 10–June 17, 1989 (30 performances).
THE INVESTIGATION OF THE MURDER IN EL SALVADOR by Charles L. Mee, Jr.; Director, David Schweizer; Set, Tom Kamm; Costumes, Gabriel Berry; Lighting, Anne Militello; Sound, Eric Liljestrand; Production Manager, William H. Lang; Stage Manager, Carol Fishman; Press, Gary Murphy CAST: Kathleen Chalfant (Lady Aitkin), Thom Christopher (D'Costa), Freddie Frankie (Bodyguard), Tom McDermott (Howard), Greg Mehrten (Peter), Leslie Nipkow (Meridee), Paul Schmidt (Stanton), Shona Tucker (Maid), Isiah Whitlock, Jr. (Butler)

A drama performed without intermission.

Gerry Goodstein, Bob Marshak, Paula Court Photos
Top: Alice Haining, Daniel Gerroll, Dan Butler, Gates McFadden in "Emerald City"
Below: Bruce Katzman, Sharon Brady, Larry Bazzell in "Mercedes"
Right: Alma Cuervo, Matt Craven, Michael Pryor (infant) in "The Nest"

Regina Taylor, Arthur Hanket, Michael Galardi in "L'Illusion"

Kathleen Chalfant, Isiah Whitlock, Jr., Thom Christopher, Shona Tucker in "Investigation of the Murder in El Salvador"

PAN ASIAN REPERTORY THEATRE

Twelfth Season

Artistic/Producing Director, Tisa Chang; Managing Director, Bonnie Hyslop; Marketing Director, Maggie Browne; Development, Mary Ann Hansen; Production Manager, Diane Freeman; Technical Director, David Von Salis; Press, G. Theodore Killmer

(Perry Street Theatre) Tuesday, June 24–July 10, 1988 (18 performances and 3 previews) Presented as part of The First New York International Festival of the Arts

BOUTIQUE LIVING & DISPOSABLE ICONS by Momoko Iko; Director, Tisa Chang; Set, Jane Epperson; Sound, Joseph Tornabene; Lighting, Clay Shirky; Costumes, Eiko Yamaguchi; Choreographer, Jane Lind; Stage Managers, Dominick Balletta, Sue Jane Stoker, Nanci Moy CAST: Michi Kobi (Ruby Oniki, mother of Glenn), Kitty Mei-Mei Chen (Mazie Kagawa, aunt of Deena), Keenan Shimizu (Perry Kagawa, nephew of Mazie), Norris M. Shimabuku (Tak Oniki, father of Glenn), Ann M. Tsuji (Deena Teraji, bride to be), Raul Aranas (Fred Teraji, father of Deena), Donald Li (Glenn Oniki, groom to be)

A play in two acts. The action takes place on a Saturday in October 1987 in the Hollywood Hills home of the Oniki family.

(Playhouse 46) Wednesday, Nov. 16–Dec. 17, 1988 (23 performances and 4 previews).

THE THREE SISTERS by Anton Chekhov; Translated by Randall Jarrell; Director, Margaret Booker; Set, David Potts; Lighting, Victor En Yu Tan; Sound, Joseph Tornabene; Costumes, Eiko Yamaguchi; Choreographer, Duyee Chang; Russian Consultant/Dramaturg, Karl Kramer; Stage Managers, Sue Jane Stoker, Gigi Rivkin CAST: Ernest Abuba (Chebutykin), Duyee Chang (Ferapont), Michael G. Chin (Fedotik), Mark W. Conklin (Andrei), Mel Duane Gionson (Vershinin), Mia Korf (Natalya), Kati Kuroda (Anfisa), Karen Tsen Lee (Various Roles), Mary Lee-Aranas (Irina), Donald Li (Tuzenbach), Philip Moon (Solyony), Ron Nakahara (Kulygin), Natsuko Ohama (Masha), Steve Park (Rode), Ginny Yang (Olga)

A drama in four acts. The action takes place in a provincial Russian town on the Siberian/Mongolian border.

(Apple Corps Theatre) Tuesday, Feb. 7–25, 1989 (18 performances).

PLAY BALL by R. A. Shiomi; Director, Ernest H. Abuba; Set, Atsushi Moriyasu; Lighting, Victor En Yu Tan; Sound, Joseph Tornabene; Costumes, Toni-Leslie James; Stage Manager, Sue Jane Stoker CAST: Ed Easton (John A. Wildman), James Jenner (Karl Warden), Ron Nakahara (Gordon Hirabayashi), Steve Park (Kazuo Yoshida), Norris M. Shimabuku (Harry Nakamura), Kelley Hinman (John Warden)

A dark comedy in three acts. The action takes place in a cabin somewhere in the Pacific Northwest in the early 1940's, early 1950's and early 1960's.

(Playhouse 46/St. Clement's) Thursday, May 4–27, 1989 (22 performances and 1 preview).

NOIRESQUE: The Fallen Angel by Ping Chong; Direction/Set, Ping Chong; Created in collaboration with the cast; Lighting, Howard Thies; Costumes, Matthew Yokobosky; Stage Managers, Arthur C. Catricala, Sue Jane Stoker CAST: Lauren Tom (Alice), Ron Nakahara (Herr Hasenpfeffer/Citoyen), Mel Duane Gionson (Katz and Jammer/Citoyan), Kati Kuroda (mme. L'Argent/Citoyen), Du-Yee Chang (The Angel/Citoyen), Norris M. Shimabuku (C. E. O'Donnell/Rag Man/Citoyen), Mary Lee (Nadine Nadine/Citoyenne)

Performed without intermission.

PEARL THEATRE COMPANY

Fifth Season

Artistic Director, Shepard Sobel; General Manager, Mary Hurd; Artistic Associate, Joanne Camp; Dramaturge, Dale Ramsey; Development, Elizabeth L. Henry; Producing Consultant, Tarquin Jay Bromley; Lighting, Douglas O'Flaherty

Friday, Sept. 30–Oct. 29, 1988 (24 performances)
SHE STOOPS TO CONQUER by Oliver Goldsmith; Director, Bob Verini; Technical Director, Gerald Grant; Props, Deborah Scott; Set, Robert Joel Schwartz; Costumes, Susan De Masi; Stage Managers, Jon Roger Clark, Nili Abrahamson CAST: Bonnie Horan (Dorothy Hardcastle), Patrick Tull (Richard Hardcastle), Tim O'Hare (Tony Lumpkin), Joanne Camp (Kate Hardcastle), Robin Leslie Brown (Constance Neville), Matthew Caldwell (Tavern Patron/Roger), Andrew Wilder (Tavern Patron/Thomas), Richard Wright (Tavern Patron), Laura Rathgeb (Barmaid/Pimple), Joseph Warren (Stingo/Sir Charles Marlowe), James Nugent (Charles Marlowe), Michael John McGuinness (George Hastings), Richard Wright (Diggory), William Christian (Jeremy)

A comedy performed with one intermission. The action takes place in and around the home of Mr. and Mrs. Hardcastle in 1773.

Friday, Nov. 4–Dec. 3, 1988 (24 performances)
BERENICE by Jean Racine; Director, Shepard Sobel; New Translation, Earle Edgerton; Set, Robert Joel Schwartz; Lighting, Vaughn Patterson; Costumes, Wallace G. Lane, Jr.; Sound, Kenn Dovel; Stage Manager, Jennifer E. Boggs CAST: Joel Swetow (Antiochus, King of Comagena), Richard Wright (Arsaces, Confidant of Antiochus), Robin Leslie Brown (Berenice, Queen of Palestine), Dawn Vanessa Brown (Phoenissa, Confidante of Berenice), Stuart Lerch (Titus, Emperor of Rome), Frank Geraci (Paulinus, Confidant of Titus)

The action takes place in Rome in a private chamber between the apartment of Titus and that of Berenice. Performed without intermission.

Friday, Dec. 9, 1988–Jan. 7, 1989 (24 performances)
THE PHILANDERER by Bernard Shaw; Director, Kent Paul; Set, Robert Joel Schwartz; Lighting, Stephen Petrilli; Costumes, Kathryn Wagner; Props, Deborah Scott; Stage Managers, Rachel Kusnetz, Michael Antonik CAST: James Nugent (Leonard Charteris), Deborah Strang (Grace Tranfield), Donnah Welby (Julia Craven), Frank Geraci (Joseph Cuthbertson), Herman Petras (Col. Daniel Craven), Michael Antonik (Page), David Omar (Dr. Percy Paramore), Laura Rathgeb (Sylvia Craven)

A play in three acts. The action takes place in London during 1893.

Friday, Jan. 13–Feb. 11, 1989 (24 performances)
HEDDA GABLER by Henrik Ibsen; Translated by Henry Beissel; Set, Robert Joel Schwartz; Lighting, Stephen Petrilli; Costumes, Barbara A. Bell; Sound, Kenn Dovel; Director, Richard Fancy; Props, Deborah Scott; Hairstylist, Randy H. Mercer; Stage Managers, Jennifer E. Boggs, Peter DiCaprio CAST: Joan Matthiessen (Juliane Tesman), Sylvia Davis (Bertha), Stuart Lerch (George Tesman), Joanne Camp (Hedda Tesman), Robin Leslie Brown (Mrs. Elvsted), Frank Geraci (Assessor Brack), James Nugent (Eilert Loevborg)

Performed with one intermission. The action takes place in the Tesmans' villa on the west side of town.

Friday, Feb. 17–March 18, 1989 (24 performances)
ALL'S WELL THAT ENDS WELL by William Shakespeare; Director, Shepard Sobel; Set, Robert Joel Schwartz; Costumes, Kathryn Wagner; Lighting, Douglas O'Flaherty; Technical Director, Stephen Petrilli; Speech/Text Coach, Robert Neff Williams; Production Assistant, Jennifer E. Boggs; Sound, Tarquin Jay Bromley; Stage Managers, C. Cameron Murphy, Marc Isaacman CAST: Joyce Sozen (Countess), Stuart Lerch (Bertram), Edward Morehouse (Lafew), Donnah Welby (Helena), Frank Geraci (Parolles), Michael Graves (King of France), Michael John McGuinness (1st Dumaine), Adrian Williams (2nd Dumaine), Jeanne LaPorta (Rynalda), James Nugent (Lavatch), Ken (Bruce) Harpster (French Lord), Marc Isaacman (Duke of Florence), Lois Raebeck (Widow), Laura Rathgeb (Diana)

Performed with one intermission.

Martha Swope Photos
Bottom Left: Donnah Welby in "All's Well That Ends Well"
Above: Joanne Camp, Robin Leslie Brown in "Hedda Gabler"
Top: Laura Rathgeb, Michael John McGuinness in "She Stoops to Conquer"
Below: Donnah Welby, James Nugent in "The Philanderer"

PLAYWRIGHTS HORIZONS

Eighteenth Season

Artistic Director, Andre Bishop; Executive Director, Paul S. Daniels; Production Manager, Carl Mulert; Development, Ruth Cohen; Business Manager, Donna M. Gearhardt; Casting, Daniel Swee; Musical Theatre, Ira Weitzman; Literary Manager, Tim Sanford; Technical Director, James E. Fuller, Jr.; Props, Susan Blume; Press, Philip Rinaldi.

Wednesday, June 1–12, 1988 (14 performances in workshop). Re-opened Tuesday, Sept. 27–Nov. 27, 1988 (72 performances)
SAVED FROM OBSCURITY by Tom Mardirosian; Director, John Ferraro; Set, Rick Dennis; Costumes, Marilyn Keith; Lighting, Jackie Manassee; Sound, Frederick Wessler; Stage Manager, Karen Armstrong CAST: Tom Mardirosian, Peter Appel, Frederica Meister, Hansford Rowe.

A comedy performed without intermission. The action takes place on the stage of the Playwrights Horizons.

Sunday, Sept. 18–Oct. 8, 1988 (30 performances) The Foundation of the Dramatists Guild (Mary Rodgers, President) presents its seventh annual:
YOUNG PLAYWRIGHTS FESTIVAL with four plays by writers under the age of 19; Producing Director, Nancy Quinn; Sets, Allen Moyer; Costumes, Jess Goldstein; Lighting, Nancy Schertier; Sound, Lia Vollack; Production Manager, Carl Mulert; Stage Managers, Stacey Fleischer, Roy Harris, Paul Warren; Press, Shirley Herz Associates/Sam Rudy, David Roggensack, Glenna Freedman, Pete Sanders, Miller Wright *"And the Air Didn't Answer"* by Robert Kerr; Director, Christopher Durang. CAST: Robert Sean Leonard (Dan Wilson), Jill Tasker (Jennifer), Debra Monk (Mother), Erica Gimpel (Renee), Richard Council (Father McLaughlin/Teacher/God/Scout Master), Jihmi Kennedy (Young Boy/Crusader/Abraham/Producer/Dante/Drunk), John Augustine (Crusader/Isaac/Salesman/Alex Trebek/Virgil/Drunk) *"Seniority"* by Eric Ziegenhagen; Director, Lisa Peterson; Advisor, Alfred Uhry. CAST: Bellina Logan (Debbie), Allison Dean (Fiona), Jihmi Kennedy (Ian). The action takes place on an autumn midnight in the living-room of a house in the suburbs. *"Women and Wallace"* by Jonathan Marc Sherman; Director, Don Scardino; Music, John Miller. CAST: Josh Hamilton (Wallace Kirkman), Mary Joy (Mother), Joan Copeland (Grandmother), Dana Behr (Victoria), Debra Monk (Psychiatrist), Bellina Logan (Sarah), Jill Tasker (Lili), Joanna Going (Nina), Erica Gimpel (Wendy) *"The Boiler Room"* by Kevin Corrigan; Director, Lawrence Sacharow; was given a staged reading for three performances.

Friday, Nov. 18, 1988–Feb. 19, 1989 (99 performances) Moved to the Plymouth Theatre Wednesday, March 1, 1989, and still playing May 31, 1989.
THE HEIDI CHRONICLES by Wendy Wasserstein; Director, Daniel Sullivan; Set, Thomas Lynch; Costumes, Jennifer von Mayrhauser; Lighting, Pat Collins; Sound, Scott Lehrer; Production Manager, Carl Mulert; Hair Stylist, Randy H. Mercer; Stage Managers, Roy Harris, Mary Fran Loftus; Props, Susan Blume; Press, Philip Rinaldi CAST: Joan Allen (Heidi Holland), Joanne Camp (Fran/Molly/Betsy), Peter Friedman (Scoop Rosenbaum), Boyd Gaines (Peter Patrone), Anne Lange (Jill/Debbie/Lisa), Drew McVety (Chris/Mark/TV Attendant/Waiter/Ray), Ellen Parker (Susan Johnston), Sarah Jessica Parker (Becky/Clara/Denise).

A play in 2 acts and 11 scenes with a prologue. The action takes place from 1968 through 1988.

Friday, Feb. 3–March 26, 1989 (32 performances)
GUS AND AL by Albert Innaurato; Director, David Warren; Set, James Youmans; Costumes, David C. Woolard; Lighting, Robert Jared; Sound, John Gromada; Musical Arrangements, Ted Sperling; Production Manager, Carl Mulert; Wardrobe, Gwena Perry; Production Assistant, Lisa Porter; Stage Managers, Allison Sommers, James Fitzsimmons CAST: Mark Blum (Al), Cara Duff-MacCormick (Natalie Bauer Lechner), Helen Hanft (Mrs. Briggs), Charles Janasz (Kafka/Freud), Christina Moore (Justine Mahler), Sam Tsoutsouvas (Gustav Mahler), Jennifer Van Dyck (Alma Schindler), Bradley White (Camillo).

A play in two acts. The play begins in 1989 in Manhattan then changes to Vienna in 1901.

Paul Kolnik, Tess Steinkolk, Gerry Goodstein Photos
Top R: Tom Mardirosian in "Saved From Obscurity"
**Below: Richard Council, Debra Monk, Robert Sean Leonard
in "And The Air Didn't Answer"**
**Right Center: Ellen Parker, Sarah Jessica Parker, Joan Allen
in "The Heidi Chronicles"**

**Charles Janasz, Jennifer Van Dyck, Sam Tsoutsouvas, Cara
Duff-MacCormick, Mark Blum in "Gus and Al"**

PUERTO RICAN TRAVELING THEATRE

Twenty-second Season

Artistic Director, Miriam Colon; Managing Director, Patricia Baldwin; Community Coordinator, Julio Martinez; Development, Vera Ryan; Press, Max Eisen, Madelon Rosen

Thursday, June 2–26, 1988 (35 performances)

FIRST CLASS by Candido Tirado; Translation, Fernando Moreno; Director, A. Dean Irby; Producer, Miriam Colon; Set, Robert Klingelhoefer; Lighting, Rachel Budin; Costumes, Laura Drawbaugh; Sound, David G. Ferdinand; Stage Manager, Sandra M. Bloom CAST: (in Spanish) Joe Gonzalez (Apache), Carlos Linares (Speedy) (in English) Paul-Felix Montez (Apache), Rico Elias (Speedy)

A drama in two acts. The action takes place at the present time on an island in the middle of an avenue in New York.

Thursday, Jan. 26–Feb. 26, 1989 (35 performances)

HAPPY BIRTHDAY, MAMA by Roberto Cossa; Translated by Myra Gann; Director, Vicente Castro; Producer, Miriam Colon Valle CAST: Marta Vidal (Esther), Mateo Gomez (Pedro), Nelson Landrieu (Osvaldo), Eugenia Cross (Graciela), Ruben Pla (Gabriel), Carmen Rosario

The action takes place at the present time in the living/dining room of a worn out apartment in an Hispanic section of New York City, about 9 P.M.

Wednesday, March 22–April 30, 1989 (35 performances)

QUINTUPLETS by Luis Rafael Sanchez; Director, Alba Oms; Translation, Alba Oms, Ivonne Coll; Set, Robert Klingelhoefer; Lighting, Bill Simmons; Costumes, Laura Drawbaugh; Sound, Gary & Timmy Harris; Stage Manager, D. C. Rosenberg CAST: Ivonne Coll (Daphne Morrison), Roberto Medina (Baby Morrison), Ivonne Coll (Bianca Morrison), Roberto Medina (Mandrake Morrison), Ivonne Coll (Carlotta Morrison), Roberto Medina (El Gran Divo Papa Morrison). The action takes place at the present time during a convention on Family Affairs. Performed with one intermission.

Thursday, May 25–June 25, 1989 (35 performances)

CONVERSATION AMONG THE RUINS by Emilio Carballido; English translation, Dr. Myra Gann; Director, Alejandra Gutierrez; Set, Robert Klingelhoefer; Lighting, Bill Simmons; Costumes, Laura Drawbaugh; Sound, Gary & Timmy Harris; Producer, Miriam Colon; Stage Manager, Mark Wagenhurst; Technical Director, Ed Bartosik; Wardrobe/Props, Bruno Aponte CAST: Elizabeth Ruiz Clemens (Anarda), Teresa Yenque (Enedian), Mark Morant (Antonio)

The action takes place during the 1950's somewhere in the jungles of Oaxaca.

Peter Krupenye Photos
Top R: Rico Elias, Paul-Felix Montez in "First Class"
Below: Eugenia Cross, Nelson Landrieu, Ruben Pla, Mateo Gomez, Marta Vidal in "Happy Birthday Mama"

Left: Ivonne Coll in "Quintuplets"
Right: Roberto Medina in "Quintuplets"

Mark Morant, Elizabeth Ruiz Clemens in "Conversation Among the Ruins"

Herman Petras in "Titus Andronicus"

RIVERSIDE SHAKESPEARE COMPANY

Artistic Director, Timothy W. Oman; Managing Director, Gus Kaikkonen; Development, Leslie Carroll; Academy Director, Laura Fine; Associate Directors, Laura Fine, Dan Johnson, Linda J. K. Masson, Robert Mooney, Austin Pendleton, Bevya Rosten, Gregory Linus Weiss

(Shakespeare Center) May 21–June 5, 1988
TITUS ANDRONICUS by William Shakespeare; Director, Timothy W. Oman; Producers, Kathleen Bishop, Buck Hobbs; Set, Peter R. Feuche; Costumes, David Pearson; Lighting, Bernadette Englert; Technical Director, Tony Rust; Props, Kelly Moorehead; Stage Manager, Timothy D. Klein. CAST: William Beckwith (Marcus), Georg Bishop (Capt. of Romans), Kathleen Bishop (Tamora), Jens Krummel (Chiron), Eric McGill (Aaron), Patrick McGuinness (Martius), Kam Metcalf (Young Lucius), Lisa Nicholas (Lavinia), Labert Owens (Quintus), Herman Petras (Titus Andronicus), Jim Pratzon (Quintus/Goth), and Jimmy Blackman, Austin Butler, Robert Freitas, David Goodman, Rick Gianasi, Tony Rust, Jack Smith, Malcolm Stephenson, Steven Zorowitz. Performed with one intermission.

(New York City Parks) Wednesday, July 20–Aug. 14, 1988 (20 performances)
LOVE'S LABOUR'S LOST by William Shakespeare; Director, Timothy W. Oman; Set, Peter R. Feuche; Costumes, David Pearson; Associate Director, John Basil; Producer, Cathleen N. Kartiganer; Composer/Musical Director, Steven Barkhimer; Stage Manager, Robert Lemieux CAST: Richard Mark Arnold (Dull), William Beckwith (Navarre), Kathleen Bishop (Katharine), Leslie Carroll (Jaquenetta), Daniel Daly (Berowne), Michael Graves (Boyet) Buck Hobbs (Don Armado), Eric Hoffman (Costard), George Holmes (Holofernes), Elizabeth Loftus (Maria), Kam Metcalf (Moth), Robin Poley (Rosaline), Angela Roberts (Princess), Christopher Roberts (Mercade), Tony Rust (Sir Nathaniel), Sturgis Warner (Longsville), David Wheeler (Dumaine)
Performed with one intermission.

(Shakespeare Center) Thursday, Dec. 15, 1989–Jan. 8, 1990. (20 performances)
MR. PICKWICK'S CHRISTMAS adapted by Thomas W. Olson from Charles Dickens' "The Pickwick Papers"; Director, Stefan Rudnicki; Costumes/Set, Kathleen Donnelly; Original Music, William Perry Morgan; Lighting, Stephen Petrilli; Producer, Kay Rothman CAST: Liz Amberly, Richar Mark Arnold, David Beckett, John F. Budzyna, Leslie Sara Carroll, Russ Cusick, James Fisk, John Haggerty, Ann Harvey, Karen Jennings, Paul Klementowicz, Jacqueline Lucid, Kari Luther, Patrick McGuinness, Deirdre Peterson, Mark Pierce, Chris Quartana, Rebecca Sayre, Irma St. Paule, Stephen Turner, Wendy Watson

Thursday, March 2–19, 1989 (12 performances)
ROMEO AND JULIET by William Shakespeare; Director, Timothy W. Oman; Assistant Director, Laura Fine; Set, Sara Edkins; Lighting, Steve Petrilli; Costumes, Ken Anders; Sound, Nathaniel Haynes; Fights, Brian Cousins; Stage Manager, Doug Shearer CAST: Richard Mark Arnold (Friar Lawrence), Steven Barkhimer (Peter), Max Brandt (Old Capulet/Apothecary), Billie Brenan (Nurse), Joanna Brown (Lady Montague), Daniel Dally (Lord Capulet), Robert Warren Davis (Lord Montague), Mark Els (Abram), Paula Eschweiler (Lady Capulet), Adriane Gage (Lady in Waiting), Mark Alan Gordon (Prince), Edward Henzel (Tybalt), Martha King (Lady in Waiting), Mark Lainer (Balthazar), Jacqueline Lucid (Juliet), Kari Luther (Lady in Waiting/Page), William D. Michie (Mercutio), Dan Perry (Paris), Mark Walthers (Samson/Watchman), David Cole Wheeler (Romeo), Earl Whitted (Gregory), Tom Williams (Friar John)

Thursday, May 18–Monday, June 5, 1989 (16 performances)
HAMLET by William Shakespeare; Director, Linda J. K. Masson; Set, Sarah Edkins; Costumes, Sasha Thayer; Lighting, Stephen Petrilli; Music, Michael Kingsley; Fights, Todd Loweth; Props, Stephen Weis; Stage Manager, Rachel S. Levine CAST: R. Bruce Elliott (Polonius), Robert Emmet (Horatio), Paula Eschweiler (Player Queen), Andrew Jarkowsky (Claudius), Richmond Johnson (Ghost/Player King), Sonja Lanzener (Gertrude), Todd Loweth (Laertes), Lisa Nicholas (Ophelia), Austin Pendleton (Hamlet), Gay Reed (Marcellus/Priest), Gene Santarelli (Guildenstern), Woody Sempliner (Rosencrantz), William Shenker (Bernardo/2nd Gravedigger), Jeff Shoemaker (Francisco/1st Gravedigger)
Performed with one intermission.

Peter R. Feuche Photos
**Top Left: Buck Hobbs, Kathleen Bishop in
"Titus Andronicus"
Below: Buck Hobbs, Leslie Carroll, Eric Hoffman in
"Love's Labour's Lost"**

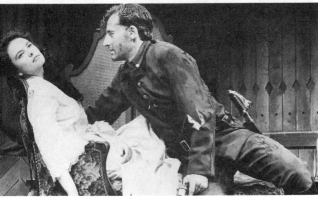

Roma Downey, Daniel Gerroll in "Arms and the Man"

ROUNDABOUT THEATRE

Twenty-third Season

Artistic Director, Gene Feist; Executive Director, Todd Haimes; General Manager, Ellen Richard; Development, Vicki Reiss; Marketing, Michael P. Lynch; Business Manager, Ellen Scrimger Gordon; Artistic Associate, Kenneth Schlesinger; Technical Director, John A. Kincaid; Musical Director/Sound Design, Philip Campanella; Casting, Jack Bowden, Barbara Hipkiss; Press, Joshua Ellis Office/Adrian Bryan-Brown, Jackie Green, Susanne Tighe, Tim Ray, Chris Boneau

Wednesday, July 20–Sept. 25, 1988 (46 performances and 16 previews)
THE MISTRESS OF THE INN by Carlo Goldoni; Translated and adapted by Mark A. Michaels; Director, Robert Kalfin; Set, Wolfgang Roth; Costumes, Andrew B. Marlay; Lighting, F. Mitchell Dana; Casting, Jay Binder; Fight Choreographer, Richard Raether; Incidental Choreography, Judith Haskell; Wardrobe, Lisa Eller; Production Assistant, Anne Raleigh; Stage Managers, Roy W. Backes, Kathy J. Faul CAST: Edward Zang (Il Marchese di Forlipopoli), George Ede (Il Conte d'Albafiorita), Gabriel Barre (Fabrizio, Mirandolina's Steward), Philip Kerr (Il Cavaliere di Ripafratta), Tovah Feldshuh (Mirandolina, Mistress of the Inn), Richard Levine (Servant to Il Cavaliere), J. Peter Adler (Second Servant)

A comedy in 2 acts and 4 scenes. The action takes place in Florence, Italy, in Mirandolina's inn during the spring of 1753.

Wednesday, Oct. 5–Nov. 27, 1988 (62 performances)
GHOSTS by Henrik Ibsen; Translated/Adapted by Lars Johannesen; Director, Stuart Vaughan; Set, David Potts; Costumes, Andrew B. Marlay; Lighting, F. Mitchell Dana; Stage Manager, Props, Keith Michl; Wardrobe, Julie Alderfer; Wigs, Bruce Geller; Stage Managers, Kathy J. Faul, Roy W. Backes CAST: Fionnula Flanagan (Mrs. Alving), Raphael Sbarge (Oswald, her son), David McCallum (Pastor Manners), Edward Seamon (Jacob Engstrand), Roma Downey (Regina Engstrand, his daughter)

The action takes place in 1881 in the home of Mrs. Alving in Norway. Performed with one intermission.

Wednesday, Dec. 21, 1988–Feb. 12, 1989 (62 performances)
ENRICO IV by Luigi Pirandello; Translated by Robert Cornthwaite; Director, J. Ranelli; Set, Marjorie Bradley Kellogg; Costumes, Andrew B. Marlay; Lighting, John Gleason; Sound, Philip Campanella; Production Assistant, Alison Ramsey; Props, Lillian Landeo; Wigs, Paul Huntley; Millinery, Arnold Levine; Stage Managers, Roy W. Backes, Kathy J. Faul CAST: Karen Chapman (Frida), Brian Cousins (Carlo di Nolli), Paul Hecht (Enrico IV), Richard Hicks (Bertholdo), Peter Francis James (Landolfo), Diane Kagan (Donna Matilde), Frank Nastasi (Giovanni), Lazaro Perez (Ordulfo), Jack Ryland (Barone Belcredi), Robert Stattel (Dr. Genoni), Joshua Worby (Arialdo)

Performed with one intermission. The action takes place in Italy during the summer of 1922.

Wednesday, March 8–May 7, 1989 (73 performances).
THE MEMBER OF THE WEDDING by Carson McCullers; Director, Harold Scott; Set, Thomas Cariello; Costumes, Andrew B. Marlay; Lighting, Shirley Prendergast; Production Assistant, Barbara Rice; Props, Janet Smith; Wigs, Paul Huntley; Hairstylist, George H. Kuhn; Assistant to Director, Jonathan Arak; Stage Manager, Kathy J. Faul CAST: Esther Rolle (Berenice Sadie Brown), Amelia Campbell (Frankie Addams), David Whalen (Jarvis Addams), Jeri Leer (Janice, his fiancee), Drew Snyder (Mr. Addams), Calvin Lennon Armitage or Lindsay Gordon (John Henry West, Frankie's cousin), Deborah Strang (Mrs. West), Donna Eskra (Helen Fletcher), Jeanne Bucci, Susan Honey (Club Members), Lou Ferguson (T. T. Williams), William Christian (Honey Camden Brown), Steven Douglas Cook (Barney MacKean), Marjorie Hawkins (Voice of Sis Laura)

A play in 3 acts and 5 scenes. The action takes place in a small town in Georgia during August of 1945.

Wednesday, May 17–July 9, 1989 (41 performances and 21 previews).
ARMS AND THE MAN by George Bernard Shaw; Director, Frank Hauser; Set, Franco Colavecchia; Costumes, A. Christina Giannini; Lighting, F. Mitchell Dana; Sound, Philip Campanella; Assistant to Director, Dan Cox; Props, Janet Smith; Production Assistant, Christine Catti; Stage Managers, Roy W. Backes, Kathy J. Faul. CAST: Barbara Andres (Catherine Petkoff), Richard Buckley (Major Plechanoff), Yusef Bulos (Nicola), Catherine Christianson (Louka), MacIntyre Dixon (Major Petkoff), Roma Downey (Raina Petkoff), Daniel Gerroll (Captain Bluntschli), Christopher Noth (Sergius Saranoff)

A comedy in 3 acts. The action takes place in a small town in Bulgaria near the Dragoman Pass from November 1885 to March 6, 1886.

Martha Swope Photos
**Top Left: George Ede, Edward Zang, Tovah Feldshuh,
Gabriel Barre, Philip Kerr in "Mistress of the Inn"
Below: Fionnula Flanagan, Raphael Sbarge, David McCallum
in "Ghosts"
Left Center: Amelia Campbell, Esther Rolle, Calvin Lennon
Armitage in "Member of the Wedding"**

SECOND STAGE

Tenth Season

Artistic Directors, Robyn Goodman, Carole Rothman; Managing Director, Rosa I. Vega; Marketing, Carol Bixler; Development, John Thew; Business Manager, Jerry Polner; Dramaturg, Anne Cattaneo; Casting, Simon & Kumin; Production Supervisor, Alfred Miller; Press, Richard Kornberg
Thursday, July 7–Aug. 6, 1988 (33 performances)
THE FILM SOCIETY by Jon Robin Baitz; Director, John Tillinger; Set, Santo Loquasto; Lighting, Dennis Parichy; Costumes, Candice Donnelly; Sound, Gary & Timmy Harris; Incidental Music, Rick Baitz; Hair, Antonio Soddu; Stage Managers, Thomas Clewell, Tammy Taylor CAST: Nathan Lane (Jonathan Balton), Dillon Evans (Hamish Fox), William Glover (Neville Sutter), Laila Robins (Nan Sinclair), Daniel Gerroll (Terry Sinclair), Margaret Hilton (Mrs. Balton)
A play in two acts. The action takes place during 1970 in Durban, Natal Province, South Africa.

Tuesday, Nov. 8–Dec. 18, 1988 (43 performances)
THE RIMERS OF ELDRITCH by Lanford Wilson; Director, Mark Brokaw; Set, Santo Loquasto; Lighting, Jennifer Tipton; Costumes, Ellen McCartney; Sound, Aural Fixation; Hairstylist, Antonio Soddu; Company Manager, Carol Bixler; Technical Director, Pat Heidenberg; Wardrobe, William Neish; Stage Manager, Carol Fishman CAST: Edward Cannan (Peck Johnson), Georgia Creighton (Wilma Atkins), Danielle DuClos (Eva Jackson), Sharon Ernster (Mavis Johnson), Georgine Hall (Mary Windrod), Deborah Hedwiall (Evelyn Jackson), Suzy Hunt (Cora Groves), Mary Jay (Martha Truitt), Kaiulani Lee (Nelly Windrod), William Mesnik (Preacher/Judge), Bill Mondy (Walter), Jennie Moreau (Patsy), Stuart Rudin (Skelly), Gary Dean Ruebsamen (Trucker), Amy Ryan (Lena Truitt), Barry Sherman (Josh Johnson), Adam Storke (Robert Conklin)
A play in two acts. The action takes place in Eldritch, a small former mining town in the middle West, population about 70, during the spring, summer and fall of the year.

Wednesday, Jan. 11–March 5, 1989 (57 performances)
IN A PIG'S VALISE with Music by August Darnell; Book/Lyrics, Eric Overmyer; Direction/Choreography, Graciela Daniele; Set, Bob Shaw; Lighting, Peggy Eisenhauer; Costumes, Jeanne Button; Musical Direction, Peter Schott; Sound, Gary & Timmy Harris; Hairstylist, Antonio Soddu; Company Manager, Carol Bixler; Technical Director, Patrick Heydenburg; Props, Janet Smith; Wardrobe, William Neish; Stage Managers, Robert Mark Kalfin, Paula Gray CAST: Nathan Lane (James Taxi), Ada Maris (Dolores Con Leche), Thom Sesma (Root Choyce), Reg E. Cathey (Bop Op), Charlie Lagond (Blind Sax), Michael McCormick (Shrimp Bucket), Lauren Tom (Mustang Sally), Dian Sorel (Dizzy Miss Lizzy), Jonathan Freeman (Zoot Alors/Gut Bucket) MUSICAL NUMBERS: Neon Heart, Kiss Me Deadly, The Skulk, Three-fingered Glove, Balkan Boogie, Mango Culo, Talent Scout, Nuevo Nuevo, Shrimp Louie, Put Your Legs on My Shoulders, Never Judge a Thriller, Prisoner of Genre, If I Was a Fool to Dream, No More Magic Kingdoms, Doin' the Denouement, Finale
A musical in two acts. The action takes place in and around the Heartbreak Hotel at the corner of Neon and Lonely.

Thursday, April 6,–May 28, 1989 (54 performances)
APPROACHING ZANZIBAR by Tina Howe; Director, Carole Rothman; Set, Heidi Landesman; Lighting, Dennis Parichy; Costumes, Susan Hilferty; Sound, Gary and Timmy Harris; Hairstylist, Antonio Soddu; Stage Managers, Pamela Edington, Ken Simmons CAST: Jane Alexander (Charlotte Blossom), Maggie Burke (Palace St. John/Dr. Sybil Wren), Angela Goethals (Pony Blossom), Damien Jackson (Fletcher St. John/Amy Childs), Clayton Barclay Jones (Turner Blossom), Bethel Leslie (Olivia Childs), Aleta Mitchell (Joy Ballad/Dalia Paz), Jamie Ross (Old Man), Harris Yulin (Wallace Blossom)
A play in 2 acts and 9 scenes. The action takes place during the first two weeks in August.

Susan Cook Photos
Top: Daniel Gerroll, Nathan Lane in
"The Film Society"
Below: Kaiulani Lee, Georgine Hall in "Rimers of Eldritch"
Right Center: Nathan Lane, Ada Maris in "In a Pig's Valise"

Bottom: Harris Yulin, Angela Goethals, Jane Alexander,
Clayton Barclay Jones in "Approaching Zanzibar"

SOHO REPERTORY THEATRE, INC.

Fourteenth Season

Artistic Director, Marlene Swartz; Associate Artistic Director, Julian Webber; Business Manager, Jeffrey R. Stevens; Production Manager, David Waggett; Resident Lighting Designer, Donald Holder; Director of Play Development, Rob Barron; Casting Directors, Brian Chavanne, Brett Goldstein; Dramaturg, Victor Gluck; Press, Bruce Cohen

(St. Bart's Playhouse) Wednesday, Sept. 14—Sunday, Oct. 9, 1988 (24 performances)

THE BLITZSTEIN PROJECT, professional stage premiere of rare works for the musical theatre by Marc Blitzstein, plus selections from Mr. Blitzstein's better-known works; Conceived and Directed by Carol Corwen; Additional Text compiled by Carol Corwen; Orchestra Conductor, Musical Reductions and Others Arrangements, Donald Sosin; Sets, Jeffrey D. McDonald; Costumes, G. A. Howard; Lighting, Donald Holder; Propmaster; John Stephenson; Choreography, Barry R. Gallo; Stage Managers, Kathryn Ballou, Deborah A. Friedman; Technical Director, Daniel D. Kirsch; Project Consultants, Leonard Lehrman, Eric Gordon.

"THE HARPIES" with Paul Binotto (Phineus), Harpies: Joanna Seaton (Aello), Loretta Giles (Ocypete), Helen Zelon (Calaeno); Argonauts: Daniel Baum (Zetes), Don Mayo (Jason); Peter Schmitz (Calais); Jennifer Lee Andrews (Iris), Mary Eileen O'Donnell (Chorus), Andre Montgomery (Chorus)

World stage premiere of a one act opera written in 1931, parodying the Jason and the Argonauts myth.

"I'VE GOT THE TUNE" with Andre Montgomery (Mr. Musiker), Joanna Seaton (Beetzie), Mary Eileen O'Donnell (Madame Arbutus), Peter Schmitz (Captain Bristlepunkt), Daniel Baum (Private Schnook), Mimi Higgins (The Mongrel), Helen Zelon (The Suicide), Don Mayo (Choral Director), Supporting Characters: Paul Binotto, Loretta Giles, Jennifer Lee Andrews

World stage premiere of a one act opera written in 1937 and set in a fictional New York City during the depression.

(Greenwich House) Thursday, Jan. 26—Sunday, Feb. 19, 1989 (24 performances)
THE CEZANNE SYNDROME by Normand Canac-Marquis, Translation, Louison Danis; Director, Liz Diamond; Sets, Anne Servanton; Costumes, Sally J. Lesser; Lighting, Donald Holder; Sound, Phil Lee; Stage Manager, Casandra Scott; Technical Director, Brian McDaniel CAST: David Strathairn (Gilbert); Caris Corfman (Suzanne); Edward Baran (Thomas Wancicovski)

American premiere of a French Canadian play. The action takes place in Montreal, Quebec; performed without intermission. Part of the New Wave of Quebec Festival made possible in part with funds from the Quebec Government and the Canadian Consulate.

(Greenwich House) Thursday, April 6—Sunday, April 30, 1989 (24 performances)
THE PHANTOM LADY by Pedro Calderon de la Barca, Translation, Edwin Honig; Director, Julian Webber; Sets, Stephen Olson; Costumes, Patricia Adshead; Lighting, Donald Holder; Fight Director, Jim Manley; Music Composed, Selected and Arranged, Jared Walker; Stage Manager, Nina L. Heller; Technical Director, David von Salis CAST: Donald Berman (Don Manuel); Gregor Paslawsky (Cosme), Monique Fowler (Dona Angela), Anne O'Sullivan (Isabel), Brian P. Glover (Don Luis), Richard McMillan, followed by Richard Karn (Don Juan), Valerie Charles (Dona Beatriz), Jared Walker (Guitar)

American premiere of a seventeenth century Spanish comedy. The play takes place in Madrid during the seventeenth century, performed in two acts.

(Greenwich House) Tuesday, May 16—Saturday, May 20, 1989. SCENES TO COME: one week festival of readings of new plays
THE MALIGNANCY OF HENRIETTA LACKS by August Baker, directed by the author; MY DAUGHTER, THE SISTER by Matt Cutugno; Director, Rob Barron; A CONFESSION & LLOYD AND LEE by Steve Monroe; Directed by Rob Barron and the author; HOME FIRES by Molly Fowler and Karen L. de Balbian Verster; Director, Collete Berge; SMITTY'S NEWS by Conrad Bishop and Elizabeth Fuller; Director, Liz Diamond; BACKWARD ANTHOLOGY by Zoe Walker; Director, David Willinger; FILTHY TALK FOR TROUBLED TIMES by Neil LaBute; Director, Julian Webber; READY FOR THE RIVER by Neil Bell; Director, David Briggs

(Greenwich House) Sunday, May 21, 1989
NEW VOICES FOR THE AMERICAN MUSICAL: SEE HOW THEY RUN, with Music and Lyrics, Tom Greenwald; Book, Tom and Leah Greenwald; POE, with Music and Lyrics, Brian Hobbs; Book, R. Vincent Razor; THE CARE AND FEEDING OF THE YOUNG, with Music, Jimmy Roberts; Lyrics, June Siegel; CROOKED LINES, with Music, Jan Mullaney, Pepi Castro; Book and Lyrics, Mary Bracken Phillips; HEROES, with Music, Douglas J. Cohen; Book and Lyrics, Tom Toce; CAPTAINS COURAGEOUS, with Music, Frederick Freyer; Book and Lyrics, Patricia Cook

Gerry Goodstein Photos
Top: Cast of "The Harpies"
Center: Caris Corfman, David Strathairn
in "Cezanne Syndrome"

Bottom: Donald Berman, Monique Fowler in "Phantom Lady"

105

Francine Beers, Reneé Taylor
in "The Grandma Plays"
Right: Diane Salinger, Elzbieta Czyzewska in "Phantasie"

VINEYARD THEATRE

Artistic Director, Doug Aibel; Executive Director, Barbara Zinn Krieger; Managing Director, Jon Nakagawa; Production Manager, Kate Mennone; Technical Director, Mark Lorenzen; Press, Bruce Cohen/Kathleen von Schmid, Victoria Lynch
(Vineyard Theatre) Wednesday, Sept. 14–Oct. 16, 1988 (33 performances)
THE GRANDMA PLAYS by Todd Graff; Director, Steve Gomer; Scenery, William Barclay; Lighting, Phil Monat; Costumes, Jennifer von Mayrhauser; Sound, Phil Lee; Stage Manager, Carol Fishman CAST: Renee Taylor (Pearl), Elzbieta Czyzewska (Rutanya), Alma Cuervo (Bibby), Francine Beers (Becky)

(Vineyard Theatre) Saturday, Dec. 10, 1988–Jan. 29, 1989 (43 performances). The Vineyard Theatre (Doug Aibel, Artistic Director; Barbara Zinn Krieger, Executive Director; Jon Nakagawa, Managing Director) presents:
PHANTASIE by Sybille Pearson; Director, John Rubinstein; Set, William Barclay; Lighting, Phil Monat; Costumes, Deborah Shaw; Sound, Phil Lee; Original Music, Frank Lindquist; Stage Managers, Shannon Graves, Michael McKinney, John Robert Reed CAST: Diane Salinger (D), Elzbieta Czyzewska (Leah), Michael French (Michael), Laurinda Barrett (Valerie), Myra Taylor (Lorraine/Maid/Mrs. Johnson/Dr. Croyers/Mom), Ryan Cutrona (Desk Clerk/Man/Danny/Dr. Prager/Tenant/Pop)
A play in two acts. The action takes place at the present in a hotel lobby in Boston, and at various locations in D's past life.

(Gertrude & Irving Dimson Theatre) Tuesday, May 16–
THE VALUE OF NAMES by Jeffrey Sweet; Director, Gloria Muzio; Set, William Barclay; Costumes, Jess Goldstein; Lighting, Phil Monat; Production Manager, Kate Mennone; Technical Director, Mark Lorenzen; Wardrobe, Melanie Hansen; Stage Manager, Crystal Huntington CAST: John Seitz (Benny), Ava Haddad (Norma), Stephen Pearlman (Leo)
The action takes place during 1982 on a patio in the Hollywood hills, and is performed without intermission.

Carol Rosegg Photos

John Seitz, Ava Haddad in "The Value of Names"

WPA THEATRE

Twelfth Season

Workshop of the Players Art: Artistic Director, Kyle Renick; Managing Director, Donna Lieberman; Resident Designer, Edward T. Gianfrancesco; Lighting, Craig Evans; General Manager, Lori Sherman; Production Manager/Technical Director, Gordon W. Brown; Press, Jeffrey Richards Associates/Ben Morse, Irene Gandy, Diane Judge, Naomi Grabel, Jillana Devine, Roger Lane

Tuesday, June 28–July 31, 1988 (28 performances)
MOROCCO written and directed by Allan Havis; Set, Bill Clarke; Costumes, Mimi Maxmen; Sound, Aural Fixation; Stage Manager, Carol Fishman CAST: Sam Freed (Mr. Kempler), George Guidall (The Colonel), Gordana Rashovich (Mrs. Kemmpler), Anthony Ruiz (Waiter)

Tuesday, Oct. 4–Nov. 6, 1988 (34 performances)
JUST SAY NO by Larry Kramer; Director, David Esbjornson; Costumes, David C. Woolard; Casting, Stanley Soble/Brian Chavanne; Wardrobe, Tracy Digesu; Stage Manager, Paul Mills Holmes CAST: Tonya Pinkins (Eustacia Vye), David Margulies (Foppy Schwartz), Julie White (Trudi Tunick), Keith Reddin (Gilbert Perch), Richard Topol (Junior), Joseph Ragno (Mayor), Richard Riehle (Herman Harrod), Kathleen Chalfant (Mrs. Potentate)
A farce in two acts. The action takes place at the present time in the townhouse of Foppy Schwartz in Georgetown, the capital city of New Columbia.

Tuesday, Jan. 10–Feb. 26, 1989 (24 performances. Re-opened Friday, March 31, 1989 in the Orpheum Theatre where it closed May 28, 1989 after 67 performances.)
THE NIGHT HANK WILLIAMS DIED by Larry L. King. Director, Christopher Ashley; Setting, Edward T. Gianfrancesco; Technical Director, Stephen Jones; Props, Janet Smith; Assistant Director, Tim Vasen; Costumes, Jess Goldstein; Stage Manager, Greta Minsky; Press, Jeffrey Richards Associates/Maria Somma CAST: Matt Mulhern succeeded by Richard McWilliams (Thurmond Stottle), Betsy Aidem (Nellie Bess Powers Clark), J. R. Horne (Moon Childers), Steve Rankin succeeded by Earl Hindman (Sheriff Royce Landon, Jr.), Phyllis Somerville (Mrs. Vida Powers), Barton Heyman succeeded by Darren McGavin, Larry L. King (Gus Gilbert)
A drama in two acts. The action takes place during the summer of 1952 in Stanley, Texas.

Sunday, April 9–30, 1989 (34 performances)
EARLY ONE EVENING AT THE RAINBOW BAR AND GRILLE by Bruce Graham; Director, Pamela Berlin; Set, Edward T. Gianfrancesco; Lighting, Craig Evans; Costumes, Mimi Maxmen; Props, Janet Smith; Fight Coordinator, Jason Kuschner; Production Assistant, John Lant; Wardrobe, Jeanne Thomas; Stage Manager, Carol Fishman; Press, Kathryn Frawley CAST: Dan Butler (Shep), Gregory Grove (Roy), Jay Patterson (Willy), Kent Broadhurst (Jake Bullard), Sharon Ernster (Shirley), Julie White (Virginia), William Wise (Joe)
A play in two acts. The action takes place at the present time in Western Pennsylvania.

Tuesday, May 30–June 25, 1989
THE GOOD COACH by Ben Siegler; Director, Michael Bloom; Set, Edward T. Gianfrancesco; Lighting, Craig Evans; Costumes, Deborah Shaw; Sound, Aural Fixation; Production Manager, Gordon W. Brown; Technical Director, Stephen Jones; Props, Janet Smith; Fight Coordinator, Jake Turner; Production Assistant, Barbara Lynne Rice; Wardrobe, Alisa Sciulli; Stage Manager, Nina Heller CAST: Jace Alexander (Man), Sal Barone (Student), Richard Council (Frank), Bill Swikowski (Chuck), Mary Kane (Sally), Tom Mardirosian (Joe LaPorte), Kathryn Rossetter (Hooker/Karen)
A play performed without intermission. The action takes place at the present time in a small town.

Friday, Nov. 18–Dec. 11, 1988 (12 performances) Presented in association with the Theatre-in-Limbo, as part of WPA's "Silly Series."
THE LADY IN QUESTION by Charles Busch; Director, Kenneth Elliott; Set, B. T. Whitehill; Costumes, Robert Locke, Jennifer Arnold; Lighting, Vivien Leone; Wigs, Elizabeth Katherine Carr; Stage Manager, Robert Vandergriff CAST: Charles Busch (Gertrude Garnet), Robert Carey (Karel), Kenneth Elliott (Baron Von Elsner), Andy Halliday (Hugo/Lotte), Julie Halston (Kitty), Mark Hamilton (Mittelhoffer), Arnie Kolodner (Erik), Theresa Marlowe (Heidi), Meghan Robinson (Augusta/Raona). Understudies: Richard Cuneo, Judith Hansen.
A comedy in two acts. The action takes place during 1940 in the Bavarian Alps, outside the Ludwigshafen train station, and the schloss of Baron Von Elsner.

Martha Swope Photos
Top Right: Gordana Rashovich, Sam Freed in "Morocco"
Below: Betsy Aidem, Matt Mulhern in "The Night Hank Williams Died"
Right Center: Julie White, Dan Butler, William Wise in "Early One Evening at the Rainbow Bar & Grille"

David Margulies, Tonya Pinkins in "Just Say No"

Ann Dowd, Benjamin White in "The Lark"

YORK THEATRE COMPANY

Twentieth Year

Producing Director, Janet Hayes Walker; Managing Director, Molly Pickering Grose; Artistic Advisers, John Newton, James Morgan; Press, Keith Sherman (Mazur Theatre/Murphy Center)

Tuesday, June 14–26, 1988 (limited 6 performances)
THE MINI-REP with Sets by Deborah Scott; Costumes, Robert Swasey; Lighting, Jack Jacobs; Production Manager, Herbert O'Dell; Stage Manager, Nicole Rosen; Technical Adviser, Sally Smith; Assistant to Directors, Kimberly Miles; Sound, Chaka Harris.
NIGHT GAMES by Jo Coudert; Director, Ralph David Westfall. CAST: Virginia Downing (Kay), John Rainer (Bennett), Jane Ives (Hilary), John Newton (Seymour), Henson Keys (Jack), David Kroll (Curtis), Michael Learned (Dr. Marianne Caldwell), Janet Hayes Walker (Muffie).

A play in two acts. The action takes place at the present in Dr. Caldwell's office in New York City.
A FROG IN HIS THROAT by Eric Conger; Freely adapted from a farce by Georges Feydeau); Director, Cash Baxter. CAST: John Newton (Pacarel), Michael Learned (His Wife), Jane Ives (Julie, their daughter), John Rainer (Landernau, their doctor, a friend), Janet Hayes Walker (Amandine, his wife), David Kroll (Curtis), Jonathan Courie (Lanoix, Julie's fiance), Henson Keys (Tiburce, the servant)

A play in two acts. The action takes place in 1888 in the drawing room of Pacarel's house in Paris.

Friday, Oct. 14–Nov. 5, 1988 (20 performances)
SING FOR YOUR SUPPER: A Rodgers and Hart Musical Celebration; Music, Richard Rodgers; Lyrics, Lorenz Hart; Original Concept, Richard Lewine, John Fearnley; Directed and Staged by Frank Wagner; Musical Director/Arranger, William Roy; Set, James Morgan; Lighting, Brian MacDevitt; Costumes, Donald Brooks; Technical Director, Brad Rosen; Costume Coordinator, Robert W. Swasey; Stage Manager, Shannon Graves CAST: Ira Hawkins, Mark Martino, Jess Richards, Melodee Savage, Lynne Stuart, Karen Ziemba

Friday, Jan. 13–29, 1989 (16 performances)
MAX AND MAXIE by James McLure; Director, D. Lynn Meyers; Sets/Costumes, Eduardo Sicangco; Lighting, Kirk Bookman, David Neville; Technical Director, Serge Hunkins; Wardrobe, Robert W. Swasey; Stage Managers, Victor Lukas, Jeffe Dorsey CAST: Robin Haynes (The Boy), John Newton (Max), Sandy Roveta (Maxie)

A play in two acts.

Friday, March 31–April 29, 1989 (24 performances).
SWEENEY TODD The Demon Barber of Fleet Street; Music/Lyrics, Stephen Sondheim; Book, Hugh Wheeler; Adaptation, Christopher Bond; Set, James Morgan; Costumes, Beba Shamash; Lighting, May Jo Dondlinger; Technical Director, James E. Fuller, Jr.; Music Director, David Krane; Choreographer, Michael Lichtefeld; Director, Susan H. Schulman CAST: Bob Gunton (Sweeney Todd), Beth Fowler (Mrs. Lovett), David Barron (Judge Turpin), SuEllen Estey (Beggar Woman), Tony Gilbert (Jonas Fogg), Ted Keegan (Bird Seller), Gretchen Kingsley-Weihe (Johanna), Eddie Korbich (Tobias Ragg), David E. Mallard (Policeman), Bill Nabel (Pirelli), Mary Ellen Phillips (Mrs. Mooney), Calvin Remsberg (The Beadle), Dawn Leigh Stone (Dora), Jim Walton (Anthony Hope) MUSICAL NUMBERS: The Ballad of Sweeney Todd, No Place Like London, The Worst Pies in London, Poor Thing, My Friends, Green Finch and Linnet Bird, Ah Miss, Johanna, Pirelli's Miracle Elixir, The Contest, Wait, Kiss Me, Ladies in Their Sensitivities, Pretty Women, Epiphany, A Little Priest, God That's Good, By the Sea, Wigmaker Sequence, Not While I'm Around, Parlour Songs, Fogg's Asylum, City on Fire, Searching, The Judge's Return, Finale.

A musical in two acts. The action takes place during the 19th Century in London on Fleet Street and environs.

(Church of the Heavenly Rest) Friday, May 19–June 3, 1989 (16 performances)
THE LARK by Jean Anouilh; Adapted by Lillian Hellman; Set, Deborah Scott; Costumes, Holly Hynes; Director, Janet Hayes Walker; Lighting, Brian MacDevitt; Technical Director, James E. Fuller, Jr.; Stage Manager, Victor Lukas, Nicole Rosen; Music, Leonard Bernstein CAST: Mel Boudrot (Cauchon), John Camera (Beaudricourt), Laura Carden (Little Queen), Ann Dowd (Joan), Lisa Fugard (Agnes Sorel), Russell Lawyer (Ladvenu), Michael McKenzie (de la Tremouille), John Newton (Archbishop), Tom Nichols (The Brother), Dennis Parlato (Warwick), Joel Swetow (Promoter), Neil Vipond (Inquisitor), Marie Wallace (Mother/Yolande), Robert Warren (Scribe/Priest), Ralph David Westfall (Father/Executioner/Priest), Benjamin White (Dauphin)

A drama in two acts that take place during the trial of Joan.

Carol Rosegg, Sandy Underwood Photos
Top Left: Ira Hawkins, Melodee Savage, Ron Raines, Lynne Stuart, Mark Martino, Karen Ziemba in "Sing For Your Supper"
Below: John Newton, Sandy Roveta in "Max and Maxie"
Left Center: Bob Gunton, Beth Fowler in "Sweeney Todd"

NATIONAL TOURING COMPANIES

ANYTHING GOES

Music/Lyrics, Cole Porter; Original Book, Guy Bolton & P. G. Wodehouse, Howard Lindsay & Russel Crouse; New Book, Timothy Crouse, John Weidman; Director, Jerry Zaks; Choreography, Michael Smuin; Settings/Costumes, Tony Walton; Lighting, Paul Gallo; Musical Supervisor, Edward Strauss; Musical Director, Jim Coleman; Orchestrations, Michael Gibson; Sound, Tony Meola; Dance Arrangements, Tom Fay; Presented by Lincoln Center Theater (Gregory Mosher, Director; Bernard Gersten, Executive Producer); General Management, Emanuel Azenberg, Eugene V. Wolsk; Company Manager, Steven Suskin; Stage Managers, Steven Beckler, Loni Ball, Thomas S. Capps; Dance Captain, Leah Brandon; Props, Alan Price, Pat Keogh; Wardrobe, Roberta Christy, Terry LaVada; Hairstylist, David H. Lawrence; Press, Merle Debuskey Associates/Jan Greenberg. Opened in New Haven's Shubert Theatre on Oct. 19, 1988 and closed in Pittsburgh's Benedum Theatre on Jan. 15, 1989. For original Broadway revival see *Theatre World* Vol. 44.

CAST

Elisha Whitney	Gordon Connell
Billy Crocker	Rex Smith
Reno Sweeney	Leslie Uggams
Captain	Kenneth Kantor
Purser	Dale O'Brien
Minister	George Riddle
Luke	Alan Muraoka
John	Ronald Yamamoto
Hope Harcourt	Rebecca Baxter
Mrs. Evangeline Harcourt	Julie Kurnitz
Lord Evelyn Oakleigh	Paul V. Ames
Erma	Susan Terry
Moonface Martin	Rip Taylor
Angels	Dianne Dilascio, J. Kathleen Lamb, Lynn Sterling, Carol Lynn Worcell
Chanty Quartet	David Earl Hart, Brad Little, Ted Jost, Bob Wrenn

ENSEMBLE: Ruth Bormann, Danielle DeCrette, Joe Deer, Dianne DiLascio, Rick Ferraro, David Earl Hart, Gib Jones, Ted Jost, Jane Labanz, J. Kathleen Lamb, Garry Q. Lewis, Brad Little, Dale O'Brien, Chris Peterson, Russell Ricard, George Riddle, Lynn Sterling, Susan Tilson, Carol Lynn Worcell, Kyle Whyte, Bob Wrenn, Swings: Leah Brandon, Russell Halley

UNDERSTUDIES: Susan Terry (Reno), Brad Little (Billy), Dale O'Brien (Moonface), Jane Labanz (Hope), Ruth Bormann (Evangeline), Kenneth Kantor (Oakleigh), George Riddle (Elisha), Susan Tilson (Erma)

MUSICAL NUMBERS: I Get a Kick out of You, No Cure Like Travel, Bon Voyage, You're the Top, Easy to Love, I Want to Row on the Crew, Sailors' Chanty, Friendship, It's Delovely, Anything Goes, Public Enemy, Blow Gabriel Blow, Be Like the Bluebird, All Through the Night, The Gypsy in Me, Buddie Beware, Finale

Martha Swope Photos

Top Left: Cast of "Anything Goes"
Below: Rex Smith, Rip Taylor, Susan Terry

Leslie Uggams, Paul V. Ames

Joe Deer, Leslie Uggams, Gary Q. Lewis

BROADWAY BOUND

By Neil Simon; Staged by Peter Lawrence after original Broadway direction by Gene Saks; Set, David Mitchell; Costumes, Joseph G. Aulisi; Lighting, Tharon Musser; Sound, Tom Morse; Casting, Simon & Kumin; Hairstylist, J. Roy Helland; Presented by Emanuel Azenberg; Company Manager, Jodi Moss; Consultant, Jose Vega; Props, Philip Adams; Wardrobe, Marilyn Knots; Stage Managers, Mindy K. Farbrother, John H. Lowe III; Press, Bill Evans & Associates/Harry Davies. Opened in St. Paul's Ordway Music Theatre on Thursday, Sept. 1, 1988 and closed in the Providence Performing Arts Center on Feb. 11, 1989. For original Broadway production, see *Theatre World* Vol. 43

CAST

Kate	Barbara Tarbuck
Ben	Ronny Graham
Eugene	Kurt Deutsch
Stanley	Brian Drillinger
Blanche	Lauren Klein
Jack	Madison Arnold
Radio Voices:	Marilyn Cooper (Mrs. Pitkin), MacIntyre Dixon (Chubby Waters), Ed Herlihy (Announcer)

STANDBYS: Faye Cameron (Kate/Blanche), Herman O. Arbeit (Ben/Jack), Michael Unger (Eugene/Stanley)

A play in two acts. The action takes place in Brighton Beach, Brooklyn, NY, during February of the late 1940's.

Martha Swope Photos

Top Right: Brian Drillinger, Madison Arnold, Kurt Deutsch
Below: Brian Drillinger, Barbara Tarbuck, Kurt Deutsch

Madison Arnold, Barbara Tarbuck, Ronny Graham, Brian Drillinger, Kurt Deutsch

DRIVING MISS DAISY

By Alfred Uhry; Winner of 1988 Pulitzer Prize; Director, Ron Lagomarsino; Set, Thomas Lynch; Costumes, Michael Krass; Lighting, Arden Fingerhut; Sound, Tony Meola; Incidental Music, Robert Waldman; Casting, Pat McCorkle; Presented by The Daisy Company in association with Playwrights Horizons, Guber/Gross Productions; General Management, Gene Wolsk; Company Manager, Charlie Willard; Technical Director, Ken Keneally; Props. Gregory Martin; Wardrobe, Cie Martin; Hairstylist, Ray Iagnocco; Wigs, Paul Huntley; Tour Direction, Roadworks; Stage Managers, Warren Crane, Danny Lewin; Press, David Powers, Morris Yuter. Opened Wednesday, Sept. 13, 1988 in Detroit's Music Hall, and still touring May 31, 1988. For original NY production, see *Theatre World* Vol. 44.

CAST

Daisy Werthan	Julie Harris
Boolie Werthan	Stephen Root
Hoke Coleburn	Brock Peters

UNDERSTUDIES: Martha Randall (Daisy), Ellis E. Williams (Hoke), Ed Steele (Boolie)

Performed without an intermission. The action takes place in Atlanta, Georgia, from 1948 to 1973.

The Chicago company opened with Sada Thompson who was succeeded by Ellen Burstyn, Dorothy Loudon, and Charlotte Rae, Bill Cobbs as "Hoke" was succeeded by Bruce Young, Ernest Perry, Mike Hodge, Bernard Mixon.

Carol Rosegg Photos
Top Right: Julie Harris
Below: Julie Harris, Brock Peters

Dorothy Loudon (Chicago Co.)

Julie Harris, Stephen Root

111

DROOD

Book/Music/Lyrics/Orchestrations by Rupert Holmes; Suggested by the unfinished novel by Charles Dickens; Director, Joe Leonardo; Set/Costumes, Neil Bierbower; Lighting, Brian MacDevitt; Musical Direction/Orchestrations/Arrangements, Hampton F. King, Jr; Technical Director, Jamie Gormley; Company Manager, Megan L. Miller; Choreography, Daniel Pelzig; Stage Manager, Joe Walsh; Production Manager, Bradford Watkins; Props/Wardrobe, John Byers; Assistant Conductor, Ross Scott Rawlings; Presented by Music Theatre Group in association with Music Theatre Association; Press, Barbara Faculjak, Lane C. Tucker. Opened Sept. 27, 1988 in Burruss Hall, Blacksburg, Va., and still touring May 31, 1989. For original Broadway production, see *Theatre World* Vol. 42.

CAST

Thomas Purcell, Maestro	Hampton F. King, Jr.
William Cartwright	Steven LeBlanc
James Throttle, stage manager	Michael Shiles
John Jasper/Clive Paget	C. M. Yates
Edwin Drood/Alice Nutting	Kris Montgomery
Rosa Bud/Deirdre Peregrine	Marie-Laurence Danvers
Wendy/Isabel Yearsley	Elizabeth Green
Beatrice/Violet Balfour	Lisa Liguori/Janet Wurst
Helena Landless/Janet Conover	Michelle Rios
Neville Landless/Victor Grinstead	Bill Lynch
Rev. Crisparkle/Cedric Moncriffe	Alan Karpe/Dell Yount
Princess Puffer/Angela Prysock	Karlah Hamilton
Mayor Thomas Sapsea/James Hitchens	George Spelvin
Durdles/Nick Cricker	Eric Burgan
Deputy/Master Cricker	Mark Aldrich
Flo/Florence Gill	Pam Mizell
Butler/Philip Bax	Mike Carruthers
Horace/Nicholas Michael	Christopher Harrod/Alan Karpe
Bazzard/Philip Bax	Mike Carruthers
Dick Datchery	???????

Citizens: Mirla Criste Agnir, Brett Alan, Richard L. Breaks, Preston Dyar, Elizabeth Green, Christopher Harrod, J. R. Hontz, Lisa Liguori, Pam Mizell, Kathy Reid, Michael Shiles

MUSICAL NUMBERS: There You Are, Two Kinsmen, Moonfall, Wages of Sin, Jasper's Vision, Ceylon, Both Sides of the Coin, Perfect Strangers, No Good Can Come from Bad, Never the Luck, Off to the Races, Private Investigation, The Name of Love, Don't Quit While You're Ahead, The Garden Path to Hell

A musical in two acts with a prologue and a solution. The action takes place in 1872.

George Whitney Photos

Top Left: Marie-Laurence Danvers, C. M. Yates and Cast
Below: Entire company

INTO THE WOODS

Music & Lyrics, Stephen Sondheim; Book, James Lapine; Director, Mr. Lapine; Presented by Tom Mallow and Pace Theatrical Group in association with Heidi Landesman, Rocco Landesman, Rick Steiner, M. Anthony Fisher, Frederick H. Mayerson, and Jujamcyn Theaters; Sets, Tony Straiges; Lighting, Richard Nelson; Costumes, Ann Hould-Ward; Based on original concepts by Patricia Zipprodt & Ann Hould-Ward; Hairstylist, Phyllis Della Illien; Orchestrations, Jonathan Tunick; Musical Staging, Lar Lubovitch; Musical Director, Randy Booth; Casting, Joanna Merlin; General Management, David Strong Warner/American Theatre Productions; Company Manager, Alan Ross Kosher; Props, Edward "Buddy" Horton, Leon B. Chenier, Jr.; Wardrobe, Bobbi Langhofer, Lucy Martinov; Stage Managers, Dan W. Langhofer, Joseph Sheridan; Press, Patt Dale Associates/Joshua Ellis Office. Opened in the Parker Playhouse, Ft. Lauderdale, Fl., on Nov. 22, 1988 and still touring May 31, 1989. For original Broadway production, see *Theatre World* Vol. 44.

CAST

Narrator/Mysterious Man .... Rex Robbins
Cinderella .... Kathleen Rowe McAllen/Jill Geddes
Jack .... Robert Duncan McNeill
Baker .... Ray Gill
Baker's Wife .... Mary Gordon Murray
Cinderella's Step-mother .... Jo Ann Cunningham
Florinda .... Susan Gordon-Clark
Lucinda .... Danette Cuming
Jack's Mother .... Charlotte Rae
Little Red Ridinghood .... Tracy Katz
Witch .... Cleo Laine
Cinderella's Father .... Don Crosby
Cinderella's Mother .... Anne Rickenbacher
Wolf/Cinderella's Prince .... Chuck Wagner
Rapunzel .... Marguerite Lowell
Rapunzel's Prince .... Douglas Sills
Grandmother/Giant .... Nora Mae Lyng
Steward .... Marcus Olson

UNDERSTUDIES: Don Crosby, Marcus Olson, Jonathan Hadley, James Weatherstone, Paul Jackel, Douglas Sills, Danette Cuming, Susan Gordon-Clark, Nora Mae Lyng, Anne Rickenbacher, Jill Geddes, Marguerite Lowell, Jody Walker-Lichtig, Jo Ann Cunningham

MUSICAL NUMBERS: see Broadway Calendar

Martha Swope Photos
Top Left: Tracy Katz, Chuck Wagner
Top Right: Charlotte Rae, Robert Duncan McNeill

Above: Ray Gill, Mary Gordon Murray, Cleo Laine

Below: Tracy Katz, Robert Duncan McNeill, Kathleen Rowe McAllen, Ray Gill, Cleo Laine

Craig Schulman
Right: Joe Locarro

LES MISÉRABLES

For original creative credits and musical numbers, see Broadway Calendar. Opened Tuesday, Dec. 15, 1987 in the Shubert Theatre in Boston, and still touring May 31, 1989. For original Broadway production, see *Theatre World* Vol. 43.

CAST

Jean Valjean	William Solo †1
Javert	Herndon Lackey †2
Bishop	Kevin McGuire †3
Fantine	Diane Fratantoni †4
Young Cosette/Young Eponine	Christina Marie DeAngelis †5, Christa Larson, Sara Nelson †6
Mme. Thenardier	Victoria Clark
Thenardier	Tom Robbins †7
Gavroche	Lantz Landry †8, Sam Brent Riegel
Eponine	Renee Veneziale
Enjolras	John Herrera †9
Marius	Hugh Panaro
Cosette	Tamara Jenkins

ENSEMBLE: Mark McVey, Michael McCormick, Scott Elliot, Andy Gale, Tom Robbins, Bjorn Johnson, Deborah Bradshaw, Willy Falk, Rick Sparks, Gary Harger, Robert DuSold, Michael Babin, Rosalyn Rahn, Olga Merediz, Carolee Carmello, Bertilla Baker, Kirsti Carnahan, Jennifer Naimo, Betsy True, Al DeCristo, Keith Rice, Kurt Johns, Barbara Walsh, Melissa Errilo, Kathy Taylor, Jill Hayman.
†succeeded by: 1. Craig Schulman, 2. Charles Pistone, 3. Claude R. Tessier, 4. Ann Crumb, 5. Marlo Landry, 6. Susannah Mulloy, 7. Michael McCormick, 8. Lantz Landry, Geoff Soffer, 9. Joe Locarro

Michael Le Poer Trench, Bob Marshak Photos

Michael McCormick

114

LES MISÉRABLES

For original creative credits and musical numbers, see Broadway Calendar. Opened Wednesday, Nov. 30, 1988 in Festival Hall, Tampa, Fl., and still touring May 31, 1989. For original Broadway production, see *Theatre World* Vol. 43.

CAST

Jean Valjean .... Gary Barker
Javert .... Peter Samuel
Bishop .... Claude R. Tessier
Fantine .... Hollis Resnik
Young Cosette/Young Eponine .... Eden Riegel, Tracy Ward
Mme. Thenardier .... Linda Kerns
Thenardier .... Paul Ainsley
Gavroche .... Andrew Harrison Leeds, Sam Brent Riegel
Eponine .... Michele Maika
Enjolras .... Greg Zerkle
Marius .... Matthew Porretta
Cosette .... Jacquelyn Piro

ENSEMBLE: Richard Poole, Jeff Gardner, Craig Wells, Rohn Seykell, Clay Guthrie, Brian Lynch, Jerry Christakos, Beth Williams, Reed Armstrong, Christopher Pecaro, Adam Heller, Jeanne Smith, Merri Sugarman, Christy Howard, Anne L. Nathan, Lisa Vroman, Dana Lynn Caruso, Cindi Page

Michael Le Poer Trench, Bob Marshak Photos

Right: Hollis Resnik

Gary Barker, Peter Samuel

Members of company
Above: Female chorus

Tim Curry, Susan Cella *(Ron Scherl)*

ME AND MY GIRL

For creative credits and musical numbers, see Broadway Calendar. Presented by the Noel Gay Organisation Ltd., Terry Allen Kramer, James M. Nederlander, Strada Entertainment; General Manager, Ralph Roseman; Company Managers, Richard Grayson, Alan R. Markinson; Stage Managers, George Martin, Harold Goldfaden, Tracy Crum; Wardrobe, Sharon Lewis, Charles C. Crutchfield; Assistant Conductor, Janet Aycock; Press, Jeffrey Richards Associates, Norman Zagier. Opened Thursday, Oct. 3, 1988 in San Francisco's Golden Gate Theatre, and still touring May 31, 1989. For original Broadway company, see *Theatre World*, Vol. 43.

CAST

Lady Jacqueline Carstone	Susan Cella
Hon. Gerald Bolingbroke	Nick Ulett †1
Stockbrokers	Cleve Asbury, John Salvatore, Roger Preston Smith
Herbert Parchester	Walter Charles †2
Lord Battersby	Ralph Farnworth
Lady Battersby	Evelyn Page
Sir Jasper Tring	Gordon Connell †3
Maria Duchess of Dene	Ursula Smith †4
Sir John Tremayne	Barrie Ingham
Charles Hethersett, butler	Keith Perry
Bill Snibson	Tim Curry
Sally Smith	Donna Bullock
Pub Pianist	Brad Moranz †5
Mrs. Worthington-Worthington	Melody Jones
Lady Diss/Clara Damming	Lou Williford
Lady Brighton	Mary Stout
Bob Barking	Peter J. Saputo
Telegraph Boy	Jamie Torcellini
Mrs. Brown	Evelyn Page †6
Constable	Michael Hayward-Jones
Swings	Kimberly Kalember, William Alan Coats

ENSEMBLE: Cleve Asbury, Stanley Bojarski, Dani Brownlee, Leigh Catlett, William Alan Coats, Scott Dainton, Michael Hayward-Jones, Melody Jones, Kimberly Kalember, Gregg Kirsopp, Ann Nieman, Tina Parise, Linda Paul, John Salvatore, Peter J. Saputo, Roger Preston Smith, Mary Stout, Peggy Taphorn, Jamie Torcellini, Lou Williford, George Wright

†Succeeded by: 1. David Cromwell, 2. Erick Devine, 3. Louis S. Crume, 4. Lenka Peterson, 5. Gregg Kirsopp, 6. Lou Williford

ME AND MY GIRL

For creative credits and musical numbers, see Broadway Calendar. General Manager, Ralph Roseman; Company Managers, Richard Grayson, Mary Miller; Stage Managers, George Martin, Harold Goldfaden, Cheryl Mintz; Props, Joseph Harris, Jr., Jack Montgomery; Wardrobe, Linda Berry, Sharon A. Lewis; Wig Master, Tiv Davenport; Associate Conductor, Robert Hirschorn; Press, Jeffrey Richards Associates/Susan Chicoine. For original Broadway production, see *Theatre World* Vol. 43.

CAST

Lady Jacqueline Carstone	Barbara Passolt
Hon. Gerald Bolingbroke	Stephen Temperley
Stockbrokers	John Salvatore, Roger Preston Smith, Jeff Williams
Herbert Parchester	Erick Devine
Sir Jasper Tring	Louis S. Crume
Maria, Duchess of Dene	Sylvia O'Brien
Sir John Tremayne	Gary Gage
Charles Hethersett	Keith Perry
Bill Snibson	James Brennan
Sally Smith	Sheri Cowart
Pub Pianist	Gregg Kirsopp
Mrs. Worthington-Worthington	Melody Jones
Clara Damming	Lou Williford
Lady Brighton	Jane Strauss
Bob Barking	Gregg Kirsopp
Telegraph Boy	Don Johanson
Mrs. Brown	Lou Williford
Lambeth Girl	Jane Strauss
Constable	Michael Hayward-Jones

ENSEMBLE: Stanley Bojarski, Danie Brownlee, Leight Catlett, William Alan Coats, Scott Dainton, Michael Hayward-Jones, Don Johanson, Melody Jones, Kimberly Kalember, Gregg Kirsopp, Ann Nieman, Donald Norris, Tina Parise, Linda Paul, John Salvatore, Roger Preston Smith, Jane Strauss, Peggy Taphorn, Jeff Williams, Lou Williford, George Wright

James Brennan, Sheri Cowart

ME AND MY GIRL

For creative credits and musical numbers, see Broadway Calendar. Presented by the Noel Gay Organisation Ltd., Terry Allen Kramer, James M. Nederlander, Strada Entertainment; Musical Director, Michael D. Biagi; General Manager, Ralph Roseman; Company Managers, Richard Grayson, Mary Miller; Technical Director, Jeremiah Harris; Stage Managers, George Martin, Harold Goldfaden, Cheryl Mintz; Associate Conductor, Jeff Conrad; Props, Keith Newton; Press, Jeffrey Richards Associates/Susan Chicoine. Opened Tuesday, Apr. 18, 1988 in the Civic Auditorium, Jacksonville, FL, and closed May 7, 1989 in St. Petersburg, Fl. For original Broadway production, see *Theatre World* Vol. 43

CAST

Lady Jacqueline Carstone	Barbara Passolt
Hon. Gerald Bolingbroke	Stephen Temperley
Stockbrokers	John Salvatore, Roger Preston Smith, Jeff Williams
Herbert Parchester	Erick Devine
Sir Jasper Tring	Louis S. Crume
Maria, Duchess of Dene	Lenka Peterson
Sir John Tremayne	Gary Gage
Charles Hethersett	Keith Perry
Bill Snibson	James Young
Sally Smith	Sheri Cowart
Pub Pianist/Bob Barking	Gregg Kirsopp
Mrs. Worthington-Worthington	Melody Jones
Clara Damming/Mrs. Brown	Lou Williford
Lady Brighton/Lambeth Girl	Bette Glenn
Constable	Michael Hayward-Jones

James Young, Sheri Cowart

Right: James Young, Barbara Passolt

Top Left: (C) Passolt, Louis Crume, Melody Jones

Ken Howard Photos

117

SOPHISTICATED LADIES

Concept, Donald McKayle; Direction/Choreography, Claudia Asbury; Originally by Donald McKayle and Michael Smuin; Music, Duke Ellington; Sets, Yuri Kuper; Costumes, Slava Zaitsev, Willa Kim; Lighting, Richard Winkler; Musical Supervision/Arrangements, Paul Chihara; Conductor, Boris Frumkin; Musical/Dance Arrangements, Lloyd Mayers; Vocal Arrangements, Malcolm Dodds, Lloyd Moyers; Sound, Christopher Bond; Assistant Choreographer, Roger Spivy; Casting, Stuart Howard, Amy Schecter; General Manager, Richard Martini; Presented by Jarvis Theatre Projects and Irving Schwartz in association with USSR Cultural Fund, Theater Worker's Union and Soyuzteatr under the auspices of the original producers Roger Berlind, Manny Fox, Sandra Gilman, Burton L. Litwin and Louise Westergaard; Company Manager, Patricia Crowe; Stage Managers, Allen McMullen, Roger Spivy, Crystal Williams; Props, Steve Callahan; Wardrobe, Donna Peck; Wigs, Howard Leonard, Jr.; Production Assistant, Mark Kornbluth; Press, Peter Cromarty & Co./Kevin P. McAnarney, David Gersten, Kevin Brockman. Tour opened Saturday, Oct. 1, 1988 in Moscow, Russia, and still touring May 31, 1989. For original Broadway production, see *Theatre World* Vol. 37.

CAST

Hinton Battle	Gregg Burge
Donna Wood	Lonette McKee
Christina Saffran	Jackie Patterson

Cleve Asbury

and Lauren Goler, Mary Frances McCatty, Elise D. Neal, Gayle Samuels, Brant Baldwin, T. Michael Dalton, Kevyn Morrow, Alan Onickel. Tim Connell, Mary Lilygren, Crystal Williams, David Washington

Gregg Burge, Lonette McKee

Top: Gregg Burge (C)

PROFESSIONAL REGIONAL COMPANIES

(Failure to submit material necessitated omission of several companies)

ACT/A CONTEMPORARY THEATRE

Seattle, Washington
Twenty-fourth Season

Founding Director, Gregory Falls; Managing Director, Susan Trapnell Moritz; Producing Director, Phil Schermer; Artistic Director, Jeff Steitzer; Stage Directors, David Ira Goldstein, Lee Shallat, Jeff Steitzer; Set Designers, Bill Forrester, Michael Olic, Shelly Henze Schermer, Scott Weldin; Costume Designers, Laura Crow, Nanrose Buchman, Frances Kenny, Michael Olich, Rose Pederson, Sally Richardson; Lighting Designers, Jody Briggs, Paulie Jenkins, Jennifer Lupton, Rick Paulsen, Phil Schermer; Stage Managers, Ten Eyck Swackhmaer, James Verdery, Craig Weindling, Manuel Zarate; Press, Michael Sande.

PRODUCTIONS & CASTS

MERRILY WE ROLL ALONG by Stephen Sondheim and George Furth. CAST: Joseph Dellger, Linda Edmond, Joseph McNally, Jo Leffingwell, Rick Tutor, Suzanne Irving, Mark Anders, Richard Farrell, Kevin Hadley, Amy Harris, Craig A. Huisenga, David Hunter Koch, Terry Palasz, Skip Roberts, Kristina Sanborn, Frankie Trevino, Diane Weyrick.
MRS. CALIFORNIA by Doris Baizley. CAST: Gun-Marie Nilsson, Cheri Sorenson, Robert Nadir, Kristina Sanborn, Sheree Galpert, Linda Emond, Rich Hawkins.
A CHORUS OF DISAPPROVAL by Alan Ayckbourn. CAST: R. Hamilton Wright, John Alward, Marianne Owen, Karen Meyer, Todd Moeller, Jo Vetter, Susan Ludlow-Corzatte, Linda Emond, Robert Nadir, Rick Tutor, Kurt Beattie, Morgan Strickland, Shellie Shulkin.
GOD'S COUNTRY by Steven Dietz. CAST: John Alward, Kurt Beattie, Gordon Carpenter, Anne Christianson, Linda Emond, Matthew Flemming, John Gilbert, Rex McDowell, Marianne Owen, Ben Prager, Michael Winters.
PRINCIPIA SCRIPTORIAE by Richard Nelson. CAST: J. Christopher O'Connor, J. Ed Araiza, Winston Jose Rocha-Castillo, Laurence Ballard, Brian Thompson, Rich Hawkins, Michael Winters.
THE VOICE OF THE PRAIRIE by John Olive. CAST: Laurence Ballard, Eric Ray Anderson, Jane Jones.
A CHRISTMAS CAROL by Charles Dickens, adapted by Gregory A. Falls. CAST: Michael Winters, J. Christopher O'Connor, Tony Soper, Michael Santo, Bill Dore, Frankie Trevino, Mark Drusch, Marc R. dela Cruz, Tawnya Pettiford-Wates, David Drummond, David P. Whitehead, Mark W. Branom, Suzanne Bouchard, Laura Kenny, Ryan O'Connor, Ina Daniels, Gretchen V. O'Connor, Claudine Wallace.

Joan Marcus Photos
Right: Joseph McNally, Kristina Sanborn, Joseph Dellger

Top: Linda Edmond, McNally, Dellger, Suzanne Irving, Rick Tutor in "Merrily We Roll Along" *(Chris Bennion Photos)*

Jane Jones, Laurence Ballard in "Voice of the Prairie"

Gun-Marie Nilsson (L) in "Mrs. California"

ACTORS THEATRE OF LOUISVILLE

Louisville, Kentucky
Twenty-fifth Season

Producing Director, Jon Jory; Administrative Director, Alexander Speer; Associate Director, Marilee Hebert-Slater; Development, Rhea Lehman; Press, James Seacat; Scenic Designer, Paul Owen; Costumes, Lewis D. Rampino; Lighting, Ralph Dressler; Sound, Mark Hendren; Props, Ron Rially; Production Manager, Frazier W. Marsh; Stage Manager, Lori M. Doyle; Asst. to the Producing Director, Zan Sawyer-Dailey; Technical Director, Steve Goodin; Wardrobe Supervisor, Melissa Canaday.

RESIDENT COMPANY: Bob Burrus, Barbara Gulan, Suzanna Hay, Ray Fry, Bill McNulty, Bob Morrisey, Adale O'Brien, Mark Sawyer-Dailey.

PRODUCTIONS: *Peter Pan* by J. M. Barrie, *Engaged* by W. S. Gilbert, *The Whore and the H'Empress*—Interviews from Henry Mayhew's London Labour and the London Poor, adapted for the stage by Jonathan Bolt, *The Nerd* by Larry Shue, *The Gift of the Magi,* adaptation, music and lyrics by Peter Ekstrom, *A Christmas Carol,* adapted by Barbara Field from the Charles Dickens novel, *Harvey* by Mary Chase, *Les Liaisons Dangereuses* by Christopher Hampton from the novel by Choderlos de Laclos, *Beehive* by Larry Gallagher, *The Tempest* by William Shakespeare.

PREMIERES: *The Bug* by Richard Strand, *Bone-the-Fish* by Arthur Kopit, *God's Country* by Steven Dietz, *Autumn Elegy* by Charlene Redick, *Tales of the Lost Formicans* by Constance Congdon, *Stained Glass* by William F. Buckley, Jr.

Top Right: Lizbeth Mackay, Barbara Gulan, Ray Fry in "Engaged" *David Talbott Photos*

Right Center: George Gerdes, Bob Burrus in "Blood Issue" *(Richard Trigg Photo)*

Marissa Chibas, Gerry Bamman in "Engaged"

Julianne Moore in "Bone-the-Fish"

Bettye Fitzpatrick, Annalee Jefferies, Eberle Thomas in
"Road to Mecca"

Right: Robin Moseley, John Spencer in
"Frankie and Johnny . . ."

"Merry Wives of Windsor, Texas"

THE ALLEY THEATRE

Houston, Texas
Forty-second Season

Interim Artistic Director, Jim Bernhard; Production Manager, Bettye Fitzpatrick;
Interim General Manager, Christopher Kawolsky; Press, Teresa Gladden.

PRODUCTIONS & CASTS

THE ROAD TO MECCA by Athol Fugard; Director, Beth Sanford; Set, Elva
Stewart; Costumes, Lauren K. Lambie; Sound, Daniel Van Pelt; Lighting, John E.
Ore; with Bettye Fitzpatrick, Annalee Jefferies, Eberle Thomas.
FRANKIE AND JOHNNY IN THE CLAIR DE LUNE by Terrence McNally;
Director, Sidney Berger; Set, Jay Michael Jagim; Costumes, Lauren K. Lambie;
Lighting, John E. Ore; Sound, Daniel Van Pelt; with Robin Moseley, John Spencer.
THE MERRY WIVES OF WINDSOR, TEXAS by John L. Haber, from William
Shakespeare's play; Music and lyrics, Tommy Thompson, Jack Herrick, Bland
Simpson, Jim Wann; Musical Director, Jack Herrick; Set, Charles S. Kadin; Cos-
tumes, Donna Kress; Director, Thomas Bullard.
THE VOICE OF THE PRAIRIE by John Olive; Director, James Martin; Set, John
E. Ore; with Bob Higgins, Annalee Jefferies, Rutherford Cravens, Adam J. Brooks,
Shauna Hicks, David Manis.
A VIEW FROM THE BRIDGE by Arthur Miller; Director, Beth Sanford; Set,
William Bloodgood; with James Belcher, James Black, Bob Marich, Philip Le-
Strange, Julie Bayer, Holly Barron, Brandon Smith, Charles Sanders, Michael David
Wright, Robert Graham, Jim McQueen, Timothy Arrington, Mary Ryan, Jonathan
Fishman, Tom Santos, Jill Brennan, Greg Schrader, Lisa McEwen.
ALFRED STIEGLITZ LOVES O'KEEFFE by Lanie Robertson; Director, Eberle
Thomas; Set, Jay Michael Jagim; Lighting, Pamela Gray Bones; with Annalee
Jefferies, Robert Strane.
HEAVEN'S HARD by Jordan Budde; Director, Allen R. Belknap; Set, Keith Belli;
Music, Brian Hurley; with Conan McCarty, Mary Doyle, Nora Chester, Calista
Flockhart.
THE WALTZ OF THE TOREADORS by Jean Anouilh; translated by Lucienne
Hill; Director, James Martin; Lighting, James Sale; Set, Jay Michael Jagim; with
Bettye Fitzpatrick, Charles Krohn, Conan McCarty, Allison Marich, Malinda
Bailey, Robert Strane, Charlene Bigham, Annalee Jefferies, Elaine L. Taylor, Jim
Bernhard, Lisa McEwen, Jill Brennan, Mary Ryan.
STEEL MAGNOLIAS by Robert Harling, Director, Beth Sanford; Lighting, Robert
Jared; with Carolyn Cope; Ellen Lauren, Marjorie Carroll, Clarinda Ross, Sally
Parrish, Bettye Fitzpatrick.

(Peter Yenne, Mark Navarro Photos)

Mary Doyle, Conan McCarty in "Heaven's Hard"

ALLIANCE THEATRE COMPANY

Atlanta, Georgia
Twentieth Season

Artistic Director, Robert J. Farley; Managing Director, Edith H. Love; Associate Artistic Director, Kenny Leon; General Manager, T. Jane Bishop; Production Manager, Rixon Hammond; Literary Manager, Sandra Deer; Resident Designer, Susan E. Mickey; Director of Marketing, Arnold; Director of Development, Betty Blondeau-Russell; Technical Director, Bob Hoffman; Stage Managers, Michael B. Paul, Dale C. Lawrence, Pat Flora, Patricia Munford, Gretchen Van Horne.

PRODUCTIONS & CASTS

ANIMAL CRACKERS: THE MARX BROTHERS MUSICAL. Director, Larry Carpenter; Choreographer, Baayork Lee; Sets, James Leonard Joy. CAST: Joel Blum, Jack Brenton, Karen Culliver, Frank Ferrante, Barry Finel, Deanna Ford, Christine Gradl, Randall Graham, Peggy Hewett, Eric Huston, Joel Imbody, Virginia King, Kurt Knudson, Judy Langfrod, Karen Lifshey, Les Marsden, Mary Frances McCatty, Ken Leigh Rogers, Jon D. Schwartz, Lise Simms, Peter Slutsker, Victoria Tabaka, Michael Watson, Christopher Wells.
DOUBLE DOUBLE by Eric Elice & Roger Rees. Director, Munson Hicks; Sets, John Falabella. CAST: Michele Farr, Francois Giroday.
PETER PAN. Director, Fran Soeder; Sets, James Leonard Joy. CAST: Sergio Aguirre, Toi Campbell, David Carlton, Melody Combs, Michael Cumpsty, Stanton Cunningham, Zack Finch, Andy Greenway, Joel Imbody, Ken Jennings, Doug Johnson, Bryan C. Jones, Jeff Kolesky, Romelle Lesada, Doug Lothes, Judge Luckey, Ann Morrison, Tommy Nowell Jr., Brian Parks, Jeff Portell, Robert Ray, Ben Reece, Judith Robinson, Jay Scovill, Jeremy Sias, Calvin Smith, Lauren Thompson, Thaddeus Valdez, Brad Wages.
JOE TURNER'S COME AND GONE by August Wilson. Director, Kenny Leon; Set, Michael Olich. CAST: Lynn Brown, Aaron Fisher, Je Nei Fleming, Michael Genet, William Jay, Carol Mitchell Leon, James Mayberry, Afemo Omilami, Chuck Paterson, Iris Little-Roberts, Sharlene Ross.
NOISES OFF by Michael Frayn. Director, Robert J. Farley; Set, Michael Stauffer. CAST: Sharon Brewer, Brenda Bynum, Monica Carr, Frank Groseclose, Larry Larson, Levi Lee, Cathy Mangrum, David Milford, Pete Shinn.
AMADEUS by Peter Shaffer. Director, Fran Soeder; Sets, James Leonard Joy. CAST: Kim Bowers-Rheay, Melody Combs, Constance Corder, George Ede, Richard Frank, Doug Johnson, Tom Key, Doug Lothes, Judge Luckey, Tess Malis, John Messenger, Brian Parks, Andrew Polk, Robert Ray, Alec Robeson, Jay Scovill, Calvin Smith, Thaddeus Valdez, Brad Wages.
DRIVING MISS DAISY by Alfred Uhry. Director, Robert J. Farley; Sets, Michael Stauffer. CAST: Al Hamacher, William Hall Jr., Mike Hodge, Mary Nell Santacroce.
TREASURE ISLAND adapted for stage by Levi Lee & Larry Larson. Director, Levi Lee; Sets, Michael Stauffer. CAST: LaLa Cochran, Bruce Evers, Al Garrison, Buck Newman, Allen O'Reilly, Simon Reynolds, Kee Strong, Ken Strong, Clayton Surratt.
BEAUTY AND THE BEAST adapted for stage by Sandra Deer. Director, Skip Foster; Sets, Victor Becker. CAST: Brad Davidorf, Jill Jackson, Terence Jenkins, Stephanie Kallos, Nancy Ann Lowery, Elizabeth Omilami, Jeff Portell, Brad Sherril, Suzanne Ventulett.

Left: Andrew Polk, Melody Combs in "Amadeus"
Above: Chuck Patterson, Iris Little-Roberts in "Joe Turner's
. . ." Top: Ann Morrison as "Peter Pan" (C), Ken Jennings
(Mr. Smee) (R)
Jonathan Burnette Photos

Mary Nell Santacroce, William Hall, Jr. in "Driving Miss Daisy"

Brad Sherrill, Jill Jackson in "Beauty and the Beast"

122

Gina Ferrall, Michael McShane in "A Funny Thing
Happened . . . ,"
Top Left: Rick Hamilton, Dennis Ludlow, Christopher
McCann, Scott Freeman in "Nothing Sacred"
Below: Kate Brickley, Lawrence Hecht in "Feathers"

AMERICAN CONSERVATORY THEATRE

San Francisco, California
Twenty-third Season

Artistic Director, Edward Hastings; Managing Director, John Sullivan; Associate Artistic Directors, Joy Carlin, Dennis Powers; Production Director, James Haire; Stage Directors, Paul Blake, Joy Carlin, Sabin Epstein, Edward Hastings, Claude Purdy, Michael Smuin, Albert Takazauckas, Laird Williamson, Robert Woodruff; Musical Directors, Dwight D. Andrews, John Johnson, Harper MacKay, Betty Anne Siu Junn Wong; Set Designers, Robert Blackman, Scott F. Bradley, Joel Fontaine, Ralph Funicello, Barbara J. Mesney, George Tsypin; Costume Designers, Beaver I. Bauer, Jovita Chow, David F. Draper, Robert Fletcher, Susan Hilferty, Pamela Peterson, Lydia Tanji, Warren Travis, Sandra Woodall; Lighting Designer, Derek Duarte; Sound & Music Designers, Barney Jones, Stephen LeGrand, Gary Schwantes; Stage Managers, Karen Van Zandt, Eugene Barcone, Bruce Elsperger, Alice Elliott Smith.

PRODUCTIONS: *Marco Millions* by Eugene O'Neill; *Woman in Mind* by Alan Ayckbourn; *A Christmas Carol* by Charles Dickens; *Side by Side by Sondheim; Joe Turner's Come and Gone* by August Wilson; *When We Are Married* by J. B. Priestley; *Saint Joan* by George Bernard Shaw; *Nothing Sacred* by George F. Walker; *A Funny Thing Happened on the Way to the Forum* by Larry Gelbart, Burt Shevelove, Stephen Sondheim.

COMPANY: Walter Addison, Dawna Bailey, Adilah Barnes, Cynthia Bassham, Velina Brown, Roscoe Lee Browne, Richard Butterfield, Mark Daniel Cade, Joy Carlin, Nancy Carlin, James Craven, George Deloy, Peter Donat, Drew Eshelman, Gina Ferrall, Jack Fletcher, Scott Freeman, John Furse, Rick Hamilton, Lawrence Hecht, Ed Hodson, Steven Anthony Jones, Martin Kildare, Randall Duk Kim, Ruth Kobart, Alan Kopischke, Barry Kraft, Kimberley LaMarque, Anne Lawder, Michael Learned, Karen Lew, Dennis Ludlow, Frances Lee McCain, Christopher McCain, Michael McShane, David Maier, Andrea Marcovicci, Paula Markovitz, Deborah May, Delores Mitchell, Fredi Olster, Luis Oropeza, Frank Ottiwell, William Paterson, Daniel Reichert, Ray Reinhardt, Amber Russ, Michael Scott Ryan, Freda Foh Shen, Garland J. Simpson, Anna Deavere Smith, Keeley Stanley, Sun Dao Lin, Howard Swain, Cathy Thomas-Grant, Tom Todoroff, Sydney Walker, Stephen Weingartner, Michael Winters, Gretchen Wyler, Kelvin Han Yee.

Left Center: Sun Dao Lin, Randall Duk Kim in
"Marco Millions"
Harry Wade, Marty Sohl Photos

Sydney Walker, Walter Addison in "Nothing Sacred"

Cherry Jones, Derek Smith, Alvin Epstein in "The Miser"
Top: Cherry Jones, Tom Hewitt in "Life Is a Dream"
Top Left: Thomas Derrah, Derek Smith in "The Serpent
Woman"

AMERICAN REPERTORY THEATRE

Cambridge, Massachusetts

Artistic Director, Robert Brustein; Managing Director, Robert J. Orchard; Associate Director, Richard Riddell; General Manager, Jonathan Seth Miller; Director of Development & Long-Range Planning, Charles Marz; Director of Communications, Jan Graham Geidt; Director of Press and Marketing, Henry Lussier; Technical Director, Max Leventhal; Technical Director (Loeb Drama Center), Donald R. Soulé; Stage Managers, Abbie H. Katz, Anne S. King; Properties Manager, Patricia Quinlan; Lighting Supervisor, Frank Butler; Resident Sound Designer/Engineer, Stephen D. Santomenna; Stage Supervisor, Steven Landry.
RESIDENT COMPANY: Michael Allart, David Asher, Joseph Daly, Thomas Derrah, John S. Drabik, Alvin Epstein, Benjamin Evett, Jeremy Geidt, Pamela Gein, Tom Hewitt, Steve Hofvendahl, Cherry Jones, John Christopher Jones, Jerome Kilty, Justine Lewis, Harry S. Murphy, Mary Lou Rosato, Sandra Shipley, Derek Smith, Daniel Von Bargen.
PRODUCTIONS: *Serpent Woman* by Carlo Gozzi, Director: Andrei Serban; *Platonov* by Anton Chekhov, adapted and directed by Liviu Ciulei; *Mastergate* (World Premiere) by Larry Gelbart; Director, Michael Engler; Sets, Philip Jung; Costumes, Candice Donnelly; Lighting, James F. Ingalls; *The Miser* by Moliere, Director, Andrei Serban; *Life Is a Dream* by Pedro Calderon de la barca, translated by Edwin Honig; Director, Anne Bogart.

Richard Feldman Photos

Cherry Jones, Daniel von Bargen, Bari Hochwald in
"Mastergate"

THE AMERICAN STAGE COMPANY

Teaneck, New Jersey
Fourth Season

Artistic Director, Paul Sorvino; Executive Producer, Theodore Rawlins; Executive Director, James R. Singer; Business Manager, Robert A. Lusko; Artistic Associate, Sheldon Epps; Press, Nikki Brown; Casting Director, Judy Henderson, Alycia Aumuller; Production Manager, Alson E. Barrett Jr.; Technical Director, Garrit Lydecker; Stage Directors, Michael Flanagan, Stuart Ross, Roderick Cook, N. Richard Nash, Bill Guske; Sets, James Morgan, Daniel Ettinger; Costumes, Barbara A. Bell, Barbara Forbes, Deborah Stein; Lighting, Stuart Duke, Kenneth Posner; Stage Managers, Mary Ellen Allison, Linda Carol Young, Peter Jablonski, Cathy White, Michael J. Chudinski.

PRODUCTIONS & CASTS

THE GLASS MENAGERIE by Tennessee Williams; Director, Michael Flanagan. CAST: Don Harvey, Ann Hillary, Jane Fleiss, Kevin Kilner.
FOREVER PLAID *(World Premiere)* by Stuart Ross; Director, Stuart Ross; Musical Supervisor and Orchestrations, James Raitt. CAST: John Caraccioli, Jason Graae, Don Kehr, Dirk Lumbard.
HOME GAMES *(World Premiere)* by Tom Ziegler; Director, Roderick Cook. CAST: John Braden, Kymberly Dakin, Michael E. Knight.
THE BLUEBIRD OF HAPPINESS (World Premiere) by N. Richard Nash; Director, N. Richard Nash. CAST: Rose Arrick, Jeffrey Hayenga, Pauline Lepore, Don Peoples, Tyagi Schwartz.
Ed Linderman's BROADWAY JUKEBOX conceived by Ed Linderman; Director, Bill Guske; Musical Arrangements & Piano, Jim Grady. CAST: Karen Culliver, Karen Jablos-Alexander, Ed Linderman, Mark McGrath, Gerry McIntyre, Jana Robbins, Ray Wills.

Right: Ray Wills, Jana Robbins, Karen Culliver, Ed Linderman, Gerry McIntyre, Karen Jablons-Alexander, Mark McGrath in "Broadway Jukebox"
Top: John Caraccioli, Jason Graae, Don Kehr, Dirk Lumbard in "Forever Plaid"

Kevin Kilner, Don Harvey, Ann Hillary
Above: Jane Fleiss in "Glass Menagerie"

Michael E. Knight, Kymberly Dakin, John Braden in "Home Games"

ARENA STAGE

Washington, D.C.
Thirty-eighth Season

Producing Director, Zelda Fischandler; Managing Director, William Stewart; Associate Producing Director, Douglas C. Wager; Press, Carla Forbes-Kelly; Directors, Liviu Ciulei, Douglas C. Wager, Tazewell Thompson, Mel Shapiro, Max Mayer, Garland Wright, Paul Weidner; Set Designers, Liviu Ciulei, George Tsypin, Adrianne Lobel, Karl Eigsti, David Glenn, John Arnone, Zack Brown, Arden Fingerhut, James Leonard Joy; Costume Designers, Smaranda Branescu, Marjorie Slaiman, Betty Siegel, Zack Brown, Tadashi Suzuki, Amanda J. Klein; Lighting Designers, Allen Lee Hughes, Frances Aronson, Nancy Schertler, Christopher Townsend, Arden Fingerhut; Stage Managers, Wendy Streeter, Maxine Krasowski Bertone, Jeffrey A. Alspaugh, Sarah Joem Bradley, Pat Cochran, Jessica Evans, Benita Hofstetter, Ruth Feldman.
RESIDENT COMPANY: Stanley Anderson, Richard Bauer, Marissa Copeland, Ralph Cosham, Terrence Currier, Mark Hammer, Tom Hewitt, Tana Hicken, Bob Kirsh, David Marks, Cary Anne Spear, Henry Strozier, John Leonard Thompson, Halo Wines
GUEST ARTISTS: Jason Adams, George Alexander, Kim Bey, Casey Biggs, Roxann Biggs, Paul Binotto, Sandra Bowie, Lucie Brightman, Leon Addison Brown, James Brown-Orleans, Ron Butler, L. Peter Callender, Karma Camp, Helen Carey, Frank Cava, Marissa Chibas, Patricia Conolly, Kevin Crawford, Abraham Dobkin, Brian Donnelly, Vladimir Ekzarkhov, John Elko, Ida Elrod Eustis, Pamela Everett, Peter Jay Fernandez, Constance Fowlkes, Mark Frawley, Inga Frederic, Deborah Geneviere, Gail Grate, Margo Hall, Bruce Harvie, Betty Henritze, Andi Hopkins, Beth Howland, Michael W. Howell, Isiah Johnson, Keith Johnson, Jean Kauffman, Ann Kittredge, Lily Knight, Danielle T. Koch, Dana Krueger, Clayton LeBouef, Adriane Lenox, LaDonna Mabry, Walt MacPherson, Kathleen Mahony-Bennett, Sarah C. Marshall, Elizabeth McGovern, Sharon Moore, Clem Moorman, Bill Mondy, Sam Morgan, Michael Noel, Michael O'Hare, Nick Olcott, Gordon Paddison, Petronia Paley, Jill Powell, Faye Richie, Tonia Rowe, John Scherer, Lorraine Serabian, Adam M. Shankman, Joshua Shirlen, Alberto Stevans, Roberta Stiehm, Victor Strengaru, Fredrick Strother, Theresa Thomas-D'Alessandro, David Toney, Laurine Towler, Keith Tyrone, Fiddle Viracola, Sullivan Walker, Amanda Waters, Kevin Winkler, Valerie Wright
PRODUCTIONS: *Six Characters in Search of an Author, Ring Round the Moon, Playboy of the West Indies, Chorus of Disapproval, Lie of the Mind, Nothing Sacred, On the Town, Walk in the Woods*
WORLD PREMIERES: *Briar Patch* by Deborah Pryor
SPECIAL EVENTS: *Tale of Lear, Abyssinia, The Fool Show*

Top Right: Paul Binotto, Valerie Wright, Kathleen Mahony-Bennett, Gordon Paddison, Adriane Lenox, John Scherer in "On the Town"
Joan Marcus Photos

Tom Hewitt, Elizabeth McGovern in "Ring Round the Moon"

Tana Hicken, Lily Knight in "A Lie of the Mind"

126

ASOLO STATE THEATRE

Sarasota, Florida
Thirtieth Season

Executive Director, Lee Warner; Associate Executive Director, Donald P. Creason; Artistic Director, John Ulmer; Stage Directors, Jamie Brown, Pat Brown, John Gulley; Sets, Ken Kurtz, Kevin Lock, Jeffrey W. Jean, Bennet Averyt, Keith Anderson; Costumes, Ainslie G. Bruneau, Howard Tsvi Kaplan; Lights, Martin Petlock; Stage Managers, Marian Wallace, Stephanie Moss, Juanita Munford, Barbara Burton; Production Supervisor, Victor Meyrich
COMPANY: R. Ward Duffy, Eric Hissom, Todd C. Johnson, Candace Dian Leverett, Rebecca Nice, Robert Patteri, David Peshek, Mary E. Proctor, David T. Shatraw, Liz Vago
ASSOCIATE COMPANY: Tobin E. Atkinson, Jack Boslet, Rick Cannon, Meghan Cary, Kristin Catherall, Susan M. Haefner, Chris Hietikko, Stephen Ivester, Joe Mannino, Dorothy McChesney, Roy McChesney, LeRoy Mitchell, Jr., Bob Mowery, Rick Norris, Grace Paige, Ann Pemberton, Frank Pennypacker, Leslie L. Rohland, Jacek Sas-Uhrynowski, Darrell Steele, Parker Jerome Swanson, Doug Wells, Kirk B. R. Woller
PRODUCTIONS: *I'm Not Rappaport, Berlin to Broadway with Kurt Weill, Side by Side by Sondheim, Towards Zero, The Boys Next Door, As You Like It, Burn This, Medea, Frankie and Johnny in the Clair de Lune, Eleemosynary, Cyrano de Bergerac*

Right: Michael James Laird, Jayne Houdyshell in "Frankie and Johnny in the Clair de Lune"
Top: Mary Fogarty, Candace Dian Leverett, Kimberly King in "Eleemosynary"
Alan Ulmer Photos

127

BARTER THEATRE

Abingdon, Virginia
Fifty-sixth Season

Artistic Director/Producer, Rex Partington; Directors, Ken Costigan, Geoffrey Hitch, Frank Lowe, Richard Major, William Van Keyser; Set Designers, Gary Aday, M. Lynne Allen, Russ Bralley, Christopher Carter, Daniel Ettinger, Daniel Gray; Costume Designers, Karen Brewster, Cyndi Orr; Lighting Designer, Timothy M. Chew; Stage Managers, Marsha Gitkind, Champe Leary, Tony Partington, Rick D. Todd, James Wood; Business Manager, Pearl Hayter; Promotions Director, Lori W. Hamm; Production Director, Marjorie Terry; Technical Director, Greg Owens
COMPANY: Richard Bowden, Gloria Boucher, Katherine Carlson, Judy Chesnutt, Joleen Fodor, Amy Danis, John Fitzgibbon, Stephen Gabis, John Hall, Stanley Harrison, Cleo Holladay, Mark Johannes, Eve Johnson, Jeff Kin, Richard Kinter, Roddy Kinter, Dane Knell, Richard Major, Sarah Melici, Valerie Mercurio, Kenny Morris, Sandra Musick, Dixie Partington, Rex Partington, Tony Partington, Frances Peter, Trip Plymale, Robert Putnam, Arleigh Richards, Janet Rollins, Christopher Shaw, Douglas Simes, Peg Small, Robin Tate, Diane Warren, Lynn Watson, Amanda Wright, Craig Wroe
PRODUCTIONS: *Relatively Speaking* by Alan Ayckbourn, *Prince and the Pauper* by Richard Kinter adapted from Mark Twain, *Dear Liar* by Jerome Kilty adapted from correspondence of G. B. Shaw and Mrs. Patrick Campbell, *Steel Magnolias* by Robert Harling, *Under Milk Wood* by Dylan Thomas, *Twelfth Night* by William Shakespeare, *Jacques Brel is Alive and Well and Living in Paris* conceived by Eric Blau and Mort Shuman, *Special Occasions* by Bernard Slade, *You Never Can Tell* by George Bernard Shaw, *Unexpected Guest* by Agatha Christie

Top: Janet Rollins, Richard Kinter, Stephen Gabis in "Twelfth Night"

Jill Patton, Steve Essner in "Gershwin by Night" (Beef & Boards)

BEEF AND BOARDS THEATRE

Indianapolis, Indiana
Sixteenth Season

Artistic Director/Producer, Douglas Stark; Managing Director/Producer, Robert Zehr; Stage Manager, Ed Stockman; Assistant Producer, Peggy Zehr; Scenic/ Lighting Director, Michael Layton; Musical Director, Richard Laughlin, Technical Director/Scenic Artist, Jeff Pajer; Sound, Steve Rivers; Public Relations/Press, Amy Jo Stark; Costumes, Livingston

PRODUCTIONS & CASTS

SOUTH PACIFIC by Richard Rodgers, Oscar Hammerstein, 2nd, Joshua Logan; Director, Robert D. Zehr; CAST: Laurie Walton, Richard Rebilas, Bob Walton, Brian Horton, Monica Cantrell, Myron E.El, Mark Heflin, Christine Hull, Doug King, Glenn Leslie, Shaune Rebilas, Cynthia Thomas, David Williams, Suzanna Park, John Park

BEST LITTLE WHOREHOUSE IN TEXAS by Carol Hall & Larry L. King; Director, Douglas E. Stark; CAST: James Anthony, Ellen McLain, Doug Holmes, Brian Horton, Eric Bohus, Nancy Edwards, Tracey Edwards, Julie Graves, Mark Heflin, Doug King, Glenn Leslie, Judi Mann, Elizabeth Anne Morgan, Kimberly Rheam, Mark Santallino, Sherry Santallino, Dan Scharbrough, Cynthia Thomas, Stephen W. Essner (Choreography)

SOUND OF MUSIC by Rodgers, Hammerstein, Howard Lindsay & Russel Crouse; Director, Douglas E. Stark; CAST: Suzanne Stark, Richard Pruitt, Dee Etta Rowe, Kathleen Conry, Doug Holmes, Julie Graves, Brian Horton, Christine Hull, Elizabeth Morgan, Ronald Dwenger, Mal Davis, Tara Holland, Nicki Kimble, Joel Lugar, Jana Lugar, Kori McComber, Matthew Miller

42nd STREET by Harry Warren, Al Dubin, Michael Stewart, Mark Bramble; Director, Robert D. Zehr; Choreography, Mike Worcell; CAST: Melodie Wolford, Douglas E. Stark, Kathy Conry, Bruce Moore, Norma Crawford, Brian Horton, Dan Scharbrough, Doug Holmes, Barbara Early, Angie Donahue, Julie Graves, Sherry Santallino, Mike Lang, Elizabeth Ward, Doug King, Glenn Leslie, Mark Heflin, Mike Worcell

SHOW BOAT by Jerome Kern & Hammerstein; Director, Douglas E. Stark; CAST: Robert McCormick, Ellen McLain, Jack Sevier, Bessie Colvin, Everett Greene, Jenifer Decker, Angie Donahue, Tracey Edwards, Kathleen Hacker, Jerry Hacker, Brian Horton, Doug King, John Patrick Lowrie, Sherry Santillano, Jacque Workman

GERSHWIN BY NIGHT arranged by Al Kiger, Ernest Coleson, David Coleson, Richard Laughlin, Andrew Cosentino; Director, Douglas E. Stark; Choreography, Stephen Essner; CAST: Stephen Essner, Suzanne Stark, Jill Patton, Brian Horton Pam Klappas, John McGinn

Right: Brian Horton, Laurie Walton in "South Pacific"
Top: Kathleen Conry, Richard Pruitt, Doug Holmes in "The
Sound of Music"

Everett Greene in "Show Boat"

James Anthony, Doug Holmes in "Best Little Whorehouse in
Texas"

CALIFORNIA MUSIC THEATRE

Pasadena, California
Second Season

Artistic Director, Gary Davis; Production Manager, Thomas Ware; Stage Directors Toby Bluth, Bonnie Evans, Gary Davis,: Choreographers, Ed Kerrigan, Randy Skinner, Patti Colombo, Dom Salinaro; Designers, David Gibson, Toby Bluth, Ken Holamon, John Brandt, Ward Carlisle, Kim Killingsworth, Michael McGivney; Press, Richard Spittel

PRODUCTIONS & CASTS

KISMET with Music & Lyrics by Robert Wright & George Forrest; Book, Charles Lederer, Luther Davis; Music Director, Steven Smith; CAST: Mark David Miller (Imam/Bangleman), Philip Chaffin (Muezzin/Servant), Gary Reynolds (Muezzin/Pearl Merchant), Dion Ramos (Muezzin), Leon Natker (Muezzin/Orange Merchant), Carl Packard (Muezzin, 1st Beggar/Prosecutor), Jeff Austin (2nd Beggar/Police Chief), Bill Odien (3rd Beggar), Ed Kerrigan (Dervish/Akbar), David Chavez (Dervish/Assiz), Kay E. Cutter (Omar), Stephen Kimbrough (Hajj) Cassandra Byram (Marsinah), Christian Nova (Fig Merchant), LaRue Palmer (Hassan-Ben), Michael Prichard (Jawan), Byron Webster (Wazir), Juliet Prowse (Lalume), Virginia Lee Latimer (Princess), Aulani (Princess), Jerri DeMars (Princess), Keith Rice (Caliph), Kelli Fish (Slave), Diana Kavilis (Slave), Jennifer Rea (Slave), Carol Winston (Slave), Victoria Dillard (Zubbediya), Suzanne Guzman (Ayah), Marie Cody (Samaris), Grace Sagara (Ayah), Carol Tammen (Widow Yussef), Elaine Houssels, Laura Lees, Lena Marie, Garen Michaels, Ann Winkowski, Leah Aldridge, Sekiya Billman

STRIKE UP THE BAND (*West Coast Premiere*) with Music by George Gershwin; Lyrics, Ira Gershwin; Book, George S. Kaufman; Restoration, Tommy Krasker; Music Director, Steven Smith; CAST: Tom Bosley (Horace J. Fletcher), Avery Schreiber (Col. Holmes), Faye DeWitt (Mrs. Draper), Donald Most (Edgar Sloane), Michael Magnusen (Jim Townsend) Roxann Parker (Joan Fletcher), Bobby Herbeck (George Spelvin), Kirby Ward (Timothy Harper), Beverly Ward (Anne Draper) Kevin Backstrom, Sherri Sperling Bannister, John Bazzell, Terrence Carey, Philip A. Chaffin, Christine Chavez, Paul Del Vecchio, Kelli Fish, Lloyd Gordon, Mark Harryman, Anita Hasten, Lawrence Hilty, Jim Hormel, Lynmarie Inge, Suzanne Kinsey, Lena Marie, Missy McGuigan, Robbi Morgan, Shelly Nichols, Christian Nova, Jim T. Ruttman, Elizabeth Stover, Lester Thompson, Christine Wisner

BABES IN TOYLAND (New Adaptation) by Victor Herbert; Reconceived by Toby Bluth; Music Direction, Roy Rogosin; CAST: Robert Morse (Toymaker), Peter Mark Richman (Barnaby), Christopher Callen (Mother Hubbard), Timothy Smith (Tom Piper), Stacy Sullivan (Bo Peep), Ernest Sarracino (Marmaduke), Chris Finch (Little Boy Blue), E. E. Bell (Gonzargo), Jeffrey Weissman (Rodrigo), Megan McGinnis-Pack (Jane), Allison McMillan (Contrary Mary), Ian Fryman (Simple Simon), Richard P. Stuart (Alan), Nick Finch (Wee Willie Winkie), Ethan Randall), Lynn Rose (Goldielocks), Doug MacArthur (Mr Dumpty), Rieka Roberta Cruz (Mr. Dumpty), Jeffrey Cornell (Fr. Christmas), Brian Norber (Ma Hag), Kevin Backstrom, Nancy Ann Doorn, David Jahn, Julie Morrical, Robert Neil, Rachelle Ottley, Gavin Ryan, Andrea Sandall, Kelly James Schmitt, Kristine Spurney, Wendy Walter

KISS ME, KATE with Music/Lyrics by Cole Porter; Book, Bella & Samuel Spewack; Music Director, Jeff Rizzo; CAST: Terry Lester (Fred Graham/Petruchio), Leslie Easterbrook (Lilli Vanessi/Katherine), Wendy Edmead (Lois Lane/Bianca), Mark Morales (Bill Calhoun/Lucentio), Len Lesser (Gangster), Tony Gaetano (Gangster), Ron Dennis (Paul), Jack Ritschel (Harry/Baptista), Rick Stockwell (Gremio), Mark Harryman (Hortensio), Kenneth Douglas (Ralph/Harrison), Carla Kendall (Lynette/Lady of Padua), Rachelle Ottley (Widow), Kevin Backstrom (Cab Driver/Gregory), Paul R. Williams (Nathaniel), Paige Price (Lady of Padua), Donna Resnick (Lady of Padua), Elizabeth Stover (Lady)

Top Left: Leslie Easterbrook, Terry Lester in "Kiss Me, Kate"

Below: Tom Bosley, Avery Schreiber in "Strike Up the Band"
Craig Schwartz, Ed Kriepe Photos

Christopher Callen, Robert Morse in "Babes in Toyland"

CAPITAL REPERTORY COMPANY

Albany, New York

Co-Producing Directors, Bruce Bouchard/Peter H. Clough; General Manager, Peter M. Kindlon; Director of Development, Christopher Lino; Business Manager, Susan Robert; Marketing & Publicity, Hilde Schuster; Associate Marketing, Vauna Bernstein; Development Associate, Julie Galloway; Production Stage Manager, Julie A. Fife; Technical Director, Patrick Ferlo; Costume Designer, Lynda L. Salsbury

PRODUCTIONS & CASTS

SAINT FLORENCE (*World Premiere*) by Elizabeth Diggs; Director, Jules Aaron; Scenic Design, Rick Dennis; Costumes, James Scott; Lighting, Victor En Yu Tan; Music, Robert Waldman; Sound, Kevin Bartlett; Choreography, Constance Valis Hill; CAST: Jim Abele, Claire Beckman, Robin Chadwick, Edmund Lewis, Emily Arnold McCully, Carole Monferdini, James Pritchett, Darcy Pulliam, Pat Timm, Jane Welch, K. Scott Coopwood, William Gurr, David Howell, Susan Pope
ROUND AND ROUND THE GARDEN by Alan Ayckbourn; Director, Michael J. Hume; Concept, Michael J. Hume; Costumes, Lynda L. Salsbury; Lighting, David Yergan; Sound, Kevin Bartlett; CAST: Mary Baird, Brad Bellamy, Kate Kelly, Anne Newhall, James Goodwin Rice, Richard Zobel
THE VOICE OF THE PRAIRIE by John Olive; Director, Gloria Muzio; Scenic Design, Pat Woodbridge,; Costumes, Martha Hally; Lighting, Jackie Manassee; Sound, Kevin Bartlett; CAST: Kathy Danzer, Rick Lawless, J. K. Simmons
GLENGARRY GLEN ROSS by David Mamet; Director, Gordon Edelstein; Scenic Design, Hugh Landwehr; Costumes, David Murin; Lighting, Pat Collins; CAST: Michael Fischetti, Jeffrey D. Kent, Michael Marcus, Terry Rabine, Toshio Sato, Allen Swift, Christopher Wynkoop
THE IMMIGRANT: A HAMILTON COUNTY ALBUM by Mark Harelik; Conceived by Harelik & Randal Myler; Director, Howard J. Millman; Scenic Design, Kevin Rupnik; Costumes, Mimi Maxmen; Lighting, Phil Monat; CAST: Carole Lockwood, Devora Millman, Bruce Nozick, Richard Thomsen
BILOXI BLUES by Neil Simon; Director, John Pynchon Holms; Scenic Design, Leslie Taylor; Costumes, Lynda L. Salsbury; Lighting, Andi Lyons; Sound, Tom Gould; CAST: Jude Ciccolella, Marc Epstein, Curt Kaplan, Todd Kimsey, Rick Lawless, Wayne Maugans, Matt Tomasino, Julie Ungerer, Carl Wade

Left: Kathy Danzer, Rick Lawless in "The Voice of the Prairie"

Top: Carole Monferdini, Jane Welch, James Pritchett, Claire Beckman in "Saint Florence"
Joseph Schuyler Photos

Brad Bellamy, Richard Zobel in "Round and Round"

Devora Millman, Carole Lockwood in "The Immigrant"

CENTER STAGE

Baltimore, Maryland

Artistic Director, Stan Wojewodski; Managing Director, Peter W. Culman; Associate Artists, Joel Agee, Colette Brooks, Michael Engler, Byron Jennings, Leon Katz, Eric Overmeyer; Artistic Administrator, Del W. Risberg; Resident Dramaturg, Rick Davies, Mona Heinze (Fellow); Production Manager, Katharyn Davies; Stage Managers, Keri Muir, Wendy Streeter, Julie Thompson; Technical Director, Tom Rupp; Costumer, F.T. Brown; Master of Properties, Julie Jordan Harrington; Master Electrician, Kent McKenzie; Sound, L. R. Smith; Associate Managing Director, Patricia Egan; Young People's Theatre Playwrights, Jim Cary, Mark Novak, Jim Sizemore, Ann G. Sjoerdsma; Development, Mary E. Howell; Marketing, Betsy Kunzelman

PRODUCTIONS & CASTS

THE IMPORTANCE OF BEING EARNEST by Oscar Wilde; Director, Stan Wojewodski, Jr, Sets, Derek McLane; Costumes, Catherine Zuber; Lighting, Pat Collins; Dramaturg, Rick Davis; CAST: Boyd Gaines (Algernon), David O. Peterson (Lane), Byron Jennings (John), Marge Redmond (Lady Bracknell), Carolyn McCormick (Gwendolen), Mary Fogarty (Prism), Pippa Pearthree (Cecily), Dillon Evans (Chasuble), Daniel Szelag (Merriman)

FOOL FOR LOVE by Sam Shepard; Director, William Foeller; Sets, Christopher Barreca; Costumes, Del W. Risberg; Lighting, James F. Ingalls; Sound, Janet Kalas; Dramturg, Colette Brooks; CAST: Peter Crombie (Eddie), Phyllis Lyons (May), William Hardy (Old Man), George Bamford (Martin)

JOE TURNER'S COME AND GONE by August Wilson; Director, Irene Lewis; Sets, Anita Stewart; Costumes, Candice Donnelly; Lighting, Pat Collins; Music, Dwight Andrews; Dramaturg, Mona Heinze; CAST: Lanyard A. Williams (Seth) Deloris Gaskins (Bertha), John Cothran, Jr. (Bynum), Burke Pearson (Rutherford), Kevin Jackson (Jeremy), Bruce A. Young (Herald), Stephanie Lansey and Jada Pinkett (Alternating perfs.) (Zonia), Shawn Judge (Mattie), Gerard Harrison and DeVron Young (Alternating perfs.) (Reuben), Lydia Hannibal (Molly), Kim Yancey (Martha)

THE TEMPEST by William Shakespeare; Director, Stan Wojewodski, Jr., Sets & Costumes, Alexander Okun; Lighting, Stephen Strawbridge; Composer, Kim D. Sherman; Speech, Timothy Monich; Dramaturg, Rick Davis; CAST: Lou Milione (Boatswain), Richard Bowden (Alonso), Armand Schultz (Antonio), Thomas Barbour (Gonzalo), Robert Jason (Sebastian), Susan Ericksen (Miranda), Byron Jennings (Prospero), Pippa Pearthree (Ariel), Larry Golden (Caliban), John Patrick Rice (Ferdinanad), Kevin Jackson (Adrian), Wil Love (Trinculo), Scott Sowers (Stephano)

THERE'S ONE IN EVERY MARRIAGE by Georges Feydeau; Translation/Adaptation, Suzanne Grossman/Paxton Whitehead; Director, Stan Wojewodski, Jr.; Sets, Derek McLane; Costumes, Catherine Zuber; Lighting, Stephen Strawbridge; Composer, Larry Delinger; Dramaturg, Rick Davis; CAST: Carolyn McCormick (Lucienne), John Hutton (Pontagnac), Robert Michael Tomlinson (Vatelin), Wil Love (Jean, Hotel Manager, Gerome), Byron Jennings (Roubillion), Jennifer Harmon (Clothilde), Cailin O'Connell (Ulla), Walt MacPherson (Soldignac), Meghan Rose Krank (Armandine), Don Harvey (Victor), Thomas Hill (Pinchard), Jill Tanner (Mme. Pinchard), Cornelia Cody (Clara), David Manis (Commissioner) Dyer Bilgrave, Janel Bosies, Shelia Childs, Christian Garretson, Chris Lamb, Charlie Wilcox

THE BROKEN PITCHER by Heinrich von Kliest; Translator, Jon Swan; Director, Michael Engler; Sets, Derek McLane; Costumes, Catherine Zuber; Lighting, James F. Ingalls; Dramaturg, Mona Heinze; CAST: Wil Love (Walter/Judge), Thomas Hill (Adam/Village Judge), David Manis (Licht), Jill Tanner (Marthe), Meghan Rose Krank (Eve), Walt MacPherson (Veit), Don Harvey (Ruprecht), Delphi Lawrence (Brigitte), Dyer Bilgrave (Constable), Robert Michael Tomlinson (Manservant), Cornelia Cody (Liese), Shelia Childs (Margaret)

THE INCREASED DIFFICULTY OF CONCENTRATION by Vaclav Havel; Translator, Vera Blackwell; Director, Stan Wojewodski, Jr.; Sets, Derek McLane; Costumes, Catherine Zuber; Lighting, Robert Wierzel; Dramaturg, Rick Davis; CAST: Caitlin O'Connell (Vlasta), Byron Jennings (Dr. Huml), Jennifer Harmon (Renata), Carolyn McCormick (Dr. Balcar), John Hutton (Karel Kriebl), David Manis (Emil), Meghan Rose Krank (Blanka), Walt MacPherson (Beck)

Top Right: Phyllis Lyons, Peter Crombie in "Fool for Love"
Below: Bruce A. Young, Shawn Judge in "Joe Turner's Come and Gone"
Center: Susan Ericksen, Byron Jennings in "The Tempest"
Richard Anderson, Stephen Spartana Photos

Carolyn McCormick, Byron Jennings in "There's One in Every Marriage"

CENTER THEATRE GROUP
AHMANSON THEATRE

Los Angeles, California
Twenty-second Season

Artistic Director, Robert Fryer; General Manager, Ellen Fay; Production General Manager, Veronica Claypool; Press, Tony Sherwood; Press Assistant, Joyce Friedmann; Assistant Production Manager, David Cipriano; Administrative Assistants, Christine Cox, Laura Bellin, Allison Sklute; Executive Associate, Joyce Zaccaro; Technical Director, Robert Routolo.

PRODUCTIONS & CASTS

LES LIAISONS DANGEREUSES by Christopher Hampton *(West Coast Premiere);* Director, Peter Wood; Design, Bob Crowley; Lighting, Beverly Emmons; Wigs, Bill Fletcher; Production Stage Manager, Joe Cappelli; Stage Manager, Arthur Gaffin; CAST: Frank Langella (Valmont), Lynn Redgrave (Marquise), Kathleen Quinlan (Tourvel), William Brown (Azolan), Paddi Edwards (Mme. de Rosemonde), Elaine Welton Hill (Emilie), Katherine McGrath (Mme. de Volanges), Si Osborne (Danceny), Elizabeth Swackhammer (Cecile), John Castellanos, Katherine Henryk, Andrew Laisser, Paul Laramore, William Wright, Jacqueline Chauvin, Jena Cole

INTO THE WOODS by Stephen Sondheim (Music/Lyrics); Book, James Lapine; Director, James Lapine; Sets, Tony Straiges; Lighting, Richard Nelson; Costumes, Ann Hould-Ward; Hair, Phyllis Della Illien; Sound, Alan Steib/James Brousseau; Orchestrations, Jonathan Tunick; Musical Director, Randy Booth; Staging, Lar Lubovitch; Company Manager, Alan Ross Kosher,; Production Stage Manager, Dan W. Langhofer; Stage Manager, Joseph Sheridan; Presented by Tom Mallow/Pace Theatrical in association with Heidi & Rocco Landesman, Rick Steiner, M. Anthony Fisher, Frederick H. Mayerson, Jujamcyn Theatres; CAST: Cleo Laine (Witch), Charlotte Rae (Jack's Mother), Ray Gill (Baker), Mary Gordon Murray (Baker's Wife), Chuck Wagner (Cinderella's Prince/Wolf), Kathleen Rowe McAllen (Cinderella) Jill Geddes (Cinderella—succeeded McAllen) Rex Robbins (Narrator/Mysterious Man): Robert Duncan McNeil (Jack), Susan Gordon-Clark (Florinda), Don Crosby (Cinderella's Father), Danette Cuming (Lucinda), Jo Ann Cunningham (Cinderella's Stepmother), Tracy Katz (Little Red Riding Hood), Marguerite Lowell (Rapunzel), Nora Mae Lyng (Grandmother/Giant), Marcus Olson (Steward), Anne Rickenbacher (Cinderella's Mother), Douglas Sills (Rapunzel's Prince), Jonathan Hadley, Paul Jackel, Jody Walker-Lichtig, James Weatherstone

HAPGOOD by Tom Stoppard; *(American Premiere)*: Director, Peter Wood; Design, Carl Toms; Lighting, David Hersey; Production Stage Manager, Joe Cappelli; Stage Manager, Arthur Gaffin; Presented in association with Michael Codron; CAST: Judy Davis (Hapgood), Roger Rees (Kerner): Simon Jones (Blair): Richard Lawson (Wates): James Lancaster (Ridley): Tim Donohue (Maggs): Morgan Strickland (Merryweather): Chris Demetral/David Tom (Joe): Tim Blough, Andrew Laisser, George C. Simms, Bryan Torfeh, Babbie Green, Roderick Horn, Paul Laramore

THE PHANTOM OF THE OPERA with Music by Andrew Lloyd Webber; Lyrics, Charles Hart, Richard Stilgoe; Book, Stilgoe & Webber; *(West Coast Premiere)*; Director, Harold Prince; Choreography, Gillian Lynne; Design, Maria Bjornson; Lighting, Andrew Bridge; Sound, Martin Levan; Musical Director, Roger Cantrell; Musical Supervision, David Caddick; Production Supervisor, Mitchell Lemsky; General Management, Alan Wasser; Casting, Johnson-Liff & Zerman; Company Manager, Martin Cohen; Production Stage Manager, David Rubinstein; Stage Managers, Sherry Cohen, Noel Stern; Presented by Cameron Mackintosh/Really Useful Theatre Co.: CAST: Michael Crawford (Phantom), Dale Kristien (Christine): Reece Holland (Raoul): Leigh Munroe (Carlotta): Norman Large (Andre): Calvin Remsberg (Firmin): Gualtiero Negrini (Piangi): Barbara Lang (Giry): Elisabeth Stringer (Meg): Mary D'Arcy (Christine-alternate) Jeffrey Amsden, D. C. Anderson, Leslie-Noriko Beadles, Karen Benjamin, Madelyn Berdes, Gene Brundage, Irene Cho, Maurizio Corbino, Joseph Dellger, Rebecca Eichenberger, Rebeca Gorostiza, Richard Gould, Rio Hibbler-Kerr, James Hogan, Gail Land Hart, Mary Alyce Laubacher, Gary Marshal, Jani Neuman, Patrice Pickering, Kris Pruet, Sylvia Rico, Candace Rogers-Adler, Brad Scott, Sean Smith, Kate Solmssen, Carlo Thomas

Right Center: Judy Davis, James Lancaster in "Hapgood"
Above: Lynn Redgrave, Frank Langella in "Les Liaisons Dangereuses"
Top: Kathleen Quinlan, Frank Langella in "Les Liaisons Dangereuses"
Jay Thompson Photos

Roger Rees, Simon Jones in "Hapgood"

CENTER THEATRE GROUP
MARK TAPER FORUM

Los Angeles, California
Twenty-second Season

Artistic Director/Producer, Gordon Davidson; Managing Director, Stephen J. Albert; Associate Producer, Madeline Puzo; Resident Director, Robert Egan; Director, ITP, Peter C. Brosius; Associate Manager, Karen S. Wood; Production Administrator, Jonathan Barlow Lee; Technical Director, Robert Routolo; Casting Director, Amy Lieberman, Stanley Sobel; Press, Nancy Hereford, Phyllis Moberly, Carol Ball Oken, Evelyn Kiyomi Emi

PRODUCTIONS & CASTS

NOTHING SACRED by George F. Walker *(United States Premiere)*: Director, Michael Lindsay-Hogg; Sets, Eugene Lee; Costumes, Robert Blackman; Lighting, Natasha Katz; Music, Nathan Birnbaum; Production Stage Manager, Jonathan Barlow Lee; Stage Manager, Dana L. Axelrod; CAST: Ned Bellamy (Bailiff), Douglas Roberts (Gregor), Corey Parker (Arkady), Tom Hulce (Bazarov), Raye Birk (Nicolai), Ford Rainey (Piotr), Mary Kohnert (fenichka), Franklyn Seales (Pavel), Gregory Cooke (Sitnikov), Margaret Gibson (Anna), Walter Olkewicz (Sergei), David Giella, Karl Wiedergott, John Warner Williams

THE SOUL OF A JEW, THE LAST NIGHT OF OTTO WEININGER by Joshua Sobol; A Haifa Municipal Theatre Co. Production; Director, Gedalia Besser; Music/Musical Direction, Yoni Rechter; Sets, Adrian Vaux; Costumes, Edna Sobel; Lighting, Yehiel Orgal; Production Stage Manager, Jonathan Barlow Lee; Stage Manager, Dana L. Axelrod; CAST: Doron Tavori (Otto), Giora Shammi (Leopld), Leora Rivlin (Adelaide/Adela), Gury Segal (Berger), Noa Goldberg (Clara), Ilan Toren (Teitz/Strindberg/Moebius), Michael Kfir (Freud), Tchia Danon (Double/prostitute)

FRANKIE AND JOHNNY IN THE CLAIR DE LUNE by Terrence McNally *(West Coast Premiere)*: Director, Paul Benedict; Sets, D. Martyn Bookwalter; Costumes, David C. Woolard; Lighting, Martin Aronstein; Sound, John Gromada; Coordinator, Pamela Singer; Production Stage Manager, James T. McDermott; Stage Manager, Jill Johnson; CAST: Kathy Bates (Frankie), Kenneth Welsh (Johnny), Dominic Cuskern (Voice of Radio Announcer)

DUTCH LANDSCAPE by Jon Robin Baitz *(World Premiere)*: Director, Gordon Davidson; Sets, Heidi Landesman; Costumes, Ann Bruice; Lighting, Tharon Musser; Music, Rick Baitz; Sound Jon Gottlieb; Assistant Director, Judy Dennis; Fights, Gary Mascaro; Production Stage Manager, Mary Michele Miner; Stage Manager, Tami Toon; CAST: Philip Reeves (Larry Cole), Penny Fuller (Rose), Todd Merrill (Alex Asch), Raphael Sbarge (Daniel), Olivia Virgil Harper (Edna Tululu), Stephen Joyce (Philip Asch), Dakin Matthews (Heine Van Broughe)

SANSEI *(World Premiere)* Created and performed by Hiroshima; Developed and Directed by Robert Egan; Sets, Mark Wendland; Costumes, Lydia Tanji; Lighting, Jeff Ravitz; Assistant Lighting, David E. Freeman; Sound Designer, Michael J. "geese" graphix (sic), Jeff Spencer, Nathan Birnbaum; Projections, Evan Mower; Assistant Director, Robin McKee; Production Stage Manager, James T. McDermott; Stage Manager, Mary K. Klinger; CAST: Marc Hayashi (D.K.), Nelson Mashita (Danny), Lane Nishikawa (Johnny), Natsuko Ohama (June), Hiroshima-Dan Kuramoto, Danny Yamamoto, Johnny Mori, June Kuramoto, Machun, Kimo Cornwell, Dean Cortez, Allen Hinds, Kevin J. O'Connor.

STAND-UP TRAGEDY *(World Premiere)*, by Bill Cain; Director, Ron Link; Sets, Yael Pardess; Costumes, Carol Brolaski; Lighting, Michael Gilliam; Sound, Jon Gottlieb; Original Music, Craig Sibley; Rap Choreography, Shabba-Doo; Associate Producer, Corey Beth Madden; Production Stage Manager, Mary Michele Miner; Stage Manager, Cari Norton; CAST: Vaughn Armstrong (Father Ed Larkin), Anthony Barrile (Marco Ruiz), Marcus Chong (Freddy), Jack Coleman (Tom Griffin), Marvin Columbus (Luis), John C. Cooke (Bob Kenter), Michael DeLorenzo (Lee Cortez), Dan Gerrity (Pierce Brennan), Ray Oriel (Henry Fernandez), Lance Slaughter (Carlos Cruz).

TEMPTATION *(West Coast Premiere)*, by Vaclav Havel; Translator, Marie Winn; Director, Richard Jordan; Set, John Iacovelli; Costumes, Csilla Marki; Lighting, Paulie Jenkins; Sound/Composition, Nathan Birnbaum; Assistant Director, Toby Reisz; Production Stage Manager, James T. McDermott; Stage Manager, Tami Toon. CAST: John Apicella (Dr. Neuwirth), Savannah Smith Boucher (Dr. Libby Lorencova), Ron Campbell (The Deputy Director), Michael Constantine (The Director), Connie Forslund (Petrushka), Robin Gammell (Fistula), Lillian Garrett (Vilma), Kate Genesius (Lover), Carol Gustafson (Mrs. Houbova), Mark Harelik (Dr. Henry Foustka), Dan Mason (Lover), Hector Mercado (Dancer), Tim Pulice (Dr. Vilem Kotrly), Keeley Stanley (Marketa), Richard Vidan (Special Secretary).

Top Left: Margaret Gibson, Tom Hulce, Corey Parker in
"Nothing Sacred"
Below: Franklyn Seales, Raye Birk in "Nothing Sacred"
Jay Thompson Photos

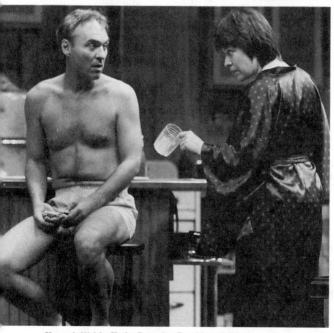

Kenneth Welsh, Kathy Bates in "Frankie and Johnny . . ."

TAPER TOO

THE DAY YOU'LL LOVE ME by Jose Ignacio Cabrujas; Translator, Eduardo Machado; Director, Lillian Garrett; Set, Deborah Raymond, Dorian Vernacchio; Costumes, Susan Denison Geller; Lighting, Liz Stillwell; Sound, Philip G. Allen; Stage Manager, Jill Ragaway. CAST: Wanda de Jesus (Maria Luisa), Miguel Sandoval (Pio), Rose Portillo (Elvira), Maritza Rivera (Matilde), Marc Tubert (Placido), Geno Silva (Le Pera), John Castellanos (Gardel).

MAKING NOISE QUIETLY (*American Premiere*) by Robert Holman; Director, Dennis Erdman; Sets, John Iacovelli; Costumes, Marianna Elliott; Lighting, Paulie Jenkins; Sound, Stephen Shaffer; Stage Manager, Cari Norton. CAST: Daniel J. O'Connor (Oliver Bell), Robert Petkoff (Eric Faber), Jeanne Hepple (May Appleton), Evan MacKenzie (Geoffrey Church), Elizabeth Hoffman (Helene Ennsslin), Christopher Grove (Alan Tadd), Chris Demetral (Sam).

STAND-UP TRAGEDY: Same credits as above, except Sound, Nathan Birnbaum; Costumes, Yael Pardess Same CAST minus Chong, Columbus.

IMPROVISATIONAL THEATRE PROJECT

¡BOCON! (*World Premiere*) by Lisa Loomer; Director, Peter C. Brosius; Movement/Choreography, Miguel Delgado; Sound, Ara Tokatlian; Music, Ara Tokatlian, John Fitzgerald; Set, Victoria Petrovich; Costumes, Lydia Tanji; Lighting, Margaret Anne Dunn; Mask Design, Alfredo Calderon; Manager, Elizabeth Harvey. CAST: Alma Martinez, Karen Maruyama, Armando Molina, Irma "Cui Cui" Rangel, Lucy Rodriguez, James Tyrone-Wallace II; Percussionist, John Fitzgerald.

SUNDAYS AT THE ITCHEY FOOT

LARKIN from Robert Phillips' Paris Review interview of 1982 and the poetry of Philip Larkin; Adapted and Directed by Ron Hutchinson; Music, Kurt Festinger; Producer, Jessica Teich. CAST: William Glover, Cristine Rose.

SAND AND STONE Israeli and Palestinian Voices. Adapted with original material by Marc Steven Dworkin. Director, Deborah La Vine; Producer, Corey Beth Madden. CAST: Stefan Gierasch, Zitto Kazann, Sam Shamshak, Rita Zohar; Musician, Rico Orell.

A CHRISTMAS MEMORY by Truman Capote. Adapted by Madeline Puzo; Director, Michael Peretzian. CAST: Mary Carver, Jay Louden; Musician, David Johnson.

THE WAY WE LIVE NOW by Susan Sontag; Adapted and Directed by Edward Parone; Producer, Corey Beth Madden. CAST: Janni Brenn, Francois Giroday, Gregory Itzen, Katherine McGrath, Cristine Rose.

SPUNK by Zora Neale Hurston. Adapted and Directed by George C. Wolfe; Producer, Corey Beth Madden. CAST: Bruce Beatty, Loretta Devine, Hawthorne James, Harry Waters Jr., Charlaine Woodard; Musician, Chic Street Man.

Top Right: June Kuramoto, Dan Kuromoto, Danny Yamamoto, Johnny Mori in "Sansei"

Below: Ray Oriel, Michael DeLorenzo, Anthony Barrile, Marcus Chong, Lance Slaughter, Marvin Columbus in "Stand-Up Tragedy"
Jay Thompson Photos

Todd Merrill, Stephen Joyce, Penny Fuller, Raphael Sbarge
in "Dutch Landscape"

Ray Oriel, Dan Gerrity in "Stand-Up Tragedy"

135

CLEVELAND PLAY HOUSE

Cleveland, Ohio
Seventy-third Season

Artistic Director, Josephine R. Abady; Managing Director, Dean R. Gladden; Resident Director, Michael Breault; Literary Manager, Roger T. Danforth; Artistic Operations, Don Roe; Company Manager, Benjamin Gutkin; Assistant Artistic Director, Paul Brown; Artistic Administrator, Susan Henry; Education Director, Marcyanne Goldman; Education Coordinator, Barbara Pullen Mingus; Design Consultant, David Potts; Casting Consultant, McCorkle Casting; Scenery, Jefferson Sage; Lighting, Clifton Taylor; Costumes, Kay Kurta; Sound, Jeffrey Montgomerie; Directors, Josephine R. Abady, Bob Baker, Robert Berlinger, Michael Breault, Roger T. Danforth, David Esbjornson, Jack Hofsiss, Tazewell Thompson; Designers, Laura Burton, Stancil Campbell, Jeff Davis, Leslie Frankish, David Jenkins, Natasha Katz, Hugh Landwehr, William Ivey Long, Mimi Maxmen, Dennis Parichy, David Potts, Ann Roth, Lia Vollack, Julie Weiss, Marc B. Weiss, Richard Winkler; Stage Managers, Robert S. Garber, Glenn Bruner, Jean Bruns, Robin Rumpf, Mark Wagenhurst; Production Assistants, Walter Baker, Karen Gironimi, Jennifer L. Grohol, Kirsten M Ludwig; Marketing Director, Nancy E. Depke; Public Relations Director, Gayle Waxman.

PRODUCTIONS & CASTS

BORN YESTERDAY by Garson Kanin; Director, Josephine R. Abady. CAST: with Madeline Kahn, Ed Asner, Franklin Cover
ON THE WATERFRONT (*World Premiere of Play Version*) by Budd Schulberg in collaboration with Stan Silverman; Director, Josphine R. Abady. CAST: included Grant Show, Robert LuPone, Kelly Curtis, Richard Herd

LES LIAISONS DANGEREUSES by Christopher Hampton; Director, Robert Berlinger. CAST: included Carol Mayo Jenkins, Anette Helde, Paul Rossilli, Nancy Hume, Tamara Daniel
CARNIVAL by Bob Merrill, Michael Stewart; Director, Jack Hofsiss; Choreography, Christopher Chadman. CAST: included Joanna Glushak, Robert Fitch, June Gabel, James Mellon
BREAKING THE CODE by Hugh Whitemore; Director, Bob Baker. CAST: included Tom Wood, Patricia Gage, Ann Turnbull, Barrie Baldaro
ITALIAN-AMERICAN RECONCILIATION by John Patrick Shanley; Director, Michael Breault. CAST: with Anette Helde, Peter Slutsker, James Andreassi, Rosemary DeAngelis
THE BOYS NEXT DOOR by Tom Griffin; Director, Josephine R. Abady. CAST: with Vasili Bogazianos, Lance Davis, Mel Winkler, Robert Machray, Jeff Dreisbach, Kristen Lowman

THE GLASS MENAGERIE (*Professional American Premiere of all-black version*) by Tennessee Williams; Director, Tazewell Thompson. CAST: with Josephine Premice, David Toney, Leon Addison Brown, Shawn Judge
THE CEMETARY CLUB by Ivan Menchell; Director, Josphine R. Abady. CAST: with Nanette Fabray, Elizabeth Franz, Doris Belack (replaced by Joyce Krempel), Eugene Troobnick

BROOKS SERIES

BROOKS COMPANY: Bob Cicchini, Charisse Coleman, Tim Conover, Kelly Gwin, William Keeler, Ted Marcoux, James Riordan, Kim Sebastian
A CHRISTMAS MEMORY by Truman Capote; Director, Roger Danforth; with Ruth Nelson
AS IS by William Hoffman; Director, Michael Breault.
REAL DREAMS by Trevor Griffiths; adapted from Revolution in Cleveland by Jeremy Pikser; Director, David Esbjornson.
BOVVER BOYS (*World Premiere*) by Willy Holtzman; Director, Michael Breault.

**Right Center: Carol Mayo Jenkins, Paul Rossilli in
"Les Liaisons Dangereuses"
Above: Kelly Curtis, Grant Show in "On the Waterfront"
Top: Doris Belack, Elizabeth Franz, Nanette Fabray in
"The Cemetery Club"
*Paul Tepley Photos***

Bob Machray, Vasili Bogazianos in "The Boys Next Door"

Rob Gomes, Kathleen McCall in "1918"
Right: Steven F. Hall in "Beggar's Opera"
Top: Full Company of "Beggar's Opera"
Richard Carter Photos

DELAWARE THEATRE COMPANY

Wilmington, Delaware
Tenth Season

Artistic Director, Cleveland Morris; Managing Director, Ralph J. Stalter, Jr.; Business Manager, Robert R. Ramirez, Donna Pody; Development, Ann Schenck; Marketing, Mary H. Johnson; Administrative Assistant, Sara Smarr, Deborah Duffey; Box Office/Student Outreach, Charles J. Conway; Assistant Artistic Director, Danny Peak; Volunteer Coordinator, Carolyn Haon; Stage Manager, Patricia Christian; Technical, Eric Schaeffer; Lighting, Bruce K. Morriss; Props, Peter J. Knecht; Sound, George Stewart; Costumes, Marla Jurglanis.

PRODUCTIONS & CASTS

THE BEGGAR'S OPERA by John Gay; Director, Cleveland Morris; Arrangements/Orchestrations, Judy Brown; Sets, Eric Schaeffer. CAST: Bill Cohen (Beggar/Lockit), Mark Baker (Player/Peachum), Franc D'Ambrosio (Filch), Susan Browning (Mrs. Peachum), Emily Loesser (Polly), Steven F. Hall (Macheath), Kristine Miller (Jenny), Maggi-Meg Reed, Diane Reick (Lucy), Terry Reamer (Diana), Peter V. Campbell (Jemmy), Ronnie Hironimus (Matt), Bob Miller (Wat), Erik Sherr (Ben), Frank P. Vignola (Ned), Brian Wells (Robin), Cynthia Charles (Suky), Jonnie Holzman (Mrs. Slammekin), Grace Kocsko (Betty), Lona Marchetti (Dolly), Melody Owens (Mrs. Vixen).
MASTER HAROLD . . . AND THE BOYS by Athol Fugard; Director, Jamie Brown; Sets, Lewis Folden. CAST: Byron Utley (Willie), Helmar Augustus Cooper (Sam), Benjamin White (Hally)
1918 by Horton Foote; Director, Cleveland Morris; Sets, Joseph A. Varga. CAST: Rob Gomes (Horace), Maurice R. Sims (Sam), Suzanne Winkler (Miss Ruth), Russ Jolly (Brother Vaughn), Kathleen McCall (Elizabeth), Aline Lathrop (Bessie), Joan Kendall (Mrs. Vaughn), Will Stutts (Vaughn), Mandy Wright (Irma), Jeffrey Bingham (Greene), Allison Hedges (Gladys), Betty Stapleford (Mrs. Boone), Brendan Pryor (Boy)
A HELL OF A TOWN by Monte Merrick; Director, Richard Hopkins; Sets, Alex Polner CAST: Carolyn Michel (Jill), Joseph Butler (Sandy)
ROSENCRANTZ & GUILDENSTERN ARE DEAD by Tom Stoppard; Director, Rick Davis; Sets, Eric Schaeffer. CAST: Anders Bolang (Rosencrantz), Peter Bradbury (Guildenstern), John Wojda (Player), Bruce A. Katlin (Alfred), Richard Geller, Eric Paul, Erik Sherr, Frank P. Vignola (Tragedians), Mary Elizabeth Smith (Ophelia), Roger Anderson (Hamlet), Warren Keith (Claudius), Carol Schultz (Gertrude), Bob Balick, Sharon FitzHenry (Courtiers), Michael Hartman (Polonius), Eric Paul, Erik Sherr (Guards), Bob Balick (Soldier), Eric Paul (Laertes), Erik Sherr (Horatio), Bob Balick (Fortinbras), Sharon FitzHenry (Ambassador)

Right Center: Peter Bradbury, John Wojda in "Rosencrantz
& Guildenstern Are Dead"

Benjamin White, Byron Utley, Helmar Augustus Cooper in
"Master Harold . . ."

DENVER CENTER THEATRE COMPANY

Denver, Colorado
Tenth Season

Artistic Director, Donovan Marley; Executive Director, Sarah Lawless; Producing Director, Barbara E. Sellers; Dean of Conservatory, Tony Church; Associate Artistic Directors, Richard L. Hay, Randal Myler, Bruce K. Sevy, Laird Williamson; Designers, John Dexter, Pavel M. Dobrusky, Richard L. Hay, Charles MacLeod, Peter Maradudin, Janet S. Morris, Daniel L. Murray, Carolyn Ross, Rodney J. Smith, Vicki Smith, Bernard Vyzga, Patricia Ann Whitelock, Andrew V. Yelusich; Associates, Bill Curley, Bruce Brisson, Judith M. Pederson, David Wallace,: Directors, Jeff Church, Larry Delinger, Carolyn Dyer, Frank Georgianna, Donovan Marley, Greg Michaels, Randal Myler, Jared Sakren, Bruce K. Sevy, Leslie Watanabe (musical dir.): Choreography, Laird Williamson; Resident Playwrights, Terry Dodd, Frank X. Hogan, Kendrew Lascelles, Molly Newman; Playwrights Workshop, Sallie Baker, Trista Conger, Kevin Kelly, Pamela Stross Kenney, Richard Morell, Lee Patton, Kevin Shancaydhe, Wayne Valero

ACTING COMPANY: Jeffrey Agnitsch, Stephen Lee Anderson, Jacqueline Antaramian, Michele Artigas, Marsha Bagwell, Jim Baker, Wayne Ballantyne, Erza Barnes, Wendy Bawmann, Tamra Benham, Elizabeth Benjamin, Craig Bierko, Kathy Brady-Garvin, William Brenner, Diana Brownstone, Riette Burdick, Jack Casperson, John Clark, Ruthay V. Coney, Kenneth Corey, Robert Covarrubias, Melinda Deane, Kay Doubleday, Rebecca Eichenberger, David Eichman, Carole B. Elmore, Donna English, Robert Eustace, Louisa Flaningam, Victor Garron, Richard R. Garvin, Frank Georgianna, David Giella, Michael Gorman, Allison Gregory, Ann Guilbert, Lydia Hannibal, Suzan Hanson, Leslie Hendrix, Gillian Hoffman, Jamie Horton, Charles Hudson, Mitchell Hudson, Leticia Jaramillo, Brian K. Jennings, Christopher Keener, Merrill Key, Barbara Reeves Kuepper, Sandra Ellis Lafferty, Kendrew Lascelles, Maurice LaMee, James J. Lawless, Alice LeCount, Blayn Lemke, Jim Litten, Kipp Lockwood, Percy Howard Lyle, Jr., Michael X. Martin, Andy McAvin, Cheryl McFarren, DeAnn Mears, Greg Michaels, John Cameron Mitchell, Burke Moses, Melinda Mounsey, Meredith Nelson, Jeffrey W. Nickelson, Ellen Noll, Scott Olson, Ann Patricio, Fred Pinkard, Scott Putman, Scott Quintard, Tracy Ray-Collins, Guy Raymond, Mick Regan, Jeffery Reid, Jamey Roberts, Mason Roberts, Ken Allen Robertson, Jim T. Ruttman, Craig Ryder, Deborah Sclar, Archie Smith, Jimmie Lee Smith, Leslie C. Smith, Robert Torres, Sharon Ullrick, Albert Valdez, Laura P. Vega, Barry Wallace, Ronnie J. Whittaker, Cara Wilder, Vernon Willet, Walker Williams, Laird Williamson, Steve Wilson, Laura Ann Worthen

PRODUCTIONS: *Carousel* by Richard Rodgers & Oscar Hammerstein, 2nd; *The Matchmaker* by Thornton Wilder; *King Lear* by William Shakespeare; *Peter Pan* by James Barrie; *I'm Not Rappaport* by Herb Gardner; *Waiting For Godot* by Samuel Beckett; *Cat on a Hot Tin Roof* by Tennessee Williams; *Company* by Stephen Sondheim and George Furth; *Child of Luck* by Donald Freed; *Exclusive Circles*

Jamie Horton, Ann Patricio in "Exclusive Circles"
Above: James J. Lawless as "King Lear"

Top Right: John Cameron Mitchell as "Peter Pan"
Top Left: Burke Moses, Jim Baker in "Cat on a Hot Tin Roof"
T. Charles Erickson Photos

138

DETROIT REPERTORY THEATRE

Detroit, Michigan
Thirty-first Season

Artistic Director, Bruce E. Millan; Advertising/Marketing Director, Reuben Yabuku; Sales, Dino A. Valdez; Outreach Director, Dee Andrus; Literary manager, Barbara Busby; Costumes, B. J. Essen; Music Director, Kelly Smith; Sets, Bruce Millan, John Knox; Stage Managers, William Boswell, Barbara Busby, Ruth Allen; Lighting, Kenneth R. Hewitt, Jr., Sound, Ron Ayers, Burr Huntington; Graphics, Barbara Barefield

PRODUCTIONS & CASTS

GONE TO GLORY by Suzanne Finlay; Director, Reuben Yabuku. CAST: Dee Andrus, Barbara Busby, Clyde T. Harper, Michael Joseph, Nancy Matejek, Jacqueline Scott

LES BLANCS by Lorraine Hansberry; Director, Bruce E. Millan. CAST: Kamal A. Amen-Ra, Shashu Amen-Ra; Dee Andrus, William Boswell, Luray Cooper, Judy Dery, Clyde T. Harper, Andrew Dunn, Thom Galasso, Armond O. Jackson, William Malachi

RHINOCEROS by Eugene Ionesco; Director, Barbara Busby. CAST: Dee Andrus, William Boswell, Harold Hogan, Terry G. Hunt, Wilton Hurtt, Charlotte Nelson, Mack Palmer, Cheryl Pouncy, John Puchalski, Jacqueline Scott, Peggy Thorp, Harry Wetzel

CHARLIE/ENCHANTED NIGHT/OUT AT SEA (3 one-act comedies) by Slawomir Mrozek; Directors, Ruth Allen, William Boswell, Charles A. Jackson. CASTS: (Charlie) Andrew Dunn, William Malachi, Gerard L. A. Smith (Enchanted Night) Paulette Brockington, Luray Cooper, Michael Joseph (Out at Sea) Paulette Brockington, Andrew Dunn, Michael Joseph, William Malachi, Gerard L. A. Smith

Left: **William Malachi, Gerard Smith in "Charlie"**
Top: **William Boswell, John Puchalski in "Rhinoceros"**
Bruce E. Millan Photos

Dee Andrus, Barbara Busby, Jacqueline Scott, Clyde Harper (kneeling) in "Gone to Glory"

Dee Andrus, Laury Cooper in "Les Blancs"

139

FLAT ROCK PLAYHOUSE

Flat Rock, North Carolina

Managing Director, Robin R. Farquhar; Marketing Director, Rita McKinley; Technical Director, Bruce R. Bailey; Business Office Manager, Becky Laughter; Publicity, William Tell Agency, Bill Mebane, Joseph Gunnels; Scenic Designer, Dennis C. Maulden; Stage Manager, Johanna Erlenbach; Costumes, Bridget Bartlett; Lighting, James W. Hunter; Sound, Hilliard Ballard, Oliver Holler; Props, Paige Posey, Luther Jones.

PRODUCTIONS & CASTS

THE FANTASTICKS by Tom Jones and Harvey Schmidt; Director, William Dreyer; Musical Director, George Wilkins. CAST: Mark Hardy (The Narrator), Kim Cozort (The Girl), Christopher Lavely (The Boy), Steve Pudenz (The Boy's Father), Doug Kaye (The Girl's Father), W. C. "Mutt" Burton (The Actor), Scott Treadway (The Man Who Dies), Jef (The Mute).

MURDER ON THE NILE by Agatha Christie; Director, Steve Carlisle. CAST: Kim Krege, Sean Parker (Beadsellers), John W. Love, Jr. (Steward), Pat Fuleihan (Miss ffoliot-ffoulkes), Glenda Chism (Christina Grant), Peter Townes (Smith), Nancy Hammill (Louise), Steve Pudenz (Dr. Bessner), Lynn Fitzpatrick (Kay Mostyn), Nick Stannard (Simon Mostyn), Michael McGuire (Canon Pennefather), Kim Cozort (Jacqueline De Severac), Scott Treadway (McNaught).

THE NERD by Larry Shue; Director, Robin Farquhar. CAST: Wayne Tetrick (William Cubbert), Barbara Kent (Tansy McGinnis), Ralph Redpath (Axel Hammond), Steve Carlisle (Warnock Waldgrave), Barbara Bradshaw (Clelia Waldgrave), Keith Salkewicz (Thor Waldgrave), Stephen Michael Ayers (Rick Steadman).

THE ROBBER BRIDEGROOM by Alfred Uhry and Robert Waldman; Adapted from the novella by Eudora Welty; Director/Choreographer, Joe Conger; Musical Director, William Dreyer. CAST: Mark Hardy (Jamie Lockhart), Michael O. Smith (Clemment Musgrove), Diana Rogers (Salome), Kim Cozort (Rosamund), Stephen Ayers (Little Harp), Steve Pudenz (Big Harp), Scott Treadway (Goat), Phoebe Hall (Goat's Mother), Kelly Eviston (Airie), John W. Love, Jr. (A Raven), Wayne Tetrick (The Innkeeper/Ship's Captain), Charles Morgan Lusk (Bayou Boy), William Dreyer (The Caller/Preacher), Wayne Demaline, Leslie Hendricks, Gregg Jones, Philip Auton, Billy Munoz, Tim Black, Paige Posey, Mark Warwick, Cindy Michaels, Carol Cloud, Eve Whittle, Susie Spear.

REMAINS TO BE SEEN by Howard Lindsay and Russel Crouse; Director, Janelle Cochrane. CAST: Wayne Tetrick (Edward Miller), Jonathan Lutz (Benjamin Goodman), Nick Stannard (Dr. Charles Gresham), Scott Treadway (Waldo Walton), William Dreyer (Dr. Chester Delapp), Charles Morgan Lusk (Robert Clark), Riley Clermont (Fred Fleming), Mark Hardy (Tony Minetti), J. Douglass Sims (Morris Rosenberg), Kim Cozort (Jody Revere), Tim Brosnan (Hideo Hayakawa), Glenda Chism (Valeska Chauvel), Mark Warwick (Al, the Porter), Doug Kaye (Lt. Casey), Wayne Demaline (Det. Davis), Billy Munoz (Det. Weiner), Janelle Cochrane (Mrs. Bright).

WEEKEND COMEDY by Jeanne and Sam Bobrick; Director, William Dreyer. CAST: J. C. Mullins (Frank), Janelle Cochrane (Peggy), Suzanne Sloan (Jill), Mark Hardy (Tony).

PUMP BOYS AND DINETTES by John Foley, Mark Hardwick, Debra Monk, Cass Morgan, John Schimmel, Jim Wann. Staged and Directed by Jason Edwards, Robin Farquhar. CAST: Matt Morrison (Jackson), Guy Strobel (Jim), Linda Edwards (Prudie Cupp), Diane Pennington (Rhetta Cup), Eric Ferguson (Eddie), Jason Edwards (Jim).

A BEDFULL OF FOREIGNERS by Dave Freeman; Director, Stephen Michael Ayers. CAST: Doug Kaye (Karak), Peter Townes (Heinz), Mark Hardy (Stanley Parker), Lauri Kempson (Brenda Parker), Nancy Hammill (Helga Philby), Nick Stannard (Claude Philby), Kim Cozort (Simone).

Mark Handy, Michael O. Smith, Diana Rogers, Kim Cozort in "Robber Bridegroom"
Top: Linda Edwards, Eric Ferguson, Guy Strobel, Diane Pennington, Jason Edwards, Matt Morrison in "Pump Boys and Dinettes"

Mark Hardy, J. Douglass Sims, Doug Kaye, Tim Brosnan (seated) in "Remains to Be Seen"

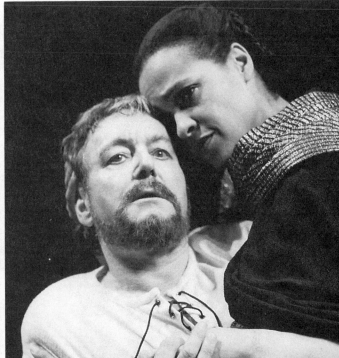

Mary Jay, Rob Woronoff in "Beggar's Opera"

FOLGER SHAKESPEARE THEATRE

Washington, D.C.

Artistic Director, Michael Kahn; Managing Director, Mary Ann de Barbieri; Business Manager, Sam Sweet; Assistant Director, Derek Jones; Director of PR/Marketing, Beth Hauptle; Production Manager, John W. Kingsbury; Technical Director, Ken Zommer.

PRODUCTIONS & CASTS

ANTONY AND CLEOPATRA by William Shakespeare; Director, Michael Kahn; Set, Robert Edward Darling; Costumes, Judith Dolan; Lighting, Dennis Parichy; Stage Manager, Pat Cochran; CAST: Kenneth Haigh, Michel R. Grill, Emery Battis, Edward Gero, Jack Ryland, Barry Mulholland, Andrew Land Prosky, Paris Peet, K. Lype O'Dell, Floyd King, Michael Forrest, Jan Notzon, Michael Forrest, D. Raymond Simonton, Katrina Van Duyn, Linda Khoury, Lisa Rhoden, Franchelle Stewart Dorn, Gayle Grate, Leah Maddrie, Robert Jason, Carlos Juan Gonzalez, Charles dUmas, Oliver Barreiro.
RICHARD II by William Shakespeare; Director, Toby Robertson; Set, Franco Colavecchia; Costumes, Judith Dolan; Lighting, John McLain; Stage Manager, Scott L. Hammar. CAST: K. Lype O'Dell, Philip Goodwin, Katherine Heasley, Clayton Corzatte, Emery Battis, Edward Gero, John Walcutt, Robert Jason, Jan Notzon, Michael Chaban, Steve Harley, Paris Peet, Floyd King, D. Raymond Simonton, James Huesz, Milledge Mosley, Andrew Land Prosky, Michael Forrest, Melanie Parrent, Lisa Rhoden, Linda Khoury, Mark Douglas, Mykal Knight.
THE BEGGAR'S OPERA by John Gay; Director, Gene Lesser; Set, Derek McLane; Costumes, Ellen McCartney; Lighting, Daniel MacLean Wagner; Stage Manager, James Latus.
AS YOU LIKE IT by William Shakespeare; Director, Michael Kahn; Set, Andrew Jackness; Costumes, Candice Donnelly; Lighting, Jeff Davis; Stage Manager, Scott L. Hammar. CAST: Emery Battis, Melissa Gallagher, Sabrina Le Beauf, Edward Gero, Mark Philpot, Steve Harley, Terry Hinz, Floyd King, Paris Peet, William Preston, Michael Forrest, James Huesz, Lawrence Redmond, Lisa Rhoden, Ted van Griethuysen, Richard Dix, Matt Bradford Sullivan, Bellina Logan, Franchelle Stewart Dorn, Mark Douglas, Jeffrey William Petersen, Jordan Young, Melanie Parrent.

Top Right: Kenneth Haigh, Franchelle Dorn in
"Antony and Cleopatra"
Below: Robert Jason, Philip Goodwin, Edward Gero in
"Richard II" *Joan Marcus Photos*

Melissa Gallagher, Floyd King, Sabrina Le Beauf in "As You
Like It"

GEORGE STREET PLAYHOUSE

New Brunswick, New Jersey

Producing Director, Gregory S. Hurst; General Manager, Michael P. Gennaro; Associate Artistic Director, Wendy Liscow; Director of Press/PR, Heidi W. Hopkins; Director of Outreach/Affiliate Director, Susan Kerner; Director of Design, Barbara Forbes; Business Manager, Karen S. Price; Development Director, Marilyn Powel; Production Manager, Dan Sedgwick; Technical Director, Kieran Kelly; Scenic Artist/Designer, Deborah Jasien.

PRODUCTIONS & CASTS

LITTLE SHOP OF HORRORS by Howard Ashman and Alan Menken; Director, Allen R. Belknap; Musical Director, Mark Goodman; Choreographer, Diana Baffa-Brill; Set, Atkin Pace; Costumes, Barbara Forbes; Lighting, Donald Holder; Stage Manager, Neal Fox; Puppet Design, Martin P. Robinson; Sound, James C. De-Rugeriis. CAST: Mone Walton, Tena Wilson, Rosemarie Jackson, Jerry Matz, Meghan Duffy, Romain Fruge, Michael Scott, Kurt Carley, Michael Mandell.
THE SUBJECT WAS ROSES by Frank D. Gilroy; Director, Stephen Rothman; Set, Atkin Pace; Special Choreography, Peter Gennaro; Costumes, Barbara Forbes; Lighting, Donald Holder; Sound, James C. DeRugeriis; Stage Manager, Sally Ann Wood. CAST: Robert DoQui, Isabel Sanford, Wendell Pierce.
TALES OF TINSELTOWN by Michael Colby and Paul Katz; Director, Larry Carpenter; Musical Direction/Dance & Vocal Arrangements, Steve Alper; Choreographer, Baayork Lee; Orchestrations, Larry Hochman; Costumes, Lindsay W. Davis; Lighting, Marcia Madeira; Sound, Jim Landis; Stage Manager, Thomas Clewell. CAST: Laura Kenyon, Patricia Ben Peterson, Evan Pappas, Robert Dorfman, Janice Lynde, Nat Chandler, Kathryn Kendall, Mark Bove.
THE EIGHTIES by Tom Cole; Director, Lamont Johnson; Set, Atkin Pace; Costumes, Barbara Forbes; Lighting, Donald Holder; Stage Manager, Sally Ann Wood. CAST: James Whitmore, Audra Lindley.
THE MYSTERY OF IRMA VEP by Charles Ludlam; Director, Sue Lawless; Set, Deborah Jasien; Costumes, Barbara Forbes; Lighting, Spencer Mosse; Stage Manager, Sally Ann Wood. CAST: Brian Reddy, Jonathan Bustle.
ALL MY SONS by Arthur Miller; Director, Wendy Liscow; Set, Deborah Jasien; Costumes, Barbara Forbes; Lighting, Michael Chybowski; Sound, Dave Mermelstein; Stage Manager, Veronica Griego. CAST: John Ramsey, Fritz Sperberg, Michael Pollard, Ellen Hulkower, Tony Carlin, Glen Kessler, Jeremy Martin, Isa Thomas, Anne Kerry Ford, Diane Gilch, Neal Lerner.
HEAVEN CAN WAIT by Harry Segall; Director, Gregory S. Hurst; Set, Atkin Pace; Costumes, Barbara Forbes; Lighting, Donald Holder; Stage Manager, Sally Ann Wood. CAST: William Cain, Robert Bender, Doug Freeburg, Peter Jay Fernandez, Edwin J. McDonough, Nancy Drumright Testa, Terry Layman, Lisby Larson, Barbara Benoit, Olivia Birkelund, Sally Vold Winters, David S. Howard, Ellen Hulkower, Michael Haney, Paul Stober, Stuart Adamo.

Left Center: Edwin McDonough, William Cain, Peter Jay
Fernandez in "Heaven Can Wait"
Top: Isabel Sanford, Wendell Pierce, Robert Do Qui in "The
Subject Was Roses"
Eddie Birch Photos

James Whitmore, Audra Lindley in "The Eighties"

GeVa THEATRE

Rochester, New York

PRODUCTIONS & CASTS

DAMES AT SEA by George Haimsohn, Robin Miller, Jim Wise; Director/Choreographer, Neal Kenyon; Musical Director, Corinne Aquilina; Set, Bob Barnett; Costumes, Mary Mease Warren; Lighting, Betsy Adams; Stage Manager, Frank Cavallo. CAST: Adinah Alexander, Karyn Quackenbush, Jeffrey Brocklin, Frank DiPasquale, Connie Kunkle, Doug Tompos.

OIL CITY SYMPHONY by Mike Craver, Mark Hardwick, Debra Monk, Mary Murfitt; Director, Larry Forde; Set, Bob Barnett; Costumes, Dana Harnish Tinsley; Lighting, Betsy Adams; Musical Director, John Miller; Stage Manager, James K. Tinsley. CAST: Mary Elhinger, G. Wayne Hoffman, Carol Sharar, Matthew M. Ward.

STEEL MAGNOLIAS by Robert Harling; Director, Walton Jones; Set, Victor Becker; Costumes, Pamela Peterson; Lighting, Tina Charney; Stage Manager, Barbara Beeching. CAST: Sally Ann Cohen, Jen Jones, Jeri Leer, Karen MacDonald, Maeve McGuire, Margot Stevenson.

EDITH STEIN by Arthur Giron; Director, Lee Sankowich; Set, Ursula Belden; Costumes, Laura Crow; Lighting, Kirk Bookman; Stage Manager, Catherine Norberg. CAST: Matthew Cowles, Ron Faber, Jack Koenig, Theresa McElwee, Devora Millman, Amanda Naughton, Susan Riskin, Sarah Sankowich, Anne Shropshire, Dolores Sutton.

A CHRISTMAS CAROL by Charles Dickens; adapted by Eberle Thomas; Director, Eberle Thomas; Music, John Franceschina; Set, Bob Barnett; Costumes, Pamela Scofield; Lighting, Nic Minetor; Choreography, Jim Hoskins; Stage Manager, Frank Cavallo. CAST: John Camera, Thomas Carson, Jeanne Cullen, Tim Douglas, Patrick Egan, Monique Morgan, Barbara Redmond, Michael Rudko, Alfred Schmitz, Dick St. George, Amy Stoller, K. C. Wilson, Christian Zwahlen.

TOMFOOLERY by Tom Lehrer; adapted by Cameron Mackintosh, Robin Ray; Director, William Roudebush; Musical Director, J. T. Smith; Set, Bob Barnett; Costumes, Dana Harnish Tinsley; Lighting, Rachel Budin; Stage Manager, Catherine Norberg. CAST: Stephen Kane, John-Charles Kelly, Mark McGrath, Laura Turnbull.

A WALK IN THE WOODS by Lee Blessing; Director, Stephen Rothman; Set, Harry Feiner; Costumes, Dana Harnish Tinsley; Lighting, Betsy Adams; Stage Manager, Frank Cavallo. CAST: Ben Hammer, Martin LaPlatney.

ITALIAN AMERICAN RECONCILIATION by John Patrick Shanley; Director, Allan Carlsen; Set, Loy Arcenas; Costumes, Jim Buff; Lighting, F. Mitchell Dana; Stage Manager, Catherine Norberg. CAST: Debra Cole, Adam Oliensis, Elizabeth Hess, Judith Scarpone, Armand Schultz.

I'M NOT RAPPAPORT by Herb Gardner; Director, Howard J. Millman; Set, Bob Barnett; Costumes, Pamela Scofield; Lighting, Nic Minetor; Stage Manager, Frank Cavallo. CAST: Thomas Martell Brimm, Saul Elkin, Michael Lewis, Richard Cottrell, Matthew Kimbrough, Carol Schultz, Donna Shanahan.

Right: John-Charles Kelly in "Tomfoolery"
Top: Karen MacDonald, Jeri Leer, Sally Ann Cohen, Margot Stevenson in "Steel Magnolias"
Gelfand-Piper Photos

Martin LaPlatney, Ben Hammer in "A Walk in the Woods"

Saul Elkin, Thomas Martell Brimm in "I'm Not Rappaport"

THE GOODMAN THEATRE

Chicago, Illinois

Artistic Director, Robert Falls; Producing Director, Roche Schulfer; Associate Directors, Frank Galati, Michael Maggio.

PRODUCTIONS & CASTS

ROMEO AND JULIET by William Shakespeare; Director, Michael Maggio; Set, Michael Merritt; Costumes, Nan Cibula; Lighting, Jennifer Tipton; Stage Manager, Lois Griffing, Alden Vasquez. CAST: Amanda Armato, Dominic Armato, Tom Benic, Larry Brandenburg, Gary Brichetto, Phoebe Cates (Juliet), Michael Cerveris (Romeo), Maurice Chasse, D. V. Devincentis, Louis DiCrescenzo, Toni Fleming, Henry Godinez, Tom Keeney, Ed Luther, Corinne Lyon, Maria Michaels, William J. Norris, Mike Nussbaum, Bob O'Donnell, Ernest Perry Jr., Steve Pickering, Gerit Quealy, John Reeger, Peggy Roeder, Stuart Joel Rosenberg, Larry Russo, Kathy Scambiatterra, Willy Schwarz, David Studwell, Kristine Thatcher, Tom Zanarini.

A CHRISTMAS CAROL by Charles Dickens; Adapted by Larry Sloan; Director, Michael Maggio; Set, Joe Nieminski; Costumes, Julie Jackson; Lighting, Robert Christen; Stage Managers, Joseph Drummond, Alden Vasquez. CAST: Miranda Kablach Bond, Pat Bowie, Anthony Bravo, Keith Byron-Kirk, Anthony Cesaretti, Christopher Creighton, Erin Creighton, Terence Gallagher, Henry Godinez, Susan Hart, Brent Hendon, Ora Jones, Dennis Kennedy, John Mohrlein, Sally Murphy, William J. Norris (Ebenezer Scrooge), James Otis, Ernest Perry Jr., Peggy Roeder, Tom Roland, Tony Russell, Robert Scogin, Kristine Thatcher, David Malcolm Thompson, Crystal R. Walker, Anthony T. Wong.

THE PIANO LESSON by August Wilson, presented in association with Yale Repertory Theatre; Director, Lloyd Richards; Sets, E. David Cosier Jr.; Costumes, Constanza Romero; Lighting, Christopher Akerlind; Stage Manager, Lois Griffing, Karen L. Carpenter. CAST: Paul Butler, Rocky Carroll, Charles S. Dutton, Tommy Hollis, S. Epatha Merkerson, Tony Pinkins, Danny Robinson-Clark, Tressa Janaee Thomas.

THE ROVER by Aphra Behn, adapted by John Barton; Director, Kyle Donnelly; Sets, John Lee Beatty; Costumes, Lindsay W. Davis; Lighting, Judy Rasmuson; Stage Managers, Joseph Drummond, Alden Vasquez. CAST: Ramiro Carillo, Ray Chapman, Randy Colborn, Bellary Darden, Henry Godinez, Kate Goehring, Sean Grennan, Timothy Grimm, Irma P. Hall, Ross Lehman, Kevin McCoy, Steve Pickering, Peggy Roeder, Peter Rybolt, Ellen Jane Smith, Marianne Tatum, Jack Wetherall, Edward Wilkerson, Lisa Zane.

THE SPEED OF DARKNESS by Steve Tesich (WORLD PREMIERE); Director, Robert Falls; Sets, Thomas Lynch; Costumes, Nan Cibula; Lighting, Michael S. Philippi; Stage Managers, Lois Griffing, Jill Larmett. CAST: Brigitte Bako, Lee Guthrie, Andy Hirsch, Stephen Lang, Bill Raymond.

MILL FIRE by Sally Nemeth (WORLD PREMIERE); Director, David Petrarca; Sets, Linda Buchanan, Laura Cunningham; Lighting, Robert Christen; Stage Manager, David P. Foti. CAST: Kate Buddeke, Kelly Coffield, Timothy Grimm, B. J. Jones, James Krag, Martha Lavey, Paul Mabon, Mary Ann Thebus, Jacqueline Williams.

A FUNNY THING HAPPENED ON THE WAY TO THE FORUM by Burt Shevelove, Larry Gelbart, Stephen Sondheim; Director, Frank Galati; Choreography, Chet Walker; Sets/Costumes, Mary Griswold, John Paoletti; Lighting, Geoffrey Bushor; Musical Director, Janet Aycock; Stage Managers, Joseph Drummond, Alden Vasquez. CAST: David Bedella, Cheridah Best, Bill Busch, Annette Calud, Shannon Cochran, Lisa Comeaux, Marietta DePrima, Louis DiCrescenzo (Pseudolus) David Girolmo, Josette Huber, Ross Lehman, Jeremy Lund, George Newbern, William J. Norris, Kristy Roy, David Studwell, Carol Swarbrick, Kelly Williams.

Left Center: "The Rover"
Above: Dennis Kennedy (C) in "A Christmas Carol"
Top: Michael Cerveris, Phoebe Cates in "Romeo and Juliet"
Photos by Charles Osgood, Tom Lascher, Kevin Horan,
Lisa Ebright

Brigitte Bako, Stephen Lang in "The Speed of Darkness"

James Krag, Kelly Coffield in "Mill Fire"

144

James Krag, B. J. Jones in "Mill Fire"
Top: (L) Lou Myers in "The Piano Lesson"
(R) Lee Guthrie, Bill Raymond in "The Speed of Darkness"

GOODSPEED OPERA HOUSE

East Haddam, Connecticut
Twenty-sixth Season

Executive Director, Michael P. Price; Associate Artistic Director, Dan Siretta; Musical Director, Lynn Crigler; Associate Producer, Sue Frost; Casting Director/ New York Representative, Warren Pincus; Stage Manager, Michael Brunner; Press, Max Eisen/Madelon Rosen

PRODUCTIONS & CASTS

WONDERFUL TOWN with Music by Leonard Bernstein; Lyrics by Betty Comden, Adolph Green; Book, Joseph Fields, Jerome Chodorov; Director, Thomas Gruenewald; Choreography, Rodney Griffin; Sets, Lowell Detweiler; Costumes, John Carver Sullivan; Lighting, Craig Miller. CAST: Jennifer Lee Andrews (Eileen), David Brand (Wreck), Roo Brown (Jane, Mrs. Wade), Catherine Cox (Ruth), Robert Frisch (Robert), Gary Gage (Appopolous), Greg Gunning (Guide, Chick), Terry Kirwin (Frank), Lori Ann Mahl (Helen), Jerry Matz (Valenti), William Ryall (Lonigan), Beth Blatt (Violet), Jerry Christakos (Villager), Kim Darwin (Villager), Lyd-Lyd Gaston (Villager) Ned Hannah (Delivery Boy), Campbell Martin (Editor), G. Eugene Moose (Editor), Len Pfluger (Patrolman), Jeff Williams (Villager), Laurie Williamson (Villager).

ANKLES AWEIGH with Music by Sammy Fain; Lyrics, Dan Shapiro; Book, Guy Bolton, Eddie Davis, adapted by Charles Busch; Director, Dan Siretta; Associate Director, Charles Busch; Choreography, Dan Siretta; Sets, Eduardo Sicangco; Costumes, Eduardo Sicangco, Jose Lengson; Lighting, Allen Lee Hughes; New Arrangements, Tom Fay; Assistant Musical Director, Patrick Vaccariello CAST: D'Jamin Bartlett (Lorraine), Peter Bartlett (Russell), Monica Carr (Gloria), Bobby Clark (Spud), Kevin Cooney (Admiral), Bob Cuccioli (Joe), Ken Lundie (Dinky), Mark McGrath (Bill), Debbie Petrino (Lucia), Maria Calabrese, Allison Gill, Steve Goodwillie, Gib Jones, Frank Kosic, Patricia Lockery, Joanne McHugh, Jeri Sager, Frank Siano, Glenn Sneed, Amiee Turner, George Wainwright.

MR. CINDERS with Music by Vivian Ellis & Richard Myers; Lyrics, Leo Robin; Book/Lyrics, Clifford Grey & Greatrex Newman; Director, Martin Connor; Choreography, Dan Siretta; Sets, James Leonard Joy; Costumes, David Toser; Lighting, Curt Ostermann; Orchestrations, Russell Warner, Lynn Crigler, Ted Kociolek (dance). CAST: Beth Austin (Jill), Tom Batten (Henry), Katy Cavanaugh (Phyllis), Pamela Clifford (Minerva), Patricia Kilgarriff (Lady Lancaster), Teresa Parente (Donna/Lucy), Charles Repole (Jim), Farnham Scott (Merks), Drew Taylor (Lumley), Ian Thomson (Smith), Bill Ullman (Guy), Iggie Wolfington (Sir George), Holly Evers (Enid), Tim Foster (Harry/Chauffeur), Gary Kirsch (Bunny), Renee Laverdiere (Becky), David Monzione (Charles), Angela Nicholas (Penelope), Ken Skrzesz (Freddie), Miki Whittles (Cynthia)

Right: "Wonderful Town"
Top: Charles Repole in "Mr. Cinders"
Diane Sobolewski, Wilson Brownell Photos

Beth Austin, Charles Repole in "Mr. Cinders"

Ken Lundie, Lynette Perry, Bobby Clark in "Ankles Aweigh"

THE GUTHRIE THEATER

Minneapolis, Minnesota
Twenty-sixth Season

Artistic Director, Garland Wright; Executive Director, Edward A. Martenson; Stage Directors, JoAnne Akalaitis, Robert Falls, Michael Maggio, Vivian Matalon, Charles Newell, Richard Ooms, Lucian Pintille, Garland Wright; Designers, John Arnone, Jack Barkla, Miruna Boruzescu, Radu Boruzescu, John Calder, Marcus Dilliard, Jack Edwards, Beverly Emmons, Jane Greenwood, Desmond Heeley, Ann Hould-Ward, James F. Ingalls, Duane Schuler, Doug Stein, Garland Wright
ACTING COMPANY: Mark Benninghofen, Peter Bernstein, Olivia Birkelund, Bruce Bohne, Jesse Borrego, John Bottoms, Elizabeth Bove, Julie Boyd, Charles Brin, David Brinkley, Sherri Bustad, Don Cheadle, Michael Countryman, Steven D'Ambrose, Bob Davis, Daniel Davis, Richard Dix, Curzon Dobell, Paul Drake, Rebecca Ellens, Tom Fervoy, Randy Fuhrmann, Nathaniel Fuller, Jennifer Harmon, Jannie Harper, Emil Herrera, Alan Hickle-Edwards, Rana Haugen, Richard Hicks, Polly Holiday, Tim Hopper, Richard S. Iglewski, Thomas Ikeda, Zeljko Ivanek, Keith Jochim, Barbara Kingsley, John Lewin, John Carroll Lynch, Ruth Maleczech, Stephen Markle, Chris McCann, Edgar Meyer, Julianne Moore, Amy Moprton, Jerry Newhouse, Andrew Hill Newman, Richard Ooms, David Ossian, Marin Osterberg, Stephen Pelinski, Lia Rivamonte, Tracy Sallows, Louis Schaefer, Buffy Sedlachek, Charles Siebert, Peter Syvertsen, Michael Tazla, Peter Thoemke, Lauren Tom, Jack Walsh, Brenda Wehle, Alan Wilder, Claudia Wilkens, Stephen Yoakam
PRODUCTIONS: *The Glass Menagerie, The Imaginary Invalid, Hamlet, The Wild Duck, A Christmas Carol*
PREMIERES: *Frankenstein: Playing With Fire (World Premiere)* adapted from Mary Shelly by Barbara Field; *Pravda: A Fleet Street Comedy* by Howard Brenton & David Hare (*U.S. Premiere*)

Right: Peter Syvertsen, John Carroll Lynch in "Frankenstein"
Michael Daniel, Joe Giannetti Photos

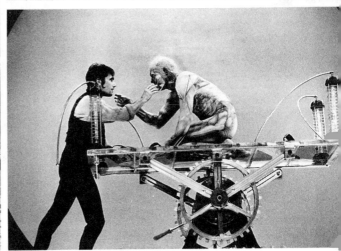

(R) Daniel Davis, Michael Countryman
Above: Davis, Nathaniel Fuller in
"Pravda—A Fleet Street Comedy"

Curzon Dobell, John Carroll Lynch in "Frankenstein"

147

HARTFORD STAGE COMPANY

Hartford, Connecticut
Twenty-sixth Season

Artistic Director, Mark Lamos; Managing Director, David Hawkanson; Resident Playwright/Literary Manager, Constance Congdon; Dramaturg/Education, Greg Leaming; General Manager/Marketing, Jeffrey Woodward; Public Relations, Howard S. Sherman; Business Manager, Michael Ross; Production Manager, Candice Chirgotis, Technical, Jim Keller; Costumer, Martha Christian; Properties/Designer, Sandy Struth

PRODUCTIONS & CASTS

A MIDSUMMER NIGHT'S DREAM by William Shakespeare; Director, Mark Lamos; Sets, Michael Yeargan; Costumes, Jess Goldstein; Lighting, Pat Collins; Stage Managers, Ruth E. Sternberg, Liz Small. CAST: Irwin Appel (Tom Snout), Meg Barone, Elizabeth DuVall (Hermia), Ken Festa, Charlie Heinemann, Keith Langsdale (Quince), Wendy Lawless (Helena), Heidi Lynne, Michelle Martin, James McDonnell (Bottom), Katlyn McNeill, Joel McKinnon Miller (Snug), Tony Morris, Howie Muir (Robin), Tom Reuel, Ali Sharaf, Daniel Nathan Spector (Lysander), Robert Stanton (Flute), Sherry Stidolph, Daniel Tamm (Puck), Bradley Whitford (Theseus/Oberon), Graham Winton (Demetrius), John Wright, Janet Zarish (Hippolyta/Titania)

OTHER PEOPLE'S MONEY by Jerry Sterner; Director, Gloria Muzio; Sets, David Jenkins; Costumes, Jess Goldstein; Lighting, F. Mitchell Dana; Sound, David Budries; Stage Managers, Stacey Fleischer. CAST: Scotty Bloch (Bea), Arch Johnson (Andrew), James Murtaugh (William), Jon Polito (Lawrence), Mercedes Ruehl (Kate)

NOTHING SACRED by George F. Walker; Director, James Simpson; Sets, Michael Yeargan; Costumes, Claudia Brown; Lighting, Frances Aronson; Composer, Michael Roth; Stage Manager, Ruth E. Sternberg. CAST: Thomas Andreson (Piotr), Charles Antalosky (Nikolai), Christian Baskous (Yevgeny), Richard M. Davidson (Pavel), Kevin Davis (Bailiff), Daryl Edwards (Gregor), Karen Evans-Kandel (Fenichka), Patrick Garner (Viktor), Jodi Long (Anna), Robert Stanton (Arkady), Jefferey V. Thompson (Sergei)

THE PAPER GRAMOPHONE based on a screenplay by Alexander Chervinsky, adapted by Yuri Yeremin & Alexander Chervinsky; Translation, Mary-Helen Ayres; Director, Yuri Yeremin; Sets/Costumes, Michael Yeargan; Lighting, Ken Tabachnick; Sound, David Budries; Dance, Kathryn Posin; Interpreter, Alexander Gelman; Assistant Director, Elise Thoron; Stage Manager, Wendy Cox. CAST: Jack Bittner (Oscar), Evan Blackford (Student), Kathleen Chalfant (Lidia), Ann Dowd (Victoria), Ray Virta (Semyon)

PEER GYNT by Henrik Ibsen; Translation, Gerry Bamman & Irene B. Berman; Director Mark Lamos; Sets, John Conklin; Costumes, Murrily Murry-Walsh; Lighting, Pat Collins; Sound, David Budries; Music, Mel Marvin; Wigs, Paul Huntley; Stage Managers, Ruth E. Sternberg, Gail Burns, Neal Fox. CAST: Terrence Caza, Patricia Conolly (Ase), Gregg Daniel, Ken Festa, Leslie Geraci, Philip Goodwin, Helen Harrelson, Harriette H. Holmes, Melonie Holt, Tara Hugo (Solveig), Paul Kandel, Barry Lee, Sharon Mann, David Scott Meikle, Tim Murray, Wyman Pendleton, Adina Porter, Benjamin Rayner, Stephen Rowe, Thomas Schall, Christine Shaker, Richard Thomas (Peer Gynt), Peter Von Berg, Jessica Weglein, Nancy Wolfe

A MOON FOR THE MISBEGOTTEN by Eugene O'Neill; Director, Jackson Phippin; Sets, Christopher Barreca; Costumes; Robert Wojewodski; Lighting, Ken Tabachnick; Sound, David Budries; Stage Managers, Liz Small, Robert L. Young. CAST: Maureen Anderman, Terrence Caza, James Handy, Gordon MacDonald, Robert Symonds

Left Center: Bradley Whitford, Daniel Tamm
Top: James McDonnell, Janet Zarish in "Midsummer
Night's Dream"

Jon Polito, Mercedes Ruehl in "Other People's Money"

T. Charles Erickson Photos

Patrick Garner, Christian Baskous, Jodi Long, Jeffery
Thompson in "Nothing Sacred"

148

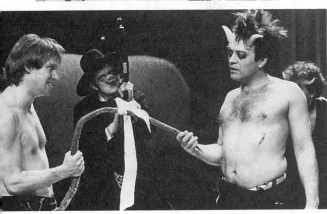

Richard Thomas, Stephen Rowe in "Peer Gynt"
Above: Karen Evans-Kandel, Charles Antalosky in "Nothing Sacred"
Top: Ann Dowd, Kathleen Chalfant, Ray Virta in "Paper Gramophone"

Maureen Anderman, James Handy in "A Moon for the Misbegotten"
Top: Richard Thomas, Patricia Conolly in "Peer Gynt"

149

HIPPODROME STATE THEATRE

Gainsville, Florida

Artistic Director, Mary Hausch; Sets, Carlos F. Asse; Costumes, Marilyn Wall-Asse; Lighting; Robert P. Robins: Stage Manager, Michael Johnson

PRODUCTIONS & CASTS

I'M NOT RAPPAPORT by Herb Gardner; CAST: David S. Howard, William Hall, Jr., Mark Sexton, Gregory Jones, Gus Hughes, Nell Page Sexton, Cynthia Leigh Pierson, Henry Sommerville
BLUE PLATE SPECIAL CAST: Rebecca Hoodwin, Kevin Rainsberger, Scott Isert, Gregory Jones, Jennifer Pritchett, Karen Hinton
TALK RADIO by Eric Bogosian; CAST: Kevin Rainsberger, Amanda Fry, John F. Lennon, Michael Beistle, Dan Jesse, Nell Page Sexton, Lauren Caldwell, Gregory Ray Jones, Rusty Stalling
ABSENT FRIENDS CAST: Nell Page Sexton, Dan Jesse, Sandra Langsner, Lauren Caldwell, Kevin Rainsberger, Rusty Stalling
BROADWAY BOUND by Neil Simon; CAST: Lauren Klein, Herbert Rubens, Pete Bauer, James Wren, Lynn Rudner Jamieson, Frank Biancamano
A WALK IN THE WOODS by Lee Blessing; CAST: Frank Biancamano, Kevin Rainsberger

Top: Gus Hughes, David Howard in "I'm Not Rappaport"
Gary S. Wolfson Photos

Kevin Rainsberger in "Talk Radio"

HUNTINGTON THEATRE COMPANY

Boston, Massachusetts
Seventh Season

Producing Director, Peter Altman; Managing Director, Michael Maso; Press Jennifer Maxwell

PRODUCTIONS & CASTS

AMERICAN CLOCK by Arthur Miller; Director, Jackson Phippin; Sets, Christopher Barreca; Costumes, Robert Wojewodski; Lighting, Steven Strawbridge; Stage Manager, Karen L. Carpenter. CAST: Donald Christopher, Richard Ciccarone, Lynn Cohen, Joseph Costa, Joanna Glushak, Rob Gomes, John Hutton, Bob Levine, Salem Ludwig, Tanny McDonald, Stephen Mendillo, Todd Merrill, William Parry, Chuck Patterson, Patricia Ben Peterson, Rex Robbins, Myra Taylor

DON JUAN by Moliere; Director, Jacques Cartier; Sets, John Falabella; Costumes, Robert Morgan; Lighting, Roger Meeker; Stage Manager, Sherrill deWitt-Howard. CAST: Julie Bargeron, Terrence Caza, Donald Christopher, Denise Dillard, Lisa Emery, Dunson Hicks, Leonard Kelly-Young, Scott Koh, Dick Latessa, Josh Mosby, Kathleen Mulligan, Paul Niebank, Thomas Schall, Ivan Stolze, Louis Turenne, John Vickery.

LES BLANCS by Lorraine Hansberry; Director, Harold Scott; Sets, Karl Eigsti; Costumes, Marjorie Slaiman; Lighting, Allen Lee Hughes; Stage Manager, Maxine Krasowski Bertone. CAST: Barnett Williams, Evelyn Thomas, Tony Todd, Basil Wallace, Jeffrey Wright, Patricia Hodges, Lou Ferguson, Phillip Clark, Mark Hammer, Steven Major West, Barry Boys, Lilia Skala, Orisanmi Burton, Ian Ellis Johnson, Nefertiti Burton, Craig Alan Edwards, Bob Knapp, Anthony Walker.

ALL'S WELL THAT ENDS WELL by William Shakespeare; Director, Edward Gilbert; Sets, Kate Edmunds; Costumes, John Falabella; Lighting, Nick Cernovitch; Stage Manager, Russell Johnson. CAST: David O'Brien, Michel R. Gill, Shelia Allen, Maryann Plunkett, Jack Aranson, J. K. Simmons, James Bodge, Derek Meader, Charles Tuthill, Jack Wallace, John Camera, Janet Sarno, Jennifer Roblin, Donna Sorbello, Cliff Allen, Andrew Dolan, Bob Knapp, Scott Koh, William McManus

CANDIDE with Music by Leonard Bernstein; Lyrics, Richard Wilbur, others; Book, Hugh Wheeler adap. Voltaire; Director, Larry Carpenter; Sets, Campbell Baird; Costumes, John Falabella; Lighting, Marcia Madeira; Stage Manager, Diane DiVita. CAST: Stephen Hanan, Scott Waara, Rose Mcguire, Nat Chandler, Stacey Logan, Ruth Williamson, Brian Arsenault, James Coelho, Deborah Collins, Pam Dillard, J. P. Doughtery, Carl Hieger, Susan Holmes, John Hoshko, Jeffery Korn, Frank Maio, Richard Malone, Janna Marshall, Karen Murphy, Mary Ellen Phillips, Sally Ann Swarm, Jake Webb

**Top Right: Michel Gill, Maryann Plunkett, Sheila Allen in
"All's Well That Ends Well"**
Below: Louis Turenne, John Vickery in "Don Juan"
Gerry Goodstein Photos

**Barry Boys, Bob Knapp, Mark Hammer, Anthony Walker,
Lilia Skala in "Les Blancs"**

Scott Waara, Rose McGuire in "Candide"

ILLINOIS THEATRE CENTER

Park Forest, Illinois
Thirteenth Season

Artistic Director, Steve S. Billig; Administrative Director, Etel Billig; Business Management, C. H. Associates; Dramaturg, Barbara Jean Mitchell; Public Relations, Maggie Evans; Sets, Nick DePaolo, Archway Scenic; Lighting, August Ziemann; Costumes, Henriette Swearingen, Pat Decker; Musical Director, Jonathan Roark; Choreographers, Larry Yando, Shole Milos

PRODUCTIONS & CASTS

BITTERSUITE: SONGS OF EXPERIENCE with Music by Elliot Weiss; Lyrics, Michael Champagne; Director, Steve S. Billig. CAST: David Perkovich, Norrice Raemaker, James Braet, Anne Kanengeiser
OUR LADY OF THE TORTILLA by Luis Santeiro; Director, Steve S. Billig. CAST: Carmen Roman, Carlos Sanz, Etel Billig, David Mazzafero, Siobhan Sullivan, Angela Friend
THE MYSTERY OF EDWIN DROOD by Rupert Holmes; Director, David Perkovich. CAST: Anne Kanengeiser, Brian-Mark Conover, Steve S. Billig, Etel Billig, Susan Dennis, Shelly Crosby, Shole Milos, Larry Yando, Benny P. Goodman, Ed Kross, Bob Keefe, Angela Friend, Richard Rowan, David Presby, Liz Donathan, Patrick Bednarczyk, Jonathan Roark
MAX AND MAXIE by James McClure; Director, Steve S. Billig. CAST: Mickey Vinson, Iris Lieberman, Michael Wexler
AMAZING GRACE by Sandra Deer; Director, Steve S. Billig. CAST: Paula Markovitz, Sam Sanders, Etel Billig, Matt Raftery, Alani Rosa Hicks-Bartlett
MUSICAL COMEDY MURDERS OF 1940 by John Bishop; Director, David Perkovitch. CAST: Sharon Carlson, Sally Jo Bannow, David Presby, Angela Friend, Christian Lebano, Terrance Paul Dunn, Steve S. Billig, Etel Billig, Bob Keefe, Shelly Crosby
PERSONALS with Music by William K. Dreskin, Joel Phillip Friedman, Seth Friedman, Alan Menken, Steven Schwartz, Michael Skloff; Lyrics & Book, David Crane, Seth Friedman, Marta Kaufman. CAST: David Perkovitch, Shelly Crosby, Angela Friend, Liz Donathan, Steve S. Billig, George Badecker

**Left: Sam Sanders, Alani Rosa Hicks-Bartlett, Etel Billig in
"Amazing Grace"
Top: Benny Goodman, Steve Billig, Ed Kross in "Drood"**
Peter LeGrand Photos

Carmen Roman, Etel Billig in "Our Lady of the Tortilla"

Iris Lieberman, Mickey Vinson in "Max and Maxie"

LONG ISLAND STAGE

Rockville Centre, New York

Artistic Director, Clinton J. Atkinson; Managing Director, Thomas M. Madden; Associate Managing, Jeffrey E. Ranbom; Administrative Director/Community Affairs, Sally Cohen; Corporate Development, John R. Staib; Assistant Artistic Director, Joe Heissan; Technical Manager, Chris Davis; Stage Manager, David Wahl; Artistic Associates, Dan Conway, John Hickey, Jill Hillgartner, Don Newcomb

PRODUCTIONS & CASTS

THE LION IN WINTER by James Goldman; Director, Jim Hillgartner; Sets, Steven Perry; Costumes, Gail Brassard; Lighting, John Hickey. CAST: Anthony Call (Henry II), Marcus Giamatti (Richard), Leah-Carla Gordone (Alais), Steven Haworth (Geoffrey), Edward Henzel (Philip), Spike McClure (John), June Prud'homme (Eleanor)
TALLEY'S FOLLY by Lanford Wilson; Director, Clinton J. Atkinson; Sets, Steven Perry; Costumes, Andrew Earl Jones; Lighting, John Hickey. CAST: Jane Hoppe (Sally), Joel Leffert (Matt)
BILLY BISHOP GOES TO WAR by John Gray in collaboration with Eric Peterson; Director, Clinton J. Atkinson; Sets, James Youmans; Costumes, Andrew Earl Jones; Lighting, John Hickey. CAST: Ross Bickell (Billy), Steve Liebman.
AFTERSHOCKS (World Premiere) by Doug Haverty; Director, Clinton J. Atkinson; Sets, James Youmans; Costumes, Don Newcomb; Lighting, John Hickey. CAST: Marilyn Chris (Daphne), Jane Hoppe (Beth), Ruth Livingston (Olive).
IN THE BEGINNING by Bernard Shaw; Director, Clinton J. Atkinson; Sets, James Singelis; Costumes, Gail Brassard; Lighting, John Hickey. CAST: Jim Fitzpatrick (Adam), Isabella Knight (Eve), David Snizek (Serpent), Jeffrey Spolan (Cain)
HARVEY by Mary C. Chase; Director, Clinton J. Atkinson; Sets, Daniel Ettinger; Costumes, Don Newcomb; Lighting, John Hickey. CAST: Harry Bennett (Duane), Shirley Bodtke (Veta), Ted Bouton (Lofgren), George Cavey (Judge), Jennifer Dawson (Myrtle), Celia Howard (Betty), Daniel Nalbach (Chumley), Sally Netzel (Mrs. Chauvenet), John Newton (Elwood), Susan Pingleton (Kelly), David Sitler (Sanderson)

Top Left: June Prud'homme, Anthony Call in "Lion in Winter" Top Right: Joel Leffert, Jane Hoppe in "Talley's Folly" Below: Ruth Livingston, Marilyn Chris, Jane Hoppe in "Aftershocks" *Brian Ballweg Photos*

Sally Netzel, John Newton in "Harvey"

LONG WHARF THEATRE

New Haven, Connecticut
Twenty-fourth Season

Artistic Director, Arvin Brown; Executive Director, M. Edgar Rosenblum; Literary Consultant, John Tillinger; Artistic Associate, Kenneth Frankel; General Manager, John K. Conte; Development, Pamela Tatge, Patricia Ford, Ana Silfer; Technical, Ted Zuse; Props, David Fletcher; Wardrobe, Jean Routt; Press, David Mayhew, John Kelly

PRODUCTIONS & CASTS

DINNER AT EIGHT by George S. Kaufman & Edna Ferber; Director, Arvin Brown; Sets, Hugh Landwehr; Costumes, David Murin; Lighting, Ronald Wallace; Stage Manager, Anne Keefe. CAST: James Andreassi (Ricci), Marylouise Burke (Miss Copeland/Mrs. Wendel), Beeson Carroll (Dan), Ray DeMattis (Max), Joyce Ebert (Carlotta), Patricia Englund (Hattie), Clement Fowler (Ed), Edmond Genest (Dr. Talbot), Annie Golden (Kitty), Tracy Griswold (Gustave), Charles Keating (Larry), Louise Roberts (Dora), Shelly Rogers (Lucy), Martin Rudy (Jo), Jennifer Van Dyck (Paula), Lorraine Venture (Tina), Richard Venture (Oliver), Elizabeth Wilson (Millicent)

NATIONAL ANTHEMS by Dennis McIntyre; Director, Arvin Brown; Sets, Michael H. Yeargan; Costumes, David Murin; Lighting, Ronald Wallce; Stage Manager, Robin Kevrick. CAST: Tom Berenger (Arthur), Mary McDonnell (Leslie), Kevin Spacey (Ben)

WHEN WE ARE MARRIED by J. B. Priestley; Director, Kenneth Frankel; Sets, Hugh Landwehr; Costumes, Jess Goldstein; Lighting, David F. Segal; Stage Manager, Anne Keefe. CAST: Marylouise Burke (Lottie), Patricia Conolly (Maria), Robertson Dean (Gerald Forbes), Donal Donnelly (Parker), Joyce Ebert (Mrs. Northrop), George Hearn (Henry), Margaret Hilton (Annie), Laurie Kennedy (Clara), Leslie Simons (Nancy), William Swetland (Rev.), Jill Tasker (Ruby), Ralph Williams (Herbert), Howard Witt (Alderman), William Youmans (Fred)

SOME SWEET DAY by Nancy Fales Garrett; Director, Seret Scott; Sets, Michael H. Yeargan; Costumes, David Murin; Lighting, Pat Collins; Stage Manager, Robin Kevrick. CAST: Terry Alexander (Vernard), Cynthia Belgrave (Annie), Rosanna Carter (Elizabeth), Clebert Ford (Elijah), Yvette Hawkins (Shug), Mike Hodge (Vernard, Sr.), Damien Leake (Preach), Herb Lovelle (Raymond), Cynthia Mace (Judy), Jack R. Marks (Mr. Abercrombie)

THE HEIRESS by Ruth and Augustus Goetz; Director Kenneth Frankel; Sets, Loy Arcenas; Costumes, Jess Goldstein; Lighting, David F. Segal; Stage Manager, Anne Keefe. CAST: Jayne Atkinson (Catherine), Michel R. Gill (Morris), Margaret Hilton (Mrs. Penniman), Richard Kiley (Dr. Sloper), Peter Mackenzie (Arthur), Gloria Maddox (Mrs. Almond), Wendee Pratt (Marian), Jeanne Ruskin (Mrs. Montgomery), Ann Sheehy (Maria)

LOVE LETTERS by A. R. Gurney; Director, John Tillinger; Lighting, Judy Rasmuson; Stage Manager, Beverly J. Andreozzi. CAST: John Cunningham, Joanna Gleason, George Hearn, E. Katherine Kerr, Ann McDonough, Charlotte Moore, John Rubinstein, Josef Somer (alternating in the roles of Andrew Makepeace Lad III and Melissa Gardner)

REBEL ARMIES DEEP INTO CHAD by Mark Lee; Director, John Tillinger; Sets, John Lee Beatty; Costumes, Candice Donnelly; Lighting, Marc B. Weiss; Stage Manager, Beverly J. Andreozzi. CAST: Gail Grate (Christina), Alan Scarfe (Dove), Pamela Tucker-White (Mary), Joe Urla (Neal)

FORGIVING TYPHOID MARY by Mark St. Germain; Director, Michael Bloom; Sets, Hugh Landwehr; Stage Manager, Beverly J. Andreozzi; CAST: Lynn Cohen (Mary), Daniel Nathan Spector (Father McKuen), Richard Spore (Frazier/Intern/Announcer), Lisa Spoerri (Sarah), Karen Trott (Dr. Saltzer), William Wise (Dr. Mills)

SONGS FROM DISTANT LANDS by Corinne Jacker; Director, Tina J. Ball; Sets, Hugh Landwehr; Stage Manager, Ruth Feldman. CAST: Gail Dartez (Maggie), Virginia Downing (Cettie), Laurie Heineman (Anne), Victor Love (Pete), Sarah Melici (Lucy), Thomas Nahrwold (Steve), Priscilla Shanks (Kate)

MINOR DEMONS by Bruce Graham; Director, Richard Harden; Sets, Hugh Landwehr; Stage Manager, Beverly Andreozzi. CAST: Phillip Clark (O'Brien), Kevin Cooney (O'Brien), Larry Joshua (Vince), Karen McDonald (Carmella), Barry Mulholland (Deke), Nicholas Tamarkin (Kenny), Lauren Thompson (Diane), John C. Vennema (Simmonds), Callan White (Mrs. Simmonds)

A DANCE LESSON by David Wiltse; Director, Gorgon Edelstein; Sets, Hugh Landwehr; Stage Manager, Ruth Feldman. CAST: Josh Charles (Jay), Eric Conger (Jason), Tracy Griswold (Dan), Rob Harris Kramer (Smitty), Susan Pellegrino (Susan), Ben Siegler (Jack)

Top left: Mary McDonnell, Tom Berenger in
"National Anthems"
Below: Cynthia Belgrave, Mike Hodge in
"Some Sweet Day"
T. Charles Erickson Photos

Jayne Atkinson, Margaret Hilton, Richard Kiley in
"The Heiress"

Laurie Kennedy, Margaret Hilton, Patricia Conolly in "When We Are Married"
Top: Elizabeth Wilson, Richard Venture in "Dinner at Eight"
T. Charles Erickson Photos

LOS ANGELES THEATRE CENTER

Los Angeles, California
Fifth Season

Artistic Producing Director, Bill Bushnell; Producer, Diane White; Consulting Director, Alan Mandell; Design Director, Timian Alsaker; General Manager, Carol Baker Tharp

PRODUCTIONS & CASTS

KINGFISH *(World Premiere)* by Marlane Meyer; Director, David Schweizer; CAST: Buck Henry, Sam Anderson
BOPHA! conceived and directed by Percy Mtwa of The Earth Players of South Africa; Produced by Market Theatre, Johannesburg.
THE SEAGULL by Anton Chekov; Director, Charles Marowitz. CAST: with Judd Nelson, Mary Crosby, Nan Martin
THE MODEL APARTMENT *(World Premiere)* by Donald Margulies; Director, Roberta Levitow. CAST: with Chloe Webb, Milton Selzer, Erica Yohn
STONE WEDDING *(World Premiere)* by Milcha Sanchez Scott and the Latino Theatre Lab; Director, Jose Luis Valenzuela. CAST: E. J. Castillo, Evelina Fernandez
DEMON WINE *(World Premiere)* by Thomas Babe; Director, David Schweizer. CAST: with Carol Kane, Tom Waits, Bill Pullman
STARS IN THE MORNING SKY *(English Premiere)* by Alexander Galin; Director, Bill Bushnell. CAST: with Deirdre O'Connell, Robert Beltran

Top Right: Mary Crosby, Judd Nelson in "The Seagull"
Top Left: Sam Anderson, Merritt Butrick in "Kingfish"
Chris Gulker Photos

Aubrey Molefi, Sydney Khumalo, Aubrey Radebe in
"Bopha!" also above

Chloe Webb, Zero Hubbard, Erica Yohn, Milton Selzer in
"Model Apartment"
Above: Merritt Butrick, Buck Henry in "Kingfish"
Top: Madge Sinclair, Nora Heflin in "Stars in the
Morning Sky"
Chris Gulker Photos

Tom Waits, Carol Kane in "Demon Wine"
Above: Angela Moya, Evelina Fernandez, Lupe Ontiveros in
"Stone Wedding"

McCARTER THEATRE

Princeton, N.J.

Artistic Director, Nagle Jackson; Managing Director, John Herochik; Associate Artistic Director, Robert Lanchester; Administrative Director, Laurence Capo; Business Manager, Robert Gillman; Communications Director, Kip Rosser; Press, Daniel Y. Bauer; Production Manager, David York; Stage Managers, Peter C. Cook, C. Townsend Olcott II, Megan Miller-Shields.

PRODUCTIONS & CASTS

THE MISS FIRECRACKER CONTEST by Beth Henley; Director, Robert Lanchester; Lighting, Don Ehman; Set, Ron Kadri; Costumes, Kathryn Wagner CAST: Constance Ray (Carnelle), Courtenay Collins (Popeye), Linda Miles (Elain), Kevin Chamberlin (Delmont), William Mesnick (Mac/Sam), Sharie Lynn Day (Tessy)

SMOKE ON THE MOUNTAIN by Constance Ray; Conceived and Directed by Alan Bailey; CAST: Kevin Chamberlin (Mervin Oglethorpe), Constance Ray (June Sanders), William Mesnick (Burl Sanders), Linda Miles (Vera Sanders), Dan Manning (Stanley Sanders), Courtenay Collins (Denise Sanders), Robert Olsen (Dennis Sanders)

BORN YESTERDAY by Garson Kanin; Director, Richard Risso; Lighting, Phil Monat; Set, John Jensen; Costumes, David C. Woolard CAST: Deborah Jeanne Culpin (Billie Dawn), Jim Baker (Harry Brock), Edmund Davys (Paul Verrall), G Wood (Ed Devery), Jay Doyle (Senator Hedges), Peggy Winslow (Mrs. Hedges), Kevin Chamberlin, William Richert, Cynthia Martells, Mark Brown, Rufus C. Gibson, Mary Ringstad

TARTUFFE by Moliere; English translation, Richard Wilbur; Director, Nagle Jackson; Set, Robert Perdziola; Costumes, Elizabeth Covey CAST: Jim Baker (Orgon), Kimberly King (Elmire), William Richert (Damis), Deborah Jeanne Culpin (Mariane), Robin Tate (Valere), Robert Lanchester (Cleante), Richard Risso (Tartuffe), Cynthia Martells (Iorine), Edmund Davys, Jay Doyle, Mary Ringstad, Kevin Chamberlin, Mark Brown, Shirlin Devrim Trainer

A CHRISTMAS CAROL by Charles Dickens; Adaptation, Nagle Jackson; Lighting, Richard Moore; Set, Brian Martin CAST: George Ede (Scrooge), Todd Anthony-Jackson (Bob Cratchit), Richard Risso (Marley), Reathel Bean, Edmund Davys, William Richert, Mary Martello, Robin Tate, Mary Ringstad, Kevin Chamberlin, John Nicholson, Mark Brown, Deborah Jeanne Culpin, Charles Dumas, Cynthia Martells, Jay Doyle, Kimberly King, Laurie Huntsman, Michael J. Tyger, Carrie Pettigrew, Brian Peter Wilby, Avery Willis, Gregory Wu, Desiree Amae Scott, Cassie Jones, Billy Milner, Kenny Shimizu, Brian Patrick Hedden, Matthew Burbach, Meghan Roberts

EXACT CHANGE by David Epstein; Director, Jacques Levy; Lighting, Chris Akerlind; Set, Ron Kadri; Costumes, April Curtis CAST: Paul Geier (Merola), Geoff Pierson (Botts), Ken Ryan (Bompkee)

SARCOPHAGUS by Vladimir Gubaryev; Translated by Michael Glenny; Director, Nagle Jackson; Lighting, F. Mitchell Dana; Set/Costumes, Eduard Kochergin CAST: Edmund Davys (Bessmertny), Kimberly King (Anna Petrovna), Frank Lowe (Lev Ivanovich Segeyev), Penelope Reed (Lydia Stepanovana), Mark Brown, Kevin Chamberlin, Deborah Jeanne Culpin, Jay Doyle, George Ede, Rufus Gibson, Patrick Hurley, Todd Anthony-Jackson, Richard Leighton, Mary Martello, Cynthia Martells, John Nicholson, Anne Karin Paaske, William Richert, Allan Salkin, Robin Tate

DIVIDING THE ESTATE *(World Premiere)* by Horton Foote; Director, Jamie Brown; Lighting, Phil Monat; Set, Jeff Modereger; Costumes, Pamela Scofield CAST: Thomas Martell Brimm (Doug), Edmund Davys (Son), Jane Hoffman (Stella), Annette Hunt (Lucille), Mary Martello (Mary Jo), Jerry Mayer (Bob), Julie Corby, Deborah Jeanne Culpin, Jay Doyle, Ginger Finney, Thea Perkins, Beatrice Winde

A FUNNY THING HAPPENED ON THE WAY TO THE FORUM with Book by Burt Shevelove, Larry Gelbart; Music/Lyrics, Stephen Sondheim; Director, Nagle Jackson; Choreographer, Edward Earle; Musical Director, Arthur Frank; Lighting, F. Mitchell Dana; Set, Dick Block; Costumes, Gregg Barnes CAST: David Schram (Pseudolus), Tom Lloyd (Hysterium), Peter Shawn (Lycus), Victor Raider-Wexler (Seneca), Maureen Sadusk (Domina), Deanna Wells (Philia), Ron Bohmer (Hero), Kenya V. Bennett, Richard Bitsko, Leslie Chain, Jennifer Chase, Deborah Jeanne Culpin, Jay Doyle, Blair Fell, David LaDuca, William Richert, Deborah Skally Robertson, Kyoko Takita

Top Right: George Ede in "A Christmas Carol"
Randall Hagadorn Photos

Deborah Jeanne Culpin, Edmund Davys in "Born Yesterday"

MEADOW BROOK THEATRE

Rochester, Michigan

Artistic/General Director, Terence Kilburn; Associate Director, James P. Spittle; Sets, Peter Hicks; Costumes, Mary Lynn Bonnell; Lighting, Reid G. Johnson; Stage Managers, Terry W. Carpenter, Robert Herrle; Technical Director, Daniel M. Jaffe; Props, Mary Chmelko-Jaffe; Sound, Paul A. Fox; Press, Sylvia Coughlin
PRODUCTIONS: *Amadeus, The Comedy of Errors, A Christmas Carol* (Sets, Barry Griffith), *The Andersonville Trial, I Ought to Be in Pictures, The Road to Mecca, Quilters, Murder at the Vicarage*
CASTS: names not submitted

Richard Hunt Photos

Top Left: Anne Sheldon in "Road to Mecca"
Below: "Quilters"
Top Right: Simon Brooking, Eric Tovares,
Liz Zweifler in "Amadeus"

Booth Colman, Tom Spackman in "The Andersonville Trial"

MERRIMACK REPERTORY THEATRE

Lowell, Massachusetts

Producing Director, Daniel Schay; Lighting, John Ambrosone; Costumes, Jane Alois Stein; Literary Manager, David Kent; Stage Managers, Colleen Riley, Blakeley Chowning.

PRODUCTIONS & CASTS

AS YOU LIKE IT by William Shakespeare; Director, Daniel Schay; Set Design, David Stern; Lighting, John Ambrosone; Costumes, Jane Alois Stein. CAST: David Bouvier (Charles), Allyn Burrows (Oliver), Michael Chiklis (Touchstone), Phillip C. Curry (LeBeau), Kermit Dunkelberg (Jacques), Paul D. Farwell (Amiens), Julia Flood (Phoebe), Gary-Thomas Keating (Adam), John Kooi (Silvius), Mark Lewis (Orlando), Diana Sheehan (Audrey), Troy Siegfreid (Dukes Senior/Frederick), Susan Wands (Rosalind).
NOISES OFF by Michael Frayn; Director, Michael Allosso; Set, Ed Chapin; Lighting, John Ambrosone; Costumes, Bradford Wood & Gregory A. Poplyk. CAST: Elizabeth Anne Dickinson (Poppy), William A. Kilmer (Frederick), Phyllis Lindy (Brooke), Paul Mayberry (Selsden), Thomas Ouellette (Tim), M. Lynda Robinson (Belinda), Timothy Scranton (Garry), Patrick Shea (Lloyd), Ingrid Sonnichsen (Dotty).
A CHRISTMAS CAROL by Charles Dickens, adapted by Larry Carpenter; Director: Daniel Schay; Set, Alison Ford; Costumes, Amanda Aldridge; Lighting, John Ambrosone. CAST: Robin Chadwick (Scrooge), Joseph Costa, Julia Flood, Tim Howard, Gary-Thomas Keating, Richard McElvain, Tammy Richards, M. Lynda Robinson (ensemble).
PILL HILL STORIES (COMING HOME TO SOMEPLACE NEW) *(World Premiere)*: An evening of stories written and performed by Jay O'Callahan; Director, Richard McElvain.
TO FORGIVE, DIVINE by Jack Neary *(World Premiere)*; Director, Jack Neary; Sets, Leslie Taylor; Costumes, Jane Alois Stein; Lighting, John Ambrosone; CAST: Betty Lee Bogue (Milly), Jennifer Hugus (Margaret), Matthew Kimbrough (Ralph), Josie McElroy (Katie), Sam Rush (Jerry).
BETRAYAL by Harold Pinter; Director, David G. Kent; Sets, Gary English; Lights, John Ambrosone & Sid Bennett, Costumes, Jane Alois Stein. CAST: Catherine Cooper (Emma), Jonathan Epstein (Robert), Jeremiah Kissel (Jerry), John Kooi (Waiter).
BLITHE SPIRIT by Noel Coward; Director, Richard McElvain; Sets, Lorilee Coleman; Lighting, John Ambrosone; Costumes, Jane Alois Stein. CAST: Peter Bubriski (Charles), Karen MacDonald (Elvira), Belle McDonald (Mrs. Bradman), Bill McDonald (Dr. Bradman), Dee Nelson (Ruth), Tammy Richards (Edith), Jenny Sterlin (Madame Arcati).

Top Left: Dee Nelson, Peter Bubriski in "Blithe Spirit"
Top Right: Susan Wands, Mark Lewis in "As You Like It"
Kevin Harkins Photos

Betty Lee Bogue, Sam Rush in "To Forgive, Divine"

MILWAUKEE REPERTORY THEATER

Milwaukee, Wisconsin
Twenty-fifth Season

Artistic Director, John Dillon; Associate Artistic Director, Kenneth Albers; Dramaturg, Robert Meiksins; Resident Playwright, John Leicht; Resident Composer, John Tanner; Sets, Loy Arcenas, Victor A. Becker, Art Johnson, Ken Kloth, Laura Maurer, Vicki Smith Sandra Strawn, John Story, Tamara Turchette, Scott Weldin; Lighting, William Browning, Peter Gottlieb, Allen Lee Hughes, Robert Jared, Ken Kloth, Dan Kotlowitz, Kevin Rigdon, Victor En Yu Tan, Ann Wrightson, Robert Zenoni; Costumes, Therese Donarski, Sam Fleming, Ellen M. Kozak, Cecelia Mason, Sally Richardson, John Carver Sullivan, Tamara Turchette; Sound, Brian Hallas, John Tanner; Production Supervisor, Richard Rogers; Props, Samuel A. Garst, Jeffrey Hicks; Wardrobe, Dawna Gregory; Company Manager, Betsy Corry; Stage Managers, Cynthia E. Poulson, Mark Baughman, Judy L. Berdan, Janice F. Campbell, Diane Carlin-Bartel, Connie Drew, Mark Sahba, Leslie Woodruff, Michael Schwartz; Press, Fran Serlin-Cobb.

COMPANY

Kenneth Albers, LeWan Alexander, Tom Blair, John Buck, Jr., Mark Corkins, Catherine Lynn Davis, Montgomery Davis, Joe Dempsey, Arabella Field, Jason FitzGerald, Marilyn Frank, Steven J. Gefroh, June Gibbons, Richard Halverson, Sharon Hope, Tad Ingram, Priscilla Hake Lauris, Darrie Lawrence, William Leach, Barry Lynch, John Malloy, Larry G. Malvern, Marie Mathay, Kelly Maurer, Tom McDermott, Johanna Melamed, Daniel Mooney, Norman Moses, Michael W. Nash, Christopher Noth, Ric Oquita, James Pickering, Rose Pickering, Barbara Roberts, Laurine Towler, Celeste Williams.
ACTING INTERNS: Nomi Bence, Larry Jean Birkett, Sandra Docwra-Jones, Polly Firestone, Steven Folstein, Terrance P. Flynn, David Mitchell Ghilardi, Cynthia Hewett, Heather L. Kendall, Amy Malloy, Stanley McDowell, Amy Jo Neill, Doug Rand, Joan Rater, Mary Ringstad, Holly Smith, Greg Steres, Thomas Van Voorhees, Jacqueline Nan Wade, Lisa Wahlig, Stephen D. Webber, Hunter West.
PRODUCTIONS: *The Torch* by Alberto Heiremans/Translation, Amlin Gray, *Precious Memories* by Romulus Linney, *Talley's Folly* by Lanford Wilson, *She Stoops to Conquer* by Oliver Goldsmith, *Wedding Band* by Alice Childress, *Juno and the Paycock* by Sean O'Casey, *Burning Patience* by Antonio Skarmeta/Translation, Marion Peter Holt, *Kind Ness* by Ping Chong, *And What of the Night?* by Maria Irene Fornes, *The Chastitute* by John B. Keane, *Eduardo Peralta, Laughing Wild* by Christopher Durang, *Ain't Nobody's Blues but Mine, Good Evening* by Peter Cook and Dudley Moore, *The Irish Rascal* by David O. Frazier/Joseph Garry/Kathleen Kennedy, *A Christmas Carol* by Charles Dickens/Adapted by Amlin Gray

Mark Avery Photos not submitted

Craig Dudley in "Irma Vep"
Top Right: Marc Kudisch, Craig Dudley in "Hamlet"

MINORCA PLAYHOUSE

Coral Gables, Florida

Executive Producer, Robert H. Deschamps; Artistic Director, Gail S. Deschamps; Associate Producer, John R. Briggs; Marketing Director, Herb Siegel; Public Relations, Clarice MacGarvey; Stage Manager, Suzanne Jones.

PRODUCTIONS & CASTS

HAMLET by William Shakespeare/**ROSENCRANTZ AND GUILDENSTERN ARE DEAD** by Tom Stoppard; Directors, John R. Briggs, Gail S. Deschamps; Sets, Allen D. Cornell; Costumes, Marilyn R. Skow; Lighting, Scott Stipetic. CAST: Craig Dudley (Claudis/Ghost), Judith Townsend (Gertrude), Jens Krummel (Guildenstern), Christopher Clavelli (Hamlet), John Rodaz (Horatio/Tragedian I), Marc Kudisch (Laertes), Andrea O'Connell (Ophelia), James Randolph II (Player King/Sexton/Laborer I/Player), Laird Stuart (Polonius), Randy Redd (Priest II/Player/Laborer II/Alfred), George Kapetan (Rosencrantz), Carlos Mena (Tragedian II/Osric/Player Queen/Player), Allan Louis (Tragedian/Lucianus/Priest I/English Ambassador).
THE MYSTERY OF IRMA VEP by Charles Ludlam; Director, John R. Briggs; Sets, John R. Briggs, Todd Sherman; Costumes, Dolly Quentin, Damaris Rodriguez; Lighting, Suzanne Jones; Stage Manager, Arthur Catricala. CAST: Craig Dudley (Jane Twisden/Lord Edgar Hillcrest/An Intruder), Christopher Clavelli (Nicodemus Underwood/Lady Enid Hillcrest/Alcazar).
THE TAMING OF THE SHREW by William Shakespeare; Adapted by Nilo Cruz, John Briggs; Director, Nilo Cruz; Set, Benigno Mendez; Costumes, Jeanne Cerasini; Lighting, Rolf Rombschick; Stage Manager, Erika Frankel. CAST: Victor Valle (Lucentio), Jack Ballish (Tranio), Henry Brewster (Biondello), Humberto Ponce de Leon (Baptista), Art Suskin (Gremio), Reynaldo Gonzalez (Hortensio), Marilyn Romero (Katharina), Donna Kimball (Bianca), Tom Disney (Petruchio), Chris Webb (Grumio), Art Suskin (Pedant), Henry Brewster (Tailor/Vincentio), Ariane Nicole (Widow)

David Groh, Karen Valentine, Richard Pruitt in "Beyond a Reasonable Doubt"

PAPER MILL PLAYHOUSE

Milburn, New Jersey
Forty-ninth Season

President/Executive Producer, Angelo Del Rossi; Artistic Director, Robert Johanson; General Manager, Geoffrey Cohen; Company Manager, Wade Miller; Assistant to Producer, Joseph McConnell; Casting, Philip Wm. McKinley; Resident Scenic Designer, Michael Anania; Technical Director, James P. Murphy; Stage Managers, Jeffry George, Peggy Imbrie, Doug Fogel, Randy Donaldson; Props, Bruce Pollock; Wardrobe, Ralph Fandetta; Press, Albertina Reilly, Meara Nigro

PRODUCTIONS & CASTS

LA CAGE AUX FOLLES with Music/Lyrics, Jerry Herman; Book, Harvey Fierstein; Based on play by Jean Poiret; Director, James Pentecost; Set, David Mitchell; Costumes, Theoni V. Aldredge; Lighting, Jules Fisher/Natasha Katz; Costume Coordinator, Alice S. Hughes; Musical Director, Kay Cameron; Choreographer, Linda Haberman; Stage Manager, Peggy Imbrie CAST: Walter Charles (Georges), Lee Roy Reams (Albin), Bill Badolato (Francis), Darrell Carey (Jacob), Peter Reardon (Jean-Michel), Wendy Oliver (Anne), Sheila Smith (Jacqueline), G. Eugene Moose (M. Renaud), Linda Poser (Mme. Renaud) Jack Davison (Edouard Dindon), Leigh Beery (Mme. Dindon), Les Cagelles: John Clonts (Chantal), John Crutchman (Monique), Scott Spahr (Dermah), David Enriquez (Nicole), Robert Argiro (Hanna), David Evans (Mercedes), Stephanie Paul (Bitelle), Ned Hannah (Lo Singh), Lynn Faro (Angelique), Dan Buelow (Phaedra), Townspeople: Susan Shofner, Tony Sperry, Peter Gunther, Kirsten Lind, Jane Ferrar, Russ Jones, Gregory Butler
1776 with Music/Lyrics, Sherman Edwards; Book, Peter Stone; Director/Choreographer, Robert Johanson; Musical Director/Conductor, Andrew Carl Wilk; Set, Kevin Rupnik; Costumes, Guy Geoly; Lighting, Jeff Davis CAST: Ron Parady (John Hancock), Tony Gilbert (Dr. Joseph Bartlett), William Linton (John Adams), Christopher Wynkoop (Stephen Hopkins), James Javore (Roger Sherman), James Harwood (Lewis Morris), Monte Ralstin (Robert Livingston), Larry Grey (Rev. John Witherspoon), Sam Kressen (Benjamin Franklin), Patrick Quinn (John Dickinson), Brent Maroon (James Wilson), John Remme (Caesar Rodney), Joe Leavitt (Col. Thomas McKean), Gene Sager (George Read), Graham Pollack (Samuel Chase), George Dvorsky (Richard Henry Lee), Brent Barrett (Thomas Jefferson), James Hindman (Joseph Hewes), Bob Cuccioli (Edward Rutledge), Tom Urich (Dr. Lyman Hall), Michael Waldron (Charles Thomson), William McClary (Andrew McNair), Keith Bernardo (Leather Apron), Woody Howard (Painter), John Scherer (Courier), Judith McCauley (Abigail Adams), Susan Powell (Martha Jefferson)
BROADWAY BOUND by Neil Simon; Director, Philip Minor; Set, David Mitchell; Lighting, David Kissel; Stage Manager, Jeffry George CAST: Barbara Caruso (Kate), Salem Ludwig (Ben), Marc Riffon (Eugene), Rudy Goldschmidt (Stanley), Bernice Massi (Blanche), Alan Mixon (Jack).
BEYOND A REASONABLE DOUBT by Nathan Mayer; Director, Thomas Gruenewald; Lighting, Marilyn Rennagel; Stage Manager, Jeffrey George CAST: David Groh (Kenneth Hayes), Karen Valentine (Ruth Ballard), Richard Pruitt (Jail Guard)
SHENANDOAH with Music by Gary Geld; Lyrics, Peter Udell; Book, James Lee Barrett, Peter Udell, Philip Rose; Based on screenplay by James Lee Barrett; Director, Robert Johanson; Choreographer, Susan Stroman; Musical Director, Kay Cameron; Costumes, Guy Geoly CAST: Timothy Nolen (Charlie Anderson), Michael Piontek (Jacob), George Dvorsky (James), Malcolm Gets (Nathan), Timothy Ford (John), Patricia Ben Peterson (Jenny), Ron Gibbs (Henry), Michael C. Maronna (Robert/The Boy), Tricia Witham (Anne) succeeded by Jacquey Maltby, Dule Hill Brent Barrett (Sam), Graham Pollock (Rev. Byrd), Kenneth Kantor (Sgt. Johnson), Donald Brooks Ford (Lt.), Ron Lee Savin (Tinkham), Robert Jensen (Carol), Sean McDermott (Cpl.), Craig Oldfather (Marauder), Brett C. Rosborough (Engineer), Ron Bohmer (Confederate Sniper), Frank Maio (Soldier)
SHOW BOAT with Music, Jerome Kern; Book/Lyrics, Oscar Hammerstein 2nd; Based on novel by Edna Ferber; Director, Robert Johanson; Choreographer, Sharon Halley; Musical Conductor, Peter Howard; Assistant Director, Marsha Bagwell; Associate Musical Conductor, Kay Cameron; Lighting, Ken Billington; Costumes, Bradford Wood, Gregory A. Poplyk; Hairstylist, Paul Germano CAST: Robert Jensen (Stephen Baker), Monte Ralstin (Pete), Ellia English (Queenie), Marsha Bagwell (Parthy Ann), Lawrence Vincent (Windy), Eddie Bracken (Cap'n Andy), Lenora Nemetz (Ellie May), Lee Roy Reams (Frank Schultz), Shelly Burch (Julie LaVerne), Richard White (Gaylord), Michael McCarty (Vallon), Rebecca Baxter (Magnolia), P. L. Brown (Joe), Larry Grey (Backwoodsman), Monte Ralstin (Jeb), Robert Jensen (Barker), Patti Allison (Landlady), Deborah Cole (Mother Superior), Samantha Jordan (Young Kim), Phil Hall (Jake), Larry Grey (Jim), Malcolm Gets (Guitar Player), Wardell Woodard (Charlie), Ruth Gotschall (Lottie), Patti Allison (Dolly), Rebecca Baxter (Adult Kim), Felicia Hannah (Old Lady), Fred Anderson, Henri Leon Baker, Shell Benjamin, Eva Breul, Cherly Burr, Gregory Butler, Deborah Cole, Sarah Downs, Lothair Eaton, Jeffrey C. Ferguson, Harriett D. Foy, Jerry Godfrey, David Koch, Kris Koop, Greg Lloyd, Jim Mara, Kenneth Nichols, Ken Shekski, Cynthia Thomas, Laurie Williamson, Lauren Gaffney, Eric Goodwin, LaShonda Hunt, Logan Jordan, Samantha Jordan

Top Left: Lee Roy Reams (C) in "La Cage . . ."
Below: Salem Ludwig, Marc Riffon, Rudy Goldschmidt in
"Broadway Bound"
Gerry Goodstein, Jerry Dalia Photos

Brent Barrett, William Linton, Monte Ralstin, Sam Kressen,
James Javore in "1776"
Above: P. L. Brown (C) in "Show Boat"
Top: Walter Charles (L), Patricia Ben Peterson (C) in
"Shenandoah"

Richard White, Rebecca Baxter
Top: Lee Roy Reams, Lenora Nemetz in "Show Boat"

163

PENNSYLVANIA STAGE COMPANY

Allentown, Pennsylvania
Sixth Season

Producing Director, Peter Wrenn Meleck; Associate Artistic Director/Outreach Director, Scott Edmiston; Administrative Director/Marketing & PR, Lisa K. Higgins; Dramaturge, David Scott; Development, Cynthia J. Armstrong; Business Manager, Rosalie Schreiber; Company Manager, Ted Ewing; Technical Director, Glenn Gerchman; Scenic Artist, Sarah Baptist; Costumer, Marianne Faust; Stage Managers, Thomas M. Kauffman, Elli Agosto

PRODUCTIONS & CASTS

THE IMPORTANCE OF BEING EARNEST by Oscar Wilde; Director, Gavin Cameron-Webb; Costumes, Gail Brassard. CAST: Kevin Donovan, Julia Gibson, Vera Johnson, Samuel Maupin, Marshall Mays, Margery Murray, Elizabeth Owens, Wyman Pendleton, Randolph Walker

LITTLE SHOP OF HORRORS (co-produced with George Street Playhouse) Book/Lyrics, Howard Ashman; Music, Alan Menken; Director, Allen R. Belknap; Musical Director, Ernest Lehrer; Choreographer, Diana Baffa-Brill; Set, Atkin Pace; Costumes, Barbara Forbes; Lighting, Donald Holder; Sound, Jim Landis; Puppet, Martin P. Robinson. CAST: Kurt Carley, Meghan Duffy, Romain Frugé, Rosemarie Jackson, Michael Mandell, Jerry Matz, Michael Scott, Moné Walton, Tena Wilson

KISS OF THE SPIDER WOMAN by Manuel Puig; Translation, Allan J. Baker; Director, Scott Edmiston; Set/Lighting, Curtis Dretsch; Costumes, Kathleen Egan. CAST: Jonathan Fuller, Peter Toran

THE MYSTERY OF IRMA VEP by Charles Ludlam (Co-produced with George Street Playhouse); Director, Sue Lawless; Set, Deborah Jasien; Lighting, Spencer Mosse; Costumes, Barbara Forbes. CAST: Jonathan Bustle, Brian Reddy, Marcy McGuigan

A MOON FOR THE MISBEGOTTEN by Eugene O'Neill; Director, Donald Hicken; Set, Wally Coberg; Lighting, Donald Holder; Costumes, Kathleen Egan. CAST: Robertson Carricart, Kevin Donovan, Victoria Gadsden, James Hilbrandt, Gus Rogerson

ON THE VERGE by Eric Overmyer; (Co-produced with Arkansas Repertory Theatre); Director, Veronica Brady; Set, Mike Nichols; Lighting, Spencer Mosse; Costumes, Mark Hughes; Sound, Shari Bethel. CAST: Peter Bradshaw, Evelyn Carol Case, Maggie Low, Laura MacDermott

BROADWAY BOUND by Neil Simon; Director, Scott Edmiston; Set/Lighting, Curtis Dretsch; Costumes, Kathleen Egan; Choreographer, Robin Gerchman. CAST: Charles Antalosky, Peter Bradshaw, David Breitbarth, Ann Ducati, David Kriegel, Marlena Lustik, Laura MacDermott, Gerald Richards

**Top Right: Brian Reddy, Jonathan Bustle in "Irma Vep"
Below: Vera Johnson, Samuel Maupin in "Importance of Being Earnest"**
Gregory M. Fota Photos

Jonathan Fuller, Peter Toran in "Kiss of the Spider Woman"

Marlena Lustik, Gerald Richards, Ann Ducati in "Broadway Bound"

164

PITTSBURGH PUBLIC THEATER

Pittsburgh, Pennsylvania
Fourteenth Season

Producing Director, William T. Gardner; Managing Director, Dan Fallon

PRODUCTIONS & CASTS

THE HABITATION OF DRAGONS by Horton Foote; *(World Premiere);* Director, Mr. Foote; Set, Howard Cummings; Lighting, Kirk Bookman; Costumes, Van Broughton Ramsey; Sound, James Capenos; Stage Manager, J. Barry Lewis. CAST: David Butler, Hallie Foote, Peter Francis James, Zachary Mott, Eugenia Rawls, Ben Tatar, Jenise duMaurier, Horton Foote, Jr., Ann Kittredge, Matt Mulhern, Douglas Rees; Isa Thomas, Harley Venton, Mac Fleischmann, Stephen Robert Hanna, Conrad McLaren, Emmett O'Sullivan-Moore, Marco St. John, William Thunhurst, Jr.
I'M NOT RAPPAPORT by Herb Gardner; Director, Maureen Heffernan; Set, Anne Mundell; Lighting, Kirk Bookman; Costumes, Patricia Adshead; Sound, Dirk Kuyk; Stage Manager, Jane Rothman. CAST: Michael Kelly Boone, Susan J. Coon, Suzanne Grodner, John Hall, David S. Howard, Will Osborne, Samuel E. Wright
THE IMMIGRANT by Mark Harelik; Director, Howard J. Millman; Set, Kevin Rupnick; Lighting, Phil Monat; Costumes, Mimi Maxmen; Stage Manager, Chuck Zito CAST: Carole Lockwood, Devora Millman, Bruce Nozick, Richard Thomsen
FALLEN ANGELS by Noel Coward; Director, Philip Minor; Set, Cletus Anderson; Costumes, David Toser; Stage Manager, Jane Rothman. CAST: Curzon Dobell, Simon Jutras, Alix Korey, Robin Moseley, Margery Murray
HEDDA GABLER by Henrik Ibsen; Adaptation, Corinne Jacker; Director, Lee Sankowich; Set, Harry Feiner; Costumes, Laura Crow; Stage Manager, Chuck Zito CAST: Jim Abele, Catherine Butterfield, Michael Hume, Vera Lockwood, Nann Mogg, Will Rhys, Helena Ruoti
FENCES by August Wilson; Director, Claude Purdy; Set, James D. Sandefur; Costumes, Mary Mease Warren; Sound, Martin Christoffel; Music, Dwight D. Andrews; Stage Manager, Jane Rothman. CAST: Trazana Beverley, Jewel Burgess, Robert Gossett, Di Ray James, William Jay, John Henry Redwood, Monte Russell, Wally Taylor

Top Right: Jim Abele, Helena Ruoti in "Hedda Gabler"
Ric Evans Photos

David S. Howard, Samuel E. Wright in "I'm Not Rappaport"

Robin Moseley, Samuel Maupin in "Fallen Angels"

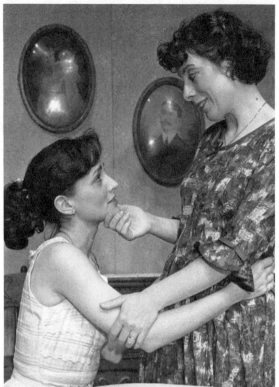

PHILADELPHIA DRAMA GUILD

Philadelphia, Pennsylvania

Producing Director, Gregory Poppi; Business Manager, Kathleen Kund Nolan; Production Manager, Edward Johnson; Marketing, Roy Wilbur; Development, Megan Riegel; Executive Assistant/Company Manager, Barbara J. Silzle; Press, Heidi Peek Jamieson; Stage Managers, Donna E. Curci, Scott Lesher

PRODUCTIONS & CASTS

THE IMMIGRANT by Mark Harelik; Director, Charles Karchmer; Set, James Noone; Costumes, Deborah Shaw; Lighting, Jeff Davis. CAST: Richard Levine, Laurinda Barrett, John Newton, Susan Gabriel

AN AMERICAN JOURNEY by Kermit Frazier and John Leicht; Director, John Dillon; Set, Daniel P. Boylen; Costumes, Sam Fleming; Lighting, William H. Grant III. CAST: Tamu Gray, Lizan Mitchell, Mark Metcalf, Christopher McHale, Rodney Creech, Drew Hanson, Tim Moyer, Tom McCarthy, Don W. Newton, Jake Turner, Isiah Whitlock, Jr., Peter DeLaurier, Johnnie Hobbs, Jr., Lex Monson, Sally Mercer, David B. Glancey, Richard Joyce, Peter Fitzkee

THE BOYS NEXT DOOR by Tom Griffin; Director, Allen R. Belknap; Set, James Fenhagen; Costumes, Gail Brassard; Lighting, Richard Winkler. CAST: Richard Levine, Michael Mandell, Guy Paul, Stephen Singer, Christopher Fields, Jay Devlin, Mary Boucher, Mary Catherine Wright, Tom McCarthy

A VIEW FROM THE BRIDGE by Arthur Miller; Director, Alex Dmitriev; Set, Rosario Provenza; Costumes, Karen Roston; Lighting, James Leitner. CAST: Anthony Scipio, Dante Giammarco, Charles Antalosky, Tony Campisi, Claire Beckman, Suzanne Toren, John Gladstein, Iocco Amato, Leland Orser, Hand DeLuca, Charles Conwell, R. E. Joyce, Peter Fitzkee, John Erlanger, Barbara Kristal, Terry Reamer, Arturo Castillo

ROCKY AND DIEGO by Roger Cornish; Director, John Henry Javis; Set, John Jensen; Costumes, Karen Roston; Lighting, F. Mitchell Dana. CAST: Robert Sean Leonard, Marco St. John, Hannah Cox, Brad Rickel, Mark Silence, John Carpenter, Allen Fitzpatrick, Amy Hoffman, Julia Meade, Mary Testa

Rodney Creech, Tamu Gray in "An American Journey"

Ken Kauffman Photos

Top Right: Stephen Singer, Mary Catherine Wright in
"The Boys Next Door"
Top Left: Claire Beckman, Suzanne Toren in "A View
from the Bridge"
Ken Kauffman Photos

166

Stephen Singer, Guy Paul, Richard Levine, Christopher Fields, Michael Mandell in "Boys Next Door"
Above: Isiah Whitlock, Jr., Tamu Gray in "American Journey"
Top: Marco St. John, Robert Sean Leonard in "Rocky & Diego"

Leland Orser, Claire Beckman in "View from the Bridge"
Top: Susan Gabriel, Richard Levine in "The Immigrant"

PLAYMAKERS REPERTORY COMPANY

Chapel Hill, North Carolina

Executive Producer, Milly S. Barranger; Artistic Director, David Hammond; Managing Director, Margaret Hahn; Production Manager, Tom Neville; Resident Director, Christian Angermann; Combat/Movement, Craig Turner; Voice, Jan Gist; Business Manager, Peter Kernan; Development, Justin Grimes; Press/Marketing, Sharon Broom; Stage Managers, Regina Lickteig, Robert Welch
RESIDENT ACTING COMPANY: Bernard Addison, Patricia Barnett, Lisa Benedict, Bess Brown, Dede Corvinus, Derek Gagnier, Thomas Garvey, Candice Milan, Demetrios Pappageorge, Susanna Rinehart, Matt Ryan, Eben Young
GUEST ARTISTS: Tobias Andersen, Terence Caza, Maury Cooper, Leslie Hicks, Johanna Jackson, Nick Kaledin, Darrie Lawrence, Mary O'Brady, Joan Potter, James Pritchett, Cal Winn

PRODUCTIONS

THE MARRIAGE OF FIGARO by Pierre Augustin Caron de Beaumarchais; Adaptation, Peter Jeffries; Director, David Hammond; Set, McKay Coble; Costumes, Marianne Custer; Lighting, Marcus Dilliard
THE ROAD TO MECCA by Athol Fugard; Director, Christian Angermann; Set, Michael Miller; Costumes, Bobbi Owen; Lighting, Mary Louise Geiger
A CHILD'S CHRISTMAS IN WALES by Dylan Thomas; Adaptation, Jeremy Brooks/Adrian Mitchell; Director, Christian Angermann; Set/Costumes, McKay Coble; Lighting, Robert Wierzel; Musical Direction, Barney Pilgrim
FOR LEASE OR SALE by Elizabeth Spencer *(World Premiere)* Director, David Hammond; Set/Costumes, McKay Coble; Lighting, Robert Wierzel
MISALLIANCE by George Bernard Shaw; Director, Maureen Heffernan; Set, Anita C. Stewart; Costumes, Kristine Kearney; Lighting, Marcus Dillard
THE TAMING OF THE SHREW by William Shakespeare; Director, David Hammond; Set/Costumes, Bill Clarke; Lighting, Robert Wierzel

**Right: Lynn Passarella, Thomas Gunning in "For Lease or Sale"
Top: Matt Ryan, Aaron Carlos, Eben Young, Tobias Andersen, Leslie Hicks, Demetrios Pappageorge in "Taming of the Shrew"**

Darrie Lawrence, Maury Cooper in "The Road to Mecca"

Terrence Caza, Bernard Addison in "The Marriage of Figaro"

PORTLAND STAGE COMPANY

Portland, Maine

Artistic Director, Richard Hamburger; Managing Director, Mark Somers; Associate Director, Lisa DiFranza; Development, Deirdre Moynihan; Marketing/Press, Monica Whitaker; Stage Manager, William Chance, Rheatha Forster

PRODUCTIONS & CASTS

A WALK IN THE WOODS by Lee Blessing; Director, Paul Moser; Set, Derek McLane; Costumes, Catherine Zuber; Lighting, Stuart Duke. CAST: Humbert Allen Astredo (Andrey Botvinnik), Hamilton Gillett (John Honeyman)

THE HOSTAGE by Brendan Behan; Director, Richard Hamburger; Set, Scott Bradley; Costumes, Martha Hally; Lighting, Peter Kaczorowski; Musical Director, Thomas Cabaniss; Choreographer, Daniel McCusker. CAST: Phil Pleasants (Pat), Joan Ulmer (Meg), John Straub (Monsewer), Kevin Dwyer (Princess Grace), Ian Trigger (Mulleady), Polly Pen (Miss Gilchrist), Simon Brooking (Leslie), Tracy Sallows (Teresa), Jennifer Berman (Colette), Suze Allen (Bobo), David C. Wyeth (IRA Officer), Clifton Bolton (Sailor/Volunteer), Phil Swegart/Jon Cooper (Fiddlers)

BENEFACTORS by Michael Frayn; Director, Charles Karchmer; Set, Michael Miller; Costumes, Deborah Shaw; Lighting, Robert Wierzel CAST: Douglas Simes (David), Ellen Tobie (Jane), Richmond Hoxie (Colin), Anne O'Sullivan (Sheila).

GHOSTS by Henrik Ibsen; Translation, Christopher Hampton; Director, Mel Marvin; Set, Michael Yeargan; Costumes, Martha Hally; Lighting, Donald Holder. CAST: Megan Cole (Mrs. Alving), Peter Birkenhead (Osvald), Mart Hulswit (Manders), Donald Christopher (Jakob Engstrand), Kitty Crooks (Regine Engstrand)

INSIDE OUT by Will Holtzman; Director, John Pynchon Holmes; Set, Philipp Jung; Costumes, Ellen McCartney; Lighting, Michael Chybowski; Sound, Tom Gould. CAST: Kimi Sung (Camille), Jacqueline Knapp (Annie), Richard Maynard (Jack), Chris Walker (Charles)

BREAKING THE SILENCE by Stephen Poliakoff; Director, Richard Hamburger; Set, Christopher Barecca; Costumes, Catherine Zuber; Lighting, Stephen Strawbridge; Sound, Stephen Santomenna. CAST: Charlotte Maier (Polya), Nicholas Strouse (Master Alexander), Ann Ducati (Eugenia Pesiakoff), Christopher McHale (Alexei Verkoff), Reno Roop (Nikolai Pesiakoff), Kevin O'Leary, Claude File (Guards)

David A. Rodgers Photos

Jacqueline Knapp, Kimi Sung in "Inside Out" Top Right: Simon Brooking, Polly Pen in "The Hostage"

REPERTORY THEATRE OF ST. LOUIS

St. Louis, Missouri

Artistic Director, Steven Woolf; Managing Director, Mark D. Bernstein; Associate Artistic Director, Susan Gregg; Technical Director, Max DeVolder; Props, John Roslevich, Jr.; Development, Nancy Forsyth; Stage Managers, Glenn Dunn, T. R. Martin, Champe Leary, Steve Marquette; Press, Judy Andrews

PRODUCTIONS & CASTS

CANDIDE adapted from Voltaire by Hugh Wheeler; Music, Leonard Bernstein; Lyrics, Richard Wilbur; Additional Lyrics, Stephen Sondheim/John Latouche; Director, Munson Hicks; Choreographer, Terry Rieser; Musical Director, Byron Grant; Set, John Falabella; Costumes, Dorothy Marshall; Lighting, Peter E. Sargent CAST: Fred Applegate (Voltaire), James Mellon (Candide), Gary Lindemann (Huntsman/Soldier), Mary Lou Shriber (Paquette), Paula Sweeney (Baroness), Joe Palmieri (Baron), Marcy DeGonge (Cunegonde), Michael Alan Gregory (Maximillian), Lawrence Patrick (Servant/Soldier), Kevin Bailey (Jew/Pirate), Charlie Serrano (Recruiter/Aristocrat), Susan Secunda, Arline Williams, Kirby Wahl, Marjie Carr-Osley, Mary Stout

BOY MEETS GIRL by Bella and Samuel Spewack; Director, Brian Murray; Set, Derel McLane; Costumes, Jennifer von Mayrhauser; Music, Bruce Pomahac CAST: Larry Green (Robert Law), Anthony Cummings (Larry Toms), Douglas Krizner (Benson), John Greenleaf (Rosetti), Martha Thompson (Miss Crews), Brian Dykstra (Friday), Gayla Finer (Peggy), Spencer Beckwith (Rodney), Alison Stair Neet (Green), David Rainey (Slade), Laura Perretta (Susie), Michael MacCauley, Ken Sawyer, James R. Carroll, Theresa McCarthy

OFFSHORE SIGNALS by Roger Cornish; Director, Edward Stern; Set, David Potts; Costumes, Dorothy Marshall; Lighting, Peter E. Sargent. CAST: Alan Clarey (Latino/Hull/Goforth), Henry Stram (Schmuel), John MacKay (Breckenridge), Steven Dennis (Harris), Ronald Wendschuh (Churchwright), Susan Pellegrino (Patricia), Peter Johl (Rabbi), BettyAnn Leeseberg-Lange (Mrs. Essex), Joneal Joplin (Essex/FDR)

STEEL MAGNOLIAS by Robert Harling; Director, Susan Gregg; Set/Costumes, Carolyn L. Ross; Lighting, Max DeVolder; Technical Adviser, Markus Bluestein. CAST: Carol Dilley (Annelle), Glynis Bell (Truvy), Mickey Hartnett (Clairee), Melissa Hurst (Shelby), Rita Gardner (M'Lynn), Billie Lou Watt (Ouiser)

SAINT JOAN by George Bernard Shaw; Director, William Woodman; Set, John Ezell CAST: Katherine Leask (Joan), Steven Rodriguez (Boudricourt), Christopher Randolph (Ladvenu), Craig Wroe (Poulengey), James Paul (Archbishop), Jeffrey Sams (La Tremouille), Spencer Humm (Page), Patrick B. Morgan (Gilles de Rais), Anthony Weaver (La Hire), Steven Dennis (Dauphin), Brannon Loomis (Duchess), Elaine Ellis (Lady), John Rensenhouse (Dunois), William Walden (Page), Ben Halley, Jr. (de Beauchamp), Joe Palmieri (de Stogumber), William Rhys (Bishop), Danny McCarthy (Page), Ronald Wendschuh (Inquisitor), Soldiers: Christopher Ross Chell, Lantz Harshbarger, Camara Nicholes, Nathaniel Sanders, Greg Werstler

NOISES OFF by Michael Frayn; Director, Donald Ewer; Set, James Wolk; Costumes, Arthur Ridley; Lighting, Phil Monat. CAST: Jenny Turner (Dotty), Douglas Wing (Lloyd), Paul DeBoy (Garry), Celine Havard (Brooke), Elaine Ellis (Poppy), Carl Schurr (Frederick), Sherry Skinker (Belinda), Norbert L. Butz (Tim), Brendan Burke (Selsdon)

HANNAH SENESH by David Schechter; Director, Mr. Schechter; Music, Steven Lutvak; Set, Kim Wilson; Costumes, Bonnie Kruger. Performed by Yvette de Botton

THE LAST GOOD MOMENT OF LILY BAKER by Russell Davis; Director, Tom Martin; Set, Bill Schmiel; Costumes, Holly Poe Durbin. CAST: Joe Barrett (Bob), Lisby Larson (Lily), Bruce Longworth (Sam), Beth Baur (Molly)

THE VOICE OF THE PRAIRIE by John Olive; Director, Steven Woolf; Set, John Roslevich, Jr. CAST: Joneal Joplin, David Holt, Susie Wall

IMPASSIONED EMBRACES by John Pielmeier; Director, Susan Gregg; Stage Manager, Jane Seiler. CAST: Carol Dilley, Joneal Joplin, BettyAnn Leeseberg-Lange, Lawrence Patrick, John Pingree, Kathleen Singleton

Top Left: James Mellon, Marcy DeGonge, Fred Applegate, Michael Alan Gregory, Mary Lou Shriber, and Below: Marcy DeGonge in "Candide"

Judy Andrews Photos

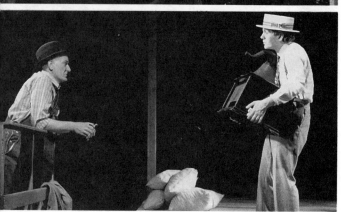

Joneal Joplin, David Holt in "The Voice of the Prairie"

Yvette de Botton is "Hannah Senesh"
Top: Paul DeBoy, Jenny Turner, Brendan Burke in
"Noises Off"

Katherine Leask, John Rensenhouse in "St. Joan"

SOUTH COAST REPERTORY

Costa Mesa, California

Producing Artistic Director, David Emmes; Artistic Director, Martin Benson; General Manager, Paula Tomei; Business Manager, Lorene Heilbrun; Development, Bonnie Brittain Hall; Marketing, John Mouledoux; Dramaturg, Jerry Patch; Literary Manager, John Glore; Production Director, Paul Hammond; Press, Cristofer Gross, Madeline Porter

ACTORS: Robert Almodovar, Michael Alvarez, Fran Bennett, Ron Boussom, Daniel Bright, Scott Burkholder, Ismael East Carlo, Kandis Chappell, Suzanne Collins, Robert Cornthwaite, Robert Crow, Keith Devaney, Mary Anne Dorward, Richard Doyle, Pamela Dunlap, John Ellington, Jennifer Flackett, Marilyn Fox, Donna Fuller, Julie Fulton, Harry Groener, Tom Harrison, Christine Healy, Katherine Hiler, I. M. Hobson, Victoria Hoffman, Jane A. Johnston, John-Frederick Jones, O-Lan Jones, Michael Kaufman, John-David Keller, Sally Kemp, Art Koustik, Annie LaRussa, Hal Landon, Jr., Hal Landon, Sr., Stuart Larson, Anni Long, Tzi Ma, Robert Machray, Alan Mandell, Nan Martin, Margaret Marx, Martha McFarland, Ron Michaelson, Jarion Monroe, Belita Moreno, Angela Moya, John Nesci, Martha J. New, Kerry Noonan, Priscilla Pointer, Annabella Price, Teri Ralston, Bryan Rasmussen, Devon Raymond, Dennis Robertson, Robin Pearson Rose, Al Ruscio, Elizabeth Ruscio, Robert Schenkkan, Mark Schneider, Howard Shangraw, Robert Sicular, Ebbe Roe Smith, Sally Spencer, Joan Stuart-Morris, James Sutorius, Dendrie Taylor, Don Took, Vic Trevino, Tom Troupe, K. T. Vogt, John Walcutt, Herta Ware, Jimmie Ray Weeks, Bruce Wright, Steve Yudson, Alexander Zale

PRODUCTIONS: THE CRUCIBLE by Arthur Miller; Director, Martin Benson; Set, Susan Tuohy; Costumes, Robert Blackman; Lighting, Tom Ruzika. A CHRISTMAS CAROL by Charles Dickens; Adaptation, Jerry Patch; Director, John-David Keller; Set, Cliff Faulkner; Costumes, Dwight Richard Odle; Lighting, Donna & Tom Ruzika. ROAD TO MECCA by Athol Fugard; Director, Martin Benson; Set, Michael Devine; Costumes, Walker Hicklin; Lighting, Paulie Jenkins. YOU NEVER CAN TELL by George Bernard Shaw; Director, David Emmes; Set, Cliff Faulkner; Costumes, Shigeru Yaji; Lighting, Peter Maradudin. SUNDAY IN THE PARK WITH GEORGE by James Lapine/Stephen Sondheim; Director, Barbara Damashek; Set, Cliff Faulkner; Costumes, Shigeru Yaji; Lighting, Tom Ruzika. IN PERPETUITY THROUGHOUT THE UNIVERSE by Eric Overmyer; Director, Roberta Levitow; Set, Cliff Faulkner; Costumes, Susan Denison Geller; Lighting, Paulie Jenkins. MOROCCO by Allan Havis; Director, David Emmes; Set, Michael Devine; Costumes, Susan Denison Geller; Lighting, Brian Gale. TALLEY'S FOLLY by Lanford Wilson; Director, Lee Shallat; Set, John Iacovelli; Costumes, Shigeru Yaji; Lighting, Cam Harvey. HARD TIMES by Charles Dickens/Adaptation, Stephen Jeffreys; Director, Robert Goldsby; Costumes/Set, Ariel Parkinson; Lighting, Peter Maradudi. WHEN I GROW UP by Jerry Patch; Director, John-David Keller; Set/Costumes, Dwight Richard Odle.

WORLD PREMIERES: AT LONG LAST LEO by Mark Stein; Set, Cliff Faulkner; Director, Steven Albrezzi; Costumes, Walter Hicklin; Lighting, Peter Maradudin. ABUNDANCE by Beth Henley; Director, Ron Lagomarsino; Set, Adrianne Lobel; Costumes, Robert Wojewodski; Lighting, Paulie Jenkins. DRAGON LADY by Robert Daseler; Director, Jerry Patch; Set, Cliff Faulkner; Costumes, Susan Denison Geller; Lighting, Tom Ruzika. GEOGRAPHY OF LUCK by Marlane Meyer; Director, Roberta Levitow; Set, Cliff Faulkner; Costumes, Susan Denison Geller; Lighting, Tom Ruzika

Top Left: Nan Martin, Christine Healy in "The Road to Mecca"
Ron Stone Photos

Ebbe Roe Smith, Al Ruscio in "The Geography of Luck"

Priscilla Pointer, Tom Troupe in "At Long Last Leo"

Tom Harrison, I. M. Hobson, Sally Spencer in "You Never Can Tell"
Top: Art Koustik, Anni Long, Jarion Monroe in "Hard Times"

STRATFORD FESTIVAL

Thirty-sixth Season

Artistic Director, John Neville; General Manager, Gary Thomas; Producer, Richard C. Dennison; Director of Music, Berthold Carriere; Development, Diana Reitberger; Communications, Ellen T. Cole, Keith Courtney; Production Director, Colleen Blake; Production Manager, Peter Lamb; Directors, Robert Beard, James deB. Domville, Jean Gascon, Jeff Huslop, Richard Monette, Peter Moss, Richard Ouzounian, Robin Phillips, Brian Rintoul, David William; Designers, Lewis Brown, Michael Eagan, Debra Hanson, Brian H. Jackson, Elis Y. Lam, Sue LePage, Andrew Murray, Christina Poddubiuk, Richard Seger, Abram Waterhouse; Composers, Louis Applebaum, Laura Burton, Alan Laing, Raymond Pannell, Allan Rae, Berthold Carriere, Andre Gagnon; Lighting, Robert Bosworth, Harry Frehner, Louise Guinand, Michael J. Whitfield; Choreography/Fights, John Broome, Patrick Crean, Jean-Pierre Fournier, Donald Saddler; Props, Frank Holte, Roy Brown, Joy Allan; Wardrobe, Gayle Larson, Jessica Blackmore, Sharrie-Ann Dial; Wigs, Clayton Shields, Dave Kerr, Richard Jarvie; Stage Managers, Peter McGuire, Michael Benoit, Margaret Palmer, Nora Polley, Catherine Russell, Hilary Graham

COMPANY

Marion Adler, Malcolm Armstrong, Ted Atherton, Alexandre Beaulieu, Andrew Binks, Mervyn Blake, James Blendick, Mary Hitch Blendick, David Brown, Daniel Buccos, Sally Cahill, Douglas Campbell, Ann Casson, Douglas Chamberlain, Juan Chioran, Antoni Cimolino, Eric Coates, Peggy Coffey, Susan Coyne, Richard Curnock, Henry Czerny, Vincent Dale, Johnny Lee Davenport, Hazel Desbarats, Keith Dinicol, Peter Donaldson, Eric Donkin, Jerry Etienne, Colm Fiore, Murray Furrow, Eli Gabay, Maurice Good, Brian Gow, Allan Gray, Kevin Gudahl, Nigel Hamer, Michael Hanrahan, Ron Hastings, Sally Heit, Sheila Helpmann, Susan Henley, Kate Hennig, Roger Honeywell, Bernard Hopkins, Kim Horsman, Ellen Horst, Doug Horst, Stuart Hughes, Scott A. Hurst, Jeffrey Hutchinson, William Hutt, John Innes, Andrew Jackson, Melanie Janzen, Nolan Jennings, David Keeley, Lorne Kennedy, Calla Krause, Michel LaFleche, Larissa Lapchinski, Anne Linden, David Lloyd-Evans, Richard March, Tony Martin, Eric McCormack, John McPherson, Dale Mieske, Melanie Miller, Michele Muzzi, William Needles, John Neville, John Ormerod, Nancy Palk, Vickie Papavs, Lucy Peacock, Nicholas Pennell, Jeffrey Prentice, Tanya Rich, Emma Richler, Christopher Robson, Bradley C. Rudy, Stephen Russell, J. Craig Sandy, Kim Scarcella, Albert Schultz, Goldie Semple, Joseph Shaw, Wenna Shaw, Robert Smith, Kent Staines, Keith Thomas, Brian Tree, William Webster, Scott Wentworth, John Wojda, Anne Wright, Susan Wright, Geraint Wyn-Davies

PRODUCTIONS: *Richard III, The Taming of the Shrew, My Fair Lady, The Three Musketeers, All's Well That Ends Well, Murder in the Cathedral, The Two Gentlemen of Verona, Not about Heroes, Irma La Douce, Twelfth Night, King Lear, Oedipus/ The Critic*

Top Right: Stephen Russell, James Blendick, Nicholas Pennell, Eric McCormack, Lorne Kennedy in "Murder in the Cathedral" Top Left: Colm Feore, Goldie Semple in "Taming of the Shrew"

John Neville, Lucy Peacock in "My Fair Lady"

Stephen Russell, Colm Feore, Lorne Kennedy in "Three Musketeers"
Above: Henry Czerny, Peggy Coffey, Kim
Horsman, John Wojda in "Two Gentlemen of Verona"
Top: William Hutt as "King Lear"

Colm Feore as "Richard III"
Top: Susan Wright, Allan Gray, Richard Curnock in "All's
Well That Ends Well"

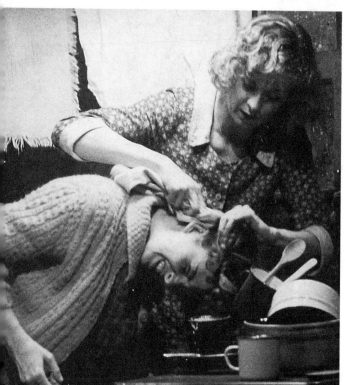

STUDIO ARENA THEATRE

Buffalo, New York
Twenty-fourth Season

Artistic Director, David Frank; Managing Director, Raymond Bonnard; Associate Director/Dramaturg, Ross Wassermann; Development, Anne E. Hayes; Marketing, Ann Marie Sanders; Press, Blossom Cohan, Susan Shaughnessy; Production Manager, Randy Engels; Sound, Rick Menke; Props, Laura A. Figueroa, Ann Blasky; Technical Director, Colin Stewart; Stage Managers, Sarah E. Donnelly, Barbara Ann O'Leary, Lisa D. Norris

PRODUCTIONS & CASTS

MEN SHOULD WEEP by Ena Lamont Stewart; Director, David Frank; Set, John Lee Beatty; Costumes, Mary Ann Powell; Lighting, Dennis Parichy. CAST: Susan Pellegrino (Maggie), Jarlath Conroy (John), Eunice Anderson (Granny), Katherine Leask (Lily), Andrew Polk (Alec), Shauna Hicks (Jenny), Michele Ragusa (Edie), William Rauch (Ernest), Kathleen McNenny (Isa), Carolyn McCarthy (Mrs. Wilson), Robyn Ross (Mrs. Harris), Michele Ragusa (Mrs. Bone), Barbara Rosenblat (Lizzie), Scott Zak, William Rauch (Removal Men), A. Sean Phelan, Lawrence T. Taylor (Neighbors)

ABINGDON SQUARE by Maria Irene Fornes; Director, Ms. Fornes; Set, Donald Eastman; Lighting, Anne Militello; Costumes, Gabriel Berry. CAST: Susan Gibney (Marion), Andrew Colteaux (Michael), Edwin Owens (Juster), Eunice Anderson (Minnie), Sarah Fleming (Mary), David Richard Bates (Frank), Joshua Moore (The Glazier), Frank Testman (Thomas)

STEEL MAGNOLIAS by Robert Harling; Director, Walton Jones; Set, Victor A. Becker; Costumes, Pamela Peterson; Lighting, Tina Charney. CAST: Sally Ann Cohen (Annelle), Karen MacDonald (Truvy), Margot Stevenson (Clairee), Jeri Leer (Shelby), Maeve McGuire (M'Lynn), Jen Jones (Ouiser)

THE BOY FRIEND by Sandy Wilson; Director, David Frank; Musical Director, Donald Rebic; Staging/Choreography, William Fleet Lively; Set, Paul Wonsek; Lighting, Judy Rasmuson; Costumes, Mary Ann Powell. CAST: Patti Perkins (Hortense), Christine Gradl (Maisie), Leigh-Anne Wencker (Dulcie), Allison Gray (Fay), Patricia Forestier (Nancy), Jennifer Jay Myers (Polly), Robert Bianca (Marcel), Christopher Nilsson (Pierre), Brian Henry (Alphonse), Barbara Andres (Mme. Dubonnet), Eric H. Kaufman (Bobby), Don Perkins (Percival), Matthew Wright (Tony), Robert Spencer (Lord Brockhurst), Jayne Houdyshell (Lady Brockhurst), Jeffrey Denman (Waiter), Christopher Nilsson (Pepe), Leigh-Anne Wencker (Lolita), Jeffrey Denman (Gendarme), Margot Davis (Original Polly/Cynthia Forsythe)

WEST MEMPHIS MOJO by Martin Jones; Director, Edward G. Smith; Set, Leonard Harman; Costumes, Catherine F. Norgren; Lighting, Shirley Prendergast; Composer/Music Consultant, Count Dabbit. CAST: Stephen McKinley Henderson (Teddy), K. Todd Freeman (Elroi), Robert Colston (Frank Jackson), Ellen Mareneck (Maxine Pettibone)

THE BEAUX' STRATAGEM by George Farquhar; Director, David Frank; Original Music, Ray Leslee; Set, Leonard Harman; Costumes, Susan Tsu; Lighting, Curt Ostermann; Choreographer, Linda H. Swiniuch; Associate Director, Ross Wassermann; Fight Choreography, Brian Cousins. CAST: Richard Hummert (Boniface), Susan Batten (Cherry/Country Woman), Mark Hymen (Aimwell), Brian Cousins (Archer), Kia Heath (Dorinda), Anne Newhall (Mrs. Sullen), Ray Collins (Sullen), Dana Mills (Gibbet), Michael Russo (Scrub), Brian LaTulip (Foigard), Nicolle Littrell (Gipsy), David Oliver (Count Bellair), Barbara Lester (Lady Bountiful), Jeff Sugarman (Sir Charles Freeman), Adrian Albino, Josh Brewster, John Kiouses (Servants, etc.)

A WALK IN THE WOODS by Lee Blessing; Director, Ross S. Wassermann; Set, Philip Jung; Costumes, Mary Ann Powell; Lighting, Peter Kaczorowski. CAST: William Glover (Andrey Botvinnik), Kenneth Gray (John Honeyman)

Jim Bush Photos

K. Todd Freeman, Stephen McKinley Henderson in "West Memphis Mojo"

Susan Gibney in "Abingdon Square"
Top: Susan Pelegrino (top), Michele Ragusa in "Men Should Weep"

176

William Glover, Kenneth Gray in "A Walk in the Woods"
Top: Mark Hymen, Dana Mills in "The Beaux Stratagem"
Jim Bush Photos

SAN JOSE REPERTORY COMPANY

San Jose, California

Artistic Director, Timothy Near; Managing Director, Shannon Yevak-Leskin; Marketing Director, Butch Coyne; Stage Managers, Doeri Welch, Peggy L. Hess; Press, Bobby Tyler

PRODUCTIONS & CASTS

ARMS AND THE MAN by George Bernard Shaw; Director, Kent Stephens; Costumes, Jeffrey Jeffrey Strukman; Set, Kate Edmunds; Lighting, Paulie Jenkins CAST: Suzanne Irving, Kate Williamson, Amy Perry, Robert Nadir, Peter Vilkin, David Pichette, Bill Striglos, John Hertzler

THE 1940's RADIO HOUR by Walton Jones; Director, Timothy Near; Musical Director, Steve Zavodnick; Choreographer, Bick Goss; Lighting, Peter Maradudin; Set/Costumes, Jeffrey Stukman. CAST: Al Blair, Skip Greer, Christa Germanson, Richard Sherman, Mark Lotito, Baomi Butts-Bhanji, John Hertzler, Will Leskin, Steve Zavodnick, Jim Newman, Michael J. Kay, Holly Near, Mike Burciullo

BENEFACTORS by Michael Frayn; Director, Skip Foster; Set, Joel Fontaine; Costumes, Deborah Weber Krahenhaul; Lighting, Derek Duarte. CAST: Lawrence Hecht, Rosemary Smith, Will Leskin, Tina Marie Goff

TALLEY'S FOLLY by Lanford Wilson; Director, Steve Albrezzi; Set, Jeffrey Stukman; Costumes, Deborah Weber Krahenbuhl; Lighting, Derek Duarte. CAST: Mitchell Greenberg, Nancy Frangione

BURNING PATIENCE directed by Tony Curiel; Set, Joel Fontaine; Costumes, Cassandra Carpenter; Lighting, Kurt Landisman. CAST: David Silva, Frank L. Lucero, Carlos Baron, Kevin Sifuentes, Vilma Silva, Anne Betancourt, Cesar E. Flores

A STREETCAR NAMED DESIRE by Tennessee Williams; Director, Steve Albrezzi; Assistant, Skip Greer; Set, Jeffrey Strukman; Costumes, Beaver Bauer; Lighting, Paulie Jenkins. CAST: Baomi Butts-Bhanji, David Dunard, Steve Ewing, Amelia Schumacher, Kathleen Stefano, Katie Mitchell, Skip Greer, Eric Castleton, Christopher Rich, Libby Boone, Kate Brickley, Tony Bennett Roque

ALL MY SONS by Arthur Miller; Director, Steve Albrezzi; Set/Costumes, Jeffrey Strukman; Lighting, Peter Maradudin; Stage Managers, Peggy Hess, Ken Barton. CAST: Howard Witt, Joyce Van Patten, Christopher Rich, Tina Marie Goff, Charles Jean, Skip Foster, Kate Brickley, Skip Greer, Cynthia Bassham, Carlos-Antonio Colon, Josh Ekblom

Right: Christopher Rich, Libby Boone in "A Streetcar Named Desire"
Top: Suzanne Irving, John Hertzler in "Arms and the Man"

Will Leskin, Michael J. Kay, Jim Newman, Mike Gurciullo in "The 1940's Radio Hour"

Kevin Sifuentes, Vilma Silva in "Burning Patience"

SYRACUSE STAGE

Syracuse, New York
Sixteenth Season

Producing Artistic Director, Arthur Storch; Managing Director, James A. Clark; Business Manager, Diana Coles; Development, Shirley Lockwood; Marketing, Barbara Beckos; Press, Barbara Haas; Company Manager, Peter Sandwall; Stage Managers, Don Buschmann, Barbara Beeching; Literary Coordinator, Howard Kerner; Production Manager, Kerro Knox 3; Technical Director, William S. Tiesi; Scenic Artist, Gary May; Lighting, Sandra Schilling; Sound, James Wildman; Props, Susan Baker, Costumer, Maria Marrero.

PRODUCTIONS & CASTS

STEEL MAGNOLIAS by Robert Harling; Director, Walton Jones; Set, Victor Becker; Costumes, Pamela Peterson; Lighting, Tina Charney. CAST: Sally Ann Cohen (Annelle), Jen Jones (Ouiser), Jeri Leer (Shelby), Karen MacDonald (Truvy), Maeve McGuire (M'Lynne), Margot Stevenson (Clairee)
LONG DAY'S JOURNEY INTO NIGHT by Eugene O'Neill; Director, William Woodman; Set, Gary May; Costumes, Maria Marrero; Lighting, Harry Feiner. CAST: P. J. Benjamin (Jamie), Pamela Campbell (Cathleen), Steven Dennis (Edmund), DeAnn Mears (Mary Tyrone), Tony Mockus (James Tyrone)
LOOK HOMEWARD, ANGEL by Ketti Frings; Director, Arthur Storch; Set, John Lee Beatty; Costumes, Nanzi Adzima; Lighting, Roger Morgan. CAST: Stephen Bradbury (Hugh Barton), Brendan Burke (Dr. Maguire), Nora Chester ("Fatty"), Emily Frankel Cullum (Eliza Gant), John Cullum (W. O. Gant), John David Cullum (Eugene Gant), Keely Eastley (Helen Gant Barton), George Hosmer (Will), Saundra McClain (Madame Elizabeth), Michael O'Shea (Jake Clatt), Jennifer Pauly (Laura), Jonathan Walker (Ben), David Whalen (Luke), Kathleen Baum, Edith Fisher, Louis Fisher, Caroline Fitzgerald, Lenore Lee, James E. Toole.
ANOTHER ANTIGONE by A. R. Gurney, Jr.; Director, Robert Berlinger; Set, Victor Becker; Lighting, Philip Monat. CAST: Pamela Burrell (Diana Eberhart), Kelly Curtis (Judy Miller), Jonathan McMurtry (Henry Harper), Andrew Myler (David Appleton)
HOW THE OTHER HALF LOVES by Alan Ayckbourn; Director, Tazewell Thompson; Set, James Noone; Costumes, Judy Dearing; Lighting, David Noling. CAST: Verna Hampton (Fiona Foster), Jack Landron (Frank Foster), Kevin Richardson (William Detweiler), David Roberson (Bob Phillips), Pamela Tyson (Teresa Phillips), Kim Weston-Moran (Mary Detweiler)
WAIT UNTIL DARK by Frederick Knott; Director, Arthur Storch; Set, Gary May; Costumes, Maria Marrero; Lighting, Phillip Monat. CAST: Clarke Bittner (Policeman 1), Jacqueline Cohen (Gloria), Timothy Davis-Reed (Sam), Munson Hicks (Harry Roat, Jr.), Jesse N. Holmes (Mike Talman), George Hosmer (Sgt. Carlino), Brenda Pentland (Susy Hendrix), Hank Unger (Policeman 2)

Top Right: Jonathan McMurtry in "Another Antigone"
Lawrence Mason, Jr. Photos

P. J. Benjamin, DeAnn Mears, Tony Mockus in "Long Day's Journey into Night"

John Cullum, Keely Eastley in "Look Homeward, Angel"

THEATRE THREE

Dallas, Texas
Twenty-seventh Season

Founding/Artistic Director, Norma Young; Executive Producer-Director, Jac Alder; General Manager, Charles Howard; Stage Manager, Terry Tittle Holman; Production Manager, Cheryl Denson; Costumier, Christopher Kovarik; Technical Director, Tristan Wilson; Associate Director, Laurence O'Dwyer; Press, Gary Yawn

PRODUCTIONS & CASTS

CLAP YO' HANDS: HOMAGE TO GEORGE AND IRA GERSHWIN devised by Jac Alder; Musical Arrangements, Terry Dobson, Jac Alder; Gowns, Victor Costa; Set, Cheryl Denson; Lighting, Robert McVay. CAST: Jac Alder, Connie Coit, Terry Dobson, Dick Dufour, Richard Hobson, Shirley McFatter, Connie Nelson
THE COLORED MUSEUM by George C. Wolfe; Director, Charles Gordone; Music, Kysia Bostic; Musical Director, Terry Dobson; Set, Charles Howard; Costumes, Charles Howard, Christopher Kovarik; Lighting, Robert McVay; Sound, Tristan Wilson. CAST: Donald Douglass, Nedra P. James, Michael Cal Stewart, Cheryle Washington, Catherine Whiteman
HUNTING COCKROACHES by Janusz Glowacki; Translation, Jadwiga Kosicka; Director, Charles Howard; Set, Cheryl Denson; Costumes, Christopher Kovarik; Lighting, Ken Hudson. CAST: Shannon Lee Avnsoe, Dwain Fail, Sharon Bunn, Vince Davis, Terry Londeree
TAKING STEPS by Alan Ayckbourn; Director, Jac Alder; Set, Jac Alder, Cheryl Denson; Costumes, Christopher Kovark; Lighting, Robert McVay; Sound, Tristan Wilson. CAST: James Harbour, Lynn Mathis, Connie Nelson, Terry Vandivort, William M. Whitehead, Donna Yeager
A QUARREL OF SPARROWS by James Duff (World Premiere) Director, Jac Alder; Set, Cheryl Denson; Costumes, Christopher Kovarik; Lighting, Ken Hudson. CAST: Jerry Crow, John Evans, John Figlmiller, Jo Haden Laurence O'Dwyer, Norma Young
THE FANTASTICKS with Words by Tom Jones; Music, Harvey Schmidt; Director, Cheryl Denson; Musical Director, Mark Miller; Set, Charles Howard; Costumes, Christopher Kovarik; Lighting, Ken Hudson. CAST: Jac Alder, Annie Biggs, Terry Dobson, Greg Dulcie, Gordon Fox, Lisa-Gabrielle Greene, Jerry Haynes, Chris Westfall
CLAPTRAP by Ken Friedman; Director, Laurence O'Dwyer; Set, Cheryl Denson; Costumes, Christopher Kovarik; Lighting, Shari Melde. CAST: Georgia Clinton, Jerry Crow, Vince Davis, Peggy Townsley, Laura Yancey
THE MIDDLE OF NOWHERE conceived and written by Tracy Friedman; Based on songs by Randy Newman; Direction/Choreography, Tracy Friedman; Musical Director, Terry Dobson; Set, Charles Howard; Costumes, Christopher Kovarik; Lighting, Ken Hudson. CAST: Keith D. Allgeier, Peggy Billo, Grover Coulson, Jr., Dennis M. Maher, Terrence Charles Rodgers

Left: Terry Vandivort, William Whitehead, Connie Nelson, James Harbour in "Taking Steps"
Top: Catherine Whiteman, Nedra James, Michael Cal Stewart, Cheryle Washington in "Colored Museum"
Susan Kandell Photos

Peggy Billo, Dennis Maher, Grover Coulson, Jr., Terrence Charles Rodgers, Keith Allgeier in "The Middle of Nowhere"

Vince Davis, Georgia Clinton, Jerry Crow in "Claptrap"

Lorraine Lanigan, Dan Hamilton and opposite: with Gerald
Richards in "A Moon for the Misbegotten"
Below: Ronald Hunter, Michael Lasswell in "A Life
in the Theatre"

THEATRE VIRGINIA

Richmond, Virginia

Executive Artistic Director, Terry Burgler; General Manager, Kathy Bateson; Business Manager, Tom Muza; Production Manager, Terry Cermak; Associate Director/ Head of Design, Charles Caldwell; Operations Manager, Sherry Jones
PRODUCTIONS: *Forum, Camelot, I'm Not Rappaport, Moon for the Misbegotten, Life in the Theatre, Tomfoolery, Pump Boys and Dinettes, Greater Tuna*. No other data included.

Michael Lasswell, Ronald Hunter in "A Life in the Theatre"

TOTEM POLE PLAYHOUSE

Fayetteville, Pennsylvania

Producing Artistic Director, Carl Shurr; Managing Director, Sue Kocek; Directors, Wil Love, Carl Schurr, Robert Spencer; Musical Director, Terrence Sherman; Sets, James Fouchard; Costumes, Patricia M. Risser; Lighting, Dave Brown; Stage Manager, Paul Mills Holmes

PRODUCTION & CASTS

THE VOICE OF THE TURTLE by John Van Druten. CAST: Brigid Cleary, Paul DeBoy, Shirleyann Kaladjian

CATCH ME IF YOU CAN by Jack Weinstock and Willie Gilbert. CAST: James Anthony, Paul DeBoy, Jayne Houdyshell, Wil Love, Jan Puffer, Sherry Skinker, Robert Spencer

A SUMMER REMEMBERED by Charles Nolte. CAST: James Anthony, Curtis Armstrong, Paul DeBoy, Johanna Ezell, Jane Houdyshell, Wil Love, Jane Lowry, Lara Lutz, Jan Puffer, Sherry Skinker, Traci Lyn Thomas, Christopher Tickner, Bart St. Clair

CARNIVAL by Bob Merrill, Michael Stewart. CAST: Melissa Bumbaugh, Thomas Colley, Bobby Dawson, Paul DeBoy, Ed Gotwalt, Rachel Hennelly, Anthony Lane Hinkle, Jayne Houdyshell, Wil Love, Lara Lutz, Ron Meier, Jan Puffer, Joe Reed, John Scott, Sherry Skinker, Robert Spencer, Traci Lyn Thomas, Christopher Tickner, Gregory Walker, Heidi White, Walter Willison, Nephi Jay Wimmer, Katrina Yaukey, Kay Yaukey

HOW THE OTHER HALF LOVES by Alan Ayckbourn. CAST: Paul DeBoy, Jayne Houdyshell, Carl Shurr, Sherry Skinker, Robert Spencer, Maggie Winn-Jones

WALLY'S CAFE by Sam Bobrick, Ron Clark. CAST: Jayne Houdyshell, Wil Love, Sherry Skinker

A CHRISTMAS CAROL by Charles Dickens; Adaptation, Wil Love, Carl Schurr. CAST: Lance Baker, Joseph Brener, Melissa Bumbaugh, Karen Cooksey, Paul DeBoy, Richert Easley, Johanna Ezell, Jayne Houdyshell, Wil Love, Charlie Mills, Elise Overcash, Francis Parkman, Michael Pedersen, Jan Puffer, Jacqueline ReBok, Joseph G. Ross, Carl Schurr, Barbara Shahpazian-DeBoy, Steven W. Shriner, Robert Spencer, Bob Tron, Gregory Walker, Katrina & Kay Yaukey

Top: Heidi White, Walter Willison in "Carnival"
Right: Robert Spencer, James Anthony in "Catch Me
If You Can"
Cellar Studio Photos

Wil Love, Richert Easley in "A Christmas Carol"

VIRGINIA STAGE COMPANY

Norfolk, Virginia
Tenth Season

Artistic Director, Charles Towers; Managing Director, Dan J. Martin; Associate Artistic Director, Christopher Hanna; General Manager, Caroline F. Turner; Development, Lexi Caswell; Marketing, Claudia Keenan; Company Manager, Marge Prendergast; Production Manager, Michael O'Connell; Technical Director, Christopher Fretts; Props, Freda Grim; Costumes, Candice Cain; Sound, Kevin Danaher; Stage Managers, Candace LoFrumento, Amanda Mengden

PRODUCTIONS & CASTS

LES LIAISONS DANGEREUSES by Christopher Hampton; Director, Charles Towers; Set/Lights, Pavel Dobrusky; Fights, David Leong. CAST: Gary Andrews, Kelly Baker, Lee Anne Beaman, Mary Jean Feton, Maureen Garrett, Marcia Gay Harden, Terry G. Jernigan, Josephine Nichols, Geoff Pierson, Kevin Thomsen
AMERICAN BUFFALO by David Mamet; Director, Charles Towers; Set, George Hillow; Lighting, Spencer Mosse; CAST: Jack Davidson, Michael Ornstein, Geoff Pierson
FOSSEY by Lois Meredith *(World Premiere)* Director, Pamela Berlin; Set, Michael Ganio; Lighting, Judy Rasmuson; Composer/Sound, Dary John Mizelle; Optics, Gayle Jeffery. CAST: Lois Meredith
MACBETH by William Shakespeare; Director, Charles Towers; Set/Lighting, Pavel Dobrusky; CAST: Gary Andrews, James G. Cadenhead, Mary Jean Feton, Bruce Gooch, George L. Hasenstab, Tom Kettells, Jack Koenig, Marty McGaw, Lachlan Macleay, Barbara March, W. T. Martin, Jim Mohr, David Penhale, Lynn Ruehlmann, Alan Sader
TOP GIRLS by Caryl Churchill; Director, Christopher Hanna; Set, Bill Clarke; Lighting, Don Holder. CAST: Gannon Daniels, Mary Lum, Roma Maffia, Lori Putnam, Sheriden Thomas, Katherine Udall, Diana Van Fossen
A WALK IN THE WOODS by Lee Blessing; Director, Christopher Hanna; Set, George Hillow; Lighting, Jon Holder; Costumes, Giva Taylor. CAST: Humbert Astredo, Mark Metcalf

Helen Anrod Jones, Mark Atkinson Photos

Mary Jean Feton, Maureen Garrett in "Les Liaisons Dangereuses"
Top Right: W. T. Martin, Barbara March in "Macbeth"

183

Kristine Nielsen, Edward Atienza, Michael Dolan
in "The Alchemist"

YALE REPERTORY THEATRE

New Haven, Connecticut

Artistic Director, Lloyd Richards; Managing Director, Benjamin Mordecai; Set Adviser, Ming Cho Lee; Costume Adviser, Jane Greenwood; Lighting Adviser, Jennifer Tipton; Speech Adviser, Barbara Somerville; Movement Adviser, Wesley Fata; Sets, Michael Yeargan; Lighting, William B. Warfel; Musical Coordinator, Craig Campbell; Dramaturge, Gitta Honegger, Joel Schecter; General Manager, Buzz Ward; Development, Ann S. Johnson; Marketing/Press, Robert Wildman; Production Supervisor, Bronislaw J. Sammler; Stage Managers, Maureen F. Gibson, Margaret Adair Quinn; Technical Director, Michael R. Van Dyke; Wardrobe, Nancy Brennan, Cyndi Orr; Props, Brian Cookson; Resident Scenic Artist, Jeffrey Crivello

PRODUCTIONS & CASTS

INTERMEZZO by Arthur Schnitzler; Translation, Robert David MacDonald; Director, Gitta Honegger; Set, James A. Schuette; Costumes, Pamela Peterson; Lighting, Jennifer Tipton; Music, Scott Davenport Richards. CAST: Philip Casnoff, Michael Countryman, Suzy Fay, Joseph Fuqua, Laura MacDermott, Jacquelyn Mari Roberts, Stephanie Roth, Mary Walden, Brendan Bloom, Joshua Evan Drumm

KISS OF THE SPIDER WOMAN by Manuel Puig; Translation, Allan Baker; Director, David Chambers; Set, Michael Yeargan; Costumes, Joel O. Thayer; Lighting, Mark London; Sound, David Budries. CAST: Richard Frank, Leon Katz, Elias Koteas, Dennis Scott

THE ALCHEMIST by Ben Jonson; Director, John Hirsch; Set, David Birn; Costumes, Wendy A. Rolfe; Lighting, Christopher Akerlind; Sound, James C. Swonger; Music, Philippe Bodin, Craig Campbell. CAST: Edward Atienza, Michael Dolan, Alexander Draper, Joshua Fardon, Claudia Feldstein, Jay P. Goede, Edward Hibbert, Bruce Katzman, William Langan, Kristine Nielsen, Stephen Ouimette, Jill Patterson, Brian Reddy, Mary Lou Rosato, Marilyn Rudnick, Frank Savino, John Shuman, Doug Spitz, Eric Swanson, Richard Woods

PHAEDRA AND HIPPOLYTUS by Elizabeth Egloff *(World Premiere)* Director, Christopher Grabowski; Set, Tony Fanning; Costumes, Melina Root; Lighting, Anita C. Stewart; Sound, John C. Huntington III. CAST: A. Benard Cummings, Joseph Fuqua, Earl Hindman, Patrick Kerr, Susan Knight, Mary Mara, Lola Pashalinski, David Stocker, Pamela Tucker-White

THE BEACH by Anthony Giardina *(World Premiere)* Director, Amy Saltz; Set, Michael Loui; Costumes, Chrisi Karvonides; Lighting, Mark London. CAST: Amy Aquino, Richard Cox, Robin Groves, Christopher McHale, Debra Monk, Deborah Offner, Michael O'Neill, Jeremy Cox, Megan Gaffney, Corey Hobbs, Lindsay McGuire

STARTING MONDAY by Anne Commire *(World Premiere)* Director, Peter Mark Schifter; Set, Sarah Lambert; Costumes, Nephelie Andonyadis; Lighting, David Birn. CAST: Charles Bartlett, Sara Botsford, Rosalyn Coleman, Babo Harrison, C. Phillips Kaufmann, Leslie Lyles, Jim MacLaren, Michael W. McCarty, Sylvia Short, Mary Louise Wilson

INTERROGATING THE NUDE by Doug Wright *(World Premiere)* Director, Gitta Honegger; Set/Costumes, James A. Schuette; Lighting, Mark London. CAST: Peter Appel, Kirk Jackson, Jerry Mayer, Brad O'Hare, David Purdham

MOON OVER MIAMI by John Guare; *(World Premiere)* Director, Andrei Belgrader; Set, Judy Gailen; Costumes, Candice Donnelly; Lighting, Scott Zielinski; Sound, G. Thomas Clark, Ann Johnson; Musical Direction/Incidental Music/Arrangements, Lawrence Yurman; Dances, Wesley Fata; Words/Music, John Guare; Music for "Osvaldo's Song" by Galt MacDermot. CAST: Frances Barney, Martin Blanco, Roger Bechtel, John R. Conway, Laurel Cronin, Julie Hagerty, Walker Jones, Susan Kellermann, Jim MacLaren, Mary Mara, Dana Morosini, Oliver Platt, Dennis Reid, Richard Riehle, Jacquelyn Mari Roberts, Robert Russell, Robin Selfridge, Tony Shalhoub, Ali Sharaf, Richard Spore, Lewis J. Stadlen, Sam Stoneburner, Stanley Tucci, Mary Walden, Ann Whitney, Lawrence Yurman, Tim Moran, Pete Derheimer

COBB by Lee Blessing *(World Premiere)* Director, Lloyd Richards; Set, Rob Greenberg; Costumes, Joel O. Thayer; Lighting, Ashley York Kennedy; Sound, G. Thomas Clark. CAST: Chris Cooper, Delroy Lindo, James E. Reynolds, Josef Somer

PLAYBOY OF THE WEST INDIES by Mustapha Matura; Director, Dennis Scott; Set, Michael Yeargan; Costumes, Mary Myers; Lighting, William B. Warfel CAST: A. Benard Cummings, Suzzanne Douglas, Richard Gant, Fanni Green, Kevin Jackson, Kathi Kennedy, Jacquelyn Mari Roberts, Michael Rogers, Vince Williams, Jeffrey Wright

Gerry Goodstein Photos

**Top: Stephanie Roth, Philip Casnoff in "Intermezzo" Below:
Richard Frank, Elias Koteas in "Kiss of the Spider Woman"**

Julie Hagerty, Oliver Platt in "Moon over Miami"

Deborah Offner, Michael O'Neill in "The Beach"

Brad O'Hare, Kirk Jackson in "Interrogating the Nude"

Pamela Tucker-White, David Stocker in "Phaedra and Hippolytus"

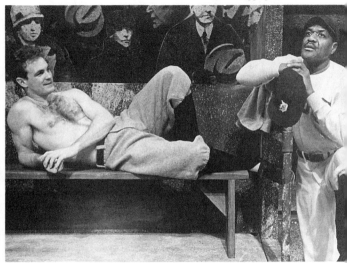

Kevin Jackson in "Playboy of the West Indies"
Above: Richard Cox, Debra Monk in "The Beach"

Sara Botsford, Leslie Lyles in "Starting Monday"
Above: James Reynolds, Delroy Lindo in "Cobb"

185

PULITZER PRIZE PRODUCTIONS

1918-Why Marry? **1919**-No award, **1920**-Beyond the Horizon, **1921**-Miss Lulu Bett, **1922**-Anna Christie, **1923**-Icebound, **1924**-Hell-Bent fer Heaven, **1925**-They Knew What They Wanted, **1926**-Craig's Wife, **1927**-In Abraham's Bosom, **1928**-Strange Interlude, **1929**-Street Scene, **1930**-The Green Pastures, **1931**-Alison's House, **1932**-Of Thee I Sing, **1933**-Both Your Houses, **1934**-Men in White, **1935**-The Old Maid, **1936**-Idiot's Delight, **1937**-You Can't Take It with You, **1938**-Our Town, **1939**-Abe Lincoln in Illinois, **1940**-The Time of Your Life, **1941**-There Shall Be No Night, **1942**-No award, **1943**-The Skin of Our Teeth, **1944**-No award, **1945**-Harvey, **1946**-State of the Union, **1947**-No award, **1948**-A Streetcar Named Desire, **1949**-Death of a Salesman, **1950**-South Pacific, **1951**-No award, **1952**-The Shrike, **1953**-Picnic, **1954**-The Teahouse of the August Moon, **1955**-Cat on a Hot Tin Roof, **1956**-The Diary of Anne Frank, **1957**-Long Day's Journey into Night, **1958**-Look Homeward, Angel, **1959**-J. B., **1960**-Fiorello!, **1961**-All the Way Home, **1962**-How to Succeed in Business without Really Trying, **1963**-No award, **1964**-No award, **1965**-The Subject Was Roses, **1966**-No award, **1967**-A Delicate Balance, **1968**-No award, **1969**-The Great White Hope, **1970**-No Place to Be Somebody, **1971**-The Effect of Gamma Rays on Man-in-the-Moon Marigolds, **1972**-No award, **1973**-That Championship Season, **1974**-No award, **1975**-Seascape, **1976**-A Chorus Line, **1977**-The Shadow Box, **1978**-The Gin Game, **1979**-Buried Child, **1980**-Talley's Folly, **1981**-Crimes of the Heart, **1982**-A Soldier's Play, **1983**-'night, Mother, **1984**-Glengarry Glen Ross, **1985**-Sunday in the Park with George, **1986**-No award, **1987**-Fences, **1988**-Driving Miss Daisy, **1989**-The Heidi Chronicles

AMERICAN THEATRE WING ANTOINETTE PERRY (TONY) AWARD PRODUCTIONS

1948-Mister Roberts, **1949**-Death of a Salesman, Kiss Me, Kate, **1950**-The Cocktail Party, South Pacific, **1951**-The Rose Tattoo, Guys and Dolls, **1952**-The Fourposter, The King and I, **1953**-The Crucible, Wonderful Town, **1954**-The Teahouse of the August Moon, Kismet, **1955**-The Desperate Hours, The Pajama Game, **1956**-The Diary of Anne Frank, Damn Yankees, **1957**-Long Day's Journey into Night, My Fair Lady, **1958**-Sunrise at Campobello, The Music Man, **1959**-J. B., Redhead, **1960**-The Miracle Worker, Fiorello! tied with The Sound of Music, **1961**-Becket, Bye Bye Birdie, **1962**-A Man for All Seasons, How to Succeed in Business without Really Trying, **1963**-Who's Afraid of Virginia Woolf?, A Funny Thing Happened on the Way to the Forum, **1964**-Luther, Hello Dolly!, **1965**-The Subject Was Roses, Fiddler on the Roof, **1966**-The Persecution and Assassination of Marat as Performed by the Inmates of the Asylum of Charenton under the Direction of the Marquis de Sade, Man of La Mancha, **1967**-The Homecoming, Cabaret, **1968**-Rosencrantz and Guildenstern Are Dead, Hallelujah Baby!, **1969**-The Great White Hope, 1776, **1970**-Borstal Boy, Applause, **1971**-Sleuth, Company, **1972**-Sticks and Bones, Two Gentlemen of Verona, **1973**-That Championship Season, A Little Night Music, **1974**-The River Niger, Raisin, **1975**-Equus, The Wiz, **1976**-Travesties, A Chorus Line, **1977**-The Shadow Box, Annie, **1978**-Da, Ain't Misbehavin', Dracula, **1979**-The Elephant Man, Sweeney Todd, **1980**-Children of a Lesser God, Evita, Morning's at Seven, **1981**-Amadeus, 42nd Street, The Pirates of Penzance, **1982**-The Life and Adventures of Nicholas Nickleby, Nine, Othello, **1983**-Torch Song Trilogy, Cats, On Your Toes, **1984**-The Real Thing, La Cage aux Folles, **1985**-Biloxi Blues, Big River, Joe Egg, **1986**-I'm Not Rappaport, The Mystery of Edwin Drood, Sweet Charity, **1987**-Fences, Les Miserables, All My Sons, **1988**-M. Butterfly, The Phantom of the Opera, Anything Goes, **1989**-The Heidi Chronicles, Jerome Robbins' Broadway, Our Town

NEW YORK DRAMA CRITICS CIRCLE AWARDS

1936-Winterset, **1937**-High Tor, **1938**-Of Mice and Men, Shadow and Substance, **1939**-The White Steed, **1940**-The Time of Your Life, **1941**-Watch on the Rhine, The Corn is Green, **1942**-Blithe Spirit, **1943**-The Patriots, **1944**-Jacobowsky and the Colonel, **1945**-The Glass Menagerie, **1946**-Carousel, **1947**-All My Sons, No Exit, Brigadoon, **1948**-A Streetcar Named Desire, The Winslow Boy, **1949**-Death of a Salesman, The Madwoman of Chaillot, South Pacific, **1950**-The Member of the Wedding, The Cocktail Party, The Consul, **1951**-Darkness at Noon, The Lady's Not for Burning, Guys and Dolls, **1952**-I Am a Camera, Venus Observed, Pal Joey, **1953**- Picnic, The Love of Four Colonels, Wonderful Town, **1954**-Teahouse of the August Moon, Ondine, The Golden Apple, **1955**-Cat on a Hot Tin Roof, Witness for the Prosecution, The Saint of Bleecker Street, **1956**-The Diary of Anne Frank, Tiger at the Gates, My Fair Lady, **1957**-Long Day's Journey into Night, The Waltz of the Toreadors, The Most Happy Fella, **1958**-Look Homeward Angel, Look Back in Anger, The Music Man, **1959**-A Raisin in the Sun, The Visit, La Plume de Ma Tante, **1960**-Toys in the Attic, Five Finger Exercise, Fiorello! **1961**-All the Way Home, A Taste of Honey, Carnival, **1962**-Night of the Iguana, A Man for All Seasons, How to Succeed in Business without Really Trying, **1963**-Who's Afraid of Virginia Woolf?, **1964**-Luther, Hello Dolly!, **1965**-The Subject Was Roses, Fiddler on the Roof, **1966**-The Persecution and Assassination of Marat as Performed by the Inmates of the Asylum of Charenton under the Direction of the Marquis de Sade, Man of La Mancha, **1967**-The Homecoming, Cabaret, **1968**-Rosencrantz and Guildenstern Are Dead, Your Own Thing, **1969**-The Great White Hope, 1776, **1970**-The Effect of Gamma Rays on Man-in-the-Moon Marigolds, Borstal Boy, Company, **1971**-Home, Follies, The House of Blue Leaves, **1972**-That Championship Season, Two Gentlemen of Verona, **1973**-The Hot 1 Baltimore, The Changing Room, A Little Night Music, **1974**-The Contractor, Short Eyes, Candide, **1975**-Equus, The Taking of Miss Janie, A Chorus Line, **1976**-Travesties, Streamers, Pacific Overtures, **1977**-Otherwise Engaged, American Buffalo, Annie, **1978**-Da, Ain't Misbehavin', **1979**-The Elephant Man, Sweeney Todd, **1980**-Talley's Folly, Evita, Betrayal, **1981**-Crimes of the Heart, A Lesson from Aloes, Special Citation to Lena Horne, The Pirates of Penzance, **1982**-The Life and Adventures of Nicholas Nickleby, A Soldier's Play, (no musical honored), **1983**-Brighton Beach Memoirs, Plenty, Little Shop of Horrors, **1984**-The Real Thing, Glengarry Glen Ross, Sunday in the Park with George, **1985**-Ma Rainey's Black Bottom, no musical, **1986**-A Lie of the Mind, Benefactors, no musical, Special to Lily Tomlin and Jane Wagner, **1987**-Fences, Les Liaisons Dangereuses, Les Miserables, **1988**-Joe Turner's Come and Gone, The Road to Mecca, Into the Woods, **1989**-The Heidi Chronicles, Aristocrats, Largely New York (Special), no musical.

1989 THEATRE WORLD AWARD RECIPIENTS
(OUTSTANDING NEW TALENT)

DYLAN BAKER
of "Eastern Standard"

JOAN CUSACK
"Road"/"Brilliant Traces"

SALLY MAYES
of "Welcome to the Club"

LOREN DEAN
of "Amulets against the Dragon Forces"

PETER FRECHETTE
of "Eastern Standard"

SHARON McNIGHT
of "Starmites"

JENNIE MOREAU
of "Eleemosynary"

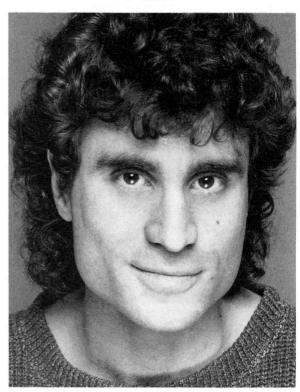

PAUL PROVENZA
of "Only Kidding"

HOWARD SPIEGEL
of "Only Kidding"

KYRA SEDGWICK
of "Ah, Wilderness!"

JOANNE WHALLEY-KILMER
of "What the Butler Saw"

ERIC STOLTZ
of "Our Town"

THEATRE WORLD AWARDS presented Thursday, June 1, 1989 in the Grand Foyer of the Beaumont Theater. Top: John Cullum, Joan Allen, Alec Baldwin, Alice Playten, Victor Garber, Carol Channing; Thom Christopher; Anita Gillette, Philip Casnoff, Nancy Dussault, Leslie Uggams, B. D. Wong, Patti Cohenour; Below: Patti Cohenour, Loren Dean; Sally Mayes; Dylan Baker; Sharon McNight, Carol Channing; Bottom: Carol Channing, John Willis; Alec Baldwin; John Cullum; Howard Spiegel
Van Williams Photos

Eric Stoltz; Martin Gottfried; Pauline Collins; B. D. Wong Below: Walter Willison, Laurie Beechman; Paul Provenza, Nancy Dussault;
Ralph Carter, Leslie Uggams;
Bottom row: Boyd Gaines; Tovah Feldshuh; Kevin Conway, Ed Evanko, Lewis J. Stadlen; Milton Goldman, John Springer, Rita Gam;
Above: Alec Baldwin, Joan Allen; Keene Curtis, Victor Garber, Patti Cohenour, Philip Casnoff; Loren Dean
Van Williams, Michael Riordan Photos

Alan
Alda

Jane
Alexander

Alec
Baldwin

Elizabeth
Ashley

Matthew
Broderick

Dixie
Carter

PREVIOUS THEATRE WORLD
AWARD RECIPIENTS

1944-45: Betty Comden, Richard Davis, Richard Hart, Judy Holliday, Charles Lang, Bambi Linn, John Lund, Donald Murphy, Nancy Noland, Margaret Phillips, John Raitt
1945-46: Barbara Bel Geddes, Marlon Brando, Bill Callahan, Wendell Corey, Paul Douglas, Mary James, Burt Lancaster, Patricia Marshall, Beatrice Pearson
1946-47: Keith Andes, Marion Bell, Peter Cookson, Ann Crowley, Ellen Hanley, John Jordan, George Keane, Dorothea MacFarland, James Mitchell, Patricia Neal, David Wayne
1947-48: Valerie Bettis, Edward Bryce, Whitfield Connor, Mark Dawson, June Lockhart, Estelle Loring, Peggy Maley, Ralph Meeker, Meg Mundy, Douglass Watson, James Whitmore, Patrice Wymore
1948-49: Tod Andrews, Doe Avedon, Jean Carson, Carol Channing, Richard Derr, Julie Harris, Mary McCarty, Allyn Ann McLerie, Cameron Mitchell, Gene Nelson, Byron Palmer, Bob Scheerer
1949-50: Nancy Andrews, Phil Arthur, Barbara Brady, Lydia Clarke, Priscilla Gillette, Don Hanmer, Marcia Henderson, Charlton Heston, Rick Jason, Grace Kelly, Charles Nolte, Roger Price
1950-51: Barbara Ashley, Isabel Bigley, Martin Brooks, Richard Burton, Pat Crowley, James Daly, Cloris Leachman, Russell Nype, Jack Palance, William Smithers, Maureen Stapleton, Marcia Van Dyke, Eli Wallach
1951-52: Tony Bavaar, Patricia Benoit, Peter Conlow, Virginia de Luce, Ronny Graham, Audrey Hepburn, Diana Herbert, Conrad Janis, Dick Kallman, Charles Proctor, Eric Sinclair, Kim Stanley, Marian Winters, Helen Wood
1952-53: Edie Adams, Rosemary Harris, Eileen Heckart, Peter Kelley, John Kerr, Richard Kiley, Gloria Marlowe, Penelope Munday, Paul Newman, Sheree North, Geraldine Page, John Stewart, Ray Stricklyn, Gwen Verdon
1953-54: Orson Bean, Harry Belafonte, James Dean, Joan Diener, Ben Gazzara, Carol Haney, Jonathan Lucas, Kay Medford, Scott Merrill, Elizabeth Montgomery, Leo Penn, Eva Marie Saint
1954-55: Julie Andrews, Jacqueline Brookes, Shirl Conway, Barbara Cook, David Daniels, Mary Fickett, Page Johnson, Loretta Leversee, Jack Lord, Dennis Patrick, Anthony Perkins, Christopher Plummer
1955-56: Diane Cilento, Dick Davalos, Anthony Franciosa, Andy Griffith, Laurence Harvey, David Hedison, Earle Hyman, Susan Johnson, John Michael King, Jayne Mansfield, Sara Marshall, Gaby Rodgers, Susan Strasberg, Fritz Weaver.

1956-57: Peggy Cass, Sydney Chaplin, Sylvia Daneel, Bradford Dillman, Peter Donat, George Grizzard, Carol Lynley, Peter Palmer, Jason Robards, Cliff Robertson, Pippa Scott, Inga Swenson
1957-58: Anne Bancroft, Warren Berlinger, Colleen Dewhurst, Richard Easton, Tim Everett, Eddie Hodges, Joan Hovis, Carol Lawrence, Jacqueline McKeever, Wynne Miller, Robert Morse, George C. Scott
1958-59: Lou Antonio, Ina Balin, Richard Cross, Tammy Grimes, Larry Hagman, Dolores Hart, Roger Mollien, France Nuyen, Susan Oliver, Ben Piazza, Paul Roebling, William Shatner, Pat Suzuki, Rip Torn
1959-60: Warren Beatty, Eileen Brennan, Carol Burnett, Patty Duke, Jane Fonda, Anita Gillette, Elisa Loti, Donald Madden, George Maharis, John McMartin, Lauri Peters, Dick Van Dyke
1960-61: Joyce Bulifant, Dennis Cooney, Sandy Dennis, Nancy Dussault, Robert Goulet, Joan Hackett, June Harding, Ron Husmann, James MacArthur, Bruce Yarnell
1961-62: Elizabeth Ashley, Keith Baxter, Peter Fonda, Don Galloway, Sean Garrison, Barbara Harris, James Earl Jones, Janet Margolin, Karen Morrow, Robert Redford, John Stride, Brenda Vaccaro
1962-63: Alan Arkin, Stuart Damon, Melinda Dillon, Robert Drivas, Bob Gentry, Dorothy Loudon, Brandon Maggart, Julienne Marie, Liza Minnelli, Estelle Parsons, Diana Sands, Swen Swenson
1963-64: Alan Alda, Gloria Bleezarde, Imelda De Martin, Claude Giraud, Ketty Lester, Barbara Loden, Lawrence Pressman, Gilbert Price, Philip Proctor, John Tracy, Jennifer West.
1964-65: Carolyn Coates, Joyce Jillson, Linda Lavin, Luba Lisa, Michael O'Sullivan, Joanna Pettet, Beah Richards, Jaime Sanchez, Victor Spinetti, Nicolas Surovy, Robert Walker, Clarence Williams III
1965-66: Zoe Caldwell, David Carradine, John Cullum, John Davidson, Faye Dunaway, Gloria Foster, Robert Hooks, Jerry Lanning, Richard Mulligan, April Shawhan, Sandra Smith, Leslie Ann Warren
1966-67: Bonnie Bedelia, Richard Benjamin, Dustin Hoffman, Terry Kiser, Reva Rose, Robert Salvio, Sheila Smith, Connie Stevens, Pamela Tiffin, Leslie Uggams, Jon Voight, Christopher Walken
1967-68: David Birney, Pamela Burrell, Jordan Christopher, Jack Crowder (Thalmus Rasulala), Sandy Duncan, Julie Gregg, Stephen Joyce, Bernadette Peters, Alice Playten, Michael Rupert, Brenda Smiley, Russ Thacker

Carol
Channing

Michael
Douglas

Faye
Dunaway

Stephen
Geoffreys

Sandy
Duncan

Richard
Gere

192

Gregory
Hines

Judy
Kaye

William
Hurt

Christine
Lahti

James Earl
Jones

Elizabeth
McGovern

1968-69: Jane Alexander, David Cryer, Blythe Danner, Ed Evanko, Ken Howard, Lauren Jones, Ron Leibman, Marian Mercer, Jill O'Hara, Ron O'Neal, Al Pacino, Marlene Warfield

1969-70: Susan Browning, Donny Burks, Catherine Burns, Len Cariou, Bonnie Franklin, David Holliday, Katharine Houghton, Melba Moore, David Rounds, Lewis J. Stadlen, Kristoffer Tabori, Fredricka Weber

1970-71: Clifton Davis, Michael Douglas, Julie Garfield, Martha Henry, James Naughton, Tricia O'Neil, Kipp Osborne, Roger Rathburn, Ayn Ruymen, Jennifer Salt, Joan Van Ark, Walter Willison

1971-72: Jonelle Allen, Maureen Anderman, William Atherton, Richard Backus, Adrienne Barbeau, Cara Duff-MacCormick, Robert Foxworth, Elaine Joyce, Jess Richards, Ben Vereen, Beatrice Winde, James Woods

1972-73: D'Jamin Bartlett, Patricia Elliott, James Farentino, Brian Farrell, Victor Garber, Kelly Garrett, Mari Gorman, Laurence Guittard, Trish Hawkins, Monte Markham, John Rubinstein, Jennifer Warren, Alexander H. Cohen (Special Award)

1973-74: Mark Baker, Maureen Brennan, Ralph Carter, Thom Christopher, John Driver, Conchata Ferrell, Ernestine Jackson, Michael Moriarty, Joe Morton, Ann Reinking, Janie Sell, Mary Woronov, Sammy Cahn (Special Award)

1974-75: Peter Burnell, Zan Charisse, Lola Falana, Peter Firth, Dorian Harewood, Joel Higgins, Marcia McClain, Linda Miller, Marti Rolph, John Sheridan, Scott Stevensen, Donna Theodore, Equity Library Theatre (Special Award)

1975-76: Danny Aiello, Christine Andreas, Dixie Carter, Tovah Feldshuh, Chip Garnett, Richard Kelton, Vivian Reed, Charles Repole, Virginia Seidel, Daniel Seltzer, John V. Shea, Meryl Streep, A Chorus Line (Special Award)

1976-77: Trazana Beverley, Michael Cristofer, Joe Fields, Joanna Gleason, Cecilia Hart, John Heard, Gloria Hodes, Juliette Koka, Andrea McArdle, Ken Page, Jonathan Pryce, Chick Vennera, Eva LeGallienne (Special Award)

1977-78: Vasili Bogazianos, Nell Carter, Carlin Glynn, Christopher Goutman, William Hurt, Judy Kaye, Florence Lacy, Armelia McQueen, Gordana Rashovich, Bo Rucker, Richard Seer, Colin Stinton, Joseph Papp (Special Award)

1978-79: Philip Anglim, Lucie Arnaz, Gregory Hines, Ken Jennings, Michael Jeter, Laurie Kennedy, Susan Kingsley, Christine Lahti, Edward James Olmos, Kathleen Quinlan, Sarah Rice, Max Wright, Marshall W. Mason (Special Award)

1979-80: Maxwell Caulfield, Leslie Denniston, Boyd Gaines, Richard Gere, Harry Groener, Stephen James, Susan Kellermann, Dinah Manoff, Lonny Price, Marianne Tatum, Anne Twomey, Dianne Wiest, Mickey Rooney (Special Award)

1980-81: Brian Backer, Lisa Banes, Meg Bussert, Michael Allen Davis, Giancarlo Esposito, Daniel Gerroll, Phyllis Hyman, Cynthia Nixon, Amanda Plummer, Adam Redfield, Wanda Richert, Rex Smith, Elizabeth Taylor (Special Award)

1981-82: Karen Akers, Laurie Beechman, Danny Glover, David Alan Grier, Jennifer Holliday, Anthony Heald, Lizbeth Mackay, Peter MacNicol, Elizabeth McGovern, Ann Morrison, Michael O'Keefe, James Widdoes, Manhatten Theatre Club (Special Award)

1982-83: Karen Allen, Suzanne Bertish, Matthew Broderick, Kate Burton, Joanne Camp, Harvey Fierstein, Peter Gallagher, John Malkovich, Anne Pitoniak, James Russo, Brian Tarantina, Linda Thorson, Natalia Makarova (Special)

1983-84: Martine Allard, Joan Allen, Kathy Whitton Baker, Mark Capri, Laura Dean, Stephen Geoffreys, Todd Graff, Glenne Headly, J. J. Johnston, Bonnie Koloc, Calvin Levels, Robert Westenberg, Ron Moody (Special)

1984-85: Kevin Anderson, Richard Chaves, Patti Cohenour, Charles S. Dutton, Nancy Giles, Whoopi Goldberg, Leilani Jones, John Mahoney, Laurie Metcalf, Barry Miller, John Turturro, Amelia White, Lucille Lortel (Special)

1985-86: Suzy Amis, Alec Baldwin, Aled Davies, Faye Grant, Julie Hagerty, Ed Harris, Mark Jacoby, Donna Kane, Cleo Laine, Howard McGillin, Marisa Tomei, Joe Urla, Ensemble Studio Theatre (Special)

1986-87: Annette Bening, Timothy Daly, Lindsay Duncan, Frank Ferrante, Robert Lindsay, Amy Madigan, Michael Maguire, Demi Moore, Molly Ringwald, Frances Ruffelle, Courtney B. Vance, Colm Wilkinson, Robert DeNiro (Special)

1987-88: Yvonne Bryceland, Philip Casnoff, Danielle Ferland, Melissa Gilbert, Linda Hart, Linzi Hateley, Brian Kerwin, Brian Mitchell, Mary Murfitt, Aidan Quinn, Eric Roberts, B. D. Wong

Laurie
Metcalf

James
Naughton

Melba
Moore

Al
Pacino

Dianne
Wiest

Ken
Page

Caroline
Aaron

Tony
Abatemarco

Barbara
Andres

Patrick
A'Hearn

Christine
Barker

Jayce
Bartok

BIOGRAPHICAL DATA ON THIS SEASON'S
CASTS

AARON, CAROLINE. Born Aug. 7, 1954 in Richmond, Va. Graduate Catholic U. Bdwy debut 1982 in "Come Back to the 5 & Dime, Jimmy Dean, Jimmy Dean," followed by "The Iceman Cometh," OB in "Flying Blind," "Last Summer at Bluefish Cove," "Territorial Rites," "Good Bargains," "The House of Bernarda Alba," "Tribute," "Social Security," "Frankie and Johnny in the Clair De Lune," "Marathon '89."

ABATEMARCO, TONY. Born Mar. 15, 1952 in Brooklyn, NY. Graduate Juilliard. OB debut 1980 in "Diary of a Madman" followed by "Slow Motion."

ABRAHAM, F. MURRAY. Born Oct. 24, 1939 in Pittsburgh, PA. Attended UTx. Debut OB 1967 in "The Fantasticks," followed by "An Opening in the Trees," "14th Dictator," "Young Abe Lincoln," "Tonight in Living Color," "Adaptation," "Survival of St. Joan," "The Dog Ran Away," "Fables," "Richard III," "Little Murders," "Scuba Duba," "Where Has Tommy Flowers Gone?," "Miracle Play," "Blessing," "Sexual Perversity in Chicago," "Landscape of the Body," "The Master and Margarita," "Biting the Apple," "The Seagull," "The Caretaker," "Antigone," "Uncle Vanya," "The Golem," "The Madwoman of Chaillot," "Twelfth Night," "Frankie and Johnny in the Clair De Lune," "A Midsummer Night's Dream," Bdwy in "The Man in the Glass Booth" (1968), "6 Rms Riv Vu," "Bad Habits," "The Ritz," "Legend," "Teibele and Her Demon," "Macbeth," "Waiting for Godot."

ABRAHAMS, JODY. Born in Chicago, IL. OB debut 1987 in "Take Me Along," followed by "Ready or Not," "The Taffetas."

ABUBA, ERNEST. Born Aug. 25, 1947 in Honolulu, HI. Attended Southwestern College. Bdwy debut 1976 in "Pacific Overtures," followed by "Loose Ends," OB in "Sunrise," "Monkey Music," "Station J.," "Yellow Fever," "Pacific Overtures," "Empress of China," "The Man Who Turned into a Stick," "Shogun Macbeth," "Three Sisters."

ACKERMAN, LONI. Born Apr. 10, 1949 in NYC. Attended New School. Bdwy debut 1968 in "George M!," followed by "No, No Nanette," "So Long 174th Street," "The Magic Show," "Evita," "Cats," OB in "Dames at Sea," "Starting Here Starting Now," "Roberta in Concert," "Brownstone," "Diamonds."

ADAMSON, ELLEN. Born July 13, 1956 in Atlanta, Ga. Neighborhood Playhouse, Stanford U. graduate. Debut 1983 OB in "The Triptych," followed by "The Park," "A Midsummer Night's Dream," "Real Family."

AHEARN, DANIEL. Born Aug. 7, 1948 in Washington, DC. Attended Carnegie-Mellon. Debut OB 1981 in "Woyzek," followed by "Brontosaurus Rex," "Billy Liar," "Second Prize Two Months in Leningrad," "No Time Flat," "Hollywood Scheherazade."

A'HEARN, PATRICK. Born Sept. 4, 1957 in Cortland, NY. Graduate Syracuse U. Debut 1985 OB in "Pirates of Penzance," followed by "Forbidden Broadway," followed by Bdwy in "Les Miserables" (1987).

AIDEM, BETSY. Born Oct. 28, 1957 in Eastmeadow, NY. Graduate NYU. Debut 1981 OB in "The Trading Post," followed by "A Different Moon," "Balm in Gilead," "Crossing the Bar," "Our Lady of the Tortilla," "Steel Magnolias," "Road."

AKERS, KAREN. Born Oct. 13, 1945 in NYC. Graduate Hunter College. Bdwy debut 1982 in "Nine" for which she received a Theatre World Award, followed by "Jacques Brel Is Alive and Well and Living in New York," "Grand Hotel."

ALDREDGE, TOM. Born Feb. 28, 1928 in Dayton, Oh. Attended Dayton U., Goodman Theatre. Bdwy debut 1959 in "The Nervous Set," followed by "UTBU," "Slapstick Tragedy," "Everything in the Garden," "Indians," "Engagement Baby," "How the Other Half Loves," "Sticks and Bones," "Where's Charley?," "Leaf People," "Rex," "Vieux Carre," "St. Joan," "Stages," "On Golden Pond," "The Little Foxes," "Into the Woods," OB in "The Tempest," "Between Two Thieves," "Henry V," "The Premise," "Love's Labour's Lost," "Troilus and Cressida," "Butter and Egg Man," "Ergo," "Boys in the Band," "Twelfth Night," "Colette," "Hamlet," "The Orphan," "King Lear," "The Iceman Cometh," "Black Angel," "Getting Along Famously," "Fool for Love," "Neon Psalms," "Richard II."

ALDRICH, JANET. (formerly Aldridge). Born Oct. 16, 1956 in Hinsdale, IL. UMiami graduate.

Debut 1979 OB in "A Funny Thing Happened on the Way to the Forum," followed by "American Princess," "The Men's Group," "Wanted Dead or Alive," "The Comedy of Errors," Bdwy in "Annie" (1982), "The Three Musketeers," "Broadway," "Starmites."

ALEANDRI, EMELISE. Born January 23 in Riva Del Garda, Italy. Attended College of New Rochelle, Hunter College. Debut OB in "Winning Hearts and Minds," followed by "Peep."

ALESSANDRINI, GERARD. Born Nov. 27, 1953 in Boston, Ma. Graduate Boston Consv. Debut 1982 OB in "Forbidden Broadway."

ALEXANDER, JACE. Born Apr. 7, 1964 in NYC. Attended NYU. Bdwy debut 1983 in "The Caine Mutiny Court Martial," OB in "I'm Not Rappaport," followed by "Wasted," "The Good Coach."

ALEXANDER, JANE. Born Oct. 28, 1939 in Boston, MA. Attended Sarah Lawrence Col., UEdinburgh. Bdwy debut 1968 in "The Great White Hope" for which she received a Theatre World Award, followed by "6 Rms Riv Vu," "Find Your Way Home," LC's "Hamlet," "The Heiress," "First Monday in October," "Monday after the Miracle," "The Night of the Iguana," OB in "Losing Time," "Goodbye Fidel," "Approaching Zanzibar."

ALEXANDER, JASON. Born Sept. 23, 1959 in Irvington, NJ. Attended Boston U. Bdwy debut 1981 in "Merrily We Roll Along," followed by "The Rink," "Broadway Bound," "Jerome Robbins' Broadway," OB in "Forbidden Broadway," "Stop the World. . . ." "D.," "Personals."

ALLEN, JOAN. Born Aug. 20, 1956 in Rochelle, IL. Attended E. Ill. U., W. Ill. U. Debut 1983 OB in "And a Nightingale Sang" for which she received a Theatre World Award, followed by "The Marriage of Bette and Boo," "Marathon '86," "Burn This," "The Heidi Chronicles," Bdwy 1987 in "Burn This," followed by "The Heidi Chronicles."

ALLEN, JONELLE. Born July 18, 1944 in NYC. Bdwy debut 1949 in "The Wisteria Trees," followed by "Hair," "George M!," "Two Gentlemen of Verona" for which she received a Theatre World Award, OB in "Someone's Coming Hungry," "5 on the Bhackhand Side," "Bury the Dead," "Moon on a Rainbow Shawl," "Etta Jenks."

ALLEN, PETER. Born Feb. 10, 1945 in Tenterfield, Australia. Bdwy debut 1970 in "Soon," followed by "Up in One," "Legs Diamond."

ALMQUIST, GREGG. Born Dec. 1, 1948 in Minneapolis, MN. Graduate UMinn. Debut 1974 OB in "Richard III," followed by "A Night at the Black Pig," "Mother Courage," "King Lear," "Algerian Romance," Bdwy in "I'm Not Rappaport" (1986)

AMBERLY, LIZ. Born Oct. 2 in Poughkeepsie, NY. Attended Syracuse U, London Academy of Music & Dramatic Art. Debut 1989 OB in "Leave it to Jane."

AMECHE, DON. Born May 31, 1908 in Kenosha, WI. Bdwy debut 1929 in "Jerry-for-Short," followed by "Silk Stockings," "Holiday for Lovers," "Goldilocks," "13 Daughters," "Henry Sweet Henry," "Our Town" (1989).

ANDERSON, CHRISTINE. Born Aug. 6 in Utica, NY. Graduate UWi. Bdwy debut in "I Love My Wife" (1980), OB in "I Can't Keep Running in Place," "On the Swing Shift," "Red, Hot and Blue," "A Night at Texas Guinan's," "Nunsense."

ANDERSON, JEAN. Born Dec. 12, 1907 in Eastbourne, Eng. Graduate RADA. Bdwy debut 1987 in the Royal Shakespeare Co.'s "Les Liasons Dangereuses," OB in "A Delicate Heart," "Dancing with Harry."

ANDERSON, JOEL. Born Nov. 19, 1955 in San Diego, CA. Graduate UUtah. Debut 1980 OB in "A Funny Thing Happened on the Way to the Forum," followed by "Joan of Lorraine," "Last of the Knucklemen," "The Widow Claire," "The Heidi Chronicles," "Fighting Light."

ANDERSON, KEVIN. Born Jan. 13, 1960 in Illinois. Attended Goodman School. Debut 1985 OB in "Orphans," for which he received a Theatre World Award, followed by "Moonchildren," "Brilliant Traces," "Orpheus Descending."

ANDRES, BARBARA. Born Feb. 11, 1939 in NYC. Catholic U graduate. Bdwy debut 1969 in "Jimmy," followed by "The Boy Friend," "Rodgers and Hart," "Rex," "On Golden Pond," "Doonesbury," OB in "Threepenny Opera," "Landscape of the Body," "Harold Arlen's Cabaret," "Suzanna Andler," "One Act Festival," "Company," "Marathon 87," "Arms and the Man."

ANDREWS, DAVID. Born in 1952 in Baton Rouge, La. Attended LSU. Debut 1985 OB in "Fool for Love," followed by "Safe Sex," "Heart Outright," "Friends in High Places."
ANDREWS, GEORGE LEE. Born Oct. 13, 1942 in Milwaukee, Wi. Debut OB 1970 in "Jacques Brel Is Alive and Well . . . ," followed by "Starting Here Starting Now," "Vamps and Rideouts," "The Fantasticks," Bdwy in "A Little Night Music" (1973), "On the 20th Century," "Merlin," "The Phantom of the Opera."
APPEL, PETER. Born Oct. 19, 1959 in NYC. Graduate BrandeisU. Debut 1987 OB in "Richard II" followed by "Henry IV Part I," "A Midsummer Night's Dream," "Saved From Obscurity," "Titus Andronicus."
AQUINO, AMY. Born Mar. 20, 1957 in Teaneck, NJ. Graduate Radcliffe, Yale. Debut 1988 OB in "Cold Sweat," followed by "Right Behind the Flag," Bdwy 1989 in "The Heidi Chronicles."
ARCARO, ROBERT (a.k.a. Bob) Born Aug. 9, 1952 in Brooklyn, NY. Graduate WesleyanU. Debut 1977 OB in "New York City Street Show," followed by "Working Theatre Festival," "Man with a Raincoat," "Working One-Acts," "Henry Lumpur."
ARLUCK, NEAL. Born Dec. 4, 1946 in Brooklyn, NY. Graduate LehighU., NYU, AADA. Debut 1981 OB in "Catch-22," followed by "Dead Giveaway," "The Hooch," "Something Old Something New," "Crazy Arnold," "Black Coffee," "American Voices."
ARMITAGE, CALVIN LENNON. Born 1982. Debut 1989 OB in "Member of the Wedding."
ARMUS, SIDNEY. Born Dec. 19, 1924 in The Bronx, NY. Attended Brooklyn Col. Credits include "South Pacific," "Wish You Were Here," "The Flowering Peach," "A Hole in the Head,": The Cold Wind and the Warm," "Harold," "A Thousand Clowns," "Never Live over a Pretzel Factory," "The Odd Couple," "Cafe Crown."
ARNOLD, VICTOR. Born July 1, 1936 in Herkimer, NY. Graduate NYU. OB in "Shadows of Heroes," "Merchant of Venice," "3×3," "Lovey," "Fortune and Men's Eyes," "Time for Bed, Take Me to Bed," "Emperor of Late Night Radio," "Macbeth," "Sign in Sidney Brustein's Window," "Cacciatore," "Maiden Stakes," "My Prince My King," "The Faithful Brethren of Pitt Street," Bdwy in "The Deputy" (1964), "Malcolm," "We Bombed in New Haven," "Fun City."
ARRAMBIDE, MARIO. Born Mar. 1, 1953 in San Antonio, Tx. Attended RADA. Debut 1985 OB in "Aunt Dan and Lemon," followed by "The Death of Garcia Lorca," "The Golem," "Hamlet," "Measure for Measure."
ASBURY, CLEVE. Born Dec. 29, 1958 in Houston, Tx. Attended L.A.Valley Col. Bdwy debut 1979 in "Peter Pan," followed by "West Side Story," "Bring Back Birdie," "Copperfield," "Harrigan 'n' Hart," "Me and My Girl."
ASHFORD, ROBERT. Born Nov. 19, 1959 in Orlando, FL. Attended Washington & Lee U. Bdwy debut 1987 in "Anything Goes."
ASNER, EDWARD. Born Nov. 15, 1929 in Kansas City, Ks. Graduate UChicago. OB in "Threepenny Opera," "Hamlet," "Ivanov," Bdwy in "Face of a Hero" (1960), "Born Yesterday" (1989)
AUBERJONOIS, RENE. Born June 1, 1940 in NYC. Graduate Carnegie Inst. With LCRep in "A Cry of Player," "King Lear," and "Twelfth Night," Bdwy in "Fire (1969)," "Coco," "Tricks," "The Good Doctor," "Break a Leg," "Every Good Boy Deserves Favor," "Big River," "Metamorphosis," BAM Co. in "The New York Idea," "Three Sisters," "The Play's the Thing," and "Julius Caesar."
AUGUSTINE, JOHN. Born Mar. 5, 1960 in Canton, OH. Attended Baldwin-White College. Debut 1988 OB in "Young Playwrights Festival '88."
AUGUSTUS, NICHOLAS. Born July 22, 1959 in NYC. Attended DenisonU. Debut 1989 OB in "Gigi," followed by "Forbidden Broadway."
AUSTRIAN, MARJORIE. Born Feb. 3, 1934 in Bronx, NY. Attended SyracuseU, UKansas. OB in "Henry V," "All's Well That Ends Well," "Sylvia Plath: A Dramatic Portrait," "Jonah," "Ivanov," "Loyalties," "The House of Bernarda Alba," "Lucky Rita," "The Diary of Anne Frank," "A Day in the Death of Elizabeth," "Dodger Blue."
AVIDON, NELSON. Born Feb. 23, 1957 in Brooklyn, NY. Debut 1987 OB in "Second Avenue," followed by "The Green Death," "Cheapside," "Chee-Chee," "Three Sisters," "Unnatural Acts."
BACHRACH, DAVID ARTHUR. Born Nov. 5, 1952 in Brunswick, Me. Graduate Harvard, UNC. Debut 1988 OB in "The Christmas Bride."
BACKUS, RICHARD. Born Mar. 28, 1945 in Goffstown, NH. Harvard graduate. Bdwy debut 1971 in "Butterflies Are Free," followed by "Promenade All," for which he received a Theatre World Award, "Ah, Wilderness!," "Camelot" (1981), OB in "Studs Edsel," "Gimme Shelter," "Sorrows of Stephen," "Missing Persons," "Henry V," "Talley and Son," "Tomorrow's Monday," "Bunker Reveries," "The Cocktail Hour."
BACON, KEVIN. Born July 8, 1958 in Philadelphia, PA. Debut OB 1978 in "Getting Out," followed by "Glad Tidings," "Album," "Flux," "Poor Little Lambs," "Slab Boys," "Men without Dates," "Loot," "The Author's Voice," "Road."
BAIRD, QUIN. Born Nov. 21, 1950 in Seattle, Wa. Graduate UCalDavis. Bdwy debut 1968 in "The Happy Time," followed by "Sweet Charity" (1986), "Legs Diamond."
BAKER, DYLAN. Born in Lackey, VA. Graduate Wm & Mary, Yale. Debut 1985 OB in "Not about Heroes," followed by "Two Gentlemen of Verona," "The Common Pursuit," "Much Ado about Nothing," "Eastern Standard," Bdwy (1989) in "Eastern Standard" for which he received a Theatre World Award.
BAKER, SCOTT. Born May 30, 1948 in Tulsa, OK. Graduate UTulsa, Northwestern U. Debut 1973 OB in "Christmas Rappings," followed by "Love's Labour's Lost," "East Lynne," "Matinee Kids," Bdwy 1978 in "Oh! Calcutta!"
BALABAN, BOB. Born Aug. 16, 1945 in Chicago, IL. Attended Colgate, NYU. Debut 1967 OB in "You're a Good Man, Charlie Brown," followed by "Up Eden," "White House Murder Case," "Basic Training of Pavlo Hummel," "The Children," "Marie and Bruce," "Three Sisters," Bdwy in "Plaza Suite" (1968), "Some of My Best Friends," "Inspector General," "Speed-the-Plow."
BAMMAN, GERRY. Born Sept. 18, 1941 in Independence, Ks. Graduate XavierU, NYU. Debut 1970 OB in "Alice in Wonderland," followed by "All Night Long," "Richard III," "Oedipus Rex," "A Midsummer Night's Dream," "He and She," "Johnny on the Spot," "Museum," "Henry V," "Our Late Night," "The Seagull," "Endgame," "Road," Bdwy "Accidental Death of an Anarchist" (1984), "Execution of Justice."
BANES, LISA. Born July 9, 1955 in Chagrin Falls, OH. Juilliard graduate. Debut OB 1980 in "Elizabeth I," followed by "A Call from the East," "Look Back in Anger," for which she received a Theatre World Award, "My Sister in This House," "Antigone," "Three Sisters," "The Cradle Will Rock," "Isn't It Romantic?," "Fighting International Fat," "Ten by Tennessee," "On the Verge," "Emily," Bdwy in "Rumors"
BANSAVAGE, LISA. Born Mar. 22, 1953 in Syracuse, NY. Graduate Carnegie-Mellon U, UPittsburgh. Debut 1983 OB in "The Changeling," followed by "As You Like It," "Revenger's Tragedy."
BARAN, EDWARD. Born May 18, 1950 in Minneapolis, Mn. Graduate Williams Col. Debut 1984 OB in "Fool's Errand," followed by "The Wonder Years," "The Sneaker Factory," "Cezanne Syndrome."
BARANSKI, CHRISTINE. Born May 2, 1952 in Buffalo, NY. Graduate Juilliard. Debut OB 1978 in "One Crack Out," followed by "Says I Says He," "The Trouble With Europe," "Coming Attractions," "Operation Midnight Climax," "Sally and Marsha," "A Midsummer Night's Dream," "It's Only a Play," "Marathon '86." Bdwy in "Hide and Seek," (1980), "The Real Thing," "Hurlyburly," "House of Blue Leaves," "Rumors."
BARBARO, CIRO. Born March 6, 1952 in Brooklyn, NY. Attended Hunter Col. Debut 1986 OB in "Girl Crazy," followed by "She Loves Me."
BARBER, ELLEN. Born in August in Brooklyn, NY. Graduate Bard Col. Debut 1970 OB in "The Mod Donna," followed by "Moonchildren," "Apple Pie," "Funeral March for a One Man Band," "Starluster," "Awake and Sing," "Occupations," "Poor Murderer," "Pantagleize," "Modern Ladies of Guanabacoa," "Poisoner of the Wells," "Souvenirs," "Haven," "Shlemiel the First," "Knepp," Bdwy in "The Good Doctor" (1973), "Fame."
BARBOUR, THOMAS. Born July 25, 1921 in NYC. Graduate Princeton, Harvard. Bdwy debut 1968 in "Portrait of a Queen," followed by "The Great White Hope," "Scratch," "Lincoln Mask," "Kingdoms," OB in "Twelfth Night," "Merchant of Venice," "Admirable Bashful," "The Lady's Not for Burning," "The Enchanted," "Antony and Cleopatra," "The Saintliness of Margery Kemp," "Dr. Willy Nilly," "Under the Sycamore Tree," "Epitaph for George Dillon," "Thracian Horses," "Old Glory," "Sgt. Musgrave's Dance," "Nestless Bird," "The Seagull," "Wayside Motor Inn," "Arthur," "The Grinding Machine," "Mr. Simian," "Sorrows of Frederick," "Terrorists," "Dark Ages," "Royal Bob," "Relatively Speaking," "Aristocrats."
BARKER, CHRISTINE. Born Nov. 26 in Jacksonville, FL. Attended UCLA. Bdwy debut 1979 in "A Chorus Line."
BARKER, MARGARET. Born Oct. 10, 1908 in Baltimore, MD. Attended Bryn Mawr. Bdwy debut 1928 in "Age of Innoecence," followed by "The Barretts of Wimpole Street," "The House of Connelly," "Men in White," "Gold Eagle Guy," "Leading Lady," "Member of the Wedding," "Autumn Garden," "See the Jaguar," "Ladies of the Corridor," "The Master Builder," OB in "Wayside Motor Inn," "The Loves of Cass McGuire," "Three Sisters," "Details without a Map," "The Inheritors," "Caligula," "The Mound Builders," "Quiet in the Land," "Uncle Vanya," "Ladies."
BARRE, GABRIEL. Born Aug. 26, 1957 in Brattleboro, VT. Graduate AADA. Debut 1977 OB in "Jabberwock," followed by "T.N.T.," "Bodo," "The Baker's Wife," "The Time of Your Life," "Children of the Sun," "Wicked Philanthropy," "Starmites," "Mistress of the Inn," "Gifts of the Magi," Bdwy in "Rags" (1986), "Starmites."
BARRETT, LAURINDA. Born 1931 in NYC. Attended Wellesley Col., RADA. Bdwy debut 1956 in "Too Late the Phalatrope," followed by "The Girls in 509," "The Milk Train Doesn't Stop Here Anymore," "UTBU," "I Never Sang for My Father," "Equus," OB in "The Misanthrope," "Palm Tree in a Rose Garden," "All is Bright," "The Carpenters," "Ah, Wilderness!," "The Other Side of Newark," "The Boys Next Door," "Phantasie."
BARRON, DAVID. Born May 11, 1938 in Pilot Point, TX. Graduate Baylor U., Yale, UIll. Debut OB 1976 in "The Fantasticks," followed by "Trouble in Tahiti," "Sound of Music," "A Doll's House," "Feathertop," "Kiss Me Quick," "Sweeney Todd."
BARTENIEFF, GEORGE. Born Jan. 24, 1933 in Berlin, Ger. Bdwy debut 1947 in "The Whole World Over," followed by "Venus Is," "All's Well That Ends Well," "Quotations from Chairman Mao Tse-Tung," "The Death of Bessie Smith," "Cop-Out," "Room Service," "Unlikely Heroes," OB in "Walking to Waldheim," "Memorandum," "The Increased Difficulty of Concentration," "Trelawny of the Wells," "Charley Chestnut Rides the IRT," "Radio (Wisdom): Sophia Part I," "Images of the Dead," "Dead End Kids," "The Blonde Leading the Blonde," "The Dispossessed," "Growing Up Gothic," "Rosetti's Apologies," "On the Lam," "Samuel Beckett Trilogy," "Quartet," "Help Wanted," "A Matter of Life and Death," "The Heart That Eats Itself," "Coney Island Kid," "Cymbeline."
BARTLETT, ROBIN. Born Apr. 22, 1951 in NYC. Graduate Boston U. Bdwy debut 1975 in "Yentl," followed by "The World of Sholem Aleichem," OB in "Agamemnon," "Fathers and Sons," "No End of Blame," "Living Quarters," "After the Fall," "Cheapside," "The Early Girl," "Reckless."
BARTOK, JAYCE. Born July 31, 1972 in Pittsburgh, PA. Debut OB 1989 in "Dalton's Back."
BARYSHNIKOV, MIKHAIL. Born Jan. 27, 1948 in Riga, Latvia. Bdwy debut 1989 in "Metamorphosis" for which he received a Theatre World Award.
BASCH, PETER. Born May 11, 1956 in NYC. Graduate Columbia Col., UCal Berkeley. Debut 1984 OB in "Hackers," followed by "Festival of One Acts."
BATES, JEROME PRESTON. Born July 20, 1954 in Augusta, GA. Attended Knoxville Col., UTn, LAMDA. Debut 1985 OB in "Jonin'," followed by "Amulets Against the Dragon Forces."
BATTISTA, LLOYD. Born May 14, 1937 in Cleveland, OH. Graduate Carnegie Tech. Bdwy debut 1966 in "Those That Play the Clowns," followed by "The Homecoming," "The Guys in the Truck," OB in "The Flame and the Rose," "Murder in the Cathedral," "The Miser," "Gorky," "Sexual Perversity in Chicago," "King of Schnorrers," "Francis," "The Keymaker," "The Guys in the Truck," "The Cost of Living," "Algerian Romance."
BAXTER, CAROL ANN. Born Dec. 31, 1953 in Syracuse, NY. Debut OB 1985 in "I Married an Angel," Bdwy in "Legs Diamond" (1988).
BAZZELL, LARRY. Born Dec. 5, 1950 in Baton Rouge, LA. Graduate LaState U. Debut 1987 OB in "Prime Time," followed by "The Signal Season of Dummy Hoy," "Mercedes."
BEECHMAN, LAURIE. Born Apr. 4, 1954 in Philadelphia, Pa. Attended NYU. Bdwy debut 1977 in "Annie," followed by "Pirates of Penzance," "Joseph and the Amazing Technicolor Dreamcoat" for which she received a Theatre World Award, "Cats," "Les Miserables," "Some Enchanted Evening" (OB), "Pal Joey in Concert."
BEERS, FRANCINE. Born Nov. 26 in NYC. Attended Hunter Col., CCNY. Debut 1962 OB in "King of the Whole Damned World," followed by "Kiss Mama," "Monopoly," "Cakes with Wine," "The Grandma Plays," Bdwy in "Cafe Crown," "6 Rms Riv Vu," "The American Clock," "Curse of an Aching Heart."

BELACK, DORIS. Born Feb. 26 in NYC. Attended AADA. Debut 1956 OB in "World of Sholem Aleichem," followed by "P.S. 193," "Letters Home," "Marathon 87," "Emerald City," Bdwy in "Middle of the Night," "Owl and the Pussycat," "The Heroine," "You Know I Can't Hear You . . .," "90 Day Mistress," "Last of the Red Hot Lovers," "Bad Habits," "The Trip Back Down," "Social Security."

BELMONTE, VICKI. Born Jan. 20, 1947 in U.S.A. Bdwy debut 1960 in "Bye Bye Birdie," followed by "Subways Are for Sleeping," "All American," "Annie Get Your Gun" (LC), OB in "Nunsense."

BENHAM, DOROTHY. Born Dec. 11, 1955 in Minneapolis, MN. Attended Lawrence U., Macalester Col. Bdwy debut 1989 in "Jerome Robbins' Broadway."

BENNETT, LYNETTE. Born Nov. 5, 1937 in Hot Springs, AK. Attended UTulsa, UCLA. Debut OB 1960 in "Absolutely Time," followed by "Gigi," Bdwy in "The Yearling," "Funny Girl."

BENSON, CINDY. Born Oct. 2, 1951 in Attleboro, Ma. Graduate St. Leo Col., UIll. Debut 1981 OB in "Some Like It Cole," followed by Bdwy "Les Miserables"(1987).

BENSON, JODI. Born Oct. 10, 1961 in Rockford, IL. Attended Millikin U. Bdwy debut 1983 in "Marilyn: An American Fable," followed by "Smile," "Welcome to the Club."

BERIS, DAVID M. Born Sept. 29, 1958 in Elizabeth, NJ. Graduate Emerson Col. Debut 1986 OB in "They're Playing Our Song," followed by "Hired Man."

BERMAN, DONALD. Born Jan. 23, 1954 in NYC. Graduate USyracuse. Debut 1977 OB in "Savages," followed by "Dona Rosita," "The Lady or the Tiger," "The Overcoat," "Steel on Steel," "Visions of Kerouac," "The Normal Heart," "Phantom Lady," "Marathon '89," "The Promise."

BERNSTEIN, DOUGLAS. Born May 6, 1958 in NYC. Amherst graduate. Debut 1982 OB in "Upstairs at O'Neals," followed by "Backer's Audition," "Mayor," "Showing Off."

BERQUE, BARBARA. Born Aug. 31, 1953 in St. Louis. MO. Debut 1983 OB in "El Salvador," followed by "The Wonder Years," "What Does a Blind Leopard See?," "The Enclave," "Measure for Measure," "The Hot 1 Baltimore," "You Never Can Tell."

BERTISH, SUZANNE. Born Aug. 7, 1951 in London, Eng. Attended London Drama School. Bdwy debut 1981 in "Nicholas Nickleby," OB in "Skirmishes," (1982) for which she received a Theatre World Award, followed by "Rosmersholm."

BISHOP, KELLY (formerly Carole). Born Feb. 28, 1944 in Colorado Springs, CO. Bdwy debut 1967 in "Golden Rainbow," followed by "Promises, Promises," "On the Town," "Rachel Lily Rosenbloom," "A Chorus Line," OB in "Piano Bar," "Changes," "The Blessing."

BLAIR, PAMELA. Born Dec. 5, 1949 in Arlington, Vt. Attended Ntl. Acad. of Ballet. Bdwy debut 1972 in "Promises, Promises," followed by "Sugar," "Seesaw," "Of Mice and Men," "Wild and Wonderful," "A Chorus Line," "The Best Little Whorehouse in Texas," "King of Hearts," "The Nerd," OB in "Ballad of Boris K," "Split," "Real Life Funnies," "Double Feature," "Hit Parade," "1-2-3-4-5."

BLAISDELL, NESBITT. Born Dec. 6, 1928 in NYC. Graduate Amherst, Columbia. Debut 1978 OB in "Old Man Joseph and His Family," followed by "Moliere in spite of Himself," "Guests of the Nation," "Ballad of Soapy Smith," "Custom of the Country," "A Cup of Coffee," "The Immigrant."

BLAXILL, PETER. Born Sept. 27, 1931 in Cambridge, MA. Graduate Bard Col. Debut 1967 OB in "Scuba Duba," followed by "The Fantasticks," "The Passion of Antigona Perez," "Oh Boy!," "From Brooks With Love," "Who's There," "The 13th Chair," Bdwy in "Marat/Sade," "The Littlest Circus," "The Innocents."

BLAZER, JUDITH. Born Oct. 22, 1956 in Dover, NJ. Graduate Manhattan School of Music. Debut 1979 OB in "Oh Boy!," followed by "Roberta in Concert," "A Little Night Music," "Company," "Babes in Arms," Bdwy in "Me and My Girl."

BLOCH, SCOTTY. Born Jan. 28 in New Rochelle, NY. Attended AADA. Debut 1945 OB in "Craig's Wife," followed by "Lemon Sky," "Battering Ram," "Richard III," "In Celebration," "An Act of Kindness," "The Price," "Grace," "Neon Psalms," "Other People's Money," Bdwy in "Children of a Lesser God."

BLOCK, LARRY. Born Oct. 30, 1942 in NYC. Graduate URI. Bdwy debut 1966 in "Hail Scrawdyke," followed by "La Turista," OB in "Eh?," "Fingernails Blue as Flowers," "Comedy of Errors," "Coming Attractions," "Henry IV Part 2," "Feuhrer Bunker," "Manhattan Love Songs," "Souvenirs," "The Golem," "Responsible Parties," "Hit Parade," "Largo Desolato," "The Square Root of 3," "Young Playwrights Festival," "Hunting Cockroaches," "Two Gentlemen of Verona," "Yellow Dog Contract," "Temptation," "Festival of 1 Acts," "The Faithful Brethren of Pitt Street," "Loman Family Picnic."

BLUM, MARK. Born May 14, 1950 in Newark, NJ. Graduate UPa. UMinn. Debut 1976 OB in "The Cherry Orchard," followed by "Green Julia," "Say Goodnight, Gracie," "Table Settings," "Key Exchange," "Loving Reno," "Messiah," "It's Only a Play," "Little Footsteps," "Cave of Life," "Gus & Al."

BLUMENFELD, ROBERT. Born Feb. 26, 1943 in NYC. Graduate Rutgers., Columbia U. Bdwy debut 1970 in "Othello," OB in "The Fall and Redemption of Man," "The Tempest," "The Dybbuk," "Count Dracula," "Nature and Purpose of the Universe," "House Music," "The Keymaker," "Epic Proportions," "Tatterdemalion," "Iolanthe," "Temple," "Friends in High Places."

BOBBIE, WALTER. Born Nov. 18, 1945 in Scranton, PA. Graduate UScranton., Catholic U. Bdwy debut 1971 in "Frank Merriwell," followed by "The Grass Harp," "Grease," "Tricks," "Going Up," "History of the American Film," "Anything Goes," OB in "Drat!," "She Loves Me," "Up from Paradise," "Goodbye Freddy," "Cafe Crown."

BODLE, JANE. Born Nov 12 in Lawrence, KS. Attended UUtah. Bdwy debut 1983 in "Cats," followed by "Les Miserables."

BOGARDUS, STEPHEN. Born Mar. 11, 1954 in Norfolk, VA. Princeton Graduate. Bdwy debut 1980 in "West Side Story," followed by "Les Miserables," OB in "March of the Falsettos," "Feathertop," "No Way to Treat a Lady," "Look on the Bright Side."

BOGOSIAN, ERIC. Born Apr. 24, 1953 in Woburn, MA. Graduate Oberlin Col. Debut 1982 OB in "Men Inside/Voices of America," followed by "Funhouse," "Drinking in America," "Talk Radio," "Sex, Drugs, Rock & Roll."

BOOCKVOR, STEVEN. Born Nov. 18 1942 in NYC. Attended Queens Col., Juilliard. Bdwy debut 1966 in "Anya," followed by "A Time for Singing," "Cabaret," "Mardi Gras," "Jimmy," "Billy," "The Rothschilds," "Follies," "Over Here," "The Lieutenant," "Musical Jubilee," "Annie," "Working," "The First," "A Chorus Line."

BOOKER, CHARLOTTE. Born Dec. 21 in Illinois. Graduate Northwestern U. Debut OB 1987 in "Psycho Beach Party," Bdwy in "Born Yesterday" (1989).

BOOTHBY, VICTORIA. Born in Chicago, IL. Graduate Barnard Col. Debut 1971 OB in "Jungle of Cities," followed by "Man's a Man," "Coarse Acting Show," "Beethoven/Karl," "False Confessions," "Professor George," "Mother Bickerdyke and Me," Bdwy in "Beethoven's Tenth" (1984), "Stepping Out," "Roza."

BORDO, EDWIN. Born Mar. 3, 1931 in Cleveland, OH. Graduate Allegheny Col., LAMDA. Bdwy debut 1964 in "The Last Analysis," followed by "Inquest," "Zalmen or the Madness of God," "Annie," OB in "The Dragon," "Waiting for Godot," "Saved," "Ten Little Indians," "King Lear," "The Sunshine Boys."

BOSCO, PHILIP. Born Sept. 26, 1930 in Jersey City, NJ. Graduate CatholicU. Credits: "Auntie Mame," "Rape of the Belt," "Ticket of Leave Man," "Donnybrook," "Man For All Seasons," "Mrs. Warren's Profession," with LCRep in "A Great Career," "In the Matter of J. Robert Oppenheimer," "The Miser," "The Time of Your Life," "Camino Real," "Operation Sidewinder," "Amphitryon," "Enemy of the People," "Playboy of the Western World," "Good Woman of Setzuan," "Antigone," "Mary Stuart," "Narrow Road to the Deep North," "The Crucible," "Twelfth Night," "Enemies," "Plough and the Stars," "Merchant of Venice," and "A Streetcar Named Desire," "Henry V," "Threepenny Opera," "Streamers," "Stages," "St. Joan," "The Biko Inquest," "Man and Superman," "Whose Life Is It Anyway?," "Major Barbara," "A Month in the Country," "Bacchae," "Hedda Gabler," "Don Juan in Hell," "Inadmissible Evidence," "Eminent Domain," "Misalliance," "Learned Ladies," "Some Men Need Help," "Ah, Wilderness!," "The Caine Mutiny Court Martial," "Heartbreak House," "Come Back, Little Sheba," "Loves of Anatol," "Be Happy For Me," "Master Class," "You Never Can Tell," "A Man For All Seasons," "Devil's Disciple," "Lend Me a Tenor."

BOUCHER, GLORIA. Born Dec. 17, 1954 in Muskegon, MI. Attended AADA, AMDA. Debut 1982 OB in "Street Scene," followed by "New Girl in Town," "Hired Man."

BOURNEUF, STEPHEN. Born Nov. 24, 1957 in St. Louis, MO. Graduate St. LouisU. Bdwy debut 1981 in "Broadway Follies," followed by "Oh, Brother!," "Dreamgirls" (1987), "A Chorus Line," "Legs Diamond."

BOVA, JOSEPH. Born May 25 in Cleveland, OH. Graduate Northwestern U. Debut 1959 OB in "On the Town," followed by "Once Upon a Mattress," "House of Blue Leaves," "Comedy," "The Beauty Part," "Taming of the Shrew," "Richard III," "Comedy of Errors," "Invitation to a Beheading," "Merry Wives of Windsor," "Henry V," "Streamers," Bdwy in "Rape of the Belt," "Irma La Douce," "Hot Spot," "The Chinese," "American Millionaire," "St. Joan," "42nd Street."

BOVASSO, JULIE. Born Aug. 1, 1930 in Brooklyn, NY. Attended CCNY. Bdwy in "Monique," "Minor Miracle," "Gloria and Esperanza," OB in "Naked," "The Maids," "The Lesson," "The Typewriter," "Screens," "Henry IV, Part I," "What I Did Last Summer," "Angelo's Wedding," "Italian American Reconciliation."

BOVE, MARK. Born Jan. 9, 1960 in Pittsburgh, Pa. Bdwy debut 1980 in "West Side Story," followed by "Woman of the Year," "A Chorus Line."

BOWDEN, RICHARD. Born May 21 in Savannah, Ga. Graduate UGa., UBristol Eng. Bdwy debut 1964 in "Don Carlos" (Schiller Theatre), followed by "Captain Brassbound's Conversion" (1972), OB in "Mlle. Colombe," "Pocahontas," "Freedom Train," "As You Like It," "The Tavern," "Revenger's Tragedy."

BOWMAN, REGIS. Born Aug. 22, 1935 in Butler, PA. Graduate WVaU. Debut 1980 OB in "Room Service," followed by "T.N.T.," "Not Now, Darling," "The Male Animal."

BOYD, JULIE. Born Jan. 2 in Kansas City, MO. Graduate UUtah, Yale. Bdwy debut 1985 in "Noises Off," followed by OB in "Only You," "Working 1 Acts."

BOYLE, ROBERT OTT. Born Mar. 28, 1950 in Spangler, PA. Graduate Carnegie-Mellon U. Debut 1980 OB in "Merton of the Movies," followed by "King of Hearts," "The Rise of David Levinsky," "Esther: A Vaudeville Megillah," "She Loves Me," Bdwy in "Alice in Wonderland" (1982), "Doubles."

BRADLEY, CAROL. Born Mar. 11, 1955 in Natick, MA. Attended Vassar Col., TuftsU in London. OB in "Cucumbers," "Siblings," "Armaggeddon Revue," "Henry Lumpur."

BRADY, ATTICUS. Born Sept. 3, 1975 in NYC. Debut OB 1988 in "Between Daylight and Boonville," Bdwy in "Our Town" (1988).

BRANDT, JAMES. Born Oct. 8, 1947 in Columbus, OH. Graduate OhioU. Debut 1975 OB in "One Cent Plain," followed by "Oh! Coward!," Bdwy in "Legs Diamond" (1988).

BRAZDA, DAVID. Born Sept. 28, 1954 in Weisbaden, Ger. Attended UVa., Circle in the Square. Debut 1985 OB in "Onlyman," followed by "Two Gentlemen of Verona," "Pericles," "Macbeth," "The Imaginary Invalid," "Electra," "All's Well That Ends Well."

BRENNAN, JAMES. Born Oct. 31, 1950 in Newark, NJ. Bdwy debut 1974 in "Good News," followed by "Rodgers and Hart," "So Long, 174th Street," "Little Me," "I Love My Wife," "Singin' in the Rain," "42nd Street," "Me and My Girl."

BRENNAN, NORA. Born Dec. 1, 1953 in East Chicago, In. Graduate PurdueU. Bdwy debut 1980 in "Camelot," followed by "Cats."

BRENNAN, TOM. Born Apr. 16, 1926 in Cleveland, OH. Graduate Oberlin, Western Reserve. Debut 1958 OB in "Synge Trilogy," followed by "Between Two Thieves," "East," "All in Love," "Under Milk Wood," "An Evening with James Purdy," "Golden Six," "Pullman Car Hiawatha," "Are You Now Or Have You Ever Been?," "Diary of Anne Frank," "Milk of Paradise," "Transcendental Love," "The Beaver Coat," "The Overcoat," "Summer," "Asian Shade," "Inheritors," "Paradise Lost," "Madwoman of Chaillot," "The Time of Your Life," Bdwy in "Play Memory" (1984), "Our Town."

BRILL, FRAN. Born Sept. 30 in PA. Attended Boston U. Bdwy debut 1969 in "Red, White and Maddox," OB in "What Every Woman Knows," "Scribes," "Naked," "Look Back in Anger," "Knuckle," "Skirmishes," "Baby with the Bathwater," "Holding Patterns," "Festival of One Acts," "Taking Steps," "Young Playwrights Festival," "Claptrap."

BROADHURST, KENT. Born Feb. 4, 1940 in St. Louis, Mo. Graduate UNe. Debut 1968 OB in "The Fourth Wall" followed by "Design For Living," "Marching Song" "Heartbreak House" "Dark of the Moon," "Hunchback of Notre Dame," "Cold Sweat," "April Snow," "Early One Evening at the Rainbow Bar and Grill," Bdwy in "The Caine Mutiny Court-Martial (1983).

BRODY, JONATHAN. Born June 16, 1963 in Englewood, NJ. Debut 1982 OB in "Shulamith," followed by "The Desk Set," Bdwy in "Me and My Girl" (1986).

BROGGER, IVAR. Born Jan. 10, in St. Paul, Mn. Graduate UMn. Debut 1979 OB in "In the Jungle of Cities," followed by "Collected Works Of Billy the Kid," "Magic Time," "Cloud 9," "Richard III," "Clarence," "Madwoman of Chaillot," "Seascapes with Sharks and Dancer," "Second Man," "Twelfth Night," "Almost Perfect," "Up 'n' Under," Bdwy in "Macbeth" (1981), "Pygmalion" (1987).

BROOKES, JACQUELINE. Born July 24, 1930 in Montclair, NJ. Graduate UIowa, RADA.

Bdwy debut 1955 in "Tiger at the Gates," followed by "Watercolor," "Abelard and Heloise," "A Meeting by the River," OB in "The Cretan Woman" for which date she received a Theatre World Award, "The Clandestine Marriage," "Measure For Measure," "Duchess of Malfi," "Ivanov," "6 Characters in Search of an Author," "An Evenings Frost," "Come Slowly, Eden," "The Increased Difficulty of Concentration," "The Persians," "Sunday Dinner," "House of Blue Leaves," "Owners," "Hallelujah," "Dream of a Blacklisted Actor," "Knuckle," "Mama Sang the Blues," "Buried Child," "On Mt. Chimorazo," "Winter Dancers," "Hamlet," "Old Flames," "The Diviners," "Richard II," "Vieux Carre," "Full Hookup," "Home Sweet Home/Crack," "Approaching Zanzibar".

BROOKS, AVERY. Born Oct. 2, in Evansville Ind. OB in "The Offering," "A Photograph," "Are You Now or Have You Ever Been," "Spell #7," Bdwy in "Paul Robeson" (1988).

BROOKS, JEFF. Born Apr. 7, 1950 in Vancouver, Can. Attended Portland State U. Debut 1976 OB in "Titanic," followed by "Fat Chances," "Nature and Purpose of the Universe," "Actor's Nightmare," "Sister Mary Ignatius Explains It All," "Marathon 84," "The Foreigner," "Talk Radio," "Washington Heights," Bdwy in "A History of the American Film" (1978), "Lend Me A Tenor."

BROWN, CHUCK. Born Oct. 16, 1959 in Cleveland, OH. Attended Baldwin-Wallace Col. Debut 1984 OB in "Pacific Overtures," followed by "The Shop on Main Street," "Vampire Lesbians of Sodom."

BROWN, GEORGIA. Born Oct. 21, 1933 in London, Eng. NYC debut 1957 OB in "Threepenny Opera," followed by "Greek," Bdwy in "Oliver!" (1962), "Side by Side by Sondheim," "Carmelina," "Roza," "3 Penny Opera."

BROWN, GRAHAM. Born Oct. 24 in NYC. Graduate Howard U. OB in "Widower's Houses" (1959), "The Emperor's Clothes," "Time of Storm," "Major Barbara," "Land Beyond the River," "The Blacks," "Firebugs," "God Is a (Guess Who?)," "Evening of 1 Acts," "Man Better Man," "Behold! Cometh the Vanderkellans," "Ride a Black Horse," "The Great MacDaddy," "Eden," "Nevis Mountain Dew," "Season Unravel," "The Devil's Tear," "Sons and Fathers of Sons," "Abercrombie Apocalypse," "Ceremonies in Dark Old Men," "Eyes of the American," "Richard II," "The Taming of the Shrew," "Winter's Tale," Bdwy in "Weekend" (1968), "Man in the Glass Booth," "River Niger," "Pericles," "Black Picture Show," "Kings."

BROWN, ROBIN LESLIE. Born Jan. 18, in Canandaigua, NY. Graduate L.I.U. Debut 1980 OB in "The Mother of Us All," followed by "Yours Truly," "Two Gentlemen of Verona," "Taming of the Shrew," "The Mollusc," "The Contrast," "Pericles," "Andromache," "Macbeth," "Electra," "She Stoops to Conquer," "Berenice," "Hedda Gabler."

BROWN, RUTH. Born Jan. 31, 1928 in Portsmouth, Va. Debut 1987 OB in "Staggerlee," followed by Broadway (1988) in "Black and Blue."

BROWN, WILLIAM SCOTT. Born Mar. 27, 1959 in Seattle, WA. Attended UWash. Debut 1986 OB in "Juba," Bdwy in "Phantom of the Opera" (1988).

BRUNNER, KEVIN. Born Feb. 8, 1957 in Fairfax, MO. Graduate Northwest Missouri StU. Debut OB 1985 in "Naughty Marietta," followed by "Gigi."

BRUTSMAN, LAURA. Born July 31, 1961 in Cheyenne, WY. Graduate Juilliard Debut 1984 OB in "Pieces of Eight," followed by "The Skin of Our Teeth," "As You Like It," "A New Way to Pay Old Debts," "Orchards," "Without Apologies," "In Circles," "Dodger Blue."

BRYANT, ADAM. (formerly Sal Biagini). Born Apr. 13 in Brooklyn, NY. Graduate USFla. Debut 1984 OB in "Sing Me Sunshine," followed by "On the Brink," "3 One Acts," "Rosemarie," "Back in the Big Time," "Jacques Brel . . .," "Gifts of the Magi," Bdwy in "Big River" (1987).

BRYANT, CRAIG. Born Sept. 13, 1961 in Aurora, IL. Graduate NYU. Debut 1986 in "Orchards," followed by "Why to Refuse," "Don Juan in New York."

BRYANT, DAVID. Born May 26, 1936 in Nashville, Tn. Attended TnStateU. Bdwy debut 1972 in "Don't Play Us Cheap," followed by "Bubbling Brown Sugar," "Amadeus," "Les Miserables," OB in "Up in Central Park," "Elizabeth and Essex," "Appear and Show Cause."

BRYGGMAN, LARRY. Born Dec. 21, 1938 in Concord, Ga. Attended CCSF., Am ThWing. Debut 1962 OB in "A Pair of Pairs," followed by "Live Like Pigs," "Stop, You're Killing Me," "Mod Donna," "Waiting for Godot," "Ballymurphy," "Marco Polo Sings a Solo," "Brownsville Raid," "Two Small Bodies," "Museum," "Winter Dancers," "Resurrection of Lady Lester," "Royal Bob," "Modern Ladies of Guanabacoa," "Rum and Coke," "Bodies, Rest and Motion," "Blood Sports," "Class 1 Acts," "Spoils of War," "Coriolanus," Bdwy in "Ulysses in Nighttown" (1974), "Checking Out," "Basic Training of Pavlo Hummel," "Richard III."

BRYNE, BARBARA. Born Apr. 1, 1929 in London, Eng. Graduate RADA. NY debut 1981 OB in "Entertaining Mr. Sloane," Bdwy in "Sunday in the Park with George" (1984), "Hay Fever," "Into the Woods."

BUELL, BILL. Born Sept. 21, 1952 in Paipai, Taiwan. Attended Portland StateU. Debut 1972 OB in "Crazy Now," followed by "Declassee," "Lorenzaccio," "Promenade," "The Common Pursuit," "Coyote Ugly," "Alias Jimmy Valentine," "Kiss Me Quick," Bdwy in "Once a Catholic" (1979), "The First," "Welcome to the Club."

BULOS, YUSEF. Born Sept. 14, 1940 in Jerusalem. Attended Beirut Am.U, AADA. Debut 1965 OB with American Savoyards in repertory, followed by "Saints," "The Trouble With Europe," "The Penultimate Problem of Sherlock Holmes," "In the Jungle of Cities," "Hernani," "Bertrano," "Duck Variations," "Insignificance," "Panache," "Arms and the Man," "The Promise," Bdwy in "Indians" (1970), "Capt. Brassbound's Conversion."

BURK, TERENCE. Born Aug. 11, 1947 in Lebanon, IL. Graduate S.Ill.U. Bdwy debut 1976 in "Equus," OB in "Religion," "The Future," "Sacred and Profane Love," "Crime and Punishment."

BURKE, MAGGIE. Born May 2, 1936 in Bay Shore, NY. Graduate Sarah Lawrence Col. OB in "Today Is Independence Day," "Lovers and Other Strangers," "Jules Feiffer's Cartoons," "Fog," "Home Is the Hero," "King John," "Rusty & Rico & Lena Louie," "Friends," "Butterfaces," "Old Times," "Man with a Raincoat," "Hall of North American Forests," "Approaching Zanzibar," Bdwy debut 1985 in "Brighton Beach Memoirs."

BURNETT, ROBERT. Born Feb. 28, 1960 in Goshen, NY. Attended HB Studio. Bdwy debut 1985 in "Cats."

BURRELL, FRED. Born Sept. 18, 1936. Graduate UNC. RADA. Bdwy debut 1964 in "Never Too Late," followed by "Illya Darling," OB in "The Memorandum," "Throckmorton," "Texas," "Voices in the Head," "Chili Queen," "The Queen's Knight."

BURSTYN, ELLEN. Born Dec. 7, 1932 in Detroit, MI. Attended Actors Studio. Bdwy debut 1957 (as Ellen MacRae) in "Fair Game," followed by "Same Time Next Year," "84 Charing Cross Road," "Shirley Valentine," OB in "Three Sisters," "Andromeda II," "Park Your Car in Harvard Yard."

BURTON, IRVING. Born Aug. 5, 1923 in NYC. Bdwy debut 1951 in "Peer Gynt," followed by "Chu Chem," OB in "Three Unnatural Acts," 24 years with Paper Bag Players, "Pal Joey," "Keegan & Lloyd Again," "One Act Festival."

BURTON, KATE. Born Sept. 10, 1957 in Geneva, Switz. Graduate BrownU, Yale. Bdwy debut 1982 in "Present Laughter," followed by "Alice in Wonderland," "Doonesbury," "Wild Honey," OB in "Winners," for which she received a 1983 Theatre World Award, "Romeo and Juliet," "The Accrington Pals," "Playboy of the Western World," "Measure for Measure."

BUSCH, CHARLES. Born Aug. 23, 1954 in NYC. Graduate NorthwesternU. Debut OB 1985 in "Vampire Lesbians of Sodom," followed by "Times Square Angel," "Pscyho Beach Party," "The Lady in Question," all of which he wrote.

BUTLER, DEAN. Born May 20, 1956 in Prince George, B.C., Canada. Graduate Uof the Pacific. Bdwy debut 1988 in "Into the Woods."

BUTT, JENNIFER. Born May 17, 1958 in Valparaiso, In. Stephens Col. graduate. Debut 1983 OB in "The Robber Bridegroom," followed by "Into the Closet," Bdwy in "Les Miserables" (1987).

BYERS, CATHERINE. Born Oct. 7 in Sioux City, IA. Graduate UIa. LAMDA. Bdwy debut 1971 in "The Philanthropist," followed by "Don't Call Back," "Equus," "M. Butterfly," OB "Petrified Forest," "All My Sons," "Murder in the Cathedral," "Grace," "The Fuehrer Bunker," "Great Days."

BYRON, JOHN. Born Jan. 5, 1920 in St. Paul, MN. Debut 1973 OB in "Venus Observed," followed by "The Hostage," "Leave It to Jane," "Put Them Out to Pasture," "Oh, Dad, Poor, Dad . . .," "Gigi."

CAHN, LARRY. Born Dec. 19, 1955 in Nassau, NY. Graduate NorthwesternU. Bdwy debut 1980 in "The Music Man," followed by "Anything Goes," OB in "Susan B!," "Jim Thorpe—All American," "Play to Win."

CAIN, WILLIAM. Born May 27, 1931 in Tuscalossa, AL. Graduate UWash., CatholicU. Debut 1962 OB in "Red Roses For Me," followed by "Jericho Jim Crow," "Henry V," "Antigone," "Relatively Speaking," "I Married an Angel in Concert," "Buddha," "Copperhead," "Forbidden City," Bdwy in "Wilson in the Promise Land" (1970), "Of the Fields Lately," "You Can't Take It with You," "Wild Honey."

CALKINS, MICHAEL. Born Apr. 27, 1948 in Chicago, IL. Graduate Webster Col. Debut 1973 OB in "Sisters of Mercy," followed by "Love! Love! Love!," "Lifesongs," "Gifts of the Magi."

CALLEN, CHRIS. Born July 14 in Fresno, CA. Graduate SanFranStateU. Bdwy debut in "Brigadoon" (1968/CC), followed by "Smeoneelse's Sandals," "1776," "Desert Song," "Over Here," "Rodgers and Hart," "Truckload," "Coolest Cat in Town," "Fiddler on the Roof" (1977), "Prince of Central Park," "Lend Me a Tenor."

CALLOW, SIMON. Born June 15, 1949 in London. Attended Queens U(Belfast). Bdwy debut 1989 as director of "Shirley Valentine."

CALLOWAY, BRIAN. Born July 17, 1934 in London, Eng. Attended HB Studio. Debut 1970 OB in "War of the Roses," followed by "Down by the River Where Waterlilies Are Disfigured Every Day," "Plough and the Stars."

CAMACHO, BLANCA. Born Nov. 19, 1956 in NYC. Graduate NYU. Debut 1984 OB in "Sarita," followed by "Maggie Magalita," "Salon," "You Can Come Back."

CAMERA, JOHN. Born in North Tarrytown, NY. Attended ColumbiaU, Tufts. Debut 1989 OB in "The Lark."

CAMP, JOANNE. Born Apr. 4, 1951 in Atlanta, GA. Graduate FlAtlanticU., GeoWashU. Debut 1981 OB in "The Dry Martini," followed by "Geniuses," for which she received a Theatre World Award, "June Moon," "Painting Churches," "Merchant of Venice," "Lady From The Sea," "The Contrast," "Coastal Disturbances," "The Rivals," "Andromache," "Electra," "Uncle Vanya," "She Stoops to Conquer," "Hedda Gabler," "The Heidi Chronicles," Bdwy in "The Heidi Chronicles" (1989).

CAMPBELL, AMELIA. Born Aug. 4, 1965 in Montreal, Canada. Graduate Syracuse U. Debut 1988 OB in "Fun," followed by "Member of the Wedding."

CAMPISI, TONY. Born May 8 in Cleveland, OH. Attended USanta Clara. Debut 1977 OB in "K," followed by "The Caseworker," "Music Hall Sidelights," "Pvt. Wars," "Frankie and Johnny in the Clair De Lune."

CANNAN, EDWARD. Born March 28, 1945 in Dallas, Tx. Graduate UTexas. Debut 1971 OB in "Basic Training of Pavlo Hummel," followed by "The Hitchikers," "Rimers of Eldritch."

CAREY, ROBERT. Born Dec 24, 1958 in Hudson County, NJ. Graduate RutgersU. Debut 1985 OB in "Vampire Lesbians of Sodom" after Theatre-in-Limbo appearances, followed by "Times Square Angel," "Psycho Beach Party," "The Lady in Question."

CARIOU, LEN. Born Sept. 30, 1939 in Winnipeg, Can. Bdwy debut 1968 in "House of Atreus," followed by "Henry V," and "Applause" (for which he received a Theatre World Award), "Night Watch," "A Little Night Music," "Cold Storage," "Sweeney Todd," "Dance A Little Closer," "Teddy and Alice" OB in "A Sorrow Beyond Dreams" "Up from Paradise," "Master Class," "Day Six," "Measure for Measure."

CARLIN, AMANDA. Born Dec. 12 in Queens, NY. Tufts U. Graduate. Bdwy debut 1980 in "Major Barbara," followed by "The Man Who Came to Dinner," "The Front Page," "The Heidi Chronicles," OB in "The Dining Room," "Twelfth Night," "The Accrington Pals," "Comedy of Errors," "Playboy of the Western World," "Waltz of the Toreadors," "The Maderati."

CARROLL, DANNY. Born May 30, 1940 in Maspeth, NY. Bdwy bow in 1957 "The Music Man," followed by "Flora the Red Menace," "Funny Girl," "George M!," "Billy," "Ballroom," "42nd Street," OB in "Boys from Syracuse," "Babes in the Woods."

CARROLL, DAVID, (formerly David-James). Born July 30, 1950 in Rockville Centre, NY. Graduate Dartmouth Col. Debut 1975 OB in "A Matter of Time," followed by "Joseph and the Amazing Technicolor Dreamcoat," "New Tunes," "La Boheme," "Company," "Cafe Crown," Bdwy in "Rodgers and Hart" (1975), "Where's Charley," "Oh Brother!," "7 Brides for 7 Brothers," "Roberta in Concert," "Wind in the Willows," "Chess," "Cafe Crown."

CARSON, THOMAS. Born May 27, 1939 in Iowa City, Io. Graduate UIo. Debut 1981 OB in "The Feuhrer Bunker," followed by "Breakfast Conversations in Miami," "Sullivan and Gilbert," "The Tempest," "Alive By Night."

CARTER, ROSANNA. Born Sept. 20 in Rolle Town, Bahamas. Bdwy debut 1980 in "The American Clock," followed by "Inacent Black," OB in "Lament of Tasta Fari," "Burghers of Callais," "Scottsboro Boys," "Les Femmes Noires," "Killings on the Last Line," "Under Heaven's Eye," "Marathon '86," "Ma Rose."

CASNOFF, PHILIP. Born Aug. 3, 1953 in Philadelphia, Pa. Graduate WesleyanU. Debut 1978 OB in "Gimme Shelter," followed by "Chincilla," "King of Schnorrers," "Mary Stuart," "Henry IV," "Marathon '89," Bdwy in "Grease" (1973), "Chess," for which he received a Theatre World Award, "Devil's Disciple."

CASSERLY, KERRY. Born Oct. 26, 1953 in Minneapolis, MN. Attended UMinn. Bdwy debut 1980 in "One Night Stand," followed by "A Chorus Line," "My One and Only."

CASSIDY, TIM. Born March 22, 1952 in Alliance, OH. Attended UCincinnati. Bdwy debut 1974 in "Good News," followed by "A Chorus Line," "Dreamgirls."

CASTLE, DIANA. Born Aug. 18, 1957 in NYC. Graduate FlaStateU. Debut 1981 OB in "Seesaw," followed by "A . . . My Name is Alice," "What's a Nice Country Like You Still Doing in a State Like This?," "Holy Ghosts," "The Middle of Nowhere."

CAVISE, JOE ANTONY. Born Jan. 7, 1958 in Syracuse, NY. Graduate Clark U. Debut 1981 OB in "Street Scene," followed by Bdwy 1984 in "Cats."

CEA, KIM. Born Apr. 15, 1964 in Pittsburgh, PA. Graduate Point Park Col. Debut 1988 OB in "On the Prowl."

CELLARIO, MARIA. Born June 19, 1948 in Buenos Aires, Arg. Graduate Ithaca Col. Bdwy debut 1975 in "The Royal Family," followed by OB in "Fugue in a Nursery," "Declassee," "Equinox," "Flatbush Faithful," "Our Lady of the Tortilla," "Half Deserted Streets," "George Washington Slept Here," "Black Hat Karma."

CERULLO, JONATHAN. Born Dec. 21, 1960 in NYC. Graduate Emerson Col. Bdwy debut 1988 in "Legs Diamond," OB in "Gigi."

CHALFANT, KATHLEEN. Born Jan. 14, 1945 in San Francisco, CA. Graduate StanfordU. Bdwy debut 1975 in "Dance with Me," followed by "M. Butterfly," OB in "Jules Feiffer's Hold Me," "Killings on the Last Line," "The Boor," "Blood Relations," "Signs of Life," "Sister Mary Ignatius Explains It All," "Actor's Nightmare," "Faith Healer," "All the Nice People," "Hard Times," "Investigation of the Murder in El Salvador."

CHAPMAN, KAREN. Born Feb. 29, 1960 in Virginia Beach, VA. Attended UDelaware, UBath, Eng. Debut OB 1989 in "Enrico IV."

CHAPPELL, KANDIS. Born July 9, 1947 in Milwaukee, WS. Graduate SanDiegoState U. Bdwy debut 1989 in "Rumors."

CHINN, LORI TAN. Born July 7 in Seattle, Wash. Bdwy debut 1970 in "Lovely Ladies, Kind Gentlemen," followed by "M. Butterfly," OB in "Coffins for Butterflies," "Hough in Blazes," "Peer Gynt," "The King and I," "Children," "The Secret Life of Walter Mitty," "Bayou Legend," "Primary English Class," "G.R. Point," "Peking Man," "Ballad of Soapy Smith."

CHRISTIAN, WILLIAM. Born Sept. 30, 1955 in Washington, D.C. Graduate CatholicU, AmericanU. OB in "She Stoops to Conquer," "A Sleep of Prisoners," "American Voices," "Member of the Wedding."

CHRISTIANSON, CATHERINE ANN. Born Feb. 10, 1957 in Evanston, IL. Graduate Vassar Col., Goodman School. Debut 1984 OB in "Romance," followed by "Arms and the Man," Bdwy in "I'm Not Rappaport."

CHRISTOPHER, THOM. Born Oct. 5, 1940 in Jackson Heights, NY. Attended Ithaca Col., Neighborhood Playhouse. Debut 1972 OB in "One Flew Over the Cuckoo's Nest," followed by "Tamara," "Investigation of the Murder in El Salvador," Bdwy in "Emperor Henry IV" (1973), "Noel Coward in Two Keys," for which he received a Theatre World Award, "Caesar and Cleopatra."

CHRYST, GARY. Born in 1959 in LaJolla, Ca. Joined Joffrey Ballet in 1968, Bdwy debut in "Dancin' " (1979), followed by "A Chorus Line," OB in "One More Song, One More Dance," "Music Moves Me."

CHUTE, LIONEL. Born Oct. 18, 1962 in NYC. Attended Carnegie-Mellon. Debut OB 1988 in "Perfect Crime."

CLARK, CHERYL. Born Dec. 7, 1950 in Boston, MA. Attended Ind. U., NYU. Bdwy debut 1972 in "Pippin," followed by "Chicago," "A Chorus Line."

CLARKE, RICHARD. Born Jan. 31, 1933 in England. Graduate UReading. With LCRep in "St. Joan" (1968), "Tiger at the Gates," "Cyrano de Bergerac," Bdwy in "Conduct Unbecoming" (1970), "The Elephant Man," "Breaking the Code," "M. Butterfly," OB in "Old Glory," "Looking-Glass."

CLAYTON, LAWRENCE. Born Oct. 10, 1956 in Mocksville, NC. Attended NC CentralU. Debut 1980 OB in "Tambourines to Glory," followed by "Skyline," "Across the Universe," "Two by Two," "Romance in Hard Times," Bdwy in "Dreamgirls" (1984).

COATS, STEVE. Born Oct. 5, 1954 in Berkeley, CA. Graduate San Fran StateU. Debut 1982 OB in "The World of Ben Caldwell," followed by "Touched," "The Last Danceman," "Stella," "Ulysses in Nighttown."

COGNETTA, PATRICK. Born Aug. 4, 1955 in Stamford, CT. Graduate NYU. OB in "The Sunshine Boys" (1989).

COHEN, BILL. Born Jan. 12, 1953 in Brooklyn, NY. Yale Graduate. Debut OB 1984 in "Child's Play," followed by "The Man Who Killed the Buddha," "Festival of 1 Acts."

COHEN, JAMIE. Born Apr. 20, 1959 in Peoria, IL. Bdwy debut 1989 in "Jerome Robbins' Broadway."

COHEN, JULIE. Born June 16, 1964 in NYC. Attended NYU. Debut 1984 OB in "The Nest of the Wild Grouse," followed by "Swing of Things."

COHENOUR, PATTI. Born Oct. 17, 1952 in Albuquerque, NMx. Attended UNMx. Bdwy debut 1982 in "A Doll's Life," followed by "Pirates of Penzance," "Big River," "The Mystery of Edwin Drood." "Phantom of the Opera," OB in "La Boheme" for which she received a Theatre World Award.

COLE, KAY. Born Jan. 13, 1948 in Miami, FL. Bdwy debut 1961 in "Bye Bye Birdie," followed by "Stop the World I Want to Get Off," "Roar of the Greasepaint . . .," "Hair," "Jesus Christ Superstar," "Words and Music," "Chorus Line," OB in "The Cradle Will Rock," "Two If By Sea," "Rainbow," "White Nights," "Sgt. Pepper's Lonely Hearts Club Band," "On the Swing Shift," "Snoopy," "Road to Hollywood," "One-man Band."

COLKER, JERRY. Born Mar. 16, 1955 in Los Angeles, CA. Attended Harvard U. Debut 1975 OB in "Tenderloin," followed by "Pal Joey," "3 Guys Naked from the Waist Down," Bdwy in "West Side Story," "Pippin," "A Chorus Line."

COLL, IVONNE. Born Nov. 4 in Fajardo, PR. Attended UPR, LACC, HB Studio. Debut 1980 OB in "Spain 1980," followed by "Animals," "Wonderful Ice Cream Suit," "Cold Air," "Fabiola," "Concerto in Hi-Fi," "Quintuplets," "A Burning Beach," "The Promise," Bdwy in "Goodbye Fidel" (1980) "Shakespeare on Broadway."

COLLINS, PAULINE. Born Sept. 3, 1940 in Exmouth, Devon, England. Graduate Central School of Speech & Drama. Broadway debut 1989 in "Shirley Valentine" for which she received a Theatre World Award.

COLLINS, RAY. Born July 20, 1949 in London, Eng. Attended LAMDA. Debut 1985 OB in "Roundheads and Peakheads," followed by "The Constant Wife," "Ragged Trousered Philanthropists," "Up 'n' Under," "Hired Man."

COLTON, CHEVI. Born Dec. 21 in NYC. Attended Hunter Col. OB in "Time of Storm," "Insect Comedy," "The Adding Machine," "O Marry Me," "Penny Change," "The Mad Show," "Jacques Brel . . .," "Bits and Pieces," "Spelling Bee," "Uncle Money," "Miami," "Come Blow Your Horn," "Almost Perfect," Bdwy in "Cabaret," "Grand Tour," "Torch Song Trilogy."

COLUMBO, JEANIE. Born Nov. 24 in Staten Island, NY. Attended AADA. Debut OB 1988 in "I've Got Ink," followed by "On the Prowl."

COMER, ANJANETTE. Born Aug. 7, 1942 in Dawson, TX. Attended BaylorU. Debut 1989 OB in "The Heart Outright."

CONNELL, JANE. Born Oct. 27, 1925 in Berkeley, CA. Attended UCal. Bdwy debut in "New Faces of 1956," followed by "Drat! The Cat!," "Mame" (1966/1983), "Dear World," "Lysistrata," "Me and My Girl," "Lend Me a Tenor," OB in "Shoestring Revue," "Threepenny Opera," "Pieces of Eight," "Demi-Dozen," "She Stoops to Conquer," "Drat!," "The Real Inspector Hound," "The Rivals," "The Rise and Rise of Daniel Rocket," "Laughing Stock," "The Singular Dorothy Parker," "No No Nanette in Concert."

CONNELL, KELLY. Born June 9, 1956 in Seneca Falls, NY. Attended Cayuga Com. Col. Debut 1982 OB in "The Butter and Egg Man," followed by "Neon Psalms," "Love's Labour's Lost," "Quiet in the Land," "The Musical Comedy Murders of 1940," "Reckless."

CONNOLLY, JOHN P. Born Sept. 1, 1950 in Philadelphia, PA. Graduate TempleU. Debut 1973 OB in "Paradise Lost," followed by "The Wizard of Oz," "Fighting Bob," "For the Use of the Hall," "The Golem," "A Step Out of Line," "For Sale," "Filthy Rich," "Colette in Love," "Sleeping Dogs," Bdwy in "Big River."

CONROY, FRANCES. Born in 1953 in Monroe, GA. Attended Dickinson Col., Juilliard, Neighborhood Playhouse. Debut 1978 OB with the Acting Co. in "Mother Courage," "King Lear," and "The Other Half," followed by "All's Well That Ends Well," "Othello," "Sorrows of Stephen," "Girls Girls Girls," "Zastrozzi," "Painting Churches," "Uncle Vanya," "Romance Language," "To Gillian on Her 37th Birthday," "Man and Superman," "Zero Positive," Bdwy in "The Lady from Dubuque" (1980), "Our Town" (1989).

CONROY, JARLATH. Born Sept. 30, 1944 in Galway, Ire. Attended RADA. Bdwy debut 1976 in "Comedians," followed by "The Elephant Man," "Macbeth," "Ghetto," OB in "Translations," "The Wind That Shook the Barley," "Gardenia," "Friends," "Playboy of the Western World," "One Act Festival."

CONWAY, KEVIN. Born May 29, 1942 in NYC. Debut 1968 OB in "Muzeeka," followed by "Saved," "The Plough and the Stars," "One Flew Over the Cuckoo's Nest," "When You Comin' Back, Red Ryder?," "Long Day's Journey Into Night," "Other Places," "King John," "Other People's Money," Bdwy in "Indians" (1969), "Moonchildren," "Of Mice and Men," "The Elephant Man."

COOK, VICTOR TRENT. Born Aug. 19, 1967 in NYC. Debut 1976 OB in "Joseph and the Amazing Technicolor Dreamcoat," followed by "The Haggadah," "Moby Dick," "Starmites," "Romance in Hard Times," Bdwy in "Don't Get God Started" (1988), "Starmites."

COOKSON, GARY. Born July 31, 1950 in Roslyn, NY. Graduate NYU. Debut 1974 OB in "Drums at Yale," followed by "The Healers," "Mad Dogs," "A Place of Springs," "Wayside Manor Inn," "Festival of 1 Acts," Bdwy in "A Streetcar Named Desire" (1988).

COOPER, MARILYN. Born Dec. 14, 1936 in NYC. Attended NYU. Bdwy in "Mr. Wonderful," "West Side Story," "Brigadoon," "Gypsy," "I Can Get it For You Wholesale," "Hallelujah Baby!," "Golden Rainbow," "Mame," "A Teaspoon Every 4 Hours," "Two by Two," "On the Town," "Ballroom," "Woman of the Year," "The Odd Couple" (1985), "Cafe Crown." OB in "The Mad Show," "Look Me Up," "The Perfect Party," "Cafe Crown."

COPELAND, JOAN. Born June 1, 1922 in NYC. Attended Brooklyn Col., AADA. Debut 1945 OB in "Romeo and Juliet," followed by "Othello," "Conversation Piece," "Delightful Season," "End of Summer," "American Clock," "The Double Game," "Isn't It Romantic?," "Hunting Cockroaches," "Young Playwrights Festival," Bdwy in "Sundown Beach," "Detective Story," "Not for Children," "Hatful of Fire," "Something More," "The Price," "Two by Two," "Pal Joey," "Checking Out," "The American Clock."

CORFMAN, CARIS. Born May 18, 1955 in Boston, MA. Graduate FlaStU. Yale. Debut 1978 OB in "Wings," followed by "Fish Riding Bikes," "Filthy Rich," "Dry Land" "All This and Moonlight," "Cezanne Syndrome," "Tea with Mommy and Jack," "Equal Wrights," Bdwy in "Amadeus" (1980).

COSGRAVE, PEGGY. Born June 23, 1946 in San Mateo, CA. Graduate San Jose St, Catholic U. Debut 1980 OB in "Come Back to the Five and Dime, Jimmy Dean," Bdwy. 1987 in "The Nerd," "Born Yesterday."

COSTA, JOSEPH. Born June 8, 1946 in Ithaca, NY. Graduate Gettysburg Col., Yale U. Debut 1978 OB in "The Show Off," followed by "The Tempest," "The Changeling," "A Map of the World," "Julius Caesar," "Titus Andronicus," "Love's Labour's Lost."

COSTEN, RUSSELL. Born May 15, 1945 in Boston, MA. Graduate St. John'sU. Bdwy debut 1970 in "J.B.," OB in "Caligula," "Danton's Death," "Othello," "Birthday Party," "Three Musketeers," "Mary Tudor," "Arsenic and Old Lace," "Gigi."

COUNCIL, RICHARD. Born Oct. 1, 1947 In Tampa, Fl. Graduate UFl. Debut 1973 OB in "Merchant of Venice," followed by "Ghost Dance," "Look, We've Come Through," "Arms and the Man," "Isadora Duncan Sleeps with the Russian Navy," "Arthur," "The Winter Dancer," "The Prevalence of Mrs. Seal," "Jane Avril," "Young Playwrights Festival 1988–89," "Sleeping Dogs," "The Good Coach," Bdwy in "Royal Family," (1975), "Philadelphia Story," "I'm Not Rappaport."

COUSINS, BRIAN. Born May 9, 1959 in Portland, Me. Graduate Tulane, UWash. Debut 1987 OB in "Death of a Buick," followed by "Taming of the Shrew," "Enrico IV."

COVER, FRANKLIN. Born Nov. 20, 1928 in Cleveland, Oh. Graduate Denison, Western Reserve U. OB in "Julius Caesar," "Henry IV," "She Stoops To Conquer," "The Plough and the Stars," "The Octoroon," "Hamlet," "Macbeth," "Kildeer," Bdwy in "Giants, Sons of Giants" (1962), "Calculated Risk," "Abraham Cochrane," "Any Wednesday," "The Investigation," "40 Carats," "A Warm Body," "Applause," "Wild Honey," "Born Yesterday."

Nora
Brennan

Eric
Bogosian

Barbara
Bryne

Stephen
Bourneuf

Karen
Chapman

Kevin
Brunner

William
Christian

Kandis
Chappell

Gary
Chryst

Catherine Ann
Christianson

Lionel
Chute

Kay
Cole

Chevi
Colton

Kelly
Connell

Kim
Criswell

Brian
Cousins

Kim
Crosby

Anthony
Crivello

Bob
Cuccioli

Gretchen
Cryer

Macaulay
Culkin

Cynthia
Darlow

Keene
Curtis

Connie
Day

Timothy
Daly

Allison
Dean

Dan
Desmond

Camille
de Ganon

Jay
Devlin

Diane
Della Piazza

COX, CATHERINE. Born Dec. 13, 1950 in Toledo, OH. Graduate Wittenberg U. Bdwy debut 1976 in "Music Is," followed by "Whoopee!," "Oklahoma!," "Shakespeare's Cabaret," "Barnum," "Baby," "Oh, Coward!," "Rumors," OB in "By Strouse," "It's Better with a Band," "In Trousers," "Crazy Arnold."

CRAIG, NOEL. Born Jan 4 in St. Louis, MO. Attended Northwestern, Goodman Theatre, London Guildhall. Bdwy debut 1967 in "Rosencrantz and Guilderstern Are Dead," followed by "A Patriot for Me," "Conduct Unbecoming," "Vivat! Vivat Regina!," "Going Up," "Dance a Little Closer," "A Chorus Line," OB in "Pygmalion," "Promenade," "Family House," "Inn at Lydda," "The Estate."

CRAMPTON, GLORY. Born Mar. 30, 1964 in Rockville Cenrer, NY. Graduate NYU. Debut 1988 OB in "The Fantasticks."

CRAVEN, MATT. Born Nov. 10, 1956 in Port Colborne, Can. Debut 1984 OB in "Blue Windows," followed by "Crackwalker," "The Nest."

CRAWFORD, MICHAEL. Born Jan. 19, 1942 in Salisbury, Wiltshire, Eng. Bdwy debut 1967 in "Black Comedy," followed by "Phantom of the Opera" (1988).

CRISWELL, KIM. Born July 19, 1957 in Hampton, Va. Graduate UCin. Bdwy debut 1981 in "The First," followed by "Nine," "Baby," "Stardust," OB in "Sitting Pretty."

CRIVELLO, ANTHONY. Born Aug. 2, 1955 in Milwaukee, Wi. Bdwy debut 1982 in "Evita," followed by "The News," "Les Miserables," OB in "The Juniper Tree,"

CROFT, PADDY. Born in Worthing, Eng. Attended Avondale Col. Debut 1961 OB in "The Hostage," followed by "Billy Liar," "Live Like Pigs," "Hogan's Goat," "Long Day's Journey into Night," "Shadow of a Gunman," "Pygmalion," "The Plough and the Stars" (LC), "Kill," "The Plough and the Stars," Bdwy in "The Killing of Sister George," "The Prime of Miss Jean Brodie," "Crown Matrimonial," "Major Barbara."

CROSBY, CATHY LEE. Born Dec. 2, 1948 in Los Angeles, CA. Graduate USCal. Debut 1988 OB in "Almost Perfect."

CROSBY, KIM. Born July 11, 1960 in Fort Smith, Ar. Attended SMU, ManSchMusic. Bdwy debut 1985 in "Jerry's Girls," followed by "Into the Woods."

CRYER, DAVID. Born Mar. 8, 1936 in Evanston, IL. Attended DePauwU. OB in "The Fantasticks," "Streets of New York," "Now Is the Time for All Good Men," "Whispers in the Wind," "The Making of Americans," "Portfolio Revue," "Paradise Lost," "The Inheritors," "Rain," "Ghosts," "Madwoman of Chaillot," "Clarence," "Mlle. Colombe," "A Little Night Music," Bdwy in "110 in the Shade," "Come Summer," for which he received a Theatre World Award, "1776," "Ari," "Leonard Bernstein's Mass," "The Desert Song," "Evita," "Chess," "Devil's Disciple."

CRYER, GRETCHEN. Born Oct. 17, 1935 in Indianapolis, IN. Graduate DePauwU. Bdwy debut 1962 in "Little Me," followed by "110 in the Shade," OB in "Now Is the Time for All Good Men," "Gallery," "Circle of Sound," "I'm Getting My Act Together . . ." "Blue Plate Special," "To Whom It May Concern," "Alterations," "Back in My Life."

CUCCIOLI, BOB. Born May 3, 1958 in Hempstead, NY. St. John's U. graduate. Debut 1982 OB in "H.M.S. Pinafore," followed by "Senor Discretion," "Gigi."

CUERVO, ALMA. Born Aug. 13, 1951 in Tampa, FL. Graduate TulaneU, YaleU. Debut 1977 in "Uncommon Women and Others," followed by "A Foot in the Door," "Put Them All Together," "Isn't It Romantic?," "Miss Julie," "Quilters," "The Sneaker Factor," "Songs on a Shipwrecked Sofa," "Uncle Vanya," "The Grandma Plays," "The Nest," Bdwy in "Once in a Lifetime," "Bedroom Farce," "Censored Scenes from King Kong," "Is There Life after High School?," "Ghetto."

CULKIN, SHANE. Born June 15, 1976 in NYC. Debut OB 1982 in "Hecuba," Bdwy 1989 in "Our Town."

CULLISON, BARRY. Born Sept. 11, 1949 in Vincennes, IN. Attended Goodman Theatre School. Bdwy debut in "Bedroom Farce" (1979), OB in "Cloud 9," "A Step Out of Line," "Bob's Guns," "Unguided Missile."

CULLITON, JOSEPH. Born Jan. 25, 1948 in Boston, MA. Attended CalStateU. Debut 1982 OB in "Francis," followed by "Flirtations," "South Pacific" (LC), "Julius Caesar," "King John," Bdwy 1987 in "Broadway."

CUNNINGHAM, JOHN. Born June 22, 1932 in Auburn, NY. Graduate Yale, Dartmouth. OB in "Love Me a Little," "Pimpernel," "The Fantasticks," "Love and Let Love," "The Bone Room," "Dancing in the Dark," "Father's Day," "Snapshot," "Head over Heels," "Quartermaine's Terms," "Wednesday," "On Approval," "Miami," "Perfect Party," "Birds of Paradise," Bdwy in "Hot Spot" (1963), "Zorba," "Company," "1776," "Rose," "Devil's Disciple."

CURLESS, JOHN. Born Sept. 16 in Wigan, Eng. Attended Central School of Speech. NY debut 1982 OB in "The Entertainer," followed by "Sus," "Up 'n' Under."

CURTIS, KEENE. Born Feb. 15, 1925 in Salt Lake City, UT. Graduate UUtah. Bdwy debut 1949 in "Shop at Sly Corner," with APA in "School for Scandal," "The Tavern," "Anatole," "Scapin," "Right You Are," "Importance of Being Earnest," "Twelfth Night," "King Lear," "Seagull," "Lower Depths," "Man and Superman," "Judith," "War and Peace," "You Can't Take It with You," "Pantaglieze," "Cherry Orchard," "Misanthrope," "Cocktail Party," "Cock-a-Doodle Dandy," and "Hamlet," "A Patriot for Me," "The Rothschilds," "Night Watch," "Via Galactica," "Annie," "Division Street," "La Cage Aux Folles," OB in "Colette," "Ride Across Lake Constance," "The Cocktail Hour."

CUSACK, JOAN. Born 1962 in NYC. Graduate UWisconsin. Debut 1988 OB in "Road," followed by "The Myth Project," "Brilliant Traces," "Cymbeline."

CWIKOWSKI, BILL. Born Aug. 4, 1945 in Newark, NJ. Graduate Smith and Monmouth Col. Debut 1972 OB in "Charlie the Chicken," followed by "Summer Brave," "Desperate Hours," "Mandrogola," "Two by Noonan," "Soft Touch," "Innocent Pleasures," "3 From the Marathon," "Two Part Harmony," "Bathroom Plays," "Little Victories," "Dolphin Position," "Cabal of Hypocrites," "Split Second," "Rose Cottages," "The Good Coach," "Marathon 88."

DALE, JIM. Born Aug 15, 1935 in Rothwell, Eng. Debut 1974 OB with Young Vic Co. in "Taming of the Shrew," "Scapino" that moved to Bdwy, followed by "Barnum," "Joe Egg," "Me and My Girl."

DALTON, LEZLIE. Born Aug. 12, 1952 in Boston, MA. Attended Pasadena Playhouse, UCLA. Debut 1980 OB in "Annie and Arthur," followed by "After Maigret," "Blessed Event," "Times and Appetites of Toulouse-Lautrec," "Good and Faithful Servant," "Unguided Missile."

DALY, TIMOTHY. Born Mar. 1, 1956 in NYC. Graduate Bennington Col. Debut 1984 OB in "Fables for Friends," followed by "Oliver Oliver," Bdwy in "Coastal Disturbances"(1987) for which he received a Theatre World Award.

DANIELLE, MARLENE. Born Aug. 16 in NYC. Bdwy debut 1979 in "Sarava," followed by "West Side Story," "Marlowe," "Damn Yankees" (JB), "Cats," OB in "Little Shop of Horrors."

DANIELLE, SUSAN. Born Jan. 30, 1949 in Englewood, NJ. Graduate Wm. Patterson Col. Debut 1979 OB in "Tip-Toes," Bdwy in "A Chorus Line" (1985).

DANIELS, LESLIE. Born May 27, 1957 in Princeton, NJ. Graduate UPa. Debut 1985 OB in "Playboy of the Western World," followed by "Touch," "The Hairy Ape."

DANNER, BLYTHE. Born Feb. 3, 1944 in Philadelphia, PA. Graduate Bard Col. Debut 1966 OB in "The Infantry," followed by "Collision Course," "Summertree," "Up Eden," "Someone's Comin' Hungry," "Cyrano," "The Miser," for which she received a Theatre World Award, "Twelfth Night," "The New York Idea," "Much Ado About Nothing," "Love Letters," Bdwy in "Butterflies Are Free," "Betrayal," "The Philadelphia Story," "Blithe Spirit," "A Streetcar Named Desire."

DANNER, BRADEN. Born in 1976 in Indianapolis, IN. Bdwy debut 1984 in "Nine," followed by "Oliver!," "Starlight Express," "Les Miserables," OB in "Genesis."

DANTUONO, MICHAEL. Born July 30, 1942 in Providence, RI. Debut 1974 OB in "How To Get Rid of It," followed by "Maggie Flynn," "Charlotte Sweet," "Berlin to Broadway," Bdwy in "Caesar and Cleopatra," "Can-Can" (1981), "Zorba" (1984), "The Three Musketeers," "42nd Street."

DANZER, KATHY. Born July 23, 1951 in Townsend, MT. Graduate UMont. Debut 1978 OB in "Curse of the Starving Class," followed by "Scientific Americans," Bdwy in "Crimes of the Heart" (1982).

DARLOW, CYNTHIA. Born June 13, 1949 in Detroit, MI. Attended NCSch of Arts, PaStateU. Debut 1974 OB in "This Property Is Condemned," followed by "Portrait of a Madonna," "Clytemnestra," "Unexpurgated Memoirs of Bernard Morgandigler," "Actors Nightmare," "Sister Mary Ignatius . . . ," "Fables for Friends," "That's It, Folks!," "Baby with the Bathwater," "Dandy Dick," Bdwy in "Grease" (1976), "Rumors."

DAVENPORT, COLLEEN. Born Sept. 2, 1958 in Beloit, KS. Graduate LaStateU. Debut 1983 OB in "The Seagull," followed by "New York Works '87," "Dalton's Back."

DAVID, KEITH. Born May 8, 1954. Juilliard graduate. Debut 1979 of in "Othello," followed by "The Haggadah," "Pirates of Penzance," "Macbeth," "Coriolanus," "Titus Andronicus."

DAVIDSON, RICHARD M. Born May 10, 1940 in Hamilton, Ont. Can. Graduate UToronto, LAMDA. Debut 1978 OB in "The Beasts," followed by "The Bacchae," "The Broken Pitcher," "Knights Errant," "The Entertainer," "Lunatic and Lover," Bdwy in "The Survivor" (1981), "Ghetto."

DAVIES, JOSEPH C. Born June 29, 1928 in Cha ton, IA. Attended Mich. State Col., Wayne U. Debut 1961 OB in "7 at Dawn," followed by "Jo," "Long Voyage Home," "Time of the Key," "Good Soldier Schweik," "Why Hanna's Skirt Won't Stay Down," "Ghandi," "Coney Island Kid," Bdwy debut 1975 in "The Skin of Our Teeth."

DAVIS, BRUCE ANTHONY. Born Mar. 4, 1959 in Dayton, Oh. Attended Juilliard. Bdwy debut 1979 in "Dancin'," followed by "Big Deal," "A Chorus Line."

DAVIS, SYLVIA. Born Apr. 10, 1910 in Philadelphia, PA. Attended TempleU. AmThWing. Debut 1949 OB in "Blood Wedding," followed by "Tobacco Road," "Orpheus Descending," "Autumn Garden," "Madwoman of Chaillot," "House of Bernarda Alba," "My Old Friends," "Max," "Pahokee Beach," "Mademoiselle," "Hot l Baltimore," "Hedda Gabler," Bdwy in "Nathan Weinstein, Mystic, CT" (1966), "Xmas in Las Vegas."

DAVISON, BRUCE. Born June 28, 1946 in Philadelphia, PA. Graduate PennState, NYU. Debut 1969 OB in "A Home Away From," followed by "Richard III," LCRep's "Tiger at the Gates," "A Cry of Players," and "King Lear," "The Cocktail Hour," Bdwy in "The Elephant Man," "The Glass Menagerie,"

DAWSON, DAVID. Born Feb. 22, 1922 in Brooklyn, NY. Graduate CCNY. Debut 1965 OB in "Hogan's Goat," followed by "Some Rain," "About Face July Festival," Bdwy in "The Freaking Out of Stephanie Blake" (1967).

DAY, CONNIE. Born Dec. 26, 1940 in NYC. Debut 1971 OB in "Look Me Up," followed by "Antigone," "Walking Papers," Bdwy in "Molly"(1973), "The Magic Show," "42nd Street."

DEAN, ALLISON. Born in NYC. Graduate SMU Univ. Debut 1988 OB in "Young Playwright's Festival."

DEAN, LOREN. Born July 31, 1969 in Las Vegas, NV. Debut 1989 OB in "Amulets against the Dragon Forces" for which he received a Theatre World Award.

deGANON, CAMILLE. Born in Springfield, OH. Appeared with several dance companies before making her Bdwy debut in 1986 in "The Mystery of Edwin Drood," followed by "Jerome Robbins' Broadway."

DeLAURENTIS, SEMINA. Born Jan. 21 in Waterbury, Ct. Graduate Southern Ct. State Col. Debut 1985 OB in "Nunsense," followed by "Have I Got a Girl for You."

DELLA PIAZZA, DIANE. Born Sept. 3, 1962 in Pittsburgh, Pa. Graduate Cincinnati Consv. Bdwy debut 1987 in "Les Miserables."

DEMPSEY, JEROME. Born Mar. 1, 1929 in St. Paul, MN. Graduate Toledo U. Bdwy debut 1959 in "West Side Story," followed by "The Deputy," "Spofford," "Room Service," "Love Suicide at Schofield Barracks," "Dracula," "Whodunit," "You Can't Take It with You," "The Mystery of Edwin Drood," "The Front Page" (LC), OB in "Cry of Players," "The Year Boston Won the Pennant," "The Crucible," "Justice Box," "Trelawny of the Wells," "Old Glory," "Six Characters in Search of an Author," "Threepenny Opera," "Johnny on the Spot," "The Barbarians," "he and she," "A Midsummer Night's Dream," "The Recruiting Officer," "Oedipus the King," "The Wild Duck," "The Fuehrer Bunker," "Entertaining Mr. Sloane," "The Clownmaker," "Two Gentlemen of Verona," "The Marry Month of May," "The Unguided Missile."

DeMUNN, JEFFREY. Born Apr. 15, 1947 in Buffalo, NY. Graduate Union Col. Debut 1975 OB in "Augusta," followed by "A Prayer for My Daughter," "Modigliani," "Chekhov Sketchbook," "A Midsummer Night's Dream," "Total Abandon," "The Country Girl," "Hands of Its Enemy," Bdwy in "Comedians" (1976), "Bent," "K2," "Sleight of Hand," "Spoils of War."

DENNISTON, LESLIE. Born May 19, 1950 in San Francisco, CA. Attended HB Studio. Bdwy debut 1976 in "Shenandoah," followed by "Happy New Year," for which she received a Theatre World Award, "To Grandmother's House We Go," "Copperfield," OB in "Class 1 Acts."

DESMOND, DAN. Born July 4, 1944 in Racine, WI. Graduate UWi, Yale. Bdwy debut 1981 in "Morning's at Seven," followed by "Othello," "All My Sons," OB in "A Perfect Diamond," "The Bear," "Vienna Notes," "On Mt. Chimborazo," "Table Settings," "Moonchildren," "Festival of 1 Acts," "Marathon '88."

DEVLIN, JAY. Born May 8, 1929 in Ft. Dodge, IA. OB in "The Mad Show," "Little Murders," "Unfair to Goliath," "Ballymurphy," "Front Page," "Fasnacht Day," "Bugles at Dawn," "A Good Year for the Roses," "Crossing the Bar," "Murder of Crows," Bdwy in "King of Hearts" (1978).

DeVRIES, JON. Born Mar. 26, 1947 in NYC. Graduate Bennington Col., Pasadena Playhouse. Debut 1977 OB in "The Cherry Orchard," followed by "Agamemnon," "The Ballad of Soapy Smith," "Titus Andronicus," "the dreamer examines his pillow." Bdwy in "The Inspector General," "Devour the Snow," "Major Barbara," "Execution of Justice."

DEWAR, JOHN. Born Jan. 24, 1953 in Evanston, Il. Graduate UMinn. Bdwy debut 1987 in "Les Miserables."

DEWHURST, COLLEEN. Born June 3, 1926 in Montreal, Can. Attended Downer Col., AADA. Bdwy debut 1952 in "Desire under the Elms," followed by "Tamburlaine the Great," "The Country Wife," "Caligula," "All the Way Home," "Great Day in the Morning," "Ballad of the Sad Cafe," "More Stately Mansions," "All Over," "Mourning Becomes Electra," "Moon for the Misbegotten," "Who's Afraid of Virginia Woolf?," "An Almost Perfect Person," "The Queen and the Rebels," "You Can't Take It with You," "Ah, Wilderness ," "Long Day's Journey into Night" (1988) OB in "The Taming of the Shrew," "The Eagle Has Two Heads," "Camille," "Macbeth," "Children of Darkness" for which she received a 1958 Theatre World Award, "Antony and Cleopatra," "Hello and Goodbye," "Good Woman of Setzuan," "Hamlet," "Are You Now or Have You Ever . . .?, "Taken in Marriage," "My Gene."

DeWOLF, CECILIA. Born May 9, 1952 in Glen Cove, NY. Graduate DenverU, PennStU, Columbia. OB in "Beautiful Dreamer" (1986), followed by "Family Life."

DIAMOND, DENNIS. Born Aug. 19, 1949 in NYC. Bdwy debut 1989 in "Largely New York."

DILLON, MIA. Born July 9, 1955 in Colorado Springs, CO. Graduate Penn State U. Bdwy debut 1977 in "Equus," followed by "Da," "Once a Catholic," "Crimes of the Heart," "The Corn Is Green," "Hay Feaver," OB in "The Crucible," "Summer," "Waiting for the Parade," "Crimes of the Heart," "Fables for Friends," "Scenes from La Vie de Boheme," "Three Sisters," "Wednesday," "Roberta in Concert," "Come Back Little Sheba," "Vienna Notes," "George White's Scandals," "Lady Moonsong, Mr. Monsoon," "Almost Perfect."

DiMEO, DONNA. Born Mar. 6, 1964 in Brooklyn, NY. Debut 1989 in "Jerome Robbins' Broadway."

DISHY, BOB. Born in Brooklyn, NY. Graduate Syracuse U. Bdwy debut 1955 in "Damn Yankees," followed by "Can-Can," "Flora the Red Menace," "Something Different," "The Goodbye People," "A Way of Life," "Creation of the World and Other Business," "American Millionaire," "Sly Fox," "Murder at the Howard Johnson's," "Grownups," "Cafe Crown," OB in "Chic," "When the Owl Screams," "Wrecking Ball," "By Jupiter," "The Unknown Soldier and His Wife," "What's Wrong with This Picture?," "Cafe Crown."

DISPENZA, JOE. Born July 18, 1961 in Buffalo, NY. Graduate SUNY. Debut OB 1988 in "Fiorello."

DIXON, MacINTYRE. Born Dec. 22, 1931 in Everett, MA. Graduate Emerson Col. Bdwy debut 1965 in "Xmas in Las Vegas," followed by "Cop-Out," "Story Theatre," "Metamorphosis," "Twigs," "Over Here!," "Once in a Lifetime," "Alice in Wonderland," OB in "Quare Fellow," "Plays for Bleecker Street," "Stewed Prunes," "Cat's Pajamas," "Three Sisters," "3×3," "Second City," "Mad Show," "Meow!," "Lotta," "Rubbers," "Conjuring an Event," "His Majesty the Devil," "Tomfoolery," "A Christmas Carol," "Times and Appetites of Toulouse-Lautrec," "Room Service," "Sills and Company," "Little Murders," "Much Ado About Nothing," "Winter's Tale," "Arms and the Man."

DODSON, COLLEEN. Born May 16, 1954 in Chicago, IL. Graduate UIl. Debut 1981 OB in "The Matinee Kids," followed by "Pal Joey," "Holding Patterns," "Breaks," Bdwy 1982 in "Nine."

DON, CARL. Born Dec. 15, 1916 in Vitebsk, Russia. Attended Western Reserve U. Bdwy debut 1954 in "Anastasia," followed by "Romanoff and Juliet," "Dear Me, the Sky Is Falling," "The Relapse," "The Tenth Man," "Zalmen," "Wings," OB in "Richard III," "Twelfth Night," "Winterset," "Arms and the Man," "Between Two Thieves," "He Who Gets Slapped," "Jacobowsky and the Colonel," "Carnival," "The Possessed," "Three Acts of Recognition," "The Golem," "Cafe Crown."

DONNELLY, DONAL. Born July 6, 1931 in Bradford, Eng. Bdwy debut 1966 in "Philadelphia, Here I Come," followed by "A Day in the Death of Joe Egg," "Sleuth," "The Faith Healer," "The Elephant Man," "Execution of Justice," "Sherlock's Last Case," "Ghetto," OB in "My Astonishing Self" (solo performance), "The Chalk Garden," "Big Maggie."

DONOHOE, ROB. Born Dec. 25, 1950 in Bossier City, LA. Graduate ENewMxU, AmThArts. Debut 1987 OB in "The Long Boat," followed by "The Last Resort," "Leave it to Jane."

DORSEY, FERN. Born Mar. 29, 1963 in NYC. Graduate NorthwesternU. Debut 1986 OB in "The Dispute," followed by "Madame Bovary."

DOWNEY, ROMA. Born in Derry, N. Ireland. Graduate Brighton Polytechnic. Debut 1987 OB in "Tamara," followed by "Ghosts," "Love's Labour's Lost," "Arms and the Man."

DOYLE, JACK. Born June 7, 1955 in Brooklyn, NY. Graduate Adelphi U. Debut 1982 OB in "New Faces of '52," followed by "Tomfoolery."

DRAPER, JASE. Born Sept. 26, 1962 in Bronxville, NY. Attended NorthwesternU. Debut 1987 OB in "Take Me Along," followed by "Madame Bovary."

DRUMMOND, ALICE. Born May 21, 1929 in Pawtucket, RI. Attended Pembroke Col. Bdwy debut 1963 in "Ballad of the Sad Cafe," followed by "Malcolm," "The Chinese," "Thieves," "Summer Brave," "Some of My Best Friends," "You Can't Take It with You," OB in "Royal Gambit," "Go Show Me a Dragon," "Sweet of You to Say So," "Gallows Humor," "American Dream," "Giants' Dance," "Carpenters," "Charles Abbot & Son," "God Says There Is No Peter Ott," "Enter a Free Man," "Memory of Two Mondays," "Secret Service," "Boy Meets Girls," "Savages," "Killings on the Last Line," "Knuckle," "Wonderland," "Endgame," "Niedecker."

DUDLEY, CRAIG. Born Jan. 22, 1945 in Sheepshead Bay, NY. Graduate AADA, AmThWing. Debut 1970 OB in "Macbeth," followed by "Zou," "I Have Always Believed in Ghosts," "Othello," "War and Peace," "Dial 'M' for Murder," "Misalliance."

DUELL, WILLIAM. Born Aug. 30, 1923 in Corinth, NY. Attended IllWesleyan, Yale. OB in "Portrait of the Artist . . .," "Barroom Monks," "A Midsummer Night's Dream," "Henry IV," "Taming of the Shrew," "The Memorandum," "Threepenny Opera," "Loves of Cass McGuire," "Romance Language," "Hamlet," Bdwy in "A Cook for Mr. General," "Ballad of the Sad Cafe," "Ilya, Darling," "1776," "Kings," "Stages," "The Inspector General," "The Marriage of Figaro," "Our Town."

DUFF-MacCORMICK, CARA. Born Dec. 12, in Woodstock, Can. Attended AADA. Debut 1969 OB in "Love Your Crooked Neighbor," followed by "The Wager," "Macbeth," "A Musical Merchant of Venice," "Ladyhouse Blues," "The Philanderer," "Bonjour, La, Bonjour," "Journey to Gdansk," "The Dining Room," "All the Nice People," "Faulkner's Bicycle," "Earthworms," "The Acting Lesson," "Craig's Wife," "Gus and Al," Bdwy in "Moonchildren" (1972) for which she received a Theatre World Award, "Out Cry," "Animals."

DUKES, DAVID. Born June 6, 1945 in San Francisco, CA. Attended Mann Col. Bdwy debut 1971 in "School for Wives," followed by "Don Juan," "The Play's the Thing," "The Visit," "Chemin de Fer," "Holiday," "Rules of the Game," "Love for Love," "Travesties," "Dracula," "Bent," "Amadeus," "M. Butterfly," OB in "Rebel Women."

DURANG, CHRISTOPHER. Born Jan. 2, 1949 in Montclair, NJ. Graduate Harvard, Yale. Debut 1976 OB in "Das Lusitania Songspiel," followed by "The Hotel Play," "Sister Mary Ignatius Explains It All," "The Birthday Present," "The Marriage of Betty and Boo," "Laughing Wild," "UBU."

DUSSAULT, NANCY. Born June 30, 1936 in Pensacola, FL. Graduate Northwestern U. Debut 1958 OB in "Diversions," followed by "Street Scene," "Dr. Willy Nilly," "The Cradle Will Rock," "No for an Answer," "Whispers on the Wind," "Trelawny of the Wells," "Detective Story," Bdwy in "Do Re Mi" (1960) for which she received a Theatre World Award, "Sound of Music," "Bajour," "Carousel," "Finian's Rainbow," "Side by Side by Sondheim," "Into the Woods."

EASTON, EDWARD. Born Oct. 21, 1942 in Moline, IL. Graduate Lincoln Col., UIll., Neighborhood Playhouse. Debut 1967 OB in "Party on Greenwich Avenue," followed by "Middle of the Night," "Summer Brave," "Sunday Afternoon," "The Education of Miss February," "The Little Foxes."

EDE, GEORGE. Born Dec. 22, 1931 in San Francisco, CA. Bdwy debut 1969 in "A Flea in Her Ear," followed by "Three Sisters," "The Changing Room," "The Visit," "Chemin de Fer," "Holiday," "Love for Love," "Rules of the Game," "Member of the Wedding," "Lady from the Sea," "A Touch of the Poet," "Philadelphia Story," "Aren't We All?," OB in "The Philanderer," "The American Clock," "The Broken Pitcher," "No End of Blame," "Sullivan and Gilbert," "Mistress of the Inn."

EDELHART, YVETTE. Born Mar. 26, 1928 in Oak Park, IL. Attended Wright Col. Debut 1984 OB in "Office Mishegoss," followed by "Home Movies," "Night Must Fall," "The Miser," "Heart of a Dog," "Peg o My Heart."

EDELMAN, GREGG. Born Sept. 12, 1958 in Chicago, IL. Graduate Northwestern U. Bdwy debut 1982 in "Evita," followed by "Oliver!," "Cats," "Cabaret," OB in "Weekend," "Shop on Main Street," "Forbidden Broadway," "She Loves Me," "Babes in Arms."

EDENFIELD, DENNIS. Born July 23, 1946 in New Orleans, LA. Debut 1970 OB in "The Evil That Men Do," followed by "I Have Always Believed in Ghosts," "Nevertheless They Laugh," "Cowboy," Bdwy in "Irene" ('73), "A Chorus Line."

EDMEAD, WENDY. Born July 6, 1956 in NYC. Graduate NYCU. Bdwy debut 1974 in "The Wiz," followed by "Stop the World . . .," "America," "Dancin'," "Encore," "Cats."

EDWARDS, ALISON. Born Aug. 7, 1953 in Jackson, MS. Graduate Boston U. Debut 1986 OB in "Night Watch," followed by "King John."

EDWARDS, BRANDT. Born Mar. 22, 1947 in Holly Springs, MS. Graduate UMiss. NY debut off and on Bdwy 1975 in "A Chorus Line," followed by "42nd Street."

EDWARDS, BURT. Born Jan. 11, 1928 in Richmond, VA. Graduate UVa. Debut 1949 OB in "Fifth Horseman of the Apocalypse," followed by "Cenci," "The Camel Has His Nose under the Tent," "Cocktail Hour," Bdwy 1985 in "The King and I."

EDWARDS, DAVID. Born Dec. 13, 1957 in NYC. Graduate NYU. Bdwy debut 1972 in "The Rothschilds," followed by "The Best Little Whorehouse in Texas," "42nd Street," "A Chorus Line," OB in "Wish You Were Here," "Bittersuite," "Bittersuite, One More Time."

EDWARDS, RANDALL. Born June 15, in Atlanta, GA. Attended CalInst of Arts. Debut 1983 OB in "Upstairs at O'Neal's," Bdwy 1985 in "Biloxi Blues," followed by "Legs Diamond."

EICHELBERGER, ETHYL. Born July 17, 1945 in Pekins, IL. Graduate AADA. Debut 1974 OB with Charles Ludlum's Ridiculous Theatre Co., followed by "Comedy of Errors," "Measure for Measure," "Herd of Buffalo."

EISENBERG, AVNER. Born Aug. 26, 1948 in Atlanta, GA. Graduate Tulane, Ga St.U., NYU. U of Washington. Debut OB 1984 in "Avner the Eccentric," Bdwy in "The Comedy of Errors," "Ghetto."

ELIO, DONNA MARIE. Born Oct. 30, 1962 in Paterson, NJ. Bdwy debut 1974 in "Gypsy," followed by "Merrily We Roll Along," "Smile," "Jerome Robbins' Broadway."

ELIOT, DREW. Born in Newark, NJ. Graduate Columbia, RADA. OB in "The Fairy Garden," "Dr. Faustus," "Servant of Two Masters," "Henry V," "Stephen D," "Sjt. Musgrave's Dance," "Deadly Game," "Taming of the Shrew," "Appear and Show Cause," "The Visit," Bdwy in "Elizabeth the Queen," "The Physicists," "Romulus."

ELLIOTT, KENNETH. Born June 15, 1955 in Indianapolis, IN. Graduate Northwestern U. Debut 1985 OB in "Vampire Lesbians of Sodom," followed by "Pyscho Beach Party," "Zero Positive," "Times Square Angel," "The Lady in Question."

ELLIOTT, R BRUCE. Born Sept. 3, 1949 in Renton, Wa. Graduate So. Meth. U. Austin Col. Debut 1984 OB in "I Am a Teacher," followed by "Leave It to Jane," "Hamlet."

ELLIS, FRASER. Born May 1, 1957 in Boulder, CO. Graduate UCo. Bdwy debut 1982 in "A Chorus Line."

ELMORE, STEVE. Born July 12, 1936 in Niangua, MO. Debut 1961 in "Madame Aphrodite," followed by "Golden Apple," "Enclave," Bdwy in "Camelot," "Jenny," "Fade in Fade Out," "Kelly," "Company," "Nash at 9," "Chicago," "42nd St."

EMERY, LISA. Born Jan. 29, in Pittsburgh, PA. Graduate Hollins Col. Debut 1981 OB in "In Connecticut," followed by "Talley & Son," "Dalton's Back," Bdwy in "Passion" (1983), "Burn This," "Rumors."

EMMET, ROBERT. Born Oct. 3, 1952 in Denver, CO. Graduate UWash. Debut 1976 OB in "The Mousetrap," followed by "The Seagull," "Blue Hotel," "Miss Jairus," "Hamlet," "Deathwatch," "Much Ado About Nothing," "Songs and Ceremonies," "Mass Appeal," "Macbeth," "Bell, Book and Candle," "Comes the Happy Hour," "The Gift," "Merchant of Venice," "Arms and the Man," "The Lady from the Sea," "Two Gentlemen from Verona," "Andromache," "Hamlet," Bdwy in "Devil's Disciple" (1988).

ENGLISH, DONNA. Born Jan. 13, 1962 in Norman, OK. Graduate NorthwesternU. Bdwy debut 1987 in "Broadway," OB in "Company," "The Last Musical Comedy," "Kiss Me Quick."

EPSTEIN, ALVIN. Born May 14, 1925 in NYC. Attended Queens Col. Appeared on Bdwy with Marcel Marceau, and in "King Lear," "Waiting for Godot" (1956), "From A to Z," "No Strings," "Passion of Josef D," "Postmark Zero," "A Kurt Weill Cabaret," OB in "Purple Dust," "Pictures in a Hallway," "Clerambard," "Endgame" (1958/1984), "Whores, Wares and Tin Pan Alley," "A Place without Doors," "Crossing Niagara," "Beckett Plays," "Kurt Weill Cabaret," "Waltz of the Toreadors," "6 Characters in Search of an Author."

ERDE, SARA. Born Mar. 18, 1970 in NYC. Debut 1987 OB in "Roosters," followed by "Dancing Feet," "A Midsummer Night's Dream," "Don Juan of Saville."

ERICKSON, DAN. Born Mar. 17, 1962 in Great Falls, MT. Graduate Mt. St. U. Debut OB 1988 in "Desire."

ESPOSITO, GIANCARLO. Born Apr. 26, 1958 in Copenhage, Den. Bdwy debut 1968 in "Maggie Flynn," followed by "The Me Nobody Knows," "Lost in the Stars," "Seesaw," "Merrily We Roll Along," "Don't Get God Started," OB in "Zooman and the Sign" for which he received a Theatre World Award, "Keyboard," "Who Loves the Dancer," "House of Ramon Iglesias," "Do Lord Remember Me," "Balm in Gilead," "Anchorman."

ESTERMAN, LAURA. Born Apr. 12 in NYC. Attended Radcliffe. LAMDA. Debut 1969 OB in "The Time of Your Life," followed by "Pig Pen," "Carpenters," "Ghosts," "Macbeth," "The Seagull," "Rubbers," "Yankees 3, Detroit 0," "Golden Boy," "Out of Our Father's House," "The Master and Margarita," "Chinchilla," "Dusa, Fish, Stas and Vi," "A Midsummer Night's Dream," "The Recruiting Officer," "Oedipus the King," "Two Fish in the Sky," "Mary Barnes," "Tamara," Bdwy in "Waltz of the Toreadors" (1973), "God's Favorite," "Teibele and Her Demon," "The Suicide," "Metamorphosis."

ESTEY, SUELLEN. Born Nov. 21, in Mason City, IA. Graduate Stephens Col., Northwestern U. Debut 1970 OB in "Some Other Time," followed by "June Moon," "Buy Bonds Buster," "Smile, Smile, Smile," "Carousel," "Lullaby of Broadway," "I Can't Keep Running," "The Guys in the Truck," "Stop the World . . .," "Bittersuite—One More Time," "Passionate Extremes," "Sweeney Todd," Bdwy in "The Selling of the President" (1972), "Barnum," "Sweethearts in Concert," "Sweeney Todd" (1989).

EVANS, DILLON. Born Jan. 2, 1921 in London, Eng. Attended RADA. Bdwy debut 1950 in "The Lady's Not for Burning," followed by "School for Scandal," "Streamers," "Hamlet," "Ivanov," "Vivat! Vivat Regina!," "Jockey Club Stakes," "Dracula," "Death and the King's Horseman" (LC), OB in "Druid's Rest," "Rondelay," "The Littles Foxes," "Playing with Fire," "The Film Society."

EVANS, HARVEY. Born Jan. 7, 1941 in Cincinnati, OH. Bdwy debut 1957 in "New Girl in Town," followed by "West Side Story," "Redhead," "Gypsy," "Anyone Can Whistle," "Hello, Dolly!," "George M!," "Our Town," "The Boy Friend," "Follies," "Barnum," "La Cage aux Folles," OB in "Sextet."

FABER, RON. Born Feb. 16, 1933 in Milwaukee, WI. Graduate Marquette U. Debut 1959 OB in "An Enemy of the People," followed by "The Exception and the Rule," "America Hurrah," "They Put Handcuffs on Flowers," "Dr. Selavy's Magic Theatre," "Troilus and Cressida," "The Beauty Part," "Woyzeck," "St. Joan of the Stockyards," "Jungle of Cities," "Scenes from Everyday Life," "Mary Stuart," "3 by Pirandello," "Times and Appetites of Toulouse-Lautrec," "Hamlet," "Johnstown Vindicator," "Don Juan of Seville," "Between the Acts," Bdwy in "Medea" (1973), "First Monday in October."

FARINA, MARILYN J. Born Apr. 9, 1947 in NYC. Graduate Sacred Heart Col. Debut 1985 OB in "Nunsense."

FARONE, FELICIA. Born Mar. 5, 1961 in Orange, NJ. Graduate Montclair St. Col. Debut 1985 OB in "Rabboni," followed by "The Pajama Game," "Fiorello!."

FASS, ROBERT. Born Aug. 15, 1958 in Wantagh, NY. Graduate MacAlester Col. Debut 1984 OB in "The Desk Set," followed by "Poland 1931," "The Male Animal."

FAYE, JOEY. Born July 12, 1910 in NYC. Bdwy debut 1938 in "Sing Out the News," followed by "Room Service," "Meet the People," "The Man Who Came to Dinner," "The Milky Way," "Boy Meets Girl," "Streets of Paris," "Allah Be Praised," "The Duchess Misbehaves," "Tidbits of 1948," "High Button Shoes," "Top Banana," "Tender Trap," "Man of La Mancha," "70 Girls 70," "Grind," OB in "Lyle," "Naomi Court," "Awake and Sing," "Coolest Cat in Town," "The Ritz," "Enter Laughing," "1-2-3-4-5."

FELDSHUH, TOVAH. Born Dec. 28, 1953 in NYC. Graduate Sarah Lawrence Col., UMn. Bdwy debut 1973 in "Cyrano," followed by "Dreyfus in Rehearsal," "Rodgers and Hart," "Yentl," for which she received a Theatre World Award, "Sarava," "Lend Me a Tenor," OB in "Yentl, the Yeshiva Boy," "Straws in the Wind," "Three Sisters," "She Stoops to Conquer," "Springtime for Henry," "The Time of Your Life," "Children of the Sun," "The Last of the Red Hot Lovers," "Mistress of the Inn."

FERGUSON, LOU. Born Aug. 8, 1944 in Trinidad, WI. Debut 1970 OB in "A Season in the Congo," followed by "Night World," "La Gente," "Shoe Shine Parlor," "The Defense," "Rum an' Coca Cola," "Remembrance," "Raisin in the Sun," "Member of the Wedding."

FERLAND, DANIELLE. Born Jan. 31, 1971 in Derby, CT. Debut 1983 OB in "Sunday in the Park with George," followed by "Paradise," Bdwy in "Sunday in the Park with George" (1984), "Into the Woods" for which she received a Theatre World Award.

FERSTENBERG, BERNARD. Born June 3, 1951 in Brooklyn, NY. Graduate SUNY. Debut 1989 OB in "The Thirteenth Chair."

FIEDLER, JOHN. Born Feb. 3, 1925 in Plateville, Wi. Attended Neighborhood Playhouse. OB in "The Seagull," "Sing Me No Lullaby," "The Terrible Swift Sword," "The Raspberry Picker," "The Frog Prince," "Raisin in the Sun," "Marathon '88," Bdwy in "One Eye Closed" (1954), "Howie," "Raisin in the Sun," "Harold," "The Odd Couple," "Our Town."

FIELD, CRYSTAL. Born Dec. 10, 1942 in NYC. Attended Juilliard. Graduate Hunter Col. Debut OB in "A Country Scandal" (1960) and most recently in "A Matter of Life and Death," "The Heart That Eats Itself," "Ruzzante Returns from the Wars," "An Evening of British Music Hall," "Ride That Never Was," "House Arrest," "Us," "Beverly's Yard Sale," "Bruno's Donuts," "Coney Island Kid."

FINKEL, FYVUSH. Born Oct. 9, 1922 in Brooklyn, NY. Bdwy debut 1970 in "Fiddler on the Roof" (also 1981 revival) followed by "Cafe Crown" (1989), OB in "Gorky," "Little Shop of Horrors," "Cafe Crown."

FITZGERALD, FERN. Born Jan. 7, 1947 in Valley Stream, NY. Bdwy debut 1976 in "Chicago," followed by "A Chorus Line."

FITZGERALD, GERALDINE. Born Nov. 24, 1914 in Dublin, Ire. Bdwy debut 1938 in "Heartbreak House," followed by "Sons and Soldiers," "Doctor's Dilemma," "King Lear," "Hide and Seek," "Ah, Wilderness," "The Shadow Box," "A Touch of the Poet," OB in "Cave Dwellers," "Pigeons," "Long Day's Journey into Night," "Everyman and Roach," "Danger: Memory!" (LC), "Streetsongs."

FLAGG, TOM. Born March 30 in Canton, OH. Attended KentState U., AADA. Debut 1975 OB in "The Fantasticks," followed by "Give Me Liberty," "The Subject Was Roses," "Lola," "Red, Hot and Blue." "Episode 26," "Dazy," "Dr. Dietrick's Process," Bdwy in "Legend" (1976), "Shenandoah," "Players."

FLANAGAN, FIONNULA. Born Dec. 10, 1941 in Dublin, Ire. Attended Fribourg U. NY debut 1968 in "Lovers" (LC), followed by "Ghosts," on Bdwy in "The Incomparable Max" (1971)., "Ulysses in Nighttown."

FLANAGAN, PAULINE. Born June 29, 1925 in Sligo, Ire. Debut 1958 OB in "Ulysses in Nighttown," followed by "Pictures in the Hallway," "Later," "Antigone," "The Crucible," "The Plough and the Stars," "Summer," "Close of Play," "In Celebration," "Without Apologies," "Yeats, a Celebration," Bdwy in "God and Kate Murphy," "The Living Room," "The Innocents," "The Father," "Medea," "Steaming," "Corpse."

FLATE, JOHN-MICHAEL. Born Aug. 24, 1959 in Framingham, MA. Attended Mass. Col. of Art. Bdwy debut 1989 in "Starmites."

FLEISS, JANE. Born Jan. 28 in NYC. Graduate NYU. Debut 1979 OB in "Say Goodnight, Gracie," followed by "Grace," "The Beaver Coat," "The Harvesting," "D.," "Second Man," "Of Mice and Men," "Niedecker," Bdwy in "5th of July" (1981), "Crimes of the Heart," "I'm Not Rappaport."

FLETCHER, SUSANN. Born Sept. 7, 1955 in Wilmington, DE. Graduate Longwood Col. Bdwy debut 1980 in "The Best Little Whorehouse in Texas," followed by "Raggedy Ann," "Jerome Robbins' Broadway."

FOGARTY, MARY. Born in Manchester, NH. Debut 1959 OB in "The Well of Saints," followed by "Shadow and Substance," "Nathan the Wise," "Bonjour La Bonjour," "Family Comedy," "Steel Magnolias," Bdwy in "The National Health," "Watch on the Rhine" (1980), "Of the Fields Lately."

FOLLANSBEE, JULIE. Born in Sept. 1919 in Chicago, IL. Graduate Bryn Mawr. Debut 1949 OB in "The Fifth Horseman," followed by "Luminosity without Radiance," "Johnny Doesn't Live Here Anymore," "Epitaph for George Dillon," "Maromichaelis," "Brothers Karamazov," "Excelsior," "In the Summer House," "Road to the Graveyard," "Day of the Dolphin," "Bell, Book and Candle," "Crime and Punishment," "Pas de Deux," "Brightness Falling," "Heathen Valley."

FOLS, CRAIG. Born Oct. 23, 1960 in Jamestown, NY. Debut OB 1986 in "Creeps," followed by "Nasty Little Secrets."

FONTAINE, LUTHER. Born Apr. 14, 1947 in Kansas City, Ks. Graduate UMo, NYU. Bdwy debut 1973 in "Two Gentlemen of Verona," followed by "Timbuktu," "The First," OB in "All Night Strut," "Feeling Good," "Dream on Monkey Mountain," "Bojangles," "Back in the Big Time," "Prizes."

FORTGANG, AMY. Born Sept. 5, 1960 on Long Island, NY. Graduate Bucknell U. Debut 1987 OB in "Too Many Girls," Bdwy in "Oh! Calcutta!" (1988).

FOSTER, FRANCES. Born June 11 in Yonkers, NY. Bdwy debut 1955 in "The Wisteria Trees," followed by "Nobody Loves an Albatross," "Raisin in the Sun," "The River Niger," "First Breeze of Summer," OB in "Take a Giant Step," "Edge of the City," "Tammy and the Doctor," "The Crucible," "Happy Ending," "Day of Absence," "An Evening of One Acts," "Man Better Man," "Brotherhood," "Akokawe," "Rosalee Pritchett," "Sty of the Blind Pig," "Ballet Behind the Bridge," "Good Woman of Setzuan" (LC), "Behold! Cometh the Vanderkellans," "Origin," "Boesman and Lena," "Do Lord Remember Me," "Henrietta," "Welcome to Black River," "House of Shadows," "Miracle Worker," "You Have Come Back."

FOSTER, GLORIA. Born Nov. 15, 1936 in Chicago, IL. Attended IllStU, Goodman Th. Debut 1963 OB in "In White America," followed by "Medea" for which she received a Theatre World Award, "Yerma," "A Hand Is on the Gate," "Black Visions," "Cherry Orchard," "Agamemnon," "Coriolanus," "Mother Courage," "Long Days Journey into Night," "Trespassing," "Forbidden City."

FOWLER, BETH. Born Nov. 1, 1940 in NJ. Graduate Caldwell Col. Bdwy debut 1970 in "Gantry," followed by "A Little Night Music," "Over Here," "1600 Pennsylvania Avenue," "Peter Pan," "Baby," "Teddy and Alice," "Sweeney Todd" (1989), OB in "Preppies" "The Blessing," "Sweeney Todd."

FOWLER, CLEMENT. Born Dec. 27, 1924 in Detroit, MI. Graduate Wayne StU. Bdwy debut 1951 in "Legend of Lovers," followed by "The Cold Wind and the Warm," "Fragile Fox," "The Sunshine Boys," "Hamlet (1964), OB in "The Eagle Has Two Heads," "House Music," "Transformation of Benno," "The Inheritors," "Paradise Lost," "The Time of Your Life," "Children of the Sun," "Highest Standard of Living," "Cymbeline."

FOWLER, SCOTT. Born March 22, 1967 in Medford, MA. Debut 1989 on Bdwy in "Jerome Robbins' Broadway."

FOX, COLIN. Born Nov. 20, 1938 in Aldershot, Can. Attended UWestern Ontario. Bdwy debut 1968 in "Soldiers," followed by "Pack Of Lies." OB in "Importance of Being Earnest," "Declassee," "Love's Labour's Lost," "Anteroom," "Resistance," "Nasty Little Secrets."

FRANCINE, ANNE. Born Aug. 8, 1917 in Philadelphia, PA. Bdwy debut in "Marriage Is for Single People," (1945), followed by "By the Beautiful Sea," "The Great Sebastians," "Tenderloin," "Mame," "A Broadway Musical," "Snow White," "Mame" (1983), "Anything Goes," OB in "Guitar," "Valmouth," "Asylum," "Are You Now or Have You Ever Been?"

FRANCIS, JOSEPH V. Born in Detroit, MI. Graduate CCNY. Debut OB 1985 in "Mark VIII:xxxvi," followed by "Four Loves in Three Acts," "Golden Leg."

FRANCIS-JAMES, PETER. Born Sept. 16, 1956 in Chicago, IL. Graduate RADA. Debut 1979 OB in "Julius Caesar," followed by "Long Day's Journey into Night," "Antigone," "Richard III," "Romeo and Juliet," "Enrico IV," "Cymbeline."

FRANKLIN, BONNIE. Born Jan. 6, 1944 in Santa Monica, CA. Attended Smith Col., UCLA. Debut OB 1968 in "Your Own Thing," followed by "Dames at Sea," "Drat!," "Carousel" (JB), "Frankie and Johnny in the Claire De Lune," Bdwy in "Applause" (1970) for which she received a Theatre World Award.

FRANZ, JOY. Born in 1944 in Modesto, Ca. Graduate UMo. Debut 1969 OB in "Of Thee I Sing," followed by "Jacques Brel Is Alive . . .," "Out of This World," "Curtains," "I Can't Keep Running in Place," "Tomfoolery," "Penelope," "Bittersuite," Bdwy in "Sweet Charity," "Lysistrata," "A Little Night Music," "Pippin," "Musical Chairs," "Into the Woods."

FRASER, BERT. Born Mar. 20, 1940 in Rocky Ford, CO. Graduate UDenver. OB in "The Real Wife Beater," "Life with Father," "The Gang's All Here," "Night of January 16," "The Baker's Wife," "The Fortunate Instant."

FRATANTONI, DIANE. Born Mar. 29, 1956 in Wilmington, DE. Bdwy debut 1979 in "A Chorus Line," followed by "Cats."

FRAZER, SUSANNA. Born Mar. 28 in NYC. Debut 1980 OB in "Kind Lady," followed by "The Enchanted," "A Doll's House," "Scenes from American Life," "Old Friends and Roommates," "Something Old, Something New," "Times and Appetites of Toulouse-Lautrec," "A Flash of Lightning," "5th of July."

FRECHETTE, PETER. Born Oct. 3, 1956 in Warwick, RI. Graduate U RI. Debut OB 1979 in "The Hornbeam Maze," followed by "Journey's End," "In Cahoots," "Harry Ruby's Songs My Mother Never Sang," "Pontifications on Pigtails and Puberty," "Scotter Thomas Makes it to the Top of the World," "We're Home," "Flora, the Red Menace," "Eastern Standard," Bdwy in "Eastern Standard," (1989) for which he received a Theatre World Award.

FREED, SAM. Born Aug. 29, 1948 in York, PA. Graduate Penn St. U. Debut 1972 OB in "The Proposition," followed by "What's a Nice Country Like You . . .," "Dance on a Country Grave," "Morocco," Bdwy in "Candide" (1974), "Torch Song Trilogy."

FREEMAN, JONATHAN. Born Feb. 5, 1950 in Bay Village, OH. Graduate Ohio U. Debut 1974 OB in "The Miser," followed by "Bil Baird Marionette Theatre," "Babes in Arms," "In a Pig's Valise," Bdwy in "Sherlock Holmes," "Platinum."

FREEMAN, MORGAN. Born June 1, 1937 in Memphis, Tn. Attended LACC. Bdwy debut 1967 in "Hello, Dolly!," followed by "The Mighty Gents," "OB in "Ostrich Feathers," "Niggerlovers," "Exhibition," "Black Visions," "Cockfight," "White Pelicans," "Julius Caesar," "Coriolanus," "Mother Courage," "The Connection," "The World of Ben Caldwell," "Buck," "The Gospel at Colonus," (also Bdwy) "Medea and the Doll," "Driving Miss Daisy."

FREEMAN, TOM. Born Jan. 3, 1964 in Seattle, WA. Debut 1987 OB in "Kismet," followed by "The Hired Man."

FRENCH, ARTHUR. Born in NYC. Attended Bklyn Col. Debut 1962 OB in "Raisin' Hell in the Sun," followed by "Ballad of Bimshire," "Day of Absence," "Happy Ending," "Brotherhood," "Perry's Mission," "Rosalee Pritchett," "Moonlight Arms," "Dark Tower," "Brownsville Raid," "Nevis Mt. Dew," "Julius Caesar," "Friends," "Court of Miracles," "The Beautiful LaSalles," "Blues for a Gospel Queen," "Black Girl," "Driving Miss Daisy," "The Spring Thing," "George Washington Slept Here," Bdwy in "Ain't Supposed to Die a Natural Death," "The Iceman Cometh," "All God's Chillun Got Wings," "The Resurrection of Lady Lester," "You Can't Take it With You," "Design for Living," "Ma Rainey's Black Bottom."

FRID, JONATHAN. Born Dec. 1924 in Hamilton, Ont., Can. Graduate McMaster U., Yale, RADA. Debut 1959 OB in "The Golem," followed by "Henry IV, Parts I & II," "The Moon in the Yellow River," "The Burning," "Murder in the Cathedral," "Fools and Fiends,"Bdwy in "Roar Like a Dove" (1964), "Arsenic and Old Lace" (1986).

FRIEDMAN, PETER. Born Apr. 24, 1949 in NYC. Debut 1971 OB in "James Joyce Memorial Theatre," followed by "Big and Little," "A Soldier's Play," "Mr. and Mrs.," "And a Nightingale Sang," "Dennis," "The Common Pursuit," "Marathon '88," "The Heidi Chronicles," Bdwy in "The Visit," "Chemin de Fer," "Love for Love," "Rules of the Game," "Piaf!," "Execution of Justice," "The Heidi Chronicles."

FUGLEI, KATE. Born Aug. 13 in Omaha, NE. Graduate Coe Col. Debut OB 1989 in "Love's Labours Lost."

FUJII, TIMM. Born May 26, 1952 in Detroit, MI. Attended CalStateU. Bdwy debut in "Pacific Overtures" (1976), followed by "Chu Chem," OB in "Pacific Overtures" (1984), "Chu Chem."

GAIL, TIM. Born in Tokyo, Japan. Attended AADA. Debut 1985 OB in "Getting Married," followed by "Murder on Broadway," "The Business of America," "Charlie Dante," "Private Wars," "The Man of Destiny," "Dirty Hands," "Thighs Like Tina Turner," "2 More by Myers," "A Circle," "Peg a Heart."

GAINES, BOYD. Born May 11, 1953 in Atlanta, GA. Graduate Juilliard. Debut 1978 OB in "Spring Awakening," followed by "A Month in the Country," for which he received a Theatre World Award, BAM Theatre Co.'s "Winter's Tale," "The Barbarians," and "Johnny on a Spot," "Vikings," "Double Bass," "The Maderati," "The Heidi Chronicles," Bdwy in "The Heidi Chronicles" (1989).

GALANTE, LORI. Born Apr. 25, 1959 in Buffalo, NY. Attended SUNY, Fla. Atlantic U. Debut 1988 OB in "The Male Animal."

GALANTICH, TOM. Born in Brooklyn, NY. Debut 1985 OB in "On the 20th Century," followed by "Mademoiselle Colombe," Bdwy in "Into the Woods" (1989).

GALINDO, RAMON. Born June 3 in San Francisco, CA. Graduate U of Calif. Berkeley. Bdwy debut 1979 in "Carmelina," followed by "Merlin," "Cats," "Song and Dance," "Jerome Robins' Broadway," OB in "Funny Feet" (1987).

GAMACHE, LAURIE. Born Sept. 25, 1959 in Mayville, ND. Graduate Stephens Col. Bdwy debut 1982 in "A Chorus Line."

GARBER, VICTOR. Born Mar. 16, 1949 in London, Canada. Debut 1973 OB in "Ghosts," for which he received a Theatre World Award, followed by "Joe's Opera," "Cracks," "Wenceslas Square," "Love Letters," Bdwy in "Tartuffe," "Deathtrap," "Sweeney Todd," "They're Playing Our Song," "Little Me," "Noises Off," "You Never Can Tell," "Devil's Disciple," "Lend Me a Tenor."

GARRICK, BARBARA. Born Feb. 3, 1962 in NYC. Debut 1986 OB in "Today I Am a Fountain Pen," followed by "A Midsummer Night's Dream," "Rosencrantz and Guildenstern Are Dead," "Eastern Standard," Bdwy in "Eastern Standard" (1988).

GARRICK, KATHY. Born Sept. 4, 1957 in Los Angeles, CA. Graduate Immaculate Heart Col Debut 1985 OB in "In Trousers," followed by "Blame it on the Movies."

GAVON, IGORS. Born Nov. 14, 1937 in Latvia. Bdwy bow 1961 in "Carnival," followed by "Hello, Dolly!" "Marat/deSade," "Billy," "Sugar," "Mack and Mabel," "Musical Jubilee," "Strider," "42 St," OB in "Your Own Thing," "Promenade," "Exchange," "Nevertheless They Laugh," "Polly," "The Boss," "Biography: A Game," "Murder in the Cathedral."

GEDRICK, JASON. Born 1965 in Chicago, IL. Graduate Drake U. Debut 1988 OB in "Mrs. Dolly," Bdwy in "Our Town" (1989).

GEFFNER, DEBORAH. Born Aug. 26, 1952 in Pittsburgh, PA. Attended Juilliard, HB Studio. Debut 1978 OB in "Tenderloin," Bdwy in "Pal Joey," "A Chorus Line."

GEHMAN, MARTHA. Born May 15, 1955 in NYC. Graduate Sarah Lawrence Col. Debut 1984 OB in "Cinders," followed by "Day Room," "Baba Goya."

GELB, JODY. Born March 11 in Cincinnatti, OH. Graduate Boston U. Debut 1983 OB in "Wild Life," followed by "36 Dramatic Situations," "Love Suicides," "Baal," "Past Lives," "Marathon '89."

GELFER, STEVEN. Born Feb. 21, 1949 in Brooklyn, NY. Graduate NYU, IndU. Debut 1968 OB and Bdwy in "The Best Little Whorehouse in Texas," followed by "Cats."

GELKE, BECKY. Born Feb. 17, 1953 in Ft. Knox, KY. Graduate WKyU. Bdwy debut 1978 in "The Best Little Whorehouse in Texas," followed by "A Streetcar Named Desire" (1988), OB in "Altitude Sickness," "John Brown's Body," "Chamber Music," "To Whom It May Concern," "Two Gentlemen of Verona," "Bob's Guns."

GERACI, FRANK. Born Sept. 8, 1939 in Brooklyn, NY. Attended Yale. Debut 1961 OB in "Color of Darkness," followed by "Mr. Grossman," "Balm in Gilead," "The Fantasticks," "Tom Paine," "End of All Things Natural," "Union Street," "Uncle Vanya," "Success Story," "Hughie," "Merchant of Venice," "Three Zeks," "Taming of the Shrew," "The Lady from the Sea," "Rivals," "Deep Swimmer," "The Imaginary Invalid," "Candida," "Uncle Vanya," "Hedda Gabler," "Serious Co.," "Berenice," "The Philanderer," "Hedda Gabler," "All's Well That Ends Well," Bdwy in "Love Suicide at Schofield Barracks" (1972).

GERAGHTY, MARITA. Born Mar. 26, 1965 in Chicago, IL. Graduate UIll. Bdwy debut 1987 in "Coastal Disturbances," followed by "The Night of the Iguana," "The Heidi Chronicles."

GERARD, DANNY. Born May 29, 1977 in NYC. Bdwy debut 1986 in "Into the Light," followed by "Les Miserables," OB in "Today I Am a Fountain Pen," "Second Hurricane."

GERETY, PETER. Born May 17, 1940 in Providence, RI. Attended URI, Boston U. Debut 1964 OB in "In the Summer House," followed by "Othello," "Baal," "Six Characters in Search of an Author," Bdwy 1982 in "The Hothouse."

GERRINGER, ROBERT. Born May 12, 1926 in NYC. Graduate Fordham U., Pasadena Playhouse. Debut 1955 OB in "Thieves Carnival," followed by "Home," "The Birthday Party," "Much Ado About Nothing," Bdwy in "Pictures in the Hallway," "A Flea in Her Ear," "Andersonville Trial," "Waltz of the Toreadors," "After the Fall," "A Doll's House," "Hedda Gabler," "Hide and Seek."

GERROLL, DANIEL. Born Oct. 16, 1951 in London, Eng. Attended Central Sch. of Speech. Debut 1980 OB in "Slab Boys," followed by "Knuckle," and "Translations," for which he received a Theatre World Award, "The Caretaker," "Scenes from La Vie de Boheme," "The Knack," "Terra Nova," "Dr. Faustus," "Second Man," "Cheapside," "Bloody Poetry," "The Common Pursuit," "Woman in Mind," "Poets' Corner," "The Film Society," "Emerald City," "Arms and the Man," Bdwy in "Plenty" (1982).

GIAMATTI, MARCUS. Born Oct. 31, 1961 in New Haven, CT. Graduate Bowdoin Col. Debut OB 1989 in "Measure for Measure," followed by "Italian American Reconciliation," "All This and Moonlight."

GIANOPOULOS, DAVID. Born Aug. 9, 1959, Long Island, NY. Attended Pacific Conserv. of Perform. Arts. Debut 1987 OB in "Richard II," followed by "Henry IV, Part I," "Shoo Bob, Freddy."

GIBSON, JULIA. Born June 8, 1962 in Norman, OK. Graduate UIowa. NYU. Debut 1987 OB in "A Midsummer Night's Dream," followed by "Love's Labor's Lost."

GIBSON, THOMAS. Born July 3, 1962 in Charleston, SC. Graduate Juilliard. Debut 1985 OB in "Map of the World," followed by "Twelfth Night," "Bloody Poetry," "Marathon '87," "Two Gentlemen of Verona," "Class 1 Acts," "Marathon '88," Bdwy in "Hay Fever" (1985).

GILBORN, STEVEN. Born in New Rochelle, NY. Graduate Swarthmore Col., Stanford U. Bdwy debut 1973 in "Creeps," followed by "Basic Training of Pavlo Hummel," "Tartuffe," OB in "Rosmersholm," "Henry V," "Measure for Measure," "Ashes," "The Dybbuk," "Museum," "Shadow of a Gunman," "It's Hard to Be a Jew," "Isn't It Romantic," "Principia Scriptoriae," "Panache," "Festival of One Acts."

GILL, RAY. Born Aug. 1, 1950 in Bayonne, NJ. Attended Rider Col. Bdwy debut 1978 in "On the 20th Century" followed by "Pirates of Penzance," "The First," "They're Playing Our Song," "Sunday in the Park with George," OB in "A Bundle of Nerves," "Driving Miss Daisy."

GILLETTE, ANITA. Born Aug. 16, 1938 in Baltimore, MD. Debut 1960 OB in "Russell Patterson's Sketchbook," for which she received a Theatre World Award, followed by "Rich and Famous," "Dead Wrong," "Road Show," "Class 1 Acts," "The Blessing," Bdwy in "Carnival," "All American," "Mr. President," "Guys and Dolls," "Don't Drink the Water," "Cabaret," "Jimmy," "Chapter Two," "They're Playing Our Song," "Brighton Beach Memoirs."

GILPIN, JACK. Born May 31, 1951 in Boyce, VA. Harvard graduate. Debut 1976 OB in "Goodbye and Keep Cold," followed by "Shay," "The Soft Touch," "Beyond Therapy," "The Lady or the Tiger," "The Middle Ages," "The Rise of Daniel Rocket," "No Happy Ending," "Strange Behavior," "The Foreigner," "Marathon '86," "The Spring Thing," Bdwy in "Lunch Hour" (1980).

GINHORN, FRED. Born Oct. 5, 1956 in NYC. Graduate SUC. Debut OB 1989 in "The Sunshine Boys."

GIONSON, MEL DUANE. Born Feb. 23, 1954 in Honolulu, HI. Graduate UHi. Debut 1979 OB in "Richard II," followed by "Sunrise," "Monkey Music," "Behind Enemy Lines," "Station J," "Teahouse," "A Midsummer Night's Dream," "Empress of China," "Chip Shot," "Manoa Valley," "Ghashiram," "Shogun Macbeth," "Life of the Land," "Noiresque," "Three Sisters."

GIOSA, SUE. Born Nov. 23, 1958 in Connecticut. Graduate Queens Col., RADA, LAMDA. Debut OB 1988 in "Tamara."

GIRARDEAU, FRANK. Born Oct. 19, 1942 in Beaumont, TX. Attended Rider Col., HB Studio. Debut 1972 OB in "22 Years," followed by "The Soldier," "Hughie," "An American Story," "El Hermano," "Dumping Ground," "Daddies," "Accounts," "Shadow Man," "Marathon '84," "Dennis," "Marathon '89."

GLEASON, JOANNA. Born June 2, 1950 in Toronto, Canada. Graduate UCLA. Bdwy debut 1977 in "I Love My Wife," for which she received a Theatre World Award, followed by "The Real Thing," "Social Security," "Into the Woods," OB in "A Hell of a Town," "Joe Egg," "It's Only a Play," "Eleemosynary."

GLENN, SCOTT. Born Jan. 26, 1942 in Pittsburgh, PA. Graduate Wm. & Mary Col. Bdwy debut 1965 in "The Impossible Years," followed by "Burn This," OB in "Collision Course," "Angelo's Wedding."

GLOVER, KEITH. Born Feb. 18, 1963 in Bessemer, AL. Graduate Bowling Green U. Debut OB 1980 in "The Sign in Sidney Brustein's Window," followed by "La Puta Vida Trilogy," "A Raisin in the Sun," "Master Harold and the Boys," "Philoctetes."

GLOVER, SAVION. Born Nov. 19, 1973 in Newark, NJ. Bdwy debut 1984 in "The Tap Dance Kid," followed by "Black and Blue."

GLUSHAK, JOANNA. Born May 27, 1958 in NYC. Attended NYU. Debut 1983 OB in "Lenny and the Heartbreakers," followed by "Lies and Legends," "Miami," Bdwy in "Sunday in the Park with George" (1984), "Rags" "Les Miserables."

GNAT, MICHAEL. Born Dec. 13, 1955 in NYC. Graduate Syracuse U. Debut 1980 OB in "The Interview," followed by "The Ballad of Bernie Babcock," "Lord Alfred's Lover," "This Property Is Condemned," "Engaged," "Courtship," "Briss," "One Night Stand," "The Tiger," "Becoming Strangers," "The Gambler."

GOELL, JULIE. Born Apr. 19, 1951 in NY. Graduate Emerson Col., HB Studios. Bdwy debut 1989 in "Ghetto."

GOETHALS, ANGELA. Born May 20, 1977. Bdwy debut 1987 in "Coastal Disturbance," OB in "Positive Me," "Approaching Zanzibar."

GOLDBERG, RUSSELL. Born Mar. 28, 1964 in Flushing, NY. Graduate Syracuse U. Debut 1988 OB in "All's Fair," followed by "Sherlock Holmes and the Red-Headed League," "The Emperor's New Clothes," "Peg o' My Heart."

GONZALEZ, ERNESTO. Born Apr. 8, 1940 in San Juan. PR. Bdwy debut 1953 in "Camino Real," followed by "Saint of Bleecker Street," "The Innkeepers," "Cut of the Axe," "Ride the Winds," "The Strong Are Lonely," "Oh Dad, Poor Dad . . .," "The Leaf People," OB in "The Kitchen," "Secret Concubine," "Life Is a Dream," "The Marquise," "Principia Scriptoriae," "Marathon '88."

GOODHEART, CAROL. Born in Chicago, IL. Graduate UCLA. Debut 1982 OB in "The Roads To Home," followed by "Valentine's Day," "The Old Friends" "Early Rains," Bdwy in "The Devil's Disciple."

GOODSPEED, DON. Born April 1, 1958 in Truro, NS, Can. Bdwy debut 1983 in "The Pirates of Penzance," followed by "Into The Woods," OB in "Diamonds," "Charley's Tale."

GOOR, CAROLYN. Born Oct. 11, 1960 in Paris, Fr. Debut 1983 OB in "The Jewish Gypsy," followed by "Oy Mama, Am I in Love," "A Little Night Music," "Singin' in the Rain," Bdwy in "Jerome Robbins' Broadway."

GORDON, LINDSAY. Born April 3, 1983 in Austin, TX. Debut 1989 OB in "Member of The Wedding."

GORDON-CLARK, SUSAN. Born Dec. 31, 1947 in Jackson, Ms. Graduate Purdue U. Debut 1984 OB in "The Nunsense Story," followed by "Chip Shot," "Nunsense."

GORDY, WAYNE. Born Dec. 26 in Philadelphia, PA. Graduate HofstraU, Richmond Col., London. Debut 1988 OB in "Fiorello."

GOTTLIEB, MATTHEW. Born Apr. 6, 1951 in Ann Arbor, MI. Graduate CalStArts. Debut 1980 OB in "Friend of the Family," followed by "Henry IV Part 2," "The Racket," "American Voices," "Blitzstein Project."

GOTTSCHALL, RUTH. Born Apr. 14, 1957 in Wilmington, DE. Bdwy debut 1981 in "The Best Little Whorehouse in Texas," followed by "Cabaret" (1987), "Legs Diamond."

GOUTMAN, CHRISTOPHER. Born Dec. 19, 1952 in Bryn Mawr, PA. Graduate Haverford Col., Carnegie-Mellon U. Debut 1978 OB in "The Promise," for which he received a Theatre World Award, followed by "Grand Magic," "The Skirmishers," "Imaginary Lovers," "Balm in Gilead," "Love's Labour's Lost," "Tamara."

GOZ, HARRY. Born June 23, 1932 in St. Louis, MO. Attended St. Louis Inst. Bdwy debut 1957 in "Utopia Limited," followed by "Bajour," "Fiddler on the Roof," "Two by Two," "Prisoner of Second Avenue," "Chess," "Cafe Crown" (1989), OB in "To Bury a Cousin," "Ferocious Kisses," "Cafe Crown."

GRAAE, JASON. Born May 15, 1958 in Chicago, IL. Graduate Cincinnati Consv. Debut 1981 OB in "Godspell," followed by "Snoopy," "Heaven on Earth," "Promenade," "Feathertop," "Tales of Tinseltown," "Living Color," "Just So," "Olympus on My Mind," "Sitting Pretty in Concert," "Babes in Arms," Bdwy 1982 in "Do Black Patent Leather Shoes Really Reflect Up?," "Stardust."

GRAFF, RANDY. Born May 23, 1955 in Brooklyn, NY. Graduate Wagner Col. Debut 1978 OB in "Pins and Needles," followed by "Station Joy," "A . . . My Name Is Alice," "Once on a Summer's Day," Bdwy in "Sarava," "Grease," "Les Miserables," "City of Angels."

GRAFF, TODD. Born Oct. 22, 1959 in NYC. Attended SUNY/Purchase. Debut 1983 OB in "American Passion," followed by "Birds of Paradise," "Grandma Plays," Bdwy in "Baby" (1983) for which he received a Theatre World Award.

GRANAROLI, TY. Born June 24, 1959 in Santa Barbara, CA. Attended John Hancock Junior Col. Debut 1988 OB in "Genesis."

GRANT, FAYE. Born July 16 in Detroit, MI. Bdwy debut 1985 in "Singin' in the Rain," for which she received a Theatre World Award, followed by "House of Blue Leaves," "Lend Me a Tenor."

GRANT, SCHUYLER. Born Apr. 29, 1970 in San Jose, CA. Attended Yale Drama School. Debut 1987 OB in "The Hooded Eye," followed by "Mortal Friends."

GRANVILLE, BERNARD. Born Nov. 8, 1923 in NYC. Attended NYU. Debut OB 1989 in "Gigi."

GRAVES, RUTHANNA. Born Sept. 14, 1957 in Philadelphia, PA. Attended NYU. Debut 1980 OB in "Mother Courage," followed by "Boogie-Woogie Rumble," "Blackamoor," Bdwy in "Uptown It's Hot" (1986).

GRAY, SAM. Born July 18, 1923 in Chicago, IL. Graduate Columbia U. Bdwy debut 1955 in "Deadfall," followed by "Six Fingers in a Five Finger Glove," "Saturday, Sunday, Monday," "Golda," "A View from the Bridge," OB in "Ascent of F-6," "Family Portrait," "One Tiger on a Hill," "Shadow of Heroes," "The Recruiting Officer," "The Wild Duck," "Jungle of Cities," "3 Acts of Recognition," "Returnings," "A Little Madness," "The Danube," "Dr. Cook's Garden," "Child's Play," "Kafka Father and Son," "D," "Dennis," "Panache!," "Marathon '89," "Bitter Friends."

GREEN, DAVID. Born June 16, 1942 in Cleveland, OH. Attended KanState U. Bdwy debut 1980

in "Annie," followed by "Evita," "Teddy and Alice," "The Pajama Game" (LC), OB in "Once on a Summer's Day," "Miami," "On the 20th Century."

GREENE, JAMES. Born Dec. 1, 1926 in Lawrence, MA. Graduate Emerson Col. OB in "The Iceman Cometh," "American Gothic," "The King and the Duke," "The Hostage," "Plays for Bleecker Street," "Moon in the Yellow River," "Misalliance," "Government Inspector," "Baba Goya," LCRep 2 years, "You Can't Take It with You," "School for Scandal," "Wild Duck," "Right You Are," "The Show-Off," "Pantagleize," "Festival of Short Plays," "Nourish the Beast," "One Crack Out," "Artichoke," "Othello," "Salt Lake City Skyline," "Summer," "Rope Dancers," "Frugal Repast," "Bella Figura," "The Freak," "Park Your Car in the Harvard Yard," "Pigeons on the Walk," "Endgame," "Great Days," "Playboy of the Western World," "Brimstone and Treacle," Bdwy "Romeo and Juliet," "Girl on the Via Flaminia," "Compulsion," "Inherit the Wind," "Shadow of a Gunman," "Andersonville Trial," "Night Life," "School for Wives," "Ring Round the Bathtub," "Great God Brown," "Don Juan," "Foxfire," "Play Memory," "The Iceman Cometh."

GREENHILL, SUSAN. Born Mar. 19 in NYC. Graduate UPa., Catholic U. Bdwy debut 1982 in "Crimes of the Heart," OB in "Hooters," "Our Lord of Lynchville," "September in the Rain," "Seascape with Sharks and Dancer," "Young Playwrights Festival," "Festival of One-Acts," "Murder of Crows," "Marathon '89."

GREGORIO, ROSE. Born in Chicago, Ill. Graduate Northwestern, Yale. Debut 1962 OB in "The Days and Nights of Beebee Fenstermaker," followed by "Kiss Mama," "The Balcony," "Bivouac at Lucca," "Journey to the Day," "Diary of Anne Frank," "Weekends Like Other People," "Curse of the Starving Class," "Dream of a Blacklisted Actor," Bdwy in "The Owl and the Pussycat," "Daphne in Cottage D," "Jimmy Shine," "The Cuban Thing," "The Shadow Box," "A View from the Bridge," "M. Butterfly."

GREGORY, MICHAEL ALAN. Born Feb. 1, 1955 in Coral Gables, FL. Graduate Wheaton Col., UWash. Debut 1985 OB in "Season's Greetings," followed by "Dracula," "Kiss Me, Kate," "A Matter of Tone," Bdwy in "Macbeth" (1988).

GREGORY, MICHAEL SCOTT. Born Mar. 13, 1962 in Ft. Lauderdale, FL. Attended Atlantic Foundation. Bdwy debut 1981 in "Sophisticated Ladies," followed by "Starlight Express," "Jerome Robbins' Broadway."

GRIESEMER, JOHN. Born Dec. 5, 1947 in Elizabeth, NJ. Graduate Dickinson Col., URI. Debut 1981 OB in "Turnbuckle," followed by "Death of a Miner," "Little Victories," "Macbeth," "A Lie of the Mind," Bdwy in "Our Town" (1989).

GRIFFITH, EDWARD. Born Jan. 8, 1949 in Osaka, Japan. Graduate Georgetown U. Debut 1980 OB in "Fugue in a Nursery," followed by "Death Takes a Holiday," "Behind a Mask," "Twelfth Night," "Othello."

GRIFFITH, LISA. Born June 18 in Honolulu, HI. Graduate Brandeis U., Trinty U. Debut 1977 OB in "The Homesickness of Capt. Rappaport," followed by "The Kennedy Play," "Chalkdust," "Murder at the Vicarage," "Ah, Wilderness!," "Stud Silo," "The Miser," "Twelfth Night," "Othello."

GRIMES, TAMMY. Born Jan. 30, 1934 in Lynn, MA. Attended Stephens Col., Neighborhood Playhouse. Debut 1956 OB in "The Littlest Revue," followed by "Clerambard," "Molly Trick," "Are You Now or Have You Ever Been," "Father's Day," "A Month in the Country," "Sunset," "Waltz of the Toreadors," "Mlle. Colombe," "Tammy Grimes in Concert," Bdwy in "Look after Lulu" (1959) for which she received a Theatre World Award, "The Unsinkable Molly Brown," "Private Lives," "High Spirits," "Rattle of a Simple Man," "The Only Game in Town," "Musical Jubilee," "California Suite," "Tartuffe," "Pal Joey in Concert," "42nd Street," "Orpheus Descending."

GROENENDAAL, CRIS. Born Feb. 17, 1948 in Erie, PA. Attended Allegheny Col., Exeter U., HB Studio. Bdwy debut 1979 in "Sweeney Todd," followed by "Sunday in the Park with George," "Brigadoon" (LC), "Desert Song" (LC), LC's "South Pacific," and "Sweeney Todd," "Phantom of the Opera," OB in "Francis," "Sweethearts in Concert," "Oh, Boy," "No No Nanette in Concert," "Sitting Pretty."

GROH, DAVID. Born May 21, 1939 in NYC. Graduate Brown U., LAMDA. Debut 1963 OB in "The Importance of Being Earnest," followed by "Elizabeth the Queen" (CC), "The Hot l Baltimore," "Be Happy for Me," "Dead Wrong," "Face to Face," "Road Show," "Tea with Mommy and Jack," Bdwy in "Chapter Two" (1978).

GROVE, GREGORY. Born Dec. 15, 1949 in Ada, OK. Graduate SMU, HB Studio. Debut 1977 OB in "K: Impressions of Kfka's Trial," "Early One Evening at the Rainbow Bar & Grill," Bdwy in "Lone Star/Private Wars" (1979).

GRUSIN, RICHARD. Born Nov. 2, 1946 in Chicago, IL. Graduate Goodman School, Yale. Debut 1978 OB in "Wings," followed by "Sganerelle," "Heat of Re-Entry," "For Sale," "The Time of Your Life," "Perfect Crime," "Terry by Terry," "Marathon '88," "Sharon and Billy."

GUAN, JAMIE H. J. Born June 19, 1950 in Beijing, China. Attended Beijing Inst. Perform. Arts. Bdwy debut 1988 in "M. Butterfly."

GUERRASIO, JOHN. Born Feb. 18, 1950 in Brooklyn, NY. Attended Bklyn Col., Boston U. Debut 1971 OB in "Hamlet," followed by "And They Put Handcuffs on Flowers," "Eros and Psyche," "The Marriage Proposal," "Macbeth," "K," "Sunday Promenade," "Family Business," "Knuckle Sandwich," "The Imperialists."

GUIDALL, GEORGE. Born June 7, 1938 in Plainfield, NJ. Attended UBuffalo, AADA. Bdwy debut 1969 in "Wrong Way Light Bulb," followed by "Cold Storage," "Cafe Crown," OB in "Counsellor-at-Law," "Taming of the Shrew," "All's Well That Ends Well," "The Art of Dining," "Biography," "After All," "Henry V," "Time of the Cuckoo," "Yours Anne," "The Perfect Party," "A Man for All Seasons," "Morocco," "Cafe Crown."

GUNDERSON, STEVE. Born June 9, 1957 in San Diego, CA. Attended SDStatU. Debut 1982 OB in "Street Scene," Bdwy in "Suds" (1989).

GUNN, MOSES. Born Oct. 2, 1929 in St. Louis, MO. Graduate UTn, AIU, UKan. OB in "Measure for Measure," "Bohikee Creek," "Day of Absence," "Happy Ending," "Baal," "Hard Travelin'," "Lonesome Train," "In White America," "The Blacks," "Titus Andronicus," "Song of the Lusitanian-Bogey," "Summer of the 17th Doll," "Kongi's Harvest," "Daddy Goodness," "Cities in Bezique," "Perfect Party," "To Be Young, Gifted and Black," "Sty of the Blind Pig," "Twelfth Night," "American Gothic," "Tapman," "King John," "Coriolanus," Bdwy in "Hand Is on the Gate," "Othello," "First Breeze of Summer," "The Poison Tree," "I Have a Dream."

Alice Drummond	William Duell	Cara Duff-MacCormick	Edward Easton	Wendy Edmead	R Bruce Elliott
Felicia Farone	John Fiedler	Pauline Flanagan	Tom Flagg	Frances Foster	Colin Fox
Jonathan Freeman	Crystal Field	Jonathan Frid	Lori Galante	Romain Frugé	Laurie Gamache
Carol Goodheart	Marcus Giomatti	Susan Gordon-Clark	Steven Gilborn	Randy Graff	Mel Gionson
Keith Glover	Ruthanna Graves	Ty Granaroli	Susan Greenhill	John Guerrasio	Rose Gregorio

GUNTON, BOB. Born Nov. 15, 1945 in Santa Monica, CA. Attended UCal. Debut 1971 OB in "Who Am I?," followed by "The Kid," "Desperate Hours," "Tip-Toes," "How I Got That Story," "Hamlet," "Death of Von Richthofen," "Man Who Could See Through Time," "Phaedra Brittanica," "Sweeney Todd," Bdwy in "Happy End" (1977), "Working," "King of Hearts," "Evita," "Passion," "Big River."

GYNGELL, PAUL. Born Jan. 26, 1963 in Church Village, South Wales. Attended Italia Conti Stage School. Bdwy debut 1988 in "Carrie."

HACK, STEVEN. Born Apr. 20, 1958 in St. Louis, MO. Attended CalArts, AADA, Debut 1978 OB in "The Coolest Cat in Town," followed by Bdwy in "Cats" (1982).

HADARY, JONATHAN. Born Oct. 11, 1948 in Chicago, IL. Attended Tufts U. Debut 1974 OB in "White Nights," followed by "El Grande de Coca Cola," "Songs from Pins and Needles," "God Bless You, Mr. Rosewater," "Pushing 30," "Scrambled Feet," "Coming Attractions," "Tom Foolery," "Charley Bacon and Family," "Road Show," "1-2-3-4-5," "Wenceslas Square," Bdwy in "Gemini," (1977/also OB), "Torch Song Trilogy," "As Is," "Gypsy."

HADDAD, AVA. Born in NYC. Debut 1986 OB in "Passover," followed by "The Milk Train Doesn't Stop Here Anymore," "A Shayna Maidel," "Value of Names."

HAFNER, JULIE J. Born June 4, 1952 in Dover, Oh. Graduate KentStateU. Debut 1976 OB in "The Club," followed by "Nunsense," Bdwy in "Nine."

HAHN, FREDRICK. Born Sept. 13, 1961 in NYC. Attended Castleton StateCol. Debut 1989 OB in "Up'n' Under."

HAILE, EVANS. Born Mar. 29, 1957 in Gainesville, FL. Graduate Juilliard. Bdwy debut 1989 in "Our Town."

HALL, DAVIS. Born Apr. 10, 1946 in Atlanta, GA. Graduate Northwestern U. Bdwy debut 1973 in "Butley," followed by "Dogg's Hamlet and Cahoot's Macbeth," OB in "The Promise," "Dreamboats," "The Taming of the Shrew," "Donkey's Years," "Love's Labour's Lost."

HALL, GEORGE. Born Nov. 19, 1916 in Toronto, Can. Attended Neighborhood Playhouse. Bdwy debut 1946 in "Call Me Mister," followed by "Lend an Ear," "Touch and Go," "Live Wire," "The Boy Friend," "There's a Girl in My Soup," "An Evening with Richard Nixon," "We Interrupt This Program," "Man and Superman," "Bent," "Noises Off," "Wild Honey," OB in "The Balcony," "Ernest in Love," "A Round with Rings," "Family Pieces," "Carousel," "The Case Against Roberta Guardino," "Marry Me!," "Arms and the Man," "The Old Glory," "Dancing for the Kaiser," "Casualties," "The Seagull," "A Stitch in Time," "Mary Stuart," "No End of Blame," "Hamlet," "Colette Collage," "The Homecoming," "And a Nightingale Sang," "The Bone Ring," "Much Ado About Nothing," "Measure for Measure."

HALL, MARGARET. Born in Richmond, VA. Graduate Wm. & Mary Col. Bdwy debut 1960 in "Becket," followed by "High Spirits," "Mame," "The Leaf People," "Sunday in the Park with George," OB in "The Boy Friend," "Fallout," "U.S.A.," "A Midsummer Night's Dream," "Little Mary Sunshine," "Just Say No."

HALLETT, JACK. Born Nov. 7, 1948 in Philadelphia, PA. Attended AADA. Debut 1972 OB in "Servant of Two Masters," followed by "Twelfth Night," "Education of Hyman Kaplan," Bdwy in "The 1940's Radio Hour," "The First."

HALLIDAY, ANDY. Born Mar. 31, 1953 in Orange, CT. Attended USIU/San Diego. Debut OB 1985 in "Vampire Lesbians of Sodom," followed by "Times Square Angel," "Psycho Beach Party," "The Lady in Question."

HALSTON, JULIE. Born Dec. 7, 1954 in NY. Graduate Hofstra U. Debut OB 1985 in "Times Square Angel," followed by "Vampire Lesbians of Sodom," "Sleeping Beauty or Coma," "The Dubliners," "The Lady in Question."

HAMILTON, LAWRENCE. Born Sept. 14, 1954 in Ashdown, AR. Graduate Henderson State U. Debut 1981 OB in "Purlie," followed by "Blues in the Night," "The River," Bdwy in "Sophisticated Ladies" (1982), "Porgy and Bess," "The Wiz," "Uptown It's Hot."

HAMLIN, MARILYN. Born Feb. 22, 1946 in West Frankfort, IL. Graduate Southern IlU. Bdwy debut 1970 in "Not Now Darling," followed by "Our Town" (1989), OB in "The Master and Margerita," "Killings on the Last Line."

HAMMOND, MICHAEL. Born Apr. 30, 1951 in Clinton, IA. Graduate UIa. LAMDA. Debut 1974 OB in "Pericles," followed by "The Merry Wives of Windsor," "A Winter's Tale," "Barbarians," "The Purging," "Romeo and Juliet," "The Merchant of Venice," Bdwy in "M. Butterfly" (1989).

HANAN, STEPHEN. Born Jan 7, 1947 in Washington, DC. Graduate Harvard, LAMDA. Debut 1978 OB in "All's Well That Ends Well," followed by "Taming of the Shrew," "Rabboni," Bdwy in "Pirates of Penzance" (1978), "Cats."

HANKET, ARTHUR. Born June 23, 1934 in Virginia. Graduate UVa., FlaStateU. Debut 1979 OB in "Cuchculain Cycle," followed by "The Boys Next Door," "In Perpetuity throughout the Universe," "L'Illusion."

HANLEY, ELLEN. Born May 15, 1926 in Lorain, OH. Attended Juilliard. Bdwy debut 1946 in "Annie Get Your Gun," followed by "Barefoot Boy with Cheek" for which she received a Theatre World Award, "High Button Shoes," "Lend an Ear," "Two's Company," "First Impressions," "Fiorello!," "The Boys from Syracuse" (OB), "The Rose Tattoo," "1776," "Anything Goes."

HARADA, ANN. Born Feb. 3, 1964 in Honolulu, HI. Attended Brown U. Debut 1987 OB in "1-2-3-4-5," Bdwy in "M. Butterfly" (1988).

HARDWICK, MARK. Born Apr. 18, 1954 in Carthage, TX. Graduate SMU. Bdwy debut 1982 in "Pump Boys and Dinettes," followed by OB's "Oil City Symphony."

HARDY, STEPHANI. Born June 13, 1957 in Dallas, TX. Graduate Baylor U. Debut 1986 OB in "What's a Nice Country Like You Still Doing in a State Like This?," followed by "The No Frills Revue," "Green Death."

HARE, WILL. Born Mar. 30, 1919 in Elkins, WVa. Attended AmActorsTh. Bdwy credits include "The Eternal Road," "The Moon is Down," "Suds in Your Eye," "Only the Heart," "The Trip to Bountiful," "Witness for the Prosecution," "Marathon '33," OB in "The Visitor," "Winter Journey," "Dylan," "Older People," "Crystal and Fox" "Long Day's Journey into Night," "Boom Boom Room," "Old Times," "Dream of a Blacklisted Actor," "Philistines," "Fighting Light."

HARMAN, PAUL. Born July 29, 1952 in Mineola, NY. Graduate Tufts U. Bdwy debut 1980 in "It's So Nice to Be Civilized," followed by "Les Miserables," "Chess," OB in "City Suite."

HARMON, JEFFREY. Born Nov. 28, 1954 in Chicago, IL. Graduate U of Chicago, Georgetown U. Debut 1988 OB in "The Winter's Tale," followed by "Hoarfrost: Fool's Gold."

HARPER, JAMES. Born Oct. 8, 1948 in Bell, CA. Attended Marin Col., Juilliard. Bdwy debut in 1973 in "King Lear," followed by "Robber Bridegroom," "Time of Your Life," "Mother Courage," "Edward II," OB in "Midsummer Night's Dream," "Recruiting Officer," "The Wild Duck," "Jungle of Cities," "Cradle Will Rock," "All the Nice People," "Cruelties of Mrs. Schnayd," "Territorial Rites," "Johnstown Vindicator," "Guadeloupe."

HARRAN, JACOB. Born July 23, 1955 in NYC. Graduate HofstraU. Debut 1984 OB in "Balm in Gilead," followed by "Awake and Sing," "Crossing Delancy," "Romeo and Juliet," "Cabbagehead," "Oklahoma Samovar," "Three Sisters."

HARRIS, JULIE. Born Dec. 2, 1925 in Grosse Pt., MI. Attended YaleU. Bdwy debut 1945 in "It's a Gift," followed by "Henry V," "Oedipus," "Playboy of the Western World," "Alice in Wonderland," "Macbeth," "Sundown Beach," for which she received a Theatre World Award, "The Young and the Fair," "Magnolia Alley," "Montserrat," "Member of the Wedding," "I Am a Camera," "Mlle. Colombe," "The Lark," "Country Wife," "Warm Peninsula," "Little Moon of Alban," "A Shot in the Dark," "Marathon '33," "Ready When You Are, CB.," "Hamlet" (CP), "Skyscraper," "40 Carats," "And Miss Reardon Drinks a Little," "Voices," "Last of Mrs. Lincoln," "Au Pair Man" (LC), "In Praise of Love," "Belle of Amherst" (Solo), "Break a Leg," "Driving Miss Daisy" (NTC).

HARRIS, VIOLA. Born Sept. 14, 1928 in NYC. Graduate Hunter Col., NorthwesternU. Bdwy debut 1948 in "On The Town," followed by "Zelda," OB in "Three Steps Down," "Berkeley Square," "Ivanov," "Waving Goodbye," "Between Friends."

HART, LINDA. Born Aug. 1, 1950 in Dallas, TX. Attended LACC. Debut 1982 OB in "Livin' Dolls," followed by "Sunday Serenade," "Gospel Rocks the Ballroom," Bdwy in "Bette Midler's Divine Madness" (1979), "Anything Goes" (1987) for which she received a Theatre World Award.

HART, ROXANNE. Born in 1952 in Trenton, NJ. Attended Skidmore, PrincetonU. Bdwy debut 1977 in "Equus," followed by "Loose Ends," "Passion," "Devil's Disciple," OB in "Winter's Tale," "Johnny On a Spot," "The Purging," "Hedda Gabler," "Waiting for the Parade," "La Brea Tarpits," "Marathon '84," "Digby."

HARTLEY, MARIETTE. Born June 21, 1940 in NYC. Debut OB 1988 in "King John."

HARTLEY, SUSAN. Born Oct. 20 in Norman, OK. Graduate AdelphiU. Bdwy Debut 1982 in "Annie," followed by "My One And Only," OB in "Leave it to Jane."

HARUM, EIVIND. Born May 24, 1944 in Stavanger, Norway. Attended Utah State U. Credits include "Sophie," "Foxy," "Baker Street," "West Side Story" ('68), "A Chorus Line," "Woman of the Year."

HARVEY, JONA. Born June 8, 1953 in Philadelphia, PA. Attended Lycoming Col., Montclair St.Col., TempleU., Hedgerow Theatre. Debut OB 1988 in "Male Animal."

HATCHER, ROBYN. Born Sept. 8, 1956 in Philadelphia, PA. Graduate AdelphiU. Debut OB 1983 in "Macbeth," followed by "Edward II," "Deep Sleep," "Flatbush Faithful," "Pardon Permission," "Welcome Signs."

HAWKES, TERRI. Born Dec. 26 in Montreal, Can. Graduate UCalgary. Debut 1986 OB in "Sorrows and Sons," followed by "The Taming of the Shrew," "The Greenhouse Keeper Died," "Tamara."

HAYNES, ROBIN. Born July 20, 1953 in Lincoln, NE. Graduate UWash. Debut 1976 OB in "Touch of the Poet," followed by "She Loves Me," "Romeo and Juliet," "Twelfth Night," "Billy Bishop Goes To War," "Comedy of Errors, (LC) "Max and Maxie," Bdwy in "Best Little Whorehouse in Texas" (1978).

HEALD, ANTHONY. Born Aug. 25, 1944 in New Rochelle, NY. Graduate MiStateU. Debut 1980 OB in "Glass Menagerie," followed by "Misalliance" for which he received a Theatre World Award, "The Caretaker," "The Fox," "Quartermaine's Terms," "The Philanthropist," "Henry V," "Digby," "Principia Scriptoriae," "Lisbon Traviata," Bdwy in "Wake of Jamey Foster" (1982), "Marriage of Figaro," "Anything Goes."

HEARD, JOHN. Born Mar. 7, 1946 in Washington, DC. Graduate ClarkU. Debut 1974 OB in "The Wager," followed by "Macbeth," "Hamlet," "Fishing," "G.R. Point" for which he received a Theatre World Award, "The Creditors," 'The Promise," "Othello," "Split," "Chekhov Sketchbook," "Love Letters," Bdwy in "Warp" (1973), "Total Abandon."

HEARN, GEORGE. Born June 18, 1934 in St. Louis, MO. Graduate Southwestern Col. OB in "Macbeth," "Antony and Cleopatra," "As You Like It," "Richard III," "Merry Wives of Windsor," "Midsummer Night's Dream," "Hamlet," "Horseman, Pass By," "The Chosen," Bdwy in "A Time for Singing," "The Changing Room," "An Almost Perfect Person," "I Remember Mama," "Watch on the Rhine," "Sweeney Todd," "A Doll's Life," "Whodunnit," "La Cage aux Folles," "Ah! Wilderness!," "Ghetto."

HECHT, PAUL. Born Aug. 16, 1941 in London, Eng. Attended McGill U. OB in "Sjt. Musgrave's Dance," "Macbird," "Phaedra," "Enrico IV," "Coriolanus," Bdwy in "Rosencrantz and Guildenstern Are Dead," "1776," "The Rothschilds," "The Ride Across Lake Constance," "The Great God Brown," "Don Juan," "Emperor Henry IV," "Herzl," "Caesar and Cleopatra," "Night and Day," "Noises Off."

HECKART, EILEEN. Born Mar. 29, 1919 in Columbus, OH. Graduate Ohio StateU. Debut OB in "Tinker's Dam" (1942) followed by "Eleemosynary," Bdwy in "Our Town," "They Knew What They Wanted," "The Traitor," "Hilda Crane," "In Any Language," "Picnic" for which she received a Theatre World Award, "Bad Seed," "View from the Bridge," "Dark at the Top of the Stairs," "Invitation to a March," "Pal Joey," "Everybody Loves Opal," "And Things That Go Bump in the Night," "Barefoot in the Park," "You Know I Can't Hear You When the Water's Running," "Mother Lover," "Butterflies Are Free," "Veronica's Room," "Ladies at the Alamo."

HEINSOHN, ELISA. Born Oct. 11, 1962 in Butler, PA. Debut 1984 OB in "Oy, Mama, Am I in Love," followed by "Scandal," Bdwy in "42nd Street" (1985), "Smile," "Phantom of the Opera."

HENIG, ANDI. Born May 6 in Washington, D.C. Attended Yale. Debut 1978 OB in "One and One," followed by "Kind Lady," "Downriver," "Romance in Hard Times," Bdwy in "Oliver!" (1984), "Big River."

HENRITZE, BETTE. Born May 23 in Betsy Layne, KY. Graduate UTenn, OB in "Lion in Love," "Abe Lincoln in Illinois," "Othello," "Baal," "Long Christmas Dinner," "Queens of France," "Rimers of Eldritch," "Displaced Person," "Acquisition," "Crime of Passion," "Happiness Cage," "Henry VI," "Richard III," "Older People," "Lotta," "Catsplay," "A Month in the Country," "The Golem," "Daughters," "Steel Magnolias," Bdwy in "Jenny Kissed Me" (1948), "Pictures in the Hallway," "Giants, Sons of Giants," "Ballad of the Sad Cafe," "The White House," "Dr. Cook's Garden," "Here's Where I Belong," "Much Ado About Nothing," "Over Here," "Angel Street," "Man and Superman," "Macbeth" (1981), "Present Laughter," "The Octette Bridge Club."

HENSLEY, DALE. Born Apr. 9, 1954 in Nevada, MO. Graduate SouthwestMoStateU. Debut 1980 OB in "Annie Get Your Gun," Bdwy in "Anything Goes" (1987).

HERNANDEZ, PHILIP. Born Dec. 12, 1959 in Queens, NY. Graduate SUNY. Debut OB 1987 in "The Gingerbread Lady," followed by "Ad Hock."

HEYMAN, BARTON. Born Jan. 24, 1937 in Washington, DC. Attended UCLA. Bdwy debut 1969 in "Indians," followed by "Trial of the Catonsville 9," "A Talent for Murder," OB in "A Midsummer Night's Dream," "Sleep," "Phantasmagoria Historia," "Enclave," "Henry V," "Signs of Life," "Coo-Coo-Shay," "Crack," "Private View."

HICKS, LAURA. Born Nov. 17, 1956 in NYC. Juilliard graduate. Debut 1978 OB in "Spring Awakening," followed by "Talking With," "The Cradle Will Rock," "Paducah," "10 by Tennessee," "On the Verge," Bdwy in "The Heidi Chronicles" (1989).

HIGGINS, JOHN F. Born Mar. 12, 1964 in NYC. Graduate SUNY. Debut 1988 OB in "Two by Two."

HIGGINS, MICHAEL. Born Jan. 20, 1926 in Brooklyn, NY. Attended AmThWing. Bdwy debut 1946 in "Antigone," followed by "Our Lan'," "Romeo and Juliet," "The Crucible," "The Lark," "Equus," "Whose Life Is It Anyway?," OB in "White Devil," "Carefree Tree," "Easter," "The Queen and the Rebels," "Sally, George and Martha," "L'Ete," "Uncle Vanya," "The Iceman Cometh," "Molly," "Artichoke," "Reunion," "Chieftans," "A Tale Told," "Richard II," "The Seagull," "Levitation," "Love's Labour's Lost," "In This Fallen City," "Murder of Crows."

HILER, KATHERINE. Born June 24, 1961 in Carson City, NV. Graduate Mt. Holyoke Col. Bdwy debut 1985 in "Hurlyburly," OB in "Liebelei" (1987), "The Year of the Duck," "A Shayna Maidel," "Temptation."

HILLARY, ANN. Born Jan. 8, 1931 in Jellico, TN. Attended Northwestern U. AADA. Bdwy debut 1953 in "Be Your Age," followed by "Separate Tables," "The Lark," OB in "Dark of the Moon," "Paradise Lost," "Total Eclipse," "The Circle," "The Immigrant."

HILLNER, NANCY. Born June 7, 1949 in Wakefield, RI. Graduate ULowell. Bdwy debut 1975 in "Dance with Me," followed by OB in "Nite Club Confidential," "Trading Places," "Nunsense."

HILTON, MARGARET. Born July 20 in Marple, Cheshire, Eng. Graduate ULondon, LAMDA. Debut 1979 OB in "Molly," followed by "Stevie," "Come Back to the Five & Dime, Jimmy Dean," "Pygmalion in Concert," "In Celebration," "Joe Egg," "The Film Society," Bdwy in "Rose" (1981), "Joe Egg."

HIRSCH, VICKI. Born Feb. 22, 1951 in Wilmington, DE. Graduate UDel., Villanova U. Debut 1985 OB in "Back County Crimes," followed by "Casualties," "Mr. Universe," "Working Magic."

HOCK, ROBERT. Born May 20, 1931 in Phoenixville, PA. Graduate Yale. Debut 1982 OB in "Romeo and Juliet," followed by "Edward II," "Macbeth," "The Adding Machine," "Caucasian Chalk Circle," "Kitty Hawk," "Heathen Valley."

HODES, GLORIA. Born Aug. 20 in Norwich, Ct. Bdwy debut in "Gantry" (1969), followed by "Me and My Girl," OB in "The Club" for which she received a Theatre World Award, "Cycles of Fancy," "The Heroine," "Pearls," "Songs of Pyre."

HOFFMAN, AVI. Born Mar. 3, 1958 in Bronx, NY. Graduate UMiami. Debut 1983 OB in "The Rise of David Levinsky," followed by "It's Hard to Be a Jew," "A Rendezvous With God," "The Golden Land," "Songs of Paradise."

HOFFMAN, PHILIP. Born May 12, 1954 in Chicago, IL. Graduate UIll. Bdwy debut 1981 in "The Moony Shapiro Songbook," followed by "Is There Life after High School?," "Baby," "Into the Woods," OB in "The Fabulous '50's," "Isn't It Romantic?," "1-2-3-4-5."

HOGAN, TESSIE. Born Aug. 23, 1957 in Chicago, IL. Graduate UIll., Yale. Debut 1985 OB in "Faulkner's Bicycle," followed by "Terry by Terry," "Festival of 1 Acts," "Lunatics and Lovers."

HOLBROOK, RUBY. Born Aug. 28, 1930 in St. John's, Nfd. Attended Denison U. Debut 1963 OB in "Abe Lincoln in Illinois," followed by "Hamlet," "James Joyce's Dubliners," "Measure for Measure," "The Farm," "Do You Still Believe the Rumor?," "The Killing of Sister George," "An Enemy of the People," "Amulets Against the Dragon Forces," Bdwy in "Da" (1979), "5th of July," "Musical Comedy Murders of 1940."

HOLGATE, RONALD. Born May 26, 1937 in Aberdeen, SD. Attended Northwestern U. NewEng Conserv. Debut 1961 OB in "Hobo," followed by "Hooray, It's a Glorious Day," "Blue Plate Special," Bdwy "A Funny Thing Happened on the Way to the Forum," "Milk and Honey," "1776," "Saturday, Sunday, Monday," "The Grand Tour," "Musical Chairs," "42nd Street," "Lend Me a Tenor."

HOLMES, GEORGE. Born June 3, 1935 in London, Eng. Graduate ULondon. Debut 1978 OB in "The Changeling," followed by "Love From a Stranger," "The Hollow," "Story of the Gadsbys," "Learned Ladies," "The Land Is Bright," "Something Old, Something New," "Oscar Wilde Solitaire," "Like Them That Dream," "Peg O' My Heart."

HOODWIN, REBECCA. Born May 14, 1949 in Miami, FL. Graduate UFla. Bdwy debut 1973 in "The Pajama Game," OB in "Fifth of July."

HOOVER, PAUL. Born June 20, 1945 in Rockford, IL. Graduate Pikeville Col., Pittsburgh Sem. Debut 1980 OB in "Kind Lady," followed by "Prizes."

HOOYMAN, BARBARA "BABS". Born May 6, 1958 in Appleton, WI. Graduate St. Norbert Col., Southern Methodist U. Debut 1989 OB in "The 13th Chair."

HOPKINS, LINDA. Born 1925 in New Orleans, LA. Bdwy in "Purlie," "Inner City," "Me and Bessie," "Black and Blue."

HORAN, BONNIE. Born Aug. 20, 1928 in Dayton, TX. Graduate UHouston, U. Paris, Geo. Wash. U. Debut 1980 OB in "The Devil's Disciple," followed by "The Meehans," "Arms and the Man," "Her Great Match," "Uncle Vanya," "She Stoops to Conquer," "Hedda Gabler," "All's Well That Ends Well."

HOREN, BOB. Born Oct. 12, 1925 in Aberdeen, SD. Graduate U Minn., U Mo. OB in "Hogan's Goat," "The 13th Chair," Bdwy in "An Enemy of the People," "A Minor Miracle," "The Great White Hope."

HORGAN, PATRICK. Born May 26, 1929 in Nottingham, Eng. Attended Stoneyhurst Col. Bdwy debut 1958 in "Redhead," followed by "Heartbreak House," "The Devil's Advocate," "Beyond the Fringe," "Baker Street," "Crown Matrimonial," "Sherlock Holmes," "My Fair Lady," "Deathtrap," "Noises Off," OB in "The Importance of Being Earnest," "Tamara."

HORMAN, MICHELLE. Born Feb. 6, 1963 in Salt Lake City, UT. Graduate UUt. Debut 1988 OB in "Oil City Symphony."

HOUGHTON, KATHARINE. Born Mar. 10, 1945 in Hartford, CT. Graduate Sarah Lawrence Col. Bdwy debut 1965 in "A Very Rich Woman," followed by "The Front Page" (1969), "Our Town" (1989), OB in "A Scent of Flowers," for which she received a Theatre World Award, "To Heaven in a Swing," "Madwoman of Chaillot," "Vivat! Vivat Regina!," "The Time of Your Life," "Children of the Sun," "Buddha," "On the Shady Side," "The Right Number," "The Hooded Eye."

HOULE, RAYMOND. Born May 16, 1950 in Colchester, VT. Graduate Champlain Col., UVt., UWash. Bdwy debut 1989 in "Largely New York."

HOWARD, KEN. Born Mar. 28, 1944 in El Centro, CA. Graduate Yale. Bdwy debut 1968 in "Promises, Promises," followed by "1776," for which he received a Theatre World Award, "Child's Play," "Seesaw," "Little Black Sheep" (LC), "The Norman Conquests," "1600 Pennsylvania Avenue," "Rumors."

HOWARD, WADE. Born Sept. 23, 1957 in Morristown, NJ. Graduate Hampden-Sydney Col. Debut OB 1988 in "Kiss Me Quick Before the Lava Reaches the Village."

HOXIE, RICHMOND. Born July 21, 1946 in NYC. Graduate Dartmouth Col., LAMDA. Debut 1975 OB in "Shaw for an Evening," followed by "The Family," "Justice," "Landscape with Waitress," "3 from the Marathon," "The Slab Boys," "Vivien," "Operation Midnight Climax," "The Dining Room," "Daddies," "To Gillian on Her 37th Birthday," "Dennis," "Traps," "Sleeping Dogs," "Equal Wrights."

HUBER, KATHLEEN. Born Mar. 3, 1947 in NYC. Graduate UCal. Debut 1969 OB in "A Scent of Flowers," followed by "The Virgin and the Unicorn," "The Constant Wife," "Milestones," "Tamara."

HUDSON, RODNEY. Born Oct. 14, 1948 in St. Louis, MO. Graduate USEMo, USDak, UMich. Debut 1977 OB in "Agamemnon," followed by "Indulgencies," "Runaways," "Dispatches," "Alice in Concert," "American Notes," "Faith/Hope/Charity."

HUDSON, TRAVIS. Born Feb. 2 in Amarillo, Tx. UTx graduate. Bdwy debut in "New Faces of 1962," followed by "Pousse Cafe," "Very Good Eddie," "The Grand Tour," OB in "Triad," "Tattooed Countess," "Young Abe Lincoln," "Get Thee to Canterbury," "The Golden Apple," "Annie Get Your Gun," "Nunsense."

HUFFMAN, CADY. Born Feb. 2, 1965 in Santa Barbara, CA. Debut 1983 OB in "They're Playing Our Song," followed by "Festival of 1 Acts," Bdwy 1985 in "La Cage aux Folles," followed by "Big Deal."

HUFFMAN, FELICITY. Born Dec. 9, 1962 in Westchester, NY. Graduate NYU. AADA., RADA, Debut 1988 in "Boys' Life," followed by "Been Taken," Bdwy in "Speed-the-Plow."

HUGHES, TRESA. Born Sept. 17, 1929 in Washington, DC. Attended Wayne U. OB in "Electra," "The Crucible," "Hogan's Goat," "Party on Greenwich Avenue," "Fragments," "Passing Through from Exotic Places," "Beggar on Horseback," "Early Morning," "The Old Ones," "Holy Places," "Awake and Sing," "Standing on My Knees," "Modern Ladies of Guanabacoa," "After the Fall," "Claptrap," "Cafe Crown," Bdwy in "The Miracle Worker," "The Devil's Advocate," "Dear Me, the Sky Is Falling," "The Last Analysis," "Spofford," "Man in the Glass Booth," "Prisoner of 2nd Avenue," "Tribute," "A View From the Bridge," "V & V Only," "Cafe Crown."

HUGOT, MARCELINE. Born Feb. 10, 1960 in Hartford, CT. Graduate Brown U., UC San Diego. Debut OB 1986 in "The Maids," followed by "Measure for Measure."

HULCE, THOMAS. Born Dec. 6, 1953 in Plymouth, MI. Graduate NCSchArts. Bdwy debut 1975 in "Equus," followed by "A Few Good Men," OB "A Memory of Two Mondays," "Julius Caesar," "Twelve Dreams," "The Rise and Rise of Daniel Rocket," "Haddock's Eyes."

HUNT, HELEN. Born in Los Angeles, CA. Debut OB 1986 in "Been Taken," Bdwy 1989 in "Our Town."

HUNT, LINDA. Born Apr. 2, 1945 in Morristown, NJ. Attended Goodman Sch. Debut 1975 OB in "Down by the River," followed by "The Tennis Game," "Metamorphosis in Miniature," "Little Victories," "Top Girls," "Aunt Dan and Lemon," "The Cherry Orchard," "Annula," Bdwy in "Ah, Wilderness!" (1975), "End of the World."

HUNTER, KIM. Born Nov. 12, 1922 in Detroit, MI. Attended Actors Studio. Bdwy debut 1947 in "A Streetcar Named Desire," followed by "Darkness at Noon," "The Chase," "The Children's Hour," "The Tender Trap," "Write Me a Murder," "Weekend," "Penny Wars," "The Women," "To Grandmother's House We Go," OB in "Come Slowly, Eden," "All Is Bright," "The Cherry Orchard," "When We Dead Awaken," "Territorial Rites," "Faulkner's Bicycle," "Man and Superman," "Murder of Crows."

HUTTON, BILL. Born Aug. 5, 1950 in Evansville, In. Graduate UEvansville. Debut 1979 OB in "Festival," followed by "Blame It on the Movies," Bdwy 1982 in "Joseph and the Amazing Technicolor Dreamcoat."

HYMAN, EARLE. Born Oct. 11, 1926 in Rocky Mount, NC. Attended New School, AmTh Wing. Bdwy debut 1943 in "Run Little Chillun," followed by "Anna Lucasta," "Climate of Eden," "Merchant of Venice," "Othello," "Julius Caesar," "The Tempest," "No Time for Sergeants," "Mr. Johnson," for which he received a Theatre World Award, "St. Joan," "Hamlet," "Waiting for Godot," "The Duchess of Malfi," "Les Blancs," "The Lady from Dubuque," "Execution of Justice," "Death of the King's Horseman," OB in "The White Rose and the Red," "Worlds of Shakespeare," "Jonah," "Life and Times of J. Walter Smintheus," "Orrin," "The Cherry Orchard," "House Party," "Carnival Dreams," "Agamemnon," "Othello," "Julius Caesar," "Coriolanus," "Remembrance," "Long Day's Journey into Night," "Sleep Beauty," "Driving Miss Daisy."

IANNUCCI, MICHAEL. Born Feb. 3, 1956 in Philadelphia, PA. Graduate TempleU., RADA. Debut 1983 OB in "Waiting For Lefty," followed by "Writers," "A Flash of Lightning," "Leave It to Jane."

INGE, MATTHEW. Born May 29, 1950 in Fitchburg, MA. Attended Boston U., Harvard. Bdwy debut 1976 in "Fiddler on the Roof," followed by "A Chorus Line."

IRVING, GEORGE S. Born Nov. 1, 1922 in Springfield, Ma. Attended Leland Powers Sch. Bdwy debut 1943 in "Oklahoma!," followed by "Call Me Mister," "Along 5th Avenue," "Two's Company," "Me and Juliet," "Can-Can," "Shinbone Alley," "Bells Are Ringing," "The Good Soup," "Tovarich," "A Murderer Among Us," "Alfie," "Anya," "Galileo," "4 on a Garden," "An Evening with Richard Nixon . . .," "Irene," "Whos Who in Hell," "All Over Town," "So Long 174th Street," "Once in a Lifetime," "I Remember Mama," "Copperfield," "Pirates of Penzance," "On Your Toes," "Rosalie in Concert," "Pal Joey in Concert," "Me and My Girl."

IRWIN, BILL. Born Apr. 11, 1950 in California. Attended UCLA, Oberlin, Clown Col. Debut 1982 OB in "The Regard of Flight," followed by "The Courtroom," "Waiting For Godot," Bdwy in "5-6-7-8 Dance" (1983), "Accidental Death of an Anarchist," "Regard of Flight" (LC), "Largely New York."

IVEY, DANA. Born Aug. 12, in Atlanta, GA. Graduate Rollins Col., LAMDA. Bdwy debut 1981 in "Macbeth" (LC), followed by "Present Laughter," "Heartbreak House," "Sunday in the Park with George," "Pack of Lies," "Marriage of Figaro," OB in "A Call From the East," "Vivien," "Candida in Concert," "Major Barbara in Concert," "Quartermaine's Terms," "Baby with the Bathwater," "Driving Miss Daisy," "Wencelas Square," "Love Letters."

JABLONS, KAREN. Born July 19, 1951 in Trenton, NJ. Juilliard graduate. Debut 1969 OB in "The Student Prince," followed by "Sound of Music," "Funny Girl," "Boys from Syracuse," "Sterling Silver," "People in Show Business Make Long Goodbyes," "In Trousers," Bdwy in "Ari," "Two Gentlemen of Verona," "Lorelei," "Where's Charley?," "A Chorus Line."

JACKS, SUSAN. Born Nov. 5, 1953 in Brooklyn, NY. Graduate SUNY. Debut 1983 OB in "Forbidden Broadway," followed by "Stages," "Nunsense," "Ad Hock."

JACKSON, ANNE. Born Sept. 3, 1926 in Allegheny, PA. Attended Neighborhood Playhouse. Bdwy debut 1945 in "Signature," followed by "Yellow Jack," "John Gabriel Borkman," "The Last Dance," "Summer and Smoke," "Magnolia Alley," "Love Me Long," "Lady from the Sea," "Never Say Never," "Oh, Men!, Oh, Women!," "Rhinoceros," "Luv," "The Exercise," "Inquest," "Promenade All," "Waltz of the Toreadors," "Twice Around the Park," "Cafe Crown," OB in "The Tiger," "The Typist," "Marco Polo Sings a Solo," "Diary of Anne Frank," "Nest of the Wood Grouse," "Madwoman of Chaillot," "Cafe Crown."

JACKSON, DAVID. Born Dec. 4, 1948 in Philadelphia, PA. Bdwy debut 1980 in "Eubie!," followed by "My One and Only," "La Cage aux Folles," OB in "Blackamoor."

JACOBS, MARC RUSTY. Born July 10, 1967 in NYC. Debut 1979 OB in "Tripletale," followed by "Glory Hallelujah!," "What a Life!," "Three Sisters," "Leave It to Jane," Bdwy in "Peter Pan" (1979).

JAFFE, JOAN. Born Dec. 23 in Wilmington, DE. Attended Boston Conserv. of Music., NYU. Debut OB 1960 in "Carousel," followed by "The Boys from Syracuse," "Once upon a Mattress," "Stage Door," "Professionally Speaking," "Young Rube," Bdwy in "Bajour," "Much Ado About Nothing."

JAMES, KELLI. Born Mar. 18, 1959 in Council Bluffs, Iowa. Bdwy debut 1987 in "Les Miserables."

JAMES, KRICKER. Born May 17, 1939 in Cleveland, OH. Graduate Denison U. Debut 1966 OB in "Winterset," followed by "Out of Control," "Rainbows for Sale," "The Firebugs," "Darkness at Noon," "The Hunting Man," "Sacraments," "Trifles," "Batting Practice."

JAMROG, JOSEPH. Born Dec. 21, 1932 in Flushing, NY. Graduate CCNY. Debut 1970 OB in "Nobody Hears a Broken Drum," followed by "Tango," "And Whose Little Boy Are You?," "When You Comin' Back, Red Ryder?," "Drums at Yale," "The Boy Friend," "Love," "Death Plays," "Too Much Johnson," "A Stitch in Time," "Pantagleize," "Final Hours," "Returnings," "Brass Birds Don't Sing," "And Things That Go Bump in the Night," "Fun," "Henry Lumpur."

JARKOWSKY, ANDREW. Born in NYC. Graduate CCNY. Debut OB 1974 in "Festival of Short Plays," followed by "Cakes with Wine," "The Boss," "The Grinding Machine," "Hamlet," "Philoctetes," Bdwy in "The Trip Back Down."

JAY, MARY. Born Dec. 23, 1939 in Brooklyn, NY. Graduate UMe, AmThWing. Debut 1962 OB in "Little Mary Sunshine," followed by "Toys in the Attic," "Telecast," "Sananda Sez," "Soul of the White Ant," "The Quilling of Prue," "Summit Conference," "Rimers of Eldritch," Bdwy in "The Student Gypsy," "Candida" (1981), "Beethoven's Tenth," "Teddy and Alice."

JAY, PENNY. Born in Chicago, IL. Graduate ButlerU. Debut OB 1987 in "Give My Regards to Broadway," followed by "Babes in Toyland," "The Merry Widow," "The Mikado," "The Desert Song," "HMS Pinafore," "Naughty Marietta," "Fiorello!"

JBARA, GREGORY. Born Sept. 28, 1961 in Wayne, MI. Graduate UMi., Juilliard. Debut 1986 OB in "Have I Got a Girl for You!," "Serious Money," Bdwy in "Serious Money" (1988), "Born Yesterday."

JENNER, JAMES. Born Mar. 5, 1953 in Houston, TX. Attended UTx, LAMDA. Debut OB 1980 in "Kind Lady," followed by "Station J," "Yellow Fever," "Comedy of Errors," "Taster's Choice," "Play Ball."

JENRETTE, RITA. Born Nov. 25, 1949 in San Antonio, Tx. Graduate UTx. Debut 1986 OB in "Girl's Guide to Chaos," followed by "Get Any Guy."

JEROME, TIMOTHY. Born Dec. 29, 1943 in Los Angeles, CA. Graduate Ithaca Col. Bdwy debut 1969 in "Man of La Mancha," followed by "The Rothschilds," "Creation of the World . . .," "Moony Shapiro Songbook," "Cats," "Me and My Girl," OB in "Beggar's Opera," "Pretzels," "Civilization and Its Discontents," "The Little Prince," "Colette Collage," "Room Service," "Romance in Hard Times."

JETER, MICHAEL. Born Aug. 26, 1952 in Lawrenceburg, TN. Graduate Memphis State U. Bdwy debut 1978 in "Once in a Lifetime," followed by "Grand Hotel," OB in "The Master and Margarita," "G.R. Point," for which he received a Theatre World Award, "Alice in Concert," "El Bravo," "Cloud 9," "Greater Tuna," "The Boys Next Door," "Only Kidding."

JILER, JOHN. Born Apr. 4, 1946 in NYC. Graduate UHartford. Debut 1982 OB in "The Frances Farmer Story," followed by "Trouble/Idle Hands," "One Room with Bath," "Emerald City," "Beverly's Yard Sale," "Sunday Promenade."

JOHANSON, DON. Born Oct. 19, 1952 in Rock Hill, SC. Graduate USC. Bdwy debut 1976 in "Rex," followed by "Cats," OB in "The American Dance Machine."

JOHNSON, ARCH. Born Mar. 14, 1931 in Minneapolis, MN. Attended UPa., Neighborhood Playhouse. Debut 1952 OB in "Down in the Valley," followed by "St. Joan," "Purple Dust," "Knucklebones," "Other People's Money," Bdwy in "Mrs. McThing," "Bus Stop," "The Happiest Millionaire," "West Side Story" (1957 & 1980).

JOHNSON, ONNI. Born Mar. 16, 1949 in NYC. Graduate Brandeis U. Debut 1964 in "Unfinished Business," followed by "She Stoops to Conquer," "22 Years," "The Master and Margarita," "Haggedah," "Fragments of a Greek Trilogy," Bdwy in "Oh, Calcutta!"

JOHNSON, PAGE. Born Aug. 25, 1930 in Welch, WV. Graduate Ithaca Col. Bdwy bow 1951 in "Romeo and Juliet," followed by "Electra," "Oedipus," "Camino Real," "In April Once," for which he received a Theatre World Award, "Red Roses for Me," "The Lovers," "Equus," "You Can't Take It With You," OB in "The Enchanted," "Guitar," "4 in 1," "Journey of the Fifth Horse," APA's "School for Scandal," "The Tavern," and "The Seagull," "Odd Couple," "Boys In The Band," "Medea," "Deathtrap," "Best Little Whorehouse in Texas," "Fool for Love."

JOHNSTON, JUSTINE. Born June 13 in Evanston, Il. Debut 1959 OB in "Little Mary Sunshine," followed by "The Time of Your Life" (CC), "The Dubliners," "The New York Idea," Bdwy in "Pajama Game," "Milk and Honey," "Follies," "Irene," "Molly," "Angel," "Me and My Girl."

JOINER, DORRIE. Born in Dublin, GA. Graduate U Southern Al. Debut 1989 OB in "Steel Magnolias."

JONES, CHERRY. Born Nov. 21, 1956 in Paris, TN. Graduate Carnegie-Mellon U. Debut 1983 OB in "The Philanthropist," followed by "he and she," "The Ballad of Soapy Smith," "The Importance of Being Earnest," "I Am a Camera," "Claptrap," "Big Time," Bdwy in "Stepping Out" (1986).

JONES, JAY AUBREY. Born Mar. 30, 1954 in Atlantic City, NJ. Graduate Syracuse U. Debut 1981 OB in "Sea Dream," followed by "Divine Hysteria," "Inacent Black and the Brothers," "La Belle Helene," Bdwy in "Cats" (1986).

JONES, LEILANI. Born May 14 in Honolulu, HI. Graduate UHi. Debut 1981 OB in "El Bravo," followed by "Little Shop of Horrors," "Blues in the Night," Bdwy in "Grind" (1985) for which she received a Theatre World Award.

JOYCE, HEIDI. Born Sept. 12, 1960 in Cleveland, OH. Graduate IndU. Debut 1986 OB in "Girl Crazy," followed by "The Shop on Main Street," "Have I Got a Girl For You!," "Leave It to Jane."

KAGAN, DIANE. Born in Maplewood, NJ. Graduate FlaStateU. Debut 1963 OB in "Asylum," followed by "Days and Nights of Beebee Fenstermaker," "Death of a Well-Loved Boy," "Mme. de Sade," "Blue Boys," "Alive and Well in Argentina," "Little Black Sheep," "The Family," "Ladyhouse Blues," "Scenes from Everyday Life," "Marvelous Gray," "Enrico IV," Bdwy in "Chinese Prime Minister" (1964), "Never Too Late," "Any Wednesday," "Venus Is," "Tiger at the Gates," "Vieux Carre."

KAHN, MADELINE. Born Sept. 29, 1942 in Boston, MA. Graduate Hofstra U. Bdwy debut in "New Faces of 1968," followed by "Two by Two," "She Loves Me," "On the 20th Century," "Born Yesterday" (1988), OB in "Promendade," "Boom Boom Room," "Marco Polo Sings a Solo," "What's Wrong with This Picture?"

KAMHI, KATHERINE. Born Feb. 15, 1964 in NYC. Debut OB 1988 in "A Shayna Maidel."

KANE, BRADLEY. Born Sept. 29, 1973 in New Rochelle, NY. Debut 1982 OB in "Scraps," followed by "A Winter's Tale," "Sunday in the Park with George," "Titus Andronicus," Bdwy in "Evita" (1983).

KANE, DONNA. Born Aug. 12, 1962 in Beacon, NY. Graduate Mt. Holyoke Col. Debut 1985 OB in "Dames at Sea," for which she received a Theatre World Award, followed by "The Vinegar Tree," "Johnny Pye and the Foolkiller," "Babes in Arms," "Young Rube."

KANSAS, JERI. Born Mar. 10, 1955 in Jersey City, NJ. Debut 1978 OB in "Gay Divorce," Bdwy 1979 in "Sugar Babies," followed by "42nd Street."

KARIBALIS, CURT. Born Feb. 24, 1947 in Superior, WI. Graduate UWis. Debut 1971 OB in "Woyzeck," followed by "The Taming of the Shrew," Bdwy in "The Great God Brown" (1972), "Don Juan," "The Visit," "Chemin de Fer," "Holiday," "Goodbye Fidel," "M. Butterfly."

KATARINA, ANNA. Born Feb. 25, 1956 in Bern, Switz. Attended Bern Consv. Debut 1987 OB in "Tamara."

KAYE, JUDY. Born Oct. 11, 1948 in Phoenix, AZ. Attended UCLA, Ariz. State U. Bdwy debut 1977 in "Grease," followed by "On the 20th Century," for which she received a Theatre World Award, "Moony Shapiro Songbook," "Oh, Brother!," "Phantom of the Opera," "The Pajama Game" (LC), OB in "Eileen in Concert," "Can't Help Singing," "Four to Make Two," "Sweethearts in Concert," "Love," "No No Nanette in Concert," "Magdalena in Concert," "Babes in Arms," "Desire Under the Elms."

KEAL, ANITA. Born in Philadelphia, PA. Graduate Syracuse U. Debut 1956 OB in "Private Life of the Master Race," followed by "Brothers Karamazov," "Hedda Gabler," "Witches Sabbath," "Six Characters in Search of an Author," "Yes, My Darling Daughter," "Speed Gets the Poppy," "You Don't Have to Tell Me," "Val Christie and Others," "Do You Still Believe the Rumor?," "Farmyard," "Merry Wives of Scarsdale," "Exiles," "Fish Riding Bikes," "Haven," "The Affair," "Mother Bickerdyke," Bdwy in "M. Butterfly" (1989).

KEATING, CHARLES. Born Oct. 22, 1941 in London, Eng. Bdwy debut 1969 in "Arturo Ui," followed by "The House of Atreus," "Loot," OB in "An Ounce of Prevention," "A Man for All Seasons," "There Is a Dream Dreaming Us," "What the Butler Saw."

KELLETT, ROBERT. Born Aug. 29, 1955 in Minneapolis, MN. Attended UIll, Goodman Theatre. Debut 1981 OB in "Oh, Johnny!," followed by "Sex Acts," Bdwy in "Anything Goes" (1987).

KELLY, MARGUERITE. Born Dec. 7, 1959 in Washington, DC. Attended Catholic U. Debut 1986 OB in "Taking Steps," Bdwy in "The Devil's Disciple."

KENER, DAVID. Born May 21, 1959 in Brooklyn, NY. Graduate NYU. Debut 1987 OB in "The Rise of David Levinsky," followed by "Songs of Paradise."

KENNY, JACK. Born Mar. 9, 1958 in Chicago, IL. Attended Juilliard. Debut 1983 OB in "Pericles," followed by "Tartuffe," "Play and Other Plays," "Normal Heart," "The Rise of David Levinsky," "Festival of 1 Acts," "Cafe Crown," Bdwy in "Cafe Crown" (1989).

KENYON, LAURA. Born Nov. 23, 1948 in Chicago, IL. Attended USCal. Debut 1970 OB in "Peace," followed by "Carnival," "Dementos," "The Trojan Women," "Have I Got a Girl For You," "Desire," Bdwy in "Man of La Mancha" (1971), "On the Town," "Nine."

KEPROS, NICHOLAS. Born Nov. 8, 1932 in Salt Lake City, UT. Graduate UUtah, RADA. Debut 1958 OB in "The Golden Six," followed by "Wars of Roses," "Julius Caesar," "Hamlet," "Henry IV," "She Stoops to Conquer," "Peer Gynt," "Octaroon," "Endicott and the Red Cross," "The Judas Applause," "Irish Hebrew Lesson," "Judgment at Havana," "The Millionairess," "Androcles and the Lion," "The Redempter," "Othello," "The Times and Appetites of Toulouse-Lautrec," "Two Fridays," "Rameau's Nephew," Bdwy in "St. Joan" (1968), "Amadeus," "Execution of Justice."

KERNER, NORBERTO. Born July 19, 1929 in Valparaiso, Chile. Attended Piscator Workshop, Goodman Theatre. Debut 1971 OB in "Yerma," followed by "I Took Panama," "The F.M. Sale," "My Old Friends," "Sharon Shashanovah," "The Blood Wedding," "Crisp," "The Great Confession," "Cold Air," "Don Juan of Seville."

KERR, PHILIP. Born Apr. 9, 1940 in NYC. Attended Harvard, LAMDA. Bdwy debut 1969 in "Tiny Alice," followed by "A Flea in Her Ear," "Three Sisters," "Jockey Club Stakes," "Macbeth" (1988), OB in "Hamlet," "The Rehearsal," "Cuchlain," "Mistress of the Inn."

KERSEY, BILLYE. Born Oct. 15, 1955 in Norfolk, VA. Bdwy debut 1981 in "42nd Street."

KERSHAW, WHITNEY. Born Apr. 10, 1962 in Orlando, FL. Attended Harkness/Joffrey Ballet Schools. Debut 1981 OB in "Francis," Bdwy in "Cats."

KEY, TOM. Born July 6, 1950 in Birmingham, AL. Graduate UTenn. Debut 1981 OB in "Cotton Patch Gospel," followed by "Revelation of John."

KHOURY, PAMELA. Born May 17, 1954 in Beirut, Lebanon. Graduate UTx. Bdwy debut 1980 in "West Side Story," followed by "Oh, Brother!," "Jerome Robbins' Broadway," OB in "Too Many Girls."

KIMMEL, MIKE. Born May 27, 1960 in NYC. Graduate Brandeis U. Debut OB 1989 in "The Thirteenth Chair."

KING, GINNY. Born May 12, 1957 in Atlanta, GA. Attended NCSch of Arts. Bdwy debut 1980 in "42nd Street."

KING, LARRY L. Born Jan. 1, 1929 in Putnam, TX. Attended Tx Tech. U, Harvard, Duke U. Bdwy debut 1979 in "The Best Little Whorehouse in Texas," OB in "The Night Hank Williams Died."

KINGSLEY-WEIHE, GRETCHEN. Born Oct. 6, 1961 in Washington, DC. Attended Tulane U. Debut 1985 OB in "Mowgli," followed by "This Could Be the Start," Bdwy in "Les Miserables" (1987), "Sweeney Todd."

KIRBY-NUNES, MIZAN. Born Oct. 8 in Port-of-Spain, Trinidad. Graduate U Chicago. OB debut 1985 in "Sherlock Holmes and the Hands of Othello," followed by "The Trial of Adam Clayton Powell," "La Mulata," "In the Beginning . . .," "The Brothers."

KIRSCH, CAROLYN. Born May 24, 1942 in Shreveport, LA. Bdwy debut 1963 in "How to Succeed . . . ," followed by "Follies Bergere," "La Grosse Valise," "Skyscraper," "Breakfast at Tiffany's," "Sweet Charity," "Hallelujah, Baby!," "Dear World," "Promises, Promises," "Coco," "Ulysses in Nighttown," "A Chorus Line," OB in "Silk Stockings," "Telecast."

KIRSTEIN, DALE. Born May 18 in Washington, DC. Graduate Ithaca Col. Bdwy debut 1981 in "Camelot," followed by "Show Boat," Radio City Music Hall Specials, "Phantom of the Opera."

KLEIN, ROBERT. Born Feb. 8, 1942 in NYC. Graduate Alfred U., Yale. OB in "Six Characters in Search of an Author," "Second City Returns," "Upstairs at the Downstairs," Bdwy in "The Apple Tree," "New Faces of 1968," "Morning Noon and Night," "They're Playing Our Song," "The Robert Klein Show," "Robert Klein on Broadway."

KLINE, KEVIN. Born Oct. 24, 1947 in St. Louis, MO. Graduate IndU, Juilliard. Debut 1970 OB in "War of Roses," followed by "School for Scandal," "Lower Depths," "The Hostage," "Women Beware Women," "Robber Bridegroom," "Edward II," "The Time of Your Life," "Beware the Jubjub Bird," "Dance on a Country Grave," "Richard III," "Henry V," "Hamlet," "Much Ado About Nothing," Bdwy in "Three Sisters," "Measure for Measure," "Beggar's Opera," "Scapin'," "On the 20th Century," "Loose Ends," "Pirates of Penzance," "Arms and the Man."

KLUNIS, TOM. Born in San Francisco, CA. Bdwy debut 1961 in "Gideon," followed by "The Devils," "Henry V," "Romeo and Juliet," "St. Joan," "Hide and Seek," "Bacchae," "Plenty," "M. Butterfly," OB in "The Immoralist," "Hamlet," "Arms and the Man," "The Potting Shed," "Measure for Measure," "Romeo and Juliet," "The Balcony," "Our Town," "The Man Who Never Died," "God Is My Ram," "Rise Marlow," "Iphigenia in Aulis," "Still Life," "The Master and Margarita," "As You Like It," "The Winter Dancers," "When We Dead Awaken," "Vieux Carre," "The Master Builder," "Richard III," "A Map of the World."

KNAPP, SARAH. Born Jan. 20, 1959 in Kansas City, MO. Graduate AADA. Debut OB 1986 in "Gifts of the Magi," followed by "The No Frills Revue," "Nunsense."

KNUDSON, KURT. Born Sept. 7, 1936 in Fargo, ND. Attended NDStateU, UMiami. Debut 1976 OB in "The Cherry Orchard," followed by "Geniuses," "Room Service," "Without Apologies," Bdwy in "Curse of an Aching Heart" (1982), "Sunday in the Park With George," "Take Me Along."

KOBI, MICHI. Born in Sacramento, CA. Graduate NYU. Bdwy debut in "One Flew Over the Cuckoo's Nest" (1965), OB in "Boutique Living and Disposable Icons."

KOKA, JULIETTE. Born Apr. 4, 1930 in Finland. Attended Helsinki School of Dramatic Arts. Debut 1977 OB in "Piaf . . . A Remembrance," for which she received a Theatre World Award, followed by "Ladies and Gentlemen Jerome Kern," "Salon," Bdwy in All Star Players Club Centennial Salute" (1989).

KOLINSKI, JOSEPH. Born June 26, 1953 in Detroit, Mi. Attended UDetroit. Bdwy debut 1980 in "Brigadoon," followed by "Dance a Little Closer," "The Three Musketeers," "Les Miserables," OB in "Hijinks!," "The Human Comedy" (also Bdwy).

KOPACHE, THOMAS. Born Oct. 17, 1945 in Manchester, NH. Graduate San Diego State U. CalInstArts. Debut 1976 OB in "The Architect and the Emperor of Assyria," followed by "Brontosaurus Rex," "Extravagant Triumph," "Caligula," "The Tempest," "Macbeth," "Measure for Measure," "Hunting Scenes from Lower Bavaria," "The Danube," "Friends Too Numerous to Mention," "Twelfth Night," "A Winter's Tale," "Working 1 Acts," Bdwy in "Our Town" (1989).

KORBICH, EDDIE. Born Nov. 6, 1960 in Washington, DC. Graduate Boston Consv. Debut 1985 OB in "A Little Night Music," followed by "Flora, the Red Menace," "No Frills Revue," "The Last Musical Comedy," "Godspell," "Sweeney Todd" (also Bdwy), Bdwy in "Singin' in the Rain" (1985).

KOREY, ALIX (formerly Alexandra). Born May 14 in Brooklyn, NY. Graduate Columbia U. Debut 1976 OB in "Fiorello!," followed by "Annie Get Your Gun," "Jerry's Girls," "Rosalie in Concert," "America Kicks Up Its Heels," "Gallery," "Feathertop," "Bittersuite," "Romance in Hard Times," Bdwy in "Hello, Dolly!" (1978), "Show Boat" (1983).

KORTHAZE, RICHARD. Born Feb. 11 in Chicago, IL. Graduate Chicago Musical Col. Bdwy debut 1953 in "Pal Joey," followed by "Wonderful Town," "Happy Hunting," "Conquering Hero," "How to Succeed in Business . . .," "Skyscraper," "Walking Happy," "Promises, Promises," "Pippin," "Chicago," "Dancin'," "Take Me Along" (1985), "Anything Goes," OB in "Phoenix '55" (1955).

KOSIS, TOM. Born Apr. 24, 1961 in Sewickley, PA. Graduate Adelphi U. Bdwy debut 1988 in "A Chorus Line."

KRAMER, BARRY. Born Oct. 4, 1959 in Chicago, IL. Graduate UIll. Debut OB 1986 in "Blind Hearts," followed by "Family Life," "Philoctetes."

KRESS, RONNA. Born Dec. 29, 1959 in Pittsburgh, PA. Graduate Boston U. Debut 1982 OB in "Twelfth Night," followed by "The Country Wife," "Pericles," "Tartuffe," "Camille/Ivanov," "No One Dances."

KRISTIEN, DALE. Born May 18 in Washington, DC. Graduate Ithaca Col. Bdwy debut 1981 in "Camelot," followed by "Show Boat," "Phantom of the Opera."

KUHN, BRUCE W. Born Dec. 7, 1955 in Davenport, IA. Graduate UWVa., UWash. Bdwy debut 1987 in "Les Miserables."

KUREK, ANNETTE. Born Feb. 6, 1950 in Chicago, IL. Graduate UWi. Debut 1976 OB in "The Hairy Ape," followed by "Isadora Duncan Sleeps with the Russian Navy," "Word of Mouth," "Coming Attractions," "The Fuehrer Bunker," "Cowboy Mouth," "An Altar to Himself."

KUROWSKI, RON. Born Mar. 14, 1953 in Philadelphia, Pa. Attended Temple U., RADA. Bdwy debut 1977 in "A Chorus Line."

KURSHAL, RAYMOND. Born in NYC. Hunter Col. graduate. Bdwy debut 1985 in "Singin' in the Rain," OB in "Garden of Earthly Delights," "Winter's Tale."

KURTH, JULIETTE. Born July 22, 1960 in Madison, WI. Graduate SUNY/Purchase. Debut 1984 OB in "The Miser," followed by "Love's Labour's Lost," "Majestic Kid," Bdwy in "La Cage aux Folles" (1986).

KURTZ, MARCIA JEAN. Born in The Bronx, NY. Graduate Juilliard. Debut 1966 OB in "Jonah," followed by "America Hurrah," "Red Cross," "Muzeeka," "Effect of Gamma Rays . . .," "The Year Boston Won the Pennant," "The Mirror," "The Orphan," "Action," "The Dybbuk," "Ivanov," "What's Wrong with This Picture?," "Today I Am a Fountain Pen," "The Chopin Playoffs," "Lowman Family Picnic," Bdwy in "The Chinese and Dr. Fish," "Thieves," "Execution of Justice."

KURTZ, SWOOSIE. Born Sept. 6 in Omaha, Ne. Attended USCal, LAMDA. Debut 1968 OB in "The Firebugs," followed by "The Effect of Gamma Rays . . .," "Enter a Free Man," "Children," "Museum," "Uncommon Women and Others," "Wine Untouched," "Summer," "The Beach House," Bdwy in "Ah, Wilderness!" (1975), "Tartuffe," "A History of the American Film," "5th of July," " House of Blue Leaves."

LABANZ, JANE. Born in Cincinnati, OH. Graduate MiamiU., Conn. Conserv. Bdwy debut 1989 in "Anything Goes."

LACKEY, SKIP. Born Sept. 28, 1961 in Baltimore, MD. Attended Ringling Bros. Clown Col. Bdwy debut 1987 in "Big River," OB in "Kiss Me Quick Before the Lava Reaches the Village" (1988), "Macbeth."

LACONI, ROBERT. Born Apr. 23, 1954 in Akron, OH. Graduate Kent StateU. Debut 1978 OB in "Gulliver's Travels," followed by "A Book of Etiquette," "cummings and goings," "Let's Face It," "Julius Caesar," "Comedy of Errors," "New Girl in Town," "The Gambler."

LAGE, JORDAN. Born Feb. 17, 1963 in Pao Alto, CA. Graduate NYU. Debut 1988 OB in "Boy's Life," Bdwy in "Our Town" (1989).

LAGERFELT, CAROLINE. Born Sept. 23 in Paris. Graduate AADA. Bdwy debut 1971 in "The Philanthropist," followed by "4 on a Garden," "Jockey Club Stakes," "The Constant Wife," "Otherwise Engaged," "Betrayal," "The Real Thing," OB in "Look Back in Anger," "Close of Play," "Sea Anchor," "Quartermaine's Terms," "Other Places," "Phaedra Britanica."

LAHTI, CHRISTINE. Born Apr. 4, 1950 in Detroit, MI. Graduate UMich., HB Studio. Debut 1979 OB in "The Wood," for which she received a Theatre World Award, followed by "Landscape of the Body," "The Country Girl," "Little Murders," Bdwy in "Loose Ends" (1980), "Division Street," "Scenes and Revelations," "Present Laughter," "The Heidi Chronicles."

LAMB, MARY ANN. Born July 4, 1959 in Seattle, WA. Attended Neighborhood Playhouse. Bdwy debut 1985 in "Song and Dance," followed by "Starlight Express," "Jerome Robbins' Broadway."

LAMBERT, BEVERLY. Born May 20, 1956 in Stamford, CT. Graduate UNH. Debut 1980 OB in "Plain and Fancy," (ELT), followed by "Sitting Pretty in Concert."

LANDES, FRANCINE. Born July 30, 1953 in San Francisco, CA. Graduate Juilliard, Columbia U. Bdwy debut 1985 in "The Mystery of Edwin Drood," OB in "Miracolo d'Amore."

LANDRON, JACK. Born June 2, 1938 in San Juan, PR. Graduate Emerson Col. Debut 1970 OB in "Ododo," followed by "Mother Courage and Her Children," "If You Promise Not to Learn," "What's a Nice Country Like You . . .," "Spell 7," "Mondongo," "Ballet Behind the Bridge," "The Garden," "Don Juan in NYC," Bdwy in "Hurry Harry" (1972), "Dr. Jazz," "Tough to Get Help," "Murderous Angels."

LANE, NANCY. Born June 16, 1951 in Passaic, NJ. Attended Va. CommonwealthU., AADA. Debut 1975 OB and Broadway in "A Chorus Line."

LANE, NATHAN. Born Feb. 3, 1956 in Jersey City, NJ. Debut 1978 OB in "A Midsummer Night's Dream," followed by "Love," "Measure for Measure," "Claptrap," "The Common Pursuit," "In a Pig's Valise," "Uncounted Blessings," "The Film Society," "The Lisbon Traviata," Bdwy in "Present Laughter" (1982), "Merlin," "Wind in the Willows."

LANG, PETER. Born Nov. 11, 1960 in Basel, Switz. Bdwy debut 1988 in "The Night of the Iguana."

LANGE, ANN. Born June 24, 1953 in Pipestone, MN. Attended Carnegie-Mellon U. Debut 1979 OB in "Rat's Nest," followed by "Hunting Scenes from Lower Bavaria," "Crossfire," "Linda Her and the Fairy Garden," "Little Footsteps," Bdwy in "The Survivor" (1981), "The Heidi Chronicles."

LANIGAN, LORRAINE. Born Mar. 10, 1956 in Long Branch, NJ. Graduate Kean Col., RutgersU. Debut OB in "My Unknown."

LANNING, JERRY. Born May 17, 1943 in Miami, FL. Graduate USCal. Bdwy debut 1966 in "Mame," for which he received a Theatre World Award, followed by "1776," "Where's Charley?," "My Fair Lady," OB in "Memphis Store Bought Teeth," "Berlin to Broadway," "Sextet," "Isn't It Romantic?," "Paradise," "Emerald City."

LANNING, NILE. Born Feb. 21, 1967 in NYC. Graduate OxfordU. Debut OB 1988 in "A Shayna Maidel."

LARSEN, LIZ. Born Jan. 16, 1959 in Philadelphia, PA. Attended HofstraU, SUNY/Purchase. Bdwy debut 1981 in "Fiddler on the Roof," followed by "Starmites," OB in "Kuni Leml," "Hamlin," "Personals," "Starmites," "Company," "After These Messages."

LARSON, LISBY. Born Oct. 23, 1951 in Washington, DC. Graduate UKs. Debut 1976 OB in "The Boys From Syracuse," followed by "Some Enchanted Evening," "Desire," "The Five O'Clock Girl," "Eileen in Concert," "The Firefly in Concert."

LAUREANO, PAUL. Born Dec. 26 in Hartford, CT. Graduate Hartt School of Music. Bdwy debut 1988 in "Chess," OB in "Fiorello!"

LAURENCE, PAULA. Born Jan. 25 in Brooklyn, NY. Bdwy debut 1936 in "Horse Eats Hat," followed by "Dr. Faustus," "Junior Miss," "Something for the Boys," "One Touch of Venus," "Cyrano de Bergerac," "The Liar," "Season in the Sun," "Tovarich," "The Time of Your Life," "Beggar's Opera," "Hotel Paradiso," "Night of the Iguana," "Have I Got a Girl For You," "Ivanov," "Rosalie in Concert," OB in "7 Days of Mourning," "Roberta in Concert," "One Touch of Venus," "Coming of Age in SoHo," "George White's Scandals," "Sitting Pretty."

LAURENSON, DIANA. Born Sept. 25, 1957 in Elmont, NY. Graduate UMass. Bdwy debut 1981 in "The Little Prince and the Aviator," followed by "Big Deal," "Sweet Charity," "Dangerous Games," OB in "No No Nanette" (1987).

LAW, MARY KATE. Born Sept. 12 in Harper, KS. Graduate Wichita StateU., Yale. Bdwy debut 1989 in "Starmites."

LAWLESS, RICK. Born Dec. 31, 1960 in Bridgeport, CT. Graduate Fairfield U. Debut 1985 OB in "Dr. Faustus," followed by "The Foreigner," "Camp Meeting," "Lady Moonsong, Mr. Monsoon," "Fun," "The Magic Act," "Uncounted Blessings."

LAYNG, KATHRYN. Born in Rockford, IL. Graduate UIllinois. Bdwy debut 1988 in "M. Butterfly."

LAZARUS, FRANK. Born May 4, 1939 in Cape Town, SAf. Graduate UCape Town. Bdwy debut 1980 in "Day in Hollywood/Night in the Ukraine," OB in "Brimstone and Treacle."

LaZEBNIK, KENNETH. Born Nov. 11, 1954 In Levitown, PA. Graduate MacAlester Col., RADA. Debut 1985 OB in "Taming of the Shrew," followed by "Camille," "Ivanov," "No One Dances."

LECESNE, JAMES. Born Nov. 24, 1954 in NJ. Debut 1982 OB in "One Man Band," followed by "Cloud 9", and revivals of "One-Man Band" in 1985 and 1988–9.

LEE, CHANDRA. Born Feb. 24, in West Virginia. Graduate SUNY. Debut 1986 OB in "The Long Goodbye," followed by "Troilus & Cressida," "Flower Palace," Bdwy in "Night of the Iguana" (1988).

LEE, KAIULANI. Born Feb. 28, 1950 in Princeton, NJ. Attended AmericanU. Bdwy debut 1975 in "Kennedy's Children," followed by "Macbeth," "Pack of Lies," OB in "Ballad of the Sad Cafe," "Museum," "Safe House," "Days to Come," "Othello," "Strange Snow," "Aristocrats," "Rimers Of Eldritch."

LEE-ARANAS, MARY. Born Sept. 23, 1959 in Taipei, Taiwan. Graduate UOttawa. Debut 1984 OB in "Empress of China," followed by "A State without Grace," "Return of the Phoenix," "Yellow Is My Favorite Color," "Man Who Turned into a Stick," "The Impostor," "Rosie's Cafe," "Three Sisters," "Noiresque."

LeFEVRE, ADAM. Born Aug. 11, 1950 in Albany, NY. Graduate Williams Col., UIowa. Debut 1981 OB in "Turnbuckle," followed by "Badgers," "Goose and Tomtom," "In the Country," "Submariners," "Boys Next Door," Bdwy in "Devil's Disciple" (1988).

LEIBMAN, RON. Born Oct. 11, 1937 in NYC. Attended Ohio Wesleyan, Actors Studio. Bdwy debut 1963 in "Dear Me, the Sky Is Falling," followed by "Bicycle Ride to Nevada," "The Deputy," "We Bombed in New Haven" for which he received a Theatre World Award, "Cop-Out," "I Ought to Be in Pictures," "Doubles," "Rumors," OB in "The Academy," "John Brown's Body," "Scapin," "The Premise," "Legend of Lovers," "Dead End," "Poker Session," "Transfers," "Room Service," "Love Two," "Rich and Famous," "Children of Darkness," "Non Pasquale."

LeMASSENA, WILLIAM. Born May 23, 1916 in Glen Ridge, NJ. Attended NYU. Bdwy debut 1940 in "Taming of the Shrew," followed by "There Shall Be No Night," "The Pirate," "Hamlet," "Call Me Mister," "Inside U.S.A.," "I Know My Love," "Dream Girl," "Nina," "Ondine," "Fallen Angels," "Redhead," "Conquering Hero," "Beauty Part," "Come Summer," "Grin and Bare It," "All Over Town," "Texas Trilogy," "Deathtrap," "Blithe Spirit," "Night of the Iguana," OB in "The Coop," "Brigadoon," "Life With Father," "F. Jasmine Addams," "The Dodge Boys," "Ivanov."

LENZ, RICK. Born Nov. 21, 1939 in Springfield, IL. Graduate UMich. Bdwy debut 1965 in "Mating Dance," followed by "Cactus Flower," OB in "The Infantry," "Calling in Crazy," "Friends."

LEON, JOSEPH. Born June 8, 1923 in NYC. Attended NYU, UCLA. Bdwy debut 1950 in "Bell, Book and Candle," followed by "Seven Year Itch," "Pipe Dream," "Fair Game," "Gazebo," "Julia, Jake and Uncle Joe," "Beauty Part," "Merry Widow," "Henry Sweet Henry," "Jimmy Shine," "All Over Town," "California Suite," "The Merchant," "Break a Leg," "Once a Catholic," "Fools," "Glengary Glen Ross," OB in "Come Share My House," "Dark Corners," "Interrogation of Havana," "Are You Now or Have You Ever," "Second Avenue Rag," "Buck," "Ah Wilderness," "Cafe Crown" (also Bdwy 1989).

LEONARD, ROBERT SEAN. Born Feb. 28, 1969 in Westwood, NJ. Debut 1985 OB in "Sally's Gone, She Left Her Name," followed by "Coming of Age in Soho," "Beach House," "Young Playwrights Festival," Bdwy in "Brighton Beach Memoirs" (1985), "Breaking The Code."

LESLIE, BETHEL. Born Aug. 3, 1929 in NYC. Bdwy debut 1944 in "Snafu," followed by "Years Ago," "Wisteria Trees," "Goodbye My Fancy," "Time of the Cuckoo," "Mary Rose," "Brass Ring," "Inherit the Wind," "Catch Me if You Can," "But Seriously," "Long Day's Journey into Night." OB in "The Aunts."

LEVINE, RICHARD S. Born July 16, 1954 in Boston, MA. Graduate Juilliard. Debut 1978 OB in "Family Business," followed by "Magic Time," "It's Better With a Band," "Emma," "Mistress of the Inn," Bdwy in "Dracula," "Rock n' Roll: First 5000 Years," "Rumors."

LEWIS, EDMUND. Born Feb. 12, 1959 in London, Eng. Attended Reading Blue Coat, RADA. Debut OB in "The Longboat," followed by "A Most Secret War," "Without Apologies," "Up 'n' Under."

LEWIS, LAURA FAY. Born July 6, 1961 in Coral Gables, FL. Attended Webster Col., Juilliard. Debut 1989 OB in "Bunnybear."

LEWIS, MARK. Born Feb. 28, 1957 in Rosario, Argentina. Graduate So.MethodistU, Portland StU. Debut 1988 OB in "Julius Caesar," followed by "Midsummer Night's Dream," "Tamara."

LEWIS, MATTHEW. Born Jan. 12, 1937 in Elizabeth, NJ. Graduate HarvardU. Debut 1970 OB in "Chicago '70," followed by "Fathers and Sons," "The Freak," "Happy Days Are Here Again," "Levitation," "The Seagull" "My Papa's Wine," "Apocalyptic Butterflies," Bdwy in "Angels Fall" (1983).

LEYDEN, LEO. Born Jan. 28, 1929 in Dublin, Ire. Attended Abbey ThSch. Bdwy debut 1960 in "Love and Libel," followed by "Darling of the Day," "Mundy Scheme," "The Rothschilds," "Capt. Brassbound's Conversion," "The Plough and the Stars" (LC), "Habeas Corpus," "Me and My Girl."

LIGHTSTONE, MARILYN. Born June 28, 1940 in Montreal, Can. Graduate McGillU. Bdwy debut 1968 in "King Lear," followed by OB's "Tamara."

LINVILLE, LARRY. Born Sept. 29, 1939 in Ojai, CA. Attended UColo., RADA. Appeared 4 seasons with APA before Bdwy debut 1967 in "More Stately Mansions," followed by "Rumors."

LIPMAN, DAVID. Born May 12, 1938 in Brooklyn, NY. Graduate LIU, Brooklyn Col. Debut 1973 OB in "Moonchildren," followed by "Devil's Disciple," "Don Juan in Hell," "Isn't It Romantic," "Kiss Me Quick," Bdwy in "Fools" (1981).

LISH, JAMES. Born Oct. 28 in NYC. Graduate Ithaca Col. Debut 1984 OB in "It's Hard To Be a Jew," followed by "Male Animal," "Solitaire," "Three Sisters."

LITTLE, JOHN. Born Aug. 12, 1956 in DeKalb, IL. Graduate Yale, NYU, Debut 1988 OB in "Moby Dick."

LIZZUL, ANTHONY JOHN. Born Jan. 11, in the Bronx, NYC. Graduate NYU. Debut 1977 OB in "Cherry Orchard," followed by "The Prophets," "Lady Windermere's Fan," "Revenger's Tragedy," "Twelfth Night," "Night Talk," "Butterfingers Angel," "Consulting Adults."

Lo BIANCO, TONY. Born Oct. 19, 1936 in NYC. Bdwy debut 1966 in "The Office," followed by "Royal Hunt of the Sun," "Rose Tattoo," "90 Day Mistress," "Goodbye People," "View From the Bridge," "Hizzoner," OB in "Threepenny Opera," "Answered the Flute," "Camino Real," "Oh Dad, Poor Dad . . ." "Journey to the Day," "Zoo Story," "Nature of the Crime," "Incident at Vichy," "Tartuffe," "Yankees 3 Detroit 0," "Big Time."

LOCKWOOD, LISA. Born Feb. 13, 1958 in San Francisco, CA. Bdwy debut 1988 in "Phantom of the Opera."

LOFTUS, ELIZABETH. Born Mar. 27, 1956 in Takoma Pk., MD. Graduate UMd, SMU. Debut 1987 OB in "Misalliance," followed by "Shooting Stars."

LOGAN, BELLINA. Born Sept. 28, 1966 in L.A., CA. Graduate Juilliard. Debut 1988 OB in "Young Playwrights Festival" "Women and Wallace"/"Seniority," followed by "For Dear Life."

LOGEN, CAROL. Born July 14 in Detroit, MI. Graduate US Int'lU. Bdwy debut 1974 in "Where's Charley," followed by "Rex," "On the 20th Century," "Evita," "Dreamgirls."

LOMBARD, MICHAEL. Born Aug. 8, 1934 In Brooklyn, NY. Graduate Brooklyn Col., BostonU. OB in "King Lear," "Merchant of Venice," "Cages," "Pinter Plays," "La Turista," "Elizabeth the Queen," "Room Service," "Mert and Phil," "Side Street Scenes," "Angelo's Wedding," "Friends in High Places," Bdwy in "Poor Bitos" (1964), "The Devils," "Gingerbread Lady," "Bad Habits," "Otherwise Engaged," "Awake and Sing."

LONDEREE, TERRY. Born June 9, 1947 in Lynchburg, VA. Graduate William & Mary. Debut 1989 OB in "Cheri."

LOPEZ, PRISCILLA. Born Feb. 26, 1948 in The Bronx, NYC. Bdwy debut 1966 in "Breakfast at Tiffany's," followed by "Henry, Sweet Henry," "Lysistrata," "Company," "Her First Roman," "Boy Friend," "Pippin," "A Chorus Line" (also OB), "Day in Hollywood/Night in the Ukraine," "Nine," OB in "What's a Nice Country Like You . . ." "Key Exchange," "Buck," "Extremites," "Non Pasquale," "Be Happy for Me," "Times and Appetites of Toulouse-Lautrec," "Marathon '88."

LORENZO. Born Sept. 22, 1925 in Beaumont, TX. Attended LACC. Debut OB in "Early Dar," followed by "Scenes from Richard III," "Requiem for Romance," "Fat Tuesday Blues," "Trouble in Mind," "Blackamoor."

LOUDON, DOROTHY. Born Sept. 17, 1933 in Boston, MA. Attended Emerson Col., Syracuse U. Debut 1961 in "World of Jules Feiffer," Bdwy 1963 in "Nowhere to Go but Up" for which she received a Theatre World Award followed by "Noel Coward's Sweet Potato," "Fig Leaves Are Falling," "Three Men on a Horse," "The Women," "Annie," "Ballroom," "West Side Waltz," "Noises Off," "Jerry's Girls."

LOVETT, FARRYL. Born Aug. 30, 1960 in Queens, NYC. Graduate SUNY/Purchase. Debut 1986 OB in "Duchess of Malfi," followed by "Bitter Friends," Bdwy in "Speed-the-Plow" (1988).

LOWERY, MARCELLA. Born Apr. 27, 1945 in Jamaica, NY. Graduate Hunter Col. Debut 1967 OB in "Day of Absence," followed by "American Pastoral," "Ballet behind the Bridge," "Jamimma," "Recent Killing," "Miracle Play," "Welcome to Black River," "Anna Lucasta," "Baseball Wives," "Louis," "Bless Me, Father," "Ladies," Bdwy in "Member of the Wedding" (1975), "Lolita."

LUCAS, J. FRANK. Born in Houston, Tx. Graduate TCU. Debut 1943 OB in "A Man's House," followed by "Coriolanus," "Edward II," "Trip to Bountiful," "Orpheus Descending," "Guitar," "Marcus in the High Grass," "Chocolates," "To Bury a Cousin," "One World at a Time," "Vinegar Tree," "Hamlet," Bdwy in "Bad Habits" (1974), "Scapino," "Best Little Whorehouse in Texas."

LUCAS, ROXIE. Born Aug. 25, 1951 In Memphis, TN. Attended UHouston. Bdwy debut 1981 in "Best Little Whorehouse in Texas," followed by "Harrigan 'n' Hart," OB in "Forbidden Broadway," "Best of Forbidden Broadway."

LUKAS, CARRENA. Born Dec. 8, 1965 in Oregon City, OR. Attended USInt'lU., Nat'l Shakespeare Conser. Debut 1989 OB in "Amulets against the Dragon Forces."

LUM, ALVIN. Born May 28, 1931 in Honolulu, HI. Attended UHI. Debut 1969 OB in "In the Bar of a Tokyo Hotel," followed by "Pursuit of Happiness," "Monkey Music," "Flowers and Household Gods," "Station J," "Double Dutch," "Teahouse," "Song for a Nisei Fisherman," "Empress of China," "Manos Valley," "Hot Sake," "Chu Chem" (also Bdwy), Bdwy in "Lovely Ladies, Kind Gentlemen" (1970), "Two Gentlemen of Verona."

LUPINO, RICHARD. Born Oct. 29, 1929 in Hollywood, CA. Attended LACC, RADA. Bdwy debut 1956 in "Major Barbara," followed by "Conduct Unbecoming," "Sherlock Holmes," OB in "The Tantalus," "Swan Song," "Hired Man."

LuPONE, ROBERT. Born July 29, 1956 in Brooklyn, NY. Juilliard graduate. Bdwy debut 1970 in "Minnie's Boys," followed by "Jesus Christ Superstar," "The Rothschilds," "Magic Show," "A Chorus Line," "St. Joan," "Late Night Comic," OB in "Charlie Was Here," "Twelfth Night," "In Connecticut," "Snow Orchid," "Lennon," "Black Angel," "The Quilling of Prue," "Time Framed," "Class 1 Acts." brance," "Children of Darkness," "Kill."

LUSTIK, MARLENA. Born Aug. 22, 1944 in Milwaukee, WI. Attended MarquetteU. Bdwy debut 1966 in "Pousse Cafe," followed by "Days in the Trees," OB in "Effect of Gamma Rays . . ." "Billy Liar," "One Flew over the Cuckoo's Nest," "Night Watch," "Othello."

LYLES, LESLIE. Born in Plainfield, NJ. Graduate Monmouth Col., RutgersU. Debut 1981 OB in "Sea Marks," followed by "Highest Standard of Living," "Vanishing Act," "I Am Who I Am," "The Arbor," "Terry by Terry," "Marathon '88," "Sleeping Dogs," Bdwy in "The Real Thing" (1985).

LYND, BETTY. Born In Los Angeles, CA. Debut 1968 OB in "Rondelay," followed by "Love Me, Love My Children," Bdwy in "The Skin of Our Teeth" (1975), "A Chorus Line."

LYNDECK, EDMUND. Born Oct. 4, 1925 in Baton Rouge, La. Graduate Montclair State Col., Fordham U. Bdwy debut 1969 in "1776," followed by "Sweeney Todd," "A Doll's Life," "Merlin,"

Robyn
Hatcher

John F.
Higgins

Vicki
Hirsch

Earle
Hyman

Ruby
Holbrook

Michael
Iannucci

George S.
Irving

Babs
Hooyman

David
Jackson

Karen
Jablons

Kricker
James

Joan
Jaffe

Kelli
James

Joseph
Jamrog

Mary
Jay

James
Jenner

Penny
Jay

Michael
Jeter

Arch
Johnson

Rita
Jenrette

Page
Johnson

Leilani
Jones

Jay Aubrey
Jones

Juliette
Koka

Diana
Laurenson

Rick
Lawless

Kaiulani
Lee

William
LeMassena

Bethel
Leslie

Joseph
Leon

211

"Into the Woods," OB in "The King and I" (JB), "Mandragola," "A Safe Place," "Amoureuse," "Piaf, A Remembrance," "Children of Darkness," "Kill."

LYNG, NORA MAE. Born Jan. 27, 1951 in Jersey City, NJ. Debut 1981 OB in "Anything Goes," followed by "Forbidden Broadway," "Road to Hollywood," "Tales of Tinseltown," Bdwy in "Wind in the Willows" (1985), "Cabaret" (1987).

MacINTOSH, JOAN E. Born Nov. 25, 1945 in NJ. Graduate Beaver Col., NYU. Debut OB 1969 in "Dionysus in '69," followed by "Macbeth," "The Beard," "Tooth of Crime," "Mother Courage," "Marilyn Project," "Seneca's Oedipus," "St. Joan of the Stockyards," "Wonderland in Concert," "Dispatches," "Endgame," "Killings on the Last Line," "Request Concert," "3 Acts of Recognition," "Consequence," "Whispers," "Cymbeline," Bdwy in "Our Town" (1989).

MacKAY, JOHN. Graduate CUNY. Bdwy debut 1960 in "Under the Yum Yum Tree," followed by "A Gift of Time," "A Man for All Seasons," "The Lovers," "Borstal Boy," OB in "Oedipus Cycle," "Gilles de Rais," "Marathon '89."

MacNICOL, PETER. Born April 10 in Dallas, Tx. Attended UMin. Bdwy debut 1981 in "Crimes of the Heart" for which he received a Theatre World Award, OB in "Found a Peanut," "Rum and Coke," "Twelfth Night," "Richard II," "The Spring Thing."

MacPHERSON, LORI. Born July 23 in Albany, NY. Attended Skidmore Col. Bdwy debut 1988 in "The Phantom of the Opera."

MACY, W. H. Born Mar. 13, 1950 in Miami, FL. Graduate Goddard Col. Debut 1980 OB in "The Man in 605," followed by "Twelfth Night," "The Beaver Coat," "A Call from the East," "Sittin'," "Sunshine," "The Dining Room," "Speakeasy," "Wild Life," "Flirtations," "Baby with the Bathwater," "Prairie/Shawl," "The Nice and the Nasty," "Bodies, Rest and Motion," Bdwy in "Our Town" (1989).

MAGLIONE, CHRISTINE. Born Aug. 24, 1964 in Orange, NJ. Graduate Cornell U. Debut 1987 OB in "Kismet," Bdwy in "A Chorus Line."

MAHER, JOSEPH. Born Dec. 29, 1933 in Westport, Ire. Bdwy debut 1964 in "The Chinese Prime Minister," followed by "The Prime of Miss Jean Brodie," "Henry V," "There's One in Every Marriage," "Who's Who in Hell," "Days in the Trees," "Spokesong," "Night and Day," "84 Charing Cross Road," "Loot," OB in "Hostage," "Live Like Pigs," "The Importance of Being Earnest," "Eh?," "Local Stigmatic," "Mary Stuart," "The Contractor," "Savages," "Entertaining Mr. Sloane," "Loot," "What the Butler Saw."

MAIER, CHARLOTTE. Born Jan. 29, 1956 in Chicago, IL. Graduate NorthwesternU. Debut 1984 OB in "Balm in Gilead."

MAILER, STEPHEN. Born Mar. 10, 1966 in NYC. Attended Middlebury Col., NYU. Debut OB 1989 in "For Dear Life."

MAJOR, CHARLES. Born Mar. 19 in NYC. Attended Bates Col., Adelphi U., Neighborhood Playhouse. Bdwy debut 1967 in "Spofford," followed by "Sly Fox," OB in "Gloria and Esperanza," "The Elizabethans," "Sports Czar," "The Iceman Cometh," "Othello," "Six Characters in Search of an Author," "An Ordinary Man," "Tribute," "Better Living," "Black Hat Karma."

MALLON, BRIAN. Born May 12, 1952 in Detroit, MI. Attended UMich. Debut 1980 OB in "Guests of the Nation," followed by "Moliere in spite of Himself," "Mr. Joyce Is Leaving Paris," "Shadow of a Gunman," "Derek."

MANCINELLI, CELESTE. Born Mar. 6, 1953 in Paterson, NJ. Graduate Rutgers U., Paterson Col. Debut 1986 OB in "A Girl's Guide to Chaos," followed by "1-2-3-4-5."

MANDRACCHIA, CHARLES. Born Mar. 29, 1962 in Brooklyn, NY. Graduate Brooklyn Col. Debut OB 1987 in "Wish You Were Here," followed by "Mr. Universe," "Philoctetes," Bdwy in "South Pacific," "Kismet," "Desert Song."

MANILOW, BARRY. Born June 17, 1946 in NYC. Bdwy debut 1976 in "Barry Manilow on Broadway," followed by 1983, 1989 concerts.

MANISCALCO, ROBERT. Born Dec. 26, 1959 in Detroit, MI. Graduate Wayne State U. UDetroit. Debut OB 1988 in "Macbeth."

MANN, JONATHAN. Born in NYC. Attended Drama Studio (London), Juilliard. Bdwy debut 1988 in "A Streetcar Named Desire," followed by "The Night of the Iguana," "Ghetto."

MANZI, WARREN. Born July 1, 1955 in Laurence, MA. Graduate Holy Cross, Yale. Bdwy debut 1980 in "Amadeus," OB in "Perfect Crime."

MARCHAND, NANCY. Born June 19, 1928 in Buffalo, NY. Graduate Carnegie Tech, Debut 1951 in CC's "Taming of the Shrew," followed by "Merchant of Venice," "Much Ado About Nothing," "Three Bags Full," "After the Rain," "The Alchemist," "Yerma," "Cyrano de Bergerac," "Mary Stuart," "Enemies," "The Plough and the Stars," "40 Carats," "And Miss Reardon Drinks a Little," "Veronica's Room," "Awake and Sing," "Morning's at Seven," "The Octette Bridge Club," OB in "The Balcony," "Children," "Taken in Marriage," "Sister Mary Ignatius Explains It All," "Elecktra," "The Cocktail Hour," "Love Letters."

MARCY, HELEN. Born June 3, 1920 in Worcester, MA. Attended Yale U. Bdwy in "Twelfth Night," "In Bed We Cry," "Dream Girl," "Love and Let Love," OB in "Lady Windemere's Fan," "Relative Values," "Verdict," "Hound of the Baskervilles," "Appointment With Death," "Ladies in Retirement," "Dr. Cook's Garden," "Murder at the Vicarage," "Black Coffee," "George Washington Slept Here."

MARDIROSIAN, TOM. Born Dec. 14, 1947 in Buffalo, NY. Graduate UBuffalo. Debut 1976 OB in "Gemini," followed by "Grand Magic," "Losing Time," "Passione," "Success and Succession," "Ground Zero Club," "Cliffhanger," "Cap and Bells," "The Normal Heart," "Measure for Measure," "Largo Desolato," "The Good Coach," Bdwy in "Happy End," "Magic Show."

MARGULIES, DAVID. Born Feb. 19, 1937 in NYC. Graduate CCNY. Debut 1958 OB in "Golden Six," followed by "Six Characters in Search of an Author," "Tragical Historie of Dr. Faustus," "Tango," "Little Murders," "Seven Days of Mourning," "Last Analysis," "An Evening with the Poet Senator," "Kid Champion," "The Man with the Flower in His Mouth," "Old Tune," "David and Paula," "Cabal of Hypocrites," "The Perfect Party," "Just Say No," Bdwy in "The Iceman Cometh" (1973), "Zalmen or the Madness of God," "Comedians," "Break a Leg," "West Side Waltz," "Brighton Beach Memoirs."

MARKELL, JODIE. Born Apr. 13, 1959 in Memphis, TN. Attended Northwestern U. Debut 1984 OB in "Balm in Gilead," followed by "Carrying School Children," "UBU," "Sleeping Dogs."

MARKS, KENNETH. Born Feb. 17, 1954 in Harwick, PA. Graduate UPa, Lehigh U. Debut 1978 OB in "Clara Bow Loves Gary Cooper," followed by "Canadian Gothic," "Time and the Conways," "Savoury Meringue," "Thrombo," "Fun," "1-2-3-4-5."

MARLOWE, THERESA. Born Aug. 20, 1958 in Monroe, Mi. Debut 1985 OB in "Vampire Lesbians of Sodom," followed by "Times Square Angel," "Psycho Beach Party," "The Lady in Question."

MARTIN, LEILA. Born Aug. 22, 1932 in NYC. Bdwy debut 1944 in "Peepshow," followed by "Two on the Aisle," "Wish You Were Here," "Guys and Dolls," "Best House in Naples," "Henry, Sweet Henry," "The Wall," "Visit to a Small Planet," "The Rothschilds," "42nd Street," "The Phantom of the Opera," OB in "Ernest in Love," "Beggar's Opera," "King of the U.S.," "Philemon," "Jerry's Girls."

MARTIN, ROBERT LEE. Born July 30, 1960 in NYC. Graduate Wagner Col. Debut 1987 OB in "The Tavern," followed by "Hamlet."

MARTIN, STEVE. Born Aug. 14, 1945 in Waco, TX. Graduate UCLA. Debut OB 1988 in "Waiting for Godot."

MASON, JACKIE. Born June 9, 1934 in Sheboygan, WI. Bdwy debut 1969 in "A Teaspoon Every Four Hours," followed by "The World according to Me."

MASON, MARSHA. Born Apr. 3, 1942 in St. Louis, MO. Attended Webster Col. Debut OB 1967 in "Deer Park," followed by "It's Called the Sugar Plum," "Happy Birthday, Wanda June," "Richard III," "Old Times," "Love Letters," Bdwy in "The Good Doctor" (1973).

MASTERS, PATRICIA. Born Dec. 8, 1952 in Washington, DC. Graduate UMd. Debut OB 1984 in "Forbidden Broadway," followed by "Tomfoolery."

MASTRONE, FRANK. Born Nov. 1, 1960 in Bridgeport, CT. Graduate CentralStStateU. Bdwy debut 1988 in "The Phantom of the Opera."

MASTROTOTARO, MICHAEL F. Born May 17, 1962 in Albany, NY. Graduate NYU. OB in "The Myth Project."

MATTHEWS, ANDERSON. Born Oct. 21, 1950 in Springfield, OH. Graduate Carnegie-Mellon U. Bdwy debut 1975 in "The Robber Bridegroom," followed by "Edward II," "The Time of Your Life," "Ten by Tennessee," "Beef," "The Sneaker Factory," "Driving Miss Daisy."

MATTHIESSEN, JOAN. Born Feb. 22, 1930 in Orange, NJ. Graduate Allegheny Co. Debut 1979 OB in "The Art of Dining," followed by "The Cocktail Party," "Hedda Gabler."

MATZ, JERRY. Born Nov. 15, 1935 in NYC. Graduate Syracuse U. Debut 1965 OB in "The Old Glory," followed by "Hefetz," "A Day Out of Time." "A Mad World, My Masters," "The Rise of David Levinsky," "The Last Danceman," "Madrid Madrid," Bdwy in "Ghetto" (1989).

MAXWELL, ROBERTA. Born in Canada. Debut 1968 OB in "Two Gentlemen of Verona," followed by "A Whistle in the Dark," "Slag," "The Plough and the Stars," "Merchant of Venice," "Ashes," "Mary Stuart," "Lydie Breeze," "Before the Dawn," "Real Estate," Bdwy in "The Prime of Miss Jean Brodie," "Henry V," "House of Atreus," "The Resistible Rise of Arturo Ui," "Othello," "Hay Fever," "There's One in Every Marriage," "Equus," "The Merchant," "Our Town."

MAYES, SALLY. Born Aug. 3 in Livingston, Tx. Attended UHouston. Broadway debut 1989 in "Welcome to the Club" for which she received a Theatre World Award.

MAYO, DON. Born Oct. 4, 1960 in Chicago, IL. Graduate Loyola U. Debut 1988 OB in "Much Ado About Nothing."

McCALL, KATHLEEN. Born Jan. 11 in Denver. CO. Graduate Moorhead State U., LAMDA. Debut 1986 OB in "Thanksgiving," followed by "Acapella Hardcore," "Class 1 Acts," "Steel Magnolias," Bdwy 1989 in "M. Butterfly."

McCALLUM, DAVID. Born Sept. 19, 1933 in Scotland. Attended Chapman Col. Bdwy debut 1968 in "The Flip Side," followed by "California Suite," OB in "After the Prize," "The Philanthropist," "Ghosts."

McCARTY, CONAN. Born Sept. 16, 1955 in Lubbock, TX. Attended USCal, AADA/West. Debut 1980 OB in "Star Treatment," followed by "Beyond Therapy," "Henry IV Part 1," "Titus Andronicus," Bdwy in "Macbeth" (1988).t OB 1988 in "Fiorello!"

McCARTY, MICHAEL. Born Sept. 7, 1946 in Evansville, IN. Graduate IndU., MiStateU. Debut 1976 OB in "Fiorello!," followed by "The Robber Bridegroom," "Sweeney Todd," Bdwy in "Dirty Linen," "King of Hearts," "Amadeus," "Oliver!," "Big River."

McCONNELL, DAVID. Born Feb. 12, 1962 in Los Alamos, NM. Graduate AADA. OB in "You Never Can Tell," "Hot l Baltimore."

McCORMICK, CAROLYN. Born Sept. 19, 1959 in Texas. Graduate Williams Col. Debut 1988 OB in "In Perpetuit Throughout the Universe."

McCORMICK, MICHAEL. Born July 24, 1951 in Gary, IN. Graduate NorthwesternU. Bdwy debut 1964 in "Oliver!," OB in "Coming Attractions," "Tomfoolery," "The Regard of Flight," "Charlotte's Secret," "Half a World Away," "In a Pig's Valise."

McCULLOH, BARBARA. Born Mar. 5 in Washington, DC. Attended Col. of William & Mary, UMd. Debut 1984 OB in "Up in Central Park," followed by "Kuni-Leml," "On the 20th Century," "1-2-3-4-5."

McCUTCHEON, BILL. Born in 1924 in Russell, KY. Attended OhioU. Bdwy credits: "New Faces of 1956," "Dandelion Wine," "Out West of Eighth," "My Daughter, Your Son," "Over Here," "West Side Story," "The Front Page," "The Man Who Came to Dinner," "You Can't Take It with You," "Anything Goes," OB in "How to Steal an Election," "Wet Paint," "One's a Crowd," "Shoestring Revue," "Upstairs at the Downstairs," "The Little Revue," "The Marriage of Bette and Boo."

McDONALD, BETH. Born May 25, 1954 in Chicago, IL. Graduate Juilliard. Debut 1981 OB in "A Midsummer Night's Dream," followed by "The Recruiting Officer," "Jungle of Cities," "Kennedy at Colonus," "Our Own Family," "Ancient History."

McDONALD, TANNY. Born Feb. 13 in Princeton, NJ. Graduate Vassar Col. Debut 1961 OB in "American Savoyards," followed by "All in Love," "To Broadway with Love," "Carricknabauna," "The Beggar's Opera," "Brand," "Goodbye Dan Bailey," "Total Eclipse," "Gorky," "Don Juan Come Back from the War," "Vera with Kate," "Francis," "On Approval," "A Definite Maybe," "Temptation," "Titus Andronicus," Bdwy in "Fiddler on the Roof," "Come Summer," "The Lincoln Mask," "Clothes for a Summer Hotel," "Macbeth" (1988).

McDONOUGH, ANN. Born in Portland, ME. Graduate Towson State U. Debut 1975 OB in "Trelawney of the Wells," followed by "Secret Service," "Boy Meets Girl," "Scribes," "Uncommon Women," "City Sugar," "Fables for Friends," "The Dining Room," "What I Did Last Summer," "The Rise of Daniel Rocket," "The Middle Ages," "Fighting International Fat," "Room Service," "The Spring Thing."

McFARLAND, ROBERT. Born May 7, 1931 in Omaha, NE. Graduate UMi, ColumbiaU. Debut 1978 OB in "The Taming of the Shrew," followed by "When the War Was Over," "Divine Fire,"

"Ten Little Indians," "The Male Animal," "Comedy of Errors," "Appointment with Death," "The Education of One Miss February," "Rule of Three," "The Male Animal."

McGAVIN, DARREN. Born May 7, 1922 in Spokane, WA. Attended Col. of Pacific. Bdwy debut 1948 in "The Old Lady Says No," followed by "Death of a Salesman," "My Three Angels," "The Rainmaker," "The Innkeepers," "The Lovers," "Tunnel of Love," "Blood, Sweat and Stanley Poole," "The King and I," "Dinner at 8," OB in "Cock-a-doodle-Doo," "The Thracian Horses," "California Dog Fight," "The Night Hank Williams Died."

McGINLEY, JOHN C. Born Aug. 3, 1959 in NYC. Graduate NYU. Debut 1984 OB in "Danny and the Deep Blue Sea," followed by "The Ballad of Soapy Smith," "Jesse and the Games," "Love as We Know It," "Talk Radio," "Florida Crackers."

McGINNIS, MAUREEN. Born Sept. 30, 1957 in Fargo, ND. Attended Noorhead State U. Debut 1983 OB in "Richard II," followed by "The Education of One Miss February," "All's Well That Ends Well."

McGOUGH, SHANNON. Born July 15, 1964 in Philadelphia, PA. Attended Point Park Col. Debut OB 1988 in "Fiorello!"

McGOWAN, TOM. Born July 26, 1959 in Neptune, NJ. Graduate Yale, Hofstra U. Debut OB 1988 in "Coriolanus," followed by "Winter's Tale."

McGREEVEY, ANNIE. Born in Brooklyn, NY. Graduate AADA. Bdwy debut 1971 in "Company," followed by "The Magic Show," "Annie," OB in "Booth Is Back in Town," "Tatterdemalion," "She Loves Me."

McGUINNESS, MICHAEL JOHN. Born May 13, 1961 in Corning, NY. Graduate NYU. Debut 1985 OB in "Brand," followed by "Frankenstein," "Wakefield/Chester Mystery Play Cycle," "The Real Inspector Hound," "Richard II," "Andromache," "She Stoops to Conquer," "All's Well That Ends Well."

McGUIRE, MAEVE. Born in Cleveland, OH. Graduate Sarah Lawrence Col., Cleveland Playhouse. Debut 1968 with LCRep in "Cyrano de Bergerac," followed by "The Miser," "Charades," OB in "Vera with Kate," "Light Up the Sky," "Steel Magnolias."

McHATTIE, STEPHEN. Born Feb. 3 in Antigosh, NS. Graduate Arcadia U, AADA. Bdwy debut 1969 in "The American Dream," followed by "The Misanthrope," "Heartbreak House," "You Never Can Tell," "Ghetto," OB in "Henry IV," "Richard III," "The Persians," "Pictures in the Hallway," "Now There's Just the Three of Us," "Anna K," "Twelfth Night," "Mourning Becomes Electra," "Alive and Well in Argentina," "The Iceman Cometh," "Winter Dancers," "Casualties," "Three Sisters," "Mensch Meier," "Haven."

McINTYRE, GERRY. Born May 31, 1962 in Grenada, West Indies. Graduate Montclair-StateCol. Debut 1985 OB in "Joan of Arc at the Stake," followed by "Homeseekers," Bdwy in "Anything Goes" (1987).

McKENNA, CHRISTIANE. Born Mar. 14, 1952 in San Francisco, CA. Attended Juilliard, Pacific Conservatory. Debut 1980 OB in "Merton of the Movies," followed by "Madwoman of Chaillot," "A Midsummer Night's Dream," "Sjt. Musgrave's Dance," "Boys in the Backroom," "Lust and the Unicorn," "Festival of 1 Acts."

McKENZIE, MICHAEL. Born Jan. 18, 1955 in Lincoln, NE. Graduate Webster Col. Debut OB in "Orchards," followed by "Much Ado About Nothing," "The Lark," Bdwy in "Eastern Standard" (1989).

McKEOWN, DAVID. Born May 27, 1956 in Upper Darby, PA. Graduate SUNY. Debut OB 1988 in "Fiorello!"

McLACHLAN, RODERICK. Born Sept. 9, 1960 in Detroit, MI. Graduate Northwestern U. Debut 1987 in "Death and the King's Horseman" (LC) followed by Bdwy in "Our Town," OB in "Madame Bovary."

McMANUS, DON R. Born in 1960 in Sylacauga, AL. Graduate Yale U. Debut 1987 OB in "Holy Ghosts," followed by "Titus Andronicus."

McNABB, BARRY. Born Aug. 26, 1960 in Toronto, CAN. Graduate UOre. Bdwy debut 1986 in "Me and My Girl," followed by "The Phantom of the Opera."

McNAMARA, MAUREEN. Born Mar. 17, 1957 in NYC. Studied at HB Studio. Debut 1978 OB in "Company," followed by "Festival," "The Ziegfeld Girl."

McNAMARA, PAT. Born July 22, 1938 in Astoria, NY. Attended Columbia U, AADA. Debut 1961 OB in "Red Roses For Me," followed by "Crystal and Fox," "Nobody Hears a Broken Drum," "The Passing Game," "Killings on the Last Line," Bdwy in "The Poison Tree" (1976), "Brothers," "The Iceman Cometh" (1985), "Sherlock's Last Case," "Legs Diamond."

McNAUGHTON, STEPHEN (formerly Steve Scott). Born Oct. 11, 1949 in Denver, CO. Graduate UDenver. Debut 1971 OB in "The Drunkard," followed by "Summer Brave," "Monsters," "Chase a Rainbow," "Two on the Isles," "Hamlet," "Ed/Kaplan," Bdwy in "The Ritz" (1976), "Shenandoah," "Cheaters," "Da," "Best Little Whorehouse in Texas," "Joseph and the Amazing Technicolor Dreamcoat."

McNIGHT, SHARON. Born Dec. 18 in Modesto, CA. Graduate SanFranStateCol. Debut 1987 OB in "Murder at the Rutherford House," Bdwy 1989 in "Starmites" for which she received a Theatre World Award.

McROBBIE, PETER. Born Jan. 31, 1943 in Hawick, Scotland. Graduate Yale U. Debut 1976 OB in "The Wobblies," followed by "The Devil's Disciple," "Cinders," "The Ballad of Soapy Smith," "Rosmersholm," Bdwy in "Whose Life is it Anyway?" (1979), "Macbeth" (1981), "The Mystery of Edwin Drood."

McVETY, DREW. Born Apr. 16, 1965 in Port Huron, MI. Graduate NYU. Debut OB 1988 in "The Heidi Chronicles," Bdwy in "The Heidi Chronicles" (1989).

McWILLIAMS, RICHARD. Born June 27, 1950 in Baytown, TX. Graduate Sam Houston State U. Debut 1983 OB in "Except in My Memory," followed by "Why Marry?", "Get Any Guy," "The Night Hank Williams Died."

MEANS, JOHN. Born Sept. 8, 1935 in Pittsburgh, PA. Graduate Washington & Jefferson Col. Debut 1984 OB in "Delirious," followed by "I've Got Ink."

MEARA, ANNE. Born Sept. 20, 1929 in Brooklyn, NY. Attended HB Studios. OB in "The Silver Tassie," "Dandy Dick," "A Month in the Country," "Spookhouse," "Eastern Standard," Bdwy in "Eastern Standard" (1989).

MEDINA, HAZEL. Born Oct. 8 in Colon, Panama. Attended LACC. Debut 1982 OB in "Brixton Recovery," followed by "Time Out of Time," "Street Sounds," "The Beautiful LaSalles," "State of the Union," "Two Can Play," "Time Out of Time," "Prince."

MEISTER, FREDERICA. Born Aug. 18, 1951 in San Francisco, CA. Graduate NYU. Debut 1978 OB in "Museum," followed by "Dolphin Position," "Waiting for the Parade," "Dream of a Blacklisted Actor," "No Damn Good," "The Magic Act."

MELLOR, STEPHEN. Born Oct. 17, 1954 in New Haven, CT. Graduate Boston U. Debut 1980 OB in "Paris Lights," followed by "Coming Attractions," "Plenty," "Tooth of Crime," "Shepard Sets," "A Country Doctor," "Harm's Way," "Brightness Falling," Bdwy in "Big River."

MEREDIZ, OLGA. Born Feb. 15, 1956 in Guantanamo, Cuba. Graduate Tulane U. Bdwy in "The Human Comedy," OB in "El Bravo!," "Women Without Men," "El Grande de Coca-Cola," "The Blessing."

MERRITT, GEORGE. Born July 10, 1942 in Raleigh, NC. Graduate Catholic U. Bdwy debut 1976 in "Porgy and Bess," followed by its 1983 revival, "Ain't Misbehavin'," "Big River," OB in "Step Into My World."

MERRYMAN, MONICA. Born June 2, 1950 in Sao Paulo, Brazil. Graduate EMichU. Debut 1975 OB in "East Lynne," followed by "A Night at the Black Pig," "Vanities," "The Voice of the Turtle," "Rhapsody Tachiste."

METZO, WILLIAM. Born June 21, 1937 in Wilkes-Barre, PA. Graduate King's Col. Debut 1963 OB in "The Bald Soprano," followed by "Papers," "A Moon for the Misbegotten," "Arsenic and Old Lace," "Super Spy," "Hamlet," "Cradle Song," Bdwy in "Cyrano" (1973).

MEYERS, T. J. Born July 18, 1953 in Pittsburgh, PA. Graduate Mesa Col. Bdwy debut 1984 in "Sunday in the Park with George," followed by "Metamorphosis."

MICHAELS, DEVON. Born Oct. 22, 1973 in NYC. Bdwy debut 1986 in "Rags," OB in "Passover," "The Knife," "King John," "1-2-3-4-5," "Cymbeline."

MILES, SYLVIA. Born Sept. 9, 1934 in NYC. Attended Pratt Inst., Actors Studio. Debut 1954 OB in "A Stone for Danny Fisher," followed by "The Iceman Cometh," "The Balcony," "Chekov Skerchbook," "Matty, Moron and Madonna," "The Kitchen," "Rosenbloom," "Nellie Toole & Co.," "American Night Cry," "It's Me, Sylvia," "Ameri/Cain Gothic," "Tea with Mommy and Jack," Bdwy in "The Riot Act," "Night of the Iguana."

MILLER, BARRY. Born Feb. 6, 1958 in Los Angeles, CA. Debut 1981 OB in "Forty Deuce," followed by "The Tempest," "1 Act Festival," Bdwy in "Biloxi Blues" (1985) for which he received a Theatre World Award.

MILLER, DEBRA ELISE. Born June 29, 1951 in San Francisco, CA. Graduate UCSC. Debut 1986 OB in "Patience and Sarah," Bdwy in "Largely New York" (1989).

MILLER, MARJORIE ANN. Born July 6, 1959 in Margaretville, NY. Graduate Syracuse U. Debut OB 1988 in "Peg o' My Heart."

MILLER, PENELOPE ANN. Born Jan. 13, 1964 in Santa Monica, CA. Attended Menlo Col. Bdwy debut 1985 in "Biloxi Blues," followed by "Our Town," OB in "Moonchildren."

MINOFF, TAMMY. Born Oct. 4, 1979 in NYC. Debut OB 1988 in "The Travelling Man," followed by "1-2-3-4-5."

MINOT, ANNA. Born in Boston, MA. Attended Vassar Col. Bdwy debut 1942 in "The Strings, My Lord, Are False," followed by "The Russian People," "The Visitor," "The Iceman Cometh," "An Enemy of the People," "Love of Four Colonels," "Trip to Bountiful," "Tunnel of Love," "Ivanov," OB in "Sands of the Niger," "Getting Out," "Vieux Carre," "State of the Union," "Her Great Match," "Rivals," "Hedda Gabler," "All's Well That Ends Well."

MISTRETTA, SAL. Born Jan. 9, 1945 in Brooklyn, NY. Graduate Ithaca Col. Bdwy debut 1976 in "Something's Afoot," followed by "On the 20th Century," "Evita," "The King and I," OB in "Charley's Tale," "The Education of Hyman Kaplan."

MITCHELL, ALETA. Born in Chicago, IL. Graduate UIowa, YaleU. Bdwy debut 1984 in "Ma Rainey's Black Bottom," OB in "Approaching Zanzibar."

MITCHELL, GREGORY. Born Dec. 9, 1951 in Brooklyn, NY. Juilliard graduate. Principal with Eliot Feld Ballet before Bdwy debut 1983 in "Merlin," followed by "Song and Dance," "Phantom of the Opera," OB in "One More Song, One More Dance," "Tango Apasionado."

MITCHELL, MELANIE. Born May 1, 1961 in Hartford, CT. Graduate NYU. Debut 1984 OB in "Bells Are Ringing," followed by "The Taffetas."

MITZMAN, MARCIA. Born Feb. 28, 1959 in NYC. Attended SUNY/Purchase, Neighborhood Playhouse. Debut 1978 OB in "Promises, Promises," followed by "Taming of the Shrew," "Around the Corner from the White House," Bdwy in "Grease" (1979), "Oliver!," "South Pacific" (LC), "Chess," "Welcome to the Club."

MOFFAT, DONALD. Born Dec. 26, 1930 in Plymouth, Eng. Attended RADA. Bdwy debut 1957 in "Under Milk Wood," followed by "Much Ado About Nothing," "The Tumbler," "Duel of Angels," "Passage to India," "The Affair," "Father's Day," "Play Memory," "The Wild Duck," "Right You Are," "You Can't Take It With You," "War and Peace," "The Cherry Orchard," "Cock-a-Doodle Dandy," "Hamlet," "The Iceman Cometh," OB in "The Bald Soprano," "Jack," "The Caretaker," "Misalliance," "Painting Churches," "Henry IV Part 1," "Titus Andronicus."

MOLNAR, ROBERT. Born June 22, 1927 in Cincinnati, OH. Attended OhNorthernU., UCin, CinConsv.of Music. Debut 1958 OB in "Hamlet of Stepney Green," followed by "The Boys from Syracuse," "Ulysses in Nighttown," Bdwy in "Camelot" (1980/81).

MONACO, MARYLIN. Born Jan. 28, 1937 in Brooklyn. NY. Graduate Queens Col. Debut OB 1989 in "Gigi."

MONDY, BILL. Born June 16, 1963 in Rochester, NY. Graduate UIll, NYU. Debut OB 1988 in "Rimers of Eldritch."

MONK, ISABELL. Born Oct. 4, 1952 in Washington, DC. Graduate TowsonStatU., Yale. Debut 1981 OB in "The Tempest," followed by "The Gospel at Colonus," "Elecktra," "Ladies," "The Spring Thing," Bdwy in "Execution of Justice" (1986).

MONTE, CHRIS. Born Jan. 8, 1963 in Philadelphia, PA. Graduate Temple U. Debut OB 1989 in "Days of Rage," followed by "Hell's Kitchen Has a Tub."

MONTGOMERY, ANDRE. Born May 17, 1959 in Toledo, OH. Graduate UToledo. Debut 1987 OB in "The No Frills Revue," followed by "The Blitzstein Project."

MOOR, BILL. Born July 13, 1931 in Toledo, OH. Attended Northwestern, Denison U. Bdwy debut 1964 in "Blues for Mr. Charlie," followed by "Great God Brown," "Don Juan," "The Visit," "Chemin de Fer," "Holiday," "P.S. Your Cat is Dead," "Night of the Tribades," "Water Engine," "Plenty," "Heartbreak House," "The Iceman Cometh," OB in "Dandy Dick," "Love Nest," "Days and Nights of Beebee Fenstermaker," "The Collection," "The Owl Answers," "Long Christmas Dinner," "Fortune and Men's Eyes," "King Lear," "Cry of Players," "Boys in the Band," "Alive and Well in Argentina," "Rosmersholm," "The Biko Inquest," "A Winter's Tale," "Johnny on a Spot," "Barbarians," "The Purging," "Potsdam Quartet," "Zones of the Spirit," "The Marriage of Bette and Boo," "Temptation," "Devil's Disciple."

MOORE, BETTY. Born Mar. 31, 1920 in Chicago, IL. Debut OB 1942 in "The First Crocus," followed by "Rimers of Eldritch," "Miss Reardon Drinks A Little," "A Tree Grows in Brooklyn," "Steel Magnolias." OB in "The Trip to Bountiful" (1958), "Face of a Hero," "Night Life," "Funny Girl."

MORAN, MARTIN. Born Dec. 29, 1959 in Denver, CO. Attended Stanford U., AmConsvTh. Debut 1983 OB in "Spring Awakening," followed by "Once on a Summer's Day," "1-2-3-4-5," Bdwy in "Oliver!" (1984), "Big River."

MOREAU, JENNIE. Born Nov. 19, 1960 in Lewisburg, PA. Graduate NCSchool of Arts. Debut 1988 OB in "Tony 'n' Tina's Wedding," followed by "Rimers of Eldritch," "Eleemosynary" for which she received a Theatre World Award.

MORENO, RENE. Born May 25, 1959 in Dallas, TX. Graduate SMU. Bdwy debut 1982 in "Amadeus," followed by "Shakespeare on Broadway," OB in "Bits and Pieces," "The Man of Destiny," "And That's the Way It Is," "The Promise."

MORFOGEN, GEORGE. Born Mar. 30, 1933 in NYC. Graduate Brown U., Yale. Debut 1957 OB in "The Trial of D. Karamazov," followed by "Christmas Oratorio," "Othello," "Good Soldier Schweik," "Cave Dwellers," "Once in a Lifetime," "Total Eclipse," "Ice Age," "Prince of Homburg," "Biography: A Game," "Mrs. Warren's Profession," "Principia Scriptoriae." "Tamara," Bdwy in "The Fun Couple," "Kingdoms," "Arms and the Man."

MORGENSTERN, SUSAN. Born May 13, 1954 in Glenn Falls, NY. Graduate UCal. Debut 1981 OB in "The Killing of Sister George," followed by "Female Transport," "The Sea Horse," "Ball," "The Christmas Bridge."

MORIN-TORRE, LORRAINE. Born in Houston, TX. Debut 1987 OB in "El Salvador," followed by "George Washington Slept Here."

MORRIS, MARK JAMES. Born Sept. 17 in Miami, FL. Graduate FlStateU, NYU. Debut OB 1988 in "Fiorello!"

MORSE, ROBIN. Born July 8, 1963 in NYC. Bdwy debut 1981 in "Bring Back Birdie," followed by "Brighton Beach Memoirs," OB in "Green Fields," "Dec. 7th," "Class 1 Acts," "Eleemosynary," "One Act Festival."

MORTON, JOE. Born Oct. 18, 1947 in NYC. Attended Hofstra U. Debut 1968 OB in "A Month of Sundays," followed by "Salvation," "Charlie Was Here and Now He's Gone," "G. R. Point," "Crazy Horse," "A Winter's Tale," "Johnny on a Spot," "Midsummer Night's Dream," "The Recruiting Officer," "Oedipus the King," "The Wild Duck," "Rhinestone," "Souvenirs," "Cheapside," "King John," Bdwy in "Hair," "Two Gentlemen of Verona," "Tricks," "Raisin," for which he received a Theatre World Award, "Oh, Brother!," "Honky Tonk Nights."

MOSES, MARK. Born Feb. 24, 1960 in NYC. Graduate Northwestern U, NYU. Debut 1983 OB in "The Slab Boys," followed by "Fraternity," "Home Remedies," "The Lady and the Clarinet," "Fantod," "Love's Labour's Lost."

MUENZ, RICHARD. Born in 1948 in Hartford, CT. Attended Eastern Baptist Col. Bdwy debut 1976 in "1600 Pennsylvania Avenue," followed by "The Most Happy Fella," "Camelot," "Rosalie in Concert," "Chess," "The Pajama Game" (LC).

MULHERN, MATT. Born July 21, 1960 in Philadelphia, PA. Graduate RutgersU. Bdwy debut 1985 in "Biloxi Blues," OB in "Wasted" (1986), "The Night Hank Williams Died."

MUNGER, MARY. Born Oct. 31, 1955 in Topeka, KS. Graduate UNC/Chapel Hill. Debut 1986 OB in "Angry Housewives," followed by "Internal Combustion," "Plainsong," "Genesis," Bdwy in "Cabaret" (1987).

MURCH, ROBERT. Born Apr. 17, 1935 in Jefferson Barracks, MO. Graduate Wash. U. Bdwy debut 1966 in "Hostile Witness," followed by "The Harangues," "Conduct Unbecoming," "The Changing Room," "Born Yesterday," OB in "Charles Abbot & Son," "She Stoops to Conquer," "Transcendental Love," "Julius Caesar."

MURFITT, MARY. Born Mar. 29, 1954 in Kansas City, MO. Graduate Marymount Col. Debut 1987 OB in "Oil City Symphony" for which she received a Theatre World Award.

MURPHY, DONNA. Born Mar. 7, 1959 in Corona, NY. Attended NYU. Bdwy debut 1979 in "They're Playing Our Song," followed by "The Human Comedy," "The Mystery of Edwin Drood," OB in "Francis," "Portable Pioneer and Prairie Show," "Little Shop of Horrors," "A . . . My Name is Alice," "Showing Off."

MURPHY, DREW. Born Apr. 19, 1966 in Walnut, CA. Graduate Grossmont Col. Debut 1987 OB in "Fortune and Men's Eyes," followed by "Macbeth."

MURPHY, ROSEMARY. Born Jan. 13, 1927 in Munich, Ger. Attended Neighborhood Playhouse, Actors Studio. Bdwy debut 1950 in "Tower Beyond Tragedy," followed by "Look Homeward, Angel," "Period of Adjustment," "Any Wednesday," "Delicate Balance," "Weekend," "Death of Bessie Smith," "Butterflies Are Free," "Ladies at the Alamo," "Cheaters," "John Gabriel Borkman," "Coastal Disturbances," "The Devil's Disciple," OB in "Are You Now or Have You Ever Been?," "Learned Ladies," "Coastal Disturbances."

MURRAY, BRIAN. Born Oct. 9, 1939 in Johannesburg, SA. Debut 1964 OB in "The Knack," followed by "King Lear," "Ashes," "The Jail Diary of Albie Sachs," "A Winter's Tale," "Barbarians," "The Purging," "Midsummer Night's Dream," "The Recruiting Officer," "The Arcata Promise," "Candida in Concert," "Much Ado About Nothing," Bdwy in "All in Good Time," "Rosencrantz and Guildenstern Are Dead," "Sleuth," "Da," "Noises Off."

MURRAY, LELAND. Born Nov. 13, 1929 in NYC. Attended CCNY. Debut 1988 OB in "Tamara."

MURTAUGH, JAMES. Born Oct. 28, 1942 in Chicago, IL. Debut OB in "The Firebugs," followed by "Highest Standard of Living," "Marathon '87," "Other People's Money," "Marathon '88."

MUSANTE, TONY. Born June 30, 1936 in Bridgeport, CT. Graduate Oberlin Col. Debut 1960 OB in "Borak," followed by "The Balcony," "Theatre of the Absurd," "Half-Past Wednesday," "The Collection," "Tender Heel," "Kiss Mama," "Mme. Mouse," "Zoo Story," "Match-Play," "Night of the Dunce," "Gun Play," "A Memory of Two Mondays," "27 Wagons Full of Cotton," "Grand Magic," "Cassatt," "Frankie and Johnnie in the Claire De Lune," Bdwy in "P.S. Your Cat is Dead" (1975), "The Lady From Dubuque."

NAJIMY, KATHY. Born Feb. 6, 1957 in San Diego, CA. Attended San Diego StateU. Debut 1986 OB in "The Kathy and Mo Show: Parallel Lives."

NAKAHARA, RON. Born July 20, 1947 in Honolulu, HI. Attended UHI., Tenri U. Debut 1981 OB in "Danton's Death," followed by "Flowers and Household Gods," "A Few Good Men," "Rohwer," "A Midsummer Night's Dream," "Teahouse," "Song for Nisei Fisherman," "Eat a Bowl of Tea," "Once is Never Enough," "Noiresque," "Play Ball," "Three Sisters."

NALBACH, DANIEL. Born May 20, 1937 in Buffalo, NY. Graduate Canisius Col., UPittsburg. Debut OB 1986 in "Murder on Broadway," followed by "Thirteenth Chair."

NASTASI, FRANK. Born Jan. 7, 1923 in Detroit, MI. Graduate WayneU, NYU. Bdwy debut 1963 in "Lorenzo," followed by "Avanti," OB in "Bonds of Interest," "One Day More," "Nathan the Wise," "The Chief Things," "Cindy," "Escurial," "The Shrinking Bride," "Macbird," "Cakes with the Wine," "Metropolitan Madness," "Rockaway Boulevard," "Scenes from La Vie de Boheme," "Agamemnon," "Happy Sunset Inc.," "3 Last Plays of O'Neill," "Taking Steam," "Lulu," "Body! Body?," "Legend of Sharon Shashanova," "Enrico IV."

NEENAN, MARIA. Born July 14, 1965 in Boston, MA. Bdwy debut 1989 in "Jerome Robbins' Broadway."

NELSON, BILL. Born Apr. 11, 1931 in Brooklyn, NY. Graduate Adelphi U. AADA. Debut OB 1986 in "Lies My Father Told Me," followed by "Almost Perfect," "Bitter Friends."

NELSON, MARK. Born Sept. 26, 1955 in Hackensack, NJ. Graduate Princeton U. Debut 1977 OB in "The Dybbuk," followed by "Green Fields," "The Keymaker," "The Common Pursuit," Bdwy in "Amadeus" (1981), "Brighton Beach Memoirs," "Biloxi Blues," "Broadway Bound," "Rumors."

NEUBERGER, JAN. Born Jan. 21, 1953 in Amityville, NY. Attended NYU. Bdwy debut 1975 in "Gypsy," OB in "Silk Stockings," "Chase a Rainbow," "Anything Goes," "A Little Madness," "Forbidden Broadway," "After These Messages," "Ad Hock."

NEWMAN, ANDREW HILL. Born Oct. 23, 1959 in Scarsdale, NY. Graduate UVt., Brandeis U. Bdwy debut 1982 in "Merlin," followed by "Big Riber," OB in "Little Shop of Horrors," "Bird of Paradise," "Only Kidding."

NEWTON, JOHN. Born Nov. 2, 1925 in Grand Junction, CO. Graduate UWash. Debut 1951 OB in "Othello," followed by "As You Like It," "Candida," "Candaules Commissioner," "Sextet," LCRep's "The Crucible," and "Streetcar Named Desire," "The Rivals," "The Subject Was Roses," "The Brass Ring," "Hadrian VII," "The Best Little Whorehouse in Texas," "A Midsummer Night's Dream," "Night Games," "A Frog in His Throat," "Max and Maxie," "The Lark," Bdwy in "Weekend," "First Monday in October," "Present Laughter."

NICCORE, VALORIE. Born Mar. 2, 1950 in Detroit, MI. Graduate Wayne StateU. Debut OB 1985 in "Carolyn," followed by "The Gambler."

NICHOLS, ROBERT. Born July 20, 1924 in Oakland, CA. Attended Pacific Col., RADA. Debut 1978 OB in "Are You Now . . .," followed by "Heartbreak House," "Ah, Wilderness!," "Oh, Boy!," "No No Nanette in Concert," "Sitting Pretty," "Cantorial," Bdwy in "Man and Superman," "The Man Who Came to Dinner," "Einstein and the Polar Bear," "Take Me Along."

NICOLAISEN, KARI. Born Feb. 16, 1961 in San Francisco, CA. Debut 1987 OB in "Wish You Were Here," followed by "Something for the Boys," "Prizes," Bdwy in "A Chorus Line" (1987)

NIPKOW, LESLIE. Born Dec. 14, 1963 in Westminster, MD. Graduate SyracuseU. Debut OB 1989 in "The Investigation of the Murder in El Salvador."

NIXON, CYNTHIA. Born Apr. 9, 1966 in NYC. Debut 1980 in "The Philadelphia Story" (LC) for which she received a Theatre World Award, OB in "Lydie Breeze," "Hurlyburly," "Sally's Gone, She Left Her Name," "Lemon Sky," "Cleveland and Half-Way Back," "Alterations," "Young Playwrights," "Moonchildren," "Romeo and Juliet," Bdwy in "The Real Thing" (1983), "Hurlyburly," "The Heidi Chronicles."

NOLEN, TIMOTHY. Born July 9, 1941 in Rotan, TX. Graduate Trenton State Col., Manhattan School of Music. Debut in "Sweeney Todd" (1984) with NYC Opera. Bdwy in "Grind" (1985) followed by "Phantom of the Opera."

NORMAN, JOHN. Born May 13, 1961 in Detroit, Mi. Graduate Cincinnati Conservatory. Bdwy debut 1987 in "Les Miserables."

NORRIS, BRUCE. Born May 16, 1960 in Houston, TX. Graduate Northwestern U. Bdwy debut 1985 in "Biloxi Blues," OB in "A Midsummer Night's Dream," "Wenceslas Square," "The Debutante Ball," "What the Butler Saw."

NOZICK, BRUCE. Born Jan. 29, 1960 in Winchester, MA. Graduate NYU. Debut 1982 OB in "Romeo and Juliet," followed by "And That's How the Rent Gets Paid," "Too Ugly for L.A.," "Sundance," "A Shayna Maidel."

NUGENT, JAMES. Born June 22, 1940 in The Bronx, NY. Graduate UFla. Debut 1984 OB in "Air Rights," followed by "Merchant of Venice," "Arms and the Man," "Mme. Colombe," "Two Gentlemen of Verona," "Days to Come," "The Good Doctor," "Pericles," "The Rivals," "Lady From the Sea," "Deep Swimmer," "Macbeth," "The Imaginary Invalid," "Uncle Vanya," "All's Well That Ends Well," "Dodger Blue," "The Philanderer," "Hedda Gabler."

NUTE, DON. Born Mar. 13, in Connellsville, PA. Attended Denver U. Debut OB 1965 in "The Trojan Women" followed by "Boys in the Band," "Mad Theatre for Madmen," "The Eleventh Dynasty," "About Time," "The Urban Crisis," "Christmas Rappings," "The Life of a Man," "A Look at the Fifties," "Aunt Millie."

NYE, CARRIE. Born in Mississippi. Attended Stephens Col., Yale U. Bdwy debut 1960 in "Second String," followed by "Mary, Mary," "Half a Sixpence," "A Very Rich Woman," "Cop-Out," "The Man Who Came to Dinner," OB in "Ondine," "Ghosts," "The Importance of Being Earnest," "The Trojan Women," "The Real Inspector Hound," "a/k/a Tennessee," "The Wisteria Trees," "Madwoman of Chaillot," "Without Apologies."

OAKES, ALICE ANNE. Born Aug. 30, 1956 in Edison, NJ. Graduate Butler U. Bdwy debut 1981 in "Broadway Follies," followed by "Anything Goes."

OAKES, CINDY. Born Mar. 25, 1959 in Homestead, Pa. Graduate UPittsburgh. Bdwy debut 1986 in "Me and My Girl," followed by "Smile."

O'BRIEN, AMY. Born Feb. 1, 1961 in La Jolla, CA. Attended San Diego State U. Bdwy debut 1987 in "Anything Goes."

O'BRIEN, DALE. Born Oct. 7, 1957 in Omaha, NB. Graduate Kearney State Col, UArk. Debut 1986 OB in "Rainbow," followed by "Mixed Doubles," "The Fantasticks."

O'BRIEN, SYLVIA. Born May 4 in Dublin, Ire. Debut 1961 OB in "O Marry Me," followed by "Red Roses for Me," "Every Other Evil," "3 by O'Casey," "Essence of Woman," "Dear Oscar," "Dona Rosita," "Returnings," Bdwy in "The Passion of Joseph D," "The Right Honourable Gentleman," "Loves of Cass McGuire," "Hadrian VII," "Conduct Unbecoming," "My Fair Lady," "Da," "Me and My Girl."

O'CONNELL, PATRICK. Born July 7, 1957 in Westport, CT. Graduate Juilliard. Bdwy debut

1983 in "Amadeus," OB in "A Man for All Seasons" (1987), "1000 Airplanes on the Roof."

O'CONNOR, KEVIN. Born May 7, 1939 in Honolulu, HI. Attended UHI, Neighborhood Playhouse. Debut 1964 OB in "Up to Thursday," followed by "Six from La Mama," "Rimers of Eldritch," "Tom Paine," "Boy on the Straightback Chair," "Dear Janet Rosenberg," "Eyes of Chalk," "Alive and Well in Argentina," "Duet," "Trio," "The Contractor," "Kool Aid," "The Frequency," "Chucky's Hutch," "Birdbath," "The Breakers," "Crossing the Crab Nebula," "Jane Avril," "Inserts," "3 by Beckett," "The Dicks," "A Kiss Is Just a Kiss," "Last of the Knucklemen," "Thrombo," "The Dark and Mr. Stone," "The Miser," "The Heart Outright," Bdwy in "Gloria and Esperanza," "The Morning After Optimism," "Figures in the Sand," "Devour the Snow," "The Lady From Dubuque."

ODO, CHRIS: Born Feb. 7, 1954 in Kansas City, MO. Attended SWMoStateU. Debut 1984 OB in "A Midsummer Night's Dream," followed by "Oedipus," "Sleepless City," "Summer Face Woman," Bdwy in "M. Butterfly" (1988).

O'HARA, PAIGE. Born May 10, 1956 in Ft. Lauderdale, FL. Debut 1975 OB in "The Gift of the Magi," followed by "Company," "The Great American Backstage Musical," "Oh, Boy!," "Rabboni," "Sitting Pretty," Bdwy in "Show Boat" (1983), "The Mystery of Edwin Drood."

O'HARE, TIM. Born Dec. 2, 1956 in Montclair, NJ. Graduate UMd. Debut 1981 OB in "Couples," followed by "Shadow of a Gunman," "Moonie's Kid Don't Cry," "Cain," "Troilus and Cressida," "Richard III," "Macbeth," "She Stoops to Conquer."

OLSON, JAMES. Born Oct. 8, 1930 in Evanston, IL. Attended Northwestern, Actors Studio. Bdwy debut 1955 in "The Young and the Beautiful," followed by "Sin of Pat Muldoon," "J.B.," "The Chinese Prime Minister," "Three Sisters," "Slapstick Tragedy," "Of Love Remembered," OB in "Twelve Dreams," "Winterplay," "A Winter's Tale."

OLSON, MARILYN. Born Feb. 2, 1948 in Chicago, IL. Graduate Western IllU. Bdwy debut 1974 in "Gypsy," OB in "The Christmas Bride."

OMAHEN, KAREN. Born May 28, 1958 in Evanston, IL. Graduate St. Ambrose Col. Bdwy debut 1989 in "Largely New York."

O'MALLEY, JIM. Born Oct. 18, 1958 in NYC. Graduate Bucknell U. Debut OB 1985 in "Creeps," followed by "Hooters," "Goodbye Charlie," "Incommunicado," "Three Sisters," "Disposal," "Rum & Coke," "Perfect Crime," "Simon Says . . ."

ONDREJKA, MALIA. Born Nov. 23, 1957 in Fairborn, OH. Graduate Wright State U. Debut OB 1989 in "The Thirteenth Chair."

ORCHID, ELLEN. Born Jan. 28, 1954 in Brooklyn, NY. Graduate Goucher Col., RADA. Debut OB 1989 in "The Thirteenth Chair."

O'REILLY, CIARAN. Born Mar. 13, 1959 in Ireland. Attended Carmelite Col., Juilliard. Debut 1978 OB in "Playboy of the Western World," followed by "Summer," "Freedom of the City," "Fannie," "The Interrogation of Ambrose Fogarty," "King Lear," "Shadow of a Gunman," "The Marry Month of May," "I Do Not Like Thee, Dr. Fell," "The Plough and the Stars," "Yeats: A Celebration!"

ORMAN, ROSCOE. Born June 11, 1944 in NYC. Debut 1962 OB in "If We Grow Up," followed by "Electronic Nigger," "The Great McDaddy," "The Sirens," "Every Night When the Sun Goes Down," "The Last Street Play," "Julius Caesar," "Coriolanus," "The 16th Round," "20 Year Friends," "Talented Tenth," Bdwy in "Fences" (1988).

O'ROURKE, KEVIN. Born Jan. 25, 1956 in Portland, OR. Graduate Williams Col. Debut 1981 OB in "Declassee," followed by "Sister Mary Ignatius . . .," "Submariners," "A Midsummer Night's Dream," "Visions of Kerouac," "Self Defense," "Spoils of War" (also Bdwy), "The Spring Thing," Bdwy in "Alone Together" (1984).

OSIAN, MATTE. Born June 21, 1960 in Boston, MA. Graduate Colgate U., Brandeis U. Debut OB 1989 in "Cheri."

O'SULLIVAN, ANNE. Born Feb. 6, 1952 in Limerick City, Ire. Debut 1977 OB in "Kid Champion," followed by "Hello Out There," "Fly Away Home," "The Drunkard," "Dennis," "The Three Sisters," "Another Paradise," "Living Quarters," "Welcome to the Moon," "The Dreamer Examines His Pillow," "Mama Drama," "Free Fall," "The Magic Act," "The Plough and the Stars," "Marathon '88," "Bobo's Guns."

OVERMIRE, LAURENCE. Born Aug. 17, 1957 in Rochester, NY. Graduate Muskingum Col., UMn. Debut 1982 OB in "Don Juan," followed by "Summit Conference," "Psycho Beach Party," "5th of July," Bdwy in "Amadeus."

PAGAN, PETER. Born July 24, 1921 in Sydney, Australia. Attended Scots Col. Bdwy debut 1953 in "Escapade," followed by "Portrait of a Lady," "The Dark Is Light Enough," "Child of Fortune," "Hostile Witness," "Aren't We All?," OB in "Busybody," "M. Amilcar," "Without Apologies."

PAGE, EVELYN. Born in Fremont, NE. Attended UNe. Debut 1958 OB in "The Boy Friend," followed by "Brothers," "Two," "Murder of Crows," Bdwy in "Plain and Fancy," "Mr. Wonderful," "Little Me," "On a Clear Day You Can See Forever," "Canterbury Tales."

PANKOW, JOHN. Born 1955 in St. Louis, MO. Attended St. Nichols Sch. of the Arts. Debut 1980 OB in "Merton of the Movies," followed by "Slab Boys," "Forty-Deuce," "Hunting Scenes from Lower Bavaria," "Cloud 9," "Jazz Poets at the Grotto," "Henry V," "North Shore Fish," "Two Gentlemen of Verona," "Italian American Reconciliation," "Aristocrats," Bdwy in "Amadeus" (1981), "The Iceman Cometh" (1985), "Serious Money."

PAOLUCCI, BOB. Born in Quincy, MA. Graduate Fordham U. Debut OB 1974 in "Inherit the Wind," followed by "The Taming of the Shrew," "Gigi."

PARADY, RON. Born Mar. 12, 1940 in Columbus, OH. Graduate Ohio Wesleyan U., OH State U. Bdwy debut 1981 in "Candida," followed by "Our Town," OB in "Uncle Vanya," "The Father," "The New Man," "For Sale."

PARKER, ELLEN. Born Sept. 30, 1949 in Paris, Fr. Graduate Bard Col. Debut 1971 OB in "James Joyce Liquid Theatre," followed by "Uncommon Women and Others," "Dusa, Fish, Stas and Vi," "A Day in the Life of the Czar," "Fen," "Isn't It Romantic?," "The Winter's Tale," "Aunt Dan and Lemon," "Cold Sweat," "The Heidi Chronicles," Bdwy in "Equus," "Strangers," "Plenty."

PARKER, SARAH JESSICA. Born Mar. 25, 1965. Bdwy 1978 in "Annie," OB in "The Innocents," "1-Act Festival," "To Gillian on Her 37th Birthday," "The Heidi Chronicles."

PARLATO, DENNIS. Born Mar. 30, 1947 in Los Angeles. Graduate Loyola U. Bdwy debut 1979 in "A Chorus Line," followed by "The First," "Chess," OB in Beckett," "Elizabeth and Essex," "The Fantasticks," "Moby Dick," "The Knife," "Shylock," "Have I Got a Girl For You," "Romance! Romance!," "The Lark."

PARRY, WILLIAM. Born Oct. 7, 1947 in Steubenville, OH. Graduate Mt. Union Col. Bdwy debut 1971 in "Jesus Christ Superstar," followed by "Rockabye Hamlet," "The Leaf People," "Camelot" (1980), "Sunday in the Park with George," "Into the Light," OB in "Sgt. Pepper's Lonely Hearts Club Band," "The Conjurer," "Noah," "The Misanthrope," "Joseph and the Amazing Technicolor Dreamcoat," "Agamemnon," "Coolest Cat in Town," "Dispatches," "The Derby," "The Knife," "Cymbeline."

PARSONS, ESTELLE. Born Nov. 20, 1927 in Lynn, MA. Attended Boston U., Actors Studio. Bdwy debut 1956 in "Happy Hunting," followed by "Whoop Up!," "Beg, Borrow or Steal," "Mother Courage," "Ready When You Are, C.B.," "Malcolm," "Seven Descents of Myrtle," "And Miss Reardon Drinks a Little," "The Norman Conquests," "Ladies at the Alamo," "Miss Margarida's Way," "Pirates of Penzance," OB in "Demi-Dozen," "Pieces of 8," "Threepenny Opera," "Automobile Graveyard," "Mrs. Dally Has a Lover" for which she received a 1963 Theatre World Award, "Next Time I'll Sing to You," "Come to the Palace of Sin," "In the Summer House," "Monopoly," "The East Wind," "Galileo," "Peer Gynt," "Mahagonny," "People Are Living There," "Barbary Shore," "Oh Glorious Tintinnabulation," "Mert and Paul," "Elizabeth and Essex," "Dialogue for Lovers," "New Moon in Concert," "Orgasmo Adulto Escapes from the Zoo," "The Unguided Missile."

PASSELTINER, BERNIE. Born Nov. 21, 1931 in NYC. Graduate Catholic U. OB in "Square in the Eye," "Sourball," "As Virtuously Given," "Now Is the Time for All Good Men," "Rain," "Kaddish," "Against the Sun," "End of Summer," "Yentl, the Yeshiva Boy," "Heartbreak House," "Every Place Is Newark," "Isn't It Romantic?," "Buck," "Pigeons on the Walk," "Waving Goodbye," "The Sunshine Boys," Bdwy in "The Office," "The Jar," "Yentl."

PATINKIN, MANDY. Born Nov. 30, 1952 in Chicago, IL. Attended Juilliard. OB in "Henry IV," followed by "Leave It to Beaver Is Dead," "Rebel Women," "Hamlet," "Trelawny of the Wells," "Savages," "The Split," "The Knife," "Winter's Tale." Bdwy in "The Shadow Box," "Evita," "Sunday in the Park with George."

PATTERSON, JAY. Born Aug. 22 in Cincinnati, OH. Attended OhioU. Bdwy debut 1983 in "K-2," followed by OB's "Caligula," "The Mound Builders," "Quiet in the Land," "Of Mice and Men," "Domino," "Early One Evening."

PATTERSON, KELLY. Born Feb. 22, 1964 in Midland, TX. Attended Southern Methodist U. Debut 1984 OB in "Up in Central Park," followed by "Manhattan Serenade," Bdwy in "Sweet Charity" (1986), "Jerome Robbins' Broadway."

PATTI, JOHN. Born Sept. 20, 1958 in Buffalo, NY. Graduate SUNY. Debut OB 1989 in "Gigi."

PATTISON, LIANN. Born Apr. 12, 1957 in Chico, CA. Attended CalStateU/Chico, UWash. Debut 1985 OB in "I'm Not Rappaport," followed by "A Burning Beach," Bdwy in "Serious Money" (1988).

PATTON, LUCILLE. Born in NYC. Attended Neighborhood Playhouse. Bdwy debut 1946 in "A Winter's Tale," followed by "Topaze," "Arms and the Man," "Joy to the World," "All You Need Is One Good Break," "Fifth Season," "Heavenly Twins," "Rhinoceros," "Marathon 33," "The Last Analysis," "Dinner at 8," "La Strada," "Unlikely Heroes," "Love Suicide at Schofield Barracks," OB in "Ulysses in Nighttown," "Failures," "Three Sisters," "Yes Yes No No," "Tango," "Mme. de Sade," "Apple Pie," "Follies," "Yesterday Is Over," "My Prince, My King," "I Am Who I Am," "Double Game," "Love in a Village," "1984," "A Little Night Music," "Cheri."

PATTON, WILL. Born June 14, 1954 in Charleston, SC. OB in "Kingdom of Earth," "Scenes from Country Life," "Cops," "Pedro Paramo," "Limbo Tales," "Tourists and Refugees," "Rearrangements," "Dark Ride," "Salt Lake City Skyline," "The Red Snake," "Goose and Tomtom," "Joan of Lorraine," "Fool for Love," "A Lie of the Mind," "What Did He See."

PAYTON-WRIGHT, PAMELA. Born Nov. 1, 1941 in Pittsburgh, PA. Graduate Birmingham Southern Col., RADA. Bdwy debut 1967 in "The Show-Off," followed by "Exit the King," "The Cherry Orchard," "Jimmy Shine," "Mourning Becomes Electra," "The Glass Menagerie," "Romeo and Juliet," "Night of the Iguana," "M. Butterfly," OB in "The Effect of Gamma Rays . . .," "The Crucible," "The Seagull," "Don Juan," "In the Garden."

PEACHENA, LADY. Born May 15, 1948 in Lancaster, PA. Graduate Carnegie Tech. Bdwy debut 1961 in "Bye Bye Birdie," followed by "A Teaspoon Every Four Hours," "Oliver!," OB in "The Glorious Age," "Over 40."

PEACOCK, CHIARA. Born Sept. 19, 1962 in Ann Arbor, MI. Graduate Sarah Lawrence Col. Debut 1985 OB in "Yours, Anne" followed by "Maggie Magalita," "One Step at a Time," "Octoberfest '87," "A Shayna Maidel."

PEARLMAN, STEPHEN. Born Feb. 26, 1935 in NYC. Graduate DartmouthCol. Bdwy debut 1964 in "Barefoot in the Park," followed by "La Strada," OB in "Threepenny Opera," "Time of the Key," "Pimpernel," "In White America," "Viet Rock," "Chocolates," "Bloomers," "Richie," "Isn't It Romantic," "Bloodletters," "Light Up the Sky," "Perfect Party," "Come Blow Your Horn," "A Shayna Maidel," "Value Of Names."

PELIKAN, LISA. Born July 12 in Paris, Fr. Attended Juilliard. Debut 1975 OB in "Spring's Awakening," followed by "Elephant in the House," "American Clock," "The Diviners," "Midnight Visitor," "Love's Labour's Lost," "The Immigrant," Bdwy in "Romeo and Juliet" (1977).

PELLEGRINO, SUSAN. Born June 3, 1950 in Baltimore, MD. Attended CCSan Francisco, CalStU. Debut 1982 OB in "Wisteria Trees," followed by "Steel on Steel," "Master Builder," "Equal Wrights."

PENDLETON, AUSTIN. Born Mar. 27, 1940 in Warren, OH. Attended YaleU. Debut 1962 OB in "Oh Dad, Poor Dad . . .," followed by "Last Sweet Days of Issac," "Three Sisters," "Say Goodnight, Gracie," "Office Murders," "Up From Paradise," "The Overcoat," "Two Character Play," "Master Class," "Educating Rita," "Uncle Vanya," "Serious Company," "Philotetes," "Hamlet," Bdwy in "Fiddler on the Roof," "Hail Scrawdyke," "Little Foxes," "American Millionaire," "Runner Stumbles," "Little Foxes (dir. 1981)," "Doubles."

PENNINGTON, GAIL. Born Oct. 2, 1957 in Kansas City, MO. Graduate SMU. Bdwy debut 1980 in "The Music Man," followed by "Can-Can," "America," "Little Me" (1982), "42nd Street," OB in "The Baker's Wife."

PERCASSI, DON. Born Jan. 11 in Amsterdam, NY. Bdwy debut 1964 in "High Spirits," followed by "Walking Happy," "Coco," "Sugar," "Molly," "Mack and Mabel," "A Chorus Line," "42nd Street."

PEREZ, LAZARO. Born Dec. 12, 1945 in Havana, Cuba. Bdwy debut 1969 in "Does a Tiger Wear a Necktie?" followed by "Animals," OB in "Romeo and Juliet," "12 Angry Men," "Wonderful Years," "Alive," "G.R. Point," "Primary English Class," "Man and the Fly," "Last Latin Lover," "Cabal of Hypocrites," "Balm in Gilead," "Enrico IV."

Peter MacNicol	Theresa Marlowe	Joseph Maher	Patricia Masters	Stephen Mailer	Joan Matthiessen
Shannon McGough	John C. McGinley	Barbara McCulloh	Gerry McIntyre	Monica Merryman	Roderick McLachlan
Daniel Nalbach	Anna Minot	Frank Nastasi	Aleta Mitchell	Mark Nelson	Kari Nicolaisen
Leslie Nipkow	Bruce Norris	Amy O'Brien	Don Nute	Paige O'Hara	Bernie Passeltiner
Gail Pennington	John Patti	Patricia Ben Peterson	Lazaro Perez	Mary Bracken Phillips	Ethan Phillips

PEREZ, LUIS. Born July 28, 1959 in Atlanta, GA. With Joffrey Ballet before 1986 debut in "Brigadoon" (LC) followed by "Phantom of the Opera," "Jerome Robbins' Bdwy," OB in "Wonderful Ice Cream Suit," "Tango Apasionada."

PEREZ, MERCEDES. Born Oct. 25, 1961 in Arlington, Va. Debut 1983 OB in "Skyline," followed by Bdwy in "Take Me Along" (1985), "A Chorus Line."

PEREZ, MICHAEL. Born Sept. 7, 1957 in San Jose, CA. Graduate USMC, Natl Shakespeare Conserv. Debut 1987 OB in "Women Beware Women," followed by "Don Juan of Seville."

PESATURO, GEORGE. Born July 29, 1949 in Winthrop, MA. Graduate Manhattan Col. Bdwy debut 1976 in "A Chorus Line," OB in "The Music Man" (JB).

PETERS, BERNADETTE. Born Feb. 28, 1948 in Jamaica, NY. Bdwy debut in "Girl in the Freudian Slip," followed by "Johnny No-Trump," "George M!" for which she received a Theatre World Award, "La Strada," "On the Town," "Mack and Mabel," "Sunday in the Park with George," "Song and Dance," "Into the Woods," OB in "Curley McDimple," "Penny Friend," "Most Happy Fella," "Dames at Sea," "Nevertheless They Laugh," "Sally and Marsha."

PETERS, BROCK. Born July 2, 1927 in NYC. Attended ChicagoU, CCNY. Bdwy debut 1943 in "Porgy and Bess," followed by "South Pacific," "Anna Lucasta," "My Darlin' Aida," "Mr. Johnson," "Kwamina," "Caucasian Chalk Circle" (LC), "Lost in the Stars," "Driving Miss Daisy" (NTC).

PETERSON, PATRICIA BEN. Born Sept. 11 in Portland, OR. Graduate PacifLutheranU. Debut 1985 OB in "Kuni Leml," followed by "The Chosen," "Grand Tour," Bdwy in "Into the Woods."

PETTIT, DODIE. Born Dec. 29 in Princeton, NJ. Attended Westminster Choir Col. Bdwy debut 1984 in "Cats," followed by "The Phantom of the Opera."

PHILLIPS, ETHAN. Born Feb. 8, 1950 in Rockville Center, NY. Graduate BostonU, CornellU. Debut 1979 OB in "Modigliani," followed by "Eccentricities of a Nightingale," "Nature and Purpose of the Universe," "The Beasts," "Dumb Waiter," "Indian Wants the Bronx," "Last of the Red Hot Lovers," "Only Kidding," "Almost Perfect."

PHILLIPS, LACY DARRYL. Born Feb. 24, 1963 in NYC. Attended Lehman Col. Debut 1981 OB in "Raisin," followed by "The Late Great Ladies," Bdwy in "Anything Goes" (1987).

PHILLIPS, MARY BRACKEN. Born Aug. 15, 1946 in Kansas City, MO. Attended KansU. Debut 1969 OB in "Perfect Party," followed by "Look Where I'm At," "Hot Grog," "Cradle Song," Bdwy in "1776," "Different Times," "Hurry, Hurry," "Annie."

PHILLIPS, MARY ELLEN. Born Apr. 17, 1963 in Providence, RI. Graduate RI Col. Debut OB 1989 in "Sweeney Todd," Bdwy in "Sweeney Todd" (1989).

PIERCE, DAVID. Born Apr. 3, 1959 in Albany, NY. Graduate Yale U. Debut 1982 on Bdwy in "Beyond Therapy," followed by "The Heidi Chronicles," OB in "Summer," "That's It, Folks!," "The Three Zeks," "Donuts," "Hamlet," "The Maderati," "Marathon 87," "The Cherry Orchard," "Zero Positive," "Much Ado about Nothing."

PIERROT, QUIN. Born Aug. 15 in Boston, MA. Attended HB Studio. OB debut in "Cheri."

PINKINS, TONYA. Born May 30, 1962 in Chicago, IL. Attended Carnegie-Mellon U. Bdwy debut 1981 in "Merrily We Roll Along," OB in "Five Points," "A Winter's Tale," "An Ounce of Prevention," "Just Say No."

PIONTEK, MICHAEL E. Born Jul. 31, 1956 in Canoga Park, CA. Graduate FSU-Asolo Conserv. Bdwy debut 1987 in "Into the Woods," OB in "Reckless," "The Pajama Game," "Dames at Sea," "One Act Festival," "Florida Crackers."

PLAYTEN, ALICE. Born Aug. 28, 1947 in NYC. Attended NYU. Bdwy debut 1960 in "Gypsy," followed by "Oliver!," "Hello, Dolly!," "Henry, Sweet Henry," for which she received a Theatre World Award, "George M!," "Spoils of War," "Rumors," OB in "Promenade," "The Last Sweet Days of Isaac," "National Lampoon's Lemmings," "Valentine's Day," "Pirates of Penzance," "Up From Paradise," "A Visit," "Sister Mary Ignatius Explains It All," "An Actor's Nightmare," "That's It, Folks," "1-2-3-4-5," "Spoils of War."

PLUNKETT, MARYANN. Born in 1953 in Lowell, MA. Attended UNH. Bdwy debut 1983 in "Agnes of God," followed by "Sunday in the Park with George," "Me and My Girl," OB in "Aristocrats."

POE, RICHARD. Born Jan. 25, 1946 in Portola, CA. Graduate USan Fran., UCal/Davis. Debut 1971 OB in "Hamlet," followed by "Seasons Greetings," "Twelfth Night," Bdwy in "Broadway" (1987) "M. Butterfly."

POGREBIN, ABIGAIL. Born May 17, 1965 in NYC. Bdwy debut 1981 in "Merrily We Roll Along," OB in "Behind the Heart."

POLENZ, ROBERT. Born June 9, 1953 in Trenton, NJ. Graduate Muskingam Col. Bdwy debut 1974 in "Over Here," followed by "Candide," OB in "Apple Pie," "Children of Adam," "Snapshot," "Young Rube."

POLEY, ROBIN. Born in NYC. Graduate Oberln Col. Debut OB 1988 in "Crystal Clear," followed by "Love's Labour's Lost."

POLT, GILBERT (Marc). Born Mar. 22, 1956 in Baltimore, MD. Graduate UMd., J.D.U. of Baltimore. Debut OB 1989 in "Gigi."

POMPEI, DONNA. Born May 13, 1960 in Philadelphia, PA. Graduate PaStateU. Bdwy debut 1989 in "A Chorus Line."

PONAZECKI, JOE. Born Jan. 7, 1934 in Rochester, NY. Attended Rochester U. Columbia U. Bdwy debut 1959 in "Much Ado about Nothing," followed by "Send Me No Flowers," "A Call on Kuprin," "Take Her She's Mine," "Fiddler on the Roof," "Xmas in Las Vegas," "3 Bags Full," "Love in E-Flat," "90 Day Mistress," "Harvey," "Trial of the Catonsville 9," "The Country Girl," "Freedom of the City," "Summer Brave," "Music Is," "The Little Foxes," OB in "The Dragon," "Muzeeka," "Witness," "All Is Bright," "The Dog Ran Away," "Dream of a Blacklisted Actor," "Innocent Pleasures," "The Dark at the Top of the Stairs," "36," "After the Revolution," "The Raspberry Picker," "Raisin in the Sun," "Light Up the Sky," "Marathon 86," "One Act Festival."

PONZINI, ANTHONY. Born June 1. Attended Neighborhood Playhouse, Actors Studio. Debut 1959 OB in "The Breaking Wall," followed by "Oh, Dad, Poor Dad . . .," "Glory in the Flower," "Purification," "The Understanding," Bdwy in "Arturo Ui," "P.S. Your Cat Is Dead."

PRESTON, WILLIAM. Born Aug. 26, 1921 in Columbia, PA. Graduate PaStateU. Debut 1972 OB in "We Bombed in New Haven," followed by "Hedda Gabler," "Whisper into My Good Ear," "A Nestless Bird," "Friends of Mine," "Iphigenia in Aulis," "Midsummer," "The Fantasticks," "Frozen Assets," "The Golem," "The Taming of the Shrew," "His Master's Voice," "Much Ado about Nothing," "Hamlet," "Winter Dreams," Bdwy in "Our Town."

PRICE, BRIAN. Born Mar. 6, 1966 in Washington D.C. Graduate Yale U. Debut OB 1989 in "Philoctetes."

PRICE, LONNY. Born Mar. 9, 1959 in NYC. Attended Juilliard. Debut 1979 OB in "Class Enemy," for which he received a Theatre World Award, followed by "Up from Paradise," "Rommel's Garden," "Times and Appetites of Toulouse-Lautrec," "Room Service," "Come Blow Your Horn," "The Immigrant," Bdwy in "The Survivor" (1980), "Merrily We Roll Along," "Master Harold and the Boys," "The Time of Your Life," "Children of the Sun," "Rags," "Broadway," "Burn This."

PRINCE, FAITH. Born Aug. 5, 1957 in Augusta, GA. Graduate UCincinnati. Debut OB 1981 in "Scrambled Feet," followed by "Olympus on My Mind," "Groucho," "Living Color," Bdwy in "Jerome Robbins' Broadway" (1989).

PROVAL, DAVID. Born May 20, 1942 in Brooklyn, NY. Debut 1978 OB in "Momma's Little Angels," followed by "My Unknown Son," Bdwy in "Requiem for a Heavyweight."

PROVENZA, PAUL. Born July 31, 1957 in NYC. Graduate UPa., RADA. Debut OB 1988 in "Only Kidding," for which he received a Theatre World Award.

PROVENZA, SAL. Born Sept. 21, 1946 in Brooklyn, NY. Debut 1980 OB in "The Fantasticks," folowed by "A Matter of Tone," Bdwy in "Oh! Brother!," (1981), "The King and I" (1984).

PUGH, RICHARD WARREN. Born Oct. 20, 1950 in NYC. Graduate Tarkio Col. Bdwy debut 1979 in "Sweeney Todd," followed by "The Music Man," "The Five O'Clock Girl," "Copperfield," "Zorba" (1983), "Phantom of the Opera," OB in "Chase a Rainbow."

PURI, RAJIKA. Born Sept. 14, 1945 in Daves-salaam. Tanzania. Graduate Delhi U. NYU. Debut 1986 OB in "The Transposed Heads" (LC), followed by "Phaedra Britannica," "Cymbeline."

PURSLEY, DAVID. Born July 13, 1938 in Lewisburg, PA. Graduate HarvardU, BaylorU. Debut 1969 OB in "Peace," followed by "The Faggott," "Wings," "The Three Musketeers," Bdwy in "Happy End" (1977), "Snow White," "Anything Goes."

QUINN, AIDAN. Born Mar. 8, 1959 in Chicago, IL. Debut OB 1984 in "Fool for Love," followed by "Lie of the Mind," Bdwy in "A Streetcar Named Desire" for which he received a Theatre World Award.

RACKLEFF, OWEN. Born July 16, 1934 in NYC. Graduate Columbia U, London U. Bdwy debut 1977 in "Piaf," OB in "The Lesson" (1978), "Catsplay," "Arms and the Man," "Escoffier: King of Chefs," "New Way to Pay Old Debts," "Samson Agonistes," "Enter Laughing," "The Jew of Malta," "Sunday Promenade."

RAEBECK, LOIS. Born in West Chicago, IL. Graduate Perdue U. Debut 1986 OB in "Rule of Three," followed by "Cork," "Between Time and Timbuktu," "The Women in the Family," "All's Well That Ends Well."

RAGNO, JOSEPH. Born Mar. 11, 1936 in Brooklyn, NY. Attended Allegheny Col. Debut 1960 OB in "Worm in the Horseradish," followed by "Elizabeth the Queen," "A Country Scandal," "The Shrike," "Cymbeline," "Love Me, Love My Children," "Interrogation of Havana," "The Birds," "Armenians," "Feedlot," "Every Place Is Newark," "Modern Romance," "Hunting Cockroaches," "Just Say No," Bdwy in "Indians" (1969), "The Iceman Cometh."

RAGONESI, ANGELO. Born Nov. 5, 1955 in Philadelphia, PA. Graduate Temple U. Bdwy debut 1989 in "Ghetto."

RAIDER-WEXLER, VICTOR. Born Dec. 31, 1943 in Toledo, OH. Attended UToledo. Debut 1976 OB in "The Prince of Homburg," followed by "The Passion of Dracula," "Ivanov," "Brandy Before Breakfast," "The Country Girl," "Dream of a Blacklisted Actor," "One Act Festival," "Loveplay," "Our Own Family," "The Boys Next Door," "L'Illusion," Bdwy in "Best Friend" (1976), "Ma Rainey's Black Bottom."

RAINEY, DAVID. Born Jan. 30, 1960 in Tucson, AZ. Graduate ENMex U, Juilliard. Debut 1987 OB in "Richard II," followed by "Henry IV Part 1," "Julius Caesar," "Love's Labour's Lost," "Boy Meets Girl," "The Phantom Tollbooth."

RAITER, FRANK. Born Jan. 17, 1932 in Cloquet, MN. Graduate Yale. Debut OB 1972 in "Soft Core Pornographer," followed by "Winter's Tale."

RAMSAY, REMAK. Born Feb. 2, 1937 in Baltimore, MD. Graduate Princeton U. Debut 1964 OB in "Hang Down Your Head and Die," followed by "The Real Inspector Hound," "Landscape of the Body," "All's Well That Ends Well," "Rear Column," "The Winslow Boy," "The Dining Room," "Pygmalion in Concert," "Save Grand Central," "Quartermaine's Terms," "Woman in Mind," Bdwy in "Half a Sixpence" (1965), "Sheep on the Runway," "Lovely Ladies, Kind Gentlemen," "On the Town," "Jumpers," "Private Lives," "Dirty Linen," "Every Good Boy Deserves Favor," "The Devil's Disciple."

RANDALL, TONY. Born Feb. 26, 1920 in Tulsa, OK. Attended Northwestern, Columbia, Neighborhood Playhouse. Bdwy debut 1947 in "Antony and Cleopatra," followed by "To Tell You the Truth," "Caesar and Cleopatra," "Oh, Men! Oh, Women!," "Inherit the Wind," "Oh, Captain!," "UTBU," "M. Butterfly."

RANDEL, MELISSA. Born June 16, 1955 in Portland, ME. Graduate UCal/Irvine. Bdwy debut 1980 in "A Chorus Line," OB in "Shooting Stars."

RASCHE, DAVID. Born Aug. 7, 1944 in St. Louis, MO. Graduate Elmhurst Col, UChicago. Debut 1976 OB in "John," followed by "Snow White," "Isadora Duncan Sleeps with the Russian Navy," "End of the War," "A Sermon," "Routed," "Geniuses," "Dolphin Position," "To Gillian on Her 37th Birthday," "Custom of the Country," Bdwy in "Shadow Box" (1977), "Loose Ends," "Lunch Hour," "Speed-the-Plow."

RASHOVICH, GORDANA. Born Sept. 18 in Chicago, IL. Graduate RooseveltU., RADA. Debut 1977 OB in "Fefu and Her Friends," for which she received a Theatre World Award, followed by "Selma," "Couple of the Year," "Mink Sonata," "Class One Acts," "Morocco," "A Shayna Maidel."

RATHGEB, LAURA. Born Sept. 5, 1962 in Burlington, VT. Graduate St. Michael's Col. Debut 1987 OB in "Deep Swimmer," followed by "The Imaginary Invalid," "Electra," "All's Well That Ends Well," "She Stoops to Conquer," "The Philanderer."

RAY, STACY Born in Jacksonville, FL. Graduate UNC/Greensboro, ACT. Debut 1988 OB in "Steel Magnolias."

REBHORN, JAMES. Born Sept. 1, 1948 in Philadelphia, PA. Graduate Wittenberg U, Columbia U. Debut 1972 OB in "Blue Boys," followed by "Are You Now or Have You Ever Been?," "Trouble with Europe," "Othello," "Hunchback of Notre Dame," "Period of Adjustment," "The Freak," "Half a Lifetime," "Touch Black," "To Gillian on Her 37th Birthday," "Rain," "The Hasty Heart," "Husbandry," "Isn't It Romantic?," "Blind Date," "Cold Sweat," "Spoils of War," "Marathon 88," Bdwy in "I'm Not Rappaport," "Our Town" (1989).

REDINGER, PAULA. Born Feb. 9, in Portland, OR. Graduate UNe. Bdwy debut 1985 in "The Marriage of Figaro," OB in "Family Life," "Two Good Boys."

REDWOOD, JOHN HENRY. Born Sept. 10 in Brooklyn, NY. Graduate UKs, Fordham U, St. John's U. Debut 1971 OB in "One Flew over the Cuckoo's Nest," followed by "Black Visions," "When the Sun Gets Blue," "Mark VIII," "Walkers," Bdwy in "Guys and Dolls."

REED, GAVIN. Born June 3, 1935 in Liverpool, Eng. Attended RADA. Debut 1974 OB in "The Taming of the Shrew," followed by "French without Tears," "Potsdam Quartet," "Two Fish in the Sky," Bdwy in "Scapino" (1974), "Some of My Best Friends," "Run for Your Wife."

REEHLING, JOYCE. Born Mar. 5, 1949 in Baltimore, MD. Graduate NCSchool of Arts. Debut 1976 OB in "The Hot l Baltimore," followed by "Who Killed Richard Cory?," "Lulu," "5th of July," "The Runner Stumbles," "Life and/or Death," "Back in the Race," "Time Framed," "Extremities," "Hands of Its Enemy," "Reckless," Bdwy in "A Matter of Gravity" (1976), "5th of July."

REEVE, CHRISTOPHER. Born Sept. 25, 1952 in NYC. Graduate Cornell U., Juilliard. Debut 1975 OB in "Berkeley Square," followed by "My Life," "Winter's Tale," "Love Letters," Bdwy in "A Matter of Gravity" (1976), "5th of July," "The Marriage of Figaro."

REISSA, ELEANOR. Born May 11 in Brooklyn, NY. Graduate Brooklyn Col. Debut 1979 OB in "Rebecca the Rabbi's Daughter," followed by "That's Not Funny, That's Sick," "The Rise of David Levinsky," "Match Made in Heaven," "Song for a Saturday," "No No Nanette," "Songs of Paradise."

REMME, JOHN. Born Nov. 21, in Fargo, ND. Attended UMn. Debut 1972 OB in "One for the Money," followed by "Anything Goes," "The Rise of David Levinsky," "Jubilee in Concert," "The Firefly in Concert," "Sweet Adeline in Concert," "George White's Scandals in Concert," "Tomfoolery," Bdwy in "The Ritz" (1975), "The Royal Family," "Can-Can," "Alice in Wonderland," "Teddy and Alice."

RENDERER, SCOTT. Born in Palo Alto, CA. Graduate Whitman Col. Bdwy debut 1983 in "Teaneck Tanzi," OB in "And Things That Go Bump in the Night," "Crossfire," "Just Like the Lions," "The Dreamer Examines His Pillow," "Nasty Little Secrets."

RENFROE, REBECCA. Born Nov. 9, 1951 in Alexandria, VA. Graduate UCincinnati. Bdwy debut 1981 in "Bring Back Birdie," OB in "The Gifts of the Magi."

RHYNE, SYLVIA. Born Dec. 27 in Chicago, IL. Graduate Carleton Col. OB in "Candide," "South Pacific," "La Vie Parisienne," Bdwy in "Sweeney Todd" (1989).

RICHARDS, CAROL. Born Dec. 26 in Aurora, IL. Graduate Northwestern U, Columbia U. Bdwy debut 1965 in "Half a Sixpence," followed by "Mame," "Last of the Red Hot Lovers," "Company," "Cats."

RICHARDS, JESS. Born Jan. 23, 1943 in Seattle, WA. Attended UWash. Bdwy debut 1966 in "Walking Happy," followed by "South Pacific" (LC), "Two by Two," "On the Town" for which he received a 1972 Theatre World Award, "Mack and Mabel," "Musical Chairs," "A Reel American Hero," "Barnum," OB in "One for the Money," "Lovesong," "A Musical Evening with Josh Logan," "The Lullaby of Broadway," "All Night Strut!," "Station Joy," "Sing for Your Supper."

RICHARDSON, LaTANYA. Born Oct. 21, 1949 in Atlanta, GA. Graduate Spelman Col. Debut 1976 OB in "Perdido," followed by "Unfinished Women Cry in No Man's Land," "Spell #7," "The Trial of Dr. Beck," "Charlotte's Web," "Nonsectarian Conversations with the Dead," "An Organdy Falsetto," "Boogie Woogie and Booker T," "Talented Tenth," "Ma Rose."

RICHARDSON, LEE. Born Sept. 11, 1926 in Chicago, IL. Graduate Goodman Theatre. Debut 1952 OB in "Summer and Smoke," followed by "St. Joan," "Volpone," "The American Dream," "Bartleby," "Plays for Bleecker Street," "Merchant of Venice," "King Lear," "Thieves Carnival," "Waltz of the Toreadors," Bdwy in "The Legend of Lizzie" (1959), "Lord Pengo," "House of Atreus," "Find Your Way Home," "Othello," "The Jockey Club Stakes," "The Devil's Disciple."

RICHERT, WANDA. Born Apr. 18, 1958 in Chicago, IL. Bdwy debut 1980 in "42nd Street" for which she received a Theatre World Award, followed by "Nine," "A Chorus Line."

RIEGERT, PETER. Born Apr. 11, 1947 in NYC. Graduate UBuffalo. Debut 1975 OB in "Dance with Me," followed by "Sexual Perversity in Chicago," "Sunday Runners," "Isn't It Romantic," "La Brea Tarpits," "A Hell of a Town," "Festival of One Acts," "A Rosen by Any Other Name," "The Birthday Party," Bdwy in "The Nerd" (1987).

RIEHLE, RICHARD. Born May 12, 1948 in Menomonee Falls, WI. Graduate UNotre Dame, UMn. Bdwy debut 1986 in "Execution of Justice," OB in "A Midsummer Night's Dream," "The Birthday Party," "Right Behind the Flag," "Knepp," "Just Say No," "Phaedra Britannica."

RILEY, ERIC. Born Mar. 22, 1955 in Albion, MI. Graduate UMI. Bdwy debut 1979 in "Ain't Misbehavin'," followed by "Dream Girls," "Ain't Misbehavin' " (1988).

RINEHART, ELAINE. Born Aug. 16, 1958 in San Antonio, TX. Graduate NCSchArts. Debut 1975 OB in "Tenderloin," followed by "Native Son," "Joan of Lorraine," "Dumping Ground," "Fairweather Friends," "The Color of the Evening Sky," "The Best Little Whorehouse in Texas," "The Wedding of the Siamese Twins," "Festival of 1 Acts," "Up 'n' Under," "Crystal Clear."

RIVIN, LUCILLE. Born Mar. 25 in Brooklyn, NY. Graduate SUNY. Debut OB 1982 in "The Beggar," followed by "Golden Leg."

ROBB, R. D. Born Mar. 31, 1972 in Philadelphia, Pa. Bdwy debut 1980 in "Charlie and Algernon," followed by "Oliver!," "Les Miserables."

ROBBINS, JANA. Born Apr. 18, 1947 in Johnstown, PA. Graduate Stephens Col. Bdwy debut 1974 in "Good News," followed by "I Love My Wife," "Crimes of the Heart," "Romance/Romance," OB in "Tickles by Tucholsky," "Tip-Toes," "All Night Strut," "Colette Collage," "Circus Gothic," "Ad Hock."

ROBERTS, RALPH. Born Aug. 17 in Salisbury, NC. Attended UNC. Bdwy debut 1948 in "Angel Street," followed by "4 Chekhov Comedies," "SS Glencairn," "Madwoman of Chaillot," "Witness for the Prosecution," "The Lark," "Bells Are Ringing," "The Milk Train Doesn't Stop Here Anymore," "Love Suicide at Shofield Barracks," "A Texas Trilogy," OB in "Siamese Connections," "Fishing," "Joan of Lorraine," "Rimers of Eldritch."

ROBERTSON, SCOTT. Born Jan. 4, 1954 in Stamford, CT. Bdwy debut 1976 in "Grease," followed by "The Pajama Game" (LC), OB in "Scrambled Feet," "Applause," "A Lady Needs a Change," "A Backer's Audition," "She Loves Me," "Secrets of a Lava Lamp."

ROBINS, LAILA. Born Mar. 14, 1959 in St. Paul, MN. Graduate UWis, Yale. Bdwy debut 1984 in "The Real Thing," OB in "Bloody Poetry," "The Film Society," "For Dear Life."

ROBINSON, MEGHAN. Born Aug. 11, 1955 in Wilton, CT. Graduate Bennington Col. Debut 1982 OB in "The Dubliners," followed by "The Habits of Rabbits," "Episode 26," "Macbeth," "King Lear," "Sleeping Beauty or Coma," "Vampire Lesbians of Sodom," "Psycho Beach Party," "Hunger," "3 Pieces for a Warehouse," "No One Dances," "The Lady in Question."

ROBINSON, ROGER. Born May 2, 1941 in Seattle, WA. Attended USCal. Bdwy debut 1969 in "Does a Tiger Wear a Necktie?," followed by "Amen Corner," "The Iceman Cometh," OB in "Walk in Darkness," "Jericho-Jim Crow," "Who's Got His Own," "Trials of Brother Jero," "The Miser," "The Interrogation of Havana," "Lady Day," "Do Lord Remember Me," "Of Mice and Men," "The Middle of Nowhere," "Measure for Measure."

RODERICK, CONNIE. Born Jan. 7 in Dayton, OH. Attended Northwestern U, Goodman Theatre. Bdwy debut 1983 in "The Corn is Green," followed by "The Marriage of Figaro," "Devil's Disciple."

RODRIGUEZ, AL. Born May 29, 1960 in NYC. Graduate Syracuse U. Debut 1983 OB in "The Senorita from Tacna," followed by "Savings," "Merchant of Venice," "Death of Garcia Lorca," "Don Juan of Seville," Bdwy in "Open Admissions" (1984).

ROGERS, ANNE. Born July 29, 1933 in Liverpool, Eng. Attended St. John's Col. Bdwy debut 1957 in "My Fair Lady," followed by "Zenda," "Half a Sixpence," "42nd Street."

ROLF, FREDERICK. Born Aug. 14, 1926 in Berlin, Ger. Bdwy debut 1951 in "St Joan," followed by "The Egg," "Time Remembered," OB in "Coriolanus," "The Strong Are Lonely," "The Smokeweaver's Daughter," "Between Two Thieves," "Hedda Gabler," "The Day the Whores Came Out to Play Tennis," "Hogan's Goat," "In the Matter of J. Robert Oppenheimer," "Dark Lady of the Sonnets," "Tamara."

ROLLE, ESTHER. Born Nov. 8 in Pompano Beach, FL. Attended Hunter Col. Bdwy debut 1964 in "Blues for Mr. Charlie," followed by "Purlie Victorious," "Amen Corner," "Don't Play Us Cheap," "Horowitz and Mrs. Washington," OB in "The Blacks" (1961), "Happy Ending," "Day of Absence," "Evening of One Acts," "Man Better Man," "Brotherhood," "Okakawe," "Rosalee Pritchett," "Dream on Monkey Mountain," "Ride a Black Horse," "Ballet Behind the Bridge," "Member of the Wedding" (1989).

ROSENBAUM, DAVID. Born in NYC. Debut OB in "America Hurrah" (1968), followed by "The Cave Dwellers," "Evenings with Chekhov," "Out of the Death Cart," "After Miriam," "The Indian Wants the Bronx," "Allergy," "Family Business," "Beagleman and Brackett," Bdwy in "Oh, Calcutta!," "Ghetto."

ROSENBLATT, MARCELL. Born July 1 in Baltimore, MD. Graduate UNC, Yale U. Debut 1979 OB in "Vienna Notes," followed by "Sorrows of Stephen," "The Dybbuk," "Twelfth Night," "Second Avenue Rag," "La Boheme," "Word of Mouth," "Twelve Dreams," "Don Juan," "A Midsummer Night's Dream," "Mud," "The Return of Pinocchio," Bdwy in "Stepping Out" (1986), "Macbeth" (1988), "Our Town."

ROSIN, JAMES (aka Jim). Born Oct. 20, 1946 in Philadelphia, PA. Attended Temple U. Debut 1979 OB in "A Yank in Beverly Hills," followed by "A Force of Nature," "A Boy in New York Calls His Mom in L.A.," "Batting Practice."

ROSS, JAMIE. Born May 4, 1939 in Markinch, Scot. Attended RADA. Bdwy debut 1962 in "Little Moon of Alban," followed by "Moon Beseiged," "Ari," "Different Times," "Woman of the Year," "La Cage aux Folles," "42nd Street," OB in "Penny Friend," "Oh, Coward!," "Approaching Zanzibar."

ROSS, NATALIE. Born Jun. 24, 1932 in Minneapolis, MN. Graduate UWash, RADA. Bdwy debut 1961 in "Come Blow Your Horn," OB in "Butterfly Dream" (1966), "Dietrich Process."

ROSSETTER, KATHY. Born July 31 in Abington, PA. Graduate Gettysburg Col. Debut 1982 OB in "After the Fall," followed by "The Incredibly Famous Willy Rivers," "A Midsummer Night's Dream," "How to Say Goodbye," "The Good Coach," Bdwy in "Death of a Salesman" (1984).

ROTHMAN, JOHN. Born June 3, 1949 in Baltimore, MD. Graduate Wesleyan U, Yale. Debut 1978 OB in "Rats Nest," followed by "The Impossible H.L. Mencken," "The Buddy System," "Rosario and the Gypsies," "Italian Straw Hat," "Modern Ladies of Guanabacoa," "Faith Hope Charity," Bdwy in "End of the World . . ." (1984).

ROTHSTEIN, JON. Born July 15, 1970 in Philadelphia, PA. Bdwy debut 1989 in "Ghetto."

ROUTMAN, STEVE. Born Aug. 28, 1962 in Washington, DC. Graduate Northwestern U. Bdwy debut 1987 in "Broadway," OB in "Love's Labour's Lost," "Much Ado about Nothing."

ROVETA, SANDY. Born in San Mateo, CA. Bdwy debut 1960 in "La Plum de Ma Tante," followed by "Wildcat," "Nowhere to Go But Up," "The Unsinkable Molly Brown," "Here's Love," "Ben Franklin in Paris," OB in "Max Maxie."

RUBINSTEIN, JOHN. Born Dec. 8, 1946 in Los Angeles. Attended UCLA. Bdwy debut 1972 in "Pippin," for which he received a Theatre World Award, followed by "Children of a Lesser God," "Fools," "The Soldier's Tale," "The Caine Mutiny Court-Martial," "Hurlyburly," "M. Butterfly," OB in "Rosencrantz and Guildenstern Are Dead," "Urban Blight," "Love Letters."

RUCK, PATRICIA. Born Sept. 11, 1963 in Washington, DC. Attended Goucher Col. Bdwy debut 1986 in "Cats."

RUFFELLE, FRANCES. Born in 1966 in London, Eng. Bdwy debut 1987 in "Les Miserables" for which she received a Theatre World Award.

RULE, CHARLES. Born Aug. 4, 1928 in Springfield, MO. Bdwy debut 1951 in "Courtin' Time," followed by "Happy Hunting," "Oh, Captain!," "The Conquering Hero," "Donnybrook," "Bye Bye Birdie," "Fiddler on the Roof," "Henry Sweet Henry," "Maggie Flynn," "1776," "Cry for Us All," "Gypsy," "Goodtime Charley," "On the 20th Century," "Phantom of the Opera," OB in "Family Portrait."

RUSSELL, CATHY. Born Aug. 6, 1955 in New Canaan, CT. Graduate Cornell U. Debut OB 1980 in "City Sugar," followed by "Miss Schuman's Quartet," "A Resounding Tinkle," "Right to Life," "Collective Choices," "The Lunch Girls," "Home on the Range," "Perfect Crime."

RYALL, WILLIAM. Born Sept. 18, 1954 in Binghamton, NY. Graduate AADA. Debut 1979 OB in "Canterbury Tales," followed by "Elizabeth and Essex," "He Who Gets Slapped," "The Seagull," "Tartuffe," Bdwy in "Me and My Girl" (1986).

RYAN, AMY. Born May 3, 1968 in NYC. Debut OB 1988 in "A Shayna Maidel," followed by "Rimers of Eldritch."

RYAN, STEVEN. Born June 19, 1947 in NYC. Graduate Boston U, UMn. Debut 1978 OB in "Winning Isn't Everything," followed by "The Beethoven," "September in the Rain," "Romance Language," "Love's Labor's Lost," Bdwy in "I'm Not Rappaport" (1986).

RYDER, RIC. Born Mar. 31 in Baltimore, MD. Graduate UMd., Peabody Conserv Bdwy debut in "Starmites" (1989).

RYLAND, JACK. Born July 22, 1935 in Lancaster, PA. Attended AADA. Bdwy debut 1958 in "The World of Suzie Wong," followed by "A Very Rich Woman," "Henry V," OB in "A Palm Tree in a Rose Garden," "Lysistrata," "The White Rose and the Red," "Old Glory," "Cyrano de Bergerac," "Mourning Becomes Electra," "Beside the Seaside," "Quartermaine's Terms," "The Miracle Worker," "Enrico IV."

SAMUELSON, HOWARD. Born Oct. 21, 1958 in Philadelphia, PA. Graduate NYU. Debut 1985 OB in "Measure for Measure," followed by "The Job Search," "The Emperor's New Clothes," "The Racket," "Vampire Lesbians of Sodom," "A Midsummer Night's Dream."

SANCHEZ, JAIME. Born Dec. 19, 1938 in Rincon, PR. Attended Actors Studio. Bdwy debut 1957 in "West Side Story," followed by "Oh, Dad, Poor, Dad . . .," "A Midsummer Night's Dream," "Richard III," OB in "The Toilet/Conerico Was Here to Stay" for which he received a 1963 Theatre World Award, "The Ox-Cart," "The Tempest," "Merry Wives of Windsor," "Julius Caesar," "Coriolanus," "He Who Gets Slapped," "State without Grace," "The Sun Always Shines for the Cool," "Othello," "Elektra," "Domino," "The Promise."

SANDERS, FRED. Born Feb. 24, 1955 in Philadelphia, PA. Graduate Yale. Debut 1981 OB in "Coming Attractions," followed by "The Tempest," "Responsible Parties," "An Evening With Lenny Bruce," "Green Fields," "Incident at Vichy," "The Wonder Years," "Festival of One Acts," "Roots," "The Miser," "Feast Here Tonight."

SANDERS, JAY O. Born Apr. 16, 1953 in Austin, TX. Graduate SUNY/Purchase. Debut 1976 OB in "Henry V," followed by "Measure for Measure," "Scooping," "Buried Child," "Fables for Friends," "In Trousers," "Girls Girls Girls," "Twelfth Night," "Geniuses," "The Incredibly Famous Willy Rivers," "Rommel's Garden," "Macbeth," "King John," Bdwy in "Loose Ends" (1979), "The Caine Mutiny Court Martial."

SANTARELLI, GENE. Born Feb. 20, 1946 in Kingston, PA. Graduate Wilkes Col., Bloomsbury State Col. Debut 1983 OB in "George by George by George," followed by "The Taming of the Shrew," "Holy Heist," "Hamlet."

SANTIAGO, SOCORRO. Born July 12, 1957 in NYC. Attended Juilliard. Debut 1977 OB in "Crack," followed by "Poets from the Inside," "Unfinished Women," "Family Portrait," "Domino," "The Promise," Bdwy in "The Bacchae" (1980).

SANTORIELLO, ALEX. Born Dec. 30, 1956 in Newark, NJ. Attended Ks State, Kean State. Debut 1986 OB in "La Belle Helene," followed by "A Romantic Detachment," "Passionate Extremes," Bdwy in "Les Miserables" (1987).

SAUNDERS, NICHOLAS. Born June 2, 1914 in Kiev, Russia. Bdwy debut 1942 in "Lady in the Dark," followed by "A New Life," "Highland Fling," "Happily Ever After," "The Magnificent Yankee," "Anastasia," "Take Her, She's Mine," "A Call on Krupin," "Passion of Josef D," OB in "An Enemy of the People," "End of All Things Natural," "The Unicorn in Captivity," "After the Rise," "All My Sons," "My Great Dead Sister," "The Investigation," "Past Tense," "Scenes and Revelations," "Zeks," "Blood Moon," "Family Comedy," "American Power Play," "Take Me Along," "The Tavern," "The Visit."

SAVAGE, KEITH. Born June 9, 1953 in Hampton, VA. Graduate Wm. & Mary Col. Bdwy debut 1982 in "Little Johnny Jones," followed by "Take Me Along," "Teddy and Alice," OB in "Sugar," "A Girl Singer," "Going Hollywood," "Alias Jimmy Valentine," "Young Rube."

SAXTON, WARD. Born Aug. 15, 1970 in Binghamton, NY. Bdwy debut 1982 in "Evita," OB in "Richard III," "Coming of Age in SoHo," "The Faithful Brethren of Pitt Street."

SBARGE, RAPHAEL. Born Feb. 12, 1964 in NYC. Attended HB Studio. Debut 1981 OB in "Henry IV Part I," followed by "The Red Snake," "Hamlet," "Short Change," "Ghosts," Bdwy in "The Curse of an Aching Heart," "Ah, Wilderness!"

SCARDINO, DON. Born in Feb. 1949 in NYC. Attended CCNY. Bdwy in "Loves of Cass McGuire" (1966), "Johnny No-Trump," "My Daughter, Your Son," "Godspell," "Angel," "King of Hearts," OB in "Shout from the Rooftops," "Rimers of Eldtrich," "The Unknown Soldier and His Wife," "Godspell," "Moonchildren," "Kid Champion," "Comedy of Errors," "Secret Service," "Boy Meets Girl," "Scribes," "I'm Getting My Act Together . . .," "As You Like It," "Holeville," "Sorrows of Stephen," "A Midsummer Night's Dream," "The Recruiting Officer," "Jungle of Cities," "Double Feature," "How I Got That Story," "Hang on to the Good Times," "Godspell."

SCHACT, SAM. Born Apr. 19, 1936 in The Bronx, NY. Graduate CCNY. OB in "Fortune and Men's Eyes," "Cannibals," "I Met a Man," "The Increased Difficulty of Concentration," "One Night Stands of a Noisy Passenger," "Owners," "Jack Gelber's New Play," "The Master and Margarita," "Was It Good for You?," "True West," "Today I Am a Fountain Pen," "The Chopin Playoffs," "Dream of a Blacklisted Actor," "Marathon '87," "The Magic Act," "Marathon '88," Bdwy in "The Magic Show," "Golda."

SCHANUEL, GREG. Born Mar. 17, 1958 in Oakland, CA. Attended U Pacific, NYU. Bdwy debut 1981 in "Can-Can," followed by "Jerome Robbins' Broadway," OB in "Mozez."

SCHAUT, ANN LOUISE. Born Nov. 21, 1956 in Minneapolis, MN. Attended UMn. Bdwy debut 1981 in "A Chorus Line."

SCHECHTER, DAVID. Born Apr. 12, 1956 in NYC. Graduate Bard Col., Neighborhood Playhouse. Debut 1976 OB in "Nightclub Cantata," followed by "Dispatches," "The Haggadah," "Temptation," Bdwy in "Runaways" (1978).

SCHMITZ, PETER. Born Aug. 20, 1962 in St. Louis, MO. Graduate Yale, NYU. Debut 1987 OB in "Henry IV Part I," followed by "We the People," "Blitzstein Project."

SCHNABEL, STEFAN. Born Feb. 2, 1912 in Berlin, Ger. Attended UBonn, Old Vic. Bdwy debut 1937 in "Julius Caesar," followed by "Shoemaker's Holiday," "Glamour Preferred," "Land of Fame," "Cherry Orchard," "Around the World in 80 Days," "Now I Lay Me Down to Sleep," "Idiot's Delight," "Love of Four Colonels," "Plain and Fancy," "Small War on Murray Hill," "A Very Rich Woman," "A Patriot for Me," "Teibele and Her Demon," "Social Security," OB in "Tango," "In the Matter of J. Robert Oppenheimer," "Older People," "Enemies," "Little Black Sheep," "Rosemersholm," "Passion of Dracula," "Biography," "The Firebugs," "Twelve Dreams," "Cymbeline."

SCHNEIDER, HELEN. Born Dec. 23 in NY. Bdwy debut 1989 in "Ghetto."

SCHNETZER, STEPHEN. Born June 11, 1948 in Boston, MA. Graduate UMa. Bdwy debut 1971 in "The Incomparable Max," followed by "Filumena," "A Talent for Murder," OB in "Timon of Athens," "Antony and Cleopatra," "Julius Caesar," "Fallen Angels," "Miss Julie," "Lisbon Traviata," "One Act Festival."

SCHREIBER, AVERY. Born Apr. 9, 1935 in Chicago, IL. Graduate Goodman ThSch. Debut 1965 OB in "Second City at Square East," followed by "Conerico Was Here to Stay," Bdwy in "Metamorphoses," "Dreyfus in Rehearsal," "Can-Can" (1981), "Welcome to the Club."

SCHULL, REBECCA. Born Feb. 22 in NYC. Graduate NYU. Bdwy debut 1976 in "Herzl," followed by "Golda," OB in "Mother's Day," "Fefu and Her Friends," "On Mt. Chimborazo," "Mary Stuart," "Balzamov's Wedding," "Before She Is Ever Born," "Exiles," "Nest of the Wood Grouse," "Green Fields," "Panache!," "Journey Into the Whirlwind."

SCHULTZ, ARMAND. Born May 17, 1959 in Rochester, NY. Graduate Niagara U, Catholic U. Debut OB 1988 in "Crystal Clear," followed by "Titus Andronicus."

SCHWEID, CAROLE. Born Oct. 5, 1946 in Newark, NJ. Graduate Boston U., Juilliard. Bdwy debut 1970 in "Minnie's Boys," followed by "A Chorus Line," "Street Scene," OB in "Love Me Love My Children," "How to Succeed in Business . . .," "Silk Stockings," "Children of Adam," "Upstairs at O'Neil's," "Not-So-New Faces of '82," "Unreasonable Expectations," "Funny Girl," "Cradle Song."

SCOTT, ERNIE. Born Mar. 20 in New Brunswick, NJ. Attended Fisk, Rutgers, Kean, Trenton State. Debut 1980 OB in "Jam," Bdwy in "Paul Robeson" (1988).

SCOTT, SERET. Born Sept. 1, 1949 in Washington, DC. Attended NYU. Debut 1969 OB in "Slave Ship," followed by "Ceremonies in Dark Old Men," "Black Terror," "Dream," "One Last Look," "My Sister, My Sister," "Weep Not for Me," "Meetings," "The Brothers," "Eyes of the American," "Remembrances/Mojo," "Tapman," "A Burning Beach," Bdwy in "For Colored Girls . . ."

SEAMAN, JANE. Born Nov. 18 in Bellevue, OH. Graduate StanfordU, WittenbergU. Debut 1982 OB in "Street Scene," Bdwy in "Anything Goes" (1987)

SEAMON, EDWARD. Born Apr. 15, 1937 in San Diego, CA. Attended San Diego State Col. Debut 1971 OB in "The Life and Times of J. Walter Smintheous," followed by "The Contractor," "The Family," "Fishing," "Feedlot," "Cabin 12," "Rear Column," "Devour the Snow," "Buried Child," "Friends," "Extenuating Circumstances," "Confluence," "Richard II," "Great Grandson of Jedediah Kohler," "Marvelous Gray," "Time Framed," "The Master Builder," "Full Hookup," "Fool for Love," "The Harvesting," "A Country for Old Men," "Love's Labour's Lost," "Caligula," "The Mound Builders," "Quiet the Land," "Talley and Son," "Tomorrow's Monday," "Ghosts," "Of Mice and Men," Bdwy in "The Trip Back Down" (1977), "Devour the Snow," "American Clock."

SEARCY, NICK. Born Mar. 7, 1959 in Hendersonville, NC. Graduate UNC. Debut OB 1983 in "Dogs," followed by "The Unguided Missile."

SEATON, JOANNA. Born Mar. 15, 1949 in NYC. Graduate Cornell U. Debut 1975 OB in "Boy Meets Boy," followed by "East of Kansas," "Francis," "Nymph Errant," "Blitzstein Project."

SEDGWICK, KYRA. Born Aug. 19, 1965 in New York City. Attended USC. Debut 1981 OB in "Time Was," followed by "Dakota's Belly, Wyoming," Bdwy in "Ah, Wilderness!" (1989) for which she received a Theatre World Award.

SEETOO, KEELEE. Born Sept. 17, 1960 in Seoul, Korea. Attended UOreg., UHi. Debut OB 1988 in "Blackamoor," followed by "Chu Chem," Bdwy in "Chu Chem."

SEGAL, KATHRIN KING. Born Dec. 8, 1947 in Washington, DC. Attended HB Studio. Debut 1969 OB in "Oh! Calcutta!," followed by "The Drunkard," "Alice in Wonderland," "Pirates of Penzance," "Portfolio Revue," "Philemon," "Butter and Egg Man," "Art of Self-Defense," "Camp Meeting," "Festival of One Acts."

SERBAGI, ROGER. Born July 26, 1937 in Waltham, MA. Attended AmThWing. Bdwy debut 1969 in "Henry V," followed by "Gemini," OB in "A Certain Young Man," "Awake and Sing," "The Partnership," "Monsters," "The Transfiguration of Benno Blimpie," "Family Snapshots," "Till Jason Comes," "1984," "Henry Lumpur."

SERRA, RAYMOND. Born Aug. 13, 1937 in NYC. Attended Rutgers U, Wagner Col. Debut 1975 OB in "The Shark," followed by "Mama's Little Angels," "Manny," "The Front Page" (LC), Bdwy in "The Wheelbarrow Closers," "Marlowe," "Accidental Death of an Anarchist," "Legs Diamond."

SERRECCHIA, MICHAEL. Born Mar. 26, 1951 in Brooklyn, NY. Attended Brockport State U. Teachers Col. Bdwy debut 1972 in "The Selling of the President," followed by "Heathen!," "Seesaw," "A Chorus Line," OB in "Lady Audley's Secret."

SESMA, THOM. Born June 1, 1955 in Sasebo, Japan. Graduate UCal. Bdwy debut 1983 in "La Cage aux Folles," followed by "Chu Chem" (OB & Bdwy), OB in "In a Pig's Valise."

SHAFER, PAMELA. Born Jan. 25, 1963 in Tiffin, OH. Graduate Point PKCol. Debut 1989 OB in "Gigi."

SHALHOUB, TONY. Born Oct. 9, 1953 in Green Bay, WI. Graduate YaleU. Bdwy debut 1985 in "Odd Couple," followed by "Heidi Chronicles," OB in "Richard II," "One Act Festival," "Zero Positive," "Rameau's Nephew," "For Dear Life."

SHANNON, MARK. Born Dec. 13, 1948 in Indianapolis, IN. Attended UCin. Debut 1969 OB in "Fortune and Men's Eyes," followed by "Brotherhood," "Nothing to Report," "Three Sisters."

SHAPIRO, DEBBIE. Born Sept. 29, 1954 in Los Angeles, CA. Graduate LACC. Bdwy debut 1979 in "They're Playing Our Song," followed by "Perfectly Frank," "Blues in the Night," "Zorba," "Jerome Robbin's Bdwy," OB in "They Say It's Wonderful," "New Moon in Concert."

SHARMA, BARBARA. Born Sept. 14, 1942. OB credits include "Boy Friend," "Italian Straw Hat," "Cole Porter Revisited," "Blame It on the Movies," Bdwy in "Fiorello," "Little Me," "Sweet Charity," "Hallelujah, Baby," "Her First Roman," "Come Summer," "Last of the Red Hot Lovers," "I Love My Wife."

SHEA, JOHN. Born Apr. 14, 1949. In North Conway, NH. Graduate Bates Col., YaleU. Debut 1974 OB in "Yentl," followed by "Gorky," "Battering Ram," "Safe House," "Master and Margarita," "Sorrows of Stephen," "American Days," "Dining Room," "Rosmersholm," Bdwy in "Yentl" (1975) for which he won a Theatre World Award, "Romeo and Juliet," "Soldier's Tale," "End of the World . . ."

SHELL, CLAUDIA. Born Sept. 11, 1959 in Passaic, NJ. Debut 1980 OB in "Jam," Bdwy in "Merlin," followed by "Cats."

SHELLEY, CAROLE. Born Aug. 16, 1939 in London, Eng. Bdwy debut 1965 in "Odd Couple," followed by "Astrakhan Coat," "Loot," "Noel Coward's Sweet Potato," "Hay Fever," "Absurd Person Singular," "Norman Conquests," "Elephant Man," "The Misanthrope," "Noises Off," "Stepping Out," OB in "Little Murders," "Devil's Disciple," "The Play's the Thing," "Double Feature," "Twelve Dreams," "Pygmalion in Concert," "A Christmas Carol," "Jubilee in Concert," "Waltz of the Toreadors," "What the Butler Saw."

SHELTON, SLOANE. Born Mar. 17, 1934 in Asheville, NC. Attended Bates Col., RADA. Bdwy debut 1967 in "The Imaginary Invalid," followed by "A Touch of the Poet," "Tonight at 8:30," "I Never Sang for My Father," "Sticks and Bones," "The Runner Stumbles," "Shadow Box," "Passione," "Open Admission," "Orpheus Descending," OB in "Androcles and the Lion," "The Maids," "Basic Training of Pavlo Hummel," "Play and Other Plays," "Julius Caesar," "Chieftans," "Passione," "The Chinese Viewing Pavilion," "Blood Relations," "The Great Divide," "Highest Standard of Living," "The Flower Palace," "April Snow."

SHEPARD, KATHERINE. Born Oct. 15, 1932 in Newark, NJ. Attended Vassar, UMo. Debut 1983 OB in "King Trilogy," followed by "Blood," "The Maids," "Grand Central Paradise."

SHERMAN, BARRY. Born Nov. 10, 1962 in Fontana, CA. Attended Col. of Marin, Nat'l Theatre Conserv. Debut 1988 OB in "Rimers of Eldritch."

SHEW, TIMOTHY. Born Feb. 7, 1959 in Grand Forks, ND. Graduate Millikin U., UMi. Debut 1987 OB in "The Knife," Bdwy in "Les Miserables."

SHIMONO, SAB. Born In Sacramento, CA. Graduate UCal. Bdwy debut 1965 in "South Pacific," followed by "Mame," "Lovely Ladies, Kind Gentlemen," "Pacific Overtures," "Ride the Winds," "Mame" (1983), OB in "Santa Anita," "Yankee Dawg You Die."

SHINER, MATTHEW. Born Dec. 8, 1960 in Wilkes-Barre, PA. Graduate Kings Col. Debut OB in "Revenge of the Space Pandas," followed by "Moby Dick."

SHIPLEY, SANDRA. Born Feb. 1 in Rainham, Kent, Eng. Attended New Col. of Speech and Drama, LondonU. Debut 1988 OB in "Six Characters in Search of an Author," followed by "Big Time."

SHROPSHIRE, ANNE. Born Aug. 27, 1917. Graduate Randolph Macon, UKentucky, Yale Drama. Debut 1949 OB in "The Father," followed by "The Blessing," Bdwy in "Father," "Look Homeward Angel," "Gang's All Here," "Trial of Lee Harvey Oswald."

SHULMAN, CONSTANCE. (a.k.a. Connie). Born Apr. 4, 1958 in Johnson City, TN. Graduate UTn. Debut 1985 OB in "Walking Through," followed by "Windfall," "Pas de Deux," "Steel Magnolias," "Desire," "One Act Festival."

SHULMAN, HEATHER. Born Aug. 25, 1973 in Livings on, NJ Debut 1984 OB in "Papushko" followed by Bdwy in "Sunday in the Park with George" (1984), "Into the Woods."

SIDNEY, P. JAY. Bdwy debut 1934 in "Dance with Your Gods," followed by "20th Century," "Carmen Jones," "Green Pastures," "Run, Little Chillun," "Jeb," "Cool World," "The Winner," "The Playroom," "First Monday in October," OB in "The Octoroon," "Goodnight, Grandpa," "Forbidden City."

SIEGLER, BEN. Born Apr. 9, 1958 In Queens, NYC. Attended HBStudio. Debut 1980 OB in "Innocent Thoughts, Harmless Intentions," followed by "Threads," "Many Happy Returns," "Snow Orchid," "The Diviners," "What I Did Last Summer," "Time Framed," "Gifted Children," "Levitation," "Elm Circle," "Romance Language," "Raw Youth," "Voices in the Head," "V & V Only," "Bitter Friends," Bdwy in "Fifth of July."

SIKES, CYNTHIA. Born Jan 2, 1954 in Coffetville, KS. Attended Wichita STU, S. MethodistU. Bdwy debut 1988 in "Into the Woods."

SILLS, PAWNEE. Born in Castalia, NC. Attended BrooklynCol. Debut 1962 OB in "Raisin' Hell in the Sun," followed by "Mr. Johnson," "Black Happening," "One Last Look," "NY and Who to Blame It On," "Cities in Bezique," "I'd Go to Heaven if I Was Good," "Oakville USA," "Hocus-Pocus," "And So to Bed," "Marathon '86," "Ma Rose," Bdwy in "Caesar and Cleopatra" (1977).

SILVER, JOE. Born Sept. 28, 1922 in Chicago, IL. Attended UIl., AmThWing. Bdwy debut 1942 in "Tobacco Road," followed by "Doughgirls," "Heads or Tails," "Nature's Way," "Gypsy," "Heroine," "Zulu and the Zayda," "You Know I Can't I Hear You . . .," "Lenny," "The Roast," "World of Sholom Aleichem," "Legs Diamond," OB in "Blood Wedding," "Lamp at Midnight," "Joseph and His Brethern," "Victors," "Shrinking Bride," "Family Pieces," "Cakes with Wine," "The Homecoming," "Cold Storage," "Rich Relatives," "Old Business."

SINGER, MARLA. Born Aug. 2, 1957 in Oklahoma City, OK. Graduate OkCityU. Debut 1981 OB in "Seesaw," followed by Bdwy's "42nd Street" (1985).

SISTO, ROCCO. Born Feb. 8, 1953 in Bari, Italy. Graduate UIl., NYU. Debut 1982 OB in "Hamlet," followed by "Country Doctor," "Times and Appetites of Toulouse-Lautrec," "Merchant of Venice," "What Did He See," "Winter's Tale."

SLAFF, JONATHAN. Born Oct. 29, 1950 in Wilkes-Barre, PA. Graduate YaleU, Columbia. Debut 1988 OB in "One Director against His Cast."

SLEZAK, VICTOR. Born July 7, 1957 in Youngstown, OH. Debut 1979 OB in "Electra Myth," followed by "Hasty Heart," "Ghosts," "Alice and Fred," "Widow Claire," "Miracle Worker," "Talk Radio," "Marathon '88," "One Act Festival."

SLOAN, GARY. Born July 6, 1952 in New Castle IN. Graduate WheatonCol., SMU, Debut 1982 OB in "Faust," followed by "Wild Oats," "Balloon," "Danton's Death," "Hamlet," "Big and Little," "Love's Labour's Lost."

SLOMAN, JOHN. Born June 23, 1954 in Rochester, NY. Graduate SUNY/Genasco. Debut 1977 OB in "Unsung Cole," followed by "Apple Tree," "Romance in Hard Times," Bdwy in "Whoopee," "1940's Radio Hour," "Day in Hollywood/Night in the Ukraine," "Mayor."

SMALL, LARRY. Born Oct. 6, 1947 in Kansas City, MO. Attended Manhattan School of Music. Bdwy debut 1971 in "1776," followed by "La Strada," "Wild and Wonderful," "A Doll's Life," OB in "Plain and Fancy," "Forbidden Broadway."

SMITH, CARRIE. Born in Ga. Bdwy debut 1989 in "Black and Blue."

SMITH, JENNIFER. Born Mar. 9, 1956 in Lubbock, TX. Graduate TxTechU. Debut 1981 OB in "Seesaw," followed by "Suffragette," "Henry the 8th and the Grand Old Opry," "No Frills Revue," "1-2-3-4-5," Bdwy in "La Cage aux Folles" (1983).

SMITH, LOIS. Born Nov. 3, 1930 in Topeka, KS. Attended UWVa. Bdwy debut 1952 in "Time Out for Ginger," followed by "Young and the Beautiful," "Wisteria Trees," "Glass Menagerie," "Orpheus Descending," "Stages," OB in "Midsummer Night's Dream," "Non Pasquale," "Promenade," "La Boheme," "Bodies, Rest and Motion," "Marathon '87," "Gus and Al," "Marathon '88," "Measure for Measure," "Spring Thing."

SMITH-CAMERON, J. Born Sept. 7, in Louisville, KY. Attended FlStU. Bdwy debut 1982 in "Crimes of the Heart," followed by "Wild Honey," "Lend Me A Tenor," OB in "Asian Shade," "The Knack," "Second Prize: 2 Weeks in Leningrad," "Great Divid," "Voice of the Turtle," "Women of Manhattan," "Alice and Fred."

SMITROVICH, BILL. Born May 16, 1947 in Bridgeport, CT. Graduate UBridgeport, Smith Col. Bdwy debut 1980 in "American Clock," OB in "Zeks," "Never Say Die," "Frankie and Johnny in the Clair de Lune."

SNYDER, DREW. Born Sept. 25, 1946 in Buffalo, NY. Graduate Carnegie Tech. Bdwy debut 1968 in APA's "Pantagleize," followed by "Cocktail Party," "Cock-a-Doodle Dandy," "Hamlet," OB in "Henry VI," "Richard II," "Sticks and Bones," "Cretan Bull," "Quail Southwest," "Wayside Motor INN," "Words from the Moon," "Member of the Wedding."

SOLO, WILLIAM. Born Mar. 16, 1948 in Worcester, MA. Graduate UMa. Bdwy debut 1987 in "Les Miserables."

SOREL, THEODORE/TED. Born Nov. 14, 1936 in San Francisco, CA. Graduate Col. of Pacific. Bdwy debut 1977 in "Sly Fox," followed by "Horowitz and Mrs. Washington," "A Little Family Business," OB in "Arms and the Man," "Moon Mysteries," "A Call from the East," "Hedda Gabler," "Drinks before Dinner," "Tamara."

SPAISMAN, ZIPORA. Born Jan. 2, 1920 in Lublin, Poland. Debut 1955 OB in "Lonesome Ship," followed by "In My Father's Court," "Thousand and One Nights," "Eleventh Inheritor," "Enchanting Melody," "Fifth Commandment," "Bronx Express," "Melody Lingers On," "Yoshke Muzikant," "Stempenyu," "Generations of Green Fields," "Shop," "A Play for the Devil," "Broome St. America," "Flowering Peach," "Riverside Drive," "Big Winner."

SPEROS, TIA. Born May 3, 1959 in San Francisco, CA. Graduate San Jose StU. Debut 1985 OB in "Tatterdemalion," followed by "The Taffetas."

SPIEGEL, HOWARD. Born Mar. 30, 1954 in Brooklyn, NYC. Attended Queens Col. Debut 1989 OB in "Only Kidding," for which he received a Theatre World Award.

SPIELBERG, DAVID. Born Mar. 6, 1940 in Mercedes, TX. Graduate UTex. Debut 1963 OB in "A Man's a Man," followed by "Two Executioners," "Funnyhouse of a Negro," "MacBird," "Persians," "Trial of the Catonsville 9," "Sleep," "Friends," Bdwy in "Thieves" (1974).

SPINDELL, AHVI. Born June 26, 1954 in Boston, MA. Attended Ithaca Col., UNH, Juilliard. Bdwy debut 1977 in "Something Old Something New," followed by "Ghetto," OB in "Antony and Cleopatra," "Forty Deuce," "Alexandria," "Emma."

SPINELLA, STEPHEN. Born Oct. 11, 1956 in Naples, Italy. Graduate NYU. Debut 1982 OB in "The Age of Assassins," followed by "Dance for Me, Rosetta," "Bremen Coffee," "The Taming of the Shrew," "L'Illusion."

SPIVEY, TOM. Born Jan. 28, 1951 in Richmond, VA. Graduate Wm. & Mary, Penn St. Debut OB in "The Thirteenth Chair" (1989).

SQUIRE, PAT. Born Oct. 12, 1941 in The Bronx, NY. Attended Brooklyn Col., Lehman Col. Debut 1983 OB in "Water Music," followed by "Romeo and Juliet," "Natural Causes," "An Occasion of Sin," "Hot l Baltimore."

STADLEN, LEWIS J. Born Mar. 7, 1947 in Brooklyn, NY. Attended Stella Adler Studio. Bdwy debut 1970 in "Minnie's Boys," for which he received a Theatre World Award, followed by "The Sunshine Boys," "Candide," "The Odd Couple," OB in "The Happiness Cage," "Heaven on Earth," "Barb-A-Que," "Don Juan and Non Don Juan," "Olympus on My Mind," "1-2-3-4-5," "S.J. Perelman in Person."

STAHL, MARY LEIGH. Born Aug. 29, 1946 in Madison, WI. Graduate JacksonvilleStateU. Debut 1974 OB in "Circus," followed by "Dragons," "Sullivan and Gilbert," "The World of Sholem Aleichem," Bdwy in "The Phantom of the Opera" (1988).

STARK, MOLLY. Born in NYC. Graduate Hunter Col. Debut 1969 OB in "Sacco-Vanzetti," followed by "Riders to the Sea," "Medea," "One Cent Plain," "Elizabeth and Essex," "Principally Pinter," "Toulouse," "Winds of Change," "The Education of Hyman Kaplan," Bdwy 1973 in "Molly."

STATON, DAKOTA. Born in Pittsburgh, PA. Graduate NSID. Bdwy debut 1989 in "Black and Blue."

STATTEL, ROBERT. Born Nov. 20, 1937 in Floral Park, NY. Graduate Manhattan Col. Debut 1958 OB in "Heloise," followed by "When I Was a Child," "Man and Superman," "The Storm," "Don Carlos," "Taming of the Shrew," "Titus Andronicus," "Henry IV," "Peer Gynt," "Hamlet," "C Rep's," "Damon's Death," "The Country Wife," "The Caucasian Chalk Circle," and "King Lear," "Iphigenia in Aulis," "Ergo," "The Persians," "Blue Boys," "The Minister's Black Veil," "Four Friends," "Two Character Play," "The Merchant of Venice," "Cuchulain," "Oedipus Cycle," "Gilles de Rais," "Woyzeck," "King Lear," "The Fuehrer Bunker," "Learned Ladies," "Domestic Issues," "Great Days," "The Tempest," "Brand," "A Man for All Seasons," "Bunker Reveries," "Enrico IV."

STEEFEL, JEFFREY. Born June 1, 1961 in San Francisco, CA. Graduate UC at Davis. OB debut 1988 in "Godspell."

STEHLIN, JACK. Born June 21, 1956 in Allentown, PA. Graduate Juilliard. Debut 1984 OB in "Henry V," followed by "Gravity Shoes," "Julius Caesar," "Romeo and Juliet," "Phaedra Britannica," "Don Juan of Seville."

STEIN, JUNE. Born June 13, 1950 in NYC. Debut 1979 OB in "The Runner Stumbles," followed by "Confluence," "Am I Blue," "Balm in Gilead," "Danny and the Deep Blue Sea," "The Miss Firecracker Contest," "As Is," "Acts of Faith," "Working Acts."

STENBORG, HELEN. Born Jan. 24, 1925 in Minneapolis, MN. Attended Hunter Col. OB in "A Doll's House," "A Month in the Country," "Say Nothing," "Rosmersholm," "Rimers of Eldritch," "Trial of the Catonsville 9," "The Hot l Baltimore," "Pericles," "Elephant in the House," "A Tribute to Lili Lamont," "Museum," "5th of July," "In the Recovery Lounge," "The Chisholm Trail," "Time Framed," "Levitation," "Enter a Free Man," "Talley and Son," "Tomorrow's Monday," "Niedecker," Bdwy in "Sheep on the Runway," (1970), "Da," "A Life."

STENDER, DOUG. Born Sept. 14, 1942 in Nanticoke, PA. Graduate Princeton U. RADA. Bdwy debut 1973 in "The Changing Room," "Run for Your Wife," OB in "New England Eclectic," "Hamlet," "Second Man," "How He Lied to Her Husband," "Bhutan."

STEPHENSON, DON. Born Sept. 10, 1964 in Chattanooga, TN. Graduate UTn. Debut 1986 OB in "Southern Lights," followed by "Hypothetic," "The Tavern," "Young Rube," "A Charles Dickens Christmas."

STEPHENSON, MALCOLM. Born Nov. 3, 1958 in Passaic, NJ. Graduate Swarthmore Col, Columbia U, LAMDA. Debut OB 1985 in "The Misanthrope," followed by "Philoctetes."

STERNHAGEN, FRANCES. Born Jan. 13, 1932 in Washington, DC. Graduate Vassar Col. OB in "Admirable Bashful," "Thieves' Carnival," "Country Wife," "Ulysses in Nighttown," "Saintliness of Margery Kemp," "The Room," "A Slight Ache," "Displaced Person," "Playboy of the Western World," "The Prevalence of Mrs. Seal," "Summer," "Laughing Stock," "The Return of

Jess
Richards

LaTanya
Richardson

Eric
Riley

Elaine
Rinehart

Frederick
Rolf

Lucille
Rivin

Megan
Robinson

David
Rosenbaum

Connie
Roderick

William
Ryall

Marcell
Rosenblatt

Ric
Ryder

Gene
Santarelli

Natalie
Ross

Raphael
Sbarge

Sandy
Roveta

Tony
Shalhoub

Patricia
Ruck

Pamela
Shafer

Timothy
Shew

Debbie
Shapiro

Sab
Shimono

Sloane
Shelton

Matthew
Shiner

Rocco
Sisto

Anne
Shropshire

William
Solo

Jennifer
Smith

Ted
Sorel

J.
Smith-Cameron

Herbert Bracewell," "Little Murders," "Driving Miss Daisy," Bdwy in "Great Day in the Morning," "The Right Honourable Gentleman," with APA in "The Cocktail Party," and "Cock-a-Doodle Dandy," "The Sign in Sidney Brustein's Window," "Enemies" (LC), "The Good Doctor," "Equus," "Angel," "On Golden Pond," "The Father," "Grownups," "You Can't Take It With You."

STEVENS, ALLAN. Born Nov. 30, 1949 in Los Angeles, CA. Attended LAMDA. Bdwy debut 1975 in "Shenandoah," followed by "Kings," OB in "It's Wilde!," "Frozen Assets," "Rule of Three," "Donkey's Years," "Sunday Promenade."

STILLER, JERRY. Born June 8, 1931 in NYC. Graduate USyracuse. Debut 1953 in "Coriolanus," followed by "The Power and the Glory," "Golden Apple," "Measure for Measure," "Taming of the Shrew," "Carefree Tree," "Diary of a Scoundrel," "Romeo and Juliet," "As You Like It," "Two Gentlemen of Verona," "Passione," "Hurlyburly," "Prairie/Shawl," "Much Ado about Nothing," Bdwy in "The Ritz," "Unexpected Guests," "Passione," "Hurlyburly,"

STOLLER, AMY. Born Mar. 7 in NYC. Attended Mills Col. Debut 1982 OB in "The Sea Anchor," followed by "La Belle au Bois," "Macbeth."

STOLTZ, ERIC. Born in 1961 in California. Attended USCal. Debut 1987 OB in "The Widow Claire," Bdwy 1989 in "Our Town," for which he received a Theatre World Award.

STORK, RENEE. Born Nov. 11, 1962 in St. Louis, MO. Attended NCSA, ABT. Debut 1989 on Bdwy in "Jerome Robbins' Broadway."

STORMARE, PETER. Born Aug. 27, 1953 in Arbro, Sweden. Attended Royal Dramatic Theatre. Debut OB in "Hamlet."

STOUT, MARY. Born Apr. 8, 1952 in Huntington, WVa. Graduate Marshall U. Debut 1980 OB in "Plain and Fancy," followed by "Sound of Music," "Crisp," "A Christmas Carol," "Song for a Saturday," "Prizes," Bdwy in "Copperfield" (1981).

STOUT, STEPHEN. Born May 19, 1952 in Huntington, WVa. Graduate SMU. Bdwy debut 1981 in "Kingdoms," followed by "The Heidi Chronicles," OB in "Cloud 9," "A Midsummer Night's Dream," "Loose Ends."

STRANG, DEBORAH. Born Nov. 12, 1950 in Appalachia, VA. Graduate UNC. Debut OB in "Man between Twilights" (LC), followed by "Member of the Wedding," "The Philanderer."

STRICKLER, DAN. Born Feb. 4, 1949 in Los Angeles, CA. Graduate CalState U. Temple U. Debut 1977 OB in "Jules Feiffer's Hold Me," followed by "Flying Blind," "Coming Attractions," "Suffragette," "Festival of 1 Acts."

STUART, LYNNE. Born Sept. 30, in Lakeland, FL. Attended Tampa U., NYCol. of Music. Bdwy debut 1953 in "Kismet," followed by "New Girl in Town," "Bells Are Ringing," "High Spirits," "The Women," "Some of My Best Friends," "Don't Call Back," OB in "Turn the Grand Up!," "Sing for Your Supper."

STUBBS, JIM. Born Mar. 19, 1949 in Charlotte, NC. Graduate UNCSchool of Arts. Bdwy debut 1975 in "Dance with Me," OB in "The Passion of Dracula," "Willie," "Macbeth," "Henry V."

SULLIVAN, JEREMIAH. Born Sept. 22, 1937 in NYC. Graduate Harvard. Bdwy debut 1957 in "Compulsion," followed by "The Astrakhan Coat," "Philadelphia, Here I Come!," "Lion in Winter," "House of Blue Leaves," "Gogol," "The Master and Margarita," "Breakfast Conversations in Miami," "Life Is a Dream," "Legend of Sharon Shashanova."

SULLIVAN, JO. Born Aug. 28 in Mounds, IL. Attended Columbia U. Bdwy debut 1950 in "Let's Make an Opera," followed by "Carousel," "Most Happy Fella," "Wonderful Town," "Show Boat," "Perfectly Frank," OB in "Threepenny Opera," "Together Again."

SULLIVAN, JOHNETTE. Born May 17, 1940 in Long Island, NY. Graduate Carnegie-Mellon. Debut OB 1989 in "Peg O'My Heart."

SUMMERHAYS, JANE. Born Oct. 11 in Salt Lake City, UT. Graduate UUt., Catholic U. Debut 1980 OB in "Paris Lights," followed by "On Approval," "One Act Festival," Bdwy in "Sugar Babies" (1980), "A Chorus Line," "Me and My Girl."

SUROVY, NICOLAS. Born June 30, 1944 in Los Angeles, CA. Attended Northwestern U., Neighborhood Playhouse. Debut OB 1964 in "Helen," for which he received a Theatre World Award, followed by "Sisters of Mercy," "Cloud 9," Bdwy in "Merchant," "Crucifer of Blood," "Major Barbara," "You Can't Take It with You," "The Night of the Iguana."

SWARBRICK, CAROL. Born Mar. 20, 1948 in Inglewood CA. Graduate UCLA, NYU. Debut 1971 OB in "Drat!," followed by "The Glorious Age," Bdwy in "Side by Side by Sondheim," "Whoopee!," "42nd Street."

SWETOW, JOEL. Born Dec. 30, 1951 in Kew Gardens, NY. Graduate Hamilton Col. Debut 1982 OB in "Shenandoah," followed by "Songs of the Religious Life," "Tiger at the Gates," "Switching Channels," "Three 1 Act Plays," "Macbeth," "Berenice," "The Lark."

SZYMANSKI, WILLIAM. Born May 16, 1949 in Omaha, NE. Attended UNe. Debut 1979 OB in "Big Bad Burlesque," followed by "Little Shop of Horrors," "The Winter's Tale," "Henry V," "The Serpent."

TALBOT, SHARON. Born Mar. 12, 1949 in Denver, CO. Graduate DenverU. Bdwy debut 1975 in "Musical Jubilee," OB in "Housewives Cantata," "The Angel and the Dragon," "Legend of Sharon Shashanova."

TALMAN, ANN. Born Sept. 13, 1957 in Welch, WVa. Graduate PaStateU. Debut 1980 OB in "What's So Beautiful about a Sunset over Prairie Avenue?," followed by "Louisiana Summer," "Winterplay," "Prairie Avenue," "Broken Eggs," "Octoberfest," "We're Home," "Yours, Anne," "Songs on a Shipwrecked Sofa," "House Arrest," "One Act Festival," Bdwy in "The Little Foxes" (1981), "House of Blue Leaves."

TALYN, OLGA. Born Dec. 5 in West Germany. Attended SyracuseU, UBuffalo. Debut 1973 OB in "The Proposition," followed by "Corral," "Tales of Tinseltown," "Shop on Main Street," Bdwy in "A Doll's House," "The Phantom of the Opera."

TATUM, MARIANNE. Born Feb. 18, 1951 in Houston, TX. Attended Manhattan Sch. of Music. Debut 1971 OB in "Ruddigore," followed by "The Sound of Music," "The Gilded Cage," "Charley's Tale," "Passionate Extremes," Bdwy in "Barnum" (1980) for which she received a Theatre World Award, "The Three Musketeers."

TAYLOR, GEORGE. Born Sept. 18, 1930 in London, Eng. Attended AADA. Debut 1972 OB in "Hamlet," followed by "Enemies," "The Contractor," "Scribes," "Says I, Says He," "Teeth 'n' Smiles," "Viaduct," "Translations," "Last of the Knucklemen," "The Accrington Pals," "Ragged Trousered Philanthropists," "Brightness Falling," Bdwy in "Emperor Henry IV" (1973), "The National Health."

TAYLOR, HOLLAND. Born Jan. 14, 1943 in Philadelphia, PA. Graduate Bennington Col. Bdwy debut 1965 in "The Devils," followed by "Butley," "We Interrupt This Program," "Something Old Something New," "Moose Murders," OB in "Poker Session," "The David Show," "Tonight in Living Color," "Colette," "Fashion," "Nightlight," "Children," "Breakfast with Les and Bess," "A Perfect Party," "Cocktail Hour."

TAYLOR, MYRA. Born July 9, 1960 in Ft. Motte, SC. Graduate Yale U. Debut 1985 OB in "Dennis," followed by "The Tempest," "Black Girl," "Marathon '86," "Phantasie," Bdwy in "A Streetcar Named Desire" (1988).

TAYLOR, REGINA. Born Aug. 22, 1960 in Dallas, TX. Graduate SMU. Debut 1983 OB in "Young Playwrights Festival," followed by "As You Like It," "Macbeth," "Map of the World," "The Box," "Dr. Faustus," "L'Illusion," Bdwy in "Shakespeare on Broadway" (1987).

TAYLOR, ROBIN. Born May 28 in Tacoma, Wa. Graduate UCLA. Debut 1979 OB in "Festival," followed by "On the 20th Century," Bdwy in "A Chorus Line" (1985).

TAYLOR, SCOTT. Born June 29, 1962 in Milan, Tn. Attended Ms.State U. Bdwy in "Wind in the Willows" (1985), followed by "Cats."

TAYLOR-MORRIS, MAXINE. Born June 26 in NYC. Graduate NYU. Debut 1977 OB in "Counsellor-at-Law," followed by "Manny," "The Devil's Disciple," "Fallen Angels," "Billy Liar," "Uncle Vanya," "What the Butler Saw," "The Subject Was Roses," "Goodnight, Grandpa," "The Thirteenth Chair."

TESTA, MARY. Born June 4, 1955 in Philadelphia, PA. Attended URI. Debut 1979 OB in "In Trousers," followed by "Company," "Life Is Not a Doris Day Movie," "Not-So-New Faces of '82," "American Princess," "Mandrake," "4 One Act Musicals," "Next Please!," "Daughters," "One Act Festival," "The Knife," "Young Playwrights," "Lucky Stiff," "1-2-3-4-5," Bdwy in "Barnum" (1980), "Marilyn," "The Rink."

THACKER, RUSS. Born June 23, 1946 in Washington, DC. Attended Montgomery Col. Bdwy debut 1967 in "Life with Father" followed by "Music! Music!," "The Grass Harp," "Heathen," "Home Sweet Homer," "Me Jack, You Jill," "Do Black Patent Leather Shoes Really Reflect Up?," OB in "Your Own Thing" for which he received a 1968 Theatre World Award, "Dear Oscar," "Once I Saw a Boy Laughing," "Tip-Toes," "Oh, Coward!," "New Moon in Concert," "The Firefly in Concert," "Rosalie in Concert," "Some Enchanted Evening," "Roberta in Concert," "Olio," "Genesis."

THAIN, ANDREW. Born Apr. 20, 1962 in Salem, MA. Graduate Villanova U. Debut OB 1988 in "Much Ado about Nothing," followed by "A Yankee Doodle Dandy," "Bitter Friends."

THOLE, CYNTHIA. Born Sept. 21, 1957 in Silver Spring, Md. Graduate Butler U. Debut 1982 OB in "Nymph Errant," followed by Bdwy in "42nd Street" (1985), "Me and My Girl."

THOMAS, RICHARD. Born June 13, 1951 in NYC. Bdwy debut 1958 in "Sunrise at Campobello," followed by "Member of the Wedding," "Strange Interlude," "The Playroom," "Richard III," "Everything in the Garden," "5th of July," "The Front Page" (LC), OB in "The Seagull," "Love Letters."

THOMAS, WILLIAM, JR. Born Nov. 8 in Columbus, OH. Graduate OhStateU. Debut 1972 OB in "Touch," followed by "Natural," "Godspell," "Poor Little Lambs," "Loose Joints," "Not-So-New Faces of '81," Bdwy in "Your Arm's Too Short to Box With God" (1976), "La Cage aux Folles," "Oh! Calcutta!"

THOMPSON, TRINITY. Born Oct. 4 in Greenwich, CT. Graduate AADA. Debut 1958 OB in "The Time of Your Life," followed by "Toys in the Attic," "Hot l Baltimore," "The Crucible," "Misalliance," "La Ronde," "Invitation to a March," "Age of Anxiety," "Under Milk Wood," "Half-Life," "The Beethoven," "Sunday Promenade."

THORNTON, ANGELA. Born in Leeds, Eng. Attended Webber-Douglas School. Bdwy debut 1956 in "Little Glass Clock," followed by "Nude with Violin," "Present Laughter," "Hostile Witness," "Pygmalion" (1987), OB in "The Mousetrap," "Big Broadcast," "Mary Barnes," "What the Butler Saw."

TOBIE, ELLEN. Born Mar. 26 in Chambersburg, PA. Graduate OH, Wesleyan U., Wayne State U. Debut 1981 OB in "The Chisholm Trail Went Through Here," followed by "Welded," "Talking With," "The Entertainer," "Equal Wrights."

TOLAN, KATHLEEN. Born Aug. 10, 1950 in Milwaukee, WI. Attended NYU, HB Studio. Debut 1974 OB in "Hothouse," followed by "More Than You Deserve," "Wicked Women Revue," "Museum," "The Imperialists at the Club Cave Canum."

TOLAN, MICHAEL. Born Nov. 27, 1925 in Detroit, MI. Graduate WayneU. Bdwy debut 1955 in "Will Success Spoil Rock Hunter?," followed by "A Hatful of Rain," "The Genius and the Goddess," "Romanoff and Juliet," "A Majority of One," "A Far Country," "Unlikely Heroes," OB in "Coriolanus," "Journey of the 5th Horse," "Close Relations," "Faces of Love/Portrait of America," "A Step Out of Line," "Bedroom Farce," "American Voices," "George Washington Slept Here."

TOLAN, PETER. Born July 5, 1958 in Scituate, MA. Graduate UMa/Amherst. Debut OB 1989 in "Laughing Matters."

TOM, LAUREN. Born Aug. 4, 1959 in Highland Park, IL. Graduate NYU. Debut 1980 OB in "The Music Lesson," followed by "Family Devotions," "Non Pasquale," "Dream of Kitamura," "American Notes," "Madame de Sade," "Noiresque," "In a Pig's Valise," Bdwy in "A Chorus Line" (1980), "Doonesbury," "Hurlyburly."

TOMEI, MARISA. Born Dec. 4, 1964 in Brooklyn, NY. Attended Boston U., NYU. Debut 1986 OB in "Daughters," for which she received a Theatre World Award, followed by "Class 1 Acts," "Evening Star," "What the Butler Saw," "Marathon 88," "Sharon and Billy."

TOMPOS, DOUG. Born Jan. 27, 1962 in Columbus, OH. Graduate Syracuse U., LAMDA. Debut 1985 OB in "Very Warm for May," followed by "A Midsummer Night's Dream," "Mighty Fine Music," "Muzeeks," "Wish You Were Here," "Vampire Lesbians of Sodom."

TONER, THOMAS. Born May 25, 1928 in Homestead, Pa. Graduate UCLA. Bdwy debut 1973 in "Tricks," followed by "The Good Doctor," "All Over Town," "The Elephant Man," "California Suite," "A Texas Trilogy," "The Inspector General," "Me and My Girl," OB in "Pericles," "The Merry Wives of Windsor," "A Midsummer Night's Dream," "Richard III," "My Early Years," "Life and Limb," "Measure for Measure," "Little Footsteps."

TOVATT, PATRICK. Born Dec. 11, 1940 in Garrett Ridge, CO. Attended Antioch, Harvard Col. Debut 1984 OB in "Husbandry," followed by "The Right Number," Bdwy in "Our Town" (1989).

TOWEY, JOHN MADDEN. Born Feb. 13, 1940 in Rochester, MN. Graduate St. John's U. Goodman ThSch. Debut 1970 OB in "To Be Young, Gifted and Black," followed by "God Bless You, Mr. Rosewater," "A Dream Out of Time," "Fashion," "My Heart Is in the East," "Crossing the Crab Nebula," "Talk Radio," "Julius Caesar," "Coriolanus," "Cymbeline."

TOY, CHRISTINE. Born Dec. 26, 1959 in Scarsdale, NY. Graduate Sarah Lawrence Col. Debut 1982 OB in "Oh, Johnny!," followed by "Pacific Overtures" "Genesis."

TRAY, ELI. Born July 19, 1959 in Glen Cove, NY. Graduate NYU. Debut 1983 OB in "The Rise of David Levinsky," followed by "Fiorello!."

TREAT, MARTIN. Born May 9, 1945 in Yreka, CA. Graduate UOr. Debut 1977 OB in "Heartbreak House," followed by "The Balcony," "Cuchulian Cycle," "Dr. Faustus," "A Dream Play," "The Danube," "Further Inquiry," "The Last of Hitler," "Dodger Blue."

TRICHTER, JUDD. Born May 8, 1974 in NYC. Debut OB 1989 in "The Loman Family Picnic," followed by "On Ice."

TROY, LOUISE. Born Nov. 9 in NYC. Attended AADA. Debut 1955 OB in "The Infernal Machine," followed by "Merchant of Venice," "Conversation Piece," "Salad Days," "O, Oysters!," "A Doll's House," "Last Analysis," "Judy and Jane," "Heartbreak House," "Rich Girls," Bdwy in "Pipe Dream" (1955), "A Shot in the Dark," "Tovarich," "High Spirits," "Walking Happy," "Equus," "Woman of the Year," "Design for Living," "42nd St."

TRUMBULL, ROBERT. Born Feb. 8, 1938 in San Rafael, CA. Graduate UCal/Berkeley. Debut 1983 in "Guys in the Truck" (OB and Bdwy), followed by OB's "Fever of Unknown Origin," "Bradley and Beth," "Othello."

TSOUTSOUVAS, SAM. Born Aug. 20, 1948 in Santa Barbara, CA. Attended UCal., Juilliard. Debut 1969 OB in "Peer Gynt," followed by "Twelfth Night," "Timon of Athens," "Cymbeline," "School for Scandal," "The Hostage," "Women Beware Women," "Lower Depths," "Emigre," "Hello Dali," "The Merchant of Venice," "The Leader," "The Bald Soprano," "The Taming of the Shrew," "Gus & Al," "Tamara," Bdwy in "Three Sisters," "Measure for Measure," "Beggar's Opera," "Scapin," "Dracula."

TUCCI, MARIA. Born June 19, 1941 in Florence, IT. Attended Actors Studio. Bdwy debut 1963 in "The Milk Train Doesn't Stop Here Anymore," followed by "The Rose Tattoo," "The Little Foxes," "The Cuban Thing," "The Great White Hope," "School for Wives," "Lesson from Aloes," "Kingdoms," "Requiem for a Heavyweight," "The Night of the Iguana," OB in "Corruption in the Palace of Justice," "Five Evenings," "Trojan Women," "White Devil," "Horseman, Pass By," "Yerma," "Shepherd of Avenue B," "The Gathering," "A Man for All Seasons," "Love Letters."

TULL, PATRICK. Born July 28, 1941 in Sussex, Eng. Attended LAMDA. Bdwy debut 1967 in "The Astrakhan Coat," OB in "Ten Little Indians," "The Tamer Tamed," "Brand," "Frankenstein," "What the Butler Saw," "She Stoops to Conquer."

TURNER, GLENN. Born Sept. 21, 1957 in Atlanta, GA. Bdwy debut 1984 in "My One and Only," followed by "A Chorus Line."

TURNER, PATRICK. Born Dec. 2, 1952 in Seattle, WA. Attended UWash, AmCons Theatre. Debut 1984 OB in "The Merchant of Venice," followed by "Double Inconstancy," "The Taming of the Shrew," "Lady from the Sea," "Two Gentlemen of Verona," "The Contrast," "Pericles," "The Rivals," "Rosaline," "Much Ado about Nothing," "You Never Can Tell."

TURTURRO, JOHN. Born Feb. 28, 1957 in Brooklyn, NY. Graduate SUNY/New Paltz, La U. Debut 1984 OB in "Danny and the Deep Blue Sea," for which he received a Theatre World Award, followed by "Men without Dates," "Chaos and Hard Times," "Steel on Steel," "Tooth of Crime," "Of Mice and Men," "Jamie's Gang," "Marathon 86," "The Bald Soprano/The Leader," "La Puta Vita Trilogy," "Italian American Reconciliation," Bdwy in "Death of a Salesman" (1984).

UBARRY, HECHTER. Born Sept. 5, 1946 in NYC. Bdwy debut 1965 in "Royal Hunt of the Sun," followed by "Man of La Mancha" (1970/'72/'77), OB in "Romance Language," "Chu Chem."

UGGAMS, LESLIE. Born May 25, 1943 in NYC. Bdwy debut 1967 in "Hallelujah, Baby!," for which she received a Theatre World Award, followed by "Her First Roman," "Blues in the Night," "Jerry's Girls," "Anything Goes."

ULISSEY, CATHERINE. Born Aug. 4, 1961 in NYC. Attended Ntl. Acad. of Arts. Bdwy debut 1986 in "Rags," followed by "The Mystery of Edwin Drood," "Phantom of the Opera."

ULLETT, NICK. Born Mar. 5, 1947 in London, Eng. Graduate Cambridge U. Debut 1967 OB in "Love and Let Love," followed by "The Importance of Being Earnest," Bdwy in "Loot" (1986), "Me and My Girl."

VALOR, HENRIETTA. Born Apr. 28 in New Cumberland, PA. Graduate NorthwesternU. Bdwy debut 1965 in "Half a Sixpence," followed by "Applause," "Jacques Brel is Alive . . .," "Annie," OB in "Fashion," "Jacques Brel . . .," "A Bistro Car on the CNR," "Vagabond Stars," "1-2-3-4-5."

VAN DYCK, JENNIFER. Born Dec. 23, 1962 in St. Andrews, Scotland. Graduate BrownU. Debut OB 1988 in "Gus and Al," followed by "Marathon 88."

VAN GRIETHUYSEN, TED. Born Nov. 7, 1934 in Ponca City, OK. Graduate UTx., RADA. Bdwy debut 1962 in "Romulus," followed by "Moon Beseiged," "Inadmissible Evidence," OB in "Failures," "Lute Song," "O Marry Me," "Red Roses for Me," "Basement," "Hedda Gabler," "Othello," "First Time Anywhere," "Man for All Seasons," "Rosmersholm."

VAN PATTEN, JOYCE. Born Mar. 9 in Kew Gardens, NY. Bdwy debut 1941 in "Popsy," followed by "This Rock," "Tomorrow the World," "The Perfect Marriage," "The Wind Is 90," "Desk Set," "A Hole in the Head," "Murder at the Howard Johnson's," "I Ought to Be in Pictures," "Supporting Cast," "Brighton Beach Memoirs," "Rumors," OB in "Between Two Thieves," "Spoon River Anthology," "The Seagull."

VANCE, COURTNEY B. Born Mar. 12, 1960 in Detroit, MI. Graduate Harvard. Bdwy debut 1987 in "Fences" for which he received a Theatre World Award, OB in "Temptation."

VARGAS, OVIDIO. Born Nov. 30, 1959 in Brooklyn, NY. Graduate Boston Conserv. of Music. Debut OB in "Yes Dear," followed by "Wonderful Town," "Salon," "Blood on Blood," "Greed."

VENNEMA, JOHN C. Born Aug. 24, 1948 in Houston, TX. Graduate Princeton U., LAMDA. Bdwy debut 1976 in "The Royal Family," followed by "The Elephant Man," "Otherwise Engaged," OB in "Loot," "Statements after an Arrest," "The Biko Inquest," "No End of Blame," "In Celebration," "Custom of the Country," "The Basement," "A Slight Ache," "Young Playwrights Festival," "Dandy Dick," "Nasty Little Secrets."

VENORA, DIANE. Born in 1952 in Hartford, CT. Graduate Juilliard. Debut 1981 OB in "Penguin Touquet," followed by "A Midsummer Night's Dream," "Hamlet," "Uncle Vanya," "Messiah," "Tomorrow's Monday," "Largo Desolato," "A Man for All Seasons," "Winter's Tale."

VIPOND, NEIL. Born Dec. 24, 1929 in Toronto, Can. Bdwy debut 1956 in "Tamburlaine the Great," followed by "Macbeth," OB in "Three Friends," "Sunday Runners," "Hamlet," "Routed," "Mr. Joyce Is Leaving Paris," "The Time of Your Life," "Children of the Sun," "Romeo and Juliet," "The Lark."

VIRTA, RAY. Born June 18, 1958 in L'Anse, MI. Debut 1982 OB in "Twelfth Night," followed by "The Country Wife," "Dubliners," "Pericles," "Tartuffe," "The Taming of the Shrew," "No One Dances."

VISCARDI, JOHN. Born Aug. 18, 1961 in NYC. Graduate Columbia U. Debut 1988 OB in "Cave Life," followed by "Borderlines," "Amulets against the Dragon Forces."

VIVIANO, SAL. Born July 12, 1960 in Detroit, MI. Graduate E.IllU. Bdwy debut 1984 in "The Three Musketeers," followed by "Romance/Romance," OB in "Miami" (1986), "Hot Times and Suicide," "Romance/Romance."

VOET, DOUG. Born Mar. 1, 1951 in Los Angeles, CA. Graduate BYU. Bdwy debut in "Joseph and the Amazing Technicolor Dreamcoat" (1982), OB in "Forbidden Broadway."

WAARA, SCOTT. Born June 5, 1957 in Chicago, IL. Graduate SMU. Debut 1982 OB in "The Rise of Daniel Rocket," followed by "The Dining Room," "Johnny Pye and the Foolkiller," "Gifts of the Magi," Bdwy in "The Wind in the Willows" (1985), "Welcome to the Club."

WAGNER, CHUCK. Born June 20, 1958 in Nashville, TN. Graduate USCal. Bdwy debut 1985 in "The Three Musketeers," followed by "Into the Woods."

WALKEN, CHRISTOPHER. Born Mar. 31, 1943 in Astoria, NY. Attended Hofstra U. Bdwy debut 1958 in "J.B.," followed by "High Spirits," "Baker Street," "The Lion in Winter," "Measure for Measure," "The Rose Tattoo" for which he received a Theatre World Award, "The Unknown Soldier and His Wife," "Rosencrantz and Guildenstern Are Dead," "Scenes from American Life," "Cymbeline," "Enemies," "The Plough and the Stars," "Merchant of Venice," "The Tempest," "Troilus and Cressida," "Macbeth," "Sweet Bird of Youth," OB in "Best Foot Forward" (1963), "Iphigenia in Aulis," "Lemon Sky," "Kid Champion," "The Seagull," "Cinders," "Hurlyburly," "House of Blue Leaves," "Love Letters," "Coriolanus."

WALKER, RAY. Born Aug. 13, 1963 in St. Johnsbury, VT. Graduate NYU. Debut 1985 OB in "Christmas Spectacular," followed by "Merrily We Roll Along," Bdwy 1988 in "Les Miserables."

WALKER, THOMAS S. Born May 12, 1947 in Torrington, CT. Graduate Yale Col. Debut OB 1985 in "A Beckett Trilogy," followed by "The Tablets," "VKTMS: Orestes in Scenes."

WALLACE, LEE. Born July 15, 1930 in NYC. Attended NYU. Debut 1966 OB in "Journey of the Fifth Horse," followed by "Saturday Night," "An Evening with Garcia Lorca," "Macbeth," "Booth Is Back in Town," "Awake and Sing," "Shepherd of Avenue B," "Basic Training of Pavlo Hummel," "Curtains," "Elephants," "Goodnight, Grandpa," "Jesse's Land," "The Sunshine Boys," Bdwy in "Secret Affairs of Mildred Wild," "Molly," "Zalmen, or the Madness of God," "Some of My Best Friends," "Grind."

WALLACE, MARIE. Born May 19, 1939 in NYC. Attended NYU. OB in "Electra," "Harlequinade," "Bell, Book and Candle," "Mert and Phil," "In the Boom Boom Room," "The Lark," Bdwy in "Gypsy," "The Beauty Part," "Nobody Loves an Albatross," "The Right Honorable Gentleman," "The Women," "Sweet Charity," "Last Licks."

WALLACH, ELI. Born Dec. 7, 1915 in Brooklyn, NY. Graduate UTx, CCNY. Bdwy debut 1945 in "Skydrift," followed by "Henry VIII," "Androcles and the Lion," "Alice in Wonderland," "Yellow Jack," "What Every Woman Knows," "Antony and Cleopatra," "Mr. Roberts," "Lady from the Sea," "The Rose Tattoo" for which he received a Theatre World Award, "Mlle. Colombe," "Teahouse of the August Moon," "Major Barbara," "The Cold Wind and the Warm," "Rhinoceros," "Luv," "Staircase," "Promenade All," "Waltz of the Toreadors," "Saturday, Sunday, Monday," "Every Good Boy Deserves Favor," "Twice Around the Park," "Cafe Crown," OB in "The Diary of Anne Frank," "Nest of the Wood Grouse," "Cafe Crown."

WALLEM, LINDA. Born May 29, 1961 in Madison, WI. Graduate UMinn. Debut OB 1989 in "Laughing Matters."

WALLER, KENNETH. Born Apr. 12, 1945 in Atlanta, Ga. Graduate Piedmont Col. Debut 1976 OB in "Boys from Syracuse," Bdwy in "Sarava" (1979), "Onward Victoria," "Me and My Girl," "Phantom of the Opera."

WALSH, BARBARA. Born June 3, 1955 in Washington, DC. Attended Montgomery Col. Bdwy debut 1982 in "Rock 'n' Roll: The First 5000 Years," followed by "Nine," OB in "Forbidden Broadway."

WALSH, ELIZABETH. Born Oct. 12 in Puerto Rico. Graduate UWisc, UMa. Debut 1987 OB in "Mademoiselle Colombe," followed by "She Loves Me."

WALTER, JESSICA. Born Jan. 31, 1944 in NYC. Attended Neighborhood Playhouse. Bdwy debut 1961 in "Advise and Consent," followed by "A Severed Head," "Night Life," "Photo Finish," "Rumors," OB in "The Murder of Me," "Fighting International Fat."

WALTERS, WILLIAM R. Born Sept. 6, 1936 in E. Chicago, IN. Graduate St. Joseph's Col. Debut OB in "Tropicana," followed by "Senor Discretion," "Kiss Me Quick Before the Lava Reaches the Village."

WALTON, JIM. Born July 31, 1955 in Tachikawa, Japan. Graduate UCincinnati. Debut 1979 OB in "Big Bad Burlesque," followed by "Scrambled Feet," "Stardust," "Sweeney Todd," Bdwy in "Perfectly Frank" (1980), "Merrily We Roll Along," "42nd Street," "Stardust."

WARDEN, YVONNE. Born Jan. 16, 1928 in NYC. Attended UCLA, NYU. Debut 1967 OB in "Trials of Brother Jero," followed by "The Strong Breed," "Macbeth," "Waiting for Godot," "Welfare," "Where Have All the Dreamers Gone," "Calalou," "Masque and Dacha," "Black Girl," "Prince."

WARING, WENDY. Born Dec. 7, 1960 in Melrose, MA. Attended Emerson Col., NYU. Debut 1987 OB in "Wish You Were Here," Bdwy in "Legs Diamond."

WARREN, JOSEPH. Born June 5, 1916 in Boston, MA. Graduate UDenver. Bdwy debut 1951 in "Barefoot in Athens," followed by "One Bright Day," "Love of Four Colonels," "Hidden River," "The Advocate," "Philadelphia, Here I Come," "Borstal Boy," "Lincoln Mask," OB in "Brecht on Brecht," "Jonah," "Little Black Sheep," "Black Tuesday," "The Show-Off," "Big Apple Messenger," "The Ballad of Soapy Smith," "Her Great Match," "Measure for Measure," "Hamlet," "The Rivals," "Of Mice and Men," "Uncle Vanya," "Aristocrats," "She Stoops to Conquer."

WASHINGTON, DENZEL. Born Dec. 28, 1954 in Mt. Vernon, NY. Graduate Fordham U. Debut 1975 OB in "The Emperor Jones," followed by "Othello," "Coriolanus," "Mighty Gents," "Becket," "Spell #7," "Ceremonies in Dark Old Men," "One Tiger To a Hill," "A Soldier's Play," "Every Goodbye Ain't Gone," Bdwy 1988 in "Checkmates."

WASHINGTON, MELVIN. Born Dec. 19 in Brooklyn, NY. Attended CCNY., HB Studio. Debut 1980 OB in "Streamers," followed by "Something to Live For," Bdwy in "My One and Only" (1983), "Black and Blue."

WEBER, ANDREA. Born in Midland, MI. Graduate IndU, Hunter Col. Debut OB 1981 in "Inadmissible Evidence," followed by "Childhood," "Festival of 1 Acts," Bdwy in "Macbeth" (1983).

WEIL, MELISSA. Born May 9, 1959 in Chicago, IL. Graduate UIll, Yale. OB in "Festival of 1 Acts" (1988).

WEISS, GORDON J. Born June 16, 1949 in Bismarck, ND. Attended MoorheadStateCol. Bdwy debut 1974 in "Jumpers," followed by "Goodtime Charley," "King of Hearts," "Raggedy Ann," "Ghetto," OB in "A Walk on the Wild Side."

WEISS, JEFF. Born in 1940 in Allentown, PA. Debut 1986 OB in "Hamlet," followed by "The Front Page" (LC), Bdwy in "Macbeth" (1988), "Our Town."

WELBY, DONNAH. Born May 4, 1952 in Scranton, PA. Graduate Catholic U. Debut 1981 OB in "Between Friends," followed by "Double Inconstancy," "The Taming of the Shrew," "The Contrast," "Macbeth," "Electra," "All's Well That Ends Well," "Hot 1 Baltimore," "The Philanderer."

WELLS, CHRISTOPHER. Born June 18, 1955 in Norwalk, CT. Graduate Amherst Col. Debut 1981 OB in "Big Apple Country," followed by "Broadway Jukebox," "Savage Amusement," "Overruled," "Heart of Darkness," "Ancient History," Bdwy in "Harrigan 'n' Hart" (1985), "Broadway," "Teddy and Alice."

WELLS, CRAIG. Born July 2, 1955 in Newark, NJ. Graduate Albion Col. Debut 1985 OB in "Forbidden Broadway," "The Best of Forbidden Broadway," Bdwy in "Chess" (1988).

WELLS, DEANNA. Born Aug. 7, 1962 in Milwaukee, Wi. Graduate Northwestern U. Debut 1985 OB in "On the 20th Century," followed by "After These Messages," "The Fantasticks," Bdwy in "Smile," "South Pacific" (LC).

WEST, MATT. Born Oct. 2, 1958 in Downey, CA. Attended Pfiffer-Smith School. Bdwy debut in "A Chorus Line" (1980).

WESTENBERG, ROBERT. Born Oct. 26, 1953 in Miami Beach, FL. Graduate UCal/Fresno. Debut 1981 OB in "Henry IV Part I," followed by "Hamlet," "The Death of von Richthofen," Bdwy in "Zorba" (1983) for which he received a Theatre World Award, "Sunday in the Park with George," "Into the Woods."

WESTFALL, RALPH DAVID. Born July 2, 1934 in North Lewisburg, OH. Graduate Oh WesleyanU, SUNY/New Paltz. Debut 1977 OB in "Richard III," followed by "Importance of Being Earnest," "Anyone Can Whistle," "Midsummer Night's Dream," "Macbeth," "Gift of the Magi," "A Theatre History," "The Lark."

WESTON, JACK. Born Aug. 21, 1915 in Cleveland, OH. Attended Cleveland Playhouse, Am.Thea.Wing. Bdwy debut 1950 in "Season in the Sun," followed by "South Pacific," "Bells Are Ringing," "California Suite," "The Ritz," "Cheaters," "Floating Light Bulb," OB in "Baker's Wife," "Measure For Measure."

WETHERALL, JACK. Born Aug. 5, 1950 in Sault Ste. Marie, Can. Graduate Glendon Col, York U. Bdwy debut 1979 in "The Elephant Man," followed by OB's "Tamara." (1987).

WHALLEY-KILMER, JOANNE. Born Aug. 25 in Manchester, Eng. Debut 1989 OB in "What the Butler Saw," for which she received a Theatre World Award.

WHELAN, RICHARD. Born Dec. 17, 1956 in Greenwich, CT. Graduate IthcaCol. Debut 1988 OB in "Fiorello!"

WHITE, JANE. Born Oct. 30, 1922 in NYC. Attended SmithCol. Bdwy debut 1942 in "Strange Fruit," followed by "Climate of Eden," "Take a Giant Step," "Jane Eyre," "Once Upon a Mattress" (also OB), "Cuban Thing," OB in "Razzle Dazzle," "Insect Comedy," "Power and the Glory," "Hop, Signor," "Trojan Women," "Iphigenia in Aulis," "Cymbeline," "Burnt Flowerbed," "Rosmersholm," "Jane White Who?," "Ah, Men," "Lola," "Madwoman of Chaillot," "Vivat, Vivat Regina!," "King John."

WHITE, JULIE. Born June 4, 1962 in San Diego, CA. Attended FordhamU/LC. Debut 1988 OB in "Lucky Stiff," followed by "Just Say No," "Early One Evening at the Rainbow Bar & Grill."

WHITE, PATRICK. Born Sept. 9, 1963 in Albany, NY. Graduate AADA. Debut 1988 OB in "Male Animal."

WHITE, TERRI. Born Jan. 24, 1953 in Palo Alto, CA. Attended USIU. Debut 1976 OB in "The Club," followed by Bdwy in "Barnum" (1980), "Ain't Misbehavin'," "Welcome to the Club."

WHITEHEAD, PAXTON. Born in Kent, Eng. Attended Webber-Douglas Acad. Bdwy debut 1962 in "The Affair," followed by "Beyond the Fringe," "Candida," "Habeas Corpus," "Crucifer of Blood," "Camelot," "Noises Off," "Run For Your Wife," OB in "Gallows Humor," "One Way Pendulum," "Doll's House," "Rondelay."

WILKINSON, COLM. Born June 5, 1944 in Dublin, Ire. Bdwy debut 1987 in "Les Miserables" for which he received a Theatre World Award.

WILKINSON, KATE. Born Oct. 25 in San Francisco, Ca. Attended San Jose State Col. Bdwy debut 1967 in "Little Murders," followed by "Johnny No Trump," "Watercolor," "Postcards," "Ring Round the Bathtub," "The Last of Mrs. Lincoln," "Man and Superman," "Frankenstein," "The Man Who Came to Dinner," OB in "La Madre," "Ernest in Love," "Story of Mary Surratt," "Bring Me a Warm Body," "Child Buyer," "Rimers of Eldritch," "A Doll's House," "Hedda Gabler," "The Real Inspector Hound," "The Contractor," "When the Old Man Died," "The Overcoat," "Villager," "Good Help Is Hard to Find," "Lumiere," "Rude Times," "Steel Magnolias."

WILLIAMS, ALLISON. Born Sept. 26, 1958 in NYC. Debut 1977 OB in "Guys and Dolls," followed by "Young Gifted and Broke," "Thrill a Moment," Bdwy in "The Wiz" (1977), "Dreamgirls," "Sweet Charity."

WILLIAMS, CINDY SUE. Born Nov. 8, 1959 in Albuquerque, NM. Graduate UNo. Carolina. Bdwy debut 1989 in "Largely New York."

WILLIAMS, MORGAN. Born Sept. 1, 1952 in Tulsa, OK. Graduate OhioU. Debut 1989 in "The Visit."

WILLIAMS, ROBIN. Born July 21, 1952 in Chicago, IL. Attended Juilliard, Col. of Mario, Claremont MensCol. Debut 1988 OB in "Waiting For Godot."

WILLIAMS, TREAT. Born Dec. 1, 1951 in Rowayton, CT. Bdwy debut 1974 in "Grease," followed by "Over Here," "Once in a Lifetime," "Pirates of Penzance," "Love Letters" (also OB), OB in "Maybe I'm Doing It Wrong," "Some Men Need Help."

WILLIAMS, VAN. Born Apr. 10, 1925 in PHARR, TX. Attended UTx, Yale U. Bdwy debut 1951 in "Richard II," followed by "St. Joan," "Dial'M'for Murder," "Little Moon of Alban," "No Time for Sergeants," "The Teahouse of the August Moon."

WILLISON, WALTER. Born June 24, 1947 in Monterey Park, Ca. Bdwy debut 1970 in "Norman, Is That You?," followed by "Two by Two" for which he received a Theatre World Award, "Wild and Wonderful," "A Celebration of Richard Rodgers," "Pippin," "A Tribute to Joshua Logan," "A Tribute to George Abbott," "Grand Hotel," OB in "South Pacific in Concert," "They Say It's Wonderful," "Broadway Scandals of 1928," and "Options," both of which he wrote, "Aldersgate 88."

WILLS, RAY. Born Sept. 14, 1960 in Santa Monica, CA. Graduate WichitaStU, BrandeisU. Debut 1988 OB in "Side by Side by Sondheim," followed by "Kiss Me Quick."

WILSON, JULIE. Born in 1925 in Omaha, NE. Bdwy debut 1946 in "Three to Make Ready," followed by "Kiss Me Kate," "Kismet," "Pajama Game," "Jimmy," "Park," "Legs Diamond," OB in "From Weill to Sondheim."

WILSON, K. C. Born Aug. 10, 1945 in Miami, Fl. Attended AADA. Debut 1973 OB in "Little Mahagonny," followed by "The Tempest," "Richard III," "Macbeth," "Threepenny Opera," "The Passion of Dracula," "Francis," "Robin Hood," "Tatterdemalion," "Beef," "The Art of War," "A Walk on the Wild Side," Bdwy in "Smile" (1986).

WILSON, MARY LOUISE. Born Nov. 12, 1936 in New Haven, CT. Graduate Northwestern U. Bdwy debut 1963 in "Hot Spot," followed by "Flora the Red Menace," "Criss-Crossing," "Promises, Promises," "The Women," "The Gypsy," "The Royal Family," "Importance of Being Earnest," "Philadelphia Story," "Fools," "Alice in Wonderland," "The Odd Couple," OB in "Our Town," "Upstairs at the Downstairs," "Threepenny Opera," "A Great Career," "Whispers on the Wind," "Beggar's Opera," "Buried Child," "Sister Mary Ignatius Explains It All," "Actor's Nightmare," "Baby with the Bathwater," "Musical Comedy Murders of 1940." "Macbeth."

WINDE, BEATRICE. Born Jan. 6, in Chicago, IL. Debut 1966 OB in "In White America," followed by "June Bug Graduates Tonight," "Strike Heaven on the Face," "Divine Comedy," "Crazy Horse," "My Mother, My Father and Me," "Steal Away," "The Actress," "Richard II," "1-2-3-4-5," "Le Bourgeois Gentilhomme," Bdwy in "Ain't Supposed to Die a Natural Death" (1971) for which she received a Theatre World Award.

WING, VIRGINIA. Born Nov. 9 in Marks, MS. Graduate Miss.Col. Debut 1989 OB in "Two by Two."

WINSON, SUZI. Born Feb. 28, 1962 in NYC. Bdwy debut 1980 in "Brigadoon," followed by OB in "Moondance," "Nunsense."

WINSTON, LEE. Born Mar. 14, 1941 in Great Bend, KS. Graduate UKs. Debut 1966 OB in "The Drunkard," followed by "Little Mahogonny," "Good Soldier Schweik," "Adopted Moon," "Miss Waters to You," "Christmas Bride," Bdwy in "Show Boat" (1966), "1600 Pennsylvania Ave."

WISE, WILLIAM. Born May 11, in Chicago, IL. Attended BradleyU., NorthwesternU. Debut 1970 OB in "Adaptation/Next," followed by "Him," "Hot 1 Baltimore," "Just the Immediate Family," "36," "For the Use of the Hall," "Orphans," "Working Theatre Festival," "Copperhead," "Early One Evening at the Rainbow Bar & Grill."

WISNISKI, RON. Born Aug. 11, 1957 in Pittsburg, PA. Debut 1983 OB in "Promises, Promises," followed by "Tatterdemalion," "Most Secret War," "Frankie."

WONG, B. D. (aka Bradd). Born Oct. 24, 1962 in San Francisco, CA. Debut 1981 OB in "Androcles and the Lion," followed by "Applause," Bdwy in "M. Butterfly" (1988) for which he received a Theatre World Award.

WOODARD, ALFRE. Born Nov. 8, in Tulsa, OK. Graduate BostonU. Bdwy debut 1976 in "Me and Bessie," OB in "So Nice They Named It Twice," "Two by South," "Map of the World," "Winter's Tale."

WOODS, ALLIE. Born Sept. 28 in Houston, TX. Graduate TexasSo.U. Debut 1989 OB in "Forbidden City."

WOODS, CAROL. Born Nov. 13, 1943 in Jamaica, NY. Graduate IthacaCol. Debut 1980 OB in "One Mo' Time," followed by "Stepping Out," "Blues in the Night," Bdwy in "Grind" (1985), "Big River."

WOODS, RICHARD. Born May 9, 1923 in Buffalo, NY. Graduate Ithaca Col. Bdwy in "Beg, Borrow or Steal," "Capt. Brassbound's Conversion," "Sail Away," "Coco," "Last of Mrs. Lincoln," "Gigi," "Sherlock Holmes," "Murder among Friends," "Royal Family," "Deathtrap," "Man and Superman," "Man Who Came to Dinner," "The Father," "Present Laughter," "Alice in Wonderland," "You Can't Take It with You," "Design For Living," "Smile," OB in "The Crucible," "Summer and Smoke," "American Gothic," "Four-in-One," "My Hearts in the Highlands," "Eastward in Eden," "Long Gallery," "Year Boston Won the Pennant," "In the Matter of J. Robert Oppenheimer," with APA in "You Can't Take It with You," "War and Peace," "School for Scandal," "Right You Are," "Wild Duck," "Pantagleize," "Exit the King," "Cherry Orchard," "Cock-a-doodle Dandy,"and "Hamlet," "Crimes and Dreams," "Marathon '84," "Much Ado about Nothing," "Sitting Pretty in Concert."

WORKMAN, SHANELLE. Born Aug. 3, 1978 in Fairfax, VA. Bdwy debut 1988 in "Les Miserables."

WORTH, IRENE. Born June 23, 1916 in Nebraska. Graduate UCLA. Bdwy debut 1943 in "Two Mrs. Carrolls," followed by "Cocktail Party," "Mary Stuart," "Toys in the Attic," "King Lear," "Tiny Alice," "Sweet Bird of Youth," "Cherry Orchard," "Lady from Dubuque," "John Gabriel Borkman," OB in "Happy Days," "Letters of Love and Affection," "Chalk Garden," "Golden Age," "Coriolanus."

WRIGHT, RICHARD LEON. Born Jan. 21 in Washington, D.C. Graduate BostonU. Debut 1988 OB in "She Stoops To Conquer."

WYLIE, JOHN. Born Dec. 14, 1925 in Peacock, TX. Graduate No.TxStU. Debut 1987 OB in "Lucky Spot," followed by Bdwy in "Born Yesterday" (1989).

WYMAN, NICHOLAS. Born May 18, 1950 in Portland, Me. Graduate Harvard U. Bdwy debut 1975 in "Very Good Eddie," followed by "Grease," "The Magic Show," "On the 20th Century," "Whoopee!," "My Fair Lady" (1981), "Doubles," "Musical Comedy Murders of 1940," "Phantom of the Opera," OB in "Paris Lights," "When We Dead Awaken," "Charlotte Sweet," "Kennedy at Colonus," "Once on a Summer's Day," "Angry Housewives."

YAMAMOTO, RONALD. Born Mar. 13, 1953 in Seatle, WA. Graduate QueensCol. Debut 1983 OB in "Song for a Nisei Fisherman," followed by "Pacific Overtures," "Rosie's Cafe," Bdwy in "Anything Goes" (1989).

Robert
Stattel

Lynne
Stuart

Ahvi
Spindell

Deborah
Strang

William
Szymanski

Mary
Stout

Renee
Stork

Nicolas
Surovy

Lauren
Tom

Eli
Tray

Angela
Thornton

John M.
Towey

Doug
Tompos

Myra
Taylor

Ray
Virta

Olga
Talyn

Ovidio
Vargas

Ann
Talman

Henrietta
Valor

Courtney
Vance

Catherine
Ulissey

Chuck
Wagner

Yvonne
Warden

Scott
Waara

Robert
Westenberg

Elizabeth
Walsh

Christopher
Wells

Linda
Wallem

Walter
Willison

Marie
Wallace

225

Virginia
Wing

Ron
Wisniski

Carol
Woods

Lee
Winston

Emily
Zacharias

Sam
Zap

YANCEY, KIM. Born Sept. 25, 1959 in NYC. Graduate CCNY. Debut 1978 OB in "Why Lillie Won't Spin," followed by "Escape to Freedom," "Dacha," "Blues for Mr. Charlie," "American Dreams," "Ties that Bind," "Walking Through," "Raisin in the Sun," "Don Juan of Seville."

YANG, GINNY. Born Apr. 22, 1952 in Korea. Graduate CatawbaCol. Debut 1980 OB in "F.O.B.," followed by "Peking Man," "Extenuating Circumstances," "Wha . . . Wha, Along Time Ago," "Three Sisters," Bdwy in "Plenty" (1982).

YEOMAN, JOANN. Born Mar. 19, 1948 in Phoenix, AZ. Graduate AzStateU, PurdueU. Debut 1974 OB in "The Boy Friend," followed by "Texas Starlight," "Ba Ta Clan," "A Christmas Carol."

YOUNGMAN, CHRISTINA. Born Sept. 14, 1963 in Philadelphia, PA. Attended PointPkCol. Debut 1983 OB in "Emperor of My Baby's Heart," followed by "Carouselle des Folles," Bdwy in "Starlight Express" (1987), "Largely NY."

ZACHARIAS, EMILY. Born July 27, 1953 in Memphis, TN. Graduate NorthwesternU. Debut 1980 OB in "March of the Falsettos," followed by "America Kicks Up Its Heels," "Crazy He Calls Me," "Olympus on My Mind," "Dirty Work," "3 Pieces for a Warehouse," Bdwy in "Perfectly Frank," (1980), "Chu Chem" (also OB).

ZAGNIT, STUART. Born Mar. 28 in New Brunswick, NJ. Graduate MontclairStCol. Debut 1978 OB in "The Wager," followed by "Manhattan Transference," "Women in Tune," "Enter Laughing," "Kuni Leml," "Tatterdemalion," "Golden Land," "Little Shop of Horrors," "Lucky Stiff," "Grand Tour," "Majestic Kid."

ZALOOM, JOE. Born July 30, 1944 in Utica, NY. Graduate CatholicU. Bdwy Debut 1972 in "Capt. Brassbound's Conversion," followed by "Kingdoms," OB in "Nature and the Purpose of the Universe," "Plot Counter Plot," "Midsummer Night's Dream," "Madrid, Madrid," "Much Ado about Nothing," "Cymbeline."

ZALOOM, PAUL. Born Dec. 14, 1951 in Brooklyn, NY. Graduate Goddard Col. Debut 1979 OB in "Fruit of Zaloom," followed by "Zalooming Along," "Zaloominations," "Crazy as Zaloom," "Return of the Creature From the Blue Zaloom," "Theatre of Trash," "House of Horrors."

ZANG, EDWARD. Born Aug. 19, 1934 in NYC. Graduate BostonU. OB in "Good Soldier Schweik," "St. Joan," "Boys in the Band," "Reliquary of Mr. and Mrs. Potterfield," "Last Analysis," "As You Like It," "More Than You Deserve," "Polly," "Threepenny Opera," "Largo Desolato," "New York Idea," "The Misanthrope," "Banana Box," "Pen-ultimate Problem of Sherlock Holmes," "Henry IV PtI," "Richard II," "Palace of Amateurs," "Mistress of the Inn."

ZAP, SAM. Born May 21, 1947 in NYC. Graduate CUNY. Debut 1988 OB in "Only Kidding."

ZARISH, JANET. Born Apr. 21, 1954 in Chicago, IL. Graduate Juilliard. Debut 1981 OB in "The Villager," followed by "Playing with Fire," "Royal Bob," "Enemy of the People," "Midsummer Night's Dream," "Festival of 1-Acts," "Other People's Money."

ZAY, TIM. Born Aug. 13, 1952 in Cleveland, OH. Graduate UCincinnati. Debut 1988 OB in "Moby Dick."

ZELLER, MARK. Born Apr. 20, 1932 in NYC. Attended NYU. Bdwy debut 1956 in "Shangri-La," followed by "Happy Hunting," "Wonderful Town" (CC), "Saratoga," "Ari," "Chu Chem" (also OB), OB in "Candle in the Wind," "Margaret's Bed," "Freud," "Kuni Leml," "Lies My Father Told Me," "Big Block Party."

ZIEMBA, KAREN. Born Nov. 12 in St. Joseph, MI. Graduate UAkron. Debut 1981 OB in "Seesaw," followed by "I Married an Angel in Concert," "Sing for Your Supper," Bdwy in "Chorus Line" (1982), "42nd St.," "Teddy and Alice."

ZIEN, CHIP. Born in 1947 in Milwaukee, WI. Attended UPa. OB in "You're a Good Man, Charlie Brown," followed by "Kadish," "How to Succeed . . . ," "Dear Mr. G," "Tuscaloosa's Calling," "Hot 1 Baltimore," "El Grande de Coca Cola," "Split," "Real Life Funnies," "March of the Falsettos," "Isn't It Romantic," "Diamonds," Bdwy in "All Over Town" (1974), "The Suicide," "Into the Woods."

ZISKIE, KURT. Born Apr. 16, 1956 in Oakland, CA. Graduate StanfordU., Neighborhood Playhouse. Debut 1985 OB in "Flash of Lightning," followed by "Ulysses in Nighttown," Bdwy in "Broadway" (1987).

Harry
Andrews

Lucille
Ball

Richard
Barr

Robert Ott
Boyle

Tally
Brown

John
Carradine

OBITUARIES

HARRY ANDREWS, 77, British stage, film and tv actor, died in his home of a viral infection complicated by asthma on March 7, 1989 in Salehurst, Eng. He made his stage debut in 1933 with the liverpool Rep., and his Bdwy debut in 1937 in Gielgud's *Hamlet*. Subsequent NY roles were in the Old Vic's 1946 *Oedipus*, and with the Oliviers in *Caesar and Cleopatra* and *Antony and Cleopatra*. He appeared in over 50 films.

DAVID BAKER, 62, composer, pianist, arranger, and vocal coach, died of lung cancer on July 16, 1988 in his home on Fire Island, NY. He was a native of Portland, Me. He wrote and arranged the dance music for *Do Re Mi, Flora, the Red Menace, Cabaret, The Yearling* and *Rex*, and contributed songs to *Phoenix '55, Shoestring Revue, Shoestring '57, Vintage '60*, and composed the music for *Copper and Brass, Smiling the Boy Fell Dead*, and *Come Summer*. His sister survives.

LUCILLE BALL, 77, the undisputed queen of television comedy, died in a Los Angeles hospital Apr. 26, 1989, a week after heart surgery. She was born in Celoron, NY, and began her career in NYC at the age of 15, where she was subsequently hired as a chorus girl in *Rio Rita*. She toured in *Dream Girl* and starred in Bdwy in *Wildcat*. It was Eddie Cantor's *Roman Scandals* that took her to Hollywood, and over 50 more films. Her greatest fame, however, came from her tv series *I Love Lucy, The Lucy Show* and *Here's Lucy*. She is survived by a daughter, actress-singer Luci Arnaz, and a son Desi by her first husband, the late bandleader, Desi Arnaz. Her second husband, comedian Gary Morton, also survives.

RICHARD BARR, 71, producer, director, and former actor, died of liver failure Jan. 9, 1989 in NYC. He was born in Washington, DC, and graduated from Princeton. He began his career in 1938 with the Mercury Theatre co. as an actor. After his service in the USAAF, he turned to directing and producing. He introduced such unknown playwrights as William Hanley, Lanford Wilson, Sam Shepard, Terrence McNally, Jack Richardson, John Guare, A. R. Gurney, LeRoi Jones, Jean-Claude van Itallie and Paul Zindel. He also presented U.S. premieres of Beckett and Ionesco. As president of the League of American Theatres for 21 years, he administered Bdwy's annual *Tony* Awards. His mother and two sisters survive.

ALVIN BEAM, 61, veteran Bdwy dancer-actor, died Jan. 15, 1989 of cardiopulmonary arrest in NYC. Born in Shelby, NC; trained at American Ballet Sch; appeared in original productions of *Candide, Wonderful Town, Carnival, Take Me Along*, and *Hello, Dolly!* He had appeared in several films and television shows. He was a recipient of a traditional Gypsy Robe. Surviving are his mother and two brothers.

ROBERT OTT BOYLE, 39, died May 16, 1989, of cancer in NYC. He appeared Off-Bdwy in *Merton of the Movies, Esther*, and Bdwy in Eva LeGallienne's *Alice in Wonderland, Doubles*, and *Social Security*. He is survived by his parents and a brother.

TALLY BROWN, 64, actress and cabaret singer, died after a stroke on May 6, 1989 in her native NYC. She appeared on Bdwy in *Pajama Game, Tenderloin, Mame*, and OB in *Jackass, Justice Box*, and *Medea*. No reported survivors.

ROBERT BRUBACH, 33, dancer, died of heart failure Dec. 25, 1988 in his native Pittsburgh, Pa. His credits include *The Magivc Show, Peter Pan, Perfectly Frank, King of Hearts, La Cage aux Folles* and *Cabaret*. His mother, 2 sisters and 4 brothers survive.

JOHN CARRADINE, 82, New York City-born stage, screen and tv character actor, died of heart and kidney failure in Milan, Italy, on Nov. 27, 1988. He had appeared in over 500 films and 180 plays. His Bdwy credits include *The Duchess of Malfi, Volpone, Galileo, The Cup of Trembling, Madwoman of Chaillot, A Funny Thing Happened on the Way to the Forum* and *Frankenstein*. He also toured in many plays and in his own Shakespeare company. He was married three times, and is survived by his five sons, actors David, Robert, Keith and Bruce, and architect Christopher.

WARREN CASEY, 53, a native of Yonkers, NY, who was co-author of the hit musical *Grease*, died Nov. 8, 1988 of AIDS. His mother and two brothers survive.

VERONICA CASTANG, 50, London-born stage and tv actress, died of ovarian cancer Nov. 5, 1988 in her NYC home. After her 1964 Bdwy debut in *How's the World Treating You?*, she appeared in *The National Health, Whose Life Is It Anyway?*, and OB in *The Trigon, Sjt. Musgrave's Dance, Saved, Water Hens, Self-Accusation, Kaspar, Ionescapade, Statements after and Arrest under the Immorality Act, Ride a Cock Horse, Banana Box, Bonjour La Bonjour, A Call from the East, Close of Play, Cloud 9, After the Prize, David and Paula, The Accrington Files*, and *Sea Marks*. She is survived by her step-father and an aunt in London.

RICHARD CASTELLANO, 55, Bronx-born character actor on stage, film and tv, died Dec. 10, 1988 of a heart attack. He ran a construction company until 1961 when he began his acting career, subsequently appearing on Bdwy in *The Investigation, That Summer-That Fall, Mike Downstairs, Lovers and Other Strangers, Sheep on the Runway*, and OB for 643 performances in *A View from the Bridge*. In addition to his wife, actress Ardell Sheridan, he is survived by a daughter and a sister.

WILLIAM CHALLEE, 84, stage and film actor, died March 18, 1989 of Alzheimer's disease in Woodland Hills, CA. He was one of the original Group Theatre in NYC. He appeared in such productions as *Rapid Transit, Faust, Judith, The Sea Gull, The Inspector General, The House of Connolly, Night over Taos, Success Story, Men in White, Waiting for Lefty, Paradise Lost, The Wild Duck, Rocket to the Moon, Awake and Sing!, Key Largo, First Stop to Heaven*, and *Across the Board on Tomorrow Morning*. No reported survivors.

DORT CLARK, 71, stage, film and tv actor, died March 30, 1989 of diabetes and cancer in his hometown of Wellington, Kan. He had appeared on Bdwy in *Sweet Charity, The First Million, Lower North, Snafu, Happy Birthday, South Pacific, Wonderful Town, Bells Are Ringing, Let It Ride, Take Me Along, Fiorello!*, and *Harvey*. His wife and four daughters survive.

EDWARD CHODOROV, 84, playwright and writer or producer of over 50 movies, died Oct. 9, 1989 in his native NYC. His plays include *Wonder Boy, Kind Lady, Those Endearing Young Charms, Decision, Common Ground* and *Oh, Men! Oh, Women!* He is survived by his widow, a son, a daughter, and his brother Jerome.

THOMAS COLEY, 75, Pennsylvania-born stage, film and tv actor, died of a heart attack in his home in Tyringham, MA. He made his Bdwy debut in *The Taming of the Shrew* (1935), followed by *Swingin' the Dream, Return Engagement, Cue for Passion, My Fair Ladies, Mr. Peebles and Mr. Hooker, Portrait in Black, Harvey, I Never Sang for My Father, Our Town* (1969), and OB in *A Passage to E. M. Forster*. A sister survives.

CHARLES COLLINS 46, California-born actor and stage manager, died July 29, 1988 in NYC of Burkett's lymphoma. He appeared OB in *The Last Sweet Days of Isaac, Coming Together, Soft Core Pornographer*, and on Bdwy in *Shelter* and *Platinum*. He toured with productions of *Panama Hattie, Sweeney Todd, Amadeus, They're Playing Our Song, Porgy and Bess*, and *Big River*. His parents survive.

WHITFIELD CONNOR, 71, Ireland-born radio, stage and film actor, and theatrical producer, died July 16, 1988 of respiratory complications in Norwalk, Ct. For the last 23 years he had been executive producer of the Elitch Gardens Theatre in Denver, Co. He made his Bdwy debut in Maurice Evans' *Hamlet* in 1945, followed by *Macbeth* for which he received a Theatre World Award, *The Winner, Lunatics and Lovers, There Was a Little Girl, Everything in the Garden*, and OB in *Six Characters in Search of an Author, The Makropoulos Secret, The Disenchanted* and *In the Matter of J. Robert Oppenheimer*. He is survived by his wife, actress-producer Haila Stoddard, a daughter, a step-daughter, and two step-sons.

SHEILA COONAN, 66, Canada-born character actress, died in NYC of a liver disease on March 28, 1989. During her 40 year career she frequently played Irish women, and her credits include *Seidman and Son, A Taste of Honey, Red Roses for Me, The Great White Hope, The Prime of Miss Jean Brodie*, OB in *Hogan's Goat, Macbeth, A Song for the First of May, Happy Hunter, Just the Immediate Family*, and on TV she had continuing roles in *The Guiding Light, Love of Life, Search for Tomorrow* and *All My Children*. Surviving are two sisters.

| Veronica Castang | Richard Castellano | Dort Clark | Charles Collins | Whitfield Connor | Sheila Coonan |

NICHOLAS CORTLAND, 47, stage, film and tv actor, died of AIDS in NYC on Aug. 21, 1988. He had appeared OB in *Honeymoon in Haiti*, *Suzanna Andler*, and *Goodbye Freddy*. At San Francisco's American Conservatory Theatre he played the leading roles in *General Gorgeous*, *Tiny Alice* and *This Is (An Entertainment)* written specifically for him by Tennessee Williams. On tv he appeared on *Search for Tomorrow* and *As the World Turns*. He is survived by his parents, a brother, and his longtime companion Peter Kruzan.

GEORGE COULOURIS, 85, England-born stage and screen actor, died April 25, 1989 of a heart attack in his home in Hampstead, London. For the last four years he had been disabled by Parkinson's Disease. He was one of the last surviving members of the Mercury Theatre company. He made his Bdwy debut in 1929 in *The Novice and the Duke*, followed by *The Apple Cart*, *The Late Christopher Bean*, *Best Sellers*, *Mary of Scotland*, *Valley Forge*, *Blind Alley*, *Saint Joan*, *Julius Caesar*, *Shoemaker's Holiday*, *Cue for Passion*, *Madame Capet*, *The White Steed*, *Richard III*, *The Alchemist*, *The Insect Comedy*, *Beekman Place*, *The Condemned of Altona*, and *Watch on the Rhine*. Surviving is his second wife, a son and a daughter by his first wife who died in 1976.

WILLIE COVAN, 92, tap and softshoe dancer and teacher who appeared on Bdwy and in movies, died May 7, 1989 in Los Angeles, Ca. Born in Savannah, Ga., he began his career at 12 in minstrel shows and subsequently vaudeville. Before moving to films, he appeared on Bdwy in *Shuffle Along*, *Runnin' Wild* and *Liza*, and was a headliner at the Palace. He opened his own dance school in Los Angeles, and also became dance instructor for MGM films. He continued teaching until 1985. A daughter survives.

RICHMOND CRINKLEY, 49, Virginia-born producer and former executive director of the Vivian Beaumont Theater at Lincoln Center, died of cancer Jan. 29, 1989 in Richmond, Va. He produced the award-winning *The Elephant Man*, and *Tintypes*, and *Passion*. At Lincoln Center his productions of *Macbeth*, *The Philadelphia Story* and *The Floating Light Bulb*. His parents and a brother survive.

MORTON DA COSTA, 74, Philadelphia-born director and former actor, died Jan. 29, 1989 of heart failure in the ambulance taking him to the hospital from his home in Redding, Ct. He changed his name from Tecosky when he began his theatre career in 1942's *The Skin of Our Teeth*. He subsequently appeared in *It's a Gift*, *Stovepipe Hat*, *Hamlet* with Maurice Evans, and *Man and Superman*. His directorial credits include *She Stoops to Conquer* (his first in 1949), *Capt. Brassbound's Conversion*, *Dream Girl*, *The Wild Duck*, *Plain and Fancy*, *No Time for Sergeants*, *Auntie Mame*, *The Music Man*, *Saratoga*, *The Wall*, *Hot Spot*, *Maggie Flynn* and *Doubles* in 1985. Two sisters survive.

HAZEL DAWN, 98, retired star of musicals, died Aug. 28, 1988 in her daughter's NYC home. Born Hazel LaTout in Ogden, Utah, she moved with her family to England so that she and her sisters could have voice lessons. She made her debut in London in 1909 in *Dear Little Denmark*, quickly rising to stardom. In 1911 she made her NY debut in *The Pink Lady* and was a sensation. She became the star of such musicals as *The Little Cafe*, *The Debutante*, *The Century Girl*, *Up in Mabel's Room*, *Getting Gertie's Garter*, *The Demi-Virgin*, *The Great Temptations*, and *Ziegfeld Follies*. She retired in 1927 when she married mining engineer Edward Gruelle. She returned to the stage briefly for *Wonder Boy* in 1931, and appeared in the 1946 film *Margie*. She is survived by a son, and a daughter, former actress-singer Hazel Dawn, Jr.

GABRIEL DELL (né del Vecchio), 68, Barbados-born stage and screen actor, died of leukemia on July 3, 1988 in his North Hollywood home. In 1935 while appearing on Bdwy in *Dead End*, he and 5 other young actors were taken to Hollywood and began successful careers in films as the *Dead End Kids* or the *Bowery Boys* or *Eastside Kids*. Unlike the others, he occasionally returned to Bdwy in such productions as *Tickets Please*, *Ankles Aweigh*, *Prisoner of Second Avenue*, *Marathon '33*, *Anyone Can Whistle*, *Sign in Sidney Brustein's Window*, *Luv*, *Something Different*, *Fun City*, at City Center in *Can-Can*, *Wonderful Town* and *Oklahoma!*, and OB in *Chocolates*, *Adaptation*, *Where Do We Go from Here?* Surviving are two sons Gabriel, Jr. and Michael (both actors), and a sister.

SALVATORE DELL'ISOLA, 88, Tony Award-winning Italy-born musical director, died of heart failure Mar. 13, 1989 in West Islip, NY. His 20-year association with Rodgers & Hammerstein began with *Oklahoma!* (on tour), followed by Bdwy's *South Pacific*, *Me and Juliet*, *Pipe Dreams*, and *Flower Drum Song* for which he received a 1959 Tony Award. A son survives.

DEAN DITTMAN, 57, Kansas-born singer-actor on stage, film, radio and opera, died of heart failure Jan. 28, 1989 in Los Angeles. His career began with the Kansas City Starlight Theatre. On Bdwy he appeared in *My Fair Lady*, *The Sunday Man*, *The Music Man*, *Hello, Dolly!*, *Annie* and *On the 20th Century*. He received an Obie for his performance in *The Cradle Will Rock*. No reported survivors.

DONALD DRIVER, 65, Oregon-born dancer, actor, playwright and director, died of AIDS June 27, 1988 in his NYC home. After serving in the navy in WWII, he came to NYC, became a member of Ballet Russe de Monte Carlo, leaving to act and dance in Bdwy musicals *Guys and Dolls*, *A Tree Grows in Brooklyn*, *Buttrio Square*, *Show Boat*, *Hit the Trail*, *Finian's Rainbow*. He was Tony-nominated for his first directorial effort, a revival of *Marat/Sade*, succeeded by *Jimmy Shine*, *Our Town* with Henry Fonda, wrote and directed *Status Quo Vadis*, *Oh, Brother!*, and OB's hit musical *Your Own Thing*. He is survived by a son.

ELIZABETH LOGUE DUGGAN, 56, former dancer and actress, died of cancer June 7, 1988 in Santa Monica, Ca. She was the widow of actor Andrew Duggan who predeceased her by less than a month. She began her career at 17 and appeared in *Brigadoon*, *Flahooley*, *Month of Sundays*, *New Faces of '52*, and *Paint Your Wagon*. Surviving are a son and two daughters.

VITO DURANTE, 64, dancer, choreographer, stage manager and teacher, died May 6, 1989 in NYC of AIDS. He had appeared in *Kiss Me, Kate*, *The King and I*, *The Unsinkable Molly Brown*, *My Fair Lady*, *The Pajama Game*, *Top Banana* and *Fiddler on the Roof*. He was a frequent dancer on tv shows. Two sisters and a brother survive.

JOHN EAMES, 64, stage, screen and tv actor, died June 13, 1989 in NYC. He was born in Connecticut, and appeared in regional theatres before making his NY debut OB in *Leave It to Jane*, followed by *The Boss*, and Bdwy's *1776*, *The Corn Is Green* (1983), and *Arsenic and Old Lace* with Jean Stapleton. His parents and two brothers survive.

FLORENCE ELDRIDGE, 86, Brooklyn-born stage and film actress, and widow of actor Fredric March, died Aug. 1, 1988 in a Santa Monica, Ca., hospital emergency room. After making her debut in the chorus of *Rockabye Baby* (1918), she became a versatile and respected actress in such productions as *Ambush*, *The Cat and the Canary*, *Six Characters in Search of an Author*, *The Great Gatsby*, *The Skin of Our Teeth*, *Years Ago*, *Now I Lay Me Down to Sleep*, *An Enemy of the People*, *The Swan*, *The Autumn Garden* and *Long Day's Journey into Night* with her husband. She is survived by her adopted daughter, and by two brothers.

MAURICE EVANS, 87, classical actor, producer and manager, died March 12, 1989 in a nursing home in Rottingdean, England. He made his Bdwy debut in 1935 as Romeo to Katharine Cornell's Juliet and established himself as a star, subsequently appearing in *St. Helena*, *Richard II*, *St. Joan*, *Henry IV*, *Hamlet*, *Macbeth*, *Man and Superman*, *The Browning Version*, *Harlequinade*, *The Devil's Disciple*, *The Wild Duck*, *Dian "M" for Murder*, *The Apple Cart*, *Heartbreak House*, *Tenderloin*, *The Aspern Papers*, *Program for Two Players*, and his *G. I. Hamlet* which he took to the military forces during WWII. He became an American citizen in 1941 and enlisted in the army in 1942. He was also producer of *The Teahouse of the August Moon* and *No Time for Sergeants*, and many tv productions. He received an Emmy for his *Macbeth* and a Special Tony in 1950. He returned to England in the late 1960's. A brother survives.

PETER EVANS, 38, New Jersey-born actor on stage, film and tv, died of AIDS on May 20, 1989 in Los Angeles, Ca. He made his debut OB in *Life Class* followed by *Streamers*, *A Life in the Theatre*, *Don Juan Comes Back from the War*, *The American Clock*, *Geniuses*, *The Transfiguration of Benno Blimpie*, *Endgame*, *Total Eclipse*, *Springtime for Henry*, *Company*, and on Bdwy in *Night and Day*, *Children of a Lesser God*. Surviving are his parents, a sister and brother.

Nicholas
Cortland

Morton
DaCosta

Hazel
Dawn

Gabriel
Dell

John
Eames

Florence
Eldridge

MORGAN FARLEY, 90, stage, screen and tv actor, died Oct. 11, 1988 in San Pedro, Ca. A native of Mamaroneck, NY, he made his Bdwy debut in 1918 in *Seventeen* followed by *Charm School, Deburau, The Grand Duke, Mary the Third, Home Fires, Wild Westcotts, Fata Morgana, Paolo and Francesca, Tangletoes, Candida, Unchastened Soman, Easter, An American Tragedy, Lady of the Camellias, Crime and Punishment, Julie the Great, Hamlet, Danton's Death, Outward Bound, The Distant City, Savpnarola* and *Galileo*. He was an army WWII veteran. Surviving are a nephew and two nieces.

RON FIELD, 55, Tony and Emmy Award-winning choreographer and director, died Feb. 6, 1989 of neurological impairment due to brain lesions in his native NYC. He made his stage debut in 1942 in *Lady in the Dark*, followed by *Gentlemen Prefer Blondes* and *Kismet*, He then turned to choreographing and received Tonys for *Cabaret* and *Applause*, among his others were *Zorba, On the Town, King of Hearts, Peter Pan* and *Rags*. He is survived by his parents.

BRAMWELL FLETCHER, 84, England-born stage, screen and tv actor, died June 22, 1988 in Westmoreland, NH. where he had retired. He made his Bdwy bow in 1929 in *Scotland Yard*, followed by *Ten Minute Alibi, Lady Precious Stream, Within the Gates, Storm Operation, Rebecca, The Day after Tomorrow, Maggie, The Little Glass Clock, The Lovers, Dandida, Misalliance, The Wisteria Trees, My Fair Lady, The Cherry Orchard* and his solo performance (OB) in *The Bernard Shaw Story*. His first three marriages ended in divorce. He is survived by his fourth wife, a daughter and two sons.

RON FORELLA, 50, dancer, choreographer and teacher, died of a heart attack on Jan. 18, 1989 in NYC. He appeared in *Promises Promises, Sweet Charity, Hallelujah Baby, The Unsinkable Molly Brown, How Now Dow Jones, Annie Get Your Gun*, and choreographed *A Patriot for Me*, and *Wild and Wonderful*. No reported survivors.

MARY K. FRANK, 77, Ohio-born producer, and former president of New Dramatists, died Nov. 20, 1988 in Grand View-on-the-Hudson, NY. She either produced or co-produced, *Tea and Sympathy, Too Late the Phalarope, One More River, Sponono*, and *K2*. A daughter survives.

ROSE FRANKEN (née Lewin) 92, playwright and novelist, died June 22, 1988 in Tucson, AZ. Born in Texas, she moved with her family to NYC, and at 19 she married Dr. S.W.A. Franken, a surgeon. *Another Language*, her first play, was produced in 1932, followed by *Claudia* based on her novels, *Outrageous Fortune, Soldier's Wife, Doctors Disagree*, and *The Hallams* her last play. She is survived by three sons.

LEONARD FREY, 49, Brooklyn-born stage, film and tv actor, died Aug. 24, 1988 in NYC of AIDS. After his debut OB in *Little Mary Sunshine* he appeared in *Funny House of a Negro, Coach with the Six Insides, Boys in the Band, The Time of Your Life, Beggar on Horseback, People Are Living There, Twelfth Night, Troilus and Cressida*, and on Bdwy in *Fiddler on the Roof, The National Health, Knock Knock, Kurt Weill Cabaret, The Man Who Came to Dinner*. A brother and nephew survive.

JOHN GANZER, 33, Illinois-born actor-singer, and Actors Equity Council member, died of AIDS Dec. 3, 1988 in NYC. He was an original member of Bdwy's *Joseph and the Amazing Technicolor Dreamcoat*, and appeared in many regional theatres and with national touring companies. He was active in establishing Equity Fights AIDS. Surviving are his parents, a brother and two sisters.

STEVEN GELFER, 39, Brooklyn-born dancer-actor, died of AIDS Dec. 26, 1988 in NYC. His Bdwy credits include *Whoopee, Gypsy, The American Dance Machine*, and the original cast of *Cats* and *The Best Little Whorehouse in Texas*. His parents, a sister and a brother survive.

MARK GOLDSTAUB, 37, press agent for the arts, died of AIDS Dec. 14, 1988 in his NYC home. He began handling publicity for the performing arts in 1977 subsequently opening his own company. Among his clients were Bdwy's *Dracula, Hello, Dolly!* and *Show Boat*, the Metropolitan Opera, and Westbury Music Fair. Surviving are his parents, a brother, and his companion Edmund Wojcik.

BOB GORMAN, 59, musical comedy performer and pianist, died Oct. 11, 1988 in Los Angeles after a long illness. He had appeared on Bdwy in *Li'l Abner, Sweet Charity*, and *How Now Dow Jones*, and had recurring roles on *The Carol Burnett Show*, and *The Mary Tyler Moore Show* on tv. He was also a singing coach and accompanist for many performers. No reported survivors.

BILL GUNN, 59, Philadelphia-born playwright, screenwriter, novelist and actor, died Apr. 5, 1989 of encephalitis in Nyack, NY, the day before his play *(The Forbidden City)* opened at the Public Theater. Other plays are *Marcus in the High Grass, Johnnas* and *Black Picture Show*. His Bdwy debut as an actor was in *The Immoralist*, followed by *Take a Giant Step* and *A Member of the Wedding*. His mother survives.

NEDDA HARRIGAN, 89, actress and widow of director-producer Joshua Logan, died of lung cancer Apr. 1, 1989 in her NYC home. Her Bdwy appearances include *Becky Sharp, Merry Andrew* and *Dracula*. She was the founder of the Stage Door Canteen in 1942 as well as the Actors Fund Blood Bank. She had been president of the Actors Fund of America for her last 10 years. Her first husband, actor Walter Connolly died in 1940. Surviving are a daughter and two sons.

GRACE HAYES, 93, stage and film actress-singer, and night club entertainer, died Feb. 1, 1989 in Las Vegas where she had lived since 1940 and operated a night club until her retirement. Married three times, she is survived by her son, Peter Lind Hayes.

WINSTON DeWITT HEMSLEY, 42, Brooklyn-born actor, dancer and choreographer, was found beaten to death in his Las Vegas home May 9, 1989. He was a star performer and choreographer for the Lido de Paris shows, among others. He had appeared on Bdwy in *Golden Boy, A Joyful Noise, Hallelujah, Baby, Hello, Dolly!, Rockabye Hamlet, A Chorus Line* and *Eubie*. No reported survivors.

JO HENDERSON, 54, stage, film and tv actress, died Aug. 6, 1988 in an automobile accident in Chinle, Az. on her way back to NY after an engagement at the La Jolla (CA) Playhouse. Her many OB credits include *Camille, The Little Foxes, An Evening with Merlin Finch, 20th Century Tar, A Scent of Flowers, Revival, Dandelion Wine, My Life, Ladyhouse Blues* for which she received an Obie Award, *Fallen Angels, Waiting for the Parade, Threads, Bella Figura, Details without a Map, The Middle Ages, Time Framed, Isn't It Romantic, Little Footsteps*, and Bdwy in *Rose, 84 Charing Cross Road* and *Play Memory* for which she received a Tony nomination. Her mother, a son and a brother survive.

ANTHONY HOLLAND, 60, Brooklyn-born stage and film actor, committed suicide in his Manhattan apartment on July 9, 1988 after suffering from AIDS for some time. After appearing with the original Second City comedy group, he made his Bdwy debut in *My Mother, My Father and Me* (1963), followed by *We Bombed in New Haven, Dreyfus in Rehearsal, Leaf People, Division Street, Nathan Weinstein, Mystic, Connecticut*, and OB in *Venice Preserved, Second City, Victim of Duty, New Tenant, Dynamite Tonight, Quare Fellow, White House Murder Case, Waiting for Godot, Tales of the Hasidim, Taming of the Shrew, Diary of Anne Frank, The Hunger Artist*. He is survived by his mother, a brother and a sister.

ROBERT BRUCE HOLLEY, 59, New Jersey-born actor, director, stage manager and producer, died Nov. 11, 1988 in his NYC home following a long cardiac illness. He made his Bdwy debut in *No Sex, Please, We're British!*. He subsequently appeared in *Dracula, Elephant Man, Morning's at 7* and *Amadeus*. Surviving are two sisters.

JOHN HOUSEMAN, 86, Rumania-born actor, director, producer and teacher, died of spinal cancer Oct. 31, 1988 in his home in Malibu, CA. He was a founder of the Mercury Theatre, and helped establish the drama school at Juilliard. After a career in grain trade Virgil Thomson asked him to direct his opera *Four Saints in Three Acts* and thus began his association with the performing arts. Success in theatre led to his work in radio, films and television, and his collecting many awards. Surviving are his widow, and two sons.

HENRIETTA JACOBSON, 82, Chicago-born star of Yiddish theatre, died Oct. 9, 1988 of heart failure in NYC. She made her stage debut at 3, and her NY debut in 1912 in *Israel's Hope*, followed by numerous plays and musicals, among which are *It Could Happen to You, The World of Mrs. Solomon, Go Fight City HALL*, and *Kosher Widow;* and on Bdwy in *Come Blow Your Horn*, and *70, Girls, 70*. Her husband, Julius Adler, was usually her co-star. He survives, as does her actor son Bruce.

ERROL JOHN, 64, Trinidad-born stage and film actor, and playwright, died in London July 10, 1988. His best known play is *Moon on a Rainbow Shawl*, and his most acclaimed performance was in the Old Vic production of *Othello*. His widow and two children survive.

DUANE L. JONES, 51, actor-director, died July 22, 1988 of cardiopulmonary arrest in Mineola, NY. He directed many productions including the long-run *Mama, I Want to Sing, God's Trombones* and *Black Picture Show*. He appeared in numerous off-broadway productions, films, and on tv. He was artistic director for the Richard Allen Center, and for the State University Theatre in Old Westbury, NY. Surviving are his mother, a sister, and a brother.

MICHAEL M. KATZ, 32, NYC-born actor, director, playwright, died of AIDS Sept. 14, 1988 in Los Angeles, Ca. He appeared in several off-Broadway productions both in NYC and Los Angeles. He wrote *The Immigrant, The Ladies Upstairs, Without Reservations, AIDS/Us*, and *Taking Care*. His mother and step-father survive.

RICHARD KAVANAUGH, 47, NYC-born actor, was found dead in his apartment Aug. 6, 1988 in Providence, RI. He had been ill for two weeks. His NYC credits include *Dracula, The Hot House* (for which he received a *Tony* nomination), *Learned Ladies, Bosoms and Neglect*. He had been a member of Trinity Repertory Co. for 20 years, and one of its most talented actors. Surviving are a son and a daughter, his mother and two brothers.

MANDEL J. KRAMER, 72, radio, tv and stage actor, died Jan. 29, 1989 in Delray Beach, FL. He was a police chief on *The Edge of Night* for 25 years, and appeared on stage in *Death of a Salesman, Plaza Suite*, and *Prisoner of Second Avenue*. His widow, two daughters and a son survive.

JAMES KIRKWOOD, 64, Hollywood-born son of actors James Kirkwood and Lila Lee, died of cancer in NYC on April 21, 1989. He began his acting career at 14 on Bdwy, appearing in such productions as *Panama Hattie, Wonderful Town, Welcome Darlings*. With Lee Goodman, he worked the nightclub circuit for several years, eventually becoming a writer and Pulitzer-Prize-winner for co-writing *A Chorus Line* that became Bdwy's longest running musical. He was author of several best-selling novels, including *Hit Me with a Rainbow, Good Times-Bad Times, P.S. Your Cat Is Dead* (which he adapted for the stage), *There Must Be a Pony* and *Diary of a Mad Playwright*. In addition to *A Chorus Line*, he penned *Unhealthy to Be Unpleasant* and *Legends*. He is survived by a half-sister and half-brother.

LOUISE LARABEE, 74, stage and screen actress, died Mar. 30, 1988. After leaving Bremerton, Wa., for Broadway, she appeared in such productions as *Angel Island, The Land Is Bright, Guest in the House, Junior Miss, Sleep No More, The Number, A Date with April, Picnic, Right Honourable Gentleman, Carousel* (CC), *The Last Resort*. No other details available.

WILFORD LEACH, 59, Virginia-born director, died of cancer June 18, 1988 in his home in Rocky Point, L.I., NY. After serving as artistic director at LaMama, he became the principal director for the NY Shakespeare Festival and received *Tonys* for his direction of its productions of *Pirates of Penzance* and *The Mystery of Edwin Drood*. Surviving are his mother, sister and half-sister.

BEATRICE LILLIE, 94, Canada-born actress-singer-comedienne star of stage and film, in U.S. and England, died Jan. 20, 1989 in her home in Henley-on-Thames, England. A series of strokes had silenced her voice and ended her career several years previously. Her last Bdwy appearance was in the 1964 musical *High Spirits*, adapted from Noel Coward's *Blithe Spirit*, and her last film was the 1967 musical *Thoroughly Modern Millie*. Her Bdwy debut was in *Charlot's Revue of 1924*, followed by *Oh, Please, This Year of Grace, She's My Baby, The Third Little Show, Too True to Be Good, At Home Abroad, The Show Is On, Set to Music, Seven Lively Arts, Inside U.S.A., An Evening with Beatrice Lillie, Ziegfeld Follies*, and *Auntie Mame*. She was the widow of England's Lord Robert Peel, but seldom used her title of Lady Peel. Their only child, Robert, was killed in military service in 1942. No immediate survivors.

PHILLIP LINDSAY, 64, actor-director-producer, died Oct. 22, 1988 of pneumonia in NYC. After serving the USNavy, and graduating from Chicago's Goodman Theatre School, he made his Bdwy debut in 1950's *The Member of the Wedding*, followed by *The Great White Hope, God's Favorite, The Skin of Our Teeth, Sweet Bird of Youth*, and revivals of *20th Century*, and *The Little Foxes*. A brother survives.

JOSHUA LOGAN, 79, stage and film director, and author, died July 12, 1988 of supranuclear palsy in his NYC home where he had been confined to a wheelchair. He was born in Texarkana, Tx, reared in Louisiana and Indiana, and attended Princeton U. where he became involved with the Triangle Club productions and the University Players. Subsequently he became a co-author and co-producer or producer as well as director of a long list of successes, beginning with the musical *I Married an Angel* in 1938, and followed by *Knickerbocker Holiday, Annie Get Your Gun, Picnic, Fanny, The World of Suzy Wong, South Pacific, Charley's Aunt, By Jupiter, Happy Birthday, Mr. Roberts, John Loves Mary, Wish You Were Here*, and *Kind Sir*. He is survived by his second wife, Nedda Harrigan, a son and a daughter, and a step-daughter. His first marriage to actress Barbara O'Neil ended in divorce.

CHET LONDON, 57, Massachusetts-born actor, director and puppeteer, died Sept. 15, 1988 of cancer in Kingston, NY. He had appeared in *First Love, The Deadly Game, Destry Rides Again, Hadrian VII, Woman Before Woman* and *Like Them That Dream*. Surviving are his son and daughter, and a brother.

JOHN F. LONG, 46, died April 2, 1989 of lymphoma in Los Angeles, Ca. After his 1967 debut Off Broadway in *Now Is the Time for All Good Men*, he appeared *The Last Sweet Days of Isaac, Beggar's Opera, Polly*, and *Dracula* with Frank Langella. Surviving are two sisters and a brother.

CARL LOW, 71, stage screen and tv actor, died of cancer Oct. 19, 1988 in Nyack, NY. He was born in Knoxville, Tn, and made his Bdwy debut in 1942 in *Janie*, followed by, among others, *Desire under the Elms, The Biko Conquest, The Diary of Anne Frank*. For more than 15 years he was Dr. Bob Rogers on tv's *Search for Tomorrow*. His longtime companion was Barbara Berjer. Three daughters and a sister survive.

HENRY LUHRMAN, 47, Cincinnati-born press agent and former actor, died April 11, 1989 of heart failure and pneumonia in NYC. He had promoted over 150 productions since forming his own company in 1973. He is survived by his parents.

KENNETH McMILLAN, 56, Brooklyn-born character actor of stage screen and tv, died of a liver disease on Jan. 8, 1989 in a Santa Monica, CA. hospital. After his 1970 Broadway debut in *Borstal Boy*, he appeared in *American Buffalo, Danger: Memory!*, and OB in *King of the Whole Damned World, Little Mary Sunshine, Babes in the Wood, Moonchildren, Merry Wives of Windsor, Where Do We Go from Here?, Kid Champion, Streamers, Henry IV Part II, Red Eye of Love* and *Weekends Like Other People*. He was featured in over 25 films. Surviving are his wife, a former dancer, and an actress daughter Allison.

RALPH MEEKER, 67, Minneapolis-born actor on Broadway, film and tv, died of a heart attack Aug. 5, 1988 in the Woodland Hills, Ca., hospital. He appeared on Broadway in *Strange Fruit, Cyrano de Bergerac, Mr. Roberts* (for which he received a Theatre World Award), *A Streetcar Named Desire, Picnic, Cloud 7, Rhinoceros, Something about a Soldier, Mrs. Dally, After the Fall, But for Whom Charlie*, and OB in *House of Blue Leaves*. He was seen in over 50 films, and starred in the tv series *Not for Hire*. His widow survives.

JACK MOORE, 62, Indiana-born dancer, choreographer, teacher and artist, died of lung cancer June 23, 1988 in NYC. He performed with the dance companies of Martha Graham, Merce Cunningham and Anna Sokolow before making his Broadway debut in 1955 in *Red Roses for Me* followed by *Copper and Brass*. Surviving are his companion of 30 years, Robert Van Cleave, and a brother.

KEN MURRAY, 85, star of stage, radio, screen, vaudeville and tv, died Oct. 12, 1988 in Burbank, CA. Born Kenneth Abner Doncourt in NY, he became Kent Tailor after leaving high school to work in vaudeville where his mother and father were successful stars. In a short time he changed his name to Ken Murray, and rose quickly in vaudeville, working mostly as mc. In the 1930's he turned to musicals and revues and was starred in *Earl Carroll's Sketch Book*. In 1942 he opened his long-running *Ken Murray's Blackouts*, and in 1950 launched the *Ken Murray Show* on TV. Surviving are his widow, a son, and two daughters.

BETTY OAKES, 60, Chicago-born singer, dancer, actress, died of cancer July 27, 1988 in NYC. After her Broadway debut in *Where's Charley?* (1951). She appeared in *Of Thee I Sing, The Moon Is Blue, The Most Happy Fella*, and OB in *Epitaph for George Dillon, Antiques, Sandhog*. A daughter survives.

BOB OLIVO, 51, actor known professionally as Ondine, died of a liver ailment on Apr. 27, 1989 in NYC. He had appeared in several Warhol films, and Off Bdwy in *Charles Dickens' Christmas Carol, Conquest of the Universe, Nightclub, Captain Jack's Revenge, Prussian Suite, The Life of Juanita Castro* and *Oscar*. He is survived by his mother.

STEWART PARKER, 47, Belfaat-born playwright, died of bone cancer Nov. 2, 1988 in London. He wrote plays for radio and television as well as theatre. His most acclaimed are *Spokesong* (presented at Circle in the Square), *Northern Star, Catchpenny Twist, I'm a Dreamer, Montreal, Nightshade* and *Pentecost*. Surviving are his father, a brother and a sister in Ireland.

MIGUEL PINERO, 41, Puerto Rico-born playwright and actor, died of cirrhosis of the liver on June 17, 1988 in NYC. In 1974 he received the NY Drama Critics Award for Best Play of the Season, *Short Eyes*. He began his playwriting career while serving time in Sing Sing prison for armed robbery. Other plays include *Straight from the Ghetto, Eulogy for a Small-time Thief, The Sun Always Shines for the Cool*, and *A Midnight Moon at the Greasy Spoon*. He was working on *Every Form of Refuge Has Its Price*. He is survived by seven brothers and sisters.

GILDA RADNER, 42, Detroit-born comedienne on stage, screen and tv, died of cancer May 20, 1989 in Los Angeles, Ca. She began her professional career in Toronto, Can., in *Godspell* and *Second City*, and came to NY in 1974 to appear in *The National Lampoon Radio Hour*, followed by *The National Lampoon Show*, both Off Broadway. After her success on tv's *Saturday Night Live*, she appeared in several films and made her Bdwy debut in *Gilda Radner—Live from New York*, followed by *Lunch Hour*. She is survived by her husband, actor Gene Wilder, her mother and a brother.

JOSEPH G. RAPOSO, 51, composer and creator of *Sesame Street*, died Feb. 5, 1989 of complications from lymphoma in a Bronxville, NY, hospital. He was a co-author of the hit musical *You're a Good Man, Charlie Brown*, and of the tv *Electric Company*. He is survived by his wife Pat Collins, tv's arts-and-entertainment editor, three sons, a daughter, and his parents of Chatham, MA.

JAMES RAY, 57, Oklahoma-born stage, film and tv actor, died of a heart attack in his Los Angeles home on Dec. 3, 1988. He had appeared on Broadway in *Compulsion, J.B., The Wall, Dylan, The Glass Menagerie* (1965), *All Over*, and OB in *Dark of the Moon, The Creditors, The Collection, Love's Labours Lost, Henry IV, The Basement, Sensations, The Disintegration of James Cherry, Amphitryon, King Lear, Henry V, The Tragical Historie of Dr. Faustus* and *Raw Youth*. Three sisters and a brother survive.

| Maurice Evans | Peter Evans | Ron Field | Bramwell Fletcher | Leonard Frey | Steven Gelfer |

| Bob Gorman | Bill Gunn | Nedda Harrigan | Winston DeWitt Hemsley | Jo Henderson | Anthony Holland |

| Robert Bruce Holley | John Houseman | Duane Jones | Beatrice Lillie | Phillip Lindsay | Joshua Logan |

| Chet London | Henry Luhrman | Kenneth McMillan | Ralph Meeker | Jack Moore | Ken Murray |

| Gilda Radner | Irene Rich | Richard Riddle | Wolfgang Roth | Anne Seymour | Hiram Sherman |

Joe Silver	Ann Thomas	Martin J. Walsh	Douglass Watson	Robert Webber	Joan Wetmore

JACK RECHZEIT, 85, Warsaw-born actor-composer for the Yiddish theatre, died of a heart ailment July 24, 1988 in NYC. He immigrated from Poland in 1923 and for 60 years was featured in many musicals, including *Yoshe Kalb* and *Hard to Be a Jew*. His last performance was in the 1986 production of *Broome Street, America*. Surviving are his wife, a brother, two sisters, and two daughters.

IRENE RICH, 96, star of stage, radio and films, died Apr. 22, 1988 of heart failure at her home in Hope Ranch, CA. Born Irene Luthe in Buffalo, NY, began her career as an extra in 1918 and subsequently appeared in over 100 silent films (several as the wife of Will Rogers). In vaudeville she did over 5000 performances in *Ask the Wife*, and was in the Bdwy musical hit *As the Girls Go*. She became a spokesperson for Welch's grape juice and her radio series *Dear John* was sponsored by the company. She was predeceased by her third husband, and is survived by two daughters and several grandchildren.

R. RICHARD RIDDLE, 51, Montana-born composer-lyricist, died of leukemia Apr. 30, 1988 in NYC. A protege of Frank Loesser, whose help proved invaluable as the composer-lyricist of *Cowboy*, *The Rocky Mountain Symphony*, and *The Oxbow Incident*. He composed numerous works for tv and musical groups. Surviving are his mother, two sisters, and a brother, actor Steve Riddle.

JAY FLASH RILEY, 72, actor-singer-dancer, died Sept. 20, 1988 in Los Angeles. His career began with the WPA Theatre in 1932, and he subsequently appeared in *Native Son*, *On the Town*, *Carmen Jones*, *Finian's Rainbow*, *Bubbling Brown Sugar* and *The Wiz*. Two brothers survive.

JOANNA ROOS, 88, actress on stage and tv, and a playwright, died of a ruptured aorta May 13, 1989 in Princeton, NJ. She retired from the soap opera *Love of Life* in 1979. A son survives.

WOLFGANG ROTH, 78, set designer, died Nov. 11, 1988 of bronchial pneumonia in NYC, Born in Berlin, he came to the U.S. in 1938 and worked in all media, including, stage, film, opera, interior design, costumes. He also appeared on stage talking and singing about Berlin's cabaret scene. His wife died in March 1988. A brother survives.

ANNE SEYMOUR, 79, NYC-born actress on stage, screen, radio and tv, died Dec. 8, 1988 of heart failure in Los Angeles. Her professional debut in 1928 was followed by Broadway roles in *Mr. Moneypenny*, *At the Bottom*, *School for Scandal*, *Troilus and Cressida*, *The Seagull*, and *Sunrise at Campobello*. She was heard on over 5000 radio programs and made her film debut in 1949 subsequently appearing in over 30 films and numerous tv films and series. A brother survives.

HIRAM SHERMAN, 81, Boston-born actor on stage, film and tv. After his Bdwy debut in *Horse Eats Hat* (1936), he appeared in *Shoemaker's Holiday*, *Sing Out the News*, *Very Warm for May*, *The Talley Method*, *Cyrano de Bergerac*, *The Alchemist*, *4 Twelves Are 48*, *The Moon Is Blue*, *Two's Company*, *Frogs of Spring*, *3 for Tonight*, *Goodbye Again*, *Measure for Measure*, *International Soiree*, *Mary, Mary*, *Where's Daddy?*, and *How Now Dow Jones*. He retired to Springfield, IL, where he died of a stroke on Apr. 11, 1989. No reported survivors.

JOE SILVER, 66, Wisconsin-born character actor on stage, film and tv, died Feb. 27, 1989 of liver cancer in NYC. He made his Broadway debut in 1942 in *Tobacco Road*, followed by *The Doughgirls*, *Heads or Tails*, *Nature's Way*, *Gypsy*, *Heroine*, *Zulu and the Zayda*, *You Know I Can't Hear You . . .*, *Lenny* (Tony nomination), *The Roast*, *The World of Sholem Aleichem*, *Legs Diamond*, and OB in *Blood Wedding*, *Lamp at Midnight*, *Joseph and His Brethern*, *Victors*, *Shrinking Bride*, *Family Pieces*, *Cakes with Wine*, *The Homecoming*, *Cold Storage*, *Rich Relatives*, *Old Business*. Surviving are his wife, actress Chevi Colton, a son and a daughter.

VALERIE TAYLOR, 85, British actress who appeared in several Broadway productions, died Oct. 24, 1988 in her native London. After her 1929 NYC debut in *Berkeley Square*, she was seen in *The Children's Hour*, *Peter Ibbetson*, *The Red Planet*, *Love of Women* and *The Gioconda Smile*. Twice widowed, she left no immediate survivors.

ANN THOMAS, 75, actress on stage, screen, radio and tv, died Apr. 28, 1989 of lung cancer in New Rochelle, NY. She was born in Newport, RI, and began her career at age 4 and subsequently appeared in over 4000 radio dramas, 10 films, and more than 40 Broadway productions, including *Doctors Disagree*, *A New Life*, *Having Wonderful Time*, *Man from Cairo*, *Chicken Every Sunday*, *The Would-Be Gentleman*, *Made in Heaven*, *Burlesque*, *Dance Me a Song*, *Not for Children*, *Home Is the Hero* and *Children of the Wind*. She is survived by her husband.

TED TILLER, 75, actor, playwright, director, producer, died Sept. 24, 1988 in NYC of complications from brain surgery. He was a native of Washington, DC, where he began his career, and made his debut on Broadway in *Sing Out, Sweet Land* (1944), followed by *No, No, Nanette*, *The Great White Hope*, *How Now Dow Jones*, *The Green-Eyed People*, *The Play's the Thing*, and many OB productions, including *Life with Father*, *The Zoo Story*, *The Amorous Flea*, *The Giant's Dance*, *Call It Virtue* and *The Boy Friend*. He was probably best known for his adaptation of Bram Stoker's novel *Count Dracula*. There are no immediate survivors.

BILL VEHR, 48, Ohio-born actor, playwright and filmmaker, died Aug. 2, 1988 of AIDS in NYC. He was one of the original members of Charles Ludlam's Ridiculous Theatre Company, appearing in *Bluebeard*, *Eunuchs of the Forbidden City*, *Reverse Psychology*, *Stage Blood*, and *Camille* among others, and he wrote *Whores of Babylon* for the company. He periodically gave readings of James Joyce's *Finnegan's Wake*, and made several cult films. His parents and a sister survive.

MARTIN J. WALSH, 41, Massachusetts-born actor, died of AIDS on July 7, 1988 in NYC. He made his debut Off Bdwy in *The Lark* (1970) followed by *Interview with God*, followed by Broadway in *Shenandoah*, *Canterbury Tales* and *Pirates of Penzance*. Surviving are his father, three sisters and a brother.

DOUGLASS WATSON, 68, Georgia-born actor on stage, film and tv, died May 1, 1989 of a heart attack while vacationing in Arizona. He made his Broadway debut in *The Iceman Cometh* (1947), followed by *Antony and Cleopatra* (Theatre World Award), *Leading Lady*, *Richard III*, *The Happiest Years*, *That Lady*, *The Wisteria Trees*, *Romeo and Juliet*, *Desire under the Elms*, *Sunday Breakfast*, *Cyrano de Bergerac*, *Confidential Clerk*, *Portrait of a Lady*, *The Miser*, *The Young and Beautiful*, *Little Glass Clock*, *Country Wife*, *A Man for All Seasons*, *Chinese Prime Minister*, *Marat/Sade*, *The Prime of Miss Jean Brodie*, *Pirates of Penzance*, *Over Here*, *The Philadelphia Story*, OB in *Much Ado about Nothing*, *King Lear*, *As You Like It*, *Hunger*, *Dancing for the Kaiser*, *Money*, *My Life*, *Sightlines*, *Glorious Morning*, *Hamlet*. Since 1974 he had played Mackenzie Cory on the tv series *Another World*. His widow and three children survive.

ROBERT WEBBER, 64, California-born actor of stage, screen and tv, died May 17, 1989 of Lou Gehrig's disease in Malibu, Ca. After his Broadway debut in *Two Blind Mice* (1948) he was cast in *Goodbye My Fancy*, *The Royal Family*, *No Time for Sergeants*, *Teahouse of the August Moon*, *Orpheus Descending*, *Fair Game*, *A Loss of Roses*, and *Period of Adjustment*, before going to Hollywood and a successful career in films and tv. His wife and father survive.

JOAN WETMORE, 77, Australia-born actress, died Feb. 13, 1989 of cancer in her Manhattan home. She made her Broadway debut in *The Two Bouquets* (1938) followed by *Two on an Island*, *Kind Lady*, *Counsellor-at-Law*, *A New Life*, *The Two Mrs. Carrolls*, *For Keeps*, *Hope for the Best*, *The Small Hours*, *A Girl Can Tell*, *Advise and Consent*, *A Very Rich Woman* and *The Great Indoors*. She also appeared in several tv serials. Surviving are a son, and two step-sons.

NOEL WILLMAN, 70, Ireland-born actor-director, died Dec. 24, 1988 of a heart attack in NYC. He made his Broadway acting career debut in *Legend of Lovers* (1951) followed by *Rashomon*. He directed *A Man for All Seasons* (Tony Award), *The Beauty Part*, *A Lion in Winter*, *Darling of the Day*, *A Matter of Gravity* and *West Side Waltz*. His sister survives.

TREY WILSON, 40, Texas-born stage and film actor, died of a cerebral hemorrhage on Jan. 16, 1989 in NYC. After his Broadway debut in *Peter Pan*, he appeared in *Tintypes*, *The First*, *Foxfire*, and his OB credits include *Personals*, *Custom of the Country*, *The Front Page*, *Debutante Ball*. Surviving are his widow and stepson, his mother and stepfather. Burial was in Houston, Tx.

MAGGIE WORTH, 58, singer, actress, teacher, died Oct. 20, 1988 of a stroke in North Hollywood. Born in Cleveland, Oh., she had appeared on Broadway in *Shangri-la*, *A Time for Singing*, *Mr. President*, *My Fair Lady*, and *The Girl Who Came to Supper*. Her husband, actor Darrell Sandeen, and a son survive.

INDEX

A'Hearn, Patrick, 194
AIDS Alive, 48
Aaron, Caroline, 68, 194
Aaron, Jack, 15
Aaron, Jules, 131
Abady, Josephine R., 23, 136
Abaldo, Joseph, 50, 70
Abatemarco, Tony, 47, 194
Abbott, George, 27, 82
Abel, Marybeth, 40
Abel, Ron, 66
Abel, Timothy, 40, 44
Abele, Jim, 131, 165
Abell, G. Roger, 88
Aberger, Tom, 88
Abingdon Square, 176
Abraham, F. Murray, 86, 87, 194
Abrahams, Jody, 49, 194
Abrahamson, Nili, 99
Abrams, Herman, 53
Abroms, Rachel, 44
Absent Friends, 150
Abuba, Ernest, 98, 194
Abundance, 172
Abyssinia, 126
Acabbo, Andrew, 24
Accola, Georgia, 52
Acey, Barbara, 47
Ackerman, Jennifer, 67
Ackerman, Loni, 38, 194
Ackerman, Robert Allan, 20
Acting Company, The, 68
Acting Company, The, 68
Adamo, Stuart, 142
Adams, Betsy, 75, 143
Adams, Brooke, 30
Adams, Cindy, 33
Adams, David, 56
Adams, Dianne, 34
Adams, J. B., 42
Adams, Jason, 126
Adams, Kent, 60
Adams, Lucinda, 54
Adams, Philip, 110
Adams, Ruth, 51
Adams, Todd E., 55
Adamson, Ellen, 194
Aday, Gary, 128
Addison, Bernard, 168
Addison, Virginia, 62
Addison, Walter, 123
Adena, Alana, 60
Adkins, Angelo, 82
Adkins, Walter, 56
Adler, Candace Rogers, 44
Adler, Emily, 32
Adler, J. Peter, 103
Adler, Marion, 174
Adler, Morris, 53
Adler, Richard, 27
Adolphe, Bruce, 68
Adshead, Patricia, 53, 105, 165
Adzima, Nanzi, 179
Afrion, 47
Aftershocks, 153
Agee, Joel, 132
Agnir, Mirla Criste, 64, 112
Agnitsch, Jeffrey, 138
Agosto, Elli, 164
Agreement, The, 66
Aguilar, Michael, 59
Aguirre, Sergio, 122
Ah, Wilderness!, 7, 189
Ahearn, Daniel, 194
Ahlin, Margit, 56
Ahlstedt, Borje, 78
Ahronheim, Albert, 90
Aibel, Doug, 106
Aidem, Betsy, 71, 86, 107, 194
Ain't Misbehavin', 12
Ain't Nobody's Blues but Mine, 161
Ainsley, Paul, 115
Akalaitis, JoAnne, 77, 96, 147
Akerlind, Christopher, 144, 158, 184
Akers, Dane, 56
Akers, Karen, 194
Akesson, Hans, 78
Akimova, Natalya, 47
Alabado, Humberto, 46
Alan, Brett, 112
Albers, Kenneth, 161
Albert, Stephen J., 77, 134
Albino, Adrian, 176
Albrecht, J. Grant, 17
Albrezzi, Steven, 172, 178
Alchemist, The, 184
Alda, Alan, 192
Alden, Christopher, 94
Alder, Jac, 180
Alderfer, Julie, 103

Aldredge, Theoni V., 33, 37, 93, 162
Aldredge, Tom, 39, 194
Aldrich, Janet, 34, 194
Aldrich, Mark, 112
Aldridge, Amanda, 160
Aldridge, Leah, 130
Aleandri, Emelise, 194
Aleichem, Sholom, 53
Alenius, Paige, 51
Alessandrini, Gerard, 50, 83, 194
Alexander, Adinah, 90, 143
Alexander, Erika, 96
Alexander, George, 126
Alexander, Jace, 107, 194
Alexander, Jane, 9, 104, 192, 194
Alexander, Jason, 25, 194
Alexander, LeWan, 161
Alexander, Randolph, 82
Alexander, Terry, 154
Alexandrovs, The, 13
Alexis, Alvin, 91
Alfred Stieglitz Loves O'Keeffe, 121
Alger, Jay, 40
Algerian Romance, 59
Alive By Night, 64
All My Sons, 142, 186
All's Well That Ends Well, 99, 151, 174, 175
Allan, Joy, 174
Allan, Ted, 31, 85
Allart, Michael, 124
Allen, Cliff, 151
Allen, Gregory Lamont, 62
Allen, Joan, 4, 30, 100, 190, 191, 194
Allen, John, 38
Allen, Jonelle, 194
Allen, M. Lynne, 128
Allen, Malcolm, 60, 65
Allen, Mana, 90
Allen, Peter, 20, 194
Allen, Philip G., 135
Allen, Philip, 47
Allen, Ruth, 139
Allen, Sheila, 151
Allen, Shelia, 151
Allen, Suze, 169
Allen, Thomas Michael, 73
Allen-Jones, Augusta, 93
Allgeier, Keith D., 180
Allgeier, Keith, 180
Allgood, Anne, 70
Allison, Mary Ellen, 34, 125
Allison, Patti, 162
Allmand, Claudia-Jo, 54
Allosso, Michael, 160
Alloy, Andrew, 64
Alma, 46
Almodovar, Robert, 172
Almost Perfect, 81
Almquist, Gregg, 59, 194
Almy, Brooks, 27
Alonso, Judith, 47, 48
Alper, Jonathan, 88
Alper, Steve, 142
Alper, Steven M., 55
Alsaker, Timian, 156
Alspaugh, Jeffrey A., 126
Alston, Peggy, 91
Altman, Peter, 151
Alton, Bill, 19, 87
Altuner, James, 73
Alvarez, Abraham, 77
Alvarez, Lynne, 80
Alvarez, Michael, 172
Alvarez, Monserrate, 27
Alvey, Kevin, 82
Alward, John, 119
Amadeus, 122, 159
Amaro, Richard, 25
Amato, Iocco, 166
Amazing Grace, 152
Amberly, Liz, 83, 102, 194
Ambrosone, John, 160
Ameche, Don, 19, 194
Amen-Ra, Kamal A., 139
Amen-Ra, Shashu, 139
American Buffalo, 183
American Clock, 151
American Journey, An, 166, 167
American Parlor Songs of the 19th Century, 75
American Voices, 58
Amerling, Victor, 44
Ames, Paul V., 63, 109
Amico, Robert F., 47
Amirante, Robert, 38
Amodeo, Paul, 56
Amsden, Jeffrey, 133
Amulets Against The Dragon Forces, 79, 187

Anania, Michael, 29, 57, 162
Ananta, Michael, 27
Ancient History, 67
And What of the Night?, 161
And the Air Didn't Answer, 100
Anderman, Maureen, 148, 149
Anders, Ken, 102
Anders, Mark, 119
Andersen, Tobias, 168
Anderson, Christine, 70, 194
Anderson, Cletus, 165
Anderson, Cochise, 68
Anderson, D. C., 133
Anderson, Edmund, 66
Anderson, Eleanor, 54
Anderson, Eric Ray, 119
Anderson, Ethel, 56
Anderson, Eunice, 176
Anderson, Fred, 162
Anderson, Jean, 194
Anderson, Joel, 79, 194
Anderson, Keith, 127
Anderson, Kevin, 79, 194
Anderson, Peter, 78
Anderson, Robert L., 46
Anderson, Robert, 58
Anderson, Roger, 137
Anderson, Sam, 156
Anderson, Sarah Pia, 56
Anderson, Stanley, 126
Anderson, Stephen Lee, 138
Andersonville Trial, The, 159
Andonyadis, Nephelie, 184
Andreassi, James, 136, 154
Andreoli, Gina, 68
Andreozzi, Beverly J., 154
Andres, Barbara, 103, 176, 194
Anderson, Thomas, 148
Andrew, Mark, 82
Andrews, Brian, 38
Andrews, David, 67, 194
Andrews, Dwight D., 123, 132, 165
Andrews, Gary, 183
Andrews, George Lee, 44, 195
Andrews, Harry, 227
Andrews, Jennifer Lee, 105, 146
Andrews, Judy, 170
Andrews, Mark S., 40
Andrews, Tom, 47
Andrus, Dee, 139
Andruszko, Henryk, 47
Angelo, Nico, 48
Angermann, Christian, 168
Anggawi, Dudy, 47
Animal Crackers: The Marx Brothers Musical, 122
Aniston, Jennifer, 95
Anker, Warren, 93
Ankles Aweigh, 146
Annula, An Autobiography, 52
Another Antigone, 179
Anouilh, Jean, 108, 121
Anselmo, Andy Thomas, 64
Antalosky, Charles, 148, 149, 164, 166
Antaramian, Jacqueline, 138
Antekeier, Kristopher, 67
Anthony, James, 129, 182
Anthony-Jackson, Todd, 158
Antonik, Michael, 99
Antony and Cleopatra, 141
Antoon, A. J., 94
Anything Goes!, 45, 109, 186
Anzalone, Johnny, 38
Apart from George, 92
Apicella, John, 134
Aponte, Bruno, 101
Appel, Irwin, 148
Appel, Peter, 100, 184, 195
Apple Acting, 50
Applebaum, Louis, 174
Applegate, Fred, 170
Appolito, Anne, 23
Approaching Zanzibar, 104
Aquila, Deborah, 32
Aquilina, Corinne, 143
Aquino, Amy, 30, 184, 195
Aradottir, Frida, 15
Araiza, J. Ed, 119
Arak, Jonathan, 103
Aran, 62
Aranas, Raul, 98
Aranson, Jack, 151
Arbeit, Herman O., 110
Arcade, Penny, 58
Arcaro, Robert (a.k.a. Bob), 195
Arcaro, Robert, 58
Arcenas, Loy, 46, 79, 95, 143, 154, 161
Archer, Julie, 78

Archpriest Avvakum: The Life Written By Himself, 47
Arevalo, Carlos, 46
Argiro, Robert, 162
Ariadne Obnoxious, 55
Ariano, Alan, 41
Aridjis, Homero, 60
Arif, N. Richard, 93
Aristocrats, 88, 186
Arkin, Michael, 54
Arkus, Francesca Mantani, 56, 67
Arluck, Neal, 49, 58, 195
Armato, Amanda, 144
Armato, Dominic, 144
Armento, Tony, 29, 32
Armitage, Calvin Lennon, 103, 195
Armitage, Richard, 42
Arms and the Man, 103, 178
Armstrong, Bill, 61
Armstrong, Curtis, 182
Armstrong, Cynthia J., 164
Armstrong, Karen, 39, 94, 95, 100
Armstrong, Malcolm, 174
Armstrong, Reed, 115
Armstrong, Vaughn, 134
Armus, Sidney, 15, 195
Arnault, Andrew, 60
Arnold, Caroline, 62
Arnold, Jennifer, 107
Arnold, Madison, 110
Arnold, Oliver, 62
Arnold, Richard Mark, 102
Arnold, Victor, 54, 195
Arnone, Joseph, 59
Aronica, Joseph, 59
Aronson, Boris, 25
Aronson, Frances, 59, 61, 63, 76, 77, 80, 126, 148
Aronson, Henry, 34
Aronstein, Martin, 134
Arrambide, Mario, 86, 93, 195
Arrick, Larry, 75
Arrick, Rose, 15, 125
Arrigo, Nancy, 43
Arrington, Timothy, 121
Arrucci, John, 60
Arsenault, Brian, 151
Arthur Cantor Associates, 54
Artificial Intelligence, 73
Artigas, Michele, 138
As Is, 136
As You Like It, 67, 127, 141, 160
Asano, Kazuyuki, 78
Asbury, Claudia, 118
Asbury, Cleve, 42, 116, 118, 195
Aschinger, Brian, 53
Ash, Jeffrey, 59
Asher, David, 124
Asher, Peter, 8
Ashford, Robert, 45, 195
Ashley, Christopher, 46, 107
Ashley, Elizabeth, 192
Ashman, Howard, 142, 164
Asano, Kazuyuki, 78
Asse, Carlos F., 150
Astrachan, Joshua, 62
Astredo, Humbert, 169, 183
At Long Last Leo, 172
At the Chelsea, 58
Atherlay, John M., 52, 65
Atherton, Ted, 174
Atienza, Edward, 184
Atkins, Cholly, 22
Atkinson, Clinton J., 153
Atkinson, Don, 85
Atkinson, Jayne, 154
Atkinson, Tobin E., 127
Atlee, Howard, 60, 91
Auberjonois, Rene, 28, 195
Auder, Alexandra, 58
Augustine, John, 100, 195
Augustus, Nicholas, 83, 195
Aulani, 130
Aulino, Tom, 73, 87
Aulisi, Joseph G., 18, 25, 29, 110
Aumuller, Alycia, 125
Aural Fixation, 26, 52, 54, 57, 71, 81, 89, 104, 107
Austin, Beth, 146
Austin, Ivy, 66
Austin, Jeff, 130
Austin, Lyn, 59, 62
Austin, Patti, 12
Austin, Robert, 75
Austrian, Marjorie, 50, 53, 195
Autograph, 40
Auton, Philip, 140
Autumn Elegy, 120
Avan, 60

Avedisian, Paul, 53
Averyt, Bennet, 127
Avian, Bob, 37
Avidon, Nelson, 51, 195
Avioli, Judy, 53
Avni, Ran, 85
Avnsoe, Shannon Lee, 180
Avvakum, Archpriest, 47
Axelrod, Dana L., 134
Axtell, Barry, 70
Ayckbourn, Alan, 119, 123, 128, 131, 179, 180, 182
Aycock, Janet, 116, 144
Ayers, Ron, 139
Ayers, Stephen, 140
Ayres, Mary-Helen, 148
Ayvazian, Leslie, 46
Azarian, Arminae, 37
Azarian, Seda, 88
Azenberg, Emanuel, 12, 18, 25, 109, 110
Babbitt, Rob, 50
Babe, Thomas, 62, 156
Babes in Toyland, 130
Babilla, Assurbanipal, 61
Babin, Michael, 114
Babruch, Steven, 51
Bacall, Lauren, 33
Bachrach, David Arthur, 56, 195
Back in My Life, 63
Back in the World, 52
Backes, Roy W., 103
Backstrom, Kevin, 130
Backus, Richard, 51, 62, 195
Backward Anthology, 105
Bacon, Kevin, 86, 195
Badecker, George, 152
Baden, Michael, 59
Badolato, Bill, 162
Baehr, Sonya, 55, 65
Baffa-Brill, Diana, 142, 164
Baggott, Kate, 55, 68
Bagwell, Marsha, 138, 162
Bailey, Adrian, 20, 92
Bailey, Alan, 158
Bailey, Brian, 72
Bailey, Bruce R., 140
Bailey, Dawna, 123
Bailey, Jason, 78
Bailey, Kevin, 170
Bailey, Malinda, 121
Bailey, Victoria, 88
Baird, Campbell, 131
Baird, Mary, 131
Baird, Quin, 20, 195
Baitz, Jon Robin, 104, 134
Baitz, Rick, 104, 134
Baizley, Doris, 119
Baker, Allan J., 164
Baker, Allan, 184
Baker, August, 105
Baker, Beata, 73
Baker, Bertilla, 114
Baker, Bob, 136
Baker, David, 227
Baker, Denys, 90
Baker, Douglas C., 23
Baker, Dylan, 21, 93, 187, 190, 195
Baker, Henri Leon, 162
Baker, Jim, 138, 158
Baker, Jonathan, 86
Baker, Joseph, 85
Baker, Kelly, 183
Baker, Lance, 182
Baker, Mark, 137
Baker, Robert, 27, 60
Baker, Sallie, 138
Baker, Scott, 195
Baker, Susan, 179
Baker, Tom, 42
Baker, Walter, 136
Baker, Word, 69
Bako, Brigitte, 144
Bakuradze, Besik, 13
Balaban, Bob, 195
Balcanoff, Michael, 77
Baldaro, Barrie, 136
Baldassare, Helen, 70
Baldassare, Jim, 16, 53, 63, 64, 80, 90
Baldwin, Alec, 190, 191, 192
Baldwin, Brant, 118
Baldwin, Clive, 65
Baldwin, Patricia, 101
Baldwin, Philip, 51, 52, 58, 60
Balick, Bob, 137
Balint, Stephan, 58
Ball, Loni, 109
Ball, Lucille, 227
Ball, Tina J., 154
Ball, Wilber, 82
Ballagh, Robert, 86
Ballantyne, Wayne, 138
Ballard, Hilliard, 140

Ballard, Laurence, 119
Ballet Folklorico de La Fonda, 8
Balletta, Dominick, 98
Ballish, Jack, 161
Ballou, Kathryn, 105
Baltazar, Mark, 50
Bamford, George, 58, 132
Bamman, Gerry, 86, 120, 148, 195
Banes, Lisa, 18, 195
Banewicz, Antonia, 64
Bang, Paul, 55
Bannister, Sherri Sperling, 130
Bannow, Sally Jo, 152
Bansavage, Lisa, 56, 73, 195
Baptist, Sarah, 164
Baran, Edward, 105, 195
Baranski, Christine, 18, 195
Barbaree, Bruce, 74
Barbaro, Ciro, 65, 195
Barber, Ellen, 48, 195
Barber, Michael, 36
Barbieri, Peter, Jr., 49
Barbour, Thomas, 88, 132, 195
Barcelo, Randy, 12
Barclay, Shelley, 64, 89
Barclay, William, 79, 106
Barcone, Eugene, 123
Barecca, Christopher, 169
Barefield, Barbara, 139
Bargeron, Julie, 151
Barkentin, Marjorie, 57
Barker, Christine, 194, 195
Barker, Gary, 115
Barker, Margaret, 62, 195
Barkhimer, Steven, 102
Barkla, Jack, 147
Barkley, Lynnette, 83
Barle, Gail, 57
Barnes, Adilah, 123
Barnes, Billy, 66
Barnes, Djuna, 56
Barnes, Eric, 90
Barnes, Erza, 138
Barnes, Gregg, 50, 57, 59, 158
Barnes, William Joseph, 88
Barnes, Willie C., 41
Barneson, Jeff, 73
Barnett, Barbara, 67
Barnett, Bob, 60, 143
Barnett, Bronwen, 51
Barnett, Hugh, 86
Barnett, Judith, 53
Barnett, Patricia, 168
Barnette, M. Neema, 89
Barney, Frances, 184
Baron, Alan, 49
Baron, Carlos, 178
Baron, David, 60
Baron, Sheldon, 69
Barone, Meg, 148
Barone, Sal, 107
Barr, Richard, 227
Barr, Shannon, 24, 26, 62, 66, 72
Barranger, Milly S., 168
Barre, Gabriel, 34, 55, 103, 195
Barreca, Christopher, 81, 132, 148, 151
Barreiro, Oliver, 141
Barrett, Alson E., Jr., 125
Barrett, Brent, 162, 163
Barrett, Dule Hill Brent, 162
Barrett, James Lee, 162
Barrett, Joe, 170
Barrett, Laurinda, 106, 166, 195
Barrett, Marie, 40
Barrett, Michael, 19
Barrie, Barbara, 62
Barrie, J. M., 120
Barrie, James M., 25, 138
Barrile, Anthony, 134, 135
Barrish, Seth, 65
Barriskill, Michael, 38
Barron, David, 90, 108, 195
Barron, Holly, 121
Barron, Rob, 105
Barry Manilow at the Gershwin, 33
Barry, B. H., 35, 89, 93, 94, 95
Barry, Charles, 50
Barry, Kevin, 48, 61
Barsha, Debra, 73
Bart, Lenny, 67
Bart, Roger, 73
Bartenieff, George, 56, 67, 96, 195
Barteve, Reine, 67
Bartlett, Bridget, 140
Bartlett, Charles, 184
Bartlett, D'Jamin, 146
Bartlett, Kevin, 131
Bartlett, Peter, 146
Bartlett, Robin, 79, 195
Bartok, Jayce, 79, 194, 195
Barton, John, 144
Barton, Ken, 178
Barton, Steve, 44
Bartosik, Ed, 101
Bartuccio, Michael A., 24
Baruch, Steven, 62
Baryshnikov, Mikhail, 28, 195

Basch, Peter, 57, 195
Bashari, 92
Basil, John, 102
Basile, Frank, 54
Baskous, Christian, 148
Bassham, Cynthia, 123, 178
Bassi, Leo, 62
Bassin, Richard, 58
Bate, Dana, 61
Bates, David Richard, 176
Bates, Jerome Preston, 79, 195
Bates, Kathy, 134
Bateson, Kathy, 181
Batho, Kristofer, 62
Battaglia, Lynn, 79
Batten, Susan, 176
Batten, Tom, 146
Batting Practice, 54
Battis, Emery, 141
Battista, Lloyd, 59, 195
Battle, The, 184, 185
Battley, Wade, 48
Baudet, Christine, 54
Bauer, Beaver I., 123
Bauer, Beaver, 178
Bauer, Daniel Y., 158
Bauer, Pete, 150
Bauer, Richard, 126
Baughman, Mark, 161
Baum, Daniel, 105
Baum, Kathleen, 179
Baumgardner, Holly, 93
Baur, Beth, 170
Bawmann, Wendy, 138
Baxter, Carol Ann, 20, 195
Baxter, Cash, 108
Baxter, Ernest, 92
Baxter, Rebecca, 109, 162, 163
Bayer, Julie, 121
Baylor, Matt, 55
Bazewicz, James A., 83
Bazzell, John, 130
Bazzell, Larry, 97, 195
Beach, The, 184, 185
Beacon Project, The, 56
Beadles, Leslie-Noriko, 133
Beal, Charlie, 8
Beam, Alvin, 227
Beaman, Lee Anne, 183
Bean, Reathel, 158
Beard, Robert, 174
Beattie, Kurt, 119
Beatty, Bruce, 135
Beatty, John Lee, 12, 79, 88, 89, 144, 154, 176, 179
Beaulieu, Alexandre, 174
Beauty and the Beast, 122
Beaux' Stratagem, The, 176, 177
Beaver, Kathy, 72
Bechtel, Roger, 184
Becker, Peter, 93
Becker, Randy, 82
Becker, Royce M., 80
Becker, Victor, 122, 143, 161, 176, 179
Beckett, David, 102
Beckett, Samuel, 86, 138
Beckford, Ruth, 92
Beckler, Steven, 26, 109
Beckman, Claire, 131, 166, 167
Beckos, Barbara, 179
Beckwith, Spencer, 68, 170
Beckwith, Tobias, 43
Beckwith, William, 102
Becky Flora & Company, 58
Bedella, David, 144
Bedfull of Foreigners, A, 140
Bednarczyk, Patrick, 152
Beeching, Barbara, 143, 179
Beechman, Laurie, 40, 191, 195
Beehive, 123
Beers, Francine, 106, 195
Beery, Leigh, 162
Beggar's Opera, The, 137, 141
Behan, Brendan, 169
Behind the Heart, 56
Behn, Aphra, 144
Behr, Dana, 100
Behrman, S. N., 85
Beissel, Henry, 99
Beistle, Michael, 150
Belack, Doris, 97, 136, 196
Belcher, James, 121
Belden, Ursula, 50, 143
Belgrader, Andrei, 80, 184
Belgrave, Cynthia, 154
Belknap, Allen R., 121, 142, 164, 166
Bell, Barbara A., 99, 125
Bell, Bruce, 59
Bell, E. E., 130
Bell, Gail, 14, 50
Bell, Glynis, 170
Bell, Jan, 56, 68
Bell, Jennifer, 74
Bell, Neal, 62, 68, 105
Bell, Ralph, 58
Bella, Robert, 86
Bellamy, Brad, 57, 131
Bellamy, Ned, 134

Bellamy, Terry E., 81
Belli, Keith, 121
Bellin, Laura, 133
Belmonte, Vicki, 70, 196
Belo, Antonio, 42
Belton, Marcia, 95, 96
Beltran, Robert, 156
Beltz, Jessica K., 55
Ben-Ari, Neal, 75
Bence, Nomi, 151
Bender, Robert, 142
Benedict, Lisa, 168
Benedict, Paul, 59, 60, 134
Benefactors, 169, 178
Benham, Dorothy, 25, 196
Benham, Tamra, 138
Benic, Tom, 144
Benjamin, Elizabeth, 138
Benjamin, Karen, 133
Benjamin, P. J., 179
Benjamin, Randy, 75
Benjamin, Shell, 162
Benjamin, Susan, 97
Bennett, Cherie, 51
Bennett, Fran, 172
Bennett, Harry, 153
Bennett, Kenya V., 158
Bennett, Lynette, 83, 196
Bennett, Matthew Eaton, 69
Bennett, Michael, 37
Bennett, Robert, 11
Bennett, Sid, 160
Benninghofen, Mark, 147
Bennion, Alan, 92
Benoit, Barbara, 142
Benoit, Michael, 174
Benson, Cindy, 40, 196
Benson, Jodi, 32, 196
Benson, Martin, 172
Bensussen, Melia, 66
Benton, Robert, 43
Benyo, Laura, 66
Berc, Shelley, 80
Berdan, Judy L., 161
Berdes, Madelyn, 133
Berenger, Tom, 154
Berenice, 109
Berezin, Tanya, 79
Berg, Bobby, 46
Berg, Christopher, 94
Berg, Richard, 29
Berge, Collete, 105
Berger, Howard, 66
Berger, Stanley, 121
Bergman, Ingmar, 78
Berianidze, Rusudan, 13
Beris, David M., 53, 196
Berkal, Eric, 60
Berkeley, Edward, 51, 55
Berkoff, Steven, 28, 94
Berkowitz, Betty, 82, 83
Berkowitz, I. D., 53
Berkowsky, Paul B., 32
Berlin to Broadway with Kurt Weill, 127
Berlin, Irving, 25
Berlin, Lisa, 58
Berlin, Pamela, 71, 107, 183
Berlind, John, 67
Berlind, Roger, 12, 25, 66, 195
Berlinger, Robert, 136, 179
Berman, Donald, 55, 68, 105, 196
Berman, Irene B., 148
Berman, Jennifer, 169
Berman, Matt, 49, 57
Berman, Norman L., 79
Bermejo, Luz, 60
Bern, Mina, 53
Bernardi, James, 94
Bernardo, Keith, 63, 162
Bernev, Brig, 63, 67
Bernhard, Jim, 121
Bernstein, Douglas, 67, 196
Bernstein, Jesse, 95
Bernstein, Joel, 23
Bernstein, Leonard, 25, 108, 146, 151, 170
Bernstein, Lisa, 84
Bernstein, Mark D., 170
Bernstein, Michael, 44
Bernstein, Peter, 147
Bernstein, Vauna, 131
Berque, Barbara, 48, 61, 196
Berry, Charles Joseph, 59
Berry, Denny, 44
Berry, Eliza, 55
Berry, Gabriel, 80, 97, 176
Berry, Lena, 70
Berry, Linda, 42, 116
Berry, Patricia, 10, 50, 59
Bertish, Suzanne, 56, 196
Bertone, Maxine Krasowski, 126, 151
Berzon, Jeffrey, 80
Besch, Jenny, 21
Besser, Gedalia, 35, 53, 134
Besserer, Rob, 93, 95
Best Little Whorehouse in Texas, 129
Best, Cheridah, 144
Betancourt, Anne, 178
Bethel, Shari, 164
Betrayal, 160

Beverley, Trazana, 165
Bey, Kim, 126
Beyond a Reasonable Doubt, 162
Bezzola, Anna, 63
Biagi, Michael D., 117
Bianca, Robert, 176
Biancamano, Frank, 150
Bibb, Teri, 64
Bichsel, Reinhard, 78
Bickell, Ross, 153
Biderman, Karen, 53
Biechler, Merri, 73
Biederman, Richard, 60, 73
Biegler, Gloria, 16
Bielecki, Bob, 36, 56
Bierbower, Neil, 112
Bierko, Craig, 138
Big Frogs, 68
Big Time, 77
Big Time: Scenes from a Service Economy, 77
Big Winner, The, 53
Biggs, Annie, 180
Biggs, Casey, 126
Biggs, Roxann, 126
Bigham, Charlene, 121
Bikini Snow, 60
Bilgrave, Dyer, 132
Bill Evans & Associates, 12, 18, 110
Billgren, Jean, 78
Billib, Margit, 78
Billig, Etel, 152
Billig, Pamela Caren, 62
Billig, Robert, 40
Billig, Steve S., 152
Billington, Ken, 49, 88, 89, 162
Billman, Sekiya, 130
Billo, Peggy, 180
Billy Bishop Goes to War, 153
Biloxi Blues, 131
Bimson, Wanda, 57, 72
Binder, Jay, 18, 25, 103
Bingham, Jeffrey, 137
Binkowitz, Wendy, 46
Binks, Andrew, 174
Binotto, Paul, 105, 126
Birch, Patricia, 32, 68
Bircher, Betsy, 8
Bird, Thomas, 52
Birk, Raye, 77, 134
Birkelund, Olivia, 142, 147
Birkenhead, Peter, 169
Birkett, Larry Jean, 161
Birn, David, 184
Birnbaum, Nathan, 134, 135
Birnbaum, Paul, 47
Biro, Cathy, 60
Bishop, Andre, 100
Bishop, Conrad, 105
Bishop, Georg, 102
Bishop, John, 79, 152
Bishop, Kathleen, 102
Bishop, Kelly, 76, 196
Bishop, T. Jane, 122
Bissell, Richard, 24
Bitsko, Richard, 158
Bitter Friends, 85
Bittersuite: Songs of Experience, 152
Bittner, Clarke, 179
Bittner, Jack, 148
Bixler, Carol, 104
Bjornson, Maria, 44, 133
Bjostad, John, 63
Black and Blue, 22
Black, Cheryl, 49
Black, Colette, 57
Black, James, 121
Black, Tim, 140
Blackamoor, 71
Blackford, Evan, 148
Blackman, Jimmy, 59, 102
Blackman, Robert, 123, 134, 172
Blackmore, Jessica, 174
Blackwell, Charles, 25
Blackwell, Vera, 132
Blair, Al, 178
Blair, Pamela, 88, 196
Blair, Tom, 161
Blaisdell, Nesbitt, 75, 196
Blake, Colleen, 174
Blake, Mervyn, 174
Blake, Paul, 123
Blame It on the Movies! The Reel Music of Hollywood, 66
Blanco, Martin, 184
Bland, Steven, 46
Blank, Bill, 80
Blaska, Felix, 93
Blasky, Ann, 176
Blatt, Beth, 146
Blau, Eric, 128
Blaxill, Peter, 83, 196
Blazer, Judith, 42, 196
Blazer, Judy, 42
Blecher, Hilary, 61
Blechler, Merri, 68
Blendick, James, 174
Blendick, Mary Hitch, 174
Blessing, Lee, 89, 143, 150, 169, 176, 183, 184
Blessing, The, 76

Blithe Spirit, 160
Blitzstein Project, The, 105
Blitzstein, Marc, 105
Bloch, Scotty, 59, 148, 196
Block, Dick, 158
Block, Larry, 57, 89, 96, 196
Block, Leslie, 57
Blodgette, Kristen, 44
Blommaert, Susan, 79
Blomquist, Matthew, 46
Blondeau-Russell, Betty, 122
Blood Issue, 120
Blood, Wayne, 63
Bloodgood, William, 121
Bloom, Brendan, 184
Bloom, Melinda P., 72
Bloom, Michael, 107, 154
Bloom, Sandra M., 101
Blough, Tim, 133
Blu, 46
Blue Plate Special, 150
Blue, Pete, 50
Bluebird of Happiness, The, 125
Blues in the Night, 50
Bluestein, Markus, 170
Blum, Harry, 59
Blum, Joel, 122
Blum, Mark, 100, 196
Blume, Robert R., 60, 65
Blume, Susan, 100
Blumenfeld, Robert, 196
Blumenkrantz, Jeff, 39
Blumenthal, Hilarie, 82
Bluth, Toby, 130
Boak, Michael, 48, 62
Bob's Guns, 54
Bobbie, Walter, 15, 45, 196
Bobrick, Jeanne, 140
Bobrick, Sam, 140, 182
Bock, Cynthia, 56
Bock, Jerry, 25, 65, 82
Bocon!, 135
Bodge, James, 151
Bodin, Philippe, 184
Bode, Jane, 196
Bodtke, Shirley, 153
Boese, Jody, 79
Bogardus, Stephen, 40, 94, 196
Bogart, Anne, 124
Bogazianos, Vasili, 136
Boggs, Jennifer E., 99
Bogosian, Eric, 150, 196, 199
Bogue, Betty Lee, 160
Bogyo, Peter, 34
Bohmer, Ron, 158, 162
Bohne, Bruce, 147
Bohr, Jimmy, 60, 68
Bohus, Eric, 129
Boiler Room, The, 100
Bojarski, Stanley, 116
Bokar, Hal, 47, 48
Bolang, Anders, 137
Bolger, Paul, 49
Bollinger, Tom, 46
Bolt, Jonathan, 120
Bolton, Clifton, 169
Bolton, Guy, 45, 63, 83, 109, 146
Bond, Christopher, 54, 108, 118
Bond, Cynthia, 91
Bond, Miranda Kablach, 144
Bond, Stephanie, 60
Bonds, Rufus, Jr., 96
Bone-the-Fish, 120
Boneau, Chris, 11, 14, 16, 24, 26, 39, 49, 50, 51, 52, 53, 54, 58, 59, 65, 66, 72, 103
Bones, Pamela Gray, 121
Bonnani, John, 33
Bonnard, Raymond, 176
Bonnell, Mary Lynn, 159
Boockvor, Steven, 196
Booker, Charlotte, 23, 196
Booker, Margaret, 98
Bookman, Kirk, 57, 108, 143, 165
Bookwalter, D. Martyn, 134
Boone, Debby, 33
Boone, Fontella, 57, 92
Boone, Libby, 178
Boone, Michael Kelly, 165
Booth, Lisa, 64
Booth, Randy, 113, 133
Booth, Richard, 54
Boothby, Victoria, 196
Boothe, Fred, 22
Bopha!, 156
Bordo, Edwin, 85, 196
Borenstein, Daryl, 90
Bormann, Ruth, 109
Born Yesterday, 23, 136, 158
Bornstein, Daryl, 14
Bornstein, David L., 60
Bornstein, Rocky, 46
Bornstein, Stephen L., 82
Borod, Bob, 41
Borow, Rena Berkowicz, 95
Borrego, Jesse, 77, 96, 147
Borrirra, Ron, 84
Borromeo, Venustiano, 51
Borstelmann, Jim, 27
Boruzescu, Miruna, 147
Boruzescu, Radu, 147

Bosakowski, Phil, 65
Boscardi, Bea, 48
Bosco, Philip, 17, 26, 62, 196
Bosies, Janel, 132
Boslet, Jack, 127
Bosley, James, 52
Bosley, Tom, 130
Bossone, Vincent, 48
Bostic, Kysia, 180
Bostick, Maria, 90
Boswell, William, 139
Bosworth, Robert, 174
Botchis, Paul, 70
Botsford, Sara, 72, 184, 185
Bottitta, Ron, 84, 94
Bottoms, John, 147
Boublil, Alain, 40
Bouchard, Bruce, 131
Bouchard, Suzanne, 119
Boucher, Gloria, 53, 128, 196
Boucher, Mary, 166
Boucher, Savannah Smith, 134
Boudrot, Mel, 108
Bougere, Teagle F., 94, 96
Bourbiel, Kay, 46, 67
Bourgeois, John, 72
Bourneuf, Stephen, 20, 37, 196, 199
Boussom, Ron, 172
Boutique Living & Disposable Icons, 98
Bouton, Ted, 153
Bouvier, Jacqueline, 160
Bova, Joseph, 196
Bovasso, Julie, 196
Bove, Elizabeth, 147
Bove, Mark, 142, 196
Bovver Boys, 136
Bowden, Jack, 103
Bowden, Jonny, 54
Bowden, Richard, 56, 128, 132, 196
Bowen, Angela, 49
Bowen, Ethan T., 93, 94, 96
Bowers, Frank, 50
Bowers-Rheay, Kim, 122
Bowidas, Gaye, 64
Bowie, Pat, 144
Bowie, Sandra, 126
Bowman, Regis, 59, 64, 82, 196
Bowne, Alan, 52
Boy Friend, The, 176
Boy Meets Girl, 68, 170
Boyd, Christopher, 53
Boyd, Julianne, 61
Boyd, Julie, 147, 196
Boyd, Leila, 76
Boyd, Pom, 84
Boyd, Robert, 78
Boyer, Mary, 48
Boyette, Larry, 87
Boyle, Consolata, 10
Boyle, Michael Francis, 64, 65
Boyle, Robert Ott, 196, 227
Boyle, Wickham, 56, 86
Boylen, Daniel P., 166
Boys Next Door, The, 127, 136, 166, 167
Boys, Barry, 151
Boys, Kenneth, 90
Bozdin, Wendy, 51
Bozzone, Bill, 57
Bracken, Eddie, 162
Bradbury, Peter, 137
Bradbury, Stephen, 53, 179
Braden, Bill, 17
Braden, John, 125
Bradford, Don, 82
Bradish, Barbara, 65
Bradley, Carol, 58, 196
Bradley, Sarah Joem, 126
Bradley, Scott, 123, 169
Bradshaw, Barbara, 140
Bradshaw, Deborah, 114
Bradshaw, Peter, 164
Brady, Atticus, 19, 86, 196
Brady, Sharon, 97
Brady, Veronica, 164
Brady-Garvin, Kathy, 138
Braet, James, 152
Bragg, Melvyn, 53
Brainerd, Kevin, 58, 83
Bral, Grzegorz, 47
Bralley, Russ, 128
Braman, Risa, 46
Bramble, Mark, 85, 129
Brancato, Joe, 66
Branch, Susan, 65
Brand, David, 146
Brand, Gibby, 18
Brand, Oscar, 75
Brandenberg, Jon E., 36
Brandenburg, Larry, 194
Brandner, Gerhart, 64
Brandon, Leah, 109
Brandt, James, 20, 196
Brandt, John, 130
Brandt, Max, 102
Branescu, Smaranda, 126
Brannick, Kevin, 95
Branom, Mark W., 119
Bransdorf, John, 64
Brant, Kathleen, 68
Brasch, Thomas, 97
Brassard, Gail, 153, 164, 166

Brassea, Bill, 42
Brassington, Don, 19, 45
Braugher, Andre K., 94
Braugher, Andre, 93, 94
Braun, Joshua, 94
Brauner, Deon I., 68
Bravo, Anthony, 144
Braxton, Brenda, 20
Brazda, David, 196
Breaking the Code, 136
Breaking the Silence, 169
Breaks, Richard L., 112
Breault, Michael, 136
Brechner, Stanley, 75
Breitbarth, David, 164
Brenan, Billie, 102
Brener, Joseph, 182
Brenn, Janni, 135
Brennan, James, 42, 116, 196
Brennan, Jill, 121
Brennan, Nancy, 184
Brennan, Nora, 196, 199
Brennan, Stephen Vincent, 57
Brennan, Tom, 9, 19, 196
Brenner, William, 138
Brent Peek Productions, 50
Brentano, Amy, 46
Brenton, Howard, 147
Brenton, Jack, 122
Bretl, Jeff, 55
Breuer, Lee, 78
Breul, Eva, 162
Brewer, Sharon, 122
Brewster, Henry, 161
Brewster, Josh, 176
Brewster, Karen, 128
Breyer, Chris, 76
Brichetto, Gary, 144
Brickley, Kate, 123, 178
Bridge, Andrew, 44, 133
Bridges, Mark, 43
Brielle, Jonathan, 79
Briggs, Bunny, 22
Briggs, David, 62, 115
Briggs, Jody, 119
Briggs, John, 161
Briggs, Robert, 53
Bright, Daniel, 172
Brightman, Lucie, 126
Brightman, Sarah, 44
Brightness Falling, 61
Brigleb, John, 18
Brill, Fran, 196
Brilliant Traces, 79, 187
Brimm, Thomas Martell, 143, 158
Brimmer, David, 48
Brimstone and Treacle, 63
Brin, Charles, 147
Brinkley, Bonnie, 75
Brinkley, David, 147
Brisky, Norman, 47
Brisson, Bruce, 138
Brizzi, Lori, 64
Broaddus, John-Eric, 50
Broadhurst, Jeffrey Lee, 25
Broadhurst, Kent, 107, 196
Broadway Bound, 110, 150, 162, 164
Broadway Jukebox, 125
Brock, Lee, 65
Brockington, Paulette, 139
Brocklin, Jeffrey, 143
Brockman, Kevin, 13, 16, 50, 53, 55, 59, 61, 62, 64, 66, 68, 80, 90, 118
Broda, Alison Lani, 46
Brode, David, 39
Broderick, Matthew, 192
Brodkin, Bridgett, 33
Brody, Jonathan, 196
Brogger, Ivar, 81, 196
Brogyanyl, Eugene, 62
Brohn, William D., 25
Brokaw, Mark, 104
Bromelmeier, Martha, 63, 82
Bromley, Tarquin Jay, 99
Brookes, Jacqueline, 197
Brookes, Jayne, 50
Brooking, Simon, 49, 60, 159, 169
Brooks Company, 136
Brooks, Adam J., 121
Brooks, Avery, 14, 49, 197
Brooks, Bryan, 78
Brooks, Colette, 132
Brooks, Donald, 108
Brooks, Eva C., 14, 49
Brooks, Hewitt, 83
Brooks, Jeff, 26, 197
Brooks, Jeremy, 168
Brooks, Melody, 56
Broom, Sharon, 168
Broome, John, 174
Brosius, Peter C., 134, 135
Brosnan, Tim, 140
Brothers, Carla, 91
Brousseau, James, 39, 133
Brown, Amelda, 92
Brown, Anthony M., 62
Brown, Arthur B., 50
Brown, Arvin, 7, 154
Brown, Bess, 168

Brown, Bev, 78
Brown, Bille, 96
Brown, Buck, 74
Brown, Charles, 18
Brown, Chuck, 73, 197
Brown, Claudia, 62, 97, 148
Brown, Dave, 182
Brown, David, 174
Brown, Dawn Vanessa, 99
Brown, FT., 132
Brown, Frank, 48
Brown, Geoffrey, 69
Brown, Georgia, 197
Brown, Gordon W., 107
Brown, Graham, 91, 95, 197
Brown, Jamie, 127, 137, 158
Brown, Jeffrey S., 96
Brown, Jennifer, 197
Brown, Joanna, 102
Brown, Judy, 137
Brown, Ken, 82
Brown, Leon Addison, 126, 136
Brown, Lewis, 174
Brown, Lynn, 122
Brown, Mark, 158
Brown, Nikki, 125
Brown, P. L., 162, 163
Brown, Pat, 127
Brown, Paul, 86, 136
Brown, Peter Carlton, 95
Brown, Ralph, 22
Brown, Robin Leslie, 99, 197
Brown, Roo, 146
Brown, Roy, 174
Brown, Ruth, 22, 197
Brown, Tally, 227
Brown, Tenor, 44
Brown, Tom, 83
Brown, Vanessa, 33
Brown, Velina, 123
Brown, William Scott, 44, 197
Brown, William, 133
Brown, Zack, 9, 17, 126
Brown-Orleans, James, 126
Browne, Maggie, 98
Browne, Roscoe Lee, 123
Browning, Dolph, 64
Browning, Elizabeth, 53
Browning, Susan, 137
Browning, William, 161
Brownlee, Dani, 116
Brownstone, Diana, 138
Brubach, Robert, 227
Bruce, Andrew, 40
Bruce, Susan, 15
Bruice, Ann, 134
Brulatour, Pierre, 46, 62
Brundage, Gene, 133
Brune, David, 60, 80
Bruneau, Ainslie G., 127
Bruner, Glenn, 136
Brunetti, David, 50
Brunner, Kevin, 83, 197, 199
Brunner, Michael, 146
Bruns, Jean, 136
Brustein, Robert, 77, 124
Brutsman, Laura, 50, 81, 197
Bryan-Brown, Adrian, 11, 14, 16, 24, 26, 39, 54, 65, 66, 72, 103
Bryant, Adam, 55, 197
Bryant, Craig, 197
Bryant, David, 197
Bryant, Mary, 51, 86
Brycon, Robert, 85
Brydon, W. B., 84
Bryggman, Larry, 60, 94, 197
Bryne, Barbara, 39, 197, 199
Buberl, Doris J., 43
Bubriski, Peter, 160
Bucci, Jeanne, 103
Buccos, Daniel, 174
Buch, Rene, 76
Buchanan, Linda, 144
Buchman, Nanrose, 119
Buck, John, Jr., 161
Buckley, Betty, 38
Buckley, Ralph, 51
Buckley, Richard, 103
Buckley, Robert A., 22
Budde, Jordan, 121
Buddeke, Kate, 144
Budin, Rachel, 101, 143
Budries, David, 59, 86, 148, 184
Budzyna, John F., 102
Buell, Bill, 32, 32, 90, 197
Buelow, Dan, 162
Buff, Jim, 143
Buffalo, Becke, 97
Buffaloe, Katharine, 44
Bug, The, 120
Bugbee, Charles, III, 50
Buggy, Niall, 88
Bullard, Thomas, 121
Bullock, Donna, 116
Bulos, Yusef, 55, 103, 197
Bumbaugh, Melissa, 182
Bundy, Laura, 102
Bunn, Sharon, 180
Bunnybear, 96
Bunster, Carmen, 93
Buono, Cara, 60
Buras, Milton, 8

Burbach, Matthew, 158
Burbridge, Edward, 11
Burch, Bryan, 71
Burch, Shelly, 162
Burch, Thayer Q., 90
Burciullo, Mike, 178
Burdick, Melissa L., 51
Burdick, Riette, 138
Burdui, Meghan, 65
Burdy, Megan, 81
Burgan, Eric, 112
Burge, Gregg, 118
Burgess, Granville, 64
Burgess, Jewel, 165
Burgler, Terry, 181
Burk, Terence, 197
Burke, Brendan, 170, 171, 179
Burke, James, 57
Burke, Maggie, 15, 104, 197
Burke, Marylouise, 154
Burke, Sean, 86
Burkholder, Scott, 172
Burmeister, Leo, 40
Burmester, Leo, 86
Burnett, Carol, 33
Burnett, Robert, 38, 197
Burnham, Jacqueline, 6, 47
Burning Beach, A, 76
Burning Patience, 161, 178
Burns, Donna Lynn, 64
Burns, Gail, 148
Burns, Ron, 67
Burr, Cherly, 162
Burrell, Fred, 197
Burrell, Pamela, 179
Burrell, Teresa, 39
Burrows, Allyn, 160
Burrus, Bob, 120
Burse-Mickelbury, Denise, 80
Burson, Linda, 51, 65
Burstyn, Ellen, 24, 111, 197
Burt, John, 34
Burton, Barbara, 127
Burton, Irving, 31, 85, 197
Burton, Kate, 86, 197
Burton, Laura, 136, 174
Burton, Miriam, 85
Burton, Nefertiti, 151
Burton, Orisanmi, 151
Burton, Ronald, 78
Burton, W. C. "Mutt", 140
Burtt, T. C., Jr., 55
Busby, Barbara, 139
Busch, Bill, 144
Busch, Charles, 73, 107, 146, 197
Buschmann, Don, 179
Bush, Michael, 88
Bush, Phillip, 56
Busheme, Joe, 25
Busheme, Joseph, 45
Bushnell, Bill, 156
Bushor, Geoffrey, 144
Busia, Akosua, 89
Bussanich, Rachele, 38
Bustad, Sherri, 147
Bustle, Jonathan, 142, 164
Buterbaugh, Keith, 44
Butler, Austin, 102
Butler, Can, 86, 89, 93, 97, 107
Butler, David, 90, 165
Butler, Dean, 39, 197
Butler, Frank, 77, 124
Butler, Gregory, 162
Butler, Joseph, 137
Butler, Leslie, 18
Butler, Paul Lindsay, 56
Butler, Paul, 144
Butler, Ron, 126
Butler, Sam, Jr., 78
Butleroff, Helen, 85
Butrick, Merritt, 156, 157
Butt, Jennifer, 40, 197
Butterfield, Catherine, 165
Butterfield, Richard, 123
Button, Jeanne, 67, 104
Butts-Bhanji, Naomi, 178
Butz, Norbert L., 170
Buxbaum, Lisa, 15
Buxton, Bill, 86
Buzas, Jason McConnell, 57, 67
Byerly, Cleon, 14
Byers, Bill, 37
Byers, Catherine, 197
Byers, John, 112
Bynum, Brenda, 122
Byram, Cassandra, 130
Byrd, Debra, 33
Byrne, David, 78
Byrne, Terry, 61
Byrnes, Bonni-Faith, 82
Byron, John, 83, 197
Byron-Kirk, Keith, 144
C. H. Associates, 152
Caballero, Christophe, 25
Cabaniss, Thomas, 169
Cabrujas, Jose Ignacio, 135
Caccomo, Bob, 60
Caddick, David, 38, 44, 133
Cade, Mark Daniel, 123
Cadeau, Lally, 72
Cadenhead, James G., 183

Cadora, Eric, 73
Cady, David, 54
Cafe Crown, 15
Cahan, Cora, 77
Cahan, Marla, 49
Cahill, Sally, 174
Cahn, Larry, 45, 197
Cahn, Sammy, 25
Cain, Bill, 134
Cain, Candice, 183
Cain, William, 6, 7, 96, 142, 197
Caird, John, 40
Caitlyn, Deryl, 86, 94
Calabrese, Maria, 146
Calder, John, 147
Calderon, Alfredo, 135
Calderwood, Michael, 49
Caldwell, Charles, 181
Caldwell, George, 74
Caldwell, Lauren, 150
Caldwell, Matthew, 99
Caldwell, Steve, 74
Cale, Bennett, 34
Caleffi, Fabrizio, 48
Calkins, Michael, 55, 197
Call, Anthony, 153
Call, Ivonne, 76
Callaghan, Edward, 6, 47
Callahan, Linda, 77
Callahan, Steve, 118
Callahan, Steven C., 19, 45, 86
Callen, Chris, 26, 130, 197
Callender, L. Peter, 126
Callner, Jan, 49
Callow, Simon, 24, 197
Calloway, Brian, 84, 197
Calman, Camille, 55, 88
Calud, Annette, 144
Calvin Trillin's Uncle Sam, 76
Camacho, Blanca, 197
Cambus, George, 48
Camelot, 181
Camera, John, 108, 143, 151, 197
Cameron, Faye, 110
Cameron, John, 40
Cameron, Kay, 162
Cameron-Webb, Gavin, 164
Camp, Joanne, 30, 99, 100, 197
Camp, Judson, 61
Camp, Karma, 126
Campana, Joyce, 27
Campanella, Christina, 49
Campanella, Philip, 103
Campbell, Amelia, 52, 103, 197
Campbell, Bruce, 45, 52, 86
Campbell, Craig, 184
Campbell, Donna, 52
Campbell, Douglas, 174
Campbell, Gerald, 50
Campbell, Janice F., 56
Campbell, Mark, 73
Campbell, Mary Schmidt, 93
Campbell, Mrs. Patrick, 128
Campbell, Pamela, 179
Campbell, Peter V., 137
Campbell, Ron, 134
Campbell, Sally, 19, 50
Campbell, Stancil, 136
Campbell, Toi, 122
Campbell, Yvonne, 53
Campese, Renato, 48
Campisi, Tony, 166, 197
Canaan Communications, 48
Canac-Marquis, Normand, 105
Canaday, Melissa, 120
Canary, Evan, 94
Canary, Tom, 58
Canciones de Mi Padre, 8
Candela, Peter, 66
Candide, 151, 170
Cane, Marianne, 39
Cannan, Edward, 104, 197
Cannon, Rick, 127
Canon, Joanie, 52, 65
Canter, Nina, 65
Cantier, Anne M., 52
Cantier, W. D., 52, 60
Cantorial, 85
Cantrell, Monica, 129
Cantrell, Roger, 133
Capenos, James, 165
Capitola, Jeff, 68
Capo, Laurence, 158
Caposaro, Rudy, 63
Capote, Truman, 135, 136
Cappelli, Joe, 133
Cappiello, Chris, 49
Capps, Thomas S., 109
Capron, Anne, 63
Captains Courageous, 105
Caraccioli, John, 125
Carballido, Emilio, 101
Carden, Laura, 108
Cardwell, Jay, 70
Care and Feeding of the Young, The, 105
Carell, Candace, 38
Carey, Darrell, 88, 162
Carey, Helen, 126
Carey, Kathy, 33
Carey, Robert, 73, 107, 197

Carey, Terrence, 130
Carfagno, Randy, 78
Cariello, Thomas, 103
Carillo, Ramiro, 87, 144
Cariou, Len, 86, 197
Carley, Kurt, 142, 164
Carlin, Amanda, 30, 197
Carlin, Joy, 123
Carlin, Nancy, 123
Carlin, Tony, 30, 142
Carlin-Bartel, Diane, 161
Carlisle, Steve, 140
Carlisle, Ward, 130
Carlo, Ismael East, 172
Carlos, Aaron, 168
Carlow, Richard, 53
Carlsen, Allan, 143
Carlson, Ann, 58
Carlson, Katherine, 128
Carlson, Sandra, 39
Carlson, Sharon, 152
Carlton, David, 122
Carmello, Carolee, 114
Carnahan, Kirsti, 114
Carnahert, Elisa, 83
Carnival, 136, 182
Carousel, 138
Carpenter, Cassandra, 178
Carpenter, Gordon, 119
Carpenter, John, 166
Carpenter, Karen L., 144, 151
Carpenter, Larry, 34, 122, 142, 151, 160
Carpenter, Terry W., 159
Carr, David, 73
Carr, Elizabeth Katherine, 73, 107
Carr, Judy Sabrina, 64
Carr, Monica, 122, 146
Carr, Rona, 52
Carr-Osley, Marjie, 170
Carradine, John, 227
Carrafa, John, 83
Carrellas, Barbara, 6, 47
Carricart, Robertson, 164
Carrick, Chris, 84
Carriere, Berthold, 174
Carrillo, Eduardo, 60
Carrillo, Ramiro, 87
Carroll, Barbara, 93
Carroll, Beeson, 154
Carroll, Danny, 197
Carroll, David, 15, 197
Carroll, Eddie, 65
Carroll, James R., 170
Carroll, Leslie, 68, 102
Carroll, Marjorie, 121
Carroll, Rocky, 144
Carroll, Ronn, 95
Carroll, Tom, 49, 52, 58, 61, 97
Carruthers, Mike, 112
Carryer, Tim, 87
Carson, Heather, 55
Carson, Susan Dawn, 40
Carson, Thomas, 67, 143, 197
Carter, Christopher, 128
Carter, Dan, 43, 64
Carter, Dixie, 192
Carter, Nell, 12
Carter, Paul M., 85
Carter, Paul, 60
Carter, Ralph, 191
Carter, Rosanna, 52, 91, 154, 198
Cartier, Jacques, 151
Cartlidge, Katrin, 92
Cartmell, Leah, 56
Cartwright, Jim, 86
Cartwright, Mindy, 25
Caruso, Barbara, 162
Caruso, Dana Lynn, 115
Caruso, Joseph George, 74
Carver, Mary, 135
Cary, Claiborne, 55
Cary, Jim, 132
Cary, Meghan, 127
Carzasty, Peter B., 78
Cascio, Anna Theresa, 60
Case, Evelyn Carol, 164
Casey, Warren, 227
Casidine, Ron, 64, 82
Caskey, Marilyn, 44
Casnoff, Philip, 17, 68, 184, 190, 191, 198
Casperson, Jack, 138
Cassaro, Nancy, 73
Cassation, 56
Casserly, Kerry, 198
Cassidy, Tim, 198
Casson, Ann, 174
Castang, Veronica, 227, 228
Castellano, Richard, 227, 228
Castellanos, John, 133, 135
Castelli, Victor, 25
Castells, Catalina, 49
Castillo, Arturo, 166
Castillo, E. J., 156
Castillo, Miguel Lopez, 56
Castle, Diana, 54, 198
Castleman, Margie, 90
Castleman, William, 54, 65
Castleton, Eric, 178
Casto, Jacqui, 91, 92
Castro, Pepi, 105
Castro, Vicente, 101
Caswell, Lexi, 183
Cat on a Hot Tin Roof, 138
Catanese, Charles, 54
Catch Me If You Can, 182
Cates, Phoebe, 93, 144
Catfish Loves Anna, 60
Catherall, Kristin, 127
Cathey, Reg E., 52, 104
Catlett, Leigh, 116
Caton, Karen, 30
Catricala, Arthur, 98, 161
Cats, 38
Cattaneo, Anne, 104
Catti, Christine, 83, 103
Caufield, James, 31
Cava, Frank, 20, 126
Cavallo, Frank, 143
Cavanaugh, Katy, 146
Cavargna, Barbara, 22
Cave, Lisa Dawn, 38
Cavett, Dick, 33, 39
Cavey, George, 153
Cavise, Joe Antony, 198
Cawley, Cathy Lee, 70
Caza, Terrence, 148, 151, 168
Cea, Kim, 54, 198
Cea, Patrick, 94
Ceballos, Arturo, 8
Cella, Susan, 42, 116
Cellario, Maria, 49, 198
Cemetery Club, The, 136
Cerasini, Jeanne, 161
Cermak, Terry, 181
Cernovitch, Nick, 151
Cerullo, Jonathan, 20, 83, 198
Cerveris, Michael, 144
Cesaretti, Anthony, 144
Cezanne Syndrome, The, 105
Chaban, Michael, 141
Chadman, Christopher, 14, 136
Chadwick, Robin, 131, 160
Chaffin, Philip, 130
Chaiken, Joel, 86
Chaiken, Stephen, 27
Chain, Leslie, 158
Chalfant, Kathleen, 97, 107, 148, 149, 198
Challee, William, 227
Chamberlain, Douglas, 174
Chamberlin, Kevin, 158
Chambers, David, 184
Chambers, Michael, 93, 95
Chambers, Renee, 65
Chamow, Marian, 58
Champagne, Michael, 152
Chan, Don, 56
Chan, Eric Y. L., 45
Chance, William, 169
Chandler, Nat, 142, 151
Chandler, Terry, 92
Chaney, Lon, 22
Chang, Duyee, 98
Chang, Tisa, 98
Changar, Murray, 62
Chanin, L. B., 47
Channing, Carol, 190, 192
Channing, Stockard, 62
Chao, Rosalind, 77
Chapin, Ed, 160
Chapin, Wendy, 86
Chapman, David W., 68
Chapman, Dianne-Finn, 60
Chapman, Karen, 103, 198, 199
Chapman, Ray, 144
Chappell, Kandis, 18, 172, 198, 199
Charity, 55
Charlap, Moose, 25
Charles, Cynthia, 137
Charles, Josh, 154
Charles, Keith, 90
Charles, Valerie, 105
Charles, Walter, 116, 162, 163
Charlie, 139
Charlie/Enchanted Night/Out at Sea, 139
Charlton, T. C., 34
Charney, Tina, 143, 176, 179
Charnin, Martin, 15, 63, 66
Charnin, Randy, 51
Chase, Jennifer, 158
Chase, Mary, 120, 153
Chasse, Maurice, 144
Chastain, Don, 46
Chastitute, The, 161
Chauvin, Jacqueline, 133
Chavanne, Brian, 105, 107
Chavez, Christine, 130
Chavez, David, 130
Cheadle, Don, 96, 147
Cheatham, Jamie, 48, 61
Checkmates, 11
Cheecchi, Robert, 72
Cheek, Jean, 74
Chekhov, Anton, 64, 65, 98, 124, 156
Chell, Christopher Ross, 170
Chelsea, Benjamin, 67
Chelton, Nick, 24
Chen, Kitty Mei-Mei, 98
Chenier, Leon B., Jr., 113
Chepulis, Kyle, 63
Cheri, 67
Cherry, Eagle-Eye, 68
Cherry, John T., 91
Chervinsky, Alexander, 148
Chesney, Leon, 36
Chesnutt, Judy, 128
Chesshire, Victoria Lanman, 54
Chester, Nora, 121, 179
Chew, Timothy M., 128
Chibas, Marissa, 120, 126
Chibbaro, John, 54
Chickering, Victoria, 93
Chicoine, Susan, 23, 29, 32, 50, 75, 81, 116, 117
Chihara, Paul, 118
Chiklis, Michael, 160
Child of Luck, 138
Child's Christmas in Wales, A, 168
Childress, Alice, 161
Childs, Casey, 54, 59, 67
Childs, Shelia, 132
Chin, Michael G., 98
Chinn, Kevin, 37
Chinn, Lori Tan, 41, 198
Chioran, Juan, 174
Chirgotis, Candice, 148
Chisholm, Anthony, 52
Chism, Glenda, 140
Chmelko-Jaffe, Mary, 159
Chmiel, Mark, 45
Cho, Irene, 25, 44, 133
Chodorov, Edward, 227
Chodorov, Jerome, 146
Cholet, Blanche, 63
Chong, Marcus, 134, 135
Chong, Ping, 98, 161
Chorus Line, A, 37
Chorus of Disapproval, A, 119, 126
Chow, Jovita, 123
Chowning, Blakeley, 160
Chris, Marilyn, 85, 153
Christakos, Jerry, 115, 146
Christen, Robert, 144
Christian, John, 36
Christian, Martha, 148
Christian, Patricia, 137
Christian, Troy, 65
Christian, William, 58, 99, 103, 198, 199
Christianson, Anne, 119
Christianson, Catherine Ann, 103, 198, 199
Christie, Agatha, 59, 128, 140
Christmas Bride, The, 56
Christmas Carol, A, 119, 120, 123, 143, 144, 147, 158, 159, 160, 161, 172, 182
Christmas Memory, A, 135, 136
Christoffel, Martin, 165
Christopher, Donald, 151, 169
Christopher, Thom, 72, 97, 190, 198
Christopher-Myers, Bill, 94
Christy, Donald, 96
Christy, Roberta, 109
Chryst, Gary, 37, 198, 199
CHS Productions & Stab Stab Stab Partners, 51
Chu Chem, 31, 85
Chuchran, Dru-ann, 63
Chudinski, Michael J., 125
Church, Jeff, 138
Church, Tony, 138
Churchill, Caryl, 183
Chute, Lionel, 198, 199
Chwat, Sam, 72
Chybowski, Michael, 21, 51, 142, 169
Cibula, Nan, 144
Ciccarone, Richard, 151
Cicchini, Bob, 136
Ciccolella, Jude, 131
Ciccone, Oscar, 93
Cigliano, Joseph A., 51
Cimolino, Antoni, 174
Cinnante, Kelly, 73
Cintron, Monique, 58
Cipriano, David, 133
Cissel, Charles D., 76
Ciulei, Liviu, 124, 126
Clair Bros., 16
Clancy, Janet, 57
Clanton, Rony, 89
Clap Yo' Hands: Homage to George and Ira Gershwin, 180
Claptrap, 180
Clarey, Alan, 170
Clark, Bobby, 146
Clark, C. A., 68
Clark, Cheryl, 198
Clark, Dort, 227, 228
Clark, G. Thomas, 184
Clark, J. Andrew, 65
Clark, James A., 179
Clark, John, 138
Clark, Jon Roger, 46, 75, 82, 99
Clark, Kate, 70
Clark, Phillip, 151, 154
Clark, Randy, 65
Clark, Ron, 182
Clark, Susan Gordon, 39
Clark, Victoria, 114
Clarke, Bill, 77, 107, 168, 183
Clarke, Martha, 93
Clarke, Richard, 17, 198
Clarke, Tony, 74
Clarkson, Patricia, 21
Classical Artists International, 13
Clausen, Richard, 84
Clavelli, Christopher, 161
Claypool, Veronica, 133
Clayton, Lawrence, 63, 96, 198
Cleary, Brigid, 182
Clelland, Deborah, 40
Clemens, Elizabeth Ruiz, 101
Clemente, Steve, 36
Clements, Randy, 37
Clemm, Susanna, 67
Clermont, Riley, 140
Cleveland, David, 44, 82
Clewell, Thomas, 104, 142
Clifford, Cheryl, 57
Clifford, Pamela, 146
Clifford, Yvonne, 63
Clinton, Georgia, 180
Clonts, Jeffrey, 40
Clonts, John, 162
Cloud, Carol, 140
Clough, Peter H., 131
Coates, Eric, 174
Coates, Norman, 51
Coates, Paul, 51
Coats, Steve, 57, 198
Coats, William Alan, 116
Cobb, 184, 185
Cobb, Eddie, 54
Cobbs, Bill, 111
Coberg, Wally, 164
Coble, McKay, 168
Cocca, Joanna, 73
Cochran, LaLa, 122
Cochran, Pat, 126, 141
Cochran, Shannon, 144
Cochrane, Janelle, 140
Cochren, Felix E., 60
Cockrum, Roy, 73
Cocktail Hour, The, 51
Codron, Michael, 133
Cody, Cornelia, 132
Cody, Marie, 130
Coelho, James, 60, 151
Coffey, Peggy, 174, 175
Coffield, Kelly, 144
Cognetta, Patrick, 85, 198
Cohan, Blossom, 176
Cohen, Alexander H., 6
Cohen, Aviva, 49, 58
Cohen, Bill, 57, 137, 198
Cohen, Bruce, 46, 47, 48, 58, 105, 106
Cohen, Buzz, 94, 95
Cohen, Charles, 96
Cohen, David S., 48
Cohen, Douglas J., 105
Cohen, Edward M., 85
Cohen, Esther, 97
Cohen, Geoffrey, 162
Cohen, Greg, 87
Cohen, Jacqueline, 179
Cohen, Jaffe, 57
Cohen, Jamie, 25, 198
Cohen, Jason Steven, 15, 93, 94
Cohen, Jerry L., 36
Cohen, Julie, 198
Cohen, Lynn, 151, 154
Cohen, Martin, 133
Cohen, Michael, 53
Cohen, Ruth, 100
Cohen, Sally Ann, 143, 176, 179
Cohen, Sally, 153
Cohen, Samuel D., 43
Cohen, Sherry, 133
Cohenour, Patti, 44, 190, 191, 198
Coid, Marshall, 35, 93
Coit, Connie, 180
Colaneri, Joseph, 27
Colavecchia, Franco, 103, 141
Colborn, Randy, 144
Colby, Michael, 142
Cold, Marshall, 85
Cole, Deborah, 63, 162
Cole, Debra, 86, 143
Cole, Ellen T., 174
Cole, Jena, 133
Cole, Jerry, 49
Cole, Kay, 198, 199
Cole, Matthew, 6
Cole, Megan, 169
Cole, Rainie, 46
Cole, Richard, 51
Cole, Tom, 142
Coleman, Charisse, 136
Coleman, Cy, 32
Coleman, Jack, 134
Coleman, Jim, 45, 109
Coleman, Lorilee, 160
Coleman, Rosalyn, 184
Coleman, Tony, 10
Coles, Diana, 179
Coleson, David, 129
Coleson, Ernest, 129
Colette, 67, 83
Coley, Thomas, 227
Colin, Margaret, 88
Colker, Jerry, 198
Coll, Ivonne, 55, 76, 101, 198
Collet, Christopher, 16
Colley, Thomas, 182
Collings, Nancy, 52, 65, 83
Collins, Charles, 227, 228
Collins, Courtenay, 158
Collins, Craig, 77
Collins, Deborah, 151
Collins, Elsbeth M., 66
Collins, Hayward, 11
Collins, Pat, 12, 30, 86, 88, 96, 100, 131, 132, 148, 154
Collins, Pauline, 24, 191, 198
Collins, Ray, 53, 81, 176, 198
Collins, Stephen, 62
Collins, Suzanne, 80, 172
Colman, Booth, 159
Colman, Shelly, 63
Colombo, Patti, 130
Colon, Carlos-Antonio, 178
Colon, Miriam, 101
Colored Museum, The, 180
Colston, Robert, 176
Colt, Alvin, 25
Colteaux, Andrew, 94, 95, 176
Colton, Chevi, 81, 198, 199
Colton, Kia, 73
Columbo, Jeanie, 54, 198
Columbus, Marvin, 134, 135
Colvin, Bessie, 129
Combs, Melody, 122
Comco Productions, 68
Comden, Betty, 25, 33, 146
Come and Gone, 186
Comeaux, Lisa, 144
Comedy of Errors, The, 159
Comer, Anjanette, 67, 198
Comet Messenger-Siegfried, 78
Coming Home, 57
Commire, Anne, 184
Company, 138
Compayno, Joe, 41
Compton, Gardner, 43
Condino, David, 58
Condon, Dennis, 65
Coney, Ruthay V., 138
Confession & Lloyd and Lee, A, 105
Congdon, Constance, 120, 148
Conger, Eric, 108, 154
Conger, Joe, 140
Conger, Trista, 138
Conklin, Cody, 68
Conklin, John, 86, 94, 148
Conklin, Kate, 79
Conklin, Mark W., 60, 98
Connell, Gordon, 109, 116
Connell, Jane, 26, 42, 198
Connell, Kelly, 79, 198, 199
Connell, Tim, 118
Connolly, John P., 62, 198
Connor, Geoffrey, 92
Connor, Martin, 146
Connor, Whitfield, 227, 228
Conolly, Patricia, 126, 148, 149, 154, 155
Conover, Brian-Mark, 152
Conover, Tim, 136
Conrad, Jeff, 117
Conroy, Frances, 19, 198
Conroy, Jarlath, 35, 60, 176, 198
Conroy, Kevin, 21
Conry, Kathleen, 129
Considine, Ron, 83
Constan, Victoria, 73
Constantine, Deborah, 58, 59, 67
Constantine, Michael, 134
Constantine, Scott, 79
Conte, John K., 154
Conversation Among the Ruins, 101
Converse-Roberts, William, 77, 95
Conway, Charles J., 137
Conway, Dan, 60, 153
Conway, John R., 184
Conway, Kevin, 59, 94, 191, 198
Conwell, Charles, 166
Cook, Dominique J., 65, 80
Cook, Dwight R. B., 92
Cook, James, 69
Cook, Patricia, 105
Cook, Peter, 158, 161
Cook, Roderick, 125
Cook, Steven Douglas, 103
Cook, Victor Trent, 34, 96, 198
Cooke, Gregory, 134
Cooke, John C., 134
Cooksey, Karen, 182
Cookson, Brian, 184
Cookson, Gary, 57, 198
Coombs, Amy A. C., 58
Coon, Susan J., 165
Coonan, Sheila, 227, 228
Cooney, Kevin, 146, 154
Cooney, Ray, 29
Cooper, Adrienne, 95
Cooper, Catherine, 160
Cooper, Chris, 184

Cooper, Denise, 6
Cooper, Helmar Augustus, 137
Cooper, Jon, 169
Cooper, Keith, 53
Cooper, Laury, 139
Cooper, Marilyn, 15, 110, 198
Cooper, Maury, 168
Cooper, Mindy, 94
Cooper, Reva, 93
Cooper-Hecht, Gail, 75, 76
Coopersmith, Kira, 52
Coopwood, K. Scott, 131
Cope, Carolyn, 121
Copeland, Carolyn Rossi, 55, 61, 65
Copeland, Joan, 100, 198
Copeland, Marissa, 126
Corbin, Demitri, 96
Corbino, Maurizio, 133
Corby, Julie, 158
Corcoran, Daniel, 73
Corcoran, Joseph, 73
Corder, Constance, 122
Cordovani, Roberto, 66
Corey, John, 53
Corey, Kenneth, 138
Corfman, Caris, 66, 81, 105, 198
Coriolanus, 94
Corker, John, 46
Corkins, Mark, 161
Corley, Hal, 64
Corley, Nick, 53, 74, 83
Corneille, Pierre, 97
Cornell, Allen D., 161
Cornell, Jeffrey, 130
Cornicelli, Carol, 63
Cornish, Roger, 166, 170
Cornthwaite, Robert, 103, 172
Cornwell, Kimo, 134
Corrado, Regina, 65
Correia, Amy, 52
Correia, Steve, 64
Corrigan, Kevin, 100
Corry, Betsy, 161
Cortez, Dean, 134
Corti, Jesse, 40
Cortland, Nicholas, 228, 229
Corvinus, Dede, 168
Corwen, Carol, 105
Corzatte, Clayton, 141
Cosell, Howard, 33
Cosentino, Andrew, 129
Cosgrave, Peggy, 23, 198
Cosham, Ralph, 126
Cosier, E. David, Jr., 144
Coss, Clare, 76
Cossa, Roberto, 101
Costa, Joseph, 95, 151, 160, 198
Costa, Victor, 180
Costabile, Richard, 95
Costello, Jeffrey, 82
Costen, Russell, 83, 198
Costigan, Ken, 128
Cothran, John, Jr., 132
Cottrell, Richard, 143
Coudert, Jo, 108
Coughlin, Sylvia, 159
Coulouris, George, 228
Coulson, Grover, Jr., 180
Coulter, Allen, 85
Council, Richard, 62, 100, 107, 198
Countryman, Michael, 147, 184
Courie, Jonathan, 108
Courtney, Keith, 174
Courts, Randy, 55
Cousins, Brian, 102, 103, 176, 199, 200
Covan, Willie, 228
Covarrubias, Robert, 138
Covell, Peter, 92
Cover, Franklin, 23, 136, 200
Covey, Elizabeth, 158
Coward, Noel, 160, 165
Cowart, Sheri, 116, 117
Cowles, Matthew, 143
Cox, Catherine, 18, 146, 200
Cox, Christine, 133
Cox, Dan, 103
Cox, Douglas, 83
Cox, Hannah, 166
Cox, Jeremy, 184
Cox, Kenneth, 14
Cox, Natania, 74
Cox, Richard, 184, 185
Cox, Veanne, 67
Cox, Wendy, 148
Coyle, Kate, 57
Coyne, Butch, 178
Coyne, Cyndi, 79
Coyne, Susan, 174
Cozort, Kim, 140
Cradle Song, 90
Craig, Noel, 200
Crampton, Glory, 69, 200
Crane, David, 152
Crane, Warren, 111
Cranendonk, Terence, 93
Craven, James, 123
Craven, Matt, 97, 200
Cravens, Rutherford, 121
Craver, Mike, 72, 143
Crawford, Ann, 53
Crawford, Kevin, 126
Crawford, Michael, 44, 133, 200
Crawford, Norma, 129
Crean, Patrick, 174
Creason, Donald P., 127
Creech, Rodney, 166
Creedon, Donald, 84
Cregan, Patricia, 73
Creighton, Christopher, 144
Creighton, Erin, 144
Creighton, Georgia, 104
Creswell, Saylor, 85
Crigler, Lynn, 146
Crinkley, Richmond, 228
Criswell, Kim, 63, 199, 200
Critic, The, 174
Crivello, Anthony, 40, 86, 199, 200
Crivello, Jeffrey, 184
Croft, Paddy, 84, 200
Cromarty, Peter, 8, 13, 16, 46, 47, 48, 50, 53, 55, 59, 61, 64, 65, 66, 68, 70, 75, 80, 90, 118
Crombie, Peter, 77, 88, 132
Cromwell, David, 116
Cronin, Jane, 26
Cronin, Laurel, 184
Cronson, Bridget, 57
Crooked Lines, 105
Crooks, Kitty, 169
Croom, George H., 59
Crosby, Cathy Lee, 81, 200
Crosby, Don, 113, 133
Crosby, Julie, 22
Crosby, Kim, 39, 199, 200
Crosby, Mary, 156
Crosby, Shelly, 152
Cross, Eugenia, 101
Crossin' the Line, 64, 65
Crouse, Russel, 45, 109, 129, 140
Crouse, Timothy, 45, 109
Crow, Ashley, 94
Crow, Jerry, 180
Crow, Laura, 79, 119, 143, 165
Crow, Robert, 172
Crow, Tom, 55
Crowder, Bill, 70
Crowe, Carla, 90
Crowe, Patricia, 118
Crowley, Bob, 133
Crucible, The, 172
Crum, Ann, 40, 114
Crum, Tracy, 12, 42, 116
Crume, Louis S., 116, 117
Cruse, Gilbert, 82
Crutchfield, Charles C., 116
Crutchman, John, 162
Cruz, Migdalia, 46
Cruz, Nilo, 161
Cruz, Rieka Roberta, 130
Cryer, David, 17, 26, 200
Cryer, Gretchen, 63, 199, 200
Cryer, Robin, 63
Crystal Clear, 52
Cuccioli, Bob, 83, 146, 162, 199, 200
Cucco, Patricia, 55
Cuervo, Alma, 35, 97, 106, 200
Culbreath, Lloyd, 45
Culhane, Lori, 52, 75, 83
Culkin, Macaulay, 46, 199
Culkin, Shane, 19, 200
Cullen, David, 38, 44
Cullen, Jeanne, 143
Cullen, Michael, 55
Cullison, Barry, 54, 76, 200
Culliton, Joseph, 94, 200
Culliver, Karen, 122, 125
Cullum, Emily Frankel, 179
Cullum, John David, 179
Cullum, John, 179, 190
Culman, Peter W., 132
Culpin, Deborah Jeanne, 158
Culver, Eric, 60
Cumbo, Rashamella, 22
Cuming, Carole, 82
Cuming, Danette, 113, 133
Cummings, A. Benard, 184
Cummings, Anthony, 68, 170
Cummings, Howard, 165
Cummings, Katina, 64
Cumpsty, Michael, 94, 95, 96, 122
Cuneo, Richard, 107
Cunningham, Christopher, Jr., 19
Cunningham, Jo Ann, 113, 133
Cunningham, John, 17, 62, 154, 200
Cunningham, Laura, 144
Cunningham, Stanton, 122
Curci, Donna E., 166
Curiel, Tony, 178
Curlee, Karen, 49
Curless, John, 81, 200
Curley, Bill, 138
Curnock, Richard, 174, 175
Curran, Keith, 79
Curran, Michael, 48, 53
Currie, Richard, 56, 57, 63
Currier, Terrence, 126
Curry, Margaret, 53
Curry, Phillip C., 160
Curry, Ruthann, 90
Curry, Tim, 116
Curschellas, Corin, 78
Curtin, Jane, 62
Curtin, Jim, 57
Curtis, Ann, 42
Curtis, April, 158
Curtis, Danny, 66
Curtis, Keene, 51, 191, 199, 200
Curtis, Kelly, 136, 179
Curtis, Simon, 86
Curtis-Hall, Vondie, 54
Curzon, Daniel, 51
Cusack, Joan, 79, 86, 96, 187, 200
Cusick, Russ, 102
Cuskern, Dominic, 60, 134
Cusnetz, Rachael, 50
Custer, Marianne, 168
Cutler, R. J., 97
Cutrona, Ryan, 106
Cutter, Kay E., 130
Cutugno, Matt, 57, 105
Cwikowski, Bill, 46, 200
Cygan, John, 66
Cymbeline, 96
Cyrano de Bergerac, 127
Czerny, Henry, 174, 175
Czyzewska, Elzbieta, 106
DaCosta, Morton, 228, 229
Dabbit, Count, 176
Dabney, Sheila, 46
Dahill, Frank, 51
Dahlsten, Dennis, 78
Daily, Patricia, 86
Daines, John, 81
Dainton, Scott, 116
Dakin, Kymberly, 125
Dakota's Belly, Wyoming, 60
Dale, Cynthia, 72
Dale, Grover, 25
Dale, Jim, 42, 200
Dale, Patt, 67, 113
Dale, Vincent, 174
Daley, Steven Michael, 69
Dalfo, Denise, 59, 68
D'Alistal, Donata, 48
Dallas, L. B., 60
Dally, Daniel, 102
Dalrymple, Jean, 33
Dalton's Back, 79
Dalton, Lezlie, 62, 76, 200
Dalton, T. Michael, 118
Daly, Daniel, 102
Daly, Joseph, 124
Daly, Lee, 56
Daly, Sarah, 50
Daly, Timothy, 199, 200
Damashek, Barbara, 172
d'Amboise, Charlotte, 25
D'Ambrose, Steven, 147
D'Ambrosio, Franc, 65, 137
Dame, Terry, 56
Dames at Sea, 143
Damon, Cate, 82
Damon, Mark, 9
Dana, F. Mitchell, 59, 103, 143, 148, 158, 166
Dana, Maurice, 68
Dana, Paige, 38
Danaher, Deidre, 84
Danaher, Kevin, 183
Dance Lesson, A, 154
D'Andrea, Al, 56
Dane, Dennis, 54
Danek, Michael, 37
Danforth, Roger T., 136
Dangerous Glee Club, 59
Daniel, Gregg, 148
Daniel, Tamara, 136
Daniele, Graciela, 64, 104
Danielle, Marlene, 38, 200
Danielle, Susan, 37, 200
Daniello, Lisa, 63
Daniels, Ead, 57
Daniels, Gannon, 183
Daniels, Ina, 119
Daniels, Leslie, 200
Daniels, Max, 55
Daniels, Paul S., 100
Danis, Amy, 128
Danis, Louison, 105
Dann, Elonzo, 11
Danner, Blythe, 62, 93, 200
Danner, Braden, 94, 200
Danny Curtis: Walls of Chance, 66
Danon, Tchia, 53, 134
Danta, Yasunori, 78
Dante, Nicholas, 37
Dantuono, Michael, 200
Danvers, Marie-Laurence, 112
Danzer, Kathy, 131, 200
D'Arcy, Mary, 133
Dapo, Kenwyn, 57
Dardaris, Janis, 51, 64
Darden, Bellary, 144
Darling, Robert Edward, 141
Darlow, Cynthia, 18, 199, 200
Darnell, August, 104
Darrett, Elizabeth, 82
Darrow, Harry Silverglat, 43
Dartez, Gail, 154
Darveris, George, 45
Darwin, Kim, 45, 146
Daseler, Robert, 172
Datcher, Irene, 92
Davenport, Colleen, 79, 200
Davenport, Johnny Lee, 174
Davenport, Tiv, 42, 116
Daves, Bradley, 55, 56
David Rothenberg Associates, 63, 73
David Strong Warner Inc., 39
David, Angel, 96
David, Jonathan, 56
David, Keith, 94, 200
David, Michael, 39
Davidorf, Brad, 122
Davidson, Gordon, 77, 134
Davidson, Jack, 183
Davidson, Richard M., 35, 49, 148, 200
Davies, Harry, 110
Davies, Joseph, 200
Davies, Katharyn, 132
Davies, Rick, 132
Davis, Bob, 147
Davis, Bruce Anthony, 37, 200
Davis, Catherine Lynn, 161
Davis, Charles, 60
Davis, Chris Quay, 36
Davis, Chris, 153
Davis, Daniel, 147
Davis, Eddie, 146
Davis, Elizabeth Brady, 48, 61
Davis, Gary, 130
Davis, Gerald A., 49, 73
Davis, Guy, 96
Davis, Helene, 88
Davis, Jack L., 82, 83
Davis, Jeff, 23, 136, 141, 162, 166
Davis, Judy, 133
Davis, Kevin, 46, 78, 148
Davis, Lance, 136
Davis, Lindsay W., 94, 142, 144
Davis, Lloyd, Jr., 89
Davis, Luther, 130
Davis, Mal, 129
Davis, Margot, 176
Davis, Maureen, 39
Davis, Merlyn, 38
Davis, Montgomery, 161
Davis, Penny, 18
Davis, Rick, 132, 137
Davis, Robert Warren, 102
Davis, Russell, 170
Davis, Sylvia, 48, 99, 200
Davis, Vicki R., 49
Davis, Vince, 180
Davis-Reed, Timothy, 179
Davison, Bruce, 51, 62, 200
Davison, Jack, 162
Davys, Edmund, 158
Dawes, Carol, 76, 80
Dawn, Hazel, 228, 229
Dawson, Bobby, 182
Dawson, David, 200
Dawson, James, 39
Dawson, Jennifer, 153
Day You'll Love Me, The, 135
Day, Connie, 199, 200
Day, Sharie Lynn, 158
de Angelis, Vincent, 58
de Balbian Verster, Karen L., 105
de Barbieri, Mary Ann, 141
de Beaumarchais, Pierre Augustin Caron, 168
de Botton, Yvette, 170, 171
De Carlo, Pamela, 56
de Ganon, Camille, 25, 199
de Jesus, Wanda, 135
de la Barca, Pedro Calderon, 105, 124
de la Chaume, Jacqueline, 87
de la Cruz, Sor Juana Ines, 60
de Laclos, Choderlos, 120
de Lavallade, Carmen, 33, 58, 68, 78
De Masi, Susan, 99
De Mille, Agnes, 33
de Molina, Tirso, 80
de Prume, Cathryn, 73
De Sousa, Melissa, 94
De Tecalitan, Mariachi Vargas, 8
de Trevino, Elizabeth Borton, 74
DeAngelis, Christina Marie, 114
DeAngelis, Rosemary, 136
DeArmas, Juan, 73
DeBoy, Paul, 170, 171, 182
DeCrescenzo, Loriana, 65
DeCrette, Danielle, 109
DeCristo, Al, 46, 114
DeCristofaro, Lucille, 63
DeFillipis, Jed, 33
DeForest, Charles, 74
deGanon, Camille, 200
DeGonge, Marcy, 38, 170
DeLaurentis, Semina, 70, 200
DeLaurier, Peter, 166
DeLorenzo, Michael, 134, 135
DeLuca, Hand, 166
DeMars, Jerri, 130
DeMarse, James, 85
DeMasi, Susan, 48
DeMattis, Ray, 72, 154
DeMunn, Jeffrey, 16, 201
DeNiro, Robert, 88
DePaolo, Nick, 152
DePena, Valerie, 70
DePrima, Marietta, 144
DeRugeriis, James C., 142
DeShields, Andre, 12, 33
DeSoto, Edouard, 74
DeVerne, Ellen, 74
DeVille, Dana, 84
DeVito, John, 96
DeVolder, Max, 170
DeVries, Jon, 201
DeVries, Michael, 38
DeWitt, Faye, 130
deWitt-Howard, Sherrill, 151
DeWolf, Cecilia, 201
DeWolfe, Thomas, 72
Deal, Dennis, 51
Dean, Allison, 100, 199, 200
Dean, Loren, 79, 187, 190, 191, 200
Dean, Michael-Pierre, 37
Dean, Phillip Hayes, 14, 49
Dean, Robertson, 154
Deane, Melinda, 138
Dear Liar, 128
Dearing, Judy, 11, 52, 91, 96, 179
Death of Garcia Lorca, The, 93
Debuskey, Merle, 8, 9, 10, 17, 19, 35, 37, 45, 86
Decastro, Travis, 29
Deckelbaum, Sheldon, 57
Decker, Jenifer, 129
Decker, Pat, 152
Dedrickson, Tracy, 54
Dee, Ruby, 11
Deegan, John Michael, 51
Deegan, Michael, 60
Deeney, Donagh, 10
Deer, Joe, 45, 109
Deer, Sandra, 122, 152
Dekanoidze, Soso, 13
Dekelbaum, Robbie, 7
Del Arco, Jonathan, 16
del Barrio, Raymond G., 94, 96
Del Pazzo, Bob, 49
Del Pozo, Emilio, 93
Del Rossi, Angelo, 162
Del Vecchio, Paul, 130
DelCoro, Christopher, 65
dela Cruz, Marc R., 119
Delafield, Tina, 55
Delaney, Thomas, 84
Delapenha, Denise, 62, 78
Delate, Brian, 58
Delaware Theatre Company, 137
Delgado, Jose, 8
Delgado, Margarita, 46
Delgado, Miguel, 135
D'Elia, Vincent, 65
Delinger, Larry, 132, 138
Dell'isola, Salvatore, 228
Dell, Gabriel, 228, 229
Della Piazza, Diane, 199, 200
Dellger, Joseph, 119, 133
Deloy, George, 123
Delsener, Ron, 14
Demaline, Wayne, 140
Demetral, Chris, 133, 135
Demon Wine, 156, 157
Dempsey, Eithne, 10
Dempsey, Jerome, 76, 200
Dempsey, Joe, 161
Dempster, Curt, 46, 55, 68
Denman, Jeffrey, 176
Denmark, Brenda, 91
Denmark, Leon B., 91
Dennehy, Elizabeth, 73
Dennin, Steve, 93
Dennis, Judy, 134
Dennis, Philip, 33
Dennis, Rick, 100, 131
Dennis, Robert, 43
Dennis, Ron, 130
Dennis, Steven, 170, 179
Dennis, Susan, 152
Dennison, Richard C., 174
Denniston, Leslie, 60, 201
Denny, Patricia, 68
Denson, Cheryl, 180
Deoni, Christofer, 51
Depke, Nancy E., 136
Derby, M. Afida, 78
Deren, Nancy, 63
Derheimer, Pete, 184
Derrah, Thomas, 77, 124
Dery, Judy, 139
Desbarats, Hazel, 174
Deschamps, Gail S., 161
Deschamps, Robert H., 161
Desire Under the Elms, 57
Desire, 51
Desmond, Dan, 18, 46, 57, 199, 201
Detweiler, Lowell, 34, 146
Deutchman, Lois, 72
Deutsch, Howard, 67
Deutsch, Kurt, 110

Devaney, Keith, 172
Devil's Disciple, The, 17
Devincentis, D. V., 144
Devine, Erick, 116, 117
Devine, Jillana, 29, 32, 50, 75, 81, 107
Devine, Loretta, 135
Devine, Michael, 172
Devish, Annie, 53
Devlin, Jay, 50, 166, 199, 201
Dewar, John, 40, 201
Dewhurst, Colleen, 6, 7, 201
Dexter, John, 41, 138
Dgvepadze, Pyotr, 13
Di Leone, Leon, 53
DiBenedetto, Tony, 54
DiBuono, Toni, 50
DiCaprio, Peter, 99
DiCrescenzo, Louis, 144
DiCristina, Philip Dennis, 59
DiDia, Maria, 43
DiFranza, Lisa, 169
DiGesu, Traci, 67
DiLascio, Dianne, 109
DiMeo, Donna, 25, 201
DiPaola, James, 46, 80
DiPasquale, Frank, 66, 88, 143
DiRenzo, Denise, 37
DiVita, Diane, 151
Dial, Sharrie-Ann, 174
Diamond, Dennis, 36, 201
Diamond, Elizabeth, 58, 77
Diamond, Liz, 105
Diaz, Mary Louise, 8
Diaz, Roylan, 93
Diaz-Farrar, Gabriella, 86
Dickens, Charles, 56, 102, 112, 119, 120, 123, 143, 144, 158, 160, 161, 172, 182
Dickinson, Debra, 27
Dickinson, Elizabeth Anne, 160
Diderot, Denis, 80
Diefendorf, Robert, 47
Diekmann, Nancy Kassak, 62, 97
Dietrich Process, The, 60
Dietz, Donovan, 62
Dietz, Steven, 119, 120
Digesu, Tracy, 107
Diggs, Elizabeth, 131
Dignan, Pat, 52, 97
Dilascio, Dianne, 109
Dillard, Denise, 151
Dillard, Pam, 151
Dillard, Victoria, 130
Dilley, Carol, 170
Dilliard, Marcus, 147, 168
Dillman, Jim, 73
Dillon, John, 161, 166
Dillon, Mia, 81, 201
Dillon, Rhonda, 44
Dinicol, Keith, 174
Dinner at Eight, 154, 155
Diphthong, 46
Dishy, Bob, 15, 201
Disney, Tom, 161
Dispenza, Joe, 82, 201
Dittman, Dean, 228
Diveny, Mary, 61
Dividing the Estate, 158
Dix, Richard, 141, 147
Dixon, Beth, 66
Dixon, Ed, 40
Dixon, MacIntyre, 93, 95, 103, 110, 201
Dmitriev, Alex, 166
DoQui, Robert, 142
Dobbin, Randy, 94
Dobbs, Jeffrey, 74
Dobell, Curzon, 147, 165
Dobie, Jeannie, 62
Dobkin, Abraham, 126
Dobrowolski, Patti, 36
Dobrusky, Pavel, 138, 183
Dobson, Terry, 180
Doctor, Simon, 49
Docwra-Jones, Sandra, 161
Dodd, Judy, 52
Dodd, Terry, 138
Dodds, Malcolm, 118
Dodge, Marcia Milgram, 96
Dodger Blue, 50
Dodin, Lev, 47
Dodson, Colleen, 201
Dodson, Kathleen, 64
Doemling, Brandon E., 51
Doherty, Devin, 19
Doherty, Jim, 10
Dolan, Andrew, 151
Dolan, Ellen, 57
Dolan, Judith, 141
Dolan, Michael, 184
Dominguez, Steven B., 94
Domville, James deB., 174
Don Juan of Seville, 80
Don Juan, 151
Don, Carl, 15, 201
Donahue, Angie, 129
Donald, Donald K., 22
Donaldson, Peter, 174
Donaldson, Randy, 162
Donarski, Therese, 161
Donat, Peter, 123
Donathan, Liz, 152
Donato, Vincent, 66

Dondlinger, May Jo, 108
Doney, Randy, 33
Donkin, Eric, 174
Donnelly, Brian, 126
Donnelly, Candice, 80, 104, 124, 132, 141, 154, 184
Donnelly, Donal, 35, 154, 201
Donnelly, Kathleen, 102
Donnelly, Kyle, 144
Donnelly, Sarah E., 46, 176
Donoghue, Cece, 53
Donoghue, Tom, 54
Donohoe, Rob, 83, 201
Donohue, Deirdre E., 59
Donohue, Tim, 133
Donovan, Kevin, 164
Dooley, Jeffrey, 60
Door to Cuba, 46
Doorn, Nancy Ann, 130
Dore, Bill, 119
Dorfman, Robert, 142
Dorman, Andrea, 56
Dorn, Carol, 62
Dorn, Franchelle Stewart, 141
Dorrell, Cynthia, 49
Dorsey, Fern, 201
Dorsey, Jeffe, 108
Dorsey, Kent, 50, 51
Dortch, Ron, 81
Dorward, Mary Anne, 172
Dossett, John, 79
Dostoevsky, Fyodor, 60
Doty, David, 94
Double Blessing, 85
Double Double, 122
Double Takes, 62
Doubleday, Kay, 138
Doughtery, J. P., 151
Douglas, Kenneth, 130
Douglas, Lucien, 53
Douglas, Mark, 141
Douglas, Michael, 192
Douglas, Suzzanne, 184
Douglas, Tim, 143
Douglass, Donald, 180
Doulin, Jack, 86
Dovel, Kenn, 49, 62, 99
Dowd, Ann, 108, 148, 149
Dowd, Frank, 49
Dowdy, Tony, 73
Dowling, Joe, 10
Dowling, Kevin, 50, 68
Downer, Herb, 14, 68, 94
Downey, Roger, 97
Downey, Roma, 72, 88, 95, 103, 201
Downing, Virginia, 108, 154
Downs, Arnall, 51
Downs, Sarah, 162
Doyle, Jack, 82, 201
Doyle, Jay, 158
Doyle, Lori M., 120
Doyle, Mary, 121
Doyle, Richard, 172
Doyle, William, 50
Drabik, John S., 124
Draghici, Marina, 97
Dragon Lady, 172
Drake, Alfred, 33
Drake, David, 73
Drake, Donna A., 39
Drake, Paul, 147
Draper, Alexander, 184
Draper, David F., 123
Draper, Jase, 201
Drauschke, Olaf, 78
Drawbaugh, Laura, 85, 101
Dreisbach, Bill, 87
Dreisbach, Jeff, 136
Dreskin, William K., 152
Dressler, Ralph, 120
Dretsch, Curtis, 164
Dretzel, Beverly, 58
Drew, Connie, 161
Dreyer, William, 140
Drillinger, Brian, 110
Driver, Donald, 228
Driver, John, 75
Driving Miss Daisy, 70, 111, 122, 122, 186
Drood, 112, 152
Dror, Liat, 35
Drulovic, Anya, 67
Drumm, Joshua Evan, 184
Drummond, Alice, 201, 205
Drummond, David, 119
Drummond, Joseph, 144
Drury, Ken, 92
Drusch, Mark, 119
Dryden, Dan, 56
DS Productions, 66
du Bois, Raoul Pene, 25
DuBay, Terrence, 87
DuBow, Susan, 33
DuClos, Danielle, 104
DuGay, Brian, 59
duMaurier, Jenise, 165
DuMont, James, 73
DuRae, Liliane, 73
DuSold, Robert, 114
DuVall, Elizabeth, 148
Duarte, Derek, 123, 178
Duarte, Herbert, 93
Dubin, Al, 129
Ducati, Ann, 164, 169
Dudek, Tina, 58

Dudley, Craig, 161, 201
Duell, William, 201, 205
Duer, Fred, 80
Duff, James, 180
Duff-MacCormick, Cara, 100, 201, 205
Duffey, Deborah, 137
Duffy, Meghan, 142, 164
Duffy, R. Ward, 127
Dufour, Dick, 180
Duggan, Elizabeth Logue, 228
Dukakis, Apollo, 53
Duke, O. L., 91
Duke, Stuart, 125, 169
Dukes, David, 41, 201
Dukes, Gerry, 86
Dulaine, Pierre, 64
Dulcie, Greg, 180
Dumas, Charles, 141, 158
Dumas, Debra, 59, 62, 75
Dunard, David, 118
Dunaway, Faye, 192
Dunbar, Brian, 25
Duncan, Kirk, 73
Duncan, Marc, 86
Duncan, Sandy, 192
Dundas, Jennifer, 7, 95
Dundas, Matthew, 77
Dunford, Christine, 72, 95
Dunkelberg, Kermit, 160
Dunlap, Pamela, 77, 172
Dunlea, Jack, 68
Dunlop, Tom, 94
Dunn, Andrew, 139
Dunn, Colleen, 20
Dunn, Eileen, 26, 49
Dunn, Glenn, 170
Dunn, Margaret Anne, 135
Dunn, Terrance Paul, 152
Dunn, Wally, 49
Dunning, Richard, 65
Durang, Christopher, 87, 100, 161, 201
Durante, Vito, 228
Duras, Marguerite, 48
Durbin, Holly Poe, 170
Durkin, Kevin, 55
Durrenmatt, Friedrich, 58
Dussault, Nancy, 39, 190, 191, 201
Dutch Landscape, 134, 135
Dutton, Charles S., 144
Dutweiler, Norman, 43
Dvorsky, George, 162
Dwenger, Ronald, 129
Dworkin, Marc Steven, 135
Dwyer, Kevin, 169
Dyar, Preston, 112
Dybisz, Dorothy, 37
Dyer, Carolyn, 77, 138
Dykstra, Brian, 93, 94, 95, 170
Dykun, Lawrence N., 72
Dys, Deanna, 20
Dyson, Erika, 50
Dzhikuri, Nugzer, 13
Eagan, Daisy, 40
Eagan, Michael, 174
Eagleton, Patrick, 49, 51, 58
Eames, John, 228, 229
Earle, Edward, 158
Early One Evening at the Rainbow Bar & Grille, 107
Early, Barbara, 129
Earth Players of South Africa, The, 156
Easley, Richert, 182
Easterbrook, Leslie, 130
Easterling, Benmio, 49
Eastern Standard, 21, 187, 188
Eastley, Keely, 179
Eastman, Donald, 76, 80, 81, 176
Easton, Edward, 98, 201, 205
Eaton, Lothair, 162
Ebert, Joyce, 154
Ebsary, Kelly, 73
Eckerle, James, 56
Eckhardt, Sarah, 57
Eckle, James, 68
Eckstein, Paul, 86, 94
Ed Linderman's Broadway Jukebox, 125
Eddy, Nelson, 56
Ede, George, 103, 122, 158, 201
Edelhart, Yvette, 82, 201
Edelman, Gregg, 45, 65, 201
Edelstein, Gordon, 131, 154
Edelstein, Stephen, 62
Edenfield, Dennis, 201
Edgerton, Earle, 99
Edgerton, Sandy, 66
Edholm, Geoff, 48
Edington, Pamela, 16, 104
Edith Stein, 98
Edkins, Sarah, 68, 102
Edmead, Wendy, 130, 201, 205
Edmiston, Scott, 164
Edmond, Linda, 119
Edmonds, Robert, 59, 64
Edmunds, Kate, 151, 178
Eduardo Peralta, 161

*Education of H*Y*M*A*N K*A*P*L*A*N, The*, 75
Edwards, Alison, 94, 201
Edwards, Ben, 6
Edwards, Brandt, 201
Edwards, Burt, 201
Edwards, Craig Alan, 151
Edwards, Daryl, 64, 148
Edwards, David, 201
Edwards, George, 50
Edwards, Jack, 147
Edwards, Jason, 140
Edwards, Linda, 140
Edwards, Nancy, 129
Edwards, Paddi, 133
Edwards, Randall, 20, 201
Edwards, Sherman, 162
Edwards, Tracey, 129
Egan, Donal, 57
Egan, Kathleen, 164
Egan, Michael John, 40
Egan, Michael, 10
Egan, Patricia, 132
Egan, Patrick, 143
Egan, Robert, 134
Egi, Stanford, 45
Eginton, Margaret, 36
Egloff, Elizabeth, 184
Ehlers, Heather, 23, 73
Ehlers, Michele, 41
Ehlert, Gunter, 78
Ehlinger, Mary, 72
Ehman, Don, 158
Ehmann, Jennifer, 90
Ehn, Erik, 60
Ehrenberg, Steven, 59, 62, 96
Eichelberger, Ethyl, 55, 86, 201
Eichenberger, Estelle, 78
Eichenberger, Rebecca, 133, 138
Eichler, Alan, 64
Eichman, David, 138
Eigeman, Chris, 48
Eigenberg, Julie Anne, 35
Eighties, The, 142
Eigsti, Karl, 126, 151
Einhorn, Anne, 59
Einhorn, Fred, 85
Einhorn, Susan, 48
Eiseb, Max, 92
Eisen, Max, 53, 60, 62, 92, 101, 146
Eisenberg, Avner, 35, 201
Eisenberg, Charlie, 58, 66
Eisenhauer, Peggy, 8, 104
Ekblom, Josh, 178
Ekson, Larrio, 93
Ekstrom, Peter, 90, 120
Ekzarkhov, Vladimir, 126
El Martirio del Pastor, 93
El, Myron E., 129
Elaine, Miss, 81
Elbert, Wayne, 91
Eldard, Ron, 73
Elder, Eldon, 24
Elder, Tanya, 90
Eldridge, Florence, 228, 229
Eleemosynary, 89, 127, 188
Elejalde, John, 64
Elena, 78
Elephant Man, The, 55
Elg, Taina, 67
Elhinger, Mary, 143
Elias, Rico, 101
Elice, Eric, 122
Elio, Donna Marie, 25, 201
Eliot, Drew, 58, 201
Eliot, Mark, 50
Eliot, Scott, 114
Eliot, T. S., 38
Eliozishvili, Tamara, 13
Elisha, Haim, 53
Elisha, Rina, 53
Elkin, Saul, 143
Elkins, Hilliard, 43
Elko, John, 126
Ellen Jacobs & Co., 60
Ellens, Rebecca, 147
Eller, Lisa, 103
Ellington, Duke, 118
Ellington, John, 172
Elliot, Scott, 114
Elliott, Christine, 65
Elliott, Kenneth, 73, 107, 201
Elliott, Marianna, 77, 135
Elliott, Milton, 53, 61
Elliott, Patricia, 62
Elliott, Paul, 29
Elliott, R Bruce, 68, 83, 102, 201, 205
Elliott, William, 12
Ellis, Chris, 42
Ellis, Elaine, 170
Ellis, Fraser, 37, 201
Ellis, Joshua, 11, 14, 16, 24, 26, 39, 54, 62, 66, 72, 103, 113
Ellis, Ken, 92
Ellis, Matthew, 55
Ellis, Richard, 82, 90
Ellis, Sam, 14
Ellis, Vivian, 146
Ellison, Julian, 92
Ellman, Bruce, 46, 55, 61
Elmer, George, 10, 59
Elmore, Carole B., 138

Elmore, Steve, 202
Elrod, Susan, 8, 10, 17, 35
Els, Mark, 102
Elsen Associates, 55
Elson, Steve, 59
Elsperger, Bruce, 123
Emerald City, 97
Emery, Lisa, 18, 79, 151, 202
Emi, Evelyn Kiyomi, 134
Emmes, David, 172
Emmet, Robert, 9, 17, 68, 102, 202
Emmons, Beverly, 14, 46, 95, 133, 147
Emo, Ann R., 60
Emond, Linda, 119
Empire Loisaida Escola de Samba, 78
Engaged, 120
Engelhardt, Liz, 53
Engelman, Arnold, 51, 52
Engels, Randy, 176
Engelstein, Amy, 74
Engler, Michael, 21, 124, 132
Englert, Bernadette, 122
English Mint, 48
English, Donna, 90, 138, 202
English, Ellia, 162
English, Gary, 160
Englund, Patricia, 154
Enis, Mark, 54
Enjoji, Aaya, 78
Ennis, James, 47
Eno, Mary P., 86, 87
Enrico IV, 103
Enriquez, David, 162
Ensler, Eve, 62
Entertainment Group, The, 20
Entertainment Ink, 67
Epperson, Jane, 98
Epperson, John, 50
Epps, Christian, 60
Epps, Sheldon, 50, 125
Epstein, Alvin, 77, 124, 202
Epstein, Dasha, 12
Epstein, David, 158
Epstein, Jonathan, 160
Epstein, Marc, 131
Epstein, Sabin, 123
Equal Wrights, 66
Erbach, Gregory, 83
Erde, Sara, 80, 93, 202
Erdman, Dennis, 135
Erdman, George, 93
Ericksen, Susan, 132
Erickson, Dan, 51, 202
Erickson, Michael, 68
Erickson, Mitchell, 6
Erkman, Jonas, 78
Erlanger, John, 166
Erlenbach, Johanna, 140
Ermides, Peter, 74
Ernster, Sharon, 104, 107
Errilo, Melissa, 114
Ertischek, Dana, 61
Esbjornson, David, 55, 107, 136
Eschweiler, Paula, 68, 102
Eshelman, Drew, 123
Eskolsky, Alan, 44
Eskra, Donna, 103
Esposito, Giancarlo, 202
Esposito, Mark, 25
Essen, B. J., 139
Essence of Margrovia, The, 68
Essner, Stephen W., 128, 129
Estabrook, Christine, 95
Esterly, James, 67
Esterman, Laura, 28, 72, 202
Estey, SuEllen, 90, 108
Estey, Suellen, 202
Estrada, Elsa, 8
Etcheto, Peter, 61
Ethan, Mark, 85
Etheredge, Randall, 51, 54
Etheridge, Annie Rae, 96
Etienne, Jerry, 174
Etkin, Carol, 65
Ettinger, Daniel, 125, 128, 153
Ettinger, Wendy, 62
Euphorbia Productions, 56
Eustace, Robert, 138
Eustis, Ida Elrod, 126
Evan-Yionoulis, 46
Evanko, Ed, 191
Evans, Abby, 25
Evans, Bill, 63, 64, 86
Evans, Bonnie, 130
Evans, Carl T., 49
Evans, Craig, 71, 107
Evans, David, 95, 162
Evans, Dillon, 63, 104, 132, 202
Evans, Gwyllum, 53, 56
Evans, Harvey, 202
Evans, Jessica, 126
Evans, John, 180
Evans, Maggie, 152
Evans, Maurice, 228, 231
Evans, Nancy, 33
Evans, Peter, 228, 231
Evans, Rosalyn, 63
Evans, Susana, 47
Evans, Troy, 81
Evans-Kandel, Karen, 148, 149

Evening with Robert Klein, An, 8
Everett, Pamela, 126
Everhart, Rex, 45
Evers, Bruce, 122
Evers, Holly, 146
Evett, Benjamin, 77, 124
Evins, Donny Ray (Nat King Cole), 65
Eviston, Kelly, 140
Evora, Cesar, 93
Ewer, Donald, 170
Ewing, Steve, 178
Ewing, Ted, 164
Exact Change, 158
Exclusive Circles, 138
Ezell, Johanna, 182
Ezell, John, 93, 95, 170
Faber, Ron, 80, 143, 202
Fabray, Nanette, 136
Faculjak, Barbara, 112
Fagin, Michael, 77, 124
Fail, Dwain, 180
Fain, Sammy, 146
Faison, Frankie R., 96
Faith, 55
Faith, Hope, and Charity, 55
Faithful Brethren of Pitt Street, The, 54
Falabella, John, 122, 151, 170
Falk, Christian, 78
Falk, Elizabeth, 33
Falk, Willy, 40, 114
Falkenhain, Patricia, 93
Fallen Angels, 165
Fallon, Dan, 165
Falls, Gregory A., 119
Falls, Robert, 144, 147
Fancy, Richard, 99
Fandetta, Ralph, 162
Fanning, Tony, 184
Fantasticks, The, 69, 140, 180
Farbrother, Mandy K., 110
Fardjad, Hamid, 61
Fardon, Joshua, 184
Farer, Ronnie, 72
Faria, Arthur, 12
Farina, Marilyn J., 70, 202
Farkas, Jonathan, 20
Farley, Morgan, 229
Farley, Robert J., 122
Farmer, Jim, 51
Farnworth, Ralph, 116
Faro, Lynn, 162
Farone, Felicia, 82, 202, 205
Farquhar, George, 176
Farquhar, Robin R., 140
Farr, Michele, 122
Farrar, Albert, 94, 95
Farrell, Bernard, 84
Farrell, Francine, 58
Farrell, Gordon, 59, 67
Farrell, James, 58
Farrell, Richard, 119
Farrell, Tom, 65, 90
Farwell, Paul D., 160
Farwell, Susan, 48, 53
Fass, Robert, 82, 202
Fata, Wesley, 184
Faul, Kathy I., 103
Faulkner, Cliff, 172
Faust, Marianne, 164
Faver, Cheryl, 97
Fay, Ellen, 133
Fay, Roxanne, 64
Fay, Suzy, 184
Fay, Tom, 45, 88, 109, 146
Faye, Christina, 54
Faye, Denise, 95
Faye, Joey, 202
Fayne, Danielle, 52
Feagan, Leslie, 45
Fearnley, John, 108
Feathers, 123
Fedigan, James, 6
Fedigan, Michael, 39
Feenan, Marjorie, 61
Feiffer, Jules, 43
Feigin, Andrew, 78
Feigin, Michael, 88
Feinberg, Linda, 88
Feiner, Harry, 143, 165, 179
Feingold, Michael, 94
Feinstein, Michael, 14
Feist, Gene, 103
Feld, Kenneth, 36
Felder, Chris, 39
Feldman, Dave, 65
Feldman, Jodi, 48, 53
Feldman, Richard, 68
Feldman, Ruth, 126, 154
Feldshuh, Tovah, 26, 103, 191, 202
Feldstein, Claudia, 184
Fell, Blair, 158
Feller, Peter, Sr., 26, 39
Felton, Holly, 73
Fences, 165
Fender, Michael Doyle, 23
Feng, James, 53
Fenhagen, James, 166
Fenton, James, 40
Feore, Colm, 174, 175
Ferber, Edna, 154, 162
Ferdinand, David G., 67, 101
Ferencz, George, 46

Ferguson, Eric, 140
Ferguson, Jeffrey C., 162
Ferguson, Lou, 103, 151, 202
Ferguson-Acosta, Dennis, 46
Ferland, Danielle, 39, 202
Ferlo, Patrick, 131
Fernandez, Evelina, 156, 157
Fernandez, Peter Jay, 95, 126, 142
Ferra, Max, 46, 60, 80
Ferrall, Gina, 123
Ferrand, Migdalia, 74
Ferrante, Elena, 65
Ferrante, Frank, 122
Ferrar, Jane, 162
Ferraro, John, 61, 100
Ferraro, Rick, 109
Ferre, Gianfranco, 72
Ferrer, Anthony, 57, 59, 68
Ferrer, Jose, 33
Ferstenberg, Bernard, 83, 202
Fervoy, Ton, 96, 147
Festa, John Joseph, 38
Festa, Ken, 148
Festinger, Kurt, 135
Festival Latino, 93
Festival of One Act Comedies, 57
Feton, Mary Jean, 183
Feuche, Peter R., 48, 59, 67, 68, 102
Feuer, Howard, 42
Feurzeig, Susan, 59
Feydeau, Georges, 108, 132
Feyijinmi, Asma, 78
Fibich, Felix, 15
Ficht, Peter, 81
Fickinger, Steven, 85
Fife, Julie A., 131
Fife, Michael, 56
Fifth of July, 82, 83
Figgis, Mike, 56
Figlmiller, John, 180
Figueroa, Laura A., 176
File, Claude, 169
Filimonova, Galina, 47
Film Society, The, 104
Filthy Talk for Troubled Times, 105
Finch, Chris, 130
Finch, Nick, 130
Finch, Zack, 122
Finding Donis Anne, 64
Fine, Laura, 102
Fine, Rosemary, 10
Finel, Barry, 122
Fineman, Carol, 93
Finer, Gayla, 68, 170
Fingerhut, Arden, 70, 95, 111, 126
Fink, Bert, 25, 30, 36, 38, 40, 44, 68
Finkel, Fyvush, 15, 202
Finkel, Ian, 14
Finkler, Marion, 71
Finlay, Suzanne, 139
Finn, William, 95, 96
Finney, Ginger, 158
Finnie, Leo V., III, 52
Fiore, Colm, 174
Fiorello!, 82
Fioretti, Maria Cristina, 48
Firestone, Henry, V, 93
Firestone, Polly, 161
Firment, Marilyn, 53
First Class, 101
Fischandler, Zelda, 126
Fischer, Don, 52
Fischer, Gioras, 47, 48
Fischer, Lori, 49
Fischetti, Michael, 50, 131
Fish, Kelli, 130
Fisher, Aaron, 122
Fisher, Anne, 69
Fisher, Brian, 74
Fisher, Edith, 179
Fisher, Jules, 8, 20, 162
Fisher, Louis, 179
Fisher, M. Anthony, 39, 113, 133
Fisher, Mark, 65
Fisher, Padraic Lee, 57
Fisher, Paula, 39
Fisher, Robert, 82
Fisher, Sanford H., 66
Fishman, Carol, 97, 104, 106, 107
Fishman, Jonathan, 121
Fisk, James, 102
Fitch, Robert, 136
Fitz, Peter, 78
FitzGerald, Jason, 161
FitzHenry, Sharon, 137
Fitzgerald, Caroline, 179
Fitzgerald, Ed, 88
Fitzgerald, Ella, 68

Fitzgerald, Fern, 202
Fitzgerald, Geraldine, 64, 81, 202
Fitzgerald, John, 135
Fitzgerald, Patrick, 84
Fitzgerald, Peter J., 20, 41
Fitzgibbon, John, 128
Fitzgibbon, Jean, 40
Fitzkee, Peter, 166
Fitzpatrick, Allen, 166
Fitzpatrick, Bettye, 121
Fitzpatrick, Burton, 57
Fitzpatrick, Jim, 153
Fitzpatrick, Joe, 57
Fitzpatrick, Lynn, 140
Fitzsimmons, James, 100
Flackett, Jennifer, 172
Flagg, Tom, 60, 202, 205
Flaherty, Stephen, 67
Flak, John, 82
Flakes, Susan, 64
Flanagan, Fionnula, 103, 202
Flanagan, Michael, 125
Flanagan, Pauline, 81, 84, 202, 205
Flaningam, Louisa, 138
Flate, John-Michael, 34, 202
Fleischer, Stacey, 59, 100, 148
Fleischmann, Mac, 165
Fleiss, Jane, 61, 125, 202
Fleiss, Mitchell, 49
Fleming, Cynthia, 37
Fleming, Eugene, 22
Fleming, James, 53
Fleming, Je Nei, 122
Fleming, Jill W., 63
Fleming, Sam, 52, 61, 161, 166
Fleming, Sarah, 176
Fleming, Toni, 144
Flemming, Matthew, 119
Fletcher, Bill, 133
Fletcher, Bramwell, 229, 231
Fletcher, Dan, 45
Fletcher, David, 27, 154
Fletcher, Gregg, 85
Fletcher, Jack, 123
Fletcher, Robert, 123
Fletcher, Susann, 25, 202
Flockhart, Calista, 121
Flood, Frank Hallinan, 10
Flood, Julia, 160
Flora, Pat, 122
Flores, Cesar E., 178
Floriani, Vincent, 73
Florida Crackers, 79
Flowering Peach, The, 63
Flowers, Kim, 79
Flowers, Roma, 56
Flying Cranes, The, 13
Flynn, Jimmy, 53, 61
Flynn, Juliann, 51, 54
Flynn, Patricia, 50
Flynn, Richard, 58
Flynn, Terrance P., 161
Fo, Dario, 57
Fodor, Joleen, 128
Foeller, William, 132
Fogarty, Mary, 71, 127, 132, 202
Fogel, Doug, 162
Fogel, Leone, 46
Fokine, Isabelle, 72
Folden, Lewis, 53, 55, 137
Foley, Angela, 51
Foley, Ellen, 42
Foley, John, 140
Follansbee, Julie, 56, 61, 202
Fols, Craig, 54, 202
Folstein, Steven, 161
Fontaine, Joel, 123, 178
Fontaine, Luther, 74, 202
Fonte, Henry, 48, 61
Fool Show, The, 126
Fool for Love, 132
Foote, Hallie, 165
Foote, Horton, 46, 137, 158, 165
Foote, Horton, Jr., 46, 165
Footsteps of Doves, The, 58
For Dear Life, 95
For Lease or Sale, 168
Forbes, Barbara, 125, 142, 164
Forbes-Kelly, Carla, 126
Forbidden Broadway, 50
Forbidden City, The, 96
Ford, Alison, 160
Ford, Anne Kerry, 142
Ford, Clebert, 154
Ford, Deanna, 122
Ford, Donald Brooks, 162
Ford, Jennifer, 64
Ford, Patricia, 154
Ford, Rick, 59
Ford, Timothy, 162
Forde, Larry, 72, 143
Forde, Roseann, 68
Forde, Seamus, 10
Fordiani, Francesca, 58
Forella, Ron, 229
Foreman, Richard, 94
Forest, D'Ran, 83
Forest, The, 78
Forestier, Patricia, 176
Forever Plaid, 125

Forget Him, 49
Forgiving Typhoid Mary, 154
Forman, Lisa, 75
Fornes, Maria Irene, 161, 176
Forrest, George, 130
Forrest, Michael, 141
Forrester, Alice M., 57
Forrester, Bill, 119
Forsgardh, Kaj, 78
Forslund, Connie, 134
Forster, Rheatha, 169
Forsyth, Jerold R., 96
Forsyth, Jerry, 92
Forsyth, Nancy, 170
Fortenberry, Philip, 50
Fortgang, Amy, 202
Forum, 181
Fosse, Nicole, 44
Fossey, 183
Foster, Angela, 57
Foster, Frances, 202, 205
Foster, Gloria, 96, 202
Foster, Herb, 42
Foster, Skip, 122, 178
Foster, Tim, 146
Foti, David P., 144
Fotopoulos, Mark, 48
Fouchard, James, 182
Fourcaut, Marie, 93
Fournier, Jean-Pierre, 174
Fowler, Beth, 76, 108, 202
Fowler, Clement, 96, 154, 202
Fowler, Molly, 105
Fowler, Monique, 72, 105
Fowler, Scott, 25, 202
Fowlkes, Constance, 126
Fox, Alan, 90
Fox, Colin, 46, 54, 203, 205
Fox, Dorothi, 92
Fox, Gordon, 180
Fox, Manny, 118
Fox, Marilyn, 172
Fox, Neal, 142, 148
Fox, Paul A., 159
Fox, Terry Curtis, 64
Foy, Harriet, 92
Foy, Harriett D., 162
Fraboni, Angelo H., 25
Fracchiolla, Chris, 73
Fraction, Karen E., 45
Fraggos, George, 31
Franceschina, John, 143
Francine, Anne, 45, 203
Francis, Joseph V., 75, 203
Francis-James, Peter, 203
Franck, Sandra M., 90
Franco, Beth, 81
Frangione, Nancy, 178
Frank, Arthur, 158
Frank, David, 176
Frank, Lee, 63
Frank, Marilyn, 161
Frank, Mary K., 229
Frank, Richard, 122, 184
Frankel, Erika, 161
Frankel, Kenneth, 154
Frankel, Richard, 51, 62, 70
Frankel, Scott, 25
Franken, Rose (née Lewin), 229
Frankenstein, 147
Frankenstein: Playing With Fire, 147
Frankie and Johnny in the Clair de Lune, 121, 127, 134
Frankie, Freddie, 97
Frankish, Leslie, 136
Franklin, Bonnie, 203
Franklin, Roger, 13
Frano, Carl J., 54
Franz, Elizabeth, 136
Franz, Joy, 39, 203
Fraser, Alexander, 54
Fraser, Bert, 203
Fratantoni, Diane, 114, 203
Frawley, Bernard, 84
Frawley, Kathryn, 29, 32, 75, 107
Frawley, Mark, 126
Frayn, Michael, 122, 160, 169, 170, 178
Frazer, Susanna, 82, 203
Frazier, David O., 161
Frazier, Grenoldo, 92
Frazier, Kermit, 68, 166
Frazier, Randy, 52, 58
Frechette, Peter, 21, 188, 190, 203
Fred Nathan Co., 30, 36, 40, 44, 52, 61, 68, 74, 76
Frederic, Inga, 126
Frederick, Ron, 6
Fredericks, Joel, 94
Freeburg, Doug, 142
Freed, Donald, 138
Freed, Morris, 37
Freed, Sam, 107, 203
Freedman, Gerald, 93, 95
Freedman, Glenna, 14, 20, 31, 50, 68, 70, 73, 85, 100
Freeman, Dave, 140
Freeman, David E., 134
Freeman, Diane, 98

Freeman, Jonathan, 104, 203, 205
Freeman, K. Todd, 87, 176
Freeman, Mickey, 88
Freeman, Morgan, 70, 203
Freeman, Scott, 123
Freeman, Stan, 14
Freeman, Tom, 53, 203
Frehner, Harry, 174
Freitas, Robert, 102
Fremont Associates, 36, 59, 61
French, Arthur, 49, 70, 203
French, Jacqueline, 89
French, Martha, 65
French, Michael, 66, 106
Fretts, Christopher, 183
Frey, Leonard, 229, 231
Frey, Maureen, 83
Freydberg, James B., 36, 59, 61
Freydont, Shelley, 64
Freyer, Frederick, 105
Friberg, Cynthia, 95
Frid, Jonathan, 203, 205
Fridman, Staffan, 78
Fried, Scott, 90
Fried-Miller, Gina, 89
Frieder, Sol, 54
Friedman, Deborah A., 105
Friedman, Ginger, 54
Friedman, Glenna, 34
Friedman, Joel Phillip, 152
Friedman, Ken, 180
Friedman, Lewis, 54
Friedman, Nan, 94
Friedman, Peter, 30, 46, 100, 203
Friedman, Seth, 152
Friedman, Sonia, 92
Friedman, Tracy, 54, 180
Friedmann, Joyce, 133
Friel, Brian, 88
Friend, Angela, 152
Friends, 68
Frimark, Merle, 25, 30, 36, 38, 40, 44, 52, 61
Frings, Ketti, 179
Fris, Jack, 73
Frisch, Robert, 146
Frish, Alexander, 13
Fritz, Florian, 78
Fritz, Lana, 85
Froehlich, Linda, 51
Frog in His Throat, A, 108
From the Mississippi Delta, 91
Frost, Lindsay, 41
Frost, Sue, 146
Fruge, Romain, 142, 164, 205
Frumkin, Boris, 118
Frutkoff, David, 55
Fry, Amanda, 150
Fry, Ray, 120
Fry, Stephen, 42
Frye, Dwight, 31
Fryer, Robert, 133
Fryman, Ian, 130
Fuchs, Jay H., 23
Fuentes, Ruben, 8
Fugard, Athol, 121, 137, 168, 172
Fugard, Lisa, 108
Fuglei, Kate, 95, 203
Fuhrer, David, 39, 72
Fuhrman, Debbi, 57
Fuhrmann, Randy, 147
Fujii, Timm, 31, 85, 203
Fulbright, Peter, 22
Fuleihan, Pat, 140
Fuller, Charles, 91
Fuller, Donna, 172
Fuller, Elizabeth, 105
Fuller, James E., Jr., 100, 108
Fuller, Jonathan, 164
Fuller, Nathaniel, 147
Fuller, Penny, 134, 135
Fulton, Julie, 172
Fulweiler, John, 73
Fun, 82
Funicello, Ralph, 123
Funny Thing Happened on the Way to the Forum, A, 123, 144, 158
Fuqua, Joseph, 184
Furber, Douglas, 42
Furrow, Murray, 174
Furse, John, 123
Furth, George, 119, 138
Fusco, Anthony, 85
Fyfe, Jim, 20
Gabay, Eli, 174
Gabel, June, 136
Gabeliya, Emzari, 13
Gabeliya, Vladimir, 13
Gabis, Stephen, 82, 128
Gabriel, Susan, 166, 167
Gadner, Thomas, 47
Gadsden, Victoria, 166
Gaetano, Tony, 130
Gaffin, Arthur, 133
Gaffney, Lauren, 162
Gaffney, Megan, 184
Gaffney, Mo, 59
Gage, Adriane, 102
Gage, Gary, 116, 117, 146
Gage, Patricia, 136
Gagliardi, Leon, 38

Gagnier, Derek, 168
Gagnon, Andre, 174
Gail, Mary, 52
Gail, Tim, 82, 203
Gailen, Judy, 184
Gaines, Boyd, 4, 30, 100, 132, 191, 203
Gaines, Davis, 63, 65, 88
Gaines, James E., 89
Gal, Nir Ben, 35
Galaher, Towner, 73
Galan, Sheri, 51
Galante, Lori, 82, 203, 205
Galantich, Tom, 203
Galardi, Michael, 59, 97
Galasso, Thom, 139
Galati, Frank, 144
Gale, Andy, 114
Gale, Brian, 172
Galeano, Eduardo, 60
Gales, Martron, 74
Gales, Morton, 74
Galin, Alexander, 47, 156
Galindo, Ramon, 25, 203
Gallagher, Kathleen, 28
Gallagher, Larry, 120
Gallagher, Melissa, 141
Gallagher, Terence, 144
Galligan, David, 66
Gallin, Susan Quint, 59
Gallo, Barry R., 105
Gallo, Paul, 16, 26, 45, 93, 109
Galloway, Julie, 131
Galpert, Sheree, 119
Galvan, George, 77
Gam, Rita, 191
Gamache, Laurie, 37, 203, 205
Gamba, Dolores, 22
Gambler, The, 60
Gammell, Robin, 134
Gandy, Irene, 23, 29, 32, 50, 75, 81, 107
Gang, Richard P., 56
Ganias, Eli, 73
Ganio, Michael, 183
Ganly, Kilian, 58
Gann, Dr. Myra, 101
Gannon, Joe, 33
Gans, Sharon, 51
Ganshaw, Robert, 56
Gant, Richard, 89, 184
Ganzer, John, 229
Garber, Robert S., 136
Garber, Victor, 17, 26, 62, 190, 191, 203
Garcia, Lalo, 8
Gardner, Brenda, 67
Gardner, Herb, 138, 143, 150, 165
Gardner, Jeff, 115
Gardner, Josie, 56
Gardner, Rita, 71, 170
Gardner, Robert J., 63
Gardner, Thomas, 47
Gardner, William T., 165
Garfein, Herschel, 60
Gari, Angela, 26, 32
Garner, Jay, 42
Garner, Patrick, 87, 148
Garr, Nicholas, 25
Garretson, Christian, 132
Garrett, Lillian, 76, 134, 135
Garrett, Maureen, 183
Garrett, Nancy Fales, 154
Garrick, Barbara, 21, 203
Garrick, Kathy, 66, 203
Garrison, Al, 122
Garrison, Gregorey, 25
Garrity, Paul, 59, 75, 82, 85
Garron, Victor, 138
Garry, Joseph, 161
Garst, Samuel A., 161
Garvey, Thomas, 168
Garvin, Richard R., 138
Garza, Troy, 37
Gascon, Jean, 174
Gaskins, Deloris, 132
Gasperec, Joseph, 27
Gaston, Lyd-Lyd, 146
Gatchell, R. Tyler, Jr., 16, 23, 24, 38
Gately, David, 57
Gathering, 47
Gaudet, Christine, 54
Gaughan, Jack, 38, 44
Gavon, Igors, 203
Gay, John, 137, 141
Gay, Noel, 42
Gearhardt, Donna M., 100
Geary, Robert J., 57
Gebbie, Tom, 48
Geddes, Jill, 113, 133
Geddie, James, 78
Gedrick, Jason, 19, 203
Gee, Simone, 31, 85
Geffen, David, 38, 41
Geffner, Deborah, 203
Gefroh, Steven J., 161
Gehman, Martha, 203
Geidt, Jan Graham, 124
Geidt, Jeremy, 77, 124
Geier, Paul, 158
Geiger, Mary Louise, 51, 168
Gein, Pamela, 77, 124
Gelb, Jody, 68, 203
Gelbart, Larry, 25, 88, 123, 124, 144, 158
Geld, Gary, 162
Gelfer, Steven, 203, 229, 231
Gelke, Becky, 54, 203
Geller, Bruce, 103
Geller, Richard, 137
Geller, Susan Denison, 135, 172
Gelman, Alexander, 148
Gelman, Jonathan, 57
Gemignani, Paul, 25, 39
Gender, Anna Jo, 36
Genesis, 94
Genesis: Music and Miracles, 94
Genesius, Kate, 134
Genest, Edmond, 154
Genet, Michael, 122
Geneviere, Deborah, 126
Gennaro, 48
Gennaro, Michael P., 142
Gennaro, Peter, 142
Gentile, Anthony, 58
Gentile, Cristina, 48
Geoffreys, Stephen, 192
Geoghan, Jim, 75
Geography of Luck, The, 172
Geoly, Guy, 162
George Washington Slept Here, 49
George, George W., 90
George, Jeffry, 162
George, Philip, 50
Georgian State Dancers, 13
Georgianna, Frank, 138
Geraci, Drew, 37
Geraci, Frank, 64, 99, 203
Geraci, Leslie, 93, 148
Geraci, Paul, 45
Geraghty, Marita, 9, 16, 30, 203
Gerald, Michael, 95
Gerard, Danny, 40, 203
Gerber, Anthony, 60
Gerchman, Glenn, 164
Gerchman, Robin, 164
Gerdes, George, 120
Gere, Richard, 192
Gerety, Peter, 77, 203
Germano, Paul, 162
Germanson, Christa, 178
Gero, Edward, 141
Gerou, Wayne, 56
Gerringer, Robert, 93, 203
Gerrity, Dan, 134, 135
Gerroll, Daniel, 97, 103, 104, 203
Gershwin by Night, 128, 129
Gershwin, George, 130
Gershwin, Ira, 130
Gersten, Alexandra, 62, 68
Gersten, Bernard, 19, 37, 86, 109
Gersten, David, 13, 16, 50, 53, 55, 59, 61, 64, 80, 90, 118
Gerut, Rosalie, 95
Get Any Guy Thru Psychic Mind Control or Your Money Back, 51
Gets, Malcolm, 162
Gettel, Douglas, 58
Gettinger, Don, 80
Gettysburg Sound Bite, The, 57
Getz, John, 41
Ghetto, 35
Ghilardi, David Mitchell, 161
Ghosts, 103, 169
Giamatti, Marcus, 86, 153, 203
Giammarco, Dante, 166
Gianasi, Rick, 102
Gianfrancesco, Edward T., 71, 107
Gianino, Jack, 22
Giannini, A. Christina, 103
Gianono, Joseph, 14
Gianopoulos, David, 203
Giardina, Anthony, 184
Gibbons, June, 161
Gibbs, Ron, 162
Gibney, Susan, 176
Gibson, David, 130
Gibson, Jon, 56
Gibson, Julia, 95, 164, 203
Gibson, Margaret, 96, 134
Gibson, Maureen F., 47, 184
Gibson, Michael, 31, 45, 109
Gibson, Philip, 43
Gibson, Rufus, 158
Gibson, Tanya, 22
Gibson, Thomas, 46, 203
Giddon, Pamela, 49
Giella, David, 134, 138
Gien, Pamela, 61, 77
Gierasch, Stefan, 135
Gift of the Magi, The, 120
Gifts of the Magi, The, 55
Gigi, 83
Gilb, Melinda, 50
Gilbert, Alyce, 32, 37
Gilbert, Edward, 151
Gilbert, Jennifer, 94
Gilbert, John, 119
Gilbert, Tony, 108, 162
Gilbert, W. S., 120
Gilbert, Willie, 182
Gilborn, Steven, 57, 203, 205
Gilburne, Jessica, 22
Gilch, Diane, 142
Giles, Chuck, 27
Giles, Loretta, 105
Gilford, Jack, 33
Gill, Allison, 146
Gill, James, 93, 96
Gill, Michael, 44
Gill, Michel R., 151, 154
Gill, Ray, 70, 113, 133, 203
Gillen, Maria, 97
Gillett, Hamilton, 169
Gillett, Julia, 77, 78
Gillette, Anita, 76, 190, 203
Gilliam, Gwendolyn M., 86
Gilliam, Michael, 66, 134
Gillis, Laura, 68
Gillman, Robert, 158
Gillogly, Bill, 58
Gilman, Sandra, 118
Gilpin, Jack, 204
Gilpin, Michael, 51
Gilroy, Frank D., 142
Gimenez, Carlos, 93
Gimpel, Erica, 100
Gindi, Roger Alan, 70
Ginhorn, Fred, 204
Ginsburg, Ned, 74
Giomatti, Marcus, 205
Gionson, Mel Duane, 98, 204
Gionson, Mel, 205
Giosa, Sue, 72, 204
Giovanni, Paul, 68
Girardeau, Frank, 68, 204
Giroday, Francois, 122, 135
Girolmo, David, 74, 144
Giron, Arthur, 143
Gironimi, Karen, 136
Gish, Lillian, 33
Gist, Jan, 168
Gitkind, Marsha, 128
Gladden, Dean R., 23, 136
Gladden, Teresa, 121
Gladding, Robert, 79
Gladstein, John, 166
Gladstone, Stacey, 57
Glaeser, Nicolas, 65
Glancey, David B., 166
Glant-Linden, Andrew, 82
Glass Menagerie, The, 125, 136, 147
Glass, Philip, 56, 96
Glatzer, Peter, 68
Gleason, Joanna, 39, 62, 89, 154, 204
Gleason, John, 94, 103
Gleason, Paul, 54
Glengarry Glen Ross, 131
Glenn, Bette, 117
Glenn, D. C., 58
Glenn, David, 126
Glenn, Scott, 12, 204
Glenny, Michael, 158
Glikin, David, 75
Glines, John, 54
Glockner, Eleanor, 42
Glore, John, 172
Glossop, Roger, 56
Glover, Brian P., 105
Glover, Cyd, 22
Glover, Keith, 61, 204, 205
Glover, Savion, 22, 204
Glover, William, 104, 135, 176, 177
Glovsky, Jeffrey, 66
Glowacki, Janusz, 180
Gluck, Victor, 105
Glushak, Joanna, 32, 136, 151, 204
Gnat, Michael, 60, 204
Gocher, Mary Jane, 59
God's Country, 119, 120
Godber, John, 81
Godfrey, Jerry, 162
Godinez, Henry, 144
Goede, Jay P., 184
Goehring, Jerry, 64
Goehring, Kate, 144
Goell, Julie, 35, 204
Goethals, Angela, 104, 204
Goetz, Augustus, 154
Goetz, Ruth, 154
Goff, Charles, 65
Goff, Tina Marie, 178
Goffredo, John Allen, 73
Goggin, Jan, 70
Goginava, Dzeheiran, 13
Gogoteshvili, Tamaz, 13
Going, Joanna, 100
Going, John, 24
Golaj, Mariusz, 47
Goldbaum, Mark, 82
Goldbeck, Charles, 68
Goldberg, Jerry, 37
Goldberg, Marcia, 75
Goldberg, Noa, 53, 134
Goldberg, Russell, 82, 204
Golden Glow Unlimited, 55
Golden Leg, The, 75
Golden, Annie, 7, 154
Golden, David, 68
Golden, Larry, 132
Golden, Norman, 75
Golden, Pat, 63
Goldenberg, Jorge, 48
Goldfaden, Harold, 116, 117
Goldman, Byron, 25
Goldman, James, 153
Goldman, Karen, 78
Goldman, Marcyanne, 136
Goldman, Milton, 191
Goldoni, Carlo, 103
Goldray, Martin, 56
Goldsby, Robert, 172
Goldschmidt, Rudy, 162
Goldsmith, Marc, 88
Goldsmith, Merwin, 42
Goldsmith, Oliver, 99, 161
Goldstaub, Mark, 229
Goldstein, Brett, 105
Goldstein, David Ira, 119
Goldstein, Jess, 59, 68, 89, 100, 106, 107, 148, 154
Goldstein, Steven E., 41
Goldstein, Steven, 19
Goler, Lauren, 118
Golub, Peter, 55, 68, 94
Gomer, Jamie, 67
Gomer, Steve, 106
Gomes, Rob, 137, 151
Gomez, Luis Fernando, 93
Gomez, Mateo, 9, 76, 101
Gone to Glory, 139
Gonzalez, Carlos Juan, 141
Gonzalez, Ernesto, 46, 204
Gonzalez, Guillermo, 74
Gonzalez, Joe, 101
Gonzalez, Reynaldo, 161
Gooch, Bruce, 183
Good Black, 92
Good Coach, The, 107
Good Evening, 161
Good Honest Food, 57
Good Omen Productions, 51
Good, Maurice, 174
Goodall, Howard, 53
Goodheart, Carol, 17, 204, 205
Goodin, Steve, 120
Goodman, Benny P., 152
Goodman, David, 102
Goodman, Erika, 65
Goodman, Mark, 89, 142
Goodman, Robyn, 16, 104
Goodman, Susan, 40
Goodrich, Bruce, 54, 59, 83
Goodson, Germaine, 22
Goodspeed, Don, 204
Goodwillie, Steve, 146
Goodwin, Eric, 162
Goodwin, Philip, 141, 148
Goodyear, Sam, 59
Goor, Carolyn, 25, 204
Gordon, Amy, 53, 85
Gordon, Carl, 91
Gordon, Carrie, 73
Gordon, Duran, 78
Gordon, Ellen Scrimger, 103
Gordon, Eric, 105
Gordon, George, 72
Gordon, Jeff, 36
Gordon, Lindsay, 103, 204
Gordon, Lloyd, 130
Gordon, Mark Alan, 102
Gordon, Marvin, 54
Gordon, Peter, 81
Gordon-Clark, Susan, 70, 113, 133, 204, 205
Gordone, Charles, 180
Gordone, Leah-Carla, 153
Gordy, Wayne, 82, 204
Gore, Leigh Gibbs, 57
Gorman, Bob, 229, 231
Gorman, Michael, 138
Gorman, Pat, 45
Gormley, Jamie, 112
Gorositza, Rebecca, 133
Gorton, Rob, 49
Goshert, Joseph, 66
Goss, Bick, 178
Gossett, Robert, 165
Gotschall, Ruth, 162
Gottesfeld, Jeff, 51
Gottfried, Martin, 191
Gottlieb, Jon, 66, 77, 134
Gottlieb, Matthew, 58, 204
Gottlieb, Morton, 33
Gottlieb, Peter, 161
Gottschall, Ruth, 20, 204
Gotwalt, Ed, 182
Gould, Morton, 25
Gould, Richard, 133
Gould, Robert B., 20
Gould, Tom, 52, 62, 131, 169
Gourfain, Noon, 84
Goutman, Christopher, 72, 204
Gow, Brian, 174
Goz, Harry, 15, 204
Gozzi, Carlo, 124
Graae, Jason, 63, 125, 204
Grabber, Ariel, 34
Grabel, Naomi, 47, 107
Grabowski, Christopher, 184
Graczyk, Ed, 50
Graden, David, 49
Gradl, Christine, 122, 176
Grady, Jim, 125
Graff, Lillian, 27
Graff, Randy, 40, 204, 205
Graff, Todd, 106, 204
Graham, Bruce, 107, 154
Graham, Elain, 89
Graham, Hilary, 174
Graham, Randall, 122
Graham, Robert, 121
Graham, Ronny, 110
Granaroli, Ty, 94, 204, 205
Granau, Patty, 73
Grand Central Paradise, 61
Grand Tour, The, 85
Grande Malade, The, 56
Grande, Loretta, 73
Grandma Plays, The, 106
Grant, Byron, 170
Grant, Dennis, 67
Grant, Faye, 204
Grant, Gerald, 99
Grant, Lisa Ann, 40
Grant, Micki, 74
Grant, Schuyler, 53, 204
Grant, William H., III, 91, 92, 166
Grant-Phillips, John, 77
Granville, Bernard, 83, 204
Grate, Gail, 126, 154
Grate, Gayle, 141
Graves, Julie, 129
Graves, Kathryn, 50
Graves, Michael, 99, 102
Graves, Ruthanna, 74, 204, 205
Graves, Shannon, 106, 108
Gray, Alan, 74
Gray, Allan, 174, 175
Gray, Allison, 176
Gray, Amlin, 161
Gray, Daniel, 128
Gray, Dolores, 33
Gray, John, 153
Gray, Kenneth, 176, 177
Gray, Kevin, 31, 93
Gray, Paula, 104
Gray, Sam, 68, 85, 204
Gray, Spalding, 19
Gray, Tamu, 166, 167
Grayman, Dwayne, 92
Grayson, Bobby, 51, 71, 72, 89
Grayson, Jerry, 75
Grayson, Richard, 116, 117
Greater Tuna, 181
Green Card, 77
Green Death, The, 51
Green, Adolph, 25, 33, 146
Green, Allysaon, 59
Green, Babbie, 133
Green, Brian Lane, 34
Green, David, 27, 204
Green, Elizabeth, 112
Green, Fanni, 184
Green, George, Jr., 24, 38, 86, 87
Green, Jackie, 11, 14, 16, 24, 26, 39, 54, 62, 65, 66, 72, 103
Green, Jonathan, 88, 89
Green, Julie, 60
Green, Kenneth J., 92
Green, Larry, 68, 93, 94, 170
Green, Laura, 46
Green, Mary-Pat, 70
Green, Rebecca, 76
Green, Scott, 46
Greenberg, Helen, 85
Greenberg, Jan, 109
Greenberg, Mitchell, 68, 178
Greenberg, Richard, 21, 46
Greenberg, Rob, 184
Greenburg, Dan, 43
Greene, Everett, 129
Greene, James, 204
Greene, Lisa-Gabrielle, 180
Greene, Marlene, 59
Greenhill, Susan, 50, 68, 204, 205
Greenhut, Andrew, 59
Greenleaf, John, 68, 170
Greenstein, Nancy, 72
Greenwald, Leah, 105
Greenwald, Raymond J., 32
Greenwald, Tom, 105
Greenway, Andy, 122
Greenwood, Jane, 6, 19, 88, 89, 147, 184
Greer, Darroch, 56
Greer, Maggie, 51
Greer, Skip, 178
Gregg, Stephen, 57
Gregg, Susan, 170
Gregorian, Vartan, 33
Gregorio, Rose, 41, 204, 205
Gregory, Allison, 138
Gregory, Andre, 18
Gregory, Dawna, 161
Gregory, Gillian, 42
Gregory, James, 79
Gregory, Michael Alan, 65, 170, 204
Gregory, Michael Scott, 25, 204
Greif, Michael, 60
Grenier, Zach, 46, 68
Grennan, Sean, 144
Grey, Clifford, 146
Grey, Larry, 162
Grey, Tina, 59
Gridasova, Marina, 47

Griego, Veronica, 142
Griesemer, John, 19, 204
Griffin, Rodney, 53, 94, 146
Griffin, Tom, 136, 166
Griffing, Lois, 144
Griffith, Barry, 159
Griffith, Edward, 204
Griffith, Jim, 73
Griffith, Lisa, 204
Griffiths, Trevor, 136
Griggs, Robert, 74
Grigoridis, Paul, 55
Grill, Michel R., 141
Grim, Freda, 183
Grimaldi, Dennis, 59
Grimes, Errol, 78
Grimes, Justin, 168
Grimes, Tammy, 204
Grimm, Timothy, 144
Griswold, Mary, 144
Griswold, Tracy, 154
Grizzard, George, 62
Grodner, Suzanne, 165
Groenendaal, Cris, 44, 204
Groener, Harry, 172
Groff, Nancy, 74
Groh, David, 81, 162, 204
Grohol, Jennifer L., 136
Gromada, John, 88, 97, 100, 134
Groos, Daphne, 56
Grose, Andrew, 25, 37
Grose, Molly Pickering, 108
Groseclose, Frank, 122
Gross, Alex, 67
Gross, Cristofer, 172
Gross, Lenny, 49
Grossman, Bill, 38
Grossman, Suzanne, 132
Grove, Barry, 88
Grove, Christopher, 135
Grove, Gregory, 107, 204
Groves, Robin, 66, 184
Gruber, Michael, 37
Gruenewald, Thomas, 146, 162
Grupper, Adam, 39
Grusin, Richard, 46, 52, 204
Guan, H. J., 41
Guan, Jamie H. J., 41, 204
Guare, John, 184
Gubaryev, Vladimir, 158
Guber, Zev, 66
Gudahl, Kevin, 174
Guenther, Alene, 49
Guenther, Daniel, 49
Guenther, Eric, 49
Guerrasio, John, 93, 205, 206
Guibert, Alejandre, 66
Guidall, George, 15, 107, 206
Guilbert, Ann, 138
Guilty Conscience, 48
Guinan, Patricia, 82
Guinand, Louise, 174
Gulan, Barbara, 120
Gulley, John, 127
Gunas, Gary, 20
Gunderson, Steve, 50, 206
Gunn, Bill, 96, 229, 231
Gunn, Moses, 94, 206
Gunnels, Joseph, 140
Gunning, Greg, 146
Gunning, Thomas, 168
Gunther, Peter, 162
Gunton, Bob, 80, 108, 206
Gurciullo, Mike, 178
Gurney, A. R., 51, 62, 154, 179
Gurney, A. R., Jr., 179
Gurr, William, 131
Gus and Al, 100
Guske, Bill, 125
Gustafson, Carol, 134
Gustafson, Russell, 49, 51, 54, 60
Gustafson, Susan, 51
Gutcheon, Jeffrey, 12
Guthrie, Clay, 115
Guthrie, Lee, 144, 145
Gutierrez, Alejandra, 101
Gutierrez, Gerald, 68, 88
Gutkin, Benjamin, 136
Guyton, Don, 48, 65
Guzman, Luis, 58
Guzman, Suzanne, 130
Gwin, Kelly, 136
Gyllenhaal, Kate, 55
Gyngell, Paul, 206
Haas, Barbara, 179
Haas, Lukas, 86
Haba, Yuichi, 78
Haber, John L., 121
Haberman, Linda, 162
Habitation of Dragons, The, 165
Hack, Steven, 206
Hacker, Jerry, 129
Hacker, Kathleen, 129
Hacker, Sander, 43
Hackshaw, Lark, 68
Hadary, Jonathan, 88, 206
Haddad, Ava, 106, 206
Hadley, Jonathan, 113, 133
Hadley, Kevin, 119
Haefner, Susan M., 127
Hafner, Julie J., 70, 206
Hagar, Teresa, 73
Hagen, Daniel, 57
Hageneuer, Hans-Jurgen, 78
Hagerty, Julie, 184, 185
Haggerty, John, 102
Hagman, Gerd, 78
Hahn, Fredrick, 81, 206
Hahn, Margaret, 168
Hahn, Wilhelm, 61
Haigh, Kenneth, 141
Haile, Evans, 19, 206
Haimes, Todd, 103
Haimsohn, George, 143
Haines, Jim, 31, 85
Haines, Mervyn, Jr., 93, 96
Haining, Alice, 97
Haire, James, 123
Haj, Joseph, 56
Halcott, Gary, 91
Hale & Husted, 57
Hale, Alan, 57
Halkmoun, Hassan, 78
Hall, Alan, 22
Hall, Angela, 22
Hall, Bonnie Brittain, 172
Hall, Carol, 129
Hall, Davis, 95, 206
Hall, Douglas, 83
Hall, George, 86, 93, 206
Hall, Georgine, 104
Hall, Irma P., 144
Hall, John, 128, 165
Hall, Margaret, 206
Hall, Margo, 126
Hall, Nancy, 38
Hall, Phil, 162
Hall, Phoebe, 140
Hall, Steven F., 137
Hall, Thomas, 51
Hall, Tom, 18
Hall, Vondie Curtis, 96
Hall, William, Jr., 122, 150
Hall-Smith, Pat, 78
Hallas, Brian, 161
Hallett, Jack, 75, 206
Halley, Ben, Jr., 170
Halley, Russell, 109
Halley, Sharon, 162
Halliday, Andy, 107, 206
Halliday, Jimm, 65
Hally, Martha, 53, 131, 169
Halpern, Jeff, 93
Halpern, Lauren, 52
Halston, Julie, 107, 206
Halverson, Richard, 161
Hamacher, Al, 122
Hamano, Masayuki, 78
Hamburger, Anne, 58
Hamburger, Richard, 169
Hamel, Veronica, 18
Hamer, Nigel, 174
Hamilton, Dan, 181
Hamilton, Jane, 56
Hamilton, Josh, 100
Hamilton, Karlah, 112
Hamilton, Lawrence, 50, 206
Hamilton, Mark, 73, 107
Hamilton, Mitchell, 36
Hamilton, Rick, 123
Hamilton, Sally, 48
Hamilton, Stephen, 51
Hamilton, Tim, 79
Hamilton, Trip, 87
Hamlet, 62, 68, 78, 102, 147, 161
Hamlin, Jeff, 19, 45, 86, 87
Hamlin, Marilyn, 19, 206
Hamlisch, Marvin, 37
Hamm, Lori W., 128
Hammar, Scott L., 141
Hammer, Ben, 143
Hammer, Mark, 126, 151
Hammerstein, Oscar, 2nd, 25, 129, 138, 162
Hammill, Nancy, 140
Hammond, Andrew, 64
Hammond, David, 168
Hammond, Michael, 206
Hammond, Paul, 172
Hammond, Rixon, 122
Hamner, Erich, 31
Hamptgon, Don, 51
Hampton, Christopher, 120, 133, 169, 183
Hampton, Verna, 179
Hanafin, Hope, 55
Hanan, Stephen, 38, 151, 206
Hanayagi, Suzushi, 78
Handley, David, 66
Handman, Wynn, 76
Handy, James, 148, 149
Handy, John, 6, 65
Handy, Mark, 140
Haney, Michael, 142
Hanft, Helen, 88, 100
Hanket, Arthur, 81, 97, 206
Hanley, Ellen, 45, 206
Hanna, Christopher, 183
Hanna, Stephen Robert, 165
Hannah Senesh, 170, 171
Hannah, Felicia, 162
Hannah, James, 73
Hannah, Ned, 146, 162
Hannibal, Lydia, 132, 138
Hanrahan, Michael, 174
Hansberry, Lorraine, 139, 151
Hansen, Doug, 68
Hansen, Greg, 65
Hansen, Judith, 107
Hansen, Larry, 42
Hansen, Mary Ann, 98
Hansen, Melanie, 106
Hanson, Cosmo P., 72
Hanson, Debra, 174
Hanson, Drew, 166
Hanson, Fred, 44
Hanson, Philip, 62
Hanson, Suzan, 138
Haon, Carolyn, 137
Hapgood, 133
Happy Birthday, Mama, 101
Hara, Masami, 78
Harada, Ann, 41, 206
Harborth, Mark, 55
Harbour, James, 180
Hard Times, 172, 173
Harden, Marcia Gay, 183
Harden, Richard, 154
Hardwick, Mark, 72, 140, 143, 206
Hardy, Mark, 140
Hardy, Stephani, 51, 206
Hardy, William, 132
Hare, David, 147
Hare, Will, 206
Hare, Wm., 9, 17, 35
Harelik, Mark, 75, 131, 134, 165, 166
Harger, Gary, 114
Harker, James, 16, 88
Harley, Margot, 68
Harley, Steve, 141
Harling, Robert, 71, 121, 128, 143, 170, 176, 179
Harman, Leonard, 176
Harman, Paul, 38, 206
Harmon, Jeffrey, 206
Harmon, Jennifer, 81, 132, 147
Harmon, Lewis, 82
Harmon, Mike, 63
Harmon, Richard, 92
Harner, Bud, 33
Harnick, Sheldon, 25, 65, 82
Harper, Clyde, 139
Harper, James, 54, 206
Harper, Jannie, 147
Harper, Olivia Virgil, 134
Harper, Sarah, 81
Harpies, The, 105
Harpster, Ken (Bruce), 99
Harran, Jacob, 65, 73, 206
Harrelson, Helen, 148
Harrigan, Nedda, 229, 231
Harrington, Christie, 61
Harrington, Julie Jordan, 132
Harrington, Nancy, 36
Harrington, Wendall, 30
Harris, Amy, 119
Harris, Chaka, 108
Harris, Gary and Timmy, 16
Harris, Gary, 60, 85, 89, 101, 104
Harris, Janet, 88
Harris, Jeremiah, 24, 28, 34, 41, 42, 117
Harris, Joseph, 15
Harris, Joseph, Jr., 15, 41, 42, 116
Harris, Julie, 62, 111, 206
Harris, Michael, 11
Harris, Niki, 37, 83
Harris, Rosalind, 85
Harris, Roy, 30, 100
Harris, Steven, 49
Harris, Timmy, 60, 85, 89, 101, 104
Harris, Viola, 85, 206
Harrison, Babo, 184
Harrison, Gerard, 132
Harrison, Gregory, 66
Harrison, Stanley, 128
Harrison, Tom, 172, 173
Harrison, Tony, 80
Harrod, Christopher, 112
Harryman, Mark, 130
Harshbarger, Lantz, 170
Hart, Charles, 44, 133
Hart, David Earl, 109
Hart, Gail Land, 133
Hart, J. Richard, 37
Hart, Linda, 45, 206
Hart, Lorenz, 108
Hart, Moss, 49
Hart, Natalie, 97
Hart, Roxanne, 17, 206
Hart, Susan, 144
Hartenstein, Frank, 39
Hartley, Cheryl, 43
Hartley, Mariette, 94, 206
Hartley, Susan, 83, 206
Hartman, Michael, 137
Hartnett, Mickey, 170
Hartney, Brick, 73
Hartos, Nico, 58
Hartpeng, Lucia, 78
Harum, Eivind, 206
Harvey, 120, 153
Harvey, Ann, 102
Harvey, Cam, 172
Harvey, Don, 125, 132
Harvey, Elizabeth, 135
Harvey, Jona, 82, 206
Harvey, Nate, 65
Harvie, Bruce, 126
Harwood, James, 162
Hasen, Andy, 82
Hasenstab, George L., 183
Haskell, Jimmie, 78
Haskell, Judith, 103
Haskins, James, 67
Hassett, James, 64
Hasten, Anita, 130
Hastings, Edward, 123
Hastings, John, 52, 60
Hastings, Ron, 174
Hasty, Doctor, 49
Hasty, Nancy, 49
Hatcher, Robyn, 206, 211
Haugen, Rana, 147
Hauptle, Beth, 141
Hausch, Mary, 150
Hauser, Frank, 35, 103
Havard, Celine, 170
Havel, Vaclav, 96, 132, 134
Haven, Sean, 66
Havens, Sean, 62
Haverty, Doug, 153
Havis, Allan, 107, 172
Havoc, June, 33
Hawkanson, David, 148
Hawkes, Terri, 72, 206
Hawkins, Holly, 55
Hawkins, Ira, 108
Hawkins, Marjorie, 103
Hawkins, Rich, 119
Hawkins, Yvette, 11, 154
Haworth, Steven, 153
Hay, Richard L., 138
Hay, Rosemary, 63
Hay, Suzanna, 120
Hayashi, Marc, 134
Hayenga, Jeffrey, 6, 7, 125
Hayes, Anne E., 176
Hayes, Grace, 229
Hayes, Helen, 33
Hayes, Monica M., 63
Hayes, Steve, 90
Hayman, Jill, 114
Haynes, Jayne, 86, 88
Haynes, Jerry, 180
Haynes, Nathaniel, 102
Haynes, Robin, 108, 206
Haynes, William, 49
Hays, Rex, 51
Hayter, Pearl, 128
Hayward, Bridget, 26
Hayward-Jones, Michael, 116, 117
Heacock, Richard, 92
Heafner, Carolyn, 74
Heald, Anthony, 45, 62, 89, 206
Healy, Christine, 172
Heard, John, 62, 206
Hearn, George, 7, 35, 62, 154, 206
Heart Outright, The, 67
Heasley, Katherine, 141
Heath, Kia, 176
Heathen Valley, 56
Heaven Can Wait, 142
Heaven's Hard, 121
Hebert-Slater, Marilee, 120
Hebron, Paul, 23
Hecht, Lawrence, 123, 178
Hecht, Paul, 94, 103, 206
Heckart, Eileen, 89, 207
Hedda Gabler, 99, 165
Hedden, Brian Patrick, 158
Hedges, Allison, 137
Hedwall, Deborah, 30, 79, 104
Heeden, Elizabeth, 58, 60, 63
Heeley, Desmond, 147
Heeschen, Tamara K., 22
Heffernan, Maureen, 165, 168
Heflin, Mark, 129
Heflin, Nora, 157
Heftler, Jennifer, 73
Heick, Aaron, 59
Heidenberg, Pat, 104
Heidi Chronicles, The, 4, 30, 100, 186
Heiges, Denni Lee, 68
Heilbrun, Lorene, 172
Heimann, Robert Paul, 57
Heineman, Laurie, 154
Heineman, Matthew, 76
Heinemann, Charlie, 148
Heinricher, Ann, 42
Heinsohn, Elisa, 44, 207
Heinze, Mona, 132
Heiremans, Alberto, 161
Heiress, The, 154
Heissan, Joe, 153
Heit, Sally, 174
Heitman, Patricia, 84
Helde, Anette, 136
Helferrich, Krista, 52
Hell of a Town, A, 137
Helland, J. Roy, 23, 25, 86, 110
Heller, Adam, 115
Heller, Nina, 105, 107
Hellman, Lillian, 108
Hello Out There, 58
Helm, Tom, 42
Helpern, Lauren, 49, 58, 83
Helpmann, Sheila, 174
Hemenway, David, 24
Hemsley, Winston DeWitt, 229, 231
Henderson, Gregory, 53
Henderson, Jo, 229, 231
Henderson, Judy, 59, 125
Henderson, Luther, 12, 22
Henderson, Stephen McKinley, 176
Hendon, Brent, 144
Hendren, Mark, 120
Hendricks, Leslie, 140
Hendrickson, Val, 57
Hendrix, Leslie, 138
Henig, Andi, 96, 207
Henley, Beth, 158, 172
Henley, Susan, 174
Hennelly, Rachel, 182
Hennig, Kate, 174
Henriquez, Amy, 49
Henritze, Bette, 71, 126, 207
Henry Lumper, 58
Henry, Brian, 176
Henry, Buck, 156, 157
Henry, Elizabeth L., 99
Henry, Susan, 136
Henry, Wilbur Edwin, 59
Henryk, Katherine, 133
Hensley, Dale, 45, 207
Hentschker, Frank, 78
Henzel, Edward, 102, 153
Hepner, Mireya, 77
Hepple, Jeanne, 135
Herbeck, Bobby, 130
Herber, Pete, 40
Herbert, Heather, 32
Herbert, Liam, 39
Herbert, Victor, 130
Herbst, Jeff, 54
Herd, Richard, 136
Hereford, Nancy, 134
Herko, Mark, 90
Herlihy, Ed, 110
Herman, Danny, 37
Herman, Jerry, 85, 162
Hernandez, Alina, 44
Hernandez, Ismael, 61
Hernandez, Philip, 207
Herochik, John, 158
Heroes, 105
Herrera, Emil, 147
Herrera, John, 114
Herrick, Jack, 121
Herring, Elizabeth Heffron, 50
Herring, Elizabeth, 73
Herring, Linda, 92
Herrle, Robert, 159
Herschfeld, Susan, 51
Hersey, David, 38, 40, 133
Hershman, Dara, 80
Herskovitz, David, 94
Herter, Miles, 66
Hertzler, John, 178
Herz, Shirley, 14, 15, 20, 31, 34, 50, 54, 57, 60, 63, 66, 67, 68, 70, 73, 85, 100
Hess, Alexia, 25
Hess, Bonnie, 65
Hess, Elizabeth, 143
Hess, Nancy, 25
Hess, Peggy, 178
Hess, Rodger H., 66
Hester, Richard, 26, 76, 80, 97
Heusel, Catherine A., 85
Hevner, Suzanne, 90
Hewett, Cynthia, 161
Hewett, Peggy, 96, 122
Hewitt, Kenneth R., Jr., 139
Hewitt, Tom, 124, 126
Heydenburg, Patrick, 104
Heyer, Thom, 58
Heyer, Thomas, 58
Heyman, Barton, 107, 207
Hibbard, David, 83
Hibbert, Edward, 42, 184
Hibbler-Kerr, Rio, 133
Hicken, Donald, 164
Hicken, Tana, 126
Hickey, John, 94, 153
Hickey, Louise, 25
Hickle-Edwards, Alan, 147
Hicklin, Walker, 79, 95, 172
Hicklin, Walter, 172
Hickox, A. C., 82
Hicks, Dunson, 151
Hicks, Jeffrey, 161
Hicks, Laura, 30, 207
Hicks, Leslie, 168
Hicks, Munson, 122, 170, 179
Hicks, Peter, 159
Hicks, Richard, 96, 103, 147
Hicks, Shauna, 121, 176
Hicks-Bartlett, Alani Rosa, 152
Hidden in This Picture, 49
Hiegel, Adrienne, 79
Hieger, Carl, 151
Hietikko, Chris, 127
Higgins, Bob, 121
Higgins, Gerri, 41
Higgins, John F., 63, 207, 211
Higgins, John Michael, 68
Higgins, Lisa K., 164
Higgins, Michael, 50, 207
Higgins, Mimi, 105
Higgins, Paul, 92
Higham, David, 53, 61

Highland, Kim, 57, 63
Hilbrandt, James, 164
Hild, Dan, 38
Hiler, Katherine, 96, 172, 207
Hilferty, Susan, 87, 104, 123
Hill, Constance Valis, 131
Hill, Elaine Welton, 133
Hill, Lucienne, 121
Hill, Michael, 48, 61
Hill, Thomas, 132
Hillary, Ann, 75, 125, 207
Hillgartner, Jill, 153
Hillgartner, Jim, 153
Hillner, Nancy, 70, 207
Hillow, George, 183
Hills, Kevin, 59
Hills, Randy, 42
Hillyer, Michael, 49
Hilton, Margaret, 104, 154, 155, 207
Hilty, Lawrence, 130
Himmel, Dieter, 60
Himmel, John, 63
Hindman, Earl, 96, 107, 184
Hindman, James, 90, 162
Hinds, Allen, 134
Hines, Gregory, 193
Hinkle, Anthony Lane, 182
Hinman, Kelley, 98
Hinns, Terry, 23
Hinton, Karen, 150
Hinz, Terry, 141
Hipkiss, Barbara, 103
Hired Man, The, 53
Hironimus, Ronnie, 137
Hiroshima, 134
Hirsch, Andy, 144
Hirsch, John, 184
Hirsch, Vicki, 57, 207, 211
Hirschfeld, Al, 33
Hirschfeld, Susan, 34
Hirschorn, Robert, 116
Hissom, Eric, 127
Hitch, Geoffrey, 128
Hizzoner!, 24
Hladsky, Barbara, 30
Hobbs, Brian, 105
Hobbs, Buck, 102
Hobbs, Corey, 184
Hobbs, Johnnie, Jr., 166
Hobson, I. M., 172, 173
Hobson, Jade, 66
Hobson, Richard, 180
Hochman, Larry, 14, 50, 142
Hochwald, Bari, 124
Hock, Robert, 56, 207
Hodes, Gloria, 42, 207
Hodge Taylor Associates, 33
Hodge, Mike, 111, 122, 154
Hodgen, Barbara J., 51, 62
Hodges, Patricia, 151
Hodson, Ed, 123
Hoesl, Joseph, 70
Hoffman, Amy, 166
Hoffman, Avi, 95, 207
Hoffman, Bob, 122
Hoffman, Elizabeth, 135
Hoffman, Eric, 102
Hoffman, G. Wayne, 143
Hoffman, Gillian, 138
Hoffman, Jane, 158
Hoffman, K. Robert, 67
Hoffman, Kevin J., 68
Hoffman, Mendl, 95
Hoffman, Miriam, 95
Hoffman, Philip, 39, 88, 207
Hoffman, Victoria, 172
Hoffman, William, 136
Hofsiss, Jack, 136
Hofstetter, Benita, 126
Hofvendahl, Steve, 124
Hogan, Frank X., 138
Hogan, Harold, 139
Hogan, James, 133
Hogan, Jonathan, 46
Hogan, Patrick, 75
Hogan, Tessie, 49, 57, 207
Hoglund, Per, 78
Hogue, Jim, 46
Hoisington, Eric A., 25
Holamon, Ken, 130
Holbrook, Ruby, 79, 207, 211
Holder, Donald, 21, 52, 105, 142, 164, 169, 183
Holder, Geoffrey, 33
Holder, Jon, 183
Holgate, Ronald, 26, 207
Holiday, Polly, 147
Holladay, Cleo, 128
Holland, Anthony, 229, 231
Holland, Beth, 33
Holland, Dr. Endesha Ida Mae, 91
Holland, Reece, 133
Holland, Tara, 129
Holler, Oliver, 140
Holley, Robert Bruce, 229, 231
Hollfield, Kimberly, 13
Hollis, Tommy, 144
Holman, Robert, 135
Holman, Terry Tittle, 180
Holmberg, Heather, 75
Holmes, Doug, 129
Holmes, George, 82, 102, 207
Holmes, Harriette H., 148
Holmes, Jesse N., 179
Holmes, John Pynchon, 169
Holmes, Paul Mills, 107, 182
Holmes, Rupert, 112, 152
Holmes, Susan, 151
Holms, John Pynchon, 131
Holpit, Penny, 67
Holt, David, 170
Holt, Marion Peter, 161
Holt, Melonie, 148
Holte, Frank, 174
Holtzman, Will, 136, 169
Holzman, Jonnie, 137
Homan, Mark, 67
Home Fires, 105
Home Games, 125
Honegger, Gitta, 184
Honesseau, Michel, 78
Honey, Susan, 103
Honeywell, Roger, 174
Hong, Barrett, 41
Honig, Edwin, 105, 124
Hontz, J. R., 112
Hoodwin, Rebecca, 82, 150, 207
Hoon, Barbara, 25
Hooper, Colin, 50
Hoover, Paul, 74, 207
Hooyman, Barbara "Babs", 83, 207, 211
Hope, 55
Hope, Sharon, 161
Hopkins, Andi, 126
Hopkins, Bernard, 174
Hopkins, Billy, 46
Hopkins, David, 35
Hopkins, Heidi W., 142
Hopkins, Linda, 22, 207
Hopkins, Richard, 137
Hoppe, Jane, 153
Hopper, Tim, 147
Horan, Bonnie, 99, 207
Horan, Monica, 73
Hordyk, Avril, 49
Horen, Bob, 83, 207
Horgan, Patrick, 51, 72, 207
Horman, Michelle, 72, 207
Hormel, Jim, 130
Horn, Alexander Francis, 51
Horn, Michael, 51
Horn, Roderick, 133
Horne, J. R., 107
Hornecker, Nancy, 63
Horovitz, Israel, 55, 58
Horrigan, Patrick, 28
Horsman, Kim, 174, 175
Horst, Doug, 174
Horst, Ellen, 174
Horton, Brian, 129
Horton, Edward "Buddy", 113
Horton, Jamie, 138
Horton, John, 95
Horton, Louisa, 76
Horvath, Jan, 44
Horwitz, Murray, 12
Hoshko, John, 151
Hoskins, Jim, 143
Hosmer, George, 179
Hosney, Doug, 14, 49
Hostage, The, 169
Hostetter, Paula, 27
Hot L Baltimore, The, 48
Hotchner, A. E., 32
Hoty, Dee, 42
Houdina, Mary Jane, 89
Houdyshell, Jayne, 127, 176, 182
Houghton, J. Joseph, 56
Houghton, Katharine, 19, 53, 207
Hould-Ward, Ann, 39, 88, 96, 113, 133, 147
Houle, Raymond, 36, 207
Houseman, John, 68, 229, 231
Houssels, Elaine, 130
Houston, Rita, 63
Hout, Douglas, 68
Houtrides, Rene, 67
How It Hangs, 66
How the Other Half Loves, 179, 182
Howard, Andrew, 85
Howard, Celia, 153
Howard, Charles, 180
Howard, Christy, 115
Howard, David S., 142, 150, 165
Howard, G. A., 65, 105
Howard, Jeffrey, 68
Howard, Ken, 18, 207
Howard, M. A., 79
Howard, Mel, 22
Howard, Peter, 27, 162
Howard, Stuart, 29, 73, 118
Howard, Tim, 51, 160
Howard, Wade, 90, 207
Howard, Woody, 162
Howe, Joan, 85
Howe, Tina, 104
Howell, David, 131
Howell, Fern, 92
Howell, Mary E., 132
Howell, Michael W., 126
Howland, Beth, 126
Hoxie, Richmond, 62, 66, 169, 207
Hoylen, Tony, 54
Huard, Jeffrey, 44
Hubbard, Kim, 57
Hubbard, Zero, 157
Hubbell, Jeffrey, 74
Huber, Josette, 144
Huber, Kathleen, 207
Hudson, Charles, 138
Hudson, Hal, 90
Hudson, Ken, 180
Hudson, Major, 92
Hudson, Mitchell, 138
Hudson, Rodney, 55, 207
Hudson, Travis, 70, 207
Hudson, Walter, 32
Huesz, James, 141
Huffman, Cady, 57, 207
Huffman, Elizabeth, 56
Huffman, Felicity, 207
Huggans, Amy, 51
Hughes, Alice S., 162
Hughes, Allen Lee, 126, 146, 151, 161
Hughes, Barnard, 33
Hughes, Gus, 150
Hughes, Julie, 22, 34, 35
Hughes, Mark, 164
Hughes, Michaela, 45
Hughes, Stuart, 174
Hughes, Tresa, 15, 207
Hughie, 64
Hugo, Marceline, 86
Hugo, Tara, 148
Hugo, Victor, 40
Hugot, Marceline, 86, 207
Hugus, Jennifer, 160
Huisenga, Craig A., 119
Hulce, Tom, 134, 207
Hulkower, Ellen, 142
Hull, Bryan, 69
Hull, Christine, 129
Hulswit, Mart, 169
Hults, L. R., 64
Human Gravity, 46
Hume, Michael, 131, 165
Hume, Nancy, 136
Humm, Spencer, 170
Hummel, Karen, 81, 85
Hummel, Mark, 20
Hummert, Richard, 176
Humphrey, James, 46
Hunkele, John, 58
Hunkins, Serge, 108
Hunt, Annette, 158
Hunt, Gareth, 29
Hunt, Helen, 19, 207
Hunt, LaShonda, 162
Hunt, Linda, 52, 207
Hunt, Lorraine, 60
Hunt, Margaret, 57
Hunt, Pamela, 82
Hunt, Suzy, 51, 71, 104
Hunt, Terry G., 139
Hunter, James W., 140
Hunter, JoAnn M., 25
Hunter, Kim, 50, 207
Hunter, Ronald, 181
Hunting Cockroaches, 180
Huntington, Burr, 139
Huntington, Crystal, 106
Huntington, John C., III, 184
Huntley, Paul, 15, 17, 30, 38, 42, 45, 67, 80, 86, 103, 111, 148
Huntsman, Laurie, 158
Hurd, Adrienne, 83
Hurd, Kate, 66
Hurd, Mary, 99
Hurd, Michelle, 65
Hurley, Brian, 121
Hurley, Patrick, 46, 158
Hurst, David, 54
Hurst, Deborah, 76
Hurst, Gregory S., 142
Hurst, Lon, 74
Hurst, Melissa, 170
Hurst, Scott A., 174
Hurston, Zora Neale, 135
Hurt, Mary Beth, 62
Hurt, William, 62, 193
Hurtt, Wilton, 139
Hurwitz, Rosalind, 64
Huslop, Jeff, 174
Husson, Richard, 63
Huston, Eric, 122
Hutchinson, Jeffrey, 174
Hutchinson, Ron, 135
Hutchison, Paul, 81
Hutson, Eric, 42
Hutt, William, 174, 175
Hutton, Bill, 66, 92, 207
Hutton, John, 132, 151
Hutton, William, 92
Hwang, David Henry, 41, 56
Hwong, Jason, 41
Hwong, Lucia, 41
Hyatt, Jeffrey, 58
Hyland, Leslie, 63
Hyman, Earle, 70, 208, 211
Hyman, Larry, 66, 88
Hymen, Mark, 95, 176, 177
Hynd, Ghretta, 78
Hynes, Holly, 108
Hyslop, Bonnie, 98
I Could Go On Lip-Synching, 50
I Do Not Like Thee, Dr. Fell, 84
I Ought to Be in Pictures, 159
I'll Go On, 86
I'm Not Rappaport, 127, 138, 143, 150, 165, 181
I've Got the Tune, 105
I, Juan de Pareja, 74
Iacovelli, John, 134, 135, 172
Iagnocco, Ray, 111
Iannucci, Michael, 83, 208, 211
Ibe, Anna, 47
Ibsen, Henrik, 56, 99, 103, 148, 165, 169
Iglewski, Richard S., 147
Ikeda, Thomas, 86, 147
Iko, Momoko, 98
Illien, Phyllis Della, 39, 41, 113, 133
Ilo, Angelique, 37
Imaginary Invalid, The, 147
Imbody, Joel, 122
Imbrie, Peggy, 162
Immigrant, The, 75, 131, 165, 166, 167
Immigrant: A Hamilton County Album, The, 131
Impassioned Embraces, 170
Imperialists at the Club Cave Canem, The, 93
Importance of Being Earnest, The, 46, 132, 164
In A Pig's Valise, 104
In Perpetuity Throughout the Universe, 81, 172
In a Pig's Valise, 104
In the Beginning, 153
Incidental Music, 70
Increased Difficulty of Concentration, The, 132
Indriati, Tita, 47
Ingalls, James F., 124, 132, 147
Inge, Lynmarie, 130
Inge, Matthew, 208
Ingham, Barrie, 116
Ingram, Clinton Chinyelu, 60
Ingram, Michael, 31
Ingram, Tad, 161
Innaurato, Albert, 100
Innes, John, 174
Innes, K. Craig, 20
Innes, Laura, 81
Innvar, Christopher, 74
Inside Out, 169
Inskeep, Carter, 48
Intermezzo, 184
Interrogating the Nude, 184, 185
Into the Woods, 39, 113, 133, 186
Investigation of the Murder in El Salvador, The, 97
Ionesco, Eugene, 139
Iovino, Andrea, 66
Irby, A. Dean, 101
Irish Rascal, The, 161
Irma La Douce, 174
Irun, Margarita, 93
Irving, George S., 33, 42, 208, 211
Irving, Suzanne, 119, 178
Irwin, Bill, 36, 86, 87, 208
Isaacman, Marc, 99
Isaacson, Donna, 88
Isert, Scott, 150
Ishida, Jim, 77
Ishioka, Eiko, 41
Israel, Robert, 93
Itabora, 60
Italian American Reconciliation, 88, 136, 143
Itzen, Gregory, 135
Ivanek, Zeljko, 147
Ivanoff, Alexandra, 93
Ives, David, 57, 67
Ives, Jane, 108
Ivester, Stephen, 127
Ivey, Dana, 62, 70, 208
Iwai, Masahiro, 78
Iwasaki, Hiroshi, 96
Jablons, Karen, 208, 211
Jablons-Alexander, Karen, 125
Jablonski, Peter, 125
Jablos-Alexander, Karen, 125
Jabo, Sawung, 47
Jackel, Paul, 113, 133
Jacker, Corinne, 154, 165
Jackness, Andrew, 14, 16, 141
Jacks, Susan, 208
Jacksina, Judy, 63, 67
Jackson, Andrew, 174
Jackson, Anne, 15, 208
Jackson, Armond O., 139
Jackson, Brian H., 174
Jackson, Charles A., 139
Jackson, Damien, 88, 104
Jackson, David, 74, 208, 211
Jackson, Jill, 122
Jackson, Johanna, 168
Jackson, Julie, 144
Jackson, Kevin, 132, 184, 185
Jackson, Kirk, 184, 185
Jackson, Maggie, 83
Jackson, Marsha, 11
Jackson, Nagle, 158
Jackson, Rosemarie, 142, 164
Jackson, Samuel, 91
Jacob, Abe, 22, 24, 37, 66
Jacob, Neil, 67
Jacobi, Michelle, 90
Jacobowsky and the Colonel, 85
Jacobs, Ben, 62
Jacobs, Bernard B., 25
Jacobs, Ellen, 77, 78
Jacobs, Jack, 108
Jacobs, Marc Rusty, 208
Jacobs, Rusty, 83
Jacobs, Sally J., 38
Jacobson, Henrietta, 230
Jacoby, Mark, 27
Jacques Brel Is Alive and Well and Living in Paris, 128
Jaffe, Daniel M., 159
Jaffe, Joan, 90, 208, 211
Jaffrey, Sakina, 49, 80
Jagim, Jay Michael, 121
Jahn, David, 130
Jakobshagen, Claudia, 78
James, Di Ray, 165
James, Hawthorne, 135
James, Jerry, 50
James, Joseph, 68
James, Kelli, 208, 211
James, Kricker, 54, 208, 211
James, Nedra, 180
James, Peter Francis, 96, 103, 165
James, Toni-Leslie, 55, 60, 98
Jamieson, Heidi Peek, 166
Jamieson, Lynn Rudner, 150
Jampolis, Neil Peter, 22
Jamrog, Joseph, 58, 208, 211
Janasz, Charles, 100
Janney, Allison, 62
Janzen, Melanie, 174
Jaramillo, Leticia, 138
Jared, Robert, 100, 121, 161
Jaris, Richard, 18
Jarkowsky, Andrew, 48, 61, 68, 102, 208
Jarred, Joseph, 65
Jarrell, Randall, 98
Jarry, Alfred, 87
Jarvie, Richard, 174
Jasien, Deborah, 142, 164
Jason, Mitchell, 15
Jason, Robert, 132, 141
Jasperson, Mary, 57, 63
Javis, John Henry, 166
Javore, James, 162, 163
Jay, Mary, 104, 141, 208, 211
Jay, Penny, 82, 208, 211
Jay, William, 122, 165
Jay-Alexander, Richard, 40
Jayce, Michael, 80
Jbara, Gregory, 23, 208
JD Productions, 67
Jean, Charles, 178
Jean, Jeffrey W., 127
Jefferies, Annalee, 121
Jeffery, Gayle, 183
Jeffrey Richards Associates, 32, 48, 50, 53, 61, 71, 72, 75, 81, 107, 116, 117
Jeffrey, Gayle, 68
Jeffreys, Stephen, 172
Jeffries, Kevin, 82
Jeffries, Peter, 168
Jellison, John, 42
Jenabi, Mehrdad, 61
Jenkins, Beverly, 91
Jenkins, Carol Mayo, 136
Jenkins, Cecil, 58
Jenkins, David, 32, 59, 136, 148
Jenkins, DeVida, 64
Jenkins, Paulie, 119, 134, 135, 172, 178
Jenkins, Richard, 72
Jenkins, Tamara, 114
Jenkins, Terence, 122
Jenner, James, 98, 208, 211
Jennings, Brian K., 138
Jennings, Byron, 132
Jennings, Karen, 102
Jennings, Ken, 122
Jennings, Nolan, 174
Jenrette, Rita, 51, 208, 211
Jensen, Brian, 79
Jensen, Don, 11, 51
Jensen, John, 158, 166
Jensen, Robert, 162
Jenson, Kari, 73
Jernigan, Terry G., 183
Jerome Robbins' Broadway, 25, 186
Jerome, Timothy, 42, 96, 208
Jesse, Dan, 150
Jeter, Michael, 75, 208, 211
Jeter, Victoria, 92
Jetter, Robert, 46
Jika, 92
Jiler, Hill Carrie, 58
Jiler, John, 208
Jilmer, G. Theodore, 52
Jirousek, Julie, 83
Jobes, Stephen, 58
Jochim, Keith, 147

Joe Turner's Come and Gone, 122, 123, 132
Joerder, Norb, 72
Johannes, Mark, 128
Johannesen, Lars, 103
Johanson, Don, 116, 208
Johanson, Robert, 162
Johanson, Ulf, 78
Johl, Peter, 170
John, Errol, 230
Johns, Kurt, 114
Johns, Martin, 42
Johnson, Alan, 20, 96
Johnson, Ann, 184
Johnson, Arch, 59, 148, 208, 211
Johnson, Art, 161
Johnson, Bertina, 95
Johnson, Bjorn, 114
Johnson, Bryan, 49, 53, 61
Johnson, Cindy Lou, 79
Johnson, Cullen, 58
Johnson, Dan, 102
Johnson, David, 135
Johnson, Doug, 122
Johnson, Edward, 166
Johnson, Eric, 42
Johnson, Eve, 128
Johnson, Gregory, 94
Johnson, Grey Cattell, 58
Johnson, Ian Ellis, 151
Johnson, Isiah, 126
Johnson, Jill, 134
Johnson, John, 123
Johnson, Keith, 126
Johnson, Lamont, 142
Johnson, Lynn, 54
Johnson, Mary H., 137
Johnson, Michael, 150
Johnson, Onni, 208
Johnson, Page, 208, 211
Johnson, Paul, 82, 83
Johnson, Reid G., 159
Johnson, Richmond, 68, 102
Johnson, Russell, 151
Johnson, Sy, 22, 50
Johnson, Todd C., 127
Johnson, Vera, 164
Johnson-Liff & Zerman, 12, 38, 44, 72
Johnston, David, 49
Johnston, Jane A., 172
Johnston, Justine, 42, 208
Johnston, Nancy, 70
Johnston, Ron, 23
Joiner, Dorrie, 71, 208
Jolli, Agus, 47
Jolly, Russ, 137
Jon, David, 93
Jones, Andrew Earl, 153
Jones, B. J., 144, 145
Jones, Barney, 123
Jones, Bradley, 37
Jones, Bryan C., 122
Jones, Cassie, 158
Jones, Cherry, 77, 124, 208
Jones, Clayton Barclay, 104
Jones, Denny, 16
Jones, Derek, 141
Jones, Dexter, 74
Jones, Don, 31, 85
Jones, Duane L., 230, 231
Jones, Gib, 45, 109, 146
Jones, Gregg, 140
Jones, Gregory, 150
Jones, Herman LeVern, 92
Jones, James Earl, 193
Jones, Jane, 119
Jones, Jay Aubrey, 38, 208, 211
Jones, Jeanne, 51
Jones, Jen, 143, 176, 179
Jones, John Christopher, 88, 124
Jones, John-Frederick, 172
Jones, Leilani, 50, 208, 211
Jones, Luther, 140
Jones, Mark, 59
Jones, Martin, 176
Jones, Melody, 116, 117
Jones, O-Lan, 72
Jones, Ora, 144
Jones, Russ, 162
Jones, Sherry, 181
Jones, Simon, 133
Jones, Stephen Mack, 52
Jones, Stephen, 107
Jones, Steven Anthony, 123
Jones, Suzanne, 161
Jones, Tom, 69, 140, 180
Jones, Walker, 184
Jones, Walton, 143, 176, 178, 179
Jones, William Barto, 27
Jonson, Ben, 184
Joplin, Joneal, 170
Jordan, Andy, 49
Jordan, Grace, 49
Jordan, Logan, 162
Jordan, Richard, 134
Jordan, Samantha, 162
Jory, Jon, 120
Joseph Harris Associates, 41
Joseph, Michael, 139
Joseph, Robin Anne, 55
Joshua, Larry, 154

Joslyn, Betsy, 39
Jost, Ted, 109
Jovovich, Scott, 25
Joy, James Leonard, 122, 126, 146
Joy, Mary, 100
Joyce, Heidi, 83, 208
Joyce, James, 57
Joyce, Melba, 22
Joyce, R. E., 166
Joyce, Richard, 166
Joyce, Stephen, 134, 135
Juback, John, 58
Judd, Jacqueline, 61
Judge, Diane, 23, 29, 32, 50, 75, 81, 107
Judge, Shawn, 132, 136
Julian, Pat, 52
Juliet, 46
June Moon, 58
Jung, Philipp, 21, 67, 89, 124, 169, 176
Jurglanis, Marla, 137
Just Say No, 107
Juster, Norton, 68
Justice, 64
Jutras, Simon, 165
Kaczorowski, Peter, 88, 96, 169, 176
Kadin, Charles S., 121
Kadri, Ron, 158
Kafka, 28
Kagan, Diane, 103, 208
Kagel, Bruce, 72
Kagen Lynellen, 56, 62
Kahle, Bruce R., 62
Kahmann, Tess, 63
Kahn, Jerry, 46
Kahn, Lesly, 85
Kahn, Madeline, 23, 136, 208
Kahn, Michael, 141
Kaikkonen, Gus, 102
Kain, Amber, 92
Kaladjian, Shirleyann, 182
Kalas, Janet, 68, 81, 132
Kalcheim, Lee, 68
Kaledin, Nick, 73, 168
Kalember, Kimberly, 116
Kalfin, Robert, 103, 104
Kalisher, Bonnie, 68
Kallos, Stephanie, 122
Kamhi, Katherine, 208
Kamil, Amien, 47
Kamlot, Robert, 26
Kamm, Tom, 78, 97
Kandel, Lenore, 43
Kandel, Paul, 148
Kane, Bradley, 208
Kane, Carol, 156, 157
Kane, Donna, 208
Kane, Douglas, 72
Kane, Mary, 107
Kane, Patricia, 67
Kane, Sheri, 55
Kane, Stephen, 143
Kanengeiser, Anne, 152
Kanin, Garson, 23, 33, 136, 158
Kann, Jerry, 67
Kansas, Jeri, 208
Kantor, Kenneth, 109, 162
Kantrowitz, Jason, 34
Kapetan, George, 161
Kaplan, Curt, 131
Kaplan, Cynthia, 51, 62
Kaplan, Howard Tsvi, 127
Kaplan, Michael B., 46
Kaplan, Pamela, 90
Kaplan, Shirley, 46
Kaplan, Steve, 57, 66, 68
Karcher, James, 46
Karchmer, Charles, 68, 166, 169
Karibalis, Curt, 41, 208
Karlya, Tom, 73
Karn, Richard, 105
Karp, Warren, 82
Karpe, Alan, 112
Kartiganer, Cathleen N., 102
Karvonides, Chrisi, 184
Kassel, Paul, 73
Katarina, Anna, 72, 208
Kathy and Mo Show, The, 59
Katlin, Bruce A., 57
Katona, Raissa, 44
Katsaros, Doug, 32
Katz, Abbie H., 77, 124
Katz, Howard, 58
Katz, Leon, 132, 184
Katz, Michael M., 230
Katz, Natasha, 72, 95, 134, 136, 162
Katz, Noel, 56
Katz, Paul, 142
Katz, Tracy, 113, 133
Katzman, Bruce, 97, 184
Kauahi, Norman Wendall, 20
Kauffman, Jean, 126
Kauffman, Thomas M., 164
Kauffmann, Christian, 20
Kaufman, Brian A., 59
Kaufman, Eric H., 176
Kaufman, George S., 49, 58, 130, 154
Kaufman, Marta, 152

Kaufman, Martin R., 51, 60
Kaufman, Michael, 172
Kaufmann, C. Phillips, 184
Kavanagh, John, 10
Kavanagh, Richard, 230
Kavilis, Diana, 37, 130
Kawamata, Shinobu, 78
Kawolsky, Christopher, 121
Kay, Hershly, 37
Kay, Michael J., 178
Kaye, Deena, 67
Kaye, Doug, 140
Kaye, Judy, 27, 44, 57, 193, 208
Kaye, Rik, 27
Kaye, Sylvia Fine, 33
Kaysar, Franklin, 70
Keal, Anita, 51, 208
Kean, Norman, 43
Keane, John B., 161
Kearney, Kristine, 168
Kearsley, Barry, 41
Keating, Barry, 34
Keating, Charles, 88, 154, 208
Keating, Gary-Thomas, 160
Keefe, Anne, 154
Keefe, Bob, 152
Keegan, Ted, 108
Keeler, Brian, 66
Keeler, William, 136
Keeley, David, 174
Keenan, Claudia, 183
Keener, Christopher, 138
Keeney, Tom, 143
Keever, Tom Dale, 56, 96
Kehr, Don, 125
Keil, Mary, 34
Keith, Jerry, 34
Keith, Marilyn, 100
Keith, Warren, 137
Kekana, Fana, 92
Keller, Jeff, 44
Keller, Jim, 148
Keller, John-David, 172
Keller, Martin, 123
Keller, Richard, 62, 154
Keller, Thomas Lee, 82
Kellermann, Susan, 184
Kellett, Robert, 45, 209
Kelley, Kevin, 60
Kellman, Barnet, 89
Kellogg, Christine, 66
Kellogg, Marjorie Bradley, 52, 103
Kellogg, Mary Ann, 56
Kellstron, Gail, 57, 63
Kelly, Charles, 73
Kelly, Chris, 68, 84
Kelly, David Patrick, 94
Kelly, Dawn, 77
Kelly, George B., 75
Kelly, Jean, 39
Kelly, John, 93, 154
Kelly, John-Charles, 143
Kelly, Kate, 131
Kelly, Kevin, 138
Kelly, Kieran, 142
Kelly, Lydia, 19
Kelly, Marguerite, 17, 209
Kelly, Randy, 48, 53
Kelly, Thomas A., 15
Kelly-Young, Leonard, 151
Kelmenson, Bob, 59
Kemp, Sally, 172
Kempson, Laurel, 140
Kenana, Fana, 92
Kendall, Carla, 130
Kendall, Heather L., 161
Kendall, Joan, 157
Kendall, Kathryn, 82, 142
Kendrick, Richard A., 67
Keneally, Ken, 111
Kener, David, 95, 209
Kennedy, Ashley York, 184
Kennedy, Beau, 74
Kennedy, David, 72
Kennedy, Dennis, 144
Kennedy, Janette, 47
Kennedy, Jihmi, 100
Kennedy, Kathi, 184
Kennedy, Kathleen, 161
Kennedy, Laurie, 16, 46, 154, 155
Kennedy, Lorne, 174, 175
Kennedy, Morgan, 68
Kenney, Mare, 83
Kenney, Pamela Stross, 138
Kenny Loggins on Broadway, 16
Kenny, Don, 78
Kenny, Frances, 119
Kenny, Jack, 15, 57, 209
Kenny, John, 82
Kenny, Laura, 119
Kenny, Paula, 84
Kent, Barbara, 140
Kent, David, 160
Kent, Jeffrey D., 131
Kent, Roberta, 33
Kenyon, Laura, 51, 142, 209
Kenyon, Neal, 143
Kenzle, Leila, 73
Keogh, Garrett, 10
Keogh, Pat, 109
Keough, Rosemary, 83
Kepros, Nicholas, 80, 209

Kern, Jerome, 83, 129, 162
Kern, Philip, 45
Kernaghan, Maryellen, 63
Kernan, Peter, 168
Kerner, Howard, 179
Kerner, Norberto, 80, 209
Kerner, Susan, 142
Kerns, Linda, 115
Kernsowski, Maud, 58
Kerr, Dave, 174
Kerr, E. Katherine, 154
Kerr, Gary, 55
Kerr, Katherine, 62
Kerr, Patrick, 78, 184
Kerr, Philip, 103, 209
Kerr, Robert, 100
Kerrigan, Ed, 130
Kersey, Billye, 209
Kershaw, Whitney, 209
Kessler, Glen, 142
Kessler, William H., Jr., 32
Kettells, Tom, 183
Kevoian, Keter, 44
Kevrick, Robin, 154
Key, Merrill, 138
Key, Tom, 61, 122, 209
Keys, Henson, 108
Kfir, Michael, 53, 134
Khalaf, Lamis, 67
Khazhomiya, Nelli, 13
Khoury, Linda, 141
Khoury, Pamela, 25, 209
Khozashvili, David, 13
Khozashvili, Teimuraz, 13
Khumalo, Sydney, 156
Kiara, Dorothy, 50
Kiberd, James, 82
Kidd, Billy, 33
Kidd, Charles S., 134
Kief, Garry C., 33
Kiger, Al, 129
Kijner, Janine, 94, 96
Kikuchi, Susan, 25
Kilburn, Terence, 159
Kildare, Martin, 123
Kiley, Richard, 62, 154
Kilgarriff, Patricia, 24, 146
Kilgore, John, 34, 62, 96
Kilian, Phil, 72
Killingsworth, Kim, 130
Killmer, G. Theodore, 52, 98
Killmer, Ted, 58
Kilmer, William A., 160
Kilner, Kevin, 125
Kilroy, Colette, 21
Kilty, Jerome, 124, 128
Kim, Josie, 77
Kim, Randall Duk, 123
Kim, Willa, 20, 118
Kimball, Donna, 161
Kimble, Nicki, 129
Kimbrew, Cher Ranae, 54
Kimbrough, Matthew, 143, 160
Kimbrough, Stephen, 130
Kimmel, Mike, 83, 209
Kimsey, Todd, 131
Kin, Jeff, 128
Kincaid, John A., 103
Kind Ness, 161
Kindberg, Wendell, 64
Kindlon, Peter M., 131
Kinet, Kristina, 56
King Henry IV, Part One, 48
King John, 94
King Lear, 138, 174, 175
King, Alice, 51
King, Anne S., 77, 124
King, Doug, 129
King, Floyd, 141
King, Ginny, 209
King, Hampton F., Jr., 112
King, Kimberly, 127, 158
King, Larry L., 107, 129, 209
King, Lucille, 56
King, Martha, 102
King, Sherry P., 95
King, Virginia, 122
King, Woodie, Jr., 11, Jr., 92
Kingfish, 156, 157
Kingsbury, John W., 141
Kingsley, Barbara, 147
Kingsley, Michael, 68, 102
Kingsley-Weihe, Gretchen, 40, 108, 209
Kingston, Debora E., 63
Kinney, Terry, 79
Kinsey, Suzanne, 130
Kinsley, Dan, 63
Kinter, Richard, 128
Kinter, Roddy, 128
Kiouses, John, 176
Kirby-Nunes, Mizan, 209
Kiritake, Kanju, 78
Kirkman, Tamara, 53
Kirkpatrick, Douglas, 58
Kirkwood, James, 37, 230
Kirman, John, 86
Kirsch, Carolyn, 209
Kirsch, Daniel D., 105
Kirsch, Gary, 90, 146
Kirsh, Bob, 126
Kirshner, Richard, 56
Kirsopp, Gregg, 116, 117
Kirstein, Dale, 44
Kirtley, Judith, 63
Kirwin, Terry, 146

Kismet, 130
Kiss Me Quick Before the Lava Reaches the Village, 90
Kiss Me, Kate, 130
Kiss of the Spider Woman, 164, 184
Kissel, David, 162
Kissel, Jeremiah, 160
Kitakazaki, Takashi Kitakizaki, 78
Kittner, Harriett, 40
Kittredge, Ann, 126, 165
Kladitis, Manny, 31
Klappas, Pam, 129
Klapper, Stephanie, 31, 85
Klavan, Laurence, 57, 61
Kleban, Edward, 37
Klein, Amanda J., 52, 90, 126
Klein, Lauren, 110, 150
Klein, Robert, 8, 209
Klein, Timothy D., 102
Kleinbort, Barry, 60
Klementowicz, Paul, 102
Klemperer, Werner, 33
Kletter, Debra J., 79, 89
Kliegel, Frank, 37
Klim, Cheryl, 61
Kline, Kevin, 93, 209
Kline, Tamara, 81
Klingelhoefer, Robert, 68, 101
Klinger, Cindi, 37
Klinger, Mary K., 134
Kloth, Ken, 161
Klotz, Florence, 33
Klunis, Tom, 41, 209
Knapp, Bob, 151
Knapp, Jacqueline, 169
Knapp, Sarah, 70, 90, 209
Knapp, Will, 50
Knecht, Peter J., 137
Knego, Helena, 85
Knell, Dane, 128
Knepp, 48
Knight, Isabella, 153
Knight, Jonathan, 60
Knight, Lily, 126
Knight, Michael E., 125
Knight, Mykal, 141
Knight, Susan, 184
Knight, Wayne, 86
Knots, Marilyn, 110
Knott, Frederick, 179
Knox, John, 139
Knox, Kerro, 3, 179
Knudsen, John, 27
Knudson, Kurt, 81, 122, 209
Kobart, Ruth, 123
Kobayashi, Katsuya, 78
Kobi, Michi, 98, 209
Kocek, Sue, 182
Koch, Danielle T., 126
Koch, David Hunter, 119
Koch, David, 27, 162
Koch, Edward I., 93
Kochergin, Eduard, 158
Kochman, Paul A., 49, 51, 53, 57, 61
Kociolek, Ted, 146
Kocsko, Grace, 137
Koenig, Jack, 143, 183
Koestner, Paul, 60
Koeppe, Sarah Cornelia, 92
Koh, Scott, 151
Kohler, Anita, 78
Kohnert, Mary, 134
Koka, Juliette, 33, 209, 211
Kole, Debby, 65
Kolesky, Jeff, 122
Kolinski, Joseph, 40, 209
Kolo, Fred, 76
Kolodner, Arnie, 107
Kondoleon, Harry, 68
Kondrat, Michael J., 52, 75
Konig, David, 57
Konigisor, Kate, 56, 59
Kooi, John, 160
Koop, Kris, 162
Kopache, Thomas, 19, 68, 94, 209
Kopelow, Mike, 49, 54, 58
Kopischke, Alan, 123
Kopit, Arthur, 120
Korbich, Eddie, 108, 209
Korder, Howard, 57
Korey, Alix, 96, 165, 209
Korf, Mia, 98
Korn, Jeffery, 151
Kornberg, Richard, 15, 93, 104
Kornbluth, Mark, 118
Korsgaard, Kendall, 56
Korthaze, Richard, 45, 209
Kosher, Alan Ross, 113, 133
Kosic, Frank, 146
Kosicka, Jadwiga, 180
Kosis, Tom, 37, 209
Koslow, Ira, 8
Koteas, Elias, 184
Kotlowitz, Dan, 55, 161
Kourilsky, Francoise, 67
Koustik, Art, 172, 173
Kovacs, Geza, 63
Kovarik, Christopher, 180
Kowanko, Chris, 92
Kozak, Ellen M., 161
Kozlov, Oleg, 47
Kozyrev, Sergei, 47

Kraft, Barry, 123
Kraft, Hy, 15
Krag, James, 144, 145
Krahenbuhl, Deborah Weber, 178
Kral, Stanislaw, 47
Kramer, Barry, 61, 209
Kramer, Carie, 21
Kramer, Karl, 98
Kramer, Larry, 107
Kramer, Mandel J., 230
Kramer, Rob Harris, 154
Kramer, Terry Allen, 42, 116, 117
Krane, David, 108
Krank, Meghan Rose, 93, 132
Krascella, Jed, 58, 61
Krasker, Tommy, 130
Krass, Ellen M., 59, 61
Krass, Michael, 70, 97, 111
Kratzer, Jim, 55
Krause, Calla, 174
Krauss, Marvin A., 20
Krauss, Michael, 53
Kravets, Laura, 50, 52, 60, 89
Kray, Antoinette, 51
Krebs, Eric, 14, 49, 50, 66
Krege, Kim, 140
Kreindel, Mitch, 28
Kreinen, Rebecca, 54
Krempel, Joyce, 136
Kreshka, Ruth, 88, 89
Kress, Donna, 121
Kress, Ronna, 209
Kressen, Sam, 162, 163
Kressyn, Miriam, 53
Kretzmer, Herbert, 40
Kriegel, David, 164
Krieger, Barbara Zinn, 106
Kripi, Jack, 56
Kristal, Barbara, 166
Kristien, Dale, 133, 209
Krizane, John, 72
Krizner, Douglas, 68, 170
Kroetz, Franz Xaver, 97
Kroeze, Jan, 94
Krohn, Charles, 121
Kroll, David, 108
Kromer, Helen, 74
Kronenberg, Bruce, 73
Kronenfeld, Daniel, 92
Kross, Ed, 152
Krueger, Dana, 126
Kruger, Bonnie, 170
Kruger, Norman, 54
Kruger, Simcha, 53
Krummel, Jens, 102, 161
Krupa, Olek, 87
Krupp, Jon, 48, 61
Kubala, Michael, 25
Kudisch, Marc, 72, 161
Kuepper, Barbara Reeves, 138
Kuhn, Bruce, 40, 209
Kuhn, George, 53, 103
Kuhn, Judy, 40
Kulick, Brian, 99
Kulok, Peter T., 15, 41
Kumin, Fran, 6, 16, 20, 41
Kunkle, Connie, 143
Kunzelman, Betsy, 132
Kuper, Yuri, 118
Kuperman, Hallie, 77
Kuramoto, Hiroshima-Dan, 134, 135
Kuramoto, June, 134, 135
Kurdi, Adi, 47
Kurek, Annette, 209
Kurnitz, Julie, 109
Kuroda, Kati, 98
Kurowski, Ron, 37, 209
Kurrelmeyer, Ellen, 56
Kurshal, Raymond, 95, 209
Kurta, Kay, 136
Kurth, Juliette, 55, 95, 209
Kurtz, Ken, 127
Kurtz, Marcia Jean, 89, 209
Kurtz, Rebecca, 56
Kurtz, Swoosie, 62, 209
Kuschner, Jason, 107
Kushner, June, 95
Kushner, Tony, 97
Kushnetz, Rachel, 99
Kuyk, Dirk, 165
Kuypers, Maggie, 27
Kyme, 22
L'Illusion, 97
La Cage Aux Folles, 162
La Cage Aux folles, 162
La Compagnie, 56
La Fosse, Robert, 25
La Nuotattice Turca (The Turkish Swimmer), 48
La Vine, Deborah, 135
LaBanz, Jane, 45
LaBelle, Rob, 94
LaBourdette, Katie (Marilyn Monroe), 65
LaBourdette, Katie, 65
LaBow, Hilary, 29
LaBute, Neil, 105
LaCoy, Deborah, 62
LaDuca, David, 75
LaFleche, Michel, 174
LaGuerre, Irma-Estel, 46, 60
LaMar, Diana, 49

LaMarque, Kimberley, 123
LaMee, Maurice, 138
LaPadura, Jason, 97
LaPlatney, Martin, 143
LaPointe, Tom, 47, 49
LaPorta, Gary, 65
LaPorte, Manuela, 94, 95
LaRosa, Gary, 65
LaRussa, Annie, 172
LaTulip, Brian, 176
LaVada, Terry, 109
LaVere, Morgan, 49
LaZebnik, Kenneth, 210
Labanz, Jane, 109, 209
Laboissonniere, Wade, 38
Labow, Hilary, 29
Lach, Mary Ann, 74
Lackey, Herndon, 40, 114
Lackey, Skip, 90, 209
Laconi, Robert, 49, 60, 209
Ladenson, Michael, 96
Ladies, 62
Lady in Question, The, 107
Lady, Robb, 42
Laffer, Denise, 62, 66, 68
Lafferty, Sandra Ellis, 138
Lage, Jordan, 19, 209
Lagerfelt, Caroline, 26, 80, 209
Lagomarsino, Ron, 70, 111, 172
Lagond, Charlie, 104
Lahti, Christine, 30, 193, 209
Laine, Cleo, 113, 133
Lainer, Mark, 65, 102
Laing, Alan, 174
Laird, Brendan, 10
Laird, Michael James, 127
Laisser, Andrew, 133
Lake Ivan Performance Group, 56
Lake, Randall E., 65
Lally, James, 86
Lam, Elis Y., 174
Lam, Sabado, 50
Lam, Zoie, 31, 85
Lamar, Vivian, 55
Lamb, Chris, 132
Lamb, J. Kathleen, 109
Lamb, Judith, 47, 48
Lamb, Mary Ann, 25, 209
Lamb, Peter, 174
Lamb, Philip, 54
Lambert, Beverly, 63, 209
Lambert, Juliet, 94
Lambert, Sarah, 184
Lamberton, Mike, 44
Lambie, Joseph, 95
Lambie, Lauren K., 121
Lamos, Mark, 86, 148
Lan, David, 35
Lancaster, James, 133
Lanchester, Robert, 138
Landa, Marie, 59
Landeo, Lillian, 103
Landes, Francine, 93, 209
Landesman, Heidi, 39, 104, 113, 133, 133
Landesman, Rocco, 39, 113, 133
Landfield, Timothy, 18
Landis, Errol, 84
Landis, Jim, 142, 164
Landis, Lynn, 45, 86
Landisman, Kurt, 178
Landon, David, 93
Landon, Hal, Jr., 172
Landon, Hal, Sr., 172
Landrieu, Nelson, 101
Landrine, Bryan, 38
Landron, Jack, 179, 209
Landry, Lantz, 114
Landry, Marlo, 114
Landry, Steven, 124
Landwehr, Hugh, 131, 136, 154
Lane, Allen Walker, 74
Lane, Nancy, 80, 210
Lane, Nathan, 49, 89, 104, 210
Lane, Roger, 50, 81, 107
Lane, Wallace G., Jr., 99
Lang, Barbara, 133
Lang, Mike, 129
Lang, Peter, 9, 67, 210
Lang, Stephen, 144
Lang, William H., 62, 97
Langan, William, 184
Langdon, Alan, 53
Lange, Anne, 30, 100, 210
Lange, Doug, 24
Langella, Frank, 133
Langford, Judy, 122
Langhofer, Bobbi, 113
Langhofer, Dan W., 113, 133
Langsdale, Keith, 148
Langsner, Sandra, 150
Langworthy, David, 50
Langworthy, Norma, 50
Lanier, David, 25
Lanier, Jane, 25, 45
Lanier, Jessica, 62
Lanigan, Lorraine, 51, 181, 210
Lanigan, Peter J., 43
Lannan, Nina, 16, 23, 24
Lanning, Jerry, 210

Lanning, Nile, 210
Lansbury, Angela, 33
Lansbury, Edgar, 81
Lansey, Stephanie, 132
Lant, John, 107
Lanzener, Sonja, 52, 68, 102
Lanzet, Amy, 57
Lapadura, Jason, 97
Lapchinski, Larissa, 174
Lapham, Kenneth J., 82
Lapine, James, 39, 95, 113, 133, 172
Larabee, Louise, 230
Laramore, Paul, 133
Lardner, Ring, 58
Large, Norman, 40, 133
Largely New York, 36, 186
Lark, The, 108
Larkin, 135
Larkin, Jill, 6
Larkin, Philip, 135
Larmett, Jill, 144
Larner, Elizabeth, 42
Larsen, Donna Marie, 53
Larsen, Liz, 34, 210
Larsen, Robert R., 32
Larson, Christa, 114
Larson, Gayle, 174
Larson, Jayne Amelia, 57
Larson, Larry, 122
Larson, Linda, 60
Larson, Lisby, 51, 142, 170, 210
Larson, Stuart, 172
Larson-Cardee, Kyle, 64
Larsson, Stefan, 78
Lascelles, Kendrew, 138
Lasswell, Michael, 181
Last Good Moment of Lily Baker, The, 170
Laszlo, Miklos, 105
Latessa, Dick, 18, 151
Lathrop, Aline, 137
Latimer, Virginia Lee, 130
Latouche, John, 170
Latta, Richard, 90
Latus, James, 141
Latzen, Ellen Hamilton, 46
Laubacher, Mary Alyce, 133
Laudano, Nicholas, 36
Laughing Matters, 66
Laughing Wild, 161
Laughlin, Richard, 129
Laughter, Becky, 144
Laundra, Linda, 46
Laureano, Paul, 44, 82, 210
Lauren, Ellen, 121
Laurence, Paula, 63, 210
Laurence, Stuart, 56
Laurenson, Diana, 210, 211
Laurents, Arthur, 25
Laurino, Adelaide, 24, 38, 40, 44
Laurino, John, 40
Lauris, Priscilla Hake, 161
Lavely, Christopher, 140
Laverdiere, Renee, 146
Lavey, Martha, 144
Lavine, Michael H., 56
Law, Mary Kate, 34, 210
Lawder, Anne, 123
Lawer, Lisa A., 77
Lawless, James J., 138
Lawless, Rick, 49, 61, 131, 210, 211
Lawless, Sarah, 138
Lawless, Sue, 142, 164
Lawless, Wendy, 96, 148
Lawlor, David, 75
Lawrence, Dale C., 122
Lawrence, Darrie, 161, 168
Lawrence, David H., 30, 109
Lawrence, Dela, 72
Lawrence, Delphi, 132
Lawrence, Howard, 69
Lawrence, Kirk, 59
Lawrence, Peter, 12, 18, 110
Lawrence, Reginald, 69
Lawson, David, 49, 58, 89
Lawson, Mary E., 70
Lawson, Richard, 133
Lawyer, Russell, 108
Layman, Terry, 50, 142
Layng, Kathryn, 41, 210
Layton, Michael, 129
Lazarus, Bruce, 75
Lazarus, Frank, 63, 210
Lazarus, Paul, 7
Le Beauf, Sabrina, 141
Le Auanae, Oliva, 59
LeBlanc, Steven, 112
LeBouef, Clayton, 126
LeCount, Alice, 138
LeFevre, Adam, 17, 210
LeFrak Entertainment, 15
LeFrak, Francine, 15
LeGrand, Stephen, 123
LeMassena, William, 9, 210, 211
LeNoire, Rosetta, 74
LePage, Joseph, 174
LeShae, Ed, 11
LeStrange, Philip, 121
LeVine, Marilynn, 22
Leach, Wilford, 230
Leach, William, 161

Leake, Damien, 154
Leake, Sandy Leigh, 38
Leaming, Chet, 45
Leaming, Greg, 148
Lear, Maggie, 52, 60
Learned, Michael, 108, 123
Leary, Champe, 128, 170
Leask, Katherine, 46, 68, 170, 171, 176
Leave It To Jane, 83
Leavengood, Wm. S., 79
Leavitt, Joe, 162
Lebano, Christian, 152
Leber, David, 13
Leber, Steven E., 13
Lebowsky, Stanley, 38, 42
Lecesne, James, 50, 210
Lechner, Geno, 78
Ledbetter, Sammy, 18
Ledbetter, William, 27
Lederer, Charles, 130
Ledesma, Michael, 181
Lee, Baayork, 37, 122, 142
Lee, Barbara, 70
Lee, Barry, 148
Lee, Chandra, 9, 17, 210
Lee, Dana, 77
Lee, Eugene, 134
Lee, Franne, 95
Lee, Jeff, 24, 38
Lee, Jonathan Barlow, 134
Lee, Kaiulani, 88, 104, 210, 211
Lee, Karen Tsen, 98
Lee, Lenore, 179
Lee, Levi, 122
Lee, Mark, 154
Lee, Mary, 98
Lee, Ming Cho, 184
Lee, Phil, 48, 62, 105, 106
Lee, Susan, 42
Lee, Victoria, 75
Lee-Aranas, Mary, 98, 210
Leeds, Andrew Harrison, 115
Leeds, Jordan, 40
Leeds, Michael, 67
Leer, Jeri, 103, 143, 176, 179
Lees, Laura, 130
Leeseberg-Lange, BettyAnn, 170
Lefevre, Robin, 88
Leffert, Joel, 153
Leffingwell, Jo, 119
Legend of Sharon Shashanovah, The, 51
Legends in Concert, 65
Legs Diamond, 20
Lehman, Rhea, 120
Lehman, Ross, 144
Lehrer, Ernest, 144
Lehrer, Scott, 30, 100
Lehrer, Tom, 82, 143
Lehrman, Leonard, 105
Leib, Russell, 17
Leiberman, Donna, 107
Leibman, Ron, 18, 210
Leicht, John, 161, 166
Leigh, Carolyn, 25
Leigh, Mitch, 31, 85
Leighton, Richard, 158
Leinweber, Laura, 67
Leitner, James, 166
Lemerise, Richard, 138
Lemieux, Robert, 102
Lemke, Blayn, 138
Lemsky, Mitchell, 44, 133
Lend Me a Tenor, 26
Lengson, Jose, 146
Leningrad Maly Drama Theatre, 47
Lennon, John F., 150
Lennon, John, 43
Lenox, Adriane, 126
Lenz, Matt, 83
Lenz, Richard, 68
Lenz, Rick, 210
Leon, Carol Mitchell, 122
Leon, Joseph, 210, 211
Leon, Kenny, 122
Leonard, Howard, 20, 118
Leonard, John A., 88
Leonard, Robert Sean, 100, 166, 167, 210
Leonardo, Joe, 112
Leone, Vivien, 46, 50, 107
Leong, David, 96, 183
Leonidas, Kevin A., 73
Lepore, Pauline, 125
Lerch, Stuart, 99
Lerner, Alan Jay, 83
Lerner, Neal, 57, 142
Les Blancs, 139, 151
Les Liaisons Dangereuses, 120, 133, 136, 183
Les Misérables, 40, 114, 115, 186
Lesada, Romelle, 122
Leshem, Lolita, 41
Lesher, Scott, 166
Leskin, Will, 178
Leslie, Bethel, 104, 210, 211
Leslie, Glenn, 129
Lessem, Stephanie, 79
Lessen, Stephanie, 79
Lesser, Gene, 141

Lesser, Len, 130
Lesser, Ron, 49
Lesser, Sally J., 46, 76, 105
Lessner, Joanne, 56
Lester, Barbara, 176
Lester, Terry, 130
Letang, Henry, 22
Letwin, David, 93
Levan, Martin, 38, 44, 133
Levenson, Keith, 90
Leventhal, Max, 124
Leverett, Candace Dian, 127
Leverone, Judith, 48
Levi, Susie, 56
Levin, Ira, 85
Levin, Nicholas, 75
Levin, Pete, 14
Levine, Arnold, 103
Levine, Bob, 151
Levine, Earl Aaron, 69
Levine, Ilana, 66
Levine, Marc, 33
Levine, Rachel S., 68, 102
Levine, Richard, 18, 103, 166, 167, 210
Levinson, Richard, 48
Levitin, Nicholas, 57
Levitow, Roberta, 156, 172
Levitt, Sandy, 53
Levy, Franklin R., 66
Levy, Jacques, 43, 158
Levy, Owen, 6, 47
Levy, Steven M., 56
Lew, Ted, 22
Lew, Karen, 123
Lewin, Daniel S., 70, 111
Lewin, John, 147
Lewin, Naomi, 75
Lewine, Richard, 108
Lewis, Edmund, 81, 131, 210
Lewis, Edwina, 70
Lewis, Garry Q., 45, 109
Lewis, Gilbert, 11
Lewis, Irene, 132
Lewis, J. Barry, 165
Lewis, Justine, 124
Lewis, Laura Fay, 58, 210
Lewis, Mark, 72, 160, 210
Lewis, Matthew, 210
Lewis, Michael, 143
Lewis, Rick, 49
Lewis, Sharon, 116
Lewis, Susan P., 49, 52
Lewis-Evans, Kecia, 12
Lewitin, Margot, 63
Leyden, Leo, 42, 210
Li, Donald, 98
Libertini, Richard, 95
Libin, Andrea Clark, 35
Libin, Claire, 35
Libin, Paul, 8, 10, 17, 35
Lichte, Richard, 68
Lichtefeld, Michael, 108
Lichtenstein, Harvey, 78
Lickteig, Regina, 168
Lie of the Mind, A, 126
Lieberman, Amy, 134
Lieberman, Iris, 152
Lieberson, Will, 54
Liebman, Steve, 153
Life Is a Dream, 124
Life in the Theatre, A, 181
Lifshey, Karen, 122
Lifton, Betsy, 50
Lightstone, Marilyn, 72, 210
Ligon, Jim, 56
Liguori, Lisa, 112
Liljestrand, Eric, 97
Lilly, T. Scott, 67
Lilly, Terry M., 47, 49, 51, 54, 60
Lilygren, Mary, 118
Lin, Sun Dao, 123
Linares, Carlos, 101
Lind, Jane, 98
Lind, Kirsten, 162
Lindblom, Gunnel, 78
Lindell, Johan, 78
Lindemann, Gary, 170
Linden, Anne, 174
Lindemann, Donna, 61
Linderman, Ed, 125
Lindley, Audra, 142
Lindo, Delroy, 184, 185
Lindquist, Frank, 106
Lindsay, Howard, 45, 109, 129, 140
Lindsay, Nick, 59
Lindsay, Phillip, 230, 231
Lindsay, Robert, 42
Lindsay-Hogg, Michael, 134
Lindy, Phyllis, 160
Link, Ron, 134
Link, William, 48
Linney, Romulus, 46, 56, 161
Linton, William, 162, 163
Linville, Larry, 18, 210
Lion in Winter, The, 153
Lipman, David, 210
Lippincott, Catherine, 6
Lippman, Jonathan, 56
Lisa, Pier, 68
Lisbon Traviata, The, 89
Liscow, Wendy, 142

Lish, James, 65, 82, 210
Lithgow, John, 41
Litten, Jim, 138
Little Prince Productions, 72
Little Shop of Horrors, 142, 164
Little Village, 78
Little, Brad, 109
Little, David, 48
Little, Gerard, 55
Little, John, 59, 210
Little-Roberts, Iris, 122
Littrell, Nicolle, 11
Litwin, Burton L., 118
Lively, William Fleet, 176
Livingston, 129
Livingston, Ruth, 153
Livingston, William, 57
Lizardo, Maribel, 60
Lizzul, Anthony John, 56, 210
Ljung, Oscar, 78
Lloyd, Greg, 162
Lloyd, Karen, 26
Lloyd, Robert Langdon, 80
Lloyd, Sherman, 49
Lloyd, Tom, 88, 158
Lloyd-Evans, David, 174
Llynn, Jana, 61
LoBianco, Robert, 56
LoBianco, Tony, 24, 210
LoCurto, Lisa, 49, 83
LoFrumento, Candace, 183
LoGuidice, Kathleen, 83
Lobel, Adrianne, 126, 172
Locarro, Joe, 114
Lock, Kevin, 127
Locke, Robert, 107
Lockery, Patricia, 146
Lockwood, Carole, 131, 165
Lockwood, Kipp, 138
Lockwood, Lisa, 44, 216
Lockwood, Shirley, 179
Lockwood, Vera, 165
Loeb, Leslie, 45
Loehle, Steven, 66
Loesser, Emily, 33, 60, 137
Loewe, Frederick, 83
Lofgren, Lars, 78
Loftus, Elizabeth, 53, 102, 210
Loftus, Mary Fran, 30, 100
Logan Family Picnic, The, 89
Logan, Angela, 49
Logan, Bellina, 95, 100, 141, 210
Logan, Joshua, 129, 230, 231
Logan, Stacey, 151
Logen, Carol, 210
Loggins, Kenny, 16
Loman Family Picnic, The, 89
Lombard, Jenny, 68
Lombard, Michael, 210
Londeree, Terry, 67, 180, 210
London, Chet, 230, 231
London, Chuck, 79
London, Danny, 66
London, Mark, 184
Lonergan, Michael, 28
Long Day's Journey into Night, 6, 179
Long, Anni, 172, 173
Long, Jodi, 148
Long, John F., 230
Long, Quincy, 46
Long, William Ivey, 21, 26, 32, 60, 88, 89, 136
Longbottom, Bobby, 42
Longstreet, Stephen, 25
Longworth, Bruce, 170
Looft, Richard, 78
Look Homeward, Angel, 179
Loomer, Lisa, 135
Loomis, Brannon, 170
Loos, Anita, 67
Lopez, Carlos, 37
Lopez, Priscilla, 46, 210
Lopez, Sal, 8
Loquasto, Santo, 15, 88, 104
Loranger, Jane, 79
Lord, Beth, 53
Lorenzen, Mark, 106
Lorenzo, 74, 210
Loring, David, 44
Lorman, Ron, 78
Lortel, Lucille, 33
Lorwin, Liza, 78
Lost Colony, The, 60
Lothes, Doug, 122
Lotito, Mark, 178
Lotz, Daivd, 51
Lotz, David, 47, 49, 52, 54, 60
Lou, Gail, 54
Louden, Jay, 135
Louden, Michael, 93, 94
Loudon, Dorothy, 111, 210
Loui, Michael, 184
Louis, Allan, 161
Louise, Merle, 39
Louiselle, Bryan, 90
Love Letters, 62, 154
Love's Labour's Lost, 68, 95, 102
Love, Edith H., 122
Love, Edward, 92
Love, John W., Jr., 140
Love, Victor, 154
Love, Wil, 132, 182

Lovelle, Herb, 52, 154
Lovett, Farryl, 85, 210
Lovett, Marcus, 40
Lovullo, Janene, 40
Low, Carl, 230
Low, Maggie, 164
Lowe, Frank, 128, 158
Lowe, Jackie, 11
Lowe, John H., III, 110
Lowell, Marguerite, 113, 133
Lowenstein, David, 25
Lowery, Marcella, 62, 210
Lowery, Nancy Ann, 122
Loweth, Todd, 68, 102
Lowman, Kristen, 136
Lowrie, John Patrick, 129
Lowry, Jane, 182
Lowstetter, Ken, 51, 62
Lozada, Maria Cristina, 93
LuPone, Patti, 45
LuPone, Robert, 37, 52, 60, 136, 212
Lubin, Paul, 9
Lubovitch, Lar, 39, 113, 133
MacKay, Harper, 123
Luc, Jean, 22
Lucas, Craig, 79
Lucas, J. Frank, 62, 210
Lucas, John M., 76
Lucas, Roxie, 50, 212
Lucero, F. L., 178
Lucero, Rick, 75
Lucero, Urbanie, 8
Luciano, Michael, 46
Lucid, Jacqueline, 102
Luckey, Judge, 122
Ludlam, Charles, 142, 161, 164
Ludlow, Dennis, 123
Ludlow-Corzatte, Susan, 119
Ludwig, John, 78
Ludwig, Karen, 52
Ludwig, Ken, 48
Ludwig, Kirsten M., 136
Ludwig, Salem, 151, 162
Luetters, Ray, 53
Lugar, Jana, 129
Lugar, Joel, 129
Luhrman, Henry, 47, 49, 51, 54, 60, 230, 231
Lukas, Carrena, 79, 212
Lukas, Victor, 32, 108
Lukeman, Brenda Shoshanna, 85
Luker, Rebecca, 44
Lum, Alvin, 31, 85, 212
Lum, Mary, 183
Lumbard, Dirk, 125
Lumpkin, Bruce, 7
Luna, Tony, 67
Lunatic and Lover, 49
Lund, Jeremy, 144
Lund, Jordan, 58, 94
Lundie, Ken, 146
Lundoner, George, 76
Lundy, Nicholas, 83
Lunon, Vernard, 46
Lupino, Richard, 53, 212
Lupton, Jennifer, 119
Lurenz, Betty, 65
Lusk, Charles Morgan, 140
Lusko, Robert A., 125
Lussier, Henry, 124
Lustik, Marlena, 164, 212
Luther, Ed, 144
Luther, Kari, 102
Lutvak, Steven, 170
Lutz, Jonathan, 140
Lutz, Lara, 182
Lutz, Renee, 89
Lutz, Tom, 48
Luzier, Aimee, 53
Lyall, Susan, 79
Lydecker, Garrit, 125
Lyle, Percy Howard, Jr., 138
Lyles, Leslie, 46, 62, 184, 185, 212
Lyman, Andrea, 83
Lynch, Barry, 161
Lynch, Bill, 112
Lynch, Brian, 29, 115
Lynch, Eileen, 59
Lynch, John Carroll, 147
Lynch, John, 57
Lynch, Michael P., 103
Lynch, Michael, 18, 25
Lynch, Sharon, 63
Lynch, Thomas, 30, 70, 100, 111, 144
Lynch, Victoria, 106
Lynd, Betty, 212
Lynde, Janice, 142
Lyndeck, Edmund, 39, 212
Lynes, Kristi, 38
Lyng, Nora Mae, 113, 133, 212
Lynn, Jess, 62
Lynne, Gillian, 38, 44, 133
Lynne, Heidi, 148
Lyon, Corinne, 144
Lyon, Robin, 37
Lyons, Andi, 131
Lyons, John, 88
Lyons, Phyllis, 132
M Square Entertainment, 50, 41
M. Butterfly, 186

MAMAW Productions, 64
Ma Rose, 52
Ma, Jason, 31
Ma, Tzi, 81, 172
Mabon, Paul, 144
Mabry, LaDonna, 60
MacArthur, Doug, 130
MacArthur, James, 33
MacCauley, Michael, 68, 170
MacDermot, Galt, 184
MacDermott, Laura, 164, 184
MacDevitt, Brian, 108, 112
MacDonald, Bob, 93
MacDonald, Gordon, 148
MacDonald, Jeanette, 56
MacDonald, Karen, 143, 160, 176, 179
MacDonald, Pirie, 91
MacDonald, Robert David, 184
MacGarvey, Clarice, 161
MacInniss, John, 42
MacIntosh, Joan, 19, 96
MacIntosh, Joane, 212
MacKay, John, 68, 170, 212
MacKenzie, Evan, 135
MacKinnon, Cecil, 63
MacLaren, Jim, 184
MacLeod, Charles, 138
MacLeod, Wendy, 60
MacNicol, Peter, 212, 216
MacPherson, Greg, 46, 55, 62, 68
MacPherson, Lori, 44, 212
MacPherson, Walt, 126, 132
MacVittie, Bruce, 46
Macbeth, 49, 92, 183
Macchio, Ralph, 75
Macdonald, James G., 46, 68
Mace, Cynthia, 154
Maceri, Bill, 78
Macfie, Jane, 6, 7
Machado, Eduardo, 76, 135
Machray, Robert, 136, 172
Machun, 13
Mack, Amy, 36
Mackay, Lizbeth, 120
Mackenzie, Peter, 154
Mackillip, Bruce, 53
Mackintosh, Cameron, 38, 40, 44, 82, 133, 143
Macklin, Valerie, 22
Macleay, Lachlan, 183
Macy, W. H., 19, 212
Madden, Corey Beth, 134, 135
Madden, Kevin, 48
Madden, Stephanie, 50
Madden, Thomas M., 153
Maddox, Gloria, 154
Maddrie, Leah, 141
Maddux, Jacklyn, 68
Madeira, Marcia, 142, 151
Madurga, Gonzalo, 93
Maeda, Jun, 56
Maffia, Roma, 183
Maffin, Neil, 97
Maffitt, Brian, 35
Magee, Rusty, 95
Maggio, Michael, 144, 147
Maggio, Tony, 47
Magic Act, The, 61
Maglione, Christine, 37, 212
Magner, J. Anthony, 16
Magnusen, Michael, 130
Magradey, Jack, 38
Maguire, Michael, 40
Mahady, James, 63
Mahan, Kevin, 47
Maher, Daniel, 73
Maher, Dennis, 180
Maher, Joseph, 88, 212, 216
Maher, Michael O., 58
Mahl, Lori Ann, 146
Mahn, Kevin, 48
Mahnken, Bob, 54
Mahonev, M. Ellen, 63
Mahony-Bennett, Kathleen, 45, 126
Maier, Charlotte, 58, 169, 212
Maier, David, 123
Maika, Michele, 115
Mailer, Stephen, 95, 212, 216
Maines, Julia, 56
Maio, Frank, 151, 162
Majestic Kid, The, 55
Major, Charles, 212
Major, Rebecca, 58
Major, Richard, 128
Making Noise Quietly, 135
Makkena, Wendy, 26, 89
Malachi, William, 139
Male Animal, The, 82
Maleczech, Ruth, 60, 78, 147
Malignancy of Henrietta Lacks, The, 105
Malis, Tess, 122
Mallard, David E., 108
Mallon, Brian, 212
Mallow, Tom, 113, 133
Malloy, Amy, 161
Malloy, John, 161
Malloy, Judy, 65
Malmberg, Benoit, 78
Malone, Richard, 151
Maloney, D. J., 82
Maloney, Peter, 19, 46

Maltby, Jacquey, 162
Maltby, Richard, Jr., 12, 64
Malvern, Larry G., 161
Mamet, David, 131, 183
Man Who Climbed the Pecan Trees, The, 46
Man, Chic Street, 135
Manager, Itsik, 95
Manassee, Jackie, 61, 100, 131
Mancinelli, Celeste, 88, 212
Mandarin, Udin, 47
Mandel, Johnny, 14
Mandelbaum, Ken, 42
Mandell, Alan, 156, 172
Mandell, Michael, 96, 142, 164, 166, 167
Mandracchia, Charles, 61, 212
Mango Tea, 46
Mangrum, Cathy, 122
Manicone, Carmine, 63
Manilow, Barry, 33, 212
Manis, David, 121, 132
Maniscalco, Robert, 49, 212
Mankin, Nina, 97
Manley, Jim, 105
Manley, Sandy, 12, 18
Manley, Sarah, 86, 87
Mann, Emily, 52
Mann, Joan, 82
Mann, Jonathan, 9, 35, 212
Mann, Judi, 129
Mann, Sharon, 148
Mann, Terence, 40
Mann, Theodore, 8, 9, 10, 17, 35
Manners, Bernard, 22
Manners, J. Hartley, 82
Manners, Jodi, 212
Manning, Dan, 158
Manning, Frankie, 22
Manning, Jerry, 97
Manning, Rick, 20
Mannino, Joe, 127
Mano, D. Keith, 46
Manocherian, Jennifer, 67
Manson, Bevan, 95
Mansur, Susan, 71
Mantello, Joseph, 58
Mantooth, Randy, 68
Manuel, 8
Manzi, Warren, 58, 212
Mapa, Alec, 41
Maple Interactive Entertainment Ltd., 72
Maponya, Maishe, 92
Mara, Jim, 162
Mara, Mary, 179
Maradudin, Peter, 138, 172, 178
Marasek, Jan, 25, 29
Marathon 88, 46
Marathon 89, 68
Marathons, 66
Marc, Peter, 66
Marcante, Mark, 56
Marceau, Yvonne, 64
Marcelli, Julietta, 38
March, Barbara, 183
March, Lori, 51
March, Richard, 174
Marchand, Nancy, 51, 62, 212
Marchetti, Lona, 137
Marcoux, Ted, 136
Marcovicci, Andrea, 123
Marcus, Bonnie, 73
Marcus, Michael, 54, 131
Marcus, Steven, 57
Marcy, Helen, 49, 212
Mardirosian, Tom, 100, 107, 212
Marek, Alyson, 82
Mareneck, Ellen, 176
Margolin, Sandor, 60
Margulies, David, 15, 107, 212
Margulies, Donald, 89, 156
Margulyan and Podchufarov, 13
Maria Productions, 43
Mariano, Patti, 85
Marich, Allison, 121
Marich, Bob, 121
Marie, Donna, 54, 62
Marie, Lena, 130
Marino, Peter-Michael, 49
Maris, Ada, 104
Mark, Magnus, 78
Markel, Daniel, 93
Markell, Denis, 67
Markell, Jodie, 62, 87, 212
Marki, Csilla, 134
Markinson, Alan R., 24, 116
Markinson, Brian, 56
Markle, Lois, 86
Markle, Stephen, 147
Markovitz, Paula, 123, 152
Marks, David, 126
Marks, Jack R., 154
Marks, Ken, 52, 60
Marks, Kenneth, 88, 212
Marlay, Andrew B., 103
Marley, Donovan, 138
Marlowe, Theresa, 107, 212, 216
Maroney, Denman, 60

Maronna, Michael C., 162
Maroon, Brent, 162
Marowitz, Charles, 156
Marquette, Steve, 170
Marquez, Julissa, 60
Marre, Adam A., 85
Marre, Albert, 31, 85
Marrero, Maria, 179
Marrero, Ralph, 59, 87
Marriage of Figaro, The, 168
Marriott, B. Rodney, 79
Marron-Montgomery, Ritchie, 54
Marsden, Les, 122
Marsh, Frazier W., 120
Marsh, Kathleen, 9, 18
Marshal, Gary, 133
Marshall, Dorothy, 170
Marshall, J. L., 93
Marshall, Janna, 151
Marshall, Jerry, 56
Marshall, Sarah C., 126
Marshii, William, 73
Marsolais, Ken, 6, 47, 86
Martel, Diane, 95, 96
Martel, Jenny, 58
Martel, Kenneth F., 59
Martello, Mary, 158
Martells, Cynthia, 158
Martens, Rica, 71
Martens, Wayne, 57
Martenson, Edward A., 147
Martin, Brian, 61, 158
Martin, Campbell, 82, 146
Martin, Christopher, 9
Martin, Cie, 111
Martin, Clay, 88
Martin, Dan, 62, 183
Martin, Dorothy, 69
Martin, George, 41, 116, 117
Martin, Gregory, 111
Martin, Greta, 25
Martin, Hugh, 25
Martin, James, 121
Martin, Jamie, 83
Martin, Jeremy, 142
Martin, Ken, 58
Martin, Leila, 44, 212
Martin, Michael X., 138
Martin, Michelle, 148
Martin, Nan, 156, 172
Martin, Nina, 95
Martin, Robert Lee, 212
Martin, Steve, 86, 87, 212
Martin, T. R., 170
Martin, Tom, 170
Martin, Tony, 174
Martin, W. T., 183
Martindale, Margo, 71
Martinez, Alma, 77, 135
Martinez, Barbara, 84
Martinez, Julio, 101
Martini, Richard, 118
Martini, Robert Lee, 62
Martino, Mark, 108
Martinov, Lucy, 113
Maruyama, Karen, 135
Marvin, Mel, 86, 148, 169
Marx, Ara, 88
Marx, Margaret, 172
Mary, Kathleen, 55, 67
Maryan, Charles, 85
Marz, Charles, 124
Marzan, Julio, 93
Mascaro, Gary, 72, 134
Mashita, Nelson, 134
Maslow, Jillian, 61
Maso, Michael, 151
Maso, Cecelia, 161
Mason, Dan, 134
Mason, Jackie, 212
Mason, Marsha, 62, 212
Mason, Robert, 49
Masque Productions, 55
Massa, Joseph, 53
Massaro, A. Lee, 49
Massee, Michael, 14, 49
Massi, Bernice, 162
Masson, Linda J. K., 68, 102
Master Harold . . . and the Boys, 137
Mastergate, 124
Masteroff, Joe, 57, 65
Masters, Patricia, 82, 212, 216
Masterson, John, 94, 96
Mastrocola, Frank, 38
Mastrogiovanni, Vito, 78
Mastroianni, Frank, 44, 212
Mastrosimone, William, 86
Mastrotottaro, Michael F., 212
Matalon, Vivian, 147
Matchmaker, The, 138
Matejek, Nancy, 139
Mathay, Marie, 111
Matheo, Len, 53
Mather, Jenny R., 59
Mather, Ted, 60
Mathers, Craig, 62
Mathis, Lynn, 180
Matlock, Norman, 52
Matone, Rocco, 58
Matsui, Rumi, 92
Matsuura, Sachiko, 79
Mattaliano, Peter, 51
Mattar, Steve, 90
Matter of Tone, A, 65

Matthews, Anderson, 70, 212
Matthews, Cindy, 63
Matthews, Dakin, 134
Matthews, Edward R. F., 57
Matthews, Evan, 74
Matthiessen, Joan, 99, 212, 216
Matura, Mustapha, 184
Matveev, Yuri, 13
Matz, Jerry, 35, 142, 146, 164, 212
Maugans, Wayne, 131
Maulden, Dennis C., 140
Maupin, Samuel, 164, 165
Maurer, Kelly, 161
Maurer, Laura, 161
Mawn, Gerard, 82
Max and Maxie, 108, 152
Maxie, Katie, 65
Maxmen, Mimi, 107, 131, 136, 165
Maxwell, Jennifer, 151
Maxwell, Roberta, 19, 212
Maxwell, Victoria, 50
May, Deborah, 123
May, Gary, 179
May, Maureen, 49
Maya, Frank, 58
Mayberry, James, 122
Mayberry, Paul, 160
Mayer, Jerry, 81, 158, 184
Mayer, Max, 68, 126
Mayer, Nathan, 162
Mayer, Ruth Rothbart, 55
Mayers, Lloyd, 118
Mayerson, Frederick H., 39, 113, 133
Mayes, Sally, 32, 187, 190, 212
Mayhew, David, 154
Mayhew, Henry, 120
Maynard, Richard, 53, 169
Mayo, Don, 86, 93, 105, 212
Mays, Marshall, 164
Mazzafero, David, 152
Mazzella, Neil A., 6
Mazzie, Marin, 39
Mazziotti, Tom, 49
McAllen, Kathleen Rowe, 113, 133
McAnarney, Kevin P., 55, 118
McAnarney, Kevin, 22, 39, 64, 90
McAvin, Andy, 138
McBrath, Mark, 125
McBride, Howard R., 65
McBride, Mark, 50
McBrien, Susan, 68
McBroom, Robert, 82
McCain, Christopher, 123
McCain, Frances Lee, 123
McCall, Kathleen, 137, 212
McCalla, Stanley & Jennifer, 64
McCallum, David, 103, 212
McCallum, Martin, 40
McCann, Chris, 147
McCann, Christopher, 123
McCann, Donal, 10
McCann, Mary, 19
McCarron, Gretta, 64
McCarry, Charles E., 51
McCarthy, Andrew, 46
McCarthy, Cara, 82
McCarthy, Carolyn, 176
McCarthy, Danny, 170
McCarthy, Denise, 58
McCarthy, Theresa, 68, 170
McCarthy, Tom, 166
McCartney, Ellen, 77, 104, 141, 169
McCarty, Conan, 121, 212
McCarty, Michael, 162, 184, 212
McCatty, Mary Frances, 118, 122
McCauley, Judith, 162
McCauley, William, 72
McChesney, Dorothy, 127
McChesney, Roy, 127
McClain, Saundra, 91, 179
McClary, William, 162
McClelland, Kay, 39
McClennahan, Charles, 89, 91
McClinton, Marion Isaac, 81
McClure, James, 152
McClure, Spike, 35, 95, 153
McCollister, Frier, 78
McCollough, Lynne, 57
McComb, Bill, 10, 60
McComber, Kori, 129
McConnell, David, 48, 61, 213
McConnell, Joseph, 162
McCorkle, Pat, 28, 51, 70, 111
McCormack, Eric, 174
McCormick, Carolyn, 81, 132, 213
McCormick, Edmund J., Jr., 57
McCormick, Michael, 104, 114, 213
McCormick, Robert, 129
McCown, Marjorie, 27
McCoy, Kerry, 65
McCoy, Kevin, 144
McCoy, Mark, 51
McCray, Jennifer, 68
McCready, Kevin Neil, 37
McCullers, Carson, 103
McCulloh, Barbara, 88, 213, 216
McCullum, Kim, 67
McCully, Emily Arnold, 131
McCusker, Daniel, 169
McCusker, Stella, 10
McCutcheon, Bill, 45, 213
McDaniel, Brian, 105
McDaniel, James, 46
McDaniel, John, 66
McDaniel, William, 74
McDermott, James T., 134
McDermott, Sean, 162
McDermott, Tom, 97, 161
McDonald, Belle, 160
McDonald, Beth, 67, 213
McDonald, Bill, 160
McDonald, Bonnie, 65
McDonald, David B., 50
McDonald, J. T., 33
McDonald, Jeff, 65
McDonald, Jeffrey D., 105
McDonald, Karen, 154
McDonald, Tanny, 96, 151, 213
McDonnell, James, 148
McDonnell, Mary, 154
McDonough, Ann, 154, 213
McDonough, Edwin J., 142
McDonough, Edwin, 142
McDowell, Bob, 82
McDowell, Rex, 119
McDowell, Stanley, 161
McElroy, Josie, 160
McElvain, Richard, 160
McElwaine, James, 34
McElwee, Theresa, 73, 143
McEowen, Michael, 24
McEwen, Lisa, 121
McFadden, Gates, 97
McFarland, Martha, 172
McFarland, Robert, 82, 213
McFarren, Cheryl, 138
McFatter, Shirley, 180
McGavin, Darren, 107, 213
McGaw, Marty, 183
McGill, Eric, 102
McGillicuddy, Pat, 82
McGillin, Howard, 45
McGinley, John C., 79, 213, 216
McGinn, John, 129
McGinn, Kevin, 58
McGinnis, Maureen, 213
McGinnis-Pack, Megan, 130
McGivney, Michael, 130
McGlinn, John, 63
McGough, Shannon, 82, 213, 216
McGovern, Barry, 86
McGovern, Elizabeth, 126, 193
McGowan, Tom, 94, 95, 213
McGrane, John, 68
McGrath, Jim, 54
McGrath, Katherine, 133, 135
McGrath, Mark, 125, 143, 146
McGrath, Matt, 79
McGrath, Michael, 50
McGreevey, Annie, 65, 213
McGuigan, Marcy, 164
McGuigan, Missy, 130
McGuinness, Frank, 56
McGuinness, Michael John, 99, 213
McGuinness, Patrick, 102
McGuire, Kevin, 114
McGuire, Lindsay, 184
McGuire, Maeve, 71, 143, 176, 179, 213
McGuire, Michael, 140
McGuire, Peter, 174
McGuire, Rose, 151
McGuire, Shawn, 58
McHale, Christopher, 94, 166, 169, 184
McHattie, Stephen, 35, 213
McHugh, Joanne, 146
McIlveen, John, 56
McIntyre, Dennis, 154
McIntyre, Dianne, 14, 49
McIntyre, Gerry, 45, 125, 213, 216
McIntyre, Judith, 82
McIntyre, Marilyn, 54
McKay, Robin, 86
McKayle, Donald, 118
McKeaney, Grace, 66
McKee, Lonette, 118
McKee, Robin, 134
McKenna, Christiane, 57, 213
McKenna, Joseph, 49, 57, 61, 67
McKenzie, Kent, 132
McKenzie, Lonnie, 8
McKenzie, Michael, 21, 108, 213
McKeown, David, 82, 213
McKinley, Philip Wm., 162
McKinley, Rita, 140
McKinney, Michael, 106
McKneely, Joey, 25
McKoy, Winsome, 56
McLachlan, Roderick, 19, 213, 216
McLain, Ellen, 129
McLain, John, 24, 141
McLanahan, Matt, 73
McLane, Derek, 68, 132, 141, 169
McLane, Derel, 170
McLaren, Conrad, 165
McLaughlin, Erin, 57
McLaughlin, Julia, 48, 53, 61
McLure, James, 108
McMahon, Briona, 72
McMahon, Brionna, 71
McManigal, Jay, 57, 82
McManus, Don R., 213
McManus, William, 151
McMichaels, Flynn, 37
McMillan, Allison, 130
McMillan, Kenneth, 230, 231
McMillan, Kevin, 93
McMillan, Richard, 105
McMullen, Allen, 118
McMurtry, Jonathan, 179
McNabb, Barry, 42, 44, 74, 213
McNally, Jacqueline, 49
McNally, Joseph, 119
McNally, Terrence, 55, 60, 89, 121, 134
McNamara, John C., 32
McNamara, Maureen, 213
McNamara, Pat, 20, 213
McNaughton, Stephen, 75, 213
McNeely, Anna, 38
McNeil, Robert Duncan, 133
McNeill, Katlyn, 148
McNeill, Robert Duncan, 113
McNenny, Kathleen, 95, 176
McNight, Sharon, 34, 188, 190, 213
McNulty, Bill, 120
McNutt, Kim, 83
McPherson, John, 174
McQueen, Armelia, 12
McQueen, Jim, 121
McRobbie, Peter, 56, 213
McShane, Michael, 123
McVay, Robert, 180
McVety, Drew, 30, 100, 213
McVey, Beth, 44
McVey, Mark, 114
McWilliams, Patric, 51
McWilliams, Richard, 51, 107, 213
Mcguire, Rose, 151
Me and My Girl, 42, 116, 117
Mead, William, 37
Mead, Winter, 80
Meade, Julia, 166
Meader, Derek, 151
Meadow, Lynne, 88, 89
Meadows, Pattilynne, 64
Means, John, 213
Meara, Anne, 21, 213
Mears, DeAnn, 138, 179
Measure for Measure, 86
Meaux, Jim, 85
Mebane, Bill, 140
Medea, 127
Medina, Hazel, 213
Medina, Roberto, 93, 101
Medley, Cassandra, 52
Mednikovi and Abakorovi, 13
Medoff, Mark, 55, 67
Mee, Charles L., Jr., 93, 97
Mee, Erin B., 93
Meeh, Greg, 88
Meeh, Gregory, 34
Meeker, Ralph, 230, 231
Meeker, Roger, 151
Mehmert, Steve, 46
Mehrten, Greg, 97
Meier, Ron, 82, 182
Meikle, David Scott, 148
Meiksins, Robert, 161
Meineke, Eva-Marie, 78
Meister, Brian, 28
Meister, Frederica, 61, 100, 213
Melamed, Johanna, 161
Melde, Shari, 180
Mele, Rande, 55
Meleck, Peter Wrenn, 164
Meledandri, Wayne, 37
Melfi, Leonard, 43, 55
Melia, Hector, 83
Melici, Sarah, 96, 128, 154
Melius, Nancy, 83
Mellon, James, 136, 170
Mellor, Stephen, 61, 213
Melotti, Joe, 33
Melrod, George, 57
Melville, Herman, 59
Member of the Wedding, The, 103
Men Should Weep, 176
Mena, Carlos, 161
Menchell, Ivan, 136
Mendelowitz, Iva, 66
Mendez, Benigno, 161
Mendillo, Stephen, 151
Mengden, Amanda, 183
Menke, Rick, 176
Menken, Alan, 142, 152, 164
Mennen, James G., 38
Mennone, Kate, 106
Menson, Uriel, 67
Meola, Tony, 45, 109, 111
Mercado, Hector, 134
Mercedes, 97
Mercer, Randy H., 70, 99, 100
Mercer, Sally, 166
Mercier, G. W., 89
Mercurio, Gregory, 52, 60
Mercurio, Valerie, 128
Meredith, Burgess, 33
Meredith, Lois, 183
Merediz, Olga, 40, 76, 114, 213
Merk, Ron, 43
Merkerson, S. Epatha, 144
Merkin, Robby, 54
Merkur, Jordan, 88
Merle Debuskey Associates, 109
Merlin, Joanna, 39, 113
Mermelstein, Dave, 142
Merrick, Monte, 137
Merrifield, Gail, 93
Merrill, Bob, 136, 182
Merrill, Dina, 33
Merrill, Robert, 33
Merrill, Todd, 134, 135, 151
Merrily We Roll Along, 119
Merritt, George, 213
Merritt, Michael, 144
Merry Wives of Windsor, Texas, The, 121
Merryman, Monica, 52, 213, 216
Mersky, Kres, 59
Mertes, Brian, 52, 60
Mesney, Barbara J., 123
Mesnick, William, 158
Mesnik, William, 104
Messenger, John, 122
Messina, Alfredo, 48
Metamorphosis, 28
Metcalf, Kam, 102
Metcalf, Laurie, 193
Metcalf, Mark, 166, 183
Mete, Marco, 48
Metheny, Russell, 65
Metzler, Kerry, 57
Metzo, William, 213
Meyer, Edgar, 147
Meyer, Karen, 119
Meyer, Marlane, 156, 172
Meyer, Michael, 49
Meyer, Richard, 68
Meyerhoff, Tom O., 54
Meyers, D. Lynn, 108
Meyers, Elliot, 75
Meyers, T. J., 28, 213
Meyrich, Victor, 127
Miceli, Michael, 89
Michael Feinstein in Concert, 14
Michaels, Cindy, 140
Michaels, Devon, 94, 96, 213
Michaels, Garen, 130
Michaels, Greg, 138
Michaels, Lynn, 48
Michaels, Maria, 144
Michaels, Mark A., 103
Michaelson, Ron, 172
Michel, Carolyn, 137
Michel, John, 64
Michie, William D., 102
Michl, Keith, 48, 53, 103
Mickelbury, Denise B., 80
Mickey, Susan E., 122
Middle of Nowhere, The, 54, 180
Midsummer Night's Dream, A, 46, 148
Mielziner, Jo, 25
Mieske, Dale, 174
Mihok, Andrew, 93, 96
Mike, Louise, 82
Milan, Candice, 168
Milani, Linda, 63
Miles, Ann, 19
Miles, Julia, 52, 61, 62
Miles, Kimberly, 108
Miles, Linda, 158
Miles, Robin, 46
Miles, Sylvia, 81, 213
Miley, Peggy, 67
Milford, David, 122
Milia, Hector, 83
Milian, Tomas, 60
Milione, Lou, 132
Militello, Anne, 56, 76, 94, 95, 97, 176
Mill Fire, 144, 145
Millan, Bruce, 139
Mille, Antoinette, 56
Millenbach, George, 59
Miller, Alfred, 104
Miller, Arthur, 121, 142, 151, 166, 172, 178
Miller, Barnabas, 87
Miller, Barry, 57, 213
Miller, Bob, 137
Miller, Bobby, 77, 96
Miller, Craig, 146
Miller, Debra Elise, 36, 213
Miller, Gwendolyn, 20
Miller, Joel McKinnon, 96, 148
Miller, John, 41, 100, 143
Miller, Jonathan Seth, 124
Miller, Kristine, 137
Miller, Marjorie Ann, 82, 213
Miller, Mark David, 130
Miller, Mark, 180
Miller, Mary C., 93
Miller, Mary, 116, 117
Miller, Matthew, 129
Miller, Megan L., 112
Miller, Melanie, 174
Miller, Michael, 168, 169
Miller, Monique, 57
Miller, Penelope Ann, 19, 213
Miller, Robin, 143
Miller, Susan, 95
Miller, Wade, 162
Miller-Shields, Megan, 158
Millman, Devora, 131, 143, 165
Millman, Howard J., 131, 143, 165
Mills, Charlie, 182
Mills, Cornelia, 62
Mills, Dana, 176, 177
Milner, Billy, 158
Milner, Ron, 11
Milos, Shole, 152
Milton, Jezy, 78
Minahan, Greg, 38
Mineo, Roseanna, 73
Miner, Kohl, 68
Miner, Mary Michele, 134
Minetor, Nic, 143
Minetor, Nic, 143
Mingus, Barbara Pullen, 136
Mini-Rep, The, 108
Minoff, Tammy, 88, 213
Minor Demons, 154
Minor, Philip, 162, 165
Minot, Anna, 71, 213, 216
Minsker, JoAnn, 75
Minskoff, Lee, 74
Minsky, Greta, 107
Mintz, Cheryl, 116, 117
Minucci, Ulpio, 74
Miracolo d'Amore, 93
Mironchik, James, 95
Mirvish, Ed and David, 16
Misalliance, 168
Miser, The, 124
Miskulin, John J., 94
Miss Firecracker Contest, The, 158
Mississippi Delta, 91
Mistress of the Inn, The, 103
Mistretta, Sal, 32, 213
Mitch Leigh Company, The, 31
Mitchell, Adrian, 168
Mitchell, Aleta, 104, 213, 216
Mitchell, Barbara Jean, 152
Mitchell, Bob, 85
Mitchell, David, 20, 90, 110, 162
Mitchell, Deborah, 22
Mitchell, Delores, 123
Mitchell, Gregory, 214
Mitchell, Jerry, 25
Mitchell, John Cameron, 138
Mitchell, Katie, 178
Mitchell, Lauren, 39, 88
Mitchell, LeRoy, Jr., 127
Mitchell, Lizan, 52, 166
Mitchell, Melanie, 49, 214
Mitchell, Robert, 31
Mitchell, Ruth, 33, 44
Mitler, Matt, 49
Mittenthal, Ellen, 79
Mitterhoff, Barry, 35
Mitzman, Marcia, 32, 214
Mixed Doubles, 62
Mixon, Alan, 162
Mixon, Bernard, 111
Mizell, Pam, 112
Mizelle, Dary John, 183
Mizzy, Danianne, 52, 57
Moberly, Phyllis, 134
Moby Dick, 59
Mockus, Tony, 179
Model Apartment, The, 156, 157
Modereger, Jeff, 158
Moeller, Todd, 119
Moffat, Donald, 214
Mofokeng, Jerry, 92
Mogg, Nann, 165
Mohn, Leslie, 78
Mohr, Jim, 183
Mohrlein, John, 144
Molaskey, Jessica, 40
Molefi, Aubrey, 156
Moliere, 124, 151, 158
Molina, Alex, 55
Molina, Armando, 135
Mollenhauer, Heidi, 57, 74
Molloy, Honor, 58
Molloy, Malone Dies, 86
Molnar, Robert, 57, 214
Molo, Angelo, 65
Monaco, John, 20, 33
Monaco, Marylin, 83, 214
Monaco, Neil, 73
Monagan, Susan, 57
Monat, Phil, 54, 74, 81, 106, 131, 158, 165, 170
Monat, Philip, 179
Mondy, Bill, 104, 126, 214
Monette, Richard, 174
Monferdini, Carol, 73

Monferdini, Carole, 131
Monge, Julio, 25
Monich, Timothy, 132
Monk, Debra, 72, 100, 140, 143, 184, 185
Monk, Isabell, 62, 78, 214
Monma, Toshio, 78
Montgomery, Andre, 105
Monroe, Donna, 42
Monroe, Jarion, 172, 173
Monroe, Steve, 105
Monson, Lex, 166
Montano, Jeanne, 85
Monte, Chris, 214
Monte, Marrielle, 65
Montez, Paul-Felix, 101
Montgomerie, Jeffrey, 136
Montgomery, Andre, 105, 214
Montgomery, Chuck, 93
Montgomery, Jack, 116
Montgomery, Kris, 112
Montgomery, Reggie, 86
Montgomery, Robert, 94
Monzione, David, 146
Moods Pan Groove, 78
Moody, Michael R., 88, 89
Moon for the Misbegotten, A, 148, 149, 164, 181
Moon over Miami, 184, 185
Moon, Marjorie, 60
Moon, Philip, 68, 86, 98
Mooney, Daniel, 161
Mooney, Debra, 62
Mooney, Robert, 102
Mooney, Stephanie, 68
Mooney, William, 91
Moor, Bill, 17, 96, 214
Moore, Betty, 71, 214
Moore, Bruce, 129
Moore, Charlotte, 84, 154
Moore, Christina, 100
Moore, Dana, 37
Moore, Dudley, 161
Moore, Jack, 230, 231
Moore, Joshua, 176
Moore, Julianne, 120, 147
Moore, Karen, 71
Moore, Kathleen, 37
Moore, Mary Tyler, 33
Moore, Matthew, 54
Moore, Melba, 193
Moore, Richard, 158
Moore, Sharon, 126
Moorehead, Kelly, 102
Moorman, Clem, 126
Moose, G. Eugene, 146, 162
Moprton, Amy, 147
Morales, Mark, 130
Moran, Brian, 95
Moran, Martin, 88, 214
Moran, Tim, 184
Morant, Mark, 101
Moranz, Brad, 116
Mordecai, Benjamin, 7, 184
Moreau, Jennie, 89, 104, 188, 190, 214
Morehouse, Edward, 99
Morell, Richard, 138
Morello, Tony, 65
Morena, Rene, 93
Moreno, Belita, 172
Moreno, Fernando, 101
Moreno, Rene, 55, 214
Morer, Paul, 14, 50
Morfogen, George, 72, 214
Morgan, Cass, 60, 140
Morgan, Elizabeth, 129
Morgan, James, 108, 125
Morgan, Jan, 13
Morgan, Monique, 143
Morgan, Patrick B., 170
Morgan, Robbi, 130
Morgan, Robert, 151
Morgan, Roger, 42, 179
Morgan, Sam, 126
Morgan, William Perry, 102
Morgenstern, Susan, 56, 214
Mori, Johnny, 134, 135
Morick, Jeanine, 50
Morin-Torre, Lorraine, 49, 214
Moritz, Susan Trapnell, 119
Moriyasu, Atsushi, 98
Morley, Carol, 56
Morley, Larry, 21
Morley, Ruth, 16
Morocco, 107, Dana, 184
Morrical, Julie, 130
Morrili, E. F., 67
Morrill, E. F., 60
Morris, Cleveland, 137
Morris, Gary, 40
Morris, Haviland, 88
Morris, Iona, 81
Morris, Janet S., 138
Morris, John, 93, 95
Morris, Kenny, 128
Morris, Mark James, 82, 214
Morris, Rotzo B., 60
Morris, Tony, 148
Morrisey, Bob, 120
Morrison, Adam, 67
Morrison, Ann, 122
Morrison, James, 24, 36, 38, 40, 44
Morrison, Matt, 140
Morrison, Toni, 33
Morriss, Bruce K., 137
Morrow, Charlie, 63
Morrow, Kevyn, 118
Morrow, Rob, 46
Morse, Ben, 42, 48, 50, 53, 81, 107
Morse, Douglas J., 55
Morse, Robert, 130
Morse, Robin, 60, 214
Morse, Tom, 12, 18, 110
Mortal Friends, 53
Mortensen, Art, 57
Morton, Bruce B., 60
Morton, Joe, 94, 214
Mosby, Josh, 65, 151
Moscow Circus '88, 13
Moscow Circus, 13
Moseley, Robin, 46, 88, 94, 121, 165
Moseman, Tom, 74
Moser, Paul, 169
Moses, Burke, 138
Moses, Denise, 73
Moses, Mark, 95, 214
Moses, Norman, 161
Moses, Samuel, 91
Mosher, Gregory, 19, 39, 86, 109
Mosher, Susan, 50
Mosley, Milledge, 141
Moss International, Inc., 13
Moss, Barry, 22, 34, 35
Moss, Charles B., Jr., 63
Moss, Hughes, 9, 17
Moss, Jodi, 110
Moss, John, 59, 68
Moss, Peter, 174
Moss, Stephanie, 127
Mosse, Spencer, 142, 164, 183
Most, Donald, 130
Mother Bickerdyke and Me, 51
Mott, Zachary, 165
Mouledoux, John, 172
Moulton, Charles, 59
Mounsey, Melinda, 138
Mourning, Inez, 65
Mousseau, Jeff, 68
Mower, Evan, 134
Mowery, Bob, 127
Moy, Nanci, 98
Moya, Angela, 157, 172
Moya, Bobby, 20
Moyer, Allen, 100
Moyer, Mimi, 85
Moyer, Tim, 166
Moyers, Lloyd, 118
Moynihan, Deirdre, 169
Moyser, Denny, 66
Mr. Cinders, 146
Mr. Pickwick's Christmas, 102
Mrozek, Slawomir, 139
Mrs. California, 119
Msomi, Welcome, 92
Mtwa, Percy, 156
Much Ado About Nothing, 93
Muenz, Richard, 27, 214
Muir, Howie, 148
Muir, Keri, 132
Mukai, Kaoru, 78
Mukeria, Nana, 13
Mulder, Paul, 60
Mulert, Carl, 30, 100
Mulhern, Leonard A., 73
Mulhern, Matt, 107, 165, 214
Mulholland, Barry, 141, 154
Mull, Kathe, 62, 84
Mullaney, Jan, 90, 105
Mullavey, Greg, 18
Muller, Heiner, 78
Mulligan, Kathleen, 151
Mullins, Brighde, 68
Mullins, Carol, 56
Mullins, J. C., 140
Mulloy, Susannah, 114
Mulvihill, Sandy, 83
Mumford, Peter B., 20
Mundell, Anne, 165
Munderloh, Otts, 11, 25, 32, 72, 88
Mundinger, Matthew T., 87
Munford, Juanita, 127
Munford, Patricia, 122
Munger, Mary, 31, 94, 214
Mungo, Howard, 52
Munkacsi, Kurt, 56
Munoz, Billy, 140
Munroe, Leigh, 133
Munsel, Patrice, 33
Muraoka, Alan, 109
Murch, Robert, 23, 214
Murder at the Vicarage, 159
Murder in the Cathedral, 174
Murder of Crows, A, 50
Murder on the Nile, 140
Murfitt, Mary, 72, 143, 214
Murin, David, 131, 154
Murphy, Alan, 65
Murphy, C. Cameron, 99
Murphy, Donna, 67, 214
Murphy, Drew, 49, 214
Murphy, Gary, 79, 97
Murphy, Harry S., 77, 124
Murphy, James P., 162
Murphy, John, 43
Murphy, Karen, 151
Murphy, Rob, 97
Murphy, Rosemary, 17, 214
Murphy, Sally, 144
Murphy, Thomas, 84
Murraxy, Rob, 48
Murray, Andrew, 174
Murray, Annie, 48
Murray, Brian, 68, 93, 170, 214
Murray, Daniel L., 138
Murray, Johnna, 39
Murray, Ken, 230, 231
Murray, Leland, 72, 214
Murray, Margery, 164, 165
Murray, Mary Gordon, 39, 113, 133
Murray, Rob, 8, 48
Murray, Robert, 46, 48
Murray, Rupert, 10, 86
Murray, Tim, 148
Murtaugh, James, 46, 59, 148, 214
Musante, Tony, 214
Musical Comedy Murders of 1940, 152
Musick, Michael, 52, 64
Musick, Sandra, 128
Musselman, David, 72
Musser, Tharon, 18, 32, 37, 110, 134
Musumeci, Justin, 97
Mutrie, Matthew P., 35
Muza, Tom, 181
Muzio, Gloria, 59, 106, 131, 148
Muzzi, Michele, 174
My Daughter, The Sister, 105
My Fair Lady, 174
My Unknown Son, 51
Myers, Jennifer Jay, 176
Myers, Lou, 145
Myers, Mary, 184
Myers, Richard, 146
Myers, Troy, 25
Myler, Andrew, 179
Myler, Randal, 75, 131, 138
Myrberg, Per, 78
Myslewski, Ray, 56
Mystery of Edwin Drood, The, 152
Mystery of Irma Vep, The, 142, 161, 164
Nabel, Bill, 108
Nadal, Jerry, 82
Nadareishvili, Gia, 13
Nadir, Robert, 119, 178
Nagle, Karen, 43
Nahrwold, Thomas, 46, 154
Naimo, Jennifer, 114
Najee-Ullah, Mansoor, 96
Najimy, Kathy, 59, 214
Nakagawa, Jon, 106
Nakahara, Ron, 98, 214
Nakao, Kenji, 31, 85
Nakashima, Takashi, 78
Nakauchi, Paul, 31
Nalbach, Daniel, 83, 153, 214, 216
Nance, Cortez, Jr., 96
Nanus, Susan, 68
Napier, John, 38, 40
Naro, Thomas, 25, 30
Nash, Michael W., 161
Nash, N. Richard, 125
Nash, Neil, 69
Nash, Ron, 43
Nason, Brian, 28, 85
Nassar, Mark, 73
Nassau, Paul, 75
Nastasi, Frank, 103, 214, 216
Nasty Little Secrets, 54
Natasi, Frank, 51
Nateghi, Behnam, 61
Nater, Christina Ann, 60
Nathan, Anne L., 115
Nathan, Fred, 25, 38
National Anthems, 154
Nations, Denise, 61, 65
Natker, Leon, 130
Natoli, Deborah, 82
Natoli, Gary, 19, 86
Naughton, Amanda, 143
Naughton, James, 62, 193
Navarre, Ron, 37
Naylor, Anthony, 67
Naylor, Marcus, 92
Neal, Elise D., 118
Nealon, Mary T., 72
Near, Holly, 178
Near, Timothy, 178
Neary, Jack, 160
Nebgen, Stephen W., 61
Nebgen, Stephen, 65
Nebozenko, Jan, 21
Nederlander, James L., 11, 15, 16, 20, 33
Nederlander, James M., 11, 13, 15, 16, 20, 33, 42, 116, 117
Needles, William, 174
Neenan, Maria, 25, 214
Neet, Alison Stair, 68, 170
Negrini, Gualtiero, 133
Neil, Robert, 130
Neill, Amy Jo, 161
Neill, Jeffery K., 59, 64
Neipris, Janet, 66
Neish, William, 104
Nelligan, Kate, 16
Nelson, Bill, 81, 85, 214
Nelson, Charlotte, 139
Nelson, Connie, 180
Nelson, David, 94
Nelson, Dee, 160
Nelson, Edward, 45
Nelson, Jesse, 77
Nelson, Judd, 156
Nelson, Mark, 18, 214, 216
Nelson, Meredith, 138
Nelson, Novella, 62
Nelson, Richard, 9, 15, 39, 113, 119, 133
Nelson, Ruth, 136
Nelson, Sara, 114
Nemeth, Sally, 144
Nemetz, Lenora, 27, 162, 163
Neofitou, Andreane, 40
Neptune's Hips, 46
Nerd, The, 120, 140
Nero's Last Folly, 62
Nesbit, Pat, 66
Nesci, John, 172
Nest, The, 97
Netzel, Sally, 153
Neuberger, Jan, 214
Neufeld, Peter, 16, 23, 24, 38
Neuman, Jani, 133
Neumann, David, 96
Neumann, Frederick, 61, 78, 96
Neuwirth, Bebe, 67
Nevard, Angela, 55
Neville, David, 108
Neville, John, 174
Neville, Tom, 168
Nevins, Kristine, 90
New American Theatre, 50
New Voices for the American Musical: See How They Run, 105
New, Martha J., 172
Newave Management, 72
Newbern, George, 144
Newby-Koschwitz, Simon, 78
Newcomb, Don, 71, 153
Newell, Charles, 147
Newhall, Anne, 131, 176
Newhouse, Jerry, 147
Newkirk, Eunice, 60
Newman, Andrew Hill, 75, 147, 214
Newman, Buck, 122
Newman, David, 43
Newman, Greatrex, 146
Newman, Jim, 178
Newman, Molly, 53, 138
Newman, Phyllis, 33
Newman, Randy, 54, 180
Newman, Rosalind, 85
News from St. Petersburg, The, 57
Newton, Don W., 166
Newton, John, 108, 153, 166, 214
Newton, Keith, 117
N'Gom, Aodoulaye, 61
Niccore, Valorie, 60, 214
Nice, Rebecca, 127
Nicely, Susan, 27
Nicholas, Angela, 146
Nicholas, Elena, 63
Nicholas, Fayard, 22
Nicholas, Lisa, 68, 102
Nicholason, Joan, 56
Nicholes, Camara, 170
Nichols, Jennifer, 29
Nichols, Jonathan, 86
Nichols, Josephine, 183
Nichols, Kenneth, 162
Nichols, Mike, 86, 164
Nichols, Robert, 63, 85, 214
Nichols, Shelly, 130
Nichols, Tom, 108
Nicholson, Betsy, 24
Nicholson, Joan, 56
Nicholson, John, 158
Nickelson, Jeffrey W., 138
Nicola, James C., 62, 97
Nicolaisen, Kari, 74, 214, 216
Nicole, Ariane, 161
Niebank, Paul, 151
Niedecker, 61
Niedzolkowski, Mark, 93
Nielsen, Kristine, 87, 184
Nieman, Ann, 116
Nieminski, Joe, 144
Night Games, 108
Night Hank Williams Died, The, 107
Night of the Iguana, The, 9
Nigro, Bob, 82
Nigro, Meara, 162
Niko Associates, 31
Nilsson, Christopher, 176
Nilsson, Gun-Marie, 119
1918, 137
1940s Radio Hour, The, 178
Nipkow, Leslie, 97, 214, 216
Nishikawa, Lane, 134
Nixon, Cynthia, 30, 215
Noble, Janet, 84
Nocciolino, Albert, 54
Noda, Hideki, 78
Noel, Michael, 126
Nohe, Marc, 56
Noiresque: The Fallen Angel, 98
Noises Off, 122, 160, 170, 171
Nolan, Anto, 10
Nolan, Kathleen Kund, 166
Nolen, Timothy, 44, 162, 215
Noling, David, 179
Noll, Ellen, 138
Nolte, Charles, 182
Noonan, Kerry, 172
Noonan, Patty, 64
Noonan, Tom, 46
Noone, James, 61, 90, 166, 179
Nora-Dunfee, 52
Norber, Brian, 130
Norberg, Catherine, 143
Nordling, Jeffrey, 80, 96
Nordstrom, Daniel A., 47
Norgren, Catherine F., 176
Norman, Inez, 92
Norman, John, 215
Norris, Bruce, 88, 215, 216
Norris, Donald, 116
Norris, Lisa D., 176
Norris, Rick, 127
Norris, William J., 144
Norton, Cari, 134, 135
Norton, Richard, 6
Norwick, Natalie, 67
Noseworthy, Jack, 25
Not About Heroes, 174
Noth, Christopher, 103, 161
Nothing Sacred, 123, 126, 134, 148, 149
Noto, Lore, 69
Noto, Tony, 69
Notzon, Jan, 141
Nova, Christian, 130
Novack, Ellen, 46, 56, 80
Novak, Mark, 132
Nowell, Tommy, Jr., 122
Nozick, Bruce, 131, 165, 215
Nri, Cyril, 92
Nugent, Elliott, 82
Nugent, James, 99, 215
Nugit, Andrea, 58
Nugzarov, Tamerlan, 13
Null, Panchali, 60, 90
Nunes, Paul, 20
Nunn, Trevor, 38, 40
Nunsense, 70
Nussbaum, Mike, 144
Nute, Don, 215, 216
Nye, Carrie, 81, 215
Nye, Hope, 80
O'Brady, Mary, 168
O'Briain, Colm, 86
O'Brian, Carmel, 84
O'Brien, Adale, 120
O'Brien, Amy, 45, 215, 216
O'Brien, Dale, 69, 109, 215
O'Brien, David, 151
O'Brien, Denise, 63
O'Brien, Jack, 18, 51
O'Brien, Jamie Lynn, 49
O'Brien, Joseph, 62
O'Brien, Paul, 58
O'Brien, Sylvia, 42, 116, 215
O'Callahan, Jay, 160
O'Carroll, Mike, 20, 90
O'Casey, Sean, 10, 84, 161
O'Connell, Andrea, 161
O'Connell, Cailin, 132
O'Connell, Caitlin, 132
O'Connell, David G., 56
O'Connell, Deirdre, 156
O'Connell, Lita, 10
O'Connell, Michael, 183
O'Connell, Patrick, 56, 215
O'Conner, Ricarda, 55
O'Connor, Daniel J., 135
O'Connor, Gretchen V., 119
O'Connor, J. Christopher, 119
O'Connor, Joyce, 94
O'Connor, Kevin J., 134
O'Connor, Kevin, 58, 67, 215
O'Connor, Ryan, 119
O'Connor, Suzanne, 82, 83
O'Dell, Herbert H., 54, 59, 67
O'Dell, Herbert, 108
O'Dell, K. Lype, 141
O'Donnell, Bob, 144
O'Donnell, Elaine R., 48
O'Donnell, Elaine, 56, 58
O'Donnell, Mark, 57
O'Donnell, Mary Eileen, 105
O'Donnell, Susan, 28
O'Dowd, Mary, 48
O'Dwyer, Jo Haden Laurence, 180
O'Dwyer, Laurence, 180
O'Flaherty, Douglas, 99
O'Flaherty, Michael, 63, 64
O'Gorman, Michael, 48, 72
O'Grady, Dan, 20, 66
O'Hara, Paige, 63, 215, 216
O'Hare, Brad, 184, 185
O'Hare, Michael, 126
O'Hare, Tim, 99, 215
O. Henry, 55
O'Karma, Alexandra, 29
O'Kelly, Aideen, 46

O'Leary, Barbara Ann, 176
O'Leary, Kevin, 169
O'Malley, Jim, 68, 215
O'Neil, Ellen, 74
O'Neil, Molly, 52
O'Neil, Tim, 47
O'Neill, Denis, 84
O'Neill, Eugene, 6, 7, 57, 64, 123, 148, 164, 179
O'Neill, James, 53
O'Neill, Michael, 88, 184, 185
O'Reilly, Allen, 122
O'Reilly, Ciaran, 84, 215
O'Rourke, Kevin, 16, 215
O'Shaugnessy, Bill, 47
O'Shea, Michael, 179
O'Steen, Michelle, 45
O'Sullivan, Anne, 46, 54, 61, 105, 169, 215
O'Sullivan-Moore, Emmett, 165
Oakes, Alice Anne, 45, 215
Oakes, Betty, 230
Oakes, Cindy, 215
Oakes, Melanie, 49
Oates, Enda, 10
Oberlander, Michael, 48
Obidowski, Cissy, 42
Oblinger, Melinda, 64
Obnoxious, Ethyl, 55
Ocel, Timothy J., 57
Ochlan, P. J., 95
Ochoa, Steve, 25
Ockrent, Mike, 42
Oddo, John, 14
Odets, Clifford, 63
Odien, Bill, 130
Odle, Dwight Richard, 172
Odo, Chris, 41, 215
Oedipus Rex, 67
Oedipus, 174
Oestreicher, Irma, 6
Offner, Deborah, 184, 185
Offshore Signals, 170
Oh! Calcutta!, 43
Ohama, Natsuko, 98, 134
Ohrenstein, Dora, 56
Ohye, Jan, 79
Oil City Symphony, 72, 143
Oka, Marc C., 85
Oka, Marc, 45
Okada, Kimi, 36
Okamura, Koji, 86
Okazaki, Alan, 50
Oken, Carol Ball, 134
Okerson, Doug, 74
Okun, Alexander, 132
Olcott, C. Townsend, II, 158
Olcott, Nick, 126
Oldfather, Craig, 162
Olic, Michael, 119
Olich, Michael, 119, 122
Oliensis, Adam, 143
Olim, Dorothy, 69
Olive, John, 119, 121, 131, 170
Oliver, David, 176
Oliver, Rochelle, 62
Oliver, Wendy, 83, 162
Olivo, Andrew, 47
Olivo, Bob, 230
Olkewicz, Walter, 134
Olsen, Marilyn, 56
Olsen, Robert, 158
Olson, James, 95, 215
Olson, Marcus, 113, 133
Olson, Marilyn, 215
Olson, Scott, 138
Olson, Stephen, 97, 105
Olson, Thomas W., 102
Olsson, Jan, 78
Olster, Fredi, 123
Omahen, Karen, 36, 215
Oman, Timothy W., 68, 102
Omar, David, 99
Omilami, Afemo, 122
Omilami, Elizabeth, 122
Oms, Alba, 101
On The Prowl, 54
On Tina Tuna Walk, 54, 55
On the Town, 126
On the Verge, 164
On the Waterfront, 136
Ondrejka, Malia, 83, 215
One Man Band, 50
One Monday, 57
1000 Airplanes on the Roof, 56
One Two Three Four Five, 88
One-Act Play Festival, 60
Onickel, Alan, 118
Only Kidding, 75, 188, 189
Onrubia, Cynthia, 25
Ontiveros, Lupe, 157
Ooms, Richard, 147
Opel, Nancy, 45
Open Boat, The, 68
Opper, Norman, 66
Oquita, Ric, 161
Orchard, Robert J., 77, 124
Orchid, Ellen, 83, 215
Ore, John E., 121
Orell, Rico, 135
Orezzeli, Hector, 22
Orfield, Cy, 54, 55
Orgal, Yehiel, 53, 134
Oriel, Ray, 134, 135
Origlio, Tony, 50
Orloff, Rich, 57
Orman, Roscoe, 89, 215
Ormerod, John, 174
Orner, Fredric H., 86
Ornstein, Michael, 183
Oropeza, Luis, 123
Orr, Cyndi, 128, 184
Orser, Leland, 166, 167
Orshan, Wendy, 24
Orton, Joe, 88
Osborne, Conrad L., 64
Osborne, Si, 133
Osborne, Will, 165
Osbun, Eric, 55
Osgood, Steven, 82
Osian, Matte, 67, 215
Osipchuk, Vladimir, 47
Osmond, Gordon C., 65
Ossian, David, 96, 147
Ossoinak, Ivan, 78
Ostaszewski, Jacek, 47
Osterberg, Bertil, 78
Osterberg, Marin, 147
Ostergren, Pernilla, 78
Ostermann, Curt, 17, 146, 176
Ostrow, Lisa, 88
Ostrow, Stuart, 41
Other People's Money, 59, 148
Otis, James, 144
Otis, John, 59
Ottavino, John, 68
Ottiwell, Frank, 123
Ottley, Rachelle, 130
Ouellette, Thomas, 160
Ouimette, Stephen, 184
Our Lady of the Tortilla, 152
Our Own Red Blood, 58
Our Town, 19, 186, 189
Out of This World, 64
Outside the Radio, 68
Ouzounian, Richard, 174
Over Forty, 60
Overall, Park, 46
Overcash, Elise, 182
Overmeyer, Eric, 132
Overmire, Laurence, 73, 82, 83, 215
Overmyer, Eric, 81, 104, 164, 172
Owen, Bobbi, 168
Owen, Marianne, 119
Owen, Paul, 120
Owens, Edwin, 176
Owens, Elizabeth, 164
Owens, Gordon, 37
Owens, Greg, 128
Owens, Labert, 102
Owens, Melody, 137
Owsley, Roy, 55
Oyamo, 46
Ozker, Eren, 78
Paaske, Anne Karin, 158
Pablo, 47
Pace, Atkin, 85, 142, 164
Pacino, Al, 193
Packard, Carl, 130
Paddison, Gordon, 126
Paetow, Jan, 63
Pagan, Peter, 81, 215
Page, Cindi, 115
Page, Evelyn, 50, 116, 215
Page, Ken, 12, 193
Pagliotti, Douglas, 51
Pagoota, Chris, 54
Paige, Grace, 127
Paine, Hugh, 58
Pajama Game, The, 27
Pajer, Jeff, 129
Pakis, Nyai Dewi, 47
Pakis, Otig, 47
Pakledinaz, Martin, 55, 94
Palasz, Terry, 119
Paley, Petronia, 126
Palk, Nancy, 174
Palm, Thom, 77
Palmas, Joseph, 93
Palmatier, Nancy, 53
Palmer, LaRue, 130
Palmer, Mack, 139
Palmer, Margaret, 174
Palmieri, Joe, 170
Panaro, Hugh, 40, 114
Pankin, Jordan, 49
Pankow, John, 88, 215
Pannell, Raymond, 174
Panson, Bonnie, 94
Paoletti, John, 144
Paolucci, Bob, 83, 215
Papavs, Vickie, 174
Paper Gramophone, The, 148
Papp, Joseph, 37, 93, 94, 96
Pappageorge, Demetrios, 168
Pappas, Evan, 142
Pappas, Theodore, 27, 95
Parady, Ron, 19, 162, 215
Pardede, Ria Rondang, 47
Pardess, Yael, 134, 135
Pardey, Jeanine, 65
Parente, Teresa, 146
Parichy, Dennis, 62, 79, 88, 89, 104, 136, 141, 176
Parise, Tina, 116
Parise, Tony, 42
Park, John, 129
Park, Steve, 98
Park, Suzanna, 129
Parker, Corey, 134
Parker, Ellen, 30, 100, 215
Parker, Jean, 84
Parker, Roxann, 130
Parker, Sarah Jessica, 100, 215
Parker, Sean, 140
Parker, Stewart, 230
Parkinson, Ariel, 172
Parkman, Francis, 182
Parkman, Russell, 68
Parks, Brian, 122
Parks, Wendy, 48
Parlato, Dennis, 108, 215
Parmeggiani, Frida, 78
Parnes, Joey, 20
Parone, Edward, 135
Parrent, Melanie, 141
Parrish, Sally, 121
Parrish, Sam, 87
Parry, William, 96, 151, 215
Parsons, Estelle, 76, 215
Parsons, Jennifer, 71
Partington, Dixie, 128
Partington, Rex, 128
Partington, Tony, 128
Paruolo, Biff, 49
Parva, Michael, 54
Pascoe, Pamela, 23
Pashalinski, Lola, 184
Paslawsky, Gregor, 105
Passarella, Lynn, 168
Passeltiner, Bernie, 15, 85, 215, 216
Passero, Jeffery, 57, 66
Passionate Extremes, 90
Passolt, Barbara, 116, 117
Patch, Jerry, 172
Paterson, Chuck, 122
Paterson, William, 123
Pathological Venus, 68
Patinkin, Laura, 75
Patinkin, Mandy, 95, 215
Patricio, Ann, 138
Patrick, Lawrence, 170
Patten, Caymichael, 58
Patteri, Robert, 127
Patterson, Chuck, 151, 122
Patterson, Jackie, 118
Patterson, Jamie, 38
Patterson, Jay, 215, 107
Patterson, Jill, 184
Patterson, Kelly, 25, 215
Patterson, Vaughn, 46, 99
Patti, John, 83, 215, 216
Pattison, Liann, 76, 215
Patton, Gayle, 20
Patton, Jill, 128, 129
Patton, Lee, 138
Patton, Lucille, 67, 217
Patton, Theresa, 60
Patton, Virginia D., 59
Patton, Will, 94, 217
Paul Robeson, 14, 49
Paul, Eric, 137
Paul, Frank, 38
Paul, Guy, 166, 167
Paul, James, 170
Paul, John H., III, 44
Paul, Kent, 74, 99
Paul, Linda, 116
Paul, Michael B., 122
Paul, Stephanie, 57, 162
Paul, Talia, 65
Paul, Tina, 49, 64, 93, 94, 95
Pauley, Jane, 33
Paull, John H., III, 40
Paulsen, Rick, 119
Pauly, Jennifer, 179
Pavelka, Michael, 50
Pavlenko, Nikolai, 13
Pavlovsky Marathon, 47
Pavlovsky, Eduardo, 47
Pavlovsky, Martin, 47
Payne, Emily, 47, 48
Payne, Erica, 60
Payne, Reed, 59
Payton-Wright, Pamela, 9, 41, 217
Peachena, Lady, 60, 217
Peacock, Chiara, 96, 217
Peacock, Lucy, 174
Peak, Danny, 137
Pearl, Jeffrey L., 76
Pearlman, Stephen, 106, 217
Pearson, Burke, 132
Pearson, David, 102
Pearson, Randolf, 63
Pearson, Scott, 37
Pearson, Sybille, 106
Pearthree, Pippa, 132
Peaslee, Richard, 93
Pecaro, Christopher, 115
Peck, Donna, 118
Peck, Richard, 56
Pedersen, Michael, 182
Pederson, Judith M., 138
Pederson, Rose, 36, 119
Pedley, Ron, 33
Peek, Brent, 64
Peek, Jenny, 46
Peer Gynt, 148, 149
Peet, Paris, 141
Peg O' My Heart, 82
Pehlivanian, Raffi, 74
Peil, Mary Beth, 96
Peled, Joanna, 28
Pelegrino, Susan, 176
Pelikan, Lisa, 75, 217
Pelinski, Stephen, 147
Pellegrini, Larry, 73
Pellegrino, Susan, 66, 154, 170, 176, 217
Pelletier, Carol Ann, 67
Pelzig, Daniel, 112
Pemberton, Ann, 127
Pemrick, Don, 32
Pen, Polly, 169
Pendleton, Austin, 16, 61, 64, 68, 102, 217
Pendleton, Wyman, 148, 164
Penhale, David, 183
Penn, Matthew, 68
Pennell, Nicholas, 174
Pennington, Diane, 140
Pennington, Gail, 216, 217
Penny, Rob, 92
Pennypacker, Frank, 127
Pentecost, James, 162
Pentland, Brenda, 179
Peoples, Don, 125
Percassi, Don, 217
Perdziola, Robert, 158
Pereiro, Gustavo, 60
Perelman, S. J., 68
Perelman, Wendy, 82
Peretzian, Michael, 135
Perez, Lazaro, 103, 216, 217
Perez, Luis, 25, 44, 217
Perez, Mercedes, 217
Perez, Michael, 80, 217
Perez, Tim, 93
Perez-Carrion, Edwin, 46
Perkins, Don, 176
Perkins, Patti, 176
Perkins, Thea, 158
Perkovich, David, 152
Perkovitch, David, 152
Perlman, Laura, 67
Perloff, Carey, 80
Perna, Jerry, 46
Perretta, Laura, 170
Perrotta, Laura, 68
Perry, Alvin B., 89
Perry, Amy, 178
Perry, Dan, 102
Perry, Ernest, 111, 144
Perry, Gwena, 100
Perry, Karen, 92, 94
Perry, Keith, 116, 117
Perry, Louis, 27
Perry, Lynette, 146
Perry, Steven, 91, 95, 153
Personals, 152
Pesaturo, George, 217
Peshek, David, 127
Peter Pan, 120, 122, 122, 138
Peter, Frances, 128
Peter, Martin, 78
Peters, Bernadette, 39, 217
Peters, Brock, 111, 217
Peters, Wes, 68
Petersen, Jeffrey William, 141
Peterson, Chris, 109
Peterson, David O., 132
Peterson, Deirdre, 102
Peterson, Eric, 153
Peterson, Kirk, 45
Peterson, Lenka, 59, 116, 117
Peterson, Lisa, 46, 68, 100
Peterson, Pamela, 123, 143, 176, 179, 184
Peterson, Patricia Ben, 85, 142, 151, 162, 163, 216, 217
Peterson, Peggy, 23, 38
Petkoff, Robert, 135
Petlock, Martin, 127
Petrarca, David, 144
Petras, Herman, 74, 99, 102
Petrilli, Stephen, 59, 68, 99, 102
Petrino, Debbie, 146
Petrovich, Victoria, 62, 135
Pettiford-Wates, Tawnya, 119
Pettigrew, Carrie, 158
Pettit, Dodie, 44, 217
Peyton, Ileana, 92
Pfeiffer, David, 27
Pfluger, Len, 146
Phaedra Britannica, 80
Phaedra and Hippolytus, 184, 185
Phantasie, 106
Phantom Lady, 105
Phantom Lady, The, 105
Phantom Tollbooth, The, 68
Phantom of the Opera, The, 44, 133, 186
Phelan, A. Sean, 176
Phelan, K. Sibohan, 93
Phelan, K. Siobhan, 95
Pheneger, Richard P., 33
Philanderer, The, 99
Philippi, Michael S., 144
Phillips, Andy, 41
Phillips, Bob, 52, 65
Phillips, Brad, 56
Phillips, Ethan, 75, 81, 216, 217
Phillips, Joseph C., 94
Phillips, Lacy Darryl, 45, 217
Phillips, Mary Braciten, 90
Phillips, Mary Bracken, 90, 105, 216, 217
Phillips, Mary Ellen, 108, 151, 217
Phillips, Pamela, 62
Phillips, Robert, 135
Phillips, Robin, 174
Philoctetes, 61
Philpot, Mark, 141
Phippin, Jackson, 148, 151
Phoenix, Alec, 48
Piano Lesson, The, 144, 145
Piccione, Nancy, 15
Piccirillo, Lou, 58
Pichette, David, 178
Pichette, Joe, 60
Pickering, James, 161
Pickering, Patrice, 133
Pickering, Rose, 161
Pickering, Steve, 144
Pickett, Mark Stephen, 78
Pickwick Papers, The, 102
Pielmeier, John, 170
Pierce, David, 30, 86, 93, 217
Pierce, Gary, 64
Pierce, Mark, 102
Pierce, Wendell, 96, 142
Pierre, Christophe, 74
Pierrot, Quin, 67, 217
Pierson, Cynthia Leigh, 150
Pierson, Geoff, 158, 183
Pietropinto, Angela, 21
Pigliavento, Michele, 37, 45
Pikser, Jeremy, 136
Pilbrow, Fred, 92
Pilgrim, Barney, 168
Pill Hill Stories (Coming Home to Someplace New), 160
Pillow Talk, 57
Pina, Lionel, 93
Pinckney, Darryl, 78
Pincus, David, 57
Pincus, Warren, 146
Pinero, Miguel, 230
Pingleton, Susan, 153
Pingree, John, 170
Pink, Laurie, 59
Pinkard, Fred, 138
Pinkett, Jada, 132
Pinkins, Tony, 144
Pinkins, Tonya, 107, 217
Pinkney, Mikell, 60
Pinkney, Scott, 55
Pinter, Harold, 160
Pintille, Lucian, 147
Pinto, Dan, 85
Piontek, Michael E., 79, 217
Piontek, Michael, 57, 79, 162
Pippin, Don, 37
Pippin, Nick, 48
Pippin, Stan, 50
Pirandello, Luigi, 77, 103
Piro, Jacquelyn, 115
Pistone, Charles, 114
Pitoniak, Anne, 71
Pittman, Richard, 60
Pivar, Amy, 78
Pla, Ruben, 101
Plachy, William J., 49
Plaisted, Joy, 69
Plass, Sally, 59, 66
Platonov, 124
Platt, Oliver, 87, 184, 185
Play Ball, 98
Playboy of the West Indies, 126, 184, 185
Players Club Centennial Salute, The, 33
Playten, Alice, 16, 18, 190, 217
Pleasants, Phil, 169
Pleasants, Philip, 72
Pliev, Nodar, 13
Plonka, Lavinia, 65
Plough and the Stars, The, 84
Plumb, Hudson, 58
Plunkett, Geraldine, 10
Plunkett, Maryann, 42, 88, 151, 217
Plymale, Trip, 128
Poddubiuk, Christina, 174
Pody, Donna, 137
Poe, 105
Poe, Kevin, 38
Poe, Marjorie, 51
Poe, Richard, 41, 217
Pogrebin, Abigail, 56, 217
Pogue, David, 32
Poindexter, Jay, 38
Pointer, Priscilla, 172
Poiret, Jean, 162
Poland, Albert, 34, 71, 75
Polcsa, Juliet, 54
Polenz, Robert, 90, 217
Poley, Robin, 52, 102, 217
Poliakoff, Stephen, 169
Policella, Catherine, 81
Polinsky, Joanna, 83
Polito, Jon, 148
Polk, Andrew, 122, 176
Pollack, Graham, 162
Pollard, Michael, 142
Polley, Nora, 174
Pollitt, Barbara, 60, 78

Pollock, Bruce, 162
Pollock, Graham, 162
Polner, Alex, 49, 137
Polner, Jerry, 104
Polt, Gilbert (Marc), 217
Polt, Gilbert Marc, 83
Pomahac, Bruce, 68, 170
Pomerance, Bernard, 55
Pompei, Donna M., 37
Pompei, Donna, 217
Ponazecki, Joe, 60, 217
Ponce de Leon, Humberto, 161
Ponce, LuAnne, 39
Pondel, John, 33
Ponzini, Anthony, 66, 217
Poole, Richard, 115
Pope, Deborah J., 52
Pope, Karen, 47
Pope, Peter, 54
Pope, Susan, 131
Poplyk, Gregory A., 160, 162
Popovich, Gregory, 13
Popp, Carolyn, 53
Popp, Ron, 65
Poppi, Gregory, 166
Poppleton, L. Glenn, III, 72
Porai-Koshitz, Alexei, 47
Porazzi, Arturo E., 42
Porowska, Dorota, 47
Porretta, Matthew, 115
Portell, Jeff, 122
Porter, Adina, 148
Porter, Cole, 45, 64, 68, 109, 130
Porter, Lisa, 100
Porter, Madeline, 172
Porter, Stephen, 17
Porter, Tom, 37
Porter, Van, 22
Portillo, Rose, 135
Poser, Linda, 162
Posey, Paige, 140
Posin, Kathryn, 148
Posner, Ken, 53
Posner, Kenneth, 83, 97, 125
Post, Randy, 8
Poster of the Cosmos, A, 46
Potestad, 47
Potter, Dennis, 63
Potter, Jane, 70
Potter, Joan, 168
Potter, Madeleine, 28
Potter, Maureen, 10
Potts, David, 23, 79, 98, 103, 136, 170
Poulson, Cynthia E., 161
Pouncy, Cheryl, 139
Powel, Marilyn, 142
Powell, Jill, 126
Powell, Marcus, 58, 83
Powell, Mary Ann, 176
Powell, Susan, 162
Powell, Tony, 94
Powell-Parker, Marianne, 54, 81
Powers, David, 21, 28, 51, 70, 111
Powers, Dennis, 123
Powers, Susan, 38
Powers, Winifred, 58
Powers, Wink, 54
Poyer, Lisa M., 26
Prabowo, Tonny, 47
Prager, Ben, 119
Pratt, Beth, 95
Pratt, Tina, 22
Pratt, Wendee, 154
Pratzon, Jim, 102
Pravda: A Fleet Street Comedy, 147
Precious Memories, 161
Preisser, Alfred, 48, 54
Prelude and Liebestod, 60
Premice, Josephine, 136
Prendergast, Marge, 183
Prendergast, Shirley, 14, 49, 103, 176
Prentice, Jeffrey, 174
Presby, David, 152
Prescott, Ken, 82
Press, Seymour Red, 95
Pressley, Brenda, 50, 88
Preston, Corliss, 53, 67
Preston, Lawrence, 49
Preston, Michael, 63
Preston, William, 19, 93, 141, 217
Price, Alan, 109
Price, Annabella, 172
Price, Brian, 61, 217
Price, Faye M., 81
Price, Karen S., 142
Price, Kenny, 49
Price, Leontyne, 33
Price, Lonny, 75, 217
Price, Michael P., 146
Price, Paige, 130
Price, Peggity, 66
Prichard, Michael, 130
Pride, Brian, 62
Priestley, J. B., 123, 154
Prignon, Joy, 82
Prince and the Pauper, 128
Prince, 91
Prince, Akili, 96

Prince, Daisy, 75
Prince, Faith, 25, 217
Prince, Harold, 33, 44, 133
Princess Theatre Ensemble, The, 63
Principia Scriptoriae, 119
Prinz, Rosemary, 71
Pritchard, Joe, 62
Pritchett, James, 131, 168
Pritchett, Jennifer, 150
Prizes, 74
Proctor, Mary E., 127
Promise, The, 55
Prosky, Andrew Land, 141
Prosky, Andrew, 62
Proval, David, 51, 217
Provenza, Paul, 75, 188, 190, 191, 217
Provenza, Rosario, 166
Provenza, Sal, 65, 217
Prowse, Juliet, 193
Prud'homme, June, 153
Pruet, Kris, 133
Pruitt, Richard, 129, 162
Pruitt, Robb, 75
Prymus, Ken, 12
Pryor, Brendan, 137
Pryor, Deborah, 126
Pryor, Michael, 97
Puccini, Giacomo, 41
Puchalski, John, 139
Pudenz, Steve, 27, 140
Puente, Gilberto, 8
Puffer, Jan, 182
Pugh, Richard Warren, 44, 217
Puig, Manuel, 164, 184
Pulice, Tim, 134
Pulliam, Darcy, 131
Pullman, Bill, 156
Puma, Marie, 62
Pump Boys and Dinettes, 140, 181
Purcell, Julie, 8
Purcell, Teresa, 88
Purdham, David, 184
Purdie, Bernard, 54
Purdy, Claude, 92, 123, 165
Purdy, Marshall B., 51, 60, 70
Puri, Kajika, 80
Puri, Rajika, 80, 96, 217
Pursley, David, 45, 217
Pursley, Jocelyn, 75
Putman, Scott, 138
Putnam, Lori, 183
Putnam, Robert, 128
Putri, Pipien, 47
Puzo, Madeline, 77, 134, 135
Pyecka, James, 90
Pyskacek, June, 46
Quackenbush, Karyn, 143
Quaglia, John, 34
Quarrel of Sparrows, A, 180
Quartana, Chris, 102
Quealy, Gerit, 144
Queens of France, 58
Quentin, Dolly, 161
Quezada, Alba, 44
Quigley, Chip, 50
Quilters, 159
Quincy, George Cochran, 90
Quinlan, Kathleen, 133
Quinlan, Patricia, 124
Quinlivan, Jim, 58
Quinn, Aidan, 217
Quinn, Lonnie, 59
Quinn, Margaret Adair, 184
Quinn, Nancy, 100
Quinn, Patrick, 26, 162
Quinones, Dee, 64
Quintard, Scott, 138
Quintero, Jose, 6
Quinton, Everett, 56
Quintuplets, 101
Rabaeus, Johan, 78
Raben, Larry, 64
Rabine, Terry, 131
Rachelle, Rainard, 62
Racine, Jean, 80, 99
Rackleff, Owen, 218
Racolin, Alexander E., 49, 53, 54, 58
Racolin, Alexander, 51, 59
Racolin, Dina, 49, 51, 53, 54, 58, 59
Radebe, Aubrey, 156
Radford, Wendy, 51
Radinson, Evelyn, 61
Rae, Allan, 174
Rae, Charlotte, 111, 113, 133
Raebeck, Lois, 99, 218
Rael, Elsa, 75
Raemaker, Norrice, 152
Raether, Richard, 103
Raftery, Matt, 152
Ragaway, Jill, 135
Ragno, Joseph, 107, 218
Ragonesi, Angelo, 35, 218
Ragusa, Michele, 176
Rahn, Rosalyn, 114
Raider-Wexler, Victor, 85, 97, 158, 218
Railton, Jeremy, 33
Rainbow, Harry, 50
Rainer, John, 108
Raines, Roger, 62

Raines, Ron, 108
Rainey, David, 68, 170, 218
Rainey, Ford, 134
Rainsberger, Kevin, 150
Rainwater, John, 51, 74
Raiter, Frank, 95, 218
Raitt, James, 125
Raitt, Kathleen, 20
Raleigh, Anne, 103
Raley, Wade, 94
Ralph, Alee, 73
Ralston, Monte, 162, 163
Ralston, Teri, 172
Ramach, Michael, 52
Ramage, Ed, 52
Ramage, Edmond, 48
Ramay, Steven, 81
Ramberg, Orjan, 78
Rame, Franca, 57
Rameau's Nephew, 80
Rameau, Patrick, 46
Ramin, Sid, 25
Ramirez, Robert R., 137
Ramishvili, Nina, 13
Ramont, Mark, 79
Ramos, Dion, 130
Ramos, Jesse, 63
Ramos, Jorge Luis, 93
Rampino, Lewis D., 120
Ramsay, Remak, 17, 62, 218
Ramsden, Dennis, 29
Ramsey, Alison, 103
Ramsey, Dale, 99
Ramsey, John, 142
Ramsey, Kevin, 22
Ramsey, Van Broughton, 165
Ramundo, Donna, 83
Ranbom, Jeffrey E., 153
Rand, Doug, 161
Randall, Ethan, 130
Randall, Martha, 111
Randall, Mia, 82
Randall, Tony, 41, 218
Randel, Melissa, 53, 218
Randolph, Beverley, 25
Randolph, Christopher, 170
Randolph, Dennis, 22
Randolph, James, II, 161
Randolph, Jim, 12, 18, 60
Ranelli, J., 103
Rangel, Irma "Cui Cui", 135
Rankin, Steve, 107
Ranson, Malcolm, 92
Raphael, Ellen, 54
Raphel, David, 84
Raposo, Joseph G., 230
Rasche, David, 218
Rashad, Phylicia, 39
Rashovich, Gordana, 107, 218
Rashovitch, Gordana, 60
Rasmuson, Judy, 144, 154, 176, 183
Rasmussen, Bryan, 172
Rater, Joan, 161
Rathgeb, Laura, 99, 218
Rauch, Stacie, 6
Rauch, William, 176
Raup, Kaarin, 58
Ravich, Paul, 57, 63
Ravitz, Jeff, 218
Rawlings, Ross Scott, 112
Rawlins, Theodore, 125
Rawls, Eugenia, 165
Ray, Constance, 60, 158
Ray, James, 230
Ray, Robert, 122
Ray, Robin, 82, 143
Ray, Stacy, 71, 218
Ray, Tim, 11, 14, 16, 24, 26, 39, 52, 54, 62, 65, 66, 72, 103
Ray-Collins, Tracy, 138
Rayfield, Gordon, 85
Raymond, Bill, 144, 217
Raymond, Deborah, 135
Raymond, Devon, 172
Raymond, Guy, 138
Raymond, John, 49, 58
Rayner, Benjamin, 148
Razor, R. Vincent, 105
Re, Tommy, 37
ReBok, Jacqueline, 182
Rea, Jennifer, 130
Reaching Out, 53
Ready for the River, 105
Real Dreams, 136
Reamer, Terry, 137, 166
Reams, Lee Roy, 33, 162, 163
Reardon, Peter, 83, 162
Reaux, Angelina, 94
Rebel Armies Deep into Chad, 154
Rebhorn, James, 19, 46, 218
Rebic, Donald, 176
Rebich, Cissy, 40
Rebilas, Richard, 129
Rebilas, Shaune, 129
Recht, Ray, 66, 85
Rechter, Yoni, 53, 134
Rechzeit, Jack, 232
Reckless, 79
Red Sheets, 86
Redd, Randy, 161
Reddin, Keith, 46, 77, 107
Reddy, Brian, 142, 164, 184
Redgrave, Lynn, 133

Redick, Charlene, 120
Redinger, Paula, 218
Redlin, Richard, 50
Redmond, Barbara, 143
Redmond, Lawrence, 141
Redmond, Marge, 132
Redpath, Ralph, 140
Redwood, John Henry, 81, 165, 218
Reece, Ben, 122
Reed, Gavin, 29, 218
Reed, Gay, 68, 102
Reed, Janet, 54, 59
Reed, Joe, 182
Reed, John Robert, 106
Reed, Maggi-Meg, 137
Reed, Pamela, 62
Reed, Penelope, 158
Reed, Tailer, 47
Reeger, John, 144
Reehling, Joyce, 79, 218
Rees, Douglas, 165
Rees, Roger, 122, 133
Reese, Arthur M., 64
Reese, Arthur, 91
Reeve, Christopher, 62, 95, 218
Reeves, Philip, 134
Regan, Marybeth, 67
Regan, Mick, 138
Reichert, Daniel, 123
Reick, Diane, 137
Reid, Dennis, 184
Reid, Jeffery, 138
Reid, Kathy, 112
Reilly, Albertina, 162
Reilly, Don, 93
Reilly, Robert, 37
Reiman, Clark C., 65
Reinerl, William, 60
Reinglas, Fred, 79
Reinhardt, Ray, 123
Reinhardt-Meyer, Larry, 56
Reinheimer, Cathy, 58
Reisman, Jane, 22, 55
Reiss, Vicki, 103
Reissa, Eleanor, 95, 218
Reissa, Eleanore, 91
Reisz, Toby, 134
Reitberger, Diana, 174
Reivant, Toby, 83
Relatively Speaking, 128
Remains to Be Seen, 140
Remington, Ralph, 64
Remme, John, 82, 162, 218
Remsberg, Calvin, 108, 133
Renderer, Scott, 54, 218
Rendezvous with Romance, 64
Rendra, W. S., 47
René, Norman, 79, 95
Renfield, Elinor, 58
Renfroe, Rebecca, 55, 218
Renha, Rita, 74
Renick, Kyle, 107
Rennagel, Marilyn, 29, 162
Reno, 61
Reno: In Rage and Rehab, 61
Rensenhouse, John, 170, 171
Repicci, Bill, 54
Repole, Charles, 146
Requiem for a Heavyweight, 57
Resistance, 46
Resnick, Donna, 130
Resnik, Hollis, 115
Reuel, Tom, 148
Revelation of John, The, 61
Revenger's Tragedy, The, 56
Revolution of Cleveland, 136
Reyeros, Rafael, 93
Reyes, Alexis, 46
Reynolds, Charles, 39
Reynolds, Gary, 130
Reynolds, James E., 46, 184
Reynolds, James, 185
Reynolds, Simon, 122
Rhalse, Foster, 59
Rhapsody Tachiste, 52
Rheam, Kimberly, 129
Rhinoceros, 139
Rhoden, Lisa, 141
Rhodes, Tran William, 64
Rhodes, Tran Wm., 59
Rhyne, Sylvia, 218
Rhys, Will, 165
Rhys, William, 170
Rial, Jose Antonio, 93
Rially, Ron, 120
Ricard, Russell, 109
Ricci, Vito, 63
Ricciardi, Gene, 94
Rice, Barbara Lynn, 94, 107
Rice, Barbara, 103
Rice, James Goodwin, 131
Rice, John Patrick, 132
Rice, Keith, 114, 130
Rice, Kelly, 92
Rice, Michael, 70
Rice, Thomas, 59, 68
Rich, Christopher, 178
Rich, Irene, 231, 232
Rich, Tanya, 174
Richard Frankel Productions, 62
Richard II, 141

Richard III, 174, 175
Richard, Ellen, 103
Richards, Arleigh, 128
Richards, Carol, 103
Richards, Cordelia, 58, 61
Richards, Gerald, 164, 181
Richards, Jeffrey, 23, 29, 42
Richards, Jess, 108, 218, 221
Richards, Lloyd, 7, 144, 184
Richards, Scott Davenport, 184
Richards, Tammy, 160
Richardson, Daryl, 45
Richardson, Kevin, 179
Richardson, LaTanya, 52, 89, 91, 218, 221
Richardson, Lee, 17, 218
Richardson, Marie, 78
Richardson, Sally, 119, 161
Richert, Wanda, 37, 218
Richert, William, 158
Richie, Faye, 126
Richler, Emma, 174
Richman, Peter Mark, 130
Richter, Charles, 46
Rickel, Brad, 166
Rickenbacher, Anne, 113, 133
Rickert, Skip, 16
Rickman, Allen L., 54
Rico, Sylvia, 133
Riddell, Richard, 77, 124
Riddle, Emily, 64
Riddle, George, 109
Riddle, Kate, 59, 80
Riddle, R. Richard, 232
Riddle, Richard, 231
Ridley, Arthur, 170
Riedl, Lisa, 78
Riegel, Eden, 115
Riegel, Megan, 166
Riegel, Sam Brent, 114, 115
Riegert, Peter, 218
Riehle, Richard, 48, 80, 107, 184, 218
Rieser, Terry, 170
Riffon, Marc, 162
Rigdon, Kevin, 19, 35, 86, 161
Rigg, Jonathan, 85
Righi, Camilla, 48
Riley, Colleen, 160
Riley, Eric, 12, 218, 221
Riley, Jay Flash, 232
Rimers of Eldritch, The, 104
Rinaldi, Philip, 24, 30, 40, 61, 65, 100
Rinehart, Elaine, 52, 57, 81, 218, 221
Rinehart, Susanna, 168
Ring Round the Moon, 126
Ringstad, Mary, 158, 161
Rinklin, Ruth E., 22
Rintala, Troy, 74
Rintoul, Brian, 174
Riordan, James, 136
Rios, Mary Lou, 72
Rios, Michelle, 112
Risberg, Del W., 132
Riskin, Susan, 143
Risser, Patricia M., 182
Risso, Richard, 158
Ritchie, Michael F., 19
Ritchie, Michael F., 9
Ritschel, Jack, 130
Ritual of Solomon's Children, The, 47
Rivamonte, Lia, 147
Rivas, Fernando, 46
Rivera, James, 25
Rivera, Jose, 46, 55, 58
Rivera, Maritza, 135
Rivera, Sonia, 45
Rivers, Steve, 129
Rivin, Lucille, 75, 218, 221
Rivkin, Gigi, 64, 98
Rivlin, Leora, 53, 134
Rizzo, Jeff, 130
Road to Mecca, The, 121, 159, 168, 172, 186
Road, 86
Roark, Jonathan, 152
Robards, Jason, 6, 7, 33, 62
Robb, R. D., 218
Robber Bridegroom, The, 140
Robbins, Dana, 33
Robbins, Jana, 125, 218
Robbins, Jerome, 25
Robbins, Kerri Lea, 53, 62
Robbins, Rex, 113, 133, 151
Robbins, Tom, 25, 114
Robere, R., 63
Roberson, David, 179
Roberson, Ken, 22
Roberson, Rudy, 54
Roberson, Will, 50
Robert V. Straus Productions, 66
Robert, Patricia, 13
Robert, Susan, 131
Roberts, Angela, 102
Roberts, Barbara, 161
Roberts, Christopher, 102
Roberts, Douglas, 154
Roberts, Jacquelyn Mari, 184
Roberts, Jamey, 138
Roberts, Jimmy, 105
Roberts, Judith, 72, 93

Scovill, Jay, 122
Scranton, Timothy, 160
Scully, Patrick J., 81
Scurfield, Matthew, 92
Seacat, James, 120
Seader, Richard, 32
Seago, Howie, 78
Seagull, The, 156
Seales, Franklyn, 134
Seaman, Jane, 45, 220
Seamon, Edward, 103, 220
Searcy, Nick, 54, 76, 220
Seaton, Joanna, 105, 220
Sebastian, Kim, 136
Second Hand Dance Company, 93
Secor, Jonathan D., 57
Secor, Jonathan Dimock, 66
Secret Thighs of New England Women, 63
Secunda, Susan, 170
Sedgwick, Dan, 142
Sedgwick, Kyra, 5, 7, 60, 189, 220
Sedlachek, Buffy, 147
Seeing Someone, 57
Seery, Florie, 23, 30
Seetoo, Keelee, 31, 74, 85, 220
Segal, David F., 154
Segal, Gury, 53, 134
Segal, Kathrin King, 57, 220
Segal, Martin E., 8
Segall, Harry, 142
Segan, Eleanor, 51, 62
Seger, Richard, 174
Segovia, Claudio, 22
Seidel, Katharina, 78
Seiler, Jane, 170
Seitz, John, 106
Seldes, Marian, 33
Seleznyova, Irina, 47
Self-Torture and Strenuous Exercise, 64
Selfridge, Robin, 184
Sellers, Barbara E., 138
Sellers, Lisa, 49
Selman, Matty, 90
Selzer, Milton, 156, 157
Semple, Goldie, 174
Sempliner, Woody, 68, 102
Sengoku, Noriko, 78
Seniority, 100
Sennett, David, 47
Serabian, Lorraine, 126
Serafin, Alexander, 78
Serbagi, Roger, 58, 220
Serban, Andrei, 124
Seriopoulos, Alkiviades, 82
Serious Company: An Evening of One-Act Plays, 64
Serlin-Cobb, Fran, 161
Serpent Woman, The, 124
Serra, Raymond, 20, 220
Serrano, Charlie, 170
Serrecchia, Michael, 220
Servanton, Anne, 105
Servitto, Matt, 93, 94
Sesma, Thom, 31, 85, 104, 220
Settler, Steve, 52
Sevec, Christine, 50
7½ Cents, 27
Seven Menus, 57
1776, 162, 163
Sevier, Jack, 120
Sevy, Bruce K., 138
Sewell, Laura, 50
Sex Lives of Superheroes, 57
Sexton, Mark, 150
Sexton, Nell Page, 150
Seykell, Rohn, 115
Seymour, Anne, 231, 232
Sha, Tamae, 78
Shabba-Doo, 134
Shaddock, Pamela Jean, 57
Shafer, Pamela, 83, 220, 221
Shaffer, Peter, 122
Shaffer, Stephen, 135
Shahnini, The, 13
Shahpazian-DeBoy, Barbara, 182
Shaker, Christine, 148
Shakespeare, William, 46, 48, 49, 62, 68, 78, 86, 92, 93, 94, 95, 96, 99, 102, 120, 121, 128, 132, 138, 141, 144, 148, 151, 160, 161, 168, 183
Shalhoub, Tony, 30, 80, 95, 184, 220, 221
Shallat, Lee, 119, 172
Shamash, Beba, 108
Shammai, Giora, 53
Shammi, Giora, 134
Shampain, Robert, 56, 82
Shamshak, Sam, 135
Shanahan, Donna, 143
Shancaydhe, Kevin, 138
Shangraw, Howard, 172
Shank, M. Christine, 83
Shankman, Adam M., 126
Shanks, Ann, 68
Shanks, Bob, 68
Shanks, Priscilla, 154

Shanley, John Patrick, 88, 136, 143
Shannon, Mark, 65, 220
Shapiro, Dan, 146
Shapiro, Debbie, 25, 220, 221
Shapiro, Leonardo, 63
Shapiro, Mel, 126
Shapiro, Ann, 56, 154
Shapiro, Ted, 20
Sharaf, Ali, 148, 184
Sharaff, Irene, 25
Sharar, Carol, 72, 143
Sharkskin Productions, 68
Sharma, Barbara, 66, 220
Sharon and Billy, 52
Sharp, Kim T., 57
Sharp, Larry, 91
Sharpe, Ascanio, 86
Shatraw, David T., 127
Shaud, Grant, 46
Shaughnessy, Susan, 176
Shaw, Bernard, 99, 153
Shaw, Bob, 94, 104
Shaw, Christopher, 128
Shaw, Deborah, 46, 61, 68, 76, 106, 107, 166, 169
Shaw, George Bernard, 17, 61, 103, 123, 128, 168, 170, 172, 178
Shaw, Joseph, 174
Shaw, Kris, 65
Shaw, Wenna, 174
Shawn, Peter, 158
Shay, Michelle, 91
Shayne, Tracy, 40
She Loves Me, 65
She Stoops to Conquer, 99, 161
Shea, Joey, 19
Shea, John, 56, 220
Shea, Patrick, 160
Shearer, Andy, 48
Shearer, Doug, 102
Sheehan, Diana, 160
Sheehan, John J. D., 65
Sheehan, Judy, 73
Sheehan, Maurice, 84
Sheehy, Julia, 56
Sheets, J. C., 40
Sheffield, Ann, 46, 55
Shekski, Ken, 162
Sheldon, Anne, 159
Shell, Claudia, 38, 220
Shelle, Michael, 75
Shellen Lubin in Mother/Child, 75
Shellenberger, James, 49
Shelley, Carole, 88, 220
Shelly, Mary, 147
Shelp, Woody, 57
Shelton, Sloane, 220, 221
Shen, Freda Foh, 123
Shenandoah, 162, 163
Shenker, William, 102
Shepard, Katherine, 61, 220
Shepard, Kiki, 92
Shepard, Sam, 43, 132
Sheppard, Julie, 65
Shepski, Ken, 45
Sher, Bartlett, 97
Sheridan, Jamey, 6, 7
Sheridan, Jeff, 57
Sheridan, Joseph, 113, 133
Sheridan, Kim B., 132
Sherman, Alison, 55, 56
Sherman, Barry, 48, 104, 220
Sherman, Dana, 36, 59
Sherman, Elizabeth, 93
Sherman, Geoffrey, 81
Sherman, Hiram, 231, 232
Sherman, Howard S., 148
Sherman, Jonathan Marc, 100
Sherman, Keith, 33, 108
Sherman, Kim D., 132
Sherman, Lauren, 51
Sherman, Loren, 54, 94, 96
Sherman, Lori, 107
Sherman, Richard, 178
Sherman, Terrence, 182
Sherman, Todd, 161
Sherr, Erik, 137
Sherril, Brad, 122
Sherrill, Brad, 122
Sherwood, Tony, 133
Shery, Beth G., 57
Shestakova, Tatyana, 47
Shevelove, Burt, 25, 123, 144, 158
Shew, Tim, 40
Shew, Timothy, 220, 221
Shields, Clayton, 174
Shifini, George, 73
Shiles, Bland, 121
Shimabuku, Norris M., 98
Shimberg, Hinks, 34
Shimizu, Keenan, 98
Shimizu, Kenny, 158
Shimizu, Sachi, 37
Shimono, Sab, 220, 221
Shimrock, John, 83
Shiner, Matthew, 51, 59, 220, 221
Shinn, Pete, 122
Shiomi, R. A., 98
Shionishi, Jun, 78
Shipley, Sandra, 77, 124, 220

Shipp, John Wesley, 72
Shire, David, 89
Shirky, Clay, 60, 98
Shirlen, Joshua, 126
Shirley Valentine, 24
Shlaes, Geoffrey C., 82
Shneider, Joshua, 62
Shocket, Steve, 40
Shoemaker, Craig, 16
Shoemaker, Jeff, 57, 68, 102
Shofner, Susan, 162
Shooting Stars, 53
Short, Sylvia, 184
Show Boat, 129, 162, 163
Show, Grant, 136
Showing Off, 67
Showpeople Ltd., 50
Shriber, Mary Lou, 170
Shriner, Steven W., 182
Shropshire, Anne, 76, 143, 220, 221
Shrout, Rick A., 54
Shue, Larry, 120, 144
Shuker, Allison, 54
Shulkin, Shellie, 119
Shulman, Constance (a.k.a. Connie), 220
Shulman, Constance, 51, 57, 71
Shulman, Heather, 39, 220
Shultz, Philip, 54
Shuman, John, 184
Shuman, Mort, 128
Shupeck, Ian, 52
Shurr, Carl, 182
Shuttleworth, Bill, 39, 72
Shyre, Paul, 24
Siano, Frank, 146
Sias, Jeremy, 122
Sibanda, Seth, 61
Sibley, Craig, 134
Sicangco, Eduardo, 64, 108, 146
Siccardi, Arthur, 26
Sicular, Robert, 172
Side by Side by Sondheim, 123, 127
Sideways Glance, 66
Sidney, P. Jay, 96, 220
Sidney, Sylvia, 33
Siebert, Charles, 147
Siegel, Betty, 126
Siegel, Herb, 161
Siegel, June, 105
Siegfreid, Troy, 160
Siegler, Ben, 85, 107, 154, 220
Sifuentes, Kevin, 178
Sikes, Cynthia, 39, 220
Sikharulidze, Gulnara, 13
Silberman, Betty, 95
Silberman, Joel, 14
Silence, Mark, 166
Silfer, Ana, 154
Silliman, Maureen, 91
Sills, Douglas, 113, 133
Sills, Pawnee, 52, 92, 220
Silva, David, 178
Silva, Geno, 55
Silva, Marie-Louise, 42
Silva, Vilma, 178
Silver, Joe, 20, 220, 232
Silver, Joshua, 50
Silver, Richard, 53, 95
Silver, Robert, 75
Silverman, Carol, 88
Silverman, Judd, 53
Silverman, Stan, 136
Silzle, Barbara J., 166
Simek, Vasek C., 65
Simes, Douglas, 128, 169
Simmons, Bill, 65, 101
Simmons, Bonnie, 38
Simmons, J. K., 131, 151
Simmons, Ken, 46, 52, 104
Simmons, Nancy, 41
Simms, George C., 133
Simms, Lise, 122
Simo, Ana Maria, 46
Simon & Kumin, 104, 110
Simon Says . . ., 68
Simon Shaheen Near East Ensemble, 78
Simon, Eddie, 64
Simon, Mark, 50
Simon, Meg, 6, 16, 20, 41
Simon, Neil, 18, 85, 110, 131, 150, 162, 164
Simons, David, 60, 67
Simons, Hal, 73
Simons, Leslie, 154
Simonton, D. Raymond, 141
Simpson, Bland, 121
Simpson, C. J., 45, 86
Simpson, Garland J., 123
Simpson, James, 148
Sims, J. Douglass, 140
Sims, Maurice R., 137
Sinclair, Chries, 96
Sinclair, Madge, 157
Sinclair, Thomas Lee, 55
Sing for Your Supper, 108
Singelis, James, 153
Singer, Connie, 79
Singer, James R., 125
Singer, Marla, 220

Singer, Pamela, 89, 134
Singer, Stephen, 166, 167
Singing Joy, 46
Singlar, John, 70
Singleton, Janyse M., 60
Singleton, Kathleen, 170
Siretta, Dan, 146
Sirlin, Jerome, 56
Sirois, Richard L., 48
Sisto, Rocco, 94, 95, 220, 221
Sitler, David, 53, 153
Sitting Pretty in Concert, 63
Siu Junn Wong, Betty Anne, 123
Six Characters in Search of an Author, 77, 126
Sizemore, Jim, 132
Sjoberg, Katarina, 78
Sjoerdsma, Ann G., 132
Skala, Lilia, 151
Skarmeta, Antonio, 161
Skelton, Thomas R., 64, 93
Skinker, Sherry, 170, 182
Skinner, Randy, 130
Sklar, Roberta, 76
Skloff, Michael, 152
Sklute, Allison, 133
Skow, Marilyn R., 161
Skriloff, Nina, 20
Skrzesz, Ken, 146
Skybell, Steven, 7, 15
Slaby, Elizabeth, 46
Slade, Bernard, 128
Slaff, Jonathan, 67, 220
Slaiman, Marjorie, 126, 151
Slasher, 49
Slate, Rex, 94
Slater, Sindy, 47
Slattery, John, 89
Slaughter in the Lake, 46
Slaughter, Lance, 134, 135
Sleeping Dogs, 62
Slezak, Victor, 46, 57, 60, 220
Slisky, C. E., 54
Sloan, Gary, 68, 220
Sloan, Larry, 87, 144
Sloan, Suzanne, 140
Sloman, John, 96, 220
Slowmotion, 47
Slutsker, Peter, 122, 136
Slyde, Jimmy, 22
Small, Larry, 38, 220
Small, Liz, 86, 148
Small, Peg, 128
Smarr, Sara, 137
Sminkey, Tom, 17
Smith, Alice Elliott, 123
Smith, Anna Deavere, 123
Smith, Archie, 138
Smith, Brandon, 121
Smith, Brendan, 82
Smith, C. E., 50
Smith, Calvin, 122
Smith, Carrie, 22, 220
Smith, Christian, 27
Smith, Derek, 124
Smith, Doug, 55
Smith, Ebbe Roe, 172
Smith, Ed, 91
Smith, Edward G., 176
Smith, Elizabeth, 68
Smith, Ellen Jane, 144
Smith, Felton, 70
Smith, Frances, 15
Smith, Gerard L. A., 139
Smith, Gerard, 139
Smith, Holly, 161
Smith, J. T., 143
Smith, Jack, 102
Smith, James Gregory, 79
Smith, Janet, 65, 103, 104, 107
Smith, Jeanne, 115
Smith, Jennifer, 88, 220, 221
Smith, Jimmie Lee, 138
Smith, Kelly, 139
Smith, Kendall, 90
Smith, L. R., 132
Smith, Larry, 31
Smith, Laurel, 52
Smith, Leif, 62
Smith, Leslie C., 138
Smith, Liz, 33
Smith, Lois, 46, 86, 220
Smith, Mary Ann, 66
Smith, Mary Elizabeth, 137
Smith, MaryAnn D., 49
Smith, Michael C., 55, 61, 65, 85
Smith, Michael O., 140
Smith, Nairobi, 60
Smith, Oliver, 25
Smith, Pat Hall, 60
Smith, Patrick, 73
Smith, Priscilla, 77
Smith, Rex, 109
Smith, Robert Vincent, 63, 69
Smith, Robert, 174
Smith, Robin, 53
Smith, Rodney J., 138
Smith, Roger Guenveur, 60, 94
Smith, Roger Preston, 116, 117
Smith, Rohan, 60
Smith, Rosemary, 178

Smith, Sally, 108
Smith, Sean, 133
Smith, Sheila, 162
Smith, Steven, 130
Smith, Sydney, 31
Smith, T. Ryder, 80
Smith, Timothy, 130
Smith, Ursula, 116
Smith, Valerie E., 22
Smith, Vicki, 138
Smith-Cameron, J., 26, 220, 221
Smitrovich, Bill, 220
Smitty's News, 105
Smoke on the Mountain, 158
Smolsky, Charles A., II, 66
Smuin, Michael, 8, 45, 109, 118, 123
Sneed, Glenn, 146
Snider, Lin, 83
Snizek, David, 153
Snow, Dan, 67
Snow, Helena, 46
Snowdon, Ted, 52
Snyder, Drew, 103, 220
Snyder, Roy, 8
Sobel, Edna, 53, 134
Sobel, Shepard, 99
Sobel, Stanley, 107, 134
Soboil, Maggie, 63
Sobol, Edna, 35
Sobol, Joshua, 35, 53, 134
Soddu, Antonio, 16, 67, 104
Soeder, Fran, 122
Soez, Isabel, 60
Soffer, Geoff, 114
Sokol, Marilyn, 32, 55
Sokolsky, Yosi, 53, 85
Solis, Jeffrey, 74
Solmssen, Kate, 133
Solo, William, 40, 114, 220, 221
Solomon, Madelon Rosen, 92
Solomon, Nicholas, 57
Solotaire, Ben, 58
Soloway, Leonard, 25, 29
Solters/Roskin/Friedman, 33
Some Sweet Day, 154
Somebody Else, 62
Somer, Josef, 154, 184
Somers, Mark, 169
Somerville, Barbara, 184
Somerville, Phyllis, 107
Something About Baseball, 46
Somlyo, Lauren, 11
Somlyo, Roy A., 11
Somma, Maria, 23, 29, 32, 75, 107
Sommer, Elke, 72
Sommer, Josef, 62
Sommers, Allison, 49, 100
Sommerville, Henry, 150
Soncrant, Michael, 65
Sonderskov, Robert, 63
Sondheim, Stephen, 25, 39, 108, 113, 119, 123, 133, 138, 144, 158, 170, 172
Songs from Distant Lands, 154
Songs of Paradise, 95
Sonnichsen, Ingrid, 160
Sontag, Susan, 135
Soper, Tony, 119
Sophisticated Ladies, 118
Sophocles, 61
Sorbello, Donna, 151
Sorce, Tom, 86
Sordelet, Rick, 79
Sorel, Dian, 104
Sorel, Nancy, 46
Sorel, Ted, 220, 221
Sorenson, Cheri, 119
Sorkin, Aaron, 49
Sorvino, Paul, 125
Sosin, Donald, 105
Sosnow, Pat, 21, 93, 96
Soul of a Jew, 53, 134
Sound of Music, The, 129
Soupstone Project, The, 49
South Pacific, 129
Sowers, Scott, 56, 132
Sozen, Joyce, 63, 99
Spacey, Kevin, 154
Spackman, Tom, 159
Spahr, Scott, 162
Spaisman, Zypora, 53, 222
Spalla, John, 42
Sparer, Paul, 62
Sparks, Rick, 114
Sparrman, Goran, 65
Speakman, Gary, 33
Spear, Cary Anne, 126
Spear, Susie, 140
Special Occasions, 128
Spector, Daniel Nathan, 148, 154
Speed of Darkness, The, 144, 145
Speer, Alexander, 120
Spelvin, George, 112
Spencer, Elizabeth, 168
Spencer, Jeff, 134
Spencer, John, 79, 121
Spencer, Paul, 64
Spencer, Robert, 176, 182
Spencer, Sally, 172, 173

Roberts, Louise, 6, 7, 154
Roberts, Mason, 138
Roberts, Meghan, 158
Roberts, Michael, 65
Roberts, Ralph, 218
Roberts, Skip, 119
Roberts, Tom, 55
Roberts-Frost, Gwen, 91
Robertson, Deborah Skally, 158
Robertson, Dennis, 172
Robertson, Joel, 40
Robertson, Ken Allen, 138
Robertson, Lanie, 48, 54, 121
Robertson, Scott, 27, 218
Robertson, Toby, 141
Robeson, Alec, 122
Robin, Leo, 146
Robins, Laila, 95, 104, 218
Robins, Robert P., 150
Robinson, Bernita, 57, 82
Robinson, Cindy, 39
Robinson, Jo-Anne, 38
Robinson, Judith, 122
Robinson, M. Lynda, 160
Robinson, Margarette, 92
Robinson, Martin P., 142, 164
Robinson, Megan, 221
Robinson, Meghan, 107, 218
Robinson, Roger, 54, 218
Robinson, Steve, 51
Robinson-Clark, Danny, 144
Roblin, Jennifer, 151
Robson, Christopher, 174
Rocco, Jean, 66
Rocha-Castillo, Winston Jose, 119
Rocky & Diego, 166, 167
Rodabaugh, Scott, 61, 95
Rodaz, John, 161
Rodeman, Cass, 94, 95
Roderick, Connie, 17, 218, 221
Roderick, Ray, 38
Rodgers, Chev, 31, 85
Rodgers, Mary, 100
Rodgers, Richard, 25, 63, 108, 129, 138
Rodgers, Terrence Charles, 180
Rodowicz, Jadwiga, 47
Rodowicz, Tomasz, 47
Rodriguez, Al, 80, 93, 218
Rodriguez, Damaris, 161
Rodriguez, Lucy, 135
Rodriguez, Steven, 170
Roe, Don, 136
Roeder, Chas E., 59
Roeder, Peggy, 144
Rogan, Peter, 84
Rogers, Adam, 93
Rogers, Anne, 218
Rogers, Dave Olin, 22
Rogers, Diana, 140
Rogers, Enid, 84
Rogers, Ken Leigh, 122
Rogers, Laura, 68
Rogers, Michael, 184
Rogers, Richard, 161
Rogers, Robin, 67
Rogers, Shelly, 154
Rogers-Adler, Candace, 133
Rogerson, Gus, 164
Roggensack, David, 14, 28, 50, 51, 85, 100
Rogosin, Roy, 130
Rogow, David, 53
Rogozzi, Claudio, 60
Rohland, Leslie L., 127
Roi, Tony, 65
Rojo, Jerry, 96
Roland, Tom, 144
Rolf, Frederick, 72, 219, 221
Rolfe, Mickey, 76
Rolfe, Wendy A., 184
Rolle, Esther, 103, 219
Rollins, Janet, 128
Rollnick, William D., 31
Roman, Carmen, 152
Romance in Hard Times, 96
Romano, David, 44
Rombschick, Rolf, 161
Rome, Ruth, 64
Romeo and Juliet, 102, 144
Romero, Constanza, 68, 144
Romero, Marilyn, 161
Romero, Peter, 82
Romoff, Colin, 60
Romoff, Douglas, 60
Romoff, Woody, 85
Ron Devito Dancers, 33
Rondo, George, 72
Ronstadt, Linda, 8
Room 102, 58
Room 302, 58
Rooney, Tom, 77
Roop, Reno, 169
Roos, Joanna, 232
Root, Melina, 184
Root, Stephen, 111
Roque, Tony Bennett, 178
Rosa, Julann, 48
Rosario, Carmen, 101
Rosario, Willie, 64
Rosato, Mary Lou, 124, 184
Rosborough, Brett C., 162
Rose, Christine, 135
Rose, David, 83
Rose, L. Arthur, 42
Rose, Lynn, 130
Rose, Philip, 11, 162
Rose, Richard, 72
Rose, Robin Pearson, 172
Rose, Robyn, 48
Roseman, Ralph, 24, 28, 42, 51, 116, 117
Rosen, Brad, 108
Rosen, Madelon, 53, 60, 62, 92, 101, 146
Rosen, Nicole, 108
Rosenbaum, David, 35, 219, 221
Rosenbaum, Ira, 93
Rosenbaum, Joshua, 45
Rosenberg, D. C., 85, 101
Rosenberg, Stuart Joel, 144
Rosenblat, Barbara, 176
Rosenblatt, Jana, 74
Rosenblatt, Marcell, 19, 219, 221
Rosenblum, M. Edgar, 154
Rosencrantz and Guildenstern Are Dead, 137, 161
Rosenfels, Joan, 53
Rosenfield, Bill, 33
Rosentel, Robert W., 63
Rosin, James, 54, 219
Roslevich, John, Jr., 170
Rosmersholm, 56
Ross, Carolyn, 138, 170
Ross, Clarinda, 121
Ross, Jamie, 104, 219
Ross, Jerry, 27
Ross, Joseph G., 182
Ross, Justin, 50
Ross, Michael, 148
Ross, Natalie, 60, 219, 221
Ross, Pamela C., 56
Ross, Robyn, 176
Ross, Sandra L., 91
Ross, Sharlene, 122
Ross, Stuart, 34, 54, 125
Rossensack, David, 70
Rosser, Kip, 158
Rossetter, Kathy, 107, 219
Rossilli, Paul, 136
Rost, Leo, 60
Rostand, Edmond, 69
Rosten, Bevya, 102
Rosten, Leo, 75
Roston, Karen, 166
Roth, Ann, 23, 86, 136
Roth, Michael, 148
Roth, Stephanie, 184
Roth, Susan Y., 60
Roth, Wolfgang, 103, 231, 232
Rothenberg, David, 51, 67
Rothman, Carole, 16, 104
Rothman, Jane, 165
Rothman, John, 55, 219
Rothman, Kay, 68, 102
Rothman, Stephen, 142, 143
Rothstein, Jon, 35, 219
Rothstein, Norman E., 22
Rotkowitz, Norm, 63
Roudebush, William, 60, 143
Round and Round the Garden, 131
Roussimoff, Ari, 75
Routh, Marc, 62, 70
Routman, Steve, 93, 219
Routolo, Robert, 133, 134
Routt, Jean, 154
Rover, The, 144
Roveta, Sandy, 108, 219, 221
Rowan, Richard, 152
Rowe, Dee Etta, 129
Rowe, Hansford, 100
Rowe, Robert L., 56
Rowe, Sandy, 82
Rowe, Stephen, 16, 148, 149
Rowe, Tonia, 126
Roy, Kristy, 144
Roy, William, 108
Rubens, Herbert, 150
Rubin, Arthur, 13, 15, 16, 20, 33
Rubin, Steven, 51
Rubino, Gina, 55
Rubinsky, Mark, 44
Rubinstein, David, 133
Rubinstein, John, 33, 41, 62, 106, 154, 219
Rubsam, Scott, 57
Ruck, Patricia, 38, 219, 221
Rudin, Stuart, 104
Rudko, Michael, 143
Rudnick, Marilyn, 184
Rudnicki, Stefan, 102
Rudolph, Stephanie, 96
Rudy, Bradley C., 174
Rudy, Martin, 154
Rudy, Sam, 14, 20, 31, 34, 50, 57, 63, 68, 73, 100
Ruebsamen, Gary Dean, 94, 104
Ruehl, Mercedes, 46, 59, 148
Ruehlmann, Lynn, 183
Ruffelle, Frances, 40, 219
Rug of Identity, The, 63
Ruiz, Anthony, 107
Ruiz, Richard, 25
Rule, Charles, 44, 219
Rumors, 18
Rumpf, Robin, 136
Run for Your Wife!, 29
Runolfsson, Anne Marie, 40
Ruoti, Helena, 165
Rupert, Florence, 59
Rupnick, Kevin, 165
Rupnik, Kevin, 131, 162
Rupp, Tom, 132
Ruscio, Al, 172
Ruscio, Elizabeth, 172
Rush, David, 49
Rush, Michael, 49
Rush, Sam, 160
Ruskin, Jeanne, 154
Russ, Amber, 123
Russell, Arland, 82
Russell, Catherine, 8, 58, 174
Russell, Cathy, 219
Russell, George, 25
Russell, Monte, 58, 165
Russell, Peter H., 13
Russell, Robert, 184
Russell, Stephen, 174, 175
Russell, Tony, 144
Russell, Willy, 24
Russell-Tutty, Nancy, 58
Russo, Larry, 144
Russo, Michael, 176
Russo, Ronald G., 74
Rust, Janet, 68
Rust, Steve, 68
Rust, Tony, 59, 68, 102
Rutenberg, Mike, 67
Ruter, Christopher, 78
Ruttman, Jim T., 130, 138
Ruyle, Bill, 59
Ruzika, Donna, 172
Ruzika, Tom, 172
Ryall, William, 146, 219, 221
Ryan, Amy, 104, 219
Ryan, Gavin, 130
Ryan, Jack, 49
Ryan, James, 46
Ryan, Jennie, 49, 64
Ryan, Ken, 158
Ryan, Mary, 121
Ryan, Matt, 168
Ryan, Michael Scott, 123
Ryan, Steven, 95, 219
Ryan, Vera, 101
Rybolt, Peter, 144
Ryder, Craig, 138
Ryder, Ric, 34, 219, 221
Ryland, Jack, 103, 141, 219
Rymer, Jennifer, 20
Rymer, Scott, 79
Rysuk, Mary, 53
Ryzuk, Regan, 53
S. J. Perelman in Person, 68
Sablow, Jane, 74
Sacharow, Lawrence, 81, 100
Saddler, Donald, 60, 174
Sader, Alan, 183
Sadusk, Maureen, 158
Saex, Robin, 57, 66
Saffran, Christina, 118
Sagara, Grace, 130
Sage, Jefferson, 136
Sager, Gene, 162
Sager, Jeri, 146
Sahba, Mark, 161
Saint Florence, 131
Saint Joan, 123, David, 49
Sakash, Evelyn, 49
Sakren, Jared, 138
Saks, Gene, 18, 110
Salamandyk, Tim, 21
Sale, James, 121
Salerno, Mary Jo, 76
Salinaro, Dom, 130
Salinger, Diane, 64, 106
Salkewicz, Keith, 140
Salkin, Allan, 158
Sallows, Tracy, 88, 147, 169
Sally, 91
Salsbury, Lynda L., 131
Saltz, Amy, 184
Saltzman, Avery, 27
Saltzman, Robert, 23
Salvatore, John, 116, 117
Salzman, Jacob, 54
Sambucci, Eddie, 49
Samelson, Peter, 46
Sametz, Laura, 15, 93, 94
Sammler, Bronislaw J., 184
Sams, Jeffrey, 170
Sams, Jeremy, 35
Samuel, Peter, 115
Samuels, Gayle, 118
Samuels, Peter, 40
Samuels, Steven, 56
Samuelsohn, Howard, 73
Samuelson, Howard, 54, 219
San Giacomo, Laura, 88
Sanborn, Kristina, 119
Sanchez, George Emilio, 60
Sanchez, Jaime, 55, 219
Sanchez, Luis Rafael, 101
Sand and Stone, 135
Sandall, Andrea, 130
Sande, Michael, 119
Sandefur, James D., 81, 165
Sandefur, Jim, 21
Sanders, Ann Marie, 176
Sanders, Charles, 121
Sanders, Fred, 57, 219
Sanders, Jay O., 94, 219
Sanders, Kerry, 92
Sanders, Nathaniel, 170
Sanders, Pete, 14, 20, 31, 34, 50, 68, 70, 73, 85, 100
Sanders, Sam, 152
Sanders, Scott David, 52, 57
Sanders, Scott, 13
Sandoval, Lapacazo, 50
Sandoval, Miguel, 135
Sandt, Stevern, 34
Sandwell, Peter, 179
Sandy, J. Craig, 174
Sanford, Beth, 121
Sanford, Isabel, 142
Sanford, Tim, 100
Sankowich, Lee, 143, 165
Sankowich, Sarah, 143
Sansei, 134, 135
Santacroce, Mary Nell, 122
Santallino, Mark, 129
Santallino, Sherry, 129
Santarelli, Gene, 68, 102, 219, 221
Santeiro, Luis, 152
Santiago, Manuel, 50
Santiago, Renoly, 60
Santiago, Socorro, 55, 97, 219
Santini, Bruno, 24
Santo, Michael, 119
Santo, Rocco, 58
Santomenna, Stephen D., 77, 124
Santomenna, Stephen, 169
Santora, Phil, 22
Santoriello, Alex, 219
Santoro, Susan, 37, 38
Santos, Tom, 121
Sanwani, Awan, 47
Sanz, Carlos, 152
Sappington, Margo, 43, 74
Saputo, Peter J., 116
Saraniero, Patti, 54
Sarcophagus, 158
Sardi, Vincent, 33
Sargent, Peter E., 170
Sarno, Janet, 151
Saroyan, William, 58
Sarracino, Ernest, 130
Sas-Uhrynowski, Jacek, 127
Saternow, Tim, 61
Sato, Toshio, 131
Satoi, Kenta, 78
Saunders, Nicholas, 58, 219
Savage, Keith, 90, 219
Savage, Melodee, 96, 108
Saved from Obscurity, 100
Savich, Rene, 63
Savin, Ron Lee, 162
Savino, Frank, 184
Savino, Joe, 10
Sawaryn, David, 61
Sawyer, Ken, 68, 170
Sawyer, Mark, 67
Sawyer-Dailey, Mark, 120
Sawyer-Dailey, Zan, 120
Saxon, Don, 60, 65
Saxon-Blume Productions, 65
Saxton, Ward, 54, 219
Sayre, Rebecca, 102
Sbarge, Raphael, 7, 103, 134, 135, 219, 221
Scambiatterra, Kathy, 144
Scanlan, John, 68
Scarbrough, Jan, 55
Scarcella, Kim, 174
Scardino, Don, 100, 219
Scarfe, Alan, 154
Scarfeo, John, 53
Scarpone, Judith, 143
Scatuorchio, Tee, 46
Scenes to Come, 105
Schaap, David, 85, 90
Schacht, Sam, 46, 61
Schachter, Beth A., 68
Schachter, Steven, 77
Schact, Sam, 219
Schaechter, Ben, 65
Schaefer, Louis, 147
Schaefer, Nancy, 6, 39
Schaefer, Richard, 56
Schaeffer, Eric, 137
Schaeffer, William, 35
Schaffner, William, 64
Schall, Thomas, 148, 151
Schallert, William, 72
Schanuel, Greg, 25, 219
Schapp, David, 90
Scharbrough, Dan, 129
Scharer, Jonathan, 14, 50
Scharif, Bina, 56
Schatzberg, Don, 67
Schaut, Ann Louise, 219
Schay, Daniel, 160
Schechter, David, 96, 170, 219
Schecter, Amy, 29, 118
Schecter, Ben, 53
Schecter, Joel, 184
Schecter, Les, 43
Scheeder, Louis, 57
Scheffler, Bob, 55
Scheiderman, Audrey, 42
Scheine, Raynor, 91
Schelble, William, 19, 37, 45
Schellenberg, August, 72
Schenck, Ann, 137
Schenck, Margaret, 53
Schenker, William, 68
Schenkkan, Robert, 172
Scherer, John, 126, 162
Schermer, Phil, 119
Schermer, Shelly Henze, 119
Schertler, Nancy, 36, 100, 126
Scherzer, Herbert, 53
Schick, Caryn, 77
Schickle, Peter, 43
Schifter, Peter Mark, 32, 184
Schilke, Raymond, 49
Schilling, Sandra, 179
Schimmel, John, 140
Schimmel, William, 35
Schissler, Jeffrey, 54, 61, 72
Schler, Michael, 57
Schlesinger, Kenneth, 103
Schmalz, Michael, 90
Schmidt, Harvey, 69, 140, 180
Schmidt, Jacques, 28
Schmidt, Lars, 28
Schmidt, Paul, 97
Schmiel, Bill, 170
Schmitt, Kelly James, 130
Schmitz, Alfred, 64, 143
Schmitz, Peter, 105, 219
Schnabel, Stefan, 96, 219
Schneider, Gary, 73
Schneider, Helen, 35, 219
Schneider, Jeffrey, 85
Schneider, Mark, 172
Schnell, Curt, 51
Schnetzer, Stephen, 60, 219
Schnirman, David A., 94
Schnitzler, Arthur, 184
Schocket, Steve, 40
Schoenfeld, Gerald, 25, 33
Schonberg, Claude-Michel, 40
Schott, Peter, 104
Schrader, Greg, 121
Schram, David, 158
Schrankl, Vera, 78
Schreiber, Avery, 32, 130, 219
Schreiber, Rosalie, 164
Schreier, Daniel Moses, 76, 86, 96
Schuberg, Carol, 27
Schuette, James A., 184
Schuettich, Fifi, 76
Schulberg, Budd, 136
Schuler, Duane, 147
Schuler, Hal, 82
Schulfer, Roche, 144
Schull, Rebecca, 219
Schulman, Craig, 40, 114
Schulman, Susan H., 108
Schultz, Albert, 174
Schultz, Armand, 52, 94, 132, 143, 219
Schultz, Carol, 137, 143
Schulz, Karen, 75
Schulz, Zipora, 57
Schumacher, Amelia, 178
Schurr, Carl, 170, 182
Schussel, Eric M., 74
Schuster, Hilde, 131
Schwantes, Gary, 123
Schwartz, Clifford, 26
Schwartz, Irving, 118
Schwartz, Jon D., 122
Schwartz, Ken, 85
Schwartz, Michael, 161
Schwartz, Paul, 44
Schwartz, Robert Joel, 99
Schwartz, Steven, 152
Schwartz, Suzanne J., 67
Schwartz, Tyagi, 125
Schwarz, Willy, 144
Schweid, Carole, 90, 219
Schweizer, David, 97, 156
Schwentner, Mark, 11
Schwisow, James, 57
Scilla, Maryellen, 45
Scionti, Steven, 20
Scipio, Anthony, 166
Sciulli, Alisa, 107
Sclafani, Sal, 24
Sclar, Deborah, 138
Scofield, Pamela, 60, 81, 143, 158
Scogin, Robert, 144
Scott, A. Robert, 35
Scott, Brad, 133
Scott, Bryan, 50
Scott, Campbell, 6, 7, 86
Scott, Casandra, 52, 105
Scott, David, 164
Scott, Deborah, 48, 54, 59, 99, 108
Scott, Dennis, 184
Scott, Desiree Amae, 158
Scott, Ernie, 14, 49, 220
Scott, Farnham, 146
Scott, Harold, 14, 49, 103, 151
Scott, Jacqueline, 139
Scott, James, 95, 131
Scott, John, 182
Scott, Joseph, 58, 83
Scott, Linda, 81
Scott, Maggie, 49
Scott, Michael, 142, 164
Scott, Milcha Sanchez, 156
Scott, Oz, 68
Scott, Seret, 68, 76, 154, 220

Spencer, Stuart, 46
Sperberg, Fritz, 142
Speredakos, John, 54, 55, 65
Sperling, Ted, 96, 100
Speros, Tia, 49, 222
Sperry, Tony, 162
Spewack, Bella, 68, 130, 170
Spewack, Samuel, 68, 130, 170
Spider's Web, 59
Spiegel, Barbara Joy, 53
Spiegel, Howard, 75, 189, 190, 222
Spielberg, David, 68, 222
Spindell, Ahvi, 35, 222, 225
Spinella, Stephen, 97, 222
Spittel, Richard, 130
Spittle, James P., 159
Spitz, Doug, 184
Spivak, Larry, 28, 94
Spivey, Tom, 83, 222
Spivy, Roger, 118
Spoerri, Lisa, 154
Spoils of War, 16
Spolan, Jeffrey, 153
Spong, Paul, 56
Spore, Richard, 154, 184
Sporing, Alan, 48
Spring, Barnaby, 61
Springer, Gary, 41
Springer, John, 41, 191
Springer, Larry, 79
Spulick, Stephen, 57
Spunk, 135
Spurney, Kristine, 130
Squire, Pat, 48, 222
St. Angelo, John, 73
St. Clair, Bart, 182
St. George, Dick, 143
St. Germain, Mark, 55, 154
St. Joan, 171
St. John, Marco, 166, 167
St. Paule, Irma, 51, 102
St. Thomas, Ashley, 78
Stabile, Bill, 66
Stacey Elizabeth Tries to Climb Out of Her Nightmare, 49
Stacey, Paul, 92
Stadlen, Lewis J., 68, 184, 191, 222
Stafford, Kate, 56
Stafford, Richard, 38, 54
Stafford, Ronald, 37
Stahl, Mary Leigh, 44, 222
Staib, John R., 153
Stained Glass, 120
Staines, Kent, 174
Stalling, Rusty, 150
Stallings, Heidi, 38
Stalter, Ralph J., Jr., 137
Stand-up Tragedy, 134, 135
Staniewski, Wlodzimierz, 47
Stanley, Keeley, 123, 134
Stannard, Nick, 140
Stanton, Robert, 148
Stapleford, Betty, 137
Starace, Tom, 49
Starbuck, Josh, 67, 93
Starbuck, Joshua, 46, 64, 70
Starger, Martin, 26
Stark's Cafe, 57
Stark, Amy Jo, 129
Stark, Douglas, 129
Stark, Molly, 75, 222
Stark, Suzanne, 129
Starmites, 34, 188
Starobin, Michael, 20, 95
Stars in the Morning Sky, 47, 156, 157
Starting Monday, 184, 185
Stathis, Nicholas John, 61
Staton, Dakota, 22, 222
Stattel, John R., 65
Stattel, Robert, 103, 222, 225
Stauch, Bonnie, 66
Stauffer, Michael, 122
Staunton, Kim, 86
Steber, John, 46
Stechschulte, Tom, 54
Steckler, Michele, 56, 62
Steefel, Jeffrey, 222
Steel Magnolias, 71, 121, 128, 143, 170, 176, 179
Steele, Darrell, 127
Steele, Ed, 111
Steele, Jevetta, 78
Steele, Philip, 44
Stefano, Kathleen, 178
Stehlin, Jack, 80, 222
Steib, Alan, 133
Stein, Alois Jane, 160
Stein, Bob, 8
Stein, Deborah, 125
Stein, Debra, 55, 65
Stein, Doug, 147
Stein, Douglas, 19, 36, 77, 87, 88
Stein, Jane Alois, 160
Stein, Joseph, 25
Stein, Julian, 69
Stein, June, 222
Stein, Mark, 172
Stein, Michael, 96
Stein, Susan, 51
Stein, Sylvia, 48
Steinberg, Lori, 45
Steinbrenner, George M., III, 20
Steiner, Rick, 39, 113, 133
Steiner, Steve, 45
Steinlein, Jean, 21, 36
Steitzer, Jeff, 119
Stella, Tim, 20
Stenberg, Paul, 94
Stenborg, Helen, 61, 222
Stender, Doug, 29, 222
Step into My World, 74
Stephens, Claudia, 67
Stephens, Grant, 64
Stephens, Kent, 178
Stephens, Melissa, 85
Stephenson, Don, 90, 222
Stephenson, John, 105
Stephenson, Malcolm, 48, 61, 102, 222
Steres, Greg, 161
Sterlin, Jenny, 160
Sterling, Lynn, 109
Stern, Alan, 32
Stern, David Glenn, 60
Stern, David, 160
Stern, Edward, 50, 170
Stern, Eric, 20
Stern, Henry J., 93
Stern, Leo, 8, 9, 10, 17, 35, 39, 45, 72
Stern, Noel, 133
Stern, Vivian, 60
Sternberg, Adam, 49
Sternberg, Ruth E., 148
Sterner, Jerry, 59, 148
Sterner, Steve, 85
Sternhagen, Frances, 62, 70, 222
Sterrer, Andrew, 48
Sterry, David H., 62
Stevans, Alberto, 126
Stevens, Allan, 222
Stevens, Grant, 59
Stevens, Jeffrey R., 105
Stevens, Roger L., 28, 51, 62
Stevens, Russell, 62
Stevens, Thea, 64
Stevens, Tony, 33
Stevenson, Isabelle, 33
Stevenson, Margot, 143, 176, 179
Stevenson, William "Mickey", 92
Stevlingson, Edward, 65
Stewart, Anita C., 80, 132, 168, 184
Stewart, Colin, 176
Stewart, Danny, 50
Stewart, Ellen, 56, 86
Stewart, Elva, 121
Stewart, Ena Lamont, 176
Stewart, Frank, 49
Stewart, George, 137
Stewart, Gwen, 34
Stewart, Michael Cal, 180
Stewart, Michael, 85, 129, 136, 182
Stewart, William, 126
Stickler, Sam, 40
Stidolph, Sherry, 148
Stieb, Alan, 6, 39
Stiehm, Roberta, 126
Stiles, Jed, 68
Stilgoe, Richard, 38, 44, 133
Stiller, Jerry, 93, 222
Stillwell, Liz, 135
Stimac, Anthony J., 90
Stimac, Marilyn, 90
Stimac, Nicola, 90
Stipetic, Scott, 161
Stober, Paul, 142
Stocker, David, 184, 185
Stocker, Gary M., 31
Stockman, Ed, 129
Stockwell, Rick, 130
Stoker, Sue Jane, 98
Stoll, David, 31, 85
Stoller, Amy, 143, 222
Stoltz, Eric, 19, 191, 189, 222
Stolze, Ivan, 151
Stone Wedding, 156, 157
Stone, Dawn Leigh, 44, 108
Stone, Jay, 58
Stone, Peter, 63, 162
Stoneburner, Sam, 184
Stoppard, Tom, 133, 137, 161
Storch, Arthur, 179
Storck, Michael, 50
Stork, Renee, 25, 222, 225
Storke, Adam, 104
Stormare, Peter, 78, 222
Story, John, 161
Stotter, Patricia Lee, 46
Stotts, Dale, 37
Stotts, Michael, 64
Stotz, Larry, 53
Stout, Mary, 74, 116, 170, 222, 225
Stout, Stephen, 30, 54, 222
Stovall, James, 96
Stover, Elizabeth, 130
Straiges, Tony, 18, 39, 113, 133
Stram, Henry, 170
Strand, Richard, 120
Strand, Thomas, 78
Strane, Robert, 121
Strang, Deborah, 99, 103, 222, 225
Stranger Here Myself, 94
Straniere, Jennifer, 64
Strassler, Abbie M., 31
Strathairn, David, 96, 105
Stratman, Daniel, 50
Straub, John, 169
Strauss, Edward, 26, 45, 109
Strauss, Jane, 116
Strawbridge, Stephen, 68, 81, 87, 132, 151, 169
Strawn, Judith, 56
Strawn, Vicki Smith Sandra, 161
Streetcar Named Desire, A, 178
Streeter, Wendy, 126, 132
Streetsongs, 64
Strengaru, Victor, 126
Strickland, Morgan, 119, 133
Strickler, Dan, 57, 222
Stricklin, Debra, 54, 57, 68
Striglos, Bill, 178
Strike Up the Band, 130
Strindberg, August, 64
Stringer, Elisabeth, 133
Stritch, Elaine, 62
Strobel, Guy, 140
Stroman, Susan, 49, 162
Stromberg, Bob, 50
Strong, Edward, 39
Strong, Ken, 122
Stronger, The, 64
Stronin, Michael, 47
Strother, Fredrick, 126
Strouse, Nicholas, 169
Strozier, Henry, 126
Strukman, Jeffrey, 178
Struth, Sandy, 148
Stuart, Ian, 29
Stuart, John, 65
Stuart, Laird, 161
Stuart, Lynne, 108, 222, 225
Stuart, Mary Ellen, 25
Stuart, Richard P., 130
Stuart, Sherry, 81
Stuart-Morris, Joan, 172
Stubbs, Jim, 53, 222
Studwell, David, 144
Stukman, Jeffrey, 178
Sturchio, Mal, 68
Sturm, Jason, 31, 85
Sturmer, Carl, 57
Stutts, Will, 137
Styne, Jule, 25
Styron, Paola, 93
Suardi, Lily, 47
Suarez, Carmen, 82
Suber, Kate, 69
Subject Was Roses, The, 142
Sucharetza, Marla, 96
Suds, 50
Suede, Bob, 66
Suenos, 60
Sugarman, Fred, 60
Sugarman, Jeff, 176
Sugarman, Merri, 115
Sugita, Hideyuki, 78
Sukhishvili, Iliko, 13
Sukhishvili, Tengiz, 13
Sulanowski, James Stephen, 54
Sulich, Stephen, 27
Sulka, Elaine, 46, 67
Sullivan, Alesia, 65
Sullivan, Anne, 84
Sullivan, Daniel, 30, 100
Sullivan, Dennis, 62
Sullivan, James, 57
Sullivan, Jean, 50
Sullivan, Jeremiah, 51, 222
Sullivan, Jo, 33, 60, 222
Sullivan, John Carver, 146, 161
Sullivan, John Frederick, 82, 83
Sullivan, John, 123
Sullivan, Johnette, 82, 222
Sullivan, Kitty, 84
Sullivan, Matt Bradford, 73, 94, 141
Sullivan, Nancy J., 51
Sullivan, Shan, 62
Sullivan, Siobhan, 152
Sullivan, Stacy, 130
Sullivan, Tom, 48
Sumbry, Dormeshia, 22
Summer Remembered, A, 182
Summerhays, Jane, 26, 42, 60, 222
Sunday in the Park with George, 172
Sung, Kimi, 169
Sunshine Boys, The, 85
Sunshine, Margaret, 42
Suppon, Charles, 20
Surovy, Nicolas, 9, 222, 225
Surratt, Clayton, 122
Susan Bloch Co., 56
Susan, Black-Eyed, 55
Suskin, Art, 161
Suskin, Steven, 109
Sutorius, James, 172
Sutton, Dolores, 143
Sutton, Greg, 51, 63
Suzuki, Tadashi, 126
Svensson, John, 78
Swackhammer, Elizabeth, 133
Swackhmaer, Ten Eyck, 119
Swados, Elizabeth, 80
Swain, Howard, 123
Swain, J. D., 50
Swan Song, 64
Swan, Jon, 132
Swanson, Eric, 184
Swanson, Maura, 64
Swanson, Parker Jerome, 127
Swarbrick, Carol, 144, 222
Swarm, Sally Ann, 63, 151
Swartz, Donald, 66
Swartz, Marlene, 105
Swartz, Nancy, 63
Swasey, Robert W., 108
Swasey, Robert, 108
Swash, Bob, 24
Swearingen, Beth, 37, 38
Swearingen, Henriette, 152
Swee, Daniel, 30, 100
Sweeney Todd, 108
Sweeney, Paula, 170
Sweet, Jeffrey, 106
Sweet, Sam, 141
Sweeters, Jim, 47, 48
Sweethearts, 56
Sweeting, Court, 64
Swegart, Phil, 169
Swetland, William, 154
Swetow, Joel, 99, 108, 222
Swift, Allen, 131
Swift, Anne, 72
Swift, G. Tom, 64, 82
Swift, Tom, 72
Swikowski, Bill, 107
Swindler, William, 35
Swiniuch, Linda H., 176
Swire, Willard, 33
Swonger, James C., 184
Sykes, Renee, 46, 67
Sylrich Management, 32
Symonds, Robert, 148
Synodinos, Jean, 73
Syvertsen, Peter, 147
Szczepanski, John Paul, 48
Szelag, Daniel, 132
Szymanski, William, 222, 225
Tabachnick, Ken, 27, 148
Tabaka, Victoria, 122
Tabor, Richard, 48
Taffetas, The, 49
Taffner, Don, 29
Tahal, Monika, 78
Tait, Jean, 49
Takahagi, Hiroshi, 78
Takatsu, Yukio, 78
Takazauckas, Albert, 123
Takeshita, Akiko, 78
Taking Steps, 180
Takita, Kyoko, 158
Talberth, Kenneth, 48
Talbot, Sharon, 51, 222
Talcott, Linda, 25
Tale of Lear, 126
Tale of Two Cities, A, 56
Talented Tenth, The, 89
Tales of Tinseltown, 142
Tales of the Lost Formicans, 120
Talipaksa, Endang, 47
Talk Radio, 150
Talley's Folly, 153, 161, 172, 178
Tally, Ted, 57
Talman, Ann, 57, 222, 225
Talpers, Daniel, 47
Talyn, Olga, 44, 222, 225
Tam, Yung, 58
Tamamatsu, Yoshida, 78
Tamara, 72
Tamara-Tucker-Cole, Tamika, 68
Tamarkin, Nicholas, 7, 154
Tambella, Mark, 56
Taming of the Shrew, The, 68, 161, 168, 174
Tamm, Daniel, 148
Tammen, Carol, 130
Tan, Victor En Yu, 98, 131, 161
Tancredi, Dorothy, 37
Tandet, A. Joseph, 23
Tanji, Lydia, 123, 134, 135
Tankersly, Mark, 49
Tanner, Betsy, 88
Tanner, Jill, 132
Tanner, John, 161
Taphorn, Peggy, 116
Tarbuck, Barbara, 110
Tartuffe, 158
Tasker, Jill, 100, 154
Tatar, Ben, 165
Tate, Barbara, 92
Tate, Robert, 46,
Tate, Robin, 128, 148, 158
Tatge, Pamela, 154
Tatishvili, Roland, 13
Tatna, Mehr, 80
Tatum, Marianne, 90, 144, 222
Taubes, Ethan, 54
Taverna, Patrick, 64
Tavin, Erin, 67
Tavori, Doron, 53, 134
Tayama, Ryosei, 78
Taylor, Clifton, 136
Taylor, Dendrie, 172
Taylor, Drew, 146
Taylor, Dwight, 64
Taylor, Elaine L., 121
Taylor, George, 61, 222
Taylor, Gina, 92
Taylor, Giva, 183
Taylor, Holland, 51, 62, 222
Taylor, John Wendes, 80
Taylor, Kathy, 114
Taylor, Lawrence T., 176
Taylor, Leslie, 131, 160
Taylor, Lili, 94
Taylor, Lois, 57
Taylor, Mark, 80
Taylor, Myra, 106, 151, 222, 225
Taylor, Regina, 97, 222
Taylor, Renee, 106
Taylor, Rip, 109
Taylor, Robin, 223
Taylor, Rubee, 92
Taylor, Scott, 25, 30, 36, 38, 40, 44, 74, 223
Taylor, Tammy, 21, 104
Taylor, Terry Hodge, 33
Taylor, Valerie, 232
Taylor, Wally, 165
Taylor-Corbett, Lynne, 94
Taylor-Morris, Maxine, 83, 223
Tazla, Michael, 147
Tea with Mommy and Jack, 81
Teagarden, Geraldine, 31, 85
Teich, Jessica, 135
Teitel, Martin, 67
Tejeda, Victoria, 58
Telsey, Bernard, 52, 60
Telson, Bob, 78
Temperley, Stephen, 116, 117
Tempest, The, 120, 132
Temptation, 96, 134
Ten Percent Revue, 46
Ternstrom, Paula, 78
Terrat, Charlie, 73
Terry, Ginni, 64
Terry, Jacob, 57
Terry, Jonathan G., 68
Terry, Marjorie, 128
Terry, Susan, 27, 109
Teschendorf, David, 57
Tesich, Steve, 144
Tessier, Claude R., 114, 115
Testa, Mary, 88, 166, 223
Testa, Nancy Drumright, 142
Testman, Frank, 176
Tetreault, Paul R., 79
Tetrick, Wayne, 140
Tevzadze, Inga, 13
Thacker, Russ, 94, 223
Thain, Andrew, 85, 223
Tharp, Carol Baker, 156
Thatcher, Kristine, 61, 144
Thayer, Joel O., 184
Thayer, Sasha, 68, 102
Thebus, Mary Ann, 144
There's One in Every Marriage, 132
Thew, John, 104
Thibeault, Debi, 48
Thibodeau, Marc P., 25, 30, 36, 38, 40, 44, 76
Thies, Howard, 98
Thirteenth Chair, The, 83
Thoemke, Peter, 147
Thole, Cynthia, 223
Thomas, Alain, 78
Thomas, Ann, 232
Thomas, Brenda, 64, 65
Thomas, Carlo, 133
Thomas, Cynthia, 129, 162
Thomas, Dylan, 128, 168
Thomas, Eberle, 121, 143
Thomas, Edward, 57
Thomas, Evelyn, 151
Thomas, Freda L., 91
Thomas, Gary, 174
Thomas, Isa, 142, 165
Thomas, Jeanne, 107
Thomas, John Norman, 40
Thomas, Julie Michael, 66
Thomas, Keith, 174
Thomas, Marie, 89
Thomas, Mike, 50
Thomas, Richard, 62, 148, 149, 223
Thomas, Robert, 37
Thomas, Sheriden, 183
Thomas, Thom, 81
Thomas, Timothy, 84
Thomas, Traci Lyn, 182
Thomas, Tressa Janaee, 144
Thomas, William, 43
Thomas, William, Jr., 223
Thomas-D'Alessandro, Theresa, 126
Thomas-Grant, Cathy, 123
Thompson, Brian, 119
Thompson, Darcy, 74
Thompson, David Malcolm, 144
Thompson, Don, 69
Thompson, Jeffery, 148

Thompson, John Leonard, 126
Thompson, Julie, 132
Thompson, Lauren, 122, 154
Thompson, Lester, 130
Thompson, Martha, 68, 170
Thompson, Melvin, 92
Thompson, Ron Stacker, 92
Thompson, Sada, 111
Thompson, Tazewell, 126, 136, 179
Thompson, Tommy, 121
Thompson, Trinity, 223
Thomsen, Kevin, 183
Thomsen, Richard, 131, 165
Thomson, Ian, 146
Thomson, Tommy, 25
Thorell, Bernt, 78
Thoresen, Howard, 48, 53, 61
Thorne, Joan Vail, 44
Thornton, Angela, 88, 223, 225
Thornton, Clarke W., 90
Thoron, Elise, 47, 148
Thorp, Peggy, 139
Thorpe, Teri, 74
Three Musketeers, 174, 175
Three Sisters, The, 65, 98
Threet, Ken, 61
Thrill A Moment, A, 92
Thropp, Randall, 73
Thunhurst, William, Jr., 165
Thurber, James, 82
Thurber, Robert, 29, 32
Ti Daro Quel Fiore, 48
Tichler, Rosemarie, 15, 93
Tickner, Christopher, 182
Tiesi, William S., 179
Tiffany, Patty, 66
Tighe, Susanne, 11, 14, 16, 24, 26, 39, 54, 65, 66, 103
Tight, Susanne, 72
Tilden, Leif, 60
Tiller, Ted, 232
Tillinger, John, 23, 62, 88, 89, 104, 154
Tillotson, John, 68
Tilson, Susan, 109
Time and Patience Unlimited, 54
Timerman, Alec, 45
Timm, Pat, 131
Timms, Rebecca, 38
Tinsley, Dana Harnish, 143
Tinsley, James K., 143
Tipton, Jennifer, 6, 25, 86, 104, 144, 184
Tirado, Candido, 101
'Tis The Morning, 92
Titus Andronicus, 102
Tjernlund, Ralf, 78
Tkacz, Virlana, 56
Tkatch, Peter Jack, 59
To Forgive, Divine, 160
Tobie, Ellen, 66, 169, 223
Toce, Tom, 105
Toda, Toshi, 45
Todd, Rick D., 128
Todd, Tony, 151
Todoroff, Tom, 123
Together Again for the First Time, 60
Toia, John J., 94
Tokatlian, Ara, 135
Tolan, Kathleen, 93, 223
Tolan, Michael, 49, 58, 223
Tolan, Peter, 57, 66, 223
Tom, David, 133
Tom, Lauren, 98, 104, 147, 223, 225
Tomala, Slawomir, 47
Tomarrow, Todd, 50
Tomasetti, Elissa Maria, 47
Tomasino, Matt, 131
Tomei, Marisa, 46, 52, 88, 223
Tomei, Paula, 172
Tomfoolery, 82, 143, 181
Tomlin, Cathy, 57, 66
Tomlinson, Robert Michael, 132
Tompkins, Lynette, 74
Tompos, Doug, 73, 143, 223, 225
Toms, Carl, 133
Toner, Thomas, 42, 223
Toney, David, 126, 136
Toni, Debi, 73
Tony 'N' Tina's Wedding, 73
Took, Don, 172
Toole, James E., 179
Toon, Tami, 134
Top Girls, 183
Topol, Richard, 46, 107
Toran, Peter, 164
Torcellini, Jamie, 42, 116
Torch, The, 161
Toren, Ilan, 53, 134
Toren, Suzanne, 166
Torfeh, Bryan, 133
Tornabene, Joseph, 98
Toro, Natalie, 40
Torres, Robert, 138
Torres, Tony, 44
Toser, David, 33, 146, 165
Tost, Bill, 69
Tost, William, 69
Totani, Masahiro, 78
Toth, Helen, 86

Touhey, John, 68
Tourneur, Cyril, 56
Toussaint, Lorraine, 86
Touzie, Mariam, 61
Tovares, Eric, 159
Tovatt, Patrick, 19, 223
Towers, Charles, 183
Towey, John M., 225
Towey, John Madden, 94, 96, 223
Towler, Laurine, 126, 161
Townes, Peter, 140
Townley, Sharon, 138
Townsend, Christopher, 126
Townsend, Judith, 161
Townsley, Peggy, 180
Toy, Christine, 31, 94, 223
Toyama, Toshia, 78
Trachtenberg, Lissy, 59
Trainer, Shirlin Devrim, 158
Trapani, Sal, 51
Trattner, Alison, 83
Travis, Warren, 123
Traxler, Mark, 65
Tray, Eli, 82, 223, 225
Trayer, Leslie, 25
Treadway, Scott, 140
Treat, Martin, 50, 223
Tree, Brian, 174
Treger, Caron, 49
Trent, Michael, 32, 81
Trevens, Francine L., 49, 54, 58
Trevino, Frankie, 119
Trevino, Vic, 172
Tribush, Nancy, 43
Trichter, Judd, 89, 223
Trigger, Ian, 169
Trillin, Calvin, 76
Tron, Bob, 182
Troobnick, Eugene, 136
Trott, Karen, 154
Trouille, Clovis, 43
Troupe, Tom, 172
Troy, Ellen, 25
Troy, Louise, 223
True, Betsy, 114
True, Rachel, 58
Truex, Bronwyn, 56
Trullinger, George, 65
Trumbull, Robert, 223
Tsoutsouvas, Sam, 72, 100, 223
Tsu, Susan, 176
Tsuda, Mitsumasa, 78
Tsuji, Ann M., 98
Tsuji, Yukio, 41
Tsypin, George, 96, 123, 126
Tubert, Marc, 135
Tucci, Maria, 9, 62, 223
Tucci, Stanley, 184
Tucker, Lane C., 112
Tucker, Shona, 97
Tucker, Zak, 90
Tucker-White, Pamela, 154, 184, 185
Tull, Patrick, 88, 99, 223
Tunick, Jonathan, 37, 39, 65, 113, 133
Tuohy, Susan, 172
Turchette, Tamara, 161
Turenne, Louis, 151
Turnbull, Ann, 136
Turnbull, Laura, 67, 143
Turner, Amiee, 146
Turner, Caroline F., 183
Turner, Charles, 49
Turner, Craig, 168
Turner, Glenn, 37, 223
Turner, Jake, 107, 166
Turner, Jenny, 170, 171
Turner, Kathleen, 62
Turner, Keith, 26
Turner, Lily, 154
Turner, Marisa Francesca, 60
Turner, Patrick, 61, 223
Turner, Stephen, 102
Turner, Susan Watson, 91
Turns, Ale, 91
Turturro, Aida, 73
Turturro, John, 88, 223
Tussey, Julie, 37
Tuthill, Charles, 151
Tutor, Rick, 119
TV Asahi, 70
Twelfth Night, 67, 128, 174
Twine, Linda, 33
Two by Two, 63
Two Gentlemen of Verona, 174, 175
Two for the Show, 47
Tyger, Michael J., 158
Tyler, Andi, 25
Tyler, Bobby, 178
Tynan, Kenneth, 43
Tyrone, Keith, 20, 126
Tyrone-Wallace, James, II, 135
Tyson, Pamala, 46, 179

Ubarry, Hechter, 31, 85, 223
Ubu, 87
Udall, Katherine, 183
Udell, Peter, 162
Uedi, Nobuyoshi, 78
Ueno, Watoku, 67

Uesugi, Shozo, 78
Uggams, Leslie, 45, 109, 190, 191, 223
Uhry, Alfred, 70, 100, 111, 122, 140
Ukena, Paul, Jr., 17, 85, 90
Ulett, Nick, 116
Ulissey, Catherine, 44, 223, 225
Ullett, Nick, 42, 223
Ullman, Bill, 146
Ullman, Jeffrey, 48, 75
Ullman, Robin, 36
Ullrick, Sharon, 138
Ulmer, Joan, 169
Ulmer, John, 127
Ulrike Meinhof, 81
Ulysses in Nighttown, 57
Umile, Marc, 58
Uncounted Blessings, 49
Under Milk Wood, 128
Understanding, The, 66
Unexpected Guest, 128
Unger, Hank, 179
Unger, Michael, 110
Ungerer, Julie, 131
Unguided Missile, The, 76
Unnamable, The, 86
Up 'N' Under, 81
Urbano, Maryann, 52
Uribe, Eduardo, 60
Urich, Tom, 162
Urla, Joe, 154
Utley, Byron, 137
Uttley, William, 80
Vaccariello, Patrick, 146
Vaccaro, Marion, 55
Vadino, Lori, 36
Vago, Liz, 127
Valdes, Albert, 138
Valdez, Daniel, 8
Valdez, Dino A., 139
Valdez, Luis, 8
Valdez, Thaddeus, 122
Valente, Deirdre, 64
Valentina, Joan, 51
Valentine, Karen, 162
Valenzuela, Jose Luis, 156
Valero, Wayne, 138
Valk, Steven, 78
Valle, Victor, 161
Vallillo, Stephen, 68
Valor, Henrietta, 88, 223, 225
Valsing, Elizabeth, 88, 93, 97
Value of Names, The, 106
Vamos, Miklos, 62
Vampire Lesbians of Sodom, 73
Van Ark, Joan, 62
Van Berg, Peter, 148
Van Buren, Shula, 63
Van Cleave, Carroll, 83
Van Cott, Bruce, 48
van der Merve, Paula, 61
Van Druten, John, 182
Van Duyn, Katrina, 141
Van Dyck, Jennifer, 46, 100, 154, 223
Van Dyke, Elizabeth, 11
Van Dyke, Michael R., 184
Van Fossen, Diana, 183
Van Griethuysen, Ted, 56, 141, 223
Van Horne, Gretchen, 122
Van Ingen, Elisabeth, 93
Van Keyser, William, 128
Van Patten, Joyce, 18, 178, 223
Van Pelt, Daniel, 121
Van Tieghem, David, 58
Van Voorhees, Thomas, 161
Van Zandt, Karen, 123
Vance, Courtney B., 223
Vance, Courtney, 225
Vance, Cynthia, 91
Vandergriff, Robert, 107
Vandivort, Terry, 180
Varga, Joseph, 67, 137
Vargas, Ovidio, 223, 225
Vargas, Tony, 6
Varna, Michael, 57
Varner, Michael, 57
Varnum, Steve, 57
Varon, Susan, 73
Vasen, Tim, 21, 107
Vasquez, Alden, 144
Vaughan, Stuart, 94, 103
Vaughn, Jeff, 57, 63
Vaughn, Wendy-Jo, 34
Vaux, Adrian, 35, 53, 154
Vaux, Lyn, 72
Veazey, Jeff, 73
Vedder, Joanna, 76
Vega, Cecilia, 93
Vega, Jose, 18, 110
Vega, Laura P., 138
Vega, Rosa I., 104
Vehr, Bill, 232
Veiller, Bayard, 83
Velde, Fred, 57, 63
Venesse, Nadia, 97
Venezia, Carol, 57, 82, 83
Venezia, Lisa, 93
Veneziale, Renee, 114

Vennema, John C., 54, 154, 223
Venora, Diane, 95, 223
Venton, Harley, 165
Ventulett, Suzanne, 122
Ventura, Frank, 90
Venture, Lorraine, 154
Venture, Richard, 94, 154, 155
Verderber, William, 35
Verdery, James, 119
Verdier, Paul, 47, 48
Verdon, Gwen, 33
Verini, Bob, 48, 61, 99
Verleny, Christine, 80
Vernacchio, Dorian, 135
Verner, Vickie, 49
Vernet, Paul, 68
Vetter, Jo, 119
Vichi, Gerry, 45
Vickery, John, 151
Vidal, Marta, 101
Vidan, Richard, 134
Video D Studios, 36
Viertel, Thomas, 51, 62
Vignola, Frank P., 137
Vilanch, Bruce, 14
Vilkin, Peter, 178
Village Theatre Company, The, 61
Vincent, A. J., 73
Vincent, David, 83
Vincent, Irving, 52
Vincent, Lawrence, 162
Vincent, Robert, 69
Vinsa, Michael, 78
Vinson, Mickey, 152
Vipond, Mathew, 52
Vipond, Neil, 108, 223
Viracola, Fiddle, 126
Virsaladze, Simon, 13
Virta, Ray, 148, 149, 223, 225
Viscardi, John, 79, 223
Visconti, Michael, 73
Visit, The, 58
Vito, Don, 22
Viverito, Suzanne, 38
Viverta, Joanna, 59
Viviano, Sal, 223
Vivino, Donna, 40
Voet, Doug, 224
Vogeley, Mark, 50
Vogt, K. T., 172
Voice of the Prairie, The, 119, 121, 131, 170
Voice of the Turtle, The, 182
Vollack, Lia, 23, 60, 100, 136
Voltaire, 151, 170
Von Bargen, Daniel, 124
Von Berg, Peter, 148
Von Brandenstein, Patrizia, 24
von Kliest, Heinrich, 132
von Mayrhauser, Jennifer, 9, 30, 52, 68, 100, 106, 170
von Pilchau, Beate Pilar, 78
Von Salis, David, 98, 105
von Schmid, Kathleen, 46, 47, 48, 58, 106
Vos, Richard, 75
Vroman, Lisa, 115
Vyzga, Bernard, 138
Waara, Scott, 32, 55, 151, 224, 225
Wade, Carl, 131
Wade, Jacqueline Nan, 161
Wagenhurst, Mark, 82, 101, 136
Wager, Douglas C., 126
Wages, Brad, 122
Waggett, David, 105
Wagner, Christien, 48
Wagner, Chuck, 39, 113, 133, 224, 225
Wagner, Dan, 48
Wagner, Daniel MacLean, 141
Wagner, Daryl (Liberace), 65
Wagner, Frank, 108
Wagner, George, 26
Wagner, Kathryn, 50, 99, 158
Wagner, Robert, 64
Wagner, Robin, 25, 37
Wagner, Terri, 66
Wahl, David, 153
Wahl, Kirby, 170
Wahlig, Lisa, 161
Wainwright, George, 146
Wait Until Dark, 179
Waite, John Thomas, 69
Waiting for Godot, 86, 87, 138
Waits, Tom, 156, 157
Walbye, Kay, 29, 55
Walcutt, John, 141, 172
Wald, Shelley, 20
Waldekranz, Jan, 78
Walden, Eric, 59
Walden, Mary, 184
Walden, Stanley, 43
Walden, William, 170
Waldheim, Julianne, 67
Waldman, Julie, 50
Waldman, Robert, 68, 70, 111, 131, 140
Waldren, Peter, 75
Waldron, Michael, 26, 162

Walk in the Woods, A, 126, 143, 150, 169, 176, 177, 183
Walken, Christopher, 62, 94, 224
Walker, Anthony, 151
Walker, Bill, 64
Walker, Celeste, 60
Walker, Chet, 144
Walker, Chris, 82, 169
Walker, Crystal R., 144
Walker, Dana, 38
Walker, Diane, 22
Walker, Don, 65
Walker, George F., 123, 134, 148
Walker, Gregory, 182
Walker, Janet Hayes, 108
Walker, Jared, 105
Walker, Jonathan, 179
Walker, Lissy, 93
Walker, Natalie, 84
Walker, Paul, 62
Walker, Polly, 63
Walker, Randolph, 164
Walker, Ray, 40, 224
Walker, Sullivan, 126
Walker, Sydney, 123
Walker, Thomas S., 224
Walker, Zoe, 105
Walker-Lichtig, Jody, 113, 133
Walkers, 81
Wall, Susie, 170
Wall-Asse, Marilyn, 150
Wallace, Barry, 138
Wallace, Basil, 151
Wallace, Claudine, 119
Wallace, David, 138
Wallace, Gregory, 68
Wallace, Jack, 86, 151
Wallace, Lee, 85, 224
Wallace, Marian, 127
Wallace, Marie, 108, 224, 225
Wallace, Peter, 46
Wallace, Ronald, 11, 154
Wallace, Ted Kent, 70
Wallace, Ted, 51
Wallach, Eli, 15, 33, 224
Waller, Linda, 66, 224, 225
Waller, Kenneth H., 42
Waller, Kenneth, 44, 224
Wally's Cafe, 182
Walnut, Dawn, 34
Walsh, Barbara, 114, 224
Walsh, Elizabeth, 65, 224, 225
Walsh, Jack, 147
Walsh, James, 30
Walsh, Joe, 112
Walsh, Martin J., 232
Walsh, Seth, 56
Walsh, Shela, 81
Walter, Jessica, 18, 224
Walter, Wendy, 130
Walters, Bill, 90
Walters, Don, 23
Walters, Melora, 60
Walters, William R., 224
Walthers, Mark, 102
Walton, Bob, 129
Walton, Jim, 108, 224
Walton, Laurie, 129
Walton, Mone, 142, 164
Walton, Tony, 8, 25, 26, 45, 86, 109
Waltz of the Toreadors, The, 121
Wands, Susan, 160
Wann, Jim, 121, 140
Wantland, Dan, 79
Ward, Bethe, 44
Ward, Beverly, 130
Ward, Buzz, 184
Ward, Christian, 78
Ward, Diane, 89
Ward, Douglas Turner, 91
Ward, Elizabeth, 129
Ward, Elsa, 81
Ward, Kirby, 130
Ward, MaryBeth, 56
Ward, Matthew M., 143
Ward, Michael, 94
Ward, Nick, 92
Ward, Tracy, 115
Warden, Yvonne, 224, 225
Ware, Herta, 172
Ware, Thomas, 130
Warehime, David, 65
Warfel, William B., 184
Waring, Wendy, 20, 224
Warner, David Strong, 113
Warner, Lee, 127
Warner, Phillip, 55
Warner, Russell, 146
Warner, Sherman, 39
Warner, Sturgis, 102
Warnick, Steven, 34
Waromi, Johnie, 47
Warren, David, 96, 100
Warren, Diane, 128
Warren, Harry, 129
Warren, Joseph, 88, 99, 224
Warren, Marc, 55
Warren, Mary Mease, 143, 165
Warren, Paul, 100
Warren, Robert, 108
Warrior Ant, The, 78

Wartnik, Adam, 50
Warwick, Mark, 140
Washington, Alicia Rene, 92
Washington, Cheryle, 180
Washington, David, 118
Washington, Denzel, 11, 224
Washington, John Ann, 50
Washington, Melvin, 22, 224
Washington, Sharon, 94, 96
Wassberg, Goran, 78
Wasser, Alan, 40, 44, 133
Wasser, Jane, 82
Wassermann, Ross, 176
Wasserstein, Wendy, 30, 100
Wasson, David, 66
Watanabe, Leslie, 138
Watanabe, Sugie, 78
Water Music, 68
Waterhouse, Abram, 174
Waterman, Mark, 67
Waters, Amanda, 126
Waters, Harry, Jr., 135
Waters, Mary Ellen, 81, 82
Watkins, Bradford, 112
Watkins, Steve, 90
Watling, E. F., 61
Watson, Douglass, 232
Watson, Lisa, 92
Watson, Lynda, 11
Watson, Lynn, 128
Watson, Michael, 122
Watson, Robert Keith, 65
Watson, Tom, 57
Watson, Warren, 56
Watson, Wendy, 102
Watt, Billie Lou, 170
Watt, Eloise, 48, 96
Watt, Nina, 93
Waxman, Gayle, 136
Way We Live Now, The, 135
Waymon, Sam, 96
Weatherly, Michael, 32
Weatherstone, James, 113, 133
Weaver, Anthony, 170
Weaver, Fritz, 62
Webb, Chloe, 156, 157
Webb, Chris, 161
Webb, Jake, 151
Webber, Andrew Lloyd, 26, 38, 44, 133
Webber, Julian, 105
Webber, Robert, 232
Webber, Stephen D., 161
Weber, Andrea, 57, 224
Weber, Jake, 86
Weber, Kathleen, 82
Weber, Steven, 46
Webster, Albert, 70, 93
Webster, Byron, 130
Webster, Lynn Alice, 64
Webster, William, 174
Wedding Band, 161
Weeden, Amanda, 19
Weekend Comedy, 140
Weekes, Laura Delano, 68
Weeks, Jimmie Ray, 172
Weeks, Todd, 19
Weferling, Myra Oney, 49
Weglein, Jessica, 148
Wehle, Brenda, 147
Weidman, Jerome, 82
Weidman, John, 45, 109
Weidmann, Ginnie, 69
Weidner, Paul, 126
Weil, Melissa, 57, 224
Weil, Tim, 43
Weill, Kurt, 94
Weinberg, Tom Wilson, 46
Weindling, Craig, 119
Weiner, Zane, 75
Weingartner, Stephen, 123
Weingust, Don, 82
Weinstock, Jack, 182
Weinstock, Kenneth M., 59
Weis, Stephen, 102
Weiser, Steve, 48
Weiss, Adrienne J., 86
Weiss, Elliot, 152
Weiss, Gordon J., 35, 224
Weiss, Greg, 56, 67
Weiss, Gregory Linus, 102
Weiss, Jeff, 19, 224
Weiss, Julie, 136
Weiss, Marc B., 33, 136, 154
Weiss, Mitchell A., 34
Weiss, Paul, 55
Weiss, Suzanne Hauser, 97
Weissman, Jeffrey, 130
Weissman, Neile, 49
Weitz, Paul, 46
Weitzenhoffer, Max, 36
Weitzman, Ira, 100
Weitzman, Joshua, 93
Welby, Donnah, 48, 99, 224
Welch, Celeste, 92
Welch, Doeri, 178
Welch, Jane, 131
Welch, Ken, 33
Welch, Mitzie, 33
Welch, Robert, 168
Welcome Back to Salamanca, 46
Welcome to the Club, 32, 187
Weldin, Scott, 119, 161
Weldon, 60
Weldon, Kevin, 20
Weller, Michael, 16
Wellman, Mac, 63
Wells, Brian, 137
Wells, Christopher, 67, 122, 224, 225
Wells, Craig, 115, 224
Wells, Deanna, 158, 224
Wells, Doug, 127
Wells, Neville, 84
Welsh, Kenneth, 134
Welty, Eudora, 33, 140
Wencker, Leigh-Anne, 176
Wendland, Mark, 134
Wendschuh, Ronald, 170
Wennerberg, Tomas, 78
Wentworth, Scott, 32, 174
Weppner, Christina, 63
Werbacher, Don, 53
Werbacher, Rich, 53
Werfel, Franz, 85
Werner, Stewart, 79
Wernick, Adam, 96
Wernick, Nancy, 49
Werstler, Greg, 170
Wesley, Richard, 89
Wessler, Frederick, 100
West Memphis Mojo, 176
West, Hunter, 161
West, Matt, 224
West, Rachel, 46
West, Ronnie, 96
West, Steven Major, 151
West, Susan, 36, 56
Westenberg, Robert, 39, 224, 225
Westergaard, Louise, 118
Westfall, Chris, 180
Westfall, Ralph David, 108, 224
Weston, Jack, 86, 224
Weston, Robert J., 54
Weston-Moran, Kim, 179
Wetherall, Jack, 72, 144, 224
Weths, Stephen, 68
Wetmore, Joan, 232
Wetzel, Harry, 139
Wewton, Robert J., 49
Wexler, Barrie, 72
Wexler, Michael, 152
Weyrick, Diane, 119
Whalen, David, 103, 179
Whalley-Kilmer, Joanne, 88, 189, 224
What Did He See?, 94
What Would Esther Williams Do in a Situation Like This?, 53
What the Butler Saw, 88, 189
Wheeler, Bill, 49
Wheeler, David Cole, 102
Wheeler, David, 94, 102
Wheeler, Ed, 91
Wheeler, Harold, 88
Wheeler, Hugh, 108, 151, 170
Wheeler, Ivery, 22
Wheeler, Jedediah, 56
Whelan, Richard, 82, 224
When I Grow Up, 172
When We Are Married, 123, 154, 155
Whiip, Carmen, 92
Whipple, Patti, 70
Whirligig, 63
Whistle in the Dark, A, 84
Whitaker, Monica, 169
Whitbell Productions, Inc., 14
White, Benjamin, 108, 137
White, Bernard, 93
White, Bob D., 56
White, Bradley, 100
White, Callan, 154
White, Cathy, 125
White, Diane, 156
White, Elizabeth D., 6, 47
White, Heidi, 182
White, Jacob, 96
White, Jane, 94, 224
White, Julie, 107, 224
White, Lillias, 96
White, Miles, 25
White, Patrick, 82, 224
White, Richard, 162, 163
White, Susan A., 50, 70, 75
White, Terri, 12, 32, 224
White, Toby, 78
White, Welker, 65, 79
Whitehead, David P., 119
Whitehead, Paxton, 29, 132, 224
Whitehead, William, 180
Whitehill, B. T., 107
Whitehill, Jane, 75
Whitelaw, Arthur, 33, 49
Whitelock, Patricia Ann, 138
Whiteman, Catherine, 180
Whitemore, Hugh, 136
Whitesell, John P., 46
Whitfield, Michael J., 174
Whitford, Bradley, 46, 148
Whitlock, Isiah, Jr., 97, 166, 167
Whitlock, Margay, 50
Whitmore, James, 142
Whitney, Ann, 184
Whittaker, Ronnie J., 138
Whitted, Earl, 102
Whittle, Eve, 140
Whittles, Miki, 90, 146
Whore and the H'Empress, The, 120
Whyte, Kyle, 109
Wicken, Jessica, 54
Wideman, Beverly, 62
Wiedergott, Karl, 134
Wiederrecht, Carol, 63
Wierzel, Robert, 56, 80, 132, 168, 169
Wiest, Dianne, 193
Wietrzychowski, Stanley, 64
Wiggins, Elaine N., 38
Wilbur, Richard, 151, 158, 170
Wilbur, Roy, 166
Wilby, Brian Peter, 158
Wilcox, Charlie, 132
Wilcox, John, 29, 81
Wilcox, Patricia, 50, 51
Wild Duck, The, 147
Wilde, Oscar, 46, 132, 164
Wilder, Alan, 147
Wilder, Andrew, 90, 99
Wilder, Cara, 138
Wilder, Carrie, 63
Wilder, Thornton, 19, 58, 138
Wildman, James, 179
Wildman, Robert, 184
Wiley, Paul, 58
Wilk, Andrew Carl, 162
Wilkens, Bob, 53
Wilkens, Claudia, 147
Wilkerson, Edward, 144
Wilkins, George, 140
Wilkinson, Colm, 40, 224
Wilkinson, Kate, 71, 93, 224
Wilkner, Pierre, 78
Will You Remember Productions, 56
Will, Ethyl, 70, 83
Willard, Charlie, 111
Willard, George C., 42
Willet, Vernon, 138
William Tell Agency, 140
William, David, 174
Williams, Adrian, 99
Williams, Allan, 40
Williams, Allison, 92, 224
Williams, Arline, 170
Williams, Barnett, 151
Williams, Beth, 115
Williams, Celeste, 161
Williams, Cindy Sue, 36, 224
Williams, Crystal, 118
Williams, Cynda, 63
Williams, Darnell, 11
Williams, David, 129
Williams, Ellis E., 111
Williams, Freida, 34
Williams, Jacqueline, 144
Williams, James A., 81
Williams, Jeff, 116, 117, 146
Williams, Jill, 80
Williams, John Warner, 134
Williams, Judi Ann, 92
Williams, Kelly, 144
Williams, Lanyard A., 132
Williams, Morgan, 58, 224
Williams, Paul R., 130
Williams, Ralph, 154
Williams, Rhys, 78
Williams, Robert Neff, 99
Williams, Robin, 86, 87, 224
Williams, Sarah, 80
Williams, Tennessee, 9, 125, 136, 138, 178
Williams, Tom, 102
Williams, Treat, 224
Williams, Van, 224
Williams, Vince, 184
Williams, Walker, 138
Williamson, David, 97
Williamson, Kate, 178
Williamson, Laird, 123, 138
Williamson, Laurie, 146, 162
Williamson, Ruth, 151
Williford, Lou, 116, 117
Willinger, David, 105
Willis, Avery, 158
Willis, John, 190
Willison, Walter, 182, 191, 224, 225
Willman, Noel, 232
Wills, Ray, 85, 90, 125, 226
Wilson, August, 122, 123, 132, 144, 165
Wilson, Daniel, 60
Wilson, Elizabeth, 7, 154, 155
Wilson, Erin Cressida, 60
Wilson, James Jay, 72
Wilson, Julie, 20, 33, 226
Wilson, K. C., 143, 226
Wilson, Kim, 170
Wilson, Lanford, 46, 48, 65, 82, 104, 153, 161, 172, 178
Wilson, Laurel Ann, 78
Wilson, Martha, 23
Wilson, Mary Louise, 184, 226
Wilson, Moira, 73
Wilson, Neil, 81
Wilson, Robert, 78
Wilson, Sandy, 176
Wilson, Steve, 138
Wilson, Tena, 142, 164
Wilson, Tracy Lee, 53, 56, 61
Wilson, Trey, 232
Wilson, Tristan, 180
Wilson, Tyrone, 68
Wiltberger, John M., 42
Wiltse, David, 154
Wimmer, Nephi Jay, 31, 182
Winbar, Geri, 50
Wincott, Michael, 86
Winde, Beatrice, 158, 226
Wines, Halo, 126
Winfield, Paul, 11
Wing, Douglas, 170
Wing, Virginia, 63, 226
Wingfield, Betsy J., 57
Wink-Dah, 68
Winkler, Andrew, 57
Winkler, Kevin, 126
Winkler, Mel, 92, 136
Winkler, Richard, 118, 136, 166
Winkler, Suzanne, 137
Winkowski, Ann, 130
Winn, Cal, 168
Winn, Marie, 96, 134
Winn-Jones, Maggie, 182
Winslow, Aaron, 51, 52
Winslow, Michele, 57
Winslow, Pamela, 39
Winslow, Peggy, 158
Winson, Suzi, 70, 226
Winston, Blair, 90
Winston, Carol, 130
Winston, Hattie, 91
Winston, Lee, 56, 226
Winston, Robert, 57
Winter's Tale, The, 95
Winter, Michael David, 57, 82, 83
Winters, Michael, 119, 123
Winters, Sally Vold, 142
Wintersteller, Lynne, 70
Winton, Chase, 73
Winton, Graham, 93, 94, 95, 148
Wipf, Alex, 55
Wise, J., 75
Wise, Jeffrey, 56
Wise, Jim, 143
Wise, John, 52
Wise, Scott, 25
Wise, William, 7, 107, 154, 226
Wisner, Christine, 130
Wisniski, Ron, 226
Wisti, Toni, 36
Witham, Tricia, 162
Without Apologies, 81
Witt, Howard, 154, 178
Wittstein, Ed, 69
Wodehouse, P. G., 45, 63, 83, 109
Woelzl, Susan, 27
Wohl, Jack, 31, 85
Wojda, John, 137, 174, 175
Wojewodski, Robert, 81, 148, 151, 172
Wojewodski, Stan, Jr., 81, 132
Wojtasik, George, 82
Wolf, Kelly, 52
Wolfe, Barbara, 56
Wolfe, George C., 135, 180
Wolfe, June, 24
Wolfe, Nancy, 148
Wolfeil, Scott, 53
Wolfington, Iggie, 146
Wolford, Mary, 60
Wolford, Melodie, 129
Wolfson, David, 56
Wolfson, Jennifer, 83
Wolhandler, Joe, 13
Wolk, James, 57, 170
Woller, Kirk B. R., 127
Wolpe, David, 76
Wolshonak, Derek, 55
Wolsk, Eugene V., 109
Wolsk, Gene, 111
Woman Floating Out a Window, 68
Woman in Mind, 123
Womble, Terence, 51, 73
Women Alone, 57
Women and Wallace, 100
Wonderful Party, 57
Wonderful Town, 146
Wondisford, Diane, 59
Wondsel, Ted, 42
Wong, Anthony, 50, 144
Wong, B. D., 41, 190, 191, 226
Wong, Lily-Lee, 38
Wonsek, Paul, 81, 176
Wood, Bradford, 160, 162
Wood, Donna, 118
Wood, G., 158
Wood, James, 128
Wood, Karen S., 134
Wood, Peter, 133
Wood, Sally Ann, 142
Wood, Sheila, 53
Wood, Tom, 136
Woodall, Sandra, 123
Woodard, Alfre, 95, 226
Woodard, Charlaine, 12, 135
Woodard, Wardell, 162
Woodbridge, Patricia, 55, 131
Woodman, Branch, 64
Woodman, William, 170, 179
Woodruff, Leslie, 161
Woodruff, Robert, 123
Woods, Allie, 96, 226
Woods, Carol, 50, 226
Woods, Eileen, 83
Woods, Richard, 93, 184, 226
Woodson, Deborah, 74
Woodward, Jeffrey, 148
Woolard, David C., 96, 100, 107, 134, 158
Woolf, Steven, 170
Woolley, Jim, 25
Wooten, John, 91
Worby, Joshua, 103
Worcell, Carol Lynn, 109
Worcell, Mike, 129
Working Magic, 57
Workman, Jacque, 129
Workman, Shanelle, 40, 226
Woronoff, Rob, 141
Worth, Irene, 94, 226
Worth, Maggie, 232
Worthen, Laura Ann, 138
Wren, Deborah, 63
Wren, Gayden, 47
Wren, James, 150
Wrenn, Bob, 109
Wright, Amanda, 128
Wright, Anne, 174
Wright, Anne-Marie, 51
Wright, Ben, 39
Wright, Bruce, 172
Wright, Doug, 87, 184
Wright, Elaine, 25
Wright, Garland, 126, 147
Wright, George, 116
Wright, Jeffrey, 151, 184
Wright, John, 148
Wright, Linda, 62
Wright, Mandy, 137
Wright, Mary Catherine, 166
Wright, Matthew, 176
Wright, Michael David, 121
Wright, Miller, 20, 31, 34, 50, 54, 66, 67, 68, 70, 73, 100
Wright, R. Hamilton, 119
Wright, Richard Leon, 226
Wright, Richard, 99
Wright, Robert, 130
Wright, Samuel E., 32, 165
Wright, Susan, 174, 175
Wright, Valerie, 126
Wright, William, 133
Wrightson, Ann, 161
Wrisemo, Thomas, 78
Wroe, Craig, 128, 170
Wrubel, Bill, 87
Wu, Gregory, 158
Wulp, John, 81
Wurst, Janet, 112
Wuthrich, Terry, 52
Wuttke, Martin, 78
Wyeth, David C., 169
Wyeth, Zoya, 34
Wyler, Gretchen, 123
Wylie, John, 23, 226
Wyman, Nicholas, 44, 226
Wyn-Davies, Geraint, 174
Wynkoop, Christopher, 131, 162
Xuereb, Emmanuel, 58
Xuereb, Sophie, 58
Yabuku, Reuben, 139
Yaji, Shigeru, 172
Yamaguchi, Eiko, 98
Yamamoto, Danny, 134, 135
Yamamoto, Ronald, 45, 109, 226
Yancey, Kim, 80, 132, 226
Yancey, Laura, 180
Yancey, Terence, 60
Yancy, Kim, 80
Yando, Larry, 152
Yaney, Denise, 79
Yang, Ginny, 98, 226
Yarborough, Michael, 69
Yarden, Guy, 93
Yates, C. M., 112
Yates, Lauren, 91
Yaukey, Katrina, 182
Yaukey, Kay, 182
Yawn, Gary, 180
Yeager, Barbara, 25, 45
Yeager, Donna, 180
Yeargan, Michael H., 7, 77, 154
Yeargan, Michael, 148, 169, 184
Yearsley, Alice, 25
Yeats: A Celebration, 84
Yee, Kelvin Han, 123
Yellen, Sherman, 43
Yellow Robe, William, Jr., 68
Yelusich, Andrew V., 138
Yenque, Teresa, 101
Yeoman, Joann, 226
Yeremin, Yuri, 148
Yergan, David, 131
Yerxa, Alison, 78
Yeston, Maury, 88
Yevak-Leskin, Shannon, 178
Yipp, Sam, 78
Yoakam, Stephen, 147

Yoder, Jerry, 51, 81
Yohn, Erica, 156, 157
Yokobosky, Matthew, 98
York, David, 158
You Never Can Tell, 61, 128, 172, 173
Youmans, James, 96, 97, 100, 153
Youmans, Jim, 52
Youmans, William, 46, 154
Young Playwrights Festival, 100
Young Rube, 90
Young, Billy Joe, 73
Young, Bruce A., 132
Young, Bruce, 111
Young, DeVron, 132
Young, Eben, 168
Young, James, 117
Young, Jordan, 141
Young, Linda Carol, 61, 125
Young, Norma, 180

Young, Phil, 52
Young, Robert L., 148
Young, Susan, 56
Youngman, Christina, 36, 226
Youngstrom, Juda, 51, 52
Yount, Dell, 112
Yount, Ken, 85
Yount, Kenneth M., 31, 43
Yudson, Steve, 172
Yuhasz, Steve, 65
Yule, Don, 27
Yulin, Harris, 104
Yuminsha, Yume no, 78
Yurman, Lawrence, 184
Yuter, Morris, 111
Zabinski, Gary M., 20, 81
Zabriskie, Grace, 47, 48
Zaccaro, Joyce, 133
Zacharias, Emily, 31, 85, 226
Zagier, Norman, 116
Zagnit, Stuart, 55, 85, 226
Zaionz, Craig R., 81

Zaitsev, Slava, 118
Zak, Scott, 176
Zakowska, Donna, 62
Zaks, Jerry, 26, 45, 109
Zale, Alexander, 172
Zaloom, Joe, 72, 93, 96, 226
Zaloom, Paul, 226
Zanarini, Tom, 144
Zane, Lisa, 144
Zanfagna, Rob, 50
Zang, Edward, 103, 226
Zap, Sam, 75, 226
Zapp, Peter, 61
Zarate, Manuel, 119
Zarish, Janet, 59, 148, 226
Zarley, Matt, 37
Zavin, Benjamin Barnard, 75
Zavodnick, Steve, 178
Zay, Tim, 59, 68, 226
Zegarsky, George, 76
Zehr, Peggy, 129
Zehr, Robert D., 129

Zehr, Robert, 129
Zeichner, Jeff, 49
Zeidman, Dale, 27
Zeig, Sande, 56
Zeisler, Ellen, 55, 56
Zelenich, Zenon, 56
Zeller, Mark, 31, 85, 226
Zelno, Christopher, 34
Zelon, Helen, 105
Zemon, Tom, 40
Zenoni, Robert, 161
Zerkle, Greg, 39, 115
Ziegenhagen, Eric, 100
Ziegler, Tom, 125
Zielinski, Scott, 184
Ziemann, August, 152
Ziemba, Karen, 27, 37, 74, 108, 226
Zien, Chip, 39, 226
Zimet, Paul, 46
Zindel, Lizabeth, 68
Zindel, Paul, 79

Zipprodt, Patricia, 25, 39, 113
Ziskie, Kurt, 57, 226
Zito, Chuck, 165
Zito, Zach, 48
Zizka, Jiri, 96
Znaimer, Moses, 72
Zobel, Richard, 131
Zohar, Rita, 135
Zoldowski, Cheryl, 52
Zolkins, The, 13
Zommer, Ken, 141
Zorich, Christina, 53
Zorowitz, Steven, 102
Zuber, Catherine, 132, 169
Zubrzycki, Anna, 47
Zucker, Grover, 48
Zuckerman, Charles, 20
Zuraida, Ken, 47
Zuse, Ted, 154
Zwahlen, Christian, 143
Zweifler, Liz, 159
Zweigbaum, Steven, 42